DOCUMENT ENGINEERING

DOCUMENT ENGINEERING

ANALYZING AND DESIGNING DOCUMENTS FOR BUSINESS INFORMATICS & WEB SERVICES

Robert J. Glushko and Tim McGrath

The MIT Press
Cambridge, Massachusetts
London, England

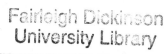

This book was set in Bauer Bodoni and Eurostile by Andrea R. Nelson.
Printed and bound in the United States of America.

Library of Congress Cataloging-in-Publication Data

Glushko, Robert J.
Document engineering: analyzing and designing documents for business informatics and Web services / Robert J. Glushko and Tim McGrath.
p. cm.
Includes bibliographical references and index.
ISBN0-262-07261-0 (alk. paper)
1. Text processing (Computer science). 2. Electronic data interchange.
3. Commercial documents—Data processing. I. McGrath, Tim. II. Title.

QA76.9.T48 G54 2005 2001030659
005—dc22

CONTENTS

PART II FOUNDATIONS

CHAPTER TWO XML FOUNDATIONS

CHAPTER THREE MODELS, PATTERNS, AND REUSE

CHAPTER SIX WHEN MODELS DON'T MATCH: THE INTEROPERABILITY CHALLENGE

PART III THE DOCUMENT ENGINEERING APPROACH

CHAPTER SEVEN THE DOCUMENT ENGINEERING APPROACH

CHAPTER TEN DESIGNING BUSINESS PROCESSES WITH PATTERNS

CHAPTER ELEVEN ANALYZING DOCUMENTS

CHAPTER TWELVE ANALYZING DOCUMENT COMPONENTS

CHAPTER THIRTEEN ASSEMBLING DOCUMENT COMPONENTS

Preface

For nearly three thousand years information has been organized in the purposeful and self-contained package that we call a document. The technology for encoding and exchanging documents has profoundly changed, but the concept of a document has remained surprisingly stable. Documents formalize the interactions between enterprises and their customers or clients, and it natural and intuitive to view documents as the input requirements and as the output results from many kinds of processes. These document exchanges follow common patterns. Models of business organization like supply chains, business-to-business marketplaces, and auctions can be composed from simpler two-party patterns of document exchanges.

The Internet and its supporting technologies like XML and web services give us great efficiencies and flexibility in how we create, manage and share information to conduct business and collaborate with others. But taking full advantage of these new technologies requires that we continue to think of documents in an abstract and technology-neutral way. When a seller asks, "What will you order from my catalog?" or the buyer asks, "Will you take this check as payment?" they are focusing on what they want to accomplish through their interactions, not on how to do it. Similarly, enterprise applications that automate business processes involving document exchanges should expose their interfaces as abstract document models so they can operate in heterogeneous technology environments.

Document Engineering helps us specify, design, and implement these documents and the processes that create and consume them. It synthesizes complementary ideas from information and systems analysis, electronic publishing, business process analysis, and business informatics to ensure that the documents and processes make sense to the people and applications that need them. A document-centric philosophy unifies these different analysis and modeling perspectives. Using patterns for document exchanges and document components ensures we can build applications and services that are robust but adaptable when technology or business conditions change (as they inevitably will).

About the Authors

Bob Glushko spent many years in industrial research and development, technology transfer, and consulting with a focus that evolved from human factors in computing systems, to electronic publishing, and then to Internet commerce. He founded or co-founded three companies, the last of which was Veo Systems in 1997, which pioneered the use of XML for electronic commerce before its 1999 acquisition by

Commerce One. From 1999-2002 he headed Commerce One's XML architecture and technical standards activities and was named an "Engineering Fellow" in 2000. In 2002 he became an Adjunct Professor in the School of Information Management and Systems at the University of California, Berkeley where he is the Director of the Center for Document Engineering.

Tim McGrath has a background in information systems design, specifically in the area of trade and transport systems. In 1990 he co-founded Transport EDI Services (TEDIS), which grew to be a leader in innovative Internet services for EDI in Australia. Apart from spending the past three years writing this book he has been the chair of the Universal Business Language Library Content subcommittee.

Bob and Tim met in 2000 as members of the Quality Review Committee in the ebXML standards initiative. This committee exercised broad technical oversight over the entire suite of ebXML standards, including information and process models, methodologies, and technical architecture for Internet business applications.

Bob's work in Silicon Valley in the "new economy" of moving bits around the Internet was perfectly complemented by Tim's expertise in the "old economy" of moving real stuff around in the physical world. Bob's efforts with SGML and XML for document analysis were matched by Tim's with EDI and data modeling. It seemed natural to work together to create a coherent and comprehensive approach for Document Engineering that builds on their unique combination of perspectives and expertise.

Acknowledgments

Many people have contributed to this book. Lecture notes for the Document Engineering course at UC Berkeley became the outline for the first draft, and students in that and other courses read versions of many chapters. This final version of the book barely resembles those lecture notes and early drafts, which means that we received much useful feedback, but it also means that early generations of Berkeley students suffered at our hands and for that we apologize. In particular, we thank Patrick Garvey, Calvin Smith, Bill French, and Carolyn Cracraft for serving as the teaching assistants in Document Engineering courses. Students Kate Ahern, Alison Billings, Aaron Brick, Peter Charles, Bob Daly, Lisa de Larios-Heiman, Marc Gratacos, Denise Green, Kristine Gual, Ryan Huebsch, Sonia Klemperer-Johnson,

John Leon, Justin Makeig, Vam Makam, and Amy Todenhagen also contributed to improving the book.

We are grateful to Allison Bloodworth, Adam Blum, Ron Bourret, David Burdett, Hank Chesbrough, Larry Downes, Robert M. Glushko, Brian Hayes, Mary Loomis, Scott McMullan, Alex Milowski, Hari Reddy, Pamela Samuelson, Anno Saxenian, and Hal Varian for their careful reviews of draft chapters. Our book is much better because of their insights and frankness.

We thank Allison Bloodworth (again), Nadine Fiebrich, Myra Liu, and Zhanna Shamis for allowing us to use their Berkeley Event Calendar Network project as an extended case study.

The concepts and methods in this book partly evolved from our work in the ebXML and Universal Business Language initiatives. There are far too many individuals who have contributed to our ideas through these projects to name them all; we hope they will feel acknowledged when they see their collective insights in the text. But we would like to specifically recognize Joe Baran, Jon Bosak, Toufic Boubez, Bill Burcham, Stuart Campbell, Dave Carlson, Chin Chee-Kai, Klaus-Dieter Naujok, Stephen Green, Arofan Gregory, Eduardo Gutentag, Eve Maler, Duane Nickull, Sue Probert, Dick Raman, Mike Rawlins, Karsten Riemer, Marion Royal, Gunther Stuhec, David Webber, and last but by no means least, the late Mike Adcock.

Our work intersects with research at the University of Hong Kong and we would like to thank David Cheung and Thomas Lee from the Center for E-Commerce Infrastructure Development (CECID) for their valuable feedback and support.

We also thank Jon Conhaim, Paul Gray, Patrick McGrath, Helen Norris, JR Schulden and Shel Waggener of the University of California, Berkeley for their organizational and financial contributions to our work and especially for allowing us to use the e-Berkeley program and campus IT projects as a testbed for many of our ideas.

IBMers Sharon Adler, David Cohn, Rob Guttman, Paul Maglio, Bob Schloss, and especially Jim Spohrer inspired us by their own work in web services, business informatics, and services science to try to pull it all together here.

We couldn't have written this book without the indirect help of many colleagues with or from whom we learned much of what it is in it. These include Terry Allen, Liora Alschuler, Mike Bianchi, Peter Brown, Brian Caporlette, Ian Crawford, Matthew Fuchs, Clive Gregory, Sue Helper, Kevin Hughes, Russ Hunt, Ken Kershner, Eliot Kimber, Mary Laplante, Michael Leventhal, Tom Malone, John Mashey, John May, Bart Meltzer, Murray Maloney, Jeff Suttor, Bill Rouse, Marty Tenenbaum, Marcy Thompson, Ben Wolin and Vincent Vuong.

Loralee Windsor copyedited the book and Andrea Nelson designed its look and feel. Carolyn Cracraft created the index and glossary of terms. Naturally, any errors in content, structure or presentation are ours.

Doug Sery and MIT Press have been remarkably patient.

And finally, we want to thank Pamela Samuelson (again) and Isabelle, Hannah and Duncan McGrath for their self-sacrifice and inestimable encouragement to us while we wrote this book. Perhaps they knew better than we did what it would take, but never let on.

How This Book is Organized

This book is organized in four parts.

I "INTRODUCTION" is just that.

II "FOUNDATIONS" consists of five chapters that discuss XML, modeling, business patterns, and XML vocabularies to establish an intellectual baseline for the rest of the book. Some of this material will be familiar to practitioners but has proven essential for students, so we've separated it so that each can attend to it as needed.

III "THE DOCUMENT ENGINEERING APPROACH" begins with Chapter 7, which summarizes the end-to-end phases of Document Engineering. Each phase is treated in depth in a separate chapter. Chapter 16, "Management and Strategy," discusses considerations that span all of Document Engineering but which would be more difficult to explain if this chapter appeared earlier.

IV "THE END OF THE BEGINNING" contains a short epilogue, notes, glossary, and index.

We wrote this book for consultants, practitioners and advanced university students in information systems, industrial engineering, business informatics or related professional disciplines. The book strives to present enough theory and concepts to frame issues but is aggressively practical where the material allows us to be. The balance between theory and reality also shows in our notes, which are more extensive than in most business or trade books but which make no attempt to be as rigorous as those in academic literature. We also mix in archival and academic sources with web citations when the latter are likely to be more current or accessible. These notes appear in a separate section near the end of the book rather than at the bottom of each page or the end of each chapter so that readers are not confronted by them if they choose not to read them.

Applications, technologies, and issues for Document Engineering frequently appear in news stories and technical journals – but are not yet categorized that way. The companion web site for this book that collects and organizes them, and provides teaching materials and other useful resources is www.docengineering.com.

Bob Glushko (San Francisco, California)
Tim McGrath (Fremantle, Western Australia)

Foreword

David L. Cohn

In its early days, information technology focused on the capture, processing, storage and transfer of data. For each step, structures and standards were established and served as the foundation for subsequent phases. IBM's universal punched cards captured data in volume, preparing it for processing. Electronics and programming languages established mechanisms and disciplines for that processing. Databases and query languages formalized data storage, and communication protocols led to widely accepted data communication.

Classical information technology has focused on processing data. Indeed, when I was young (which some are not sure was ever the case), the field was called Data Processing. It has primarily dealt with the applications that did the processing (defined by Glushko and McGrath as "software artifacts that present, collect, and manipulate information"). We have a vast literature on modeling, creating, defining, testing and describing these processes. They are important because, without them, nothing would happen.

However, as we move comfortably into the 21st century, information technology is evolving into Business Informatics. This term recalls the dramatic transformation information technology brought to biology through bioinformatics. We'll likely see similar impact on business.

With Business Informatics, we deal directly with the very concepts of data: what it means, how it is represented and which elements are related. These meanings, representations and relationships are present when data is structured into documents.

Documents have long been important, but HTML and the World Wide Web dramatically increase their value. They've accelerated document exchange and emphasized the need for structures and discipline. These structures and disciplines are what Document Engineering is about, and the document-centric view is where this book is leading us.

Applications are to information technology as verbs (the action words) are to human language. But human language would be useless without nouns (the actor words). In fact, nouns play a larger role in language than verbs. According to Princeton University's Cognitive Science Laboratory, the English language has 114,648 distinct nouns but only 11,306 verbs (see wordnet.princeton.edu for a neat online lexical reference system). However, language depends on both and on their close relationship.

Glushko and McGrath understand the dualism of information technology's nouns and verbs. They note, "it is undeniable that documents and processes have an inseparable and complementary relationship." However, the evolution of information technology has not supported this duality. If it had, we would have the tools to model, create, define, test and describe documents, just as we do for processes. Where are they?

They are in Document Engineering.

Unfortunately, the problem of creating these tools is hard. Just as there ten times as many nouns in English as verbs, we seem to have ten times as many ways of representing information as of processing it. Glushko and McGrath have laid down an organized approach to identify the key documents, canonize their representations and leverage these to solve the larger problem. They have begun to develop the structure that will lead us to the needed tool set.

And there is good news along the way.

The document view of Business Informatics may be more natural than the process view. Documents are concrete entities, and people are comfortable agreeing on their description and meaning; processes are abstract, and consensus is difficult. In the work described in this book, and in related efforts covered elsewhere, document-based analysis is proving to be a powerful technique for designing, building and managing information systems.

The journey is, indeed, the proverbial thousand miles; this book has begun it with well more than the usual single step. Fortunately, we don't have to reach the final destination to reap substantial rewards.

David L. Cohn
Director, Business Informatics
IBM Research
Yorktown Heights, New York

INTRODUCTION

1

Introduction to Document Engineering

1.0 INTRODUCTION

Twenty-four hundred years ago, a Middle Eastern farmer named Halfat paid his taxes by giving barley and wheat to King Artaxerces. The receipt that documented this transaction was recorded on a fragment of pottery.[1]

We don't use pottery, papyrus, and parchment anymore, and although paper hasn't gone away, electronic documents have replaced much of it. A corresponding evolution has taken place in the nature of document exchanges and the business processes they enable. Every major advance in transportation, communications, manufacturing, or financial technology has brought a need for different kinds of information flow. People have met these needs by developing specialized types of documents containing the required information. Letters of credit, bills of lading, paper currency, promissory notes, checks, and other new types of documents came into being in response to a business opportunity made possible by some advance in technology.

In the 19th century the telegraph and telephone made it possible to exchange information electronically and coordinate business activities at a scale vastly larger than before, leading to the rise of the modern corporation. The late 20th and early 21st centuries have witnessed the equally profound impact of the Internet (and related technologies such as the World Wide Web, electronic mail, and XML) on how businesses work. Now the web-based virtual enterprise can be open for business 24 hours a day, 7 days a week, with a global presence enabled by distributing people and resources wherever they are needed in either physical space or cyberspace.

Clearly, companies can't reliably achieve new business value by facing inward and focusing on efficiency. But they can't succeed in the dynamic 21st century global economy just by getting on the web either—they need to fundamentally rethink what they do and how they do it. Then they can begin to exploit their own strengths and start to rely on those of other organizations that may be halfway around the world but because of abundant bandwidth seem to be next door. When they face outward to create richer relationships with suppliers, customers, and business service providers and integrate their internal business processes with those of their business partners, they create value they could not produce on their own.

And behind this flexible, adaptive business architecture remains the very simple and natural idea of document exchange. Documents organize business interactions and package the information needed to carry out transactions. The notion of documents as the inputs and outputs of business processes wherever they reside in the network is a technology-independent abstraction perfectly suited for the heterogeneous technology environment of the Internet.

We don't need to understand the technical nuts and bolts of XML and web services to appreciate the revolutionary power of this approach. Any business service that is invoked with an XML document and sends an XML document as its response can be a component in a service oriented business architecture. That business component can then be plugged into a new business model that may never have existed before.

But although the web services standards tell us how to package information into documents and where and how to route them, they don't tell us what any of the documents mean. We need Document Engineering to help us specify, design, and implement the documents that are the inputs and outputs of business services.

Document Engineering synthesizes complementary ideas from information and systems analysis, electronic publishing, business process analysis, and business informatics. Its unifying document-centric perspective helps us conceive and understand the new network-based business models made possible by the Internet and supporting technologies.

The essence of Document Engineering is the analysis and design methods that yield:

- Precise specifications or models for the information that business processes require.

- Rules by which related processes are coordinated, whether between different firms to create composite services or virtual enterprises or within a firm to streamline information flow between organizations.

Document Engineering provides the concepts and methods needed to align business strategy and information technology, to bridge the gap between what we want to do and how to do it. Describing business processes in terms of the more abstract notion of document exchanges makes it easier to understand the constraints imposed by legacy systems and technologies and to recognize the opportunities created by new ones if we focus on conceptual models of the exchanges rather than on how they are implemented. The expressiveness of XML for implementation models bridges the traditional gap between business strategy and its technology realization.

1.1 A SIMPLE BUSINESS TRANSACTION?

Imagine that you go into your local bookstore and notice a new book with an intriguing title, "Document Engineering" by Glushko & McGrath. You hand the clerk your credit card, and a few moments later you leave the store with your copy of the book. To describe what just took place, you might say that you purchased a book, using the single word purchased because the experience seemed like a single economic event or transaction taking place between you and the bookstore.

Now imagine that you are browsing the website at an Internet bookstore, GlushkoMcGrathBooks.com (from now on we'll just call it GMBooks.com). You navigate a few screens to select that new book with the intriguing title, "Document Engineering" by Glushko & McGrath. You add your credit card information and shipping address to the shopping cart form, and a few days later the book arrives by delivery service.

How would you describe what took place at GMBooks.com? At first glance the online experience seems equivalent to the bookstore experience, so you might describe it as "buying a book online." But if you analyze the online experience more closely, you can see that it is composite service in which at least three separate transactions or exchanges of information occurred:

1. Your interaction with the GMBooks.com catalog to select the book you want to order.

2. A document exchange between GMBooks.com and a credit authority (a bank or authorization network like VISA or MasterCard) to verify your creditworthiness and charge your account.[2]

3. A document exchange between GMBooks.com and the delivery service with the instructions for picking up and delivering your book.

So what looked at first like a single event, "buying a book," turns out to be at least three separate events that have been combined in a particular sequence to create a composite business process (see Figure 1-1.)

This pattern is typical of many Internet retailers and completely invisible to you as the customer. But there may be even more involved here. The retailer taking your order doesn't have its own inventory of the books it offers in its catalog. Instead it maintains a virtual inventory, which consists of the books it can reliably obtain from distributors when a customer selects them from the online catalog. So other transactions that might take place are:

4. An exchange between GMBooks.com and the distributor to confirm that the book you selected is available so that GMBooks.com can sell it to you and promise a delivery date.

5. The order sent by GMBooks.com to the distributor to obtain the book on your behalf.

6. The request for delivery (or forwarding instructions) sent from the distributor to the delivery service with the instructions for delivering your book. This document exchange takes place instead of Exchange 3 because the order taker never has your book!

This simple example, contrasting a "bricks and mortar" bookstore and an online bookstore, illustrates the disruptive force of the Internet on traditional business models. A virtual company created by using services provided by separate businesses can be created more rapidly, more flexibly, and at a lower cost than a traditional store can.[3]

The new business model of the virtual store changes both the business processes of the traditional model and the document exchanges required to carry them out. Redesigning and realigning these into a new business model requires the concepts and methods of Document Engineering.

A virtual company can be created rapidly, flexibly, and at low cost

1.2 THE EXTENDED OR VIRTUAL ENTERPRISE

Before we go any further, we must point out that when we say things like enterprise or business model, we don't mean to rule out governments, educational institutions, or nonprofit institutions. Business is shorthand for "purposeful, systematized activity to create and exchange value" and can apply as well to government, educational, and nonprofit entities.

Unlike the physical bookstore, which might exist as a single entity in a fixed location, the online bookstore, GMBooks.com, functions as an extended or virtual enterprise. It emerges from the coordination of the activities of numerous independent businesses that collaborate to achieve their interlocking goals, as illustrated in Figure 1-1. This coordination takes place by the exchange of information between the retailer and book distributors, shippers, and credit authorities. The retailer doesn't need its own books and delivery trucks—it can replace inventory and equipment with information.

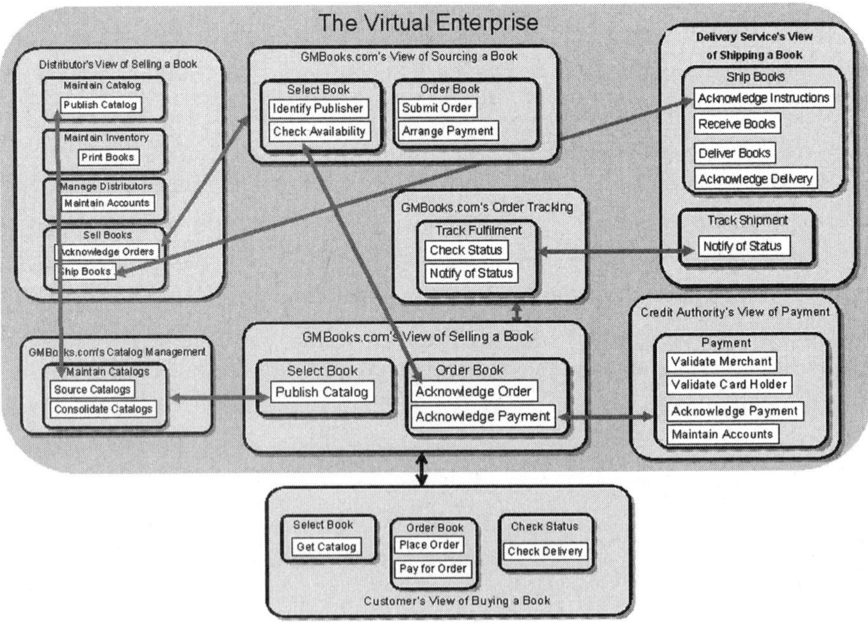

Figure 1-1. The GMBooks.com Virtual Enterprise

The business model used by GMBooks.com is a drop shipment pattern, where a retailer without inventory offers products from an aggregated catalog and routes customer orders to distributors or other firms who fulfill the orders from their own inventories.[4] While this coordination is usually invisible from the customer's perspective, it requires a complex and carefully managed series of document exchanges (often called a document choreography) over a period that may range from hours to weeks.

Independent business processes are coordinated by the exchange of information

Many dot-coms failed because their flashy websites could take orders from customers but did not implement the "back end" information exchanges with warehouses and shippers required to make reliable delivery promises to customers. Dissatisfied customers whose orders arrived late never ordered another product.

1.3 IT'S ALL ABOUT EXCHANGING DOCUMENTS

The exchange of information between GMBooks.com and the other businesses that provide services to it takes place in the form of electronic messages or documents. In the book purchase scenario it is easy to identify the information that must be exchanged to carry out the desired business processes: an identifier for the book (perhaps an ISBN), a credit card number and purchase amount, and a customer's name and shipping address.

Some people might object to classifying these relatively small pieces of information as documents. They may want to distinguish between fine-grained, structured "data" and coarse-grained, unstructured "documents" or use the latter term only where they can imagine something printed.

A chain of related documents will reuse common components

But more and more business processes involve both these ideas of "documents" and "data." A catalog might contain a mixture of description about products (text, graphics, photographs, and so on) and detailed data about their technical specifications. GMBooks.com depends on narrative documents like catalogs and book reviews as well as on transactional documents like orders, shipping notes, and payments to carry out its drop shipment business pattern. For information to flow efficiently from one type of document to another in this chain of related documents, there must be common content components that are reused. It isn't helpful to impose some arbitrary boundary between data and documents—what matters is the information components they convey.

1.3.1 THE DOCUMENT TYPE SPECTRUM

We view both documents and data on a continuum we call the Document Type Spectrum (see Figure 1-2) by analogy with the continuous rainbow formed by the visible light spectrum. It is easy to contrast highly narrative style documents from those that are highly transactionally oriented, just as it is easy to distinguish red from blue. But it can be difficult to distinguish different shades of a single color.

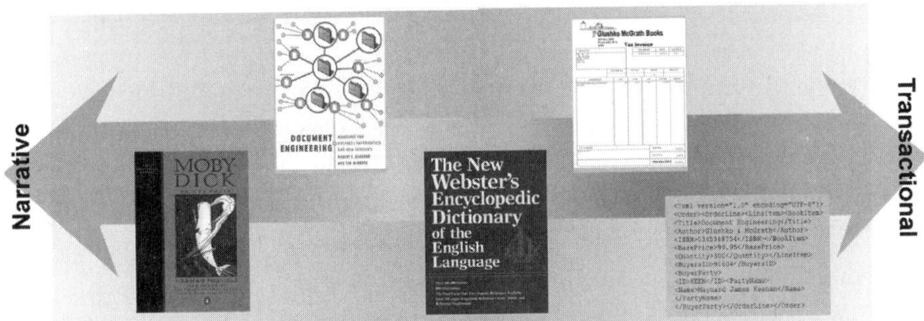

Figure 1-2. The Document Type Spectrum

These difficult distinctions arise in the middle of the Document Type Spectrum where documents contain both narrative and transactional features. This is where we find hybrid documents like catalogs, encyclopedias, and requests for quotes.

The point is that this is a continuum. We don't see a magical point in the scale of information exchange from a short string of bits to complete purchase orders where data end and documents take over.

A document is a purposeful and self-contained collection of information

Nor do we see a sharp boundary between structured sets of data designed for use by computer applications and unstructured information designed for people. Defining document in a technology-neutral way as a purposeful and self-contained collection of information seems to cover both ends of the continuum.

1.3.2 DOCUMENT EXCHANGE AS A BUILDING BLOCK IN BUSINESS MODEL PATTERNS

Doing business by document exchange is natural and intuitive. Businesses use documents to organize their interactions with each other and to package the information needed to carry out a transaction or other meaningful unit of business. The seller may ask, "What do you want to order from my catalog?" and the buyer might ask, "Will you accept my purchase order?" The buyer and seller (or their lawyers) may negotiate a detailed contract with the precise terms and conditions of their business relationship. This contract often specifies the content and timing of other documents that the parties are to exchange in the course of conducting their business with each other.

The exchanges of documents that take place to carry out business models follow common patterns. For example, the drop shipment pattern illustrated in Figure 1-1 is just one example of how a firm uses document exchanges with other firms to carry out its business model. Supply chains, business-to-business marketplaces, auctions, information brokers or aggregators, and content syndication networks are other examples of business processes that use document exchanges to combine or interconnect products or services from multiple businesses.

The document exchanges an organization uses to carry out its internal business processes also follow patterns. For example, the order management cycle can be described as ten steps that begin with order planning and end with post sales service. The complete cycle involves numerous documents that flow between sales, engineering, finance, logistics, customer service, and other divisions within the organization. The specific documents and divisions vary in different contexts, but the general pattern is ubiquitous.

There is no necessary relationship between these business process patterns and their organization within an business's management structure or their support in technology and systems. For example, the fact that a business conducts procurement processes to obtain goods and services does not imply that it has a procurement department or that it has an automated procurement system.

Of course, the business model may determine or at least constrain many decisions about how the enterprise is organized and what information technology it uses. The fit between what a business does and how it does it can be more easily assessed if the business model is defined in an abstract manner independently of its organizational and technological implementation. The foundation of the U.S. government's Federal Enterprise Architecture[5] effort is such a business reference model (BRM). Their goal is to support cross-agency collaboration, transformation, and government-wide improvement by requiring that organizational structures and technology investments be aligned with the business model.

The alignment of business models and technology is easier to achieve when an organization systematically structures its business capabilities as self-contained resources or processes so they can efficiently interact and recombine to meet changing business requirements. Using standard documents as the interfaces for business processes is a natural outcome of organizing business functions as more discrete and flexible components.

GMBooks.com is a simple example of combining component business services to create a composite application. Real-world components like the Amazon.com catalog,[6] the UPS delivery and tracking functions, and Visa payment processing are all available as document-based web services for easy integration into other business systems.

In Chapter 4, "Describing What Businesses Do and How They Do It," we compare and contrast the organizational, business model, system architecture, business process, and information architecture perspectives from which one can analyze and describe models of document exchanges. This provides a repertoire of patterns of different granularity that can be reused to devise new business solutions.

1.3.3 DOCUMENT EXCHANGE AS LOOSE COUPLING

Document exchange as a mechanism for conducting business lets the participants focus on what they want to accomplish rather than how they must do it. The seller asks, "What do you want to order from my catalog?" and hopes not to have to ask, "What kind of software do you use to arrange and send electronic orders?" A relationship is called loosely coupled when the parties avoid dependencies, so that changes by one party have no impact on the other.

It is nonsensical to imagine a business relationship that depends on the color of the file cabinets in which documents are stored, the brand of accounting software used to calculate invoices, a database or directory structure, or anything else about the technology choices involving information or documents to be exchanged. A relationship with these kinds of constraints would be too tightly coupled to cope with the ordinary evolution of business practices. But historically many approaches for integrating applications depend on screen layout, record or table structures, fine-grained application program interfaces (APIs), or other implementation details and are more tightly coupled than might be desirable.

Loose coupling is an old and familiar idea

Loose coupling is an old and familiar idea. Telephones and fax machines enable businesses anywhere in the world to exchange information with each other even if they have no existing relationship.

All they need to know is the other's phone or fax numbers, which they might find in a business directory. They don't need to know anything about the other's choice of telephone or fax equipment, and either business could buy a new phone system or fax machine and the other one wouldn't need to know and wouldn't care. Technical standards for how these devices connect to the phone network make them all look the same to the other side.

Of course, the problem with telephone messages and fax machines is that they don't make it easy for the recipient to extract the important information about the business activity in an automated way. That's why businesses (or different divisions within an organization) prefer to send computer-processable documents to each other—to improve accuracy and allow the information they exchange to grow in volume or frequency. And as with telephones and fax machines, standardization of these documents can be essential in maintaining a loosely coupled relationship.

What this all leads to is that two business organizations must agree on what the documents mean and on the business processes they expect each other to carry out with them, but they don't need to agree on or even know anything about the technology they use to create and process the documents.

Organizations must agree on what their documents mean

For example, suppose a customer sends a purchase order to GMBooks.com; if GMBooks.com can fulfill it, they respond with a purchase order acknowledgment, or perhaps with an invoice and a shipping note. As long as the customer and GMBooks.com understand each other's documents and can produce and respond with the documents appropriate for each other's business processes, they don't need to reveal how they produce the documents they send or how they process the documents they receive. The documents are the only visible interfaces to their respective business processes.

1.4 UNDERSTANDING THE MEANING OF DOCUMENTS

For most people understanding something they read in their native language is so immediate that they don't think much about it. The meaning seems to leap directly from the words on the page into their consciousness in a natural and automatic way. This is why we may feel surprised or confused if we later realize that other meanings or interpretations of the words were possible.

And we're not just talking about poetry or philosophy, where the author's intent or the inherent abstractness of the subject matter challenges readers to make sense of the words. Even in catalogs, forms, contracts, and other ordinary business documents, the relationship between words and meaning can be complex and subtle. For example, the same meaning can be described with different words (Address in one document might mean the same as Location in another one), or different concepts can be described with the same words (Address might mean the buyer's address in one document and the seller's address in another). The meaning of some words can change significantly in different business situations or contexts; consider that Next Day Delivery might mean delivery tomorrow but not if today is a weekend day or holiday because Day in Next Day Delivery means business day.

Situations like these can obviously cause misinterpretations, but people have a remarkable ability to refine or repair their understanding. However, computers and software have no such ability. We have all experienced system crashes and unexpected behavior when some bit of data was misinterpreted by application logic because it didn't mean to the program what we thought it did (an infamous example occurred in 1999 when an interplanetary mission to Mars failed because one engineering team used metric units and another one didn't).[7]

So we need to be diligent and precise when we define the meaning (or semantics) of any information content produced and consumed by business applications. But this is easier said than done, and there is a great range in how diligent and precise we can be in doing so.

We need to be diligent and precise when we define semantics

At the very least we can try to define words to create a dictionary. At the other extreme our definitions are expressed in a formal language using a controlled set of terms and relationship types between them.

In the ideal world we end up with a complete view of how information is defined and used in different business contexts—what is often called the information model—a formal representation of the structure and semantics of information. Of course, people often aren't as careful or conscientious as they should be in creating information models. They may fail to recognize the seriousness of the semantic ambiguity problem, or they may have insufficient time, expertise, resources, or incentives to attack it. In either case, there can be substantial differences in the meaning and presentation of information within a single enterprise. And this is invariably reflected in any documents they create.

1.4.1 INCOMPATIBLE INFORMATION MODELS

In large organizations it is easy to find numerous varieties of timesheets, expense reports, purchase orders, catalogs, calendars, and other types of documents. These are likely to contain incompatible information models that prevent time, expenses, and purchases from being aggregated or compared.

In Chapter 6, "When Models Don't Match: The Interoperability Challenge" we further describe the problem of multiple interpretations or formats for what is supposed to be the same information.

Even if each enterprise in a business relationship were disciplined in its own approach to modeling and describing the information it uses internally, that wouldn't be sufficient. There are at least two sides to every document exchange, and all parties need to ensure that they understand the documents in the same way.

One way to do this would be for every enterprise to adopt a common data model and use exactly the same definitions for the document components of their applications. But that's inconceivable; enterprises, applications, and people just don't stand still long enough to make it possible. It is more conceivable that two parties might each create conceptual information models to help them translate or transform the documents they receive so their applications can understand them. The Data and Information Reference Model being created as part of the U.S. government's Federal Enterprise Architecture is an exemplary and ambitious step in this direction.

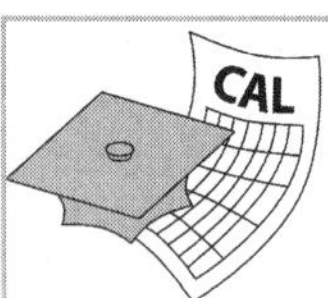

Starting in Chapter 8, we'll present a case study about the development of a standard model of an event calendar to replace dozens of incompatible ones used at the University of California, Berkeley.

1.4.2 STANDARD INFORMATION MODELS

Both the common data model and conceptual information model approaches for ensuring that parties understand each other's documents are facilitated when the syntax, structure or semantics conform to common patterns or standards. Many of these have been developed for specific vertical industries by trade associations, industry consortia, or formal standards bodies.[8] Standards efforts are often the most successful where the stakes are the highest, and it isn't surprising that standards compliance is highest for business processes like payment initiation, reconciliation, funds transfers, and statutory reporting.

Standards for information components needed in all businesses are a more recent development. For example, descriptions of organizations and individuals, basic item details, measurements, date and time, location, country codes, currencies, business classification codes, and similar reusable patterns of information components are found in a wide variety of documents.

Standards for syntax, structure, and semantics facilitate document understanding

Standard reusable patterns are especially important when designing the set of documents needed to carry out a composite business process because they encourage the assembly of documents from building blocks that are reused as information flows from one document into the next. In this regard, the Universal Business Language (UBL) effort, released in mid-2004 promises to be an extremely important standard.[9]

1.5 XML AS AN ENABLING TECHNOLOGY

To exchange documents, computers or business applications require a precise and unambiguous language for describing information models. Since its emergence in the late 1990s, XML—the Extensible Markup Language—has rapidly become the preferred format for representing information in documents both on and off the Internet.

People who work in web publishing view XML as an improvement on HTML, that enables greater automation and consistency in formatting.

Programmers see XML as an Internet-friendly, easy-to-parse, and nonproprietary data format that they can use instead of ad hoc languages for application configuration and interprocess communication.

Electronic data interchange (EDI) developers see XML as a more expressive, maintainable, and therefore lower cost syntax for creating business messages.

XML's broad impact in publishing, programming, and EDI has made it a unifying technology for implementing applications that use Internet protocols, especially for those that span enterprise boundaries, such as web services.

XML has become the preferred language for representing information in documents

Expressing information content and processing logic in a computer-friendly XML vocabulary enables robust applications to be deployed efficiently and at a reasonable cost. XML content can be taken from documents, databases, and enterprise applications, combined and treated as a single source, and delivered to multiple users, devices, or applications.

In Chapter 2, "XML Foundations," we introduce XML from the perspective of modeling and document exchange. We emphasize the conceptual innovations in XML and don't dwell on XML syntax or schema languages. There are plenty of excellent books about the latter, and these aren't what is most important about XML anyway.

1.6 USING XML-ENCODED MODELS TO DESIGN AND DRIVE APPLICATIONS

The expressiveness and flexibility with which XML encodes models makes it a powerful technology for improving software engineering. Applications that are built using models to bridge the traditional gap between design and implementation are often called model based applications or model driven applications.[10] They share information and can be integrated with others more readily. And they are vastly easier to deploy and maintain than those developed without explicit models or for which the models were left behind when coding began.

Some developers still ignore the well-known benefits of a disciplined software development methodology with controlled iteration of analysis, design, implementation, and user feedback and still employ labor intensive and ad hoc techniques that do not predictably yield quality software. The reasons (or excuses) for not following a software engineering approach are well-known: unrelenting user demands for new or revised functionality, competitive pressure for rapid application deployment and modification, or simply the difficulty of obtaining correct requirements without coding something and testing it. Unfortunately, the results are also well-known: little reuse of information or processes across applications, applications that are coupled in unpredictable ways by shared data, and business rules and workflow specifications embedded into application logic.

It doesn't have to be this way. Data dictionaries, programming language classes, database schemas, UML models, spreadsheet templates, and XML schemas can represent the rules and semantics for the documents and processes needed by software applications. These different ways of expressing models are designed for different purposes, but what is important is that each of these representations can be used in a rigorous and formal way to define models that can then be used as specifications for generating code or configuring applications.

In this book we emphasize the use of XML-encoded implementation models to design and drive applications. But, there is certainly nothing about models of documents or processes that requires them to be represented in XML.

Nevertheless, using XML to encode implementation models yields an overall rigor, reusability, and programmability unmatched by other representations. Furthermore, XML's facility for document encoding is an excellent match for the document exchange architecture of the Internet. For those who prefer other representations of data models, programming paradigms are emerging in which XML schemas, programming language objects, database schemas, and UML models can be treated as equivalent because XML schemas can be used to generate any of the other formats if required.[11]

In Chapter 15, "Implementing Models in Applications," we discuss the use of XML for document and process implementation models as explicit representations of application requirements.

1.6.1 DOCUMENT MODELS AS INTERFACES

The simplest case of model based applications is also the most common. For countless information-based activities that have moved to the web, the application is little more than a document displayed in a browser that users interact with in ways that are determined by the document's model.

On the narrative end of the Document Type Spectrum are E-books or other structured publications in which user interface features like tables of contents, hypertext links, and navigation aids are generated from the names or attributes of the information components in the document. On the transactional end of the Document Type Spectrum are E-forms in which applications collect the information specified in the document's model to automate processes that previously have relied on printed forms. We can readily imagine applications where information moves within and between companies—filling out purchase orders, submitting a budget or timesheet, seeking reimbursement for expenses, applying for a grant or job, registering for classes or events, filing income taxes, making insurance claims—the list is endless.

In our online bookstore example, a customer's order from an online catalog might be captured using a web-based E-form. Some pieces of this information, such as the customer's name and address or the title of the book being purchased may be required in other applications, such as those dealing with supply, delivery, or billing, as illustrated in Figure 1-3.

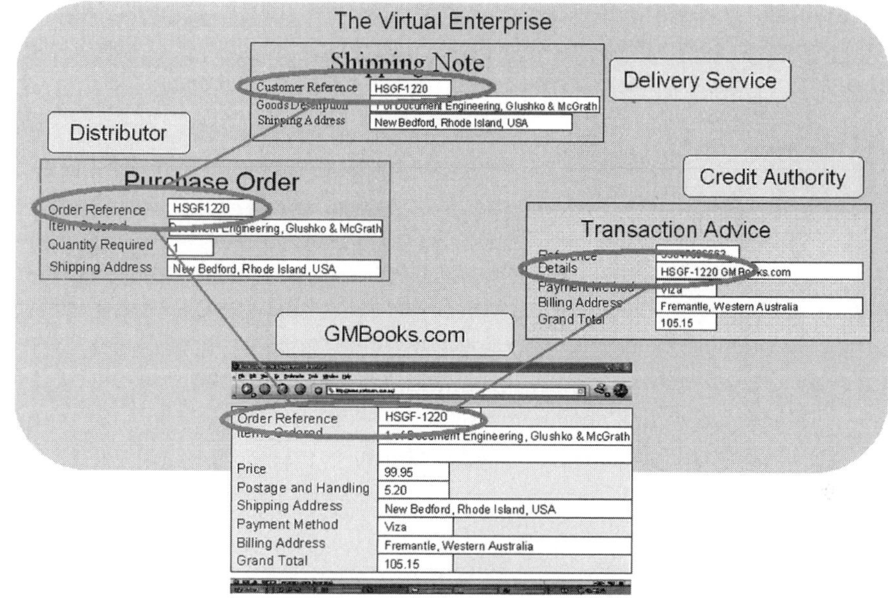

Figure 1-3. Overlapping Content Models in the Virtual Enterprise

These shared pieces of information form the glue that binds the different services to create the virtual enterprise that the customer sees as GMBooks.com. The benefits of a common model for these shared pieces of information are obvious: no data reentry and no omissions or misinterpretations. And this is a trivial example. Consider the benefits of reuse in the average cross-border trading process, which can involve up to 40 documents and 200 data elements, 30 of which are occur in at least 30 documents.

While many applications begin as user interactions with a form, the business processes that follow might be carried out by computer programs with no human involvement. But it makes sense for us to look at both kinds of model based interactions in the same way, generalizing the idea of documents as interfaces for people to the idea that documents are interfaces to business services or business processes.

Documents describe the interfaces to business processes

In both cases the document conveys or captures information in an exchange with another party or process without necessarily revealing anything about how the information is consumed or created by each participant in the exchange.

1.6.2 MODELS OF BUSINESS PROCESSES

Figure 1-3 illustrates the reuse of information between numerous documents that together carry out a business process. But the mere reuse of information from one document to another isn't sufficient to make the business process work. It is also essential for all parties in a document exchange to agree on the purpose or context of a document, which means understanding the business process in which the document exchange is taking place.

Suppose GMBooks.com sends a list of books to another business. This same list of books might appear in an order, an order response, an order change, a price and inventory check, a shipment notice, a bill of lading, an invoice, and so on.

All parties in a document exchange must agree on the context of use

But nothing in the list of books itself communicates anything about the purpose, intent, or business context with which the list should be interpreted by the organization that receives it.

If GMBooks.com sends a purchase order to a book distributor and expects a purchase order acknowledgment in return, what happens if the book distributor's normal business practice (when it can fulfill an order) is to only send an invoice and a shipping notice?

If GMBooks.com's applications are incapable of handling such an electronic response from the book distributor, the process breaks down.

In such situations, it is unlikely to be trivial for GMBooks.com to modify its order management system to dispense with its acknowledgment and accept the document that the book distributor sends. Nor could we expect the book distributor to modify its systems to produce what GMBooks.com wants. But one or the other must do this to enable an automated business exchange.

Clearly, the rules of the business process that control the pattern of document exchanges or, more generally, define the agreement or mutual understanding of the parties to the exchange, should be expressed in an explicit model.

For example, GMBooks.com could accompany the order with a business process model that defines both the documents it expects to exchange when it sends orders and the sequence of their document exchanges. This model can be defined as another document that is used to configure the software on the distributor's side, or it might even be executable and used at run time to ensure that the appropriate documents are exchanged and processed in the specified sequence.

We may not be quite there yet but many initiatives are working diligently to get us closer by developing standards for specifying processes, their composition, and their coordination. Furthermore, many software vendors are developing middleware for using the specifications to control or verify document exchanges.

How these problems of business process integration are resolved depends on what causes them. Technology mismatches are a significant factor. Also significant are the existence of industry standards or reference models, the relative power in the business relationship, the technological and process maturity of each firm, and the extent to which the firms have complementary long-term business strategies. In Chapter 16, "Management and Strategy in Document Engineering" we look at broader factors that determine the success or failure of efforts to exchange information within and between enterprises.

1.6.3 WEB SERVICES AND SERVICE ORIENTED ARCHITECTURES

Using documents as interfaces and thereby hiding implementation details underlies the idea of service oriented architectures (SOAs) as a way to create new applications or systems such as web services by integrating or combining components of other ones.

A technical definition of a web service is "an interface that describes a collection of operations that are network accessible through standardized XML messaging."[14] This means that any self-contained application functionality or information resource is turned into a service by packaging it so that it exposes only input and output XML documents. Typically, these are transported over the Internet.

But this definition, though entirely comprehensive, doesn't explain why there is so much hype about web services and SOAs. One of the most common senses of service contrasts it with products to mean some kind of activity performed by a person so if you aren't a programmer you might not realize from the definition that almost anything can be turned into a service. Because of the abstraction level introduced by document exchange, a service can be:

- Anything that can send or receive a document.
- Anything that can accept a document, process it and return a result.
- Anything that can accept a document and allow the user to act on it.
- Anything that can accept a document and forward it to some other application or destination.
- Anything that can generate a document as a result of user interaction, processing a received document, or some other event.[15]

So a service can be anything and do anything, as long as the information needed to request it and the work or results that it produces can be effectively described using XML. Note also that the way we've defined services allows them to be provided by people as well as by software or other automated means, and the document interface by itself provides no hints.[16]

Anything that takes requests and describes its results using XML can be a web service

No small set of examples can convey the range of possible services, but here are some anyway: stock quotes, tax rates, inventory levels, order tracking, payment processing, restaurant reservations, traffic conditions, sports statistics, credit ratings, algebraic expression evaluation, and language translation.[17]

While a service can carry out some useful business activities on its own, if its document interfaces are described in standard ways, it can combine with other services to create a composite application that provides additional value because of the combination and is more efficient in invocation. For example, consider how a travel information service could be created by combining separate services that provide personalized information about local news, weather, cultural events, traffic conditions, hotels, restaurants, and so on. You could request all of this interrelated information with little more than the name of the destination city, and it would be assembled invisibly by the composite service.

Adopting a flexible SOA benefits a firm in many ways. The core idea that applications should be built by assembling service components rather than repeatedly coding them, promises lower cost and a more general approach for integrating or reusing separate systems or resources within an enterprise. Duplicated functions can be consolidated; for example, in a large enterprise a single service for processing payments might replace dozens of existing applications.

SOAs also enable web services to expose inward-facing legacy systems and data repositories to external businesses or customers and thereby add value to business relationships. For example, a web service that looks up customer details in a customer database can be combined with one that knows about orders in a ERP system, creating a composite service that locates the current orders when a customer calls in.

Because web services are loosely coupled and hide implementations, document interfaces allow firms to maintain a clean and stable relationship to partners and customers. Even if an organization subsequently migrates its internal processes and data from legacy systems, users of the web service shouldn't notice.

Document interfaces maintain clean and stable relationships between business partners

By using independent components, web services also make it easier and cheaper to adopt new technologies incrementally without affecting any existing business functionality. Implementation transparency supports more objective "build vs. buy" decisions about business services and permits comparisons among alternative providers. Because document interfaces can be implemented in any technology, platform compatibility concerns are lessened. And since businesses can have nonessential processes performed by another firm without being locked into a relationship with that provider, traditional arguments for running business applications internally might now lose to those for outsourcing. But as we shall see in Chapter 4 "Describing What Businesses Do and How They Do It," such decisions may not be that simple.

Finally, as more third-party service providers adopt document interfaces for hosted services, enterprises can more quickly react to changes in business conditions and customer demand by treating software resources like utilities, using only as much as needed. The flexibility, extensibility, and responsiveness made possible by web services and service oriented business architectures are becoming central to the marketing and branding of platform vendors, consultants, and professional services firms.[18]

However, this is not a book about web services, and while we will discuss them briefly in Section 4.4, "Views of Business Architecture," we will not go into any more detail about web services specifications or technologies. Once again, there are many excellent sources that do that.[19] Instead we focus on how to understand the business context for web services and on the conceptual tasks of analyzing and designing the documents and processes that might ultimately be implemented in service oriented architectures.

1.7 DOCUMENT SPECIFICATIONS AND DOCUMENT ENGINEERING

Where do the specifications for the documents needed by the new business models come from? We propose that they should come from Document Engineering—a new discipline for specifying, designing, and implementing the documents that serve as the interfaces to business processes.

We do not mean to imply that every document or process model needs to be created from scratch—far from it. Just as with every other engineering discipline, Document Engineering emphasizes the reuse of existing specifications, standards, or patterns that work, reducing costs and risks while increasing reliability and interoperability. Useful patterns for Document Engineering include those encoded at the implementation level in the form of XML schema libraries or EDI message standards. Others are at more conceptual levels, in the form of industry reference models for common business processes, or even in more abstract patterns for the organization of activities between businesses such as supply chains, marketplaces, or straight-through processing.

Of course, no existing pattern is likely to be totally suited to the required context of use. So a business must follow an engineering approach that develops models that meet these requirements. And even then it is essential to design and implement the models in a manner that enables its subsequent modification and reuse. In Chapter 7, "The Document Engineering Approach," we introduce Document Engineering as an artifact-focused view of the classical requirements-analyze-design-refine-implement methodology.

1.8 DOCUMENT ENGINEERING— A NEW AND SYNTHETIC DISCIPLINE

The analysis and design methods of Document Engineering have their roots in other fields, primarily information and systems analysis, electronic publishing, business process analysis and business informatics, and user-centered design. Each of these disciplines looks at documents and processes differently, and while each of them is highly effective in some areas, they all have blind spots where their methods and techniques do not work well.

Many people have contrasted narrative types of documents that mostly contain text with transactional types that mostly contain data, but they typically conclude that documents and data cannot be understood with the same terminology, techniques, and tools. For example, with narrative documents, such as those that are traditionally called publications and intended for use by people, analysis and modeling techniques are usually described as document analysis.

In contrast, transactional documents are optimized for use by business applications and differ in other substantial ways from traditional user-oriented publications. The analysis and design methods used for transactional documents are often described as data analysis or object analysis.

Task analysis and related techniques for user-centered design overlap with document and data analysis to identify the intent and information requirements for the tasks people perform.

Finally, while business process analysis can be conducted in domains that involve either or both narrative and transactional document types to set the context for document or data analysis, analyzing the content of the documents required is not its primary goal.

Document Engineering synthesizes the complementary ideas from these separate fields, emphasizing what they have in common and applying it with a unified focus to a broad range of documents and processes.

Document Engineering synthesizes complementary ideas from separate disciplines

This synthesis is essential because narrative and transactional documents are often closely related, either by structural transformation or by business processes. Consider, for example, the close relationship between tax forms and the instructions for filling them out, or between product brochures and purchase orders.

1.8.1 BUSINESS PROCESS ANALYSIS

When an organization wants to improve its effectiveness and efficiency, it often conducts a business process analysis (or reengineering) to acquire a better understanding of what it does and how it does it. Often the goal is to assess business capabilities or competencies and identify processes that enable strategic opportunities or pose strategic risks for the organization.

Business analysis is also required when two organizations consider joint ventures, partnerships, or other strategic relationships that involve doing strategic business with each other. This analysis can determine the compatibility of business processes, customer and supplier relationships, accounting practices, and the day-to-day processes that define the corporate culture of each organization.

Whether within an organization or between them, business analysis usually begins with an abstract or broadly defined perspective on business activities and works from the top down through a hierarchy of business reference models, business processes, collaborations, and transactions. Because the usual goal is increased understanding of how things work from a business perspective, the process analysis often stops at the transactional level where document exchanges are visible. Often no one pays any attention to the design of the documents, their implementation, or the technical capabilities they require to design, develop, and deploy. The analysts may assume that the technology exists or will be created to implement the business decisions that emerge from the high-level process analysis. In any case, it's someone else's problem.

1.8.2 TASK ANALYSIS

Task analysis (or user analysis) is the observation of users performing the tasks or use cases when the application or system must support people and not just other applications. Task analysis identifies the specific steps and information that users need to carry out a task. Task analysis is especially important when few documents or information sources exist because user problems or errors can suggest that important information is missing.

1.8.3 DOCUMENT ANALYSIS

In contrast to the top-down approach of business and task analysis, document analysis is inherently a more bottom-up activity. This is especially true when the motivation for analyzing documents is the narrow goal of transforming existing printed documents or business forms into electronic versions, a process known as document automation. Indeed, when the business driver is a mandate to automate the exchange of documents with a dominant business partner, as Wal-Mart has done with its major suppliers,[20] the paramount goal may be to take an existing manual process and encode it in documents according to process specifications imposed by the partner. Any process or task analysis in this one-sided situation can be viewed as needing little attention or, in the extreme case, as being irrelevant.

A more typical business motivation for document analysis is an enterprise's desire to become more efficient and effective at managing and distributing its documents. A common goal is single-source publishing in which content is managed as reusable information components and assembled as needed in different types of documents or output formats. For example, the same content might appear in product catalogs, printed installation and repair manuals, a CD-ROM E-book, and web pages. Process analysis is important in this situation but still secondary to the need to analyze the existing and potential documents very carefully.

Document analysis emphasizes the study of narrative style documents as artifacts because of the complex ways in which they merge presentation with structural and content components. Making sense of this complexity requires a wide range of document analysis techniques developed by publishing, text processing, information architecture, and graphic design experts. Document analysis is typically carried out with the goal of separating a specification of a document's content and structure from its presentational characteristics such as fonts, type sizes, and formatting used to represent or highlight various structural or content distinctions.

Once this separation is accomplished, a model of the document is created, usually called a schema. The optimal prescriptive schema for a set of documents is one that best satisfies the requirements of current and prospective users for carrying out specific tasks with new instances.

Finally, one or more stylesheets can be used to assign formatting or rendering characteristics in a consistent manner to any document that conforms to this schema.

1.8.4 DATA ANALYSIS

Data analysis has its roots in philosophy and linguistics, but in its current incarnation is a set of techniques used for designing database systems. It is primarily devoted to understanding and describing the properties and relationships between information components or objects.[21] The typical goal of the data analyst is to define conceptual models that organize these components efficiently to support a broad range of contexts or applications. Because their information is often stored as large structured sets of data in databases, data analysis is a key step in database design.

Data analysis methods, like those of document analysis, are bottom-up in the sense that they are applied to existing artifacts. But in contrast to the heterogeneous narrative artifacts for which document analysis techniques are best suited, the more transactional artifacts to which data analysis methods apply best are homogeneous. Transactional documents usually exist as a limitless number of almost identical instances, often produced mechanically to represent some state of an activity or business process. Such documents are extremely regular in their structures and have strongly defined content components, but provide minimal or arbitrary presentation features.

The regularity of transactional information has enabled the development of more formal techniques for modeling its use in information systems. These techniques progressively refine and abstract information models by identifying repeating or recurring structures, removing redundancies and technology constraints, and otherwise creating a more concise and reusable representation of the information components.

1.8.5 UNIFICATION IN DOCUMENT ENGINEERING

We acknowledge that document analysis, data analysis, task analysis, and business analysis come from different intellectual traditions. In addition, the practitioners of these approaches often come from different educational backgrounds, may have little professional communication with each other, and can fail to recognize the overlap in their goals and methods. We cannot, however, just shrug our shoulders and treat documents, data, processes, and user interfaces as separate universes.

For example, the services in a service oriented architecture involve both documents and processes, and their information invariably flows between narrative documents and transactional ones. To make these services work, the businesses or business units involved must implicitly or explicitly reach a common understanding about how their processes should be designed, how they can be deconstructed into service components, the documents and information they exchange, the timing of the exchanges, and the people, organizations, or roles involved. This common understanding must be represented in models of the required documents and processes that are comparable in abstraction and satisfy the requirements for their context of use. This can happen only if document, data, task, and business process analyses can be brought together in a unified approach.

To achieve this common understanding Document Engineering proposes a document-centric reformulation of traditional data analysis. But we recast its formal and specialized methods to apply equally to narrative style documents. At the same time it takes the best practices of document analysis and applies them to understanding information components. Finally it adapts task and business process analysis techniques to identify the requirements and business rules of their context of use.

This synthesis achieves the composite goal of all four analysis methods

This synthesis achieves the composite goal of all four analysis methods—creating formal specifications of information components and classes of documents that contain them, satisfying both the business processes in which they participate and the people who create and use them.

Viewing narrative and transactional types of documents as different points on a continuous Document Type Spectrum (see Figure 1-2) is a fundamental part of the new Document Engineering approach. Likewise, it is essential to make the top-down activities of business process and task analysis meet in the middle with the bottom-up efforts of document and data analysis.

1.9 THE DOCUMENT ENGINEERING APPROACH

Commercial firms, governments, universities, and other types of organizations have different goals and conduct different kinds of Document Engineering projects. But before they undertake any project, each must make a business case that identifies its objectives and the likely return on investment. These management and strategy decisions shape the project's goals and permeate most of its activities, and we could properly view them as the first phase of Document Engineering. But it is difficult to discuss the overarching perspectives of what to do and whether to do it before explaining how to do it, so we'll defer these concerns until Chapter 16, "Management and Strategy in Document Engineering" and not treat making these decisions as a separate phase.

Document Engineering organizes its modeling approach into eight phases as shown in Figure 1-4. The figure shows a path winding its way through the phases of Document Engineering and suggests each phase is equally important. But in practice different phases may get more or less emphasis, depending on the management and strategy decisions that shape the project. Top-down or strategic efforts to align business organization and technology make the activities at the beginning of the path more essential. In contrast, bottom-up and more document-driven projects emphasize the phases near the end of the path.

We briefly outline the approach here and will explain it in detail starting in Chapter 7.

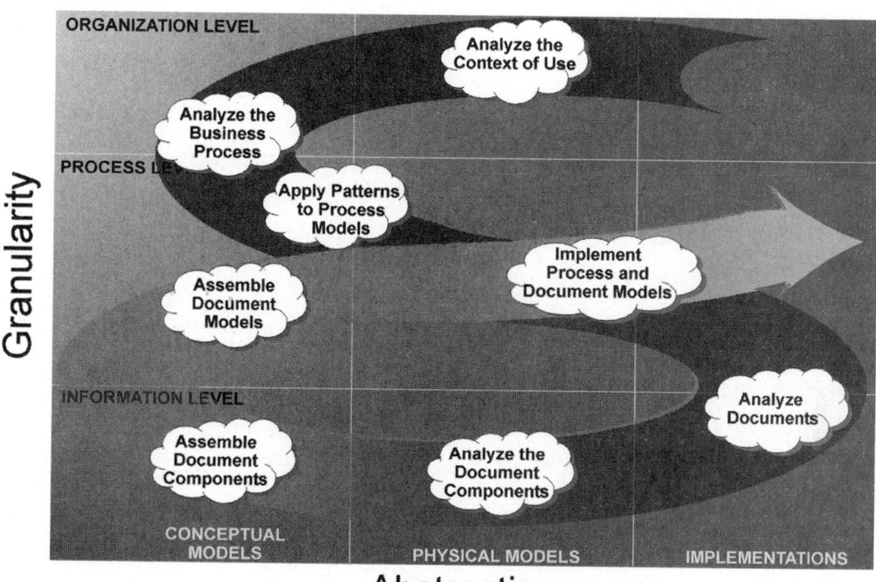

Figure 1-4. The Document Engineering Approach

In the first phase, Analyzing the Context of Use, business and task analysis techniques establish the context for a Document Engineering effort by identifying the requirements and rules that must be satisfied to provide an acceptable solution. Chapter 8, "Analyzing the Context of Use," explains this phase in detail.

In the next two phases—Analyzing Business Processes and Apply Patterns— we apply business process analysis to identify the requirements for the document exchange patterns needed to carry out the desired processes, collaborations, and transactions in the context of use. These patterns identify documents that are needed, but only generally as the payload of the transactions. The complete requirements for the documents can't be determined without analyzing existing documents and other information sources. Chapters 9, "Analyzing Business Processes" and Chapter 10, "Designing Business Processes with Patterns" describe this phase.

The next phase—Document Analysis—involves identifying a representative set of documents or information sources (including people) and analyze them to harvest all the meaningful information components and business rules. Chapter 11, "Analyzing Documents," and Chapter 12, "Analyzing Document Components," present the activities in this phase.

In the Component Assembly phase we develop a document component model that represents structures and their associations and content that define the common rules for the possible contexts of use. Chapter 13, "Assembling Document Components" presents the steps of this phase.

We then move from analysis tasks to designing new document models. In the Document Assembly phase, we use the document component model to create document assembly models for each type of document required. If possible we reuse common or standard patterns to make the documents more general and robust. Chapter 14, "Assembling Document Models" presents this phase.

The new conceptual models we have created for processes and documents can be viewed as specifications for interfaces, for generating code, or configuring an application that creates or exchanges new documents. These models represent substantial investments in understanding a context and capturing its requirements in a rigorous way. Using these models to implement a solution in an automated or semiautomated manner exploits those investments to bridge the gap between knowing what to do and actually doing it.

In the Implementation phase these conceptual models are first encoded using a suitable language to support their physical implementation. This is most likely to be

XML, but because of the technology-neutrality of our approach, the models can be implemented in languages such as UN/EDIFACT or ASN.1 if required.

Chapter 15, " Implementing Models in Applications," begins with a discussion of encoding document and process models and then reviews the issues that arise when applications are based on these models.

Why We Call It Document Engineering

Document engineering may seem a novel formulation, but we couldn't think of a more appropriate combination of terms to describe what this book is about. We want to highlight the creation of tangible end products with economic or social value (that is, documents), and we believe that process is more strongly implied by engineering than any other word.

The closest existing discipline to what we are defining is probably business informatics, which seeks to "combine the modern theory, methods and techniques of business (i.e. organization science) and informatics (i.e. information and computing science) into one integrative programme."[22] This definition certainly covers many of our goals, but it doesn't emphasize the need for conceptual modeling of the documents and processes at a granularity that is implementable, which we believe is fundamental.

In addition, while business informatics seems to have a foothold in Europe and Australia, the phrase is almost invisible in the United States (somewhat surprising given the relative familiarity there of "bioinformatics" and "medical informatics" as names for disciplines and academic departments). An exception is the Business Informatics organization at IBM's Watson Research Center headed by Dr. David Cohn, who wrote the foreword to this book.

A lawyer might say, "I'm a document engineer. I create the documents that govern business relationships, ensuring that the document handles my client's needs while getting agreement from the other side so that there are no surprises later."

A technical writer or information architect might say, "I'm a document engineer. I design documents so that they contain the information my intended audience needs. I follow company and industry practices for content, structure, and presentation to convey the information in an optimal way."

A programmer might say "I'm a software engineer, and in addition to designing programs I design the data structures, objects, or messages that convey or exchange information from one process or program to another. So I'm a document engineer, too."

Our definition of document engineering is mostly consistent with those of the lawyer and the technical writer, with some modest differences. Unlike the documents they create, the documents we want to engineer are likely to be used more often by an application or web service than by a person. And until relatively recently, most programmers were vastly more familiar with fine-grained and tightly coupled application program interfaces than with the coarse-grained, loosely-coupled document exchanges.

But all of us share the goals of conveying the right information in a mutually intelligible and standardized fashion, and we follow a disciplined approach to ensure that the documents are useful and reliable.

Nevertheless, the combination of "document" and "engineering" remains surprisingly novel. If you google the separate words "software" and "document," they have roughly the same number of results, but the results when you search for "software engineering" are orders of magnitude higher than those for "document engineering." That's good. We have a nearly blank slate on which to write, and we're confident that over time our new phrase will start to catch up.

1.10 KEY POINTS IN CHAPTER ONE

- Doing business by document exchange is natural and intuitive.
- We define document in a technology-neutral way as a purposeful and self-contained collection of information.
- We generalize the idea of documents as interfaces for people, to the idea that documents are interfaces to business processes.
- A virtual company created by using services provided by separate businesses can be created more rapidly, more flexibly, and at a lower cost than a traditional one can.
- When businesses exchange documents, they must agree on what the documents mean and on the business processes they expect each other to carry out with them, but they don't need to agree on the technology they use.
- We need to be diligent and precise when we define the meaning of any information produced and consumed by business applications.
- We emphasize XML because it has become the preferred format for representing information in documents but many other representations can be used to define models.
- Document Engineering synthesizes complementary ideas from the separate fields of business process analysis, task analysis, document analysis and data analysis.
- The essence of Document Engineering is analysis and design methods that yield precise specifications for the information and rules that business processes require.

FOUNDATIONS

2 XML Foundations

2.0 INTRODUCTION

The essence of Document Engineering is the analysis and design methods that yield precise models describing the information required by business processes and the rules by which related processes are coordinated and combined. Neither the methods nor the models have anything inherently to do with XML or any other syntax. Nevertheless, XML has rapidly become the preferred format for representing the physical models used to exchange information, so some familiarity with XML is essential.

Document Engineering has nothing inherently to do with XML

If you have a web publishing or programming background you undoubtedly have some experience with XML. But if your expertise is in systems analysis or business, you are probably new to this material. Furthermore, even though XML is an essential technology for Document Engineering, just knowing XML doesn't make you a document engineer because of the interdisciplinary nature of this new field.

The web publishing perspective on XML is incomplete in some respects compared to the perspective we take in Document Engineering. If you work in web publishing, you might view XML as an improvement on HTML that enables greater automation and consistency in formatting. This is true, but just thinking of XML as a smarter HTML misses its central ideas of document types and validation.[1] If you came to web publishing from working in technical documentation with the Standard Generalized Markup Language (SGML), of which XML is a subset, you certainly understand these key ideas. But your experience is likely to be with text-oriented or narrative types of documents, not with the transactional varieties used in applications that exchange documents.

Many programmers see XML as an Internet-friendly, easy-to-parse, and nonproprietary data format to use instead of ad hoc syntaxes for application configuration and inter-process communication. So if you have come to XML as a programmer, you appreciate the need for structured information and strong data typing and validation. But unless you've worked with applications that exchange documents, you probably build software designed for tight coupling with fine-grained APIs. You need to learn to use XML as a format for describing document models that represent entire business events, not just tiny messages. Using coarse-grained documents as interfaces is the key idea behind web services and service oriented architectures.

The syntax isn't what is most important about XML

So this chapter will introduce XML from the perspective of realizing document models and model-based applications. We will emphasize the big ideas of XML and not dwell on XML syntax and schema languages, because there are plenty of excellent books about them that cover them in more depth than this book allows.[2] If you have a business strategy interest in Document Engineering, this chapter will introduce all the XML you need to know. If you want to learn more about XML, this chapter will make it much easier for you to learn it. If you already know XML, this chapter will help you apply that knowledge in new ways.

2.1 FROM HTML TO XML

HTML, the language for publishing web pages, will go down in history as one of the most important inventions of our time. It is surely as significant to the creation and dissemination of information as the printing press. HTML and the web browser transformed the Internet, which had been around for two decades but was used primarily by scientists and engineers, into a ubiquitous publishing platform used by everyone from grade-school children to their grandmothers.

HTML took off because it was nonproprietary and because of the conceptual and technical simplicity of publishing with it. Authors used an ordinary text editor to "mark up" a document by surrounding bits of text with "pointy brackets" and tags whose name suggested their structural role or formatting, and the browser did the rest. These two ideas—using tags to enclose or surround content with labels, and relating the labels to the desired presentation of the content—are easy to understand, even for schoolchildren (see SIDEBAR).

A very simple example of an HTML document and how it appears in a browser is shown in Figure 2-1a and 2-1b.

```
<html>
<body>
 <h1>Center for Document Engineering</h1>
 <h2>Calendar of Events: January 2004</h2>
 <ul>
 <li><p>"Delivering on the Promise of XML"</p>
 <ul>
 <li>Lecture by Eve Maler, Sun Microsystems
      <li>Monday, January 12 4:00-5:00 PM
      <li>South Hall 202
      </ul>
      <p>Eve Maler will introduce the <strong>Universal Business Language
(UBL)</strong> and the <strong>Security Assertion Markup Language (SAML)</strong>
and discuss their XML design features that maximize the sharing of semantics and pro-
cessing even when the core vocabularies are customized.</p>
 </li>
 <li><p>"Adobe's XML Architecture"</p>
 <ul>
 <li>Workshop by Charles Myers, Adobe Systems
      <li>Thursday, January 22 1:00-3:00 PM
      <li>South Hall 110
          </ul>
      <p>Adobe's XML architecture combines the <strong>Portable Document Format
(PDF)</strong> with XML to combine user data and its visual presentation and data into
a common framework.
 </p>
 </li>
 </ul>
 </body>
</html>
```

Figure 2-1a. A Calendar Event in HTML

Center for Document Engineering

Calendar of Events: January 2004

- "Delivering on the Promise of XML"
  - Lecture by Eve Maler, Sun Microsystems
  - Monday, January 12 4:00-5:00 PM
  - South Hall 202

  Eve Maler will introduce the **Universal Business Language (UBL)** and the **Security Assertion Markup Language (SAML)**, both from OASIS, and discuss their XML design features that maximize the sharing of semantics and processing even when the core vocabularies are customized.

- "Adobe's XML Architecture"
  - Workshop by Charles Myers, Adobe Systems
  - Thursday, January 22 1:00-3:00 PM
  - South Hall 110

  Adobe's XML architecture combines the **Portable Document Format (PDF)** with XML to combine user data and its visual presentation and data into a common framework. This combination gives enterprises an extremely flexible method for creating and extending business processes that efficiently integrate into an organization's existing systems.

Figure 2-1b A Calendar Event in HTML viewed with a Browser

A Primer On Markup Syntax

Markup is the repertoire of characters that takes a flat or undifferentiated stream of text and turns it into a set of elements, which consist of paired text labels and the content they surround or contain. The paired text labels, called the open (or start) tag and close (or end) tag, are distinguished from the text being marked up because they are enclosed by delimiters, the most common of which are the "pointy brackets."

In the open tag, the "<" bracket is immediately followed by the element's name, perhaps one or more element properties or attributes, and the ">" bracket, which indicates the end of the tag. In attribute-value pairs the value must be surrounded by quotes. The order of attributes is not significant.

After the open tag, the element can contain ordinary text content or other elements in an order that is significant, so if the order in which information appears must be preserved, that must be conveyed by using elements.

For example, consider the element: <Event type="Lecture"> in Figure 2-2.

<Event> is the open tag, type is an attribute, and Lecture is the attribute value. The corresponding close tag </Event> follows after the element's content, which consists of elements for <Title>, <Description>, <Speaker>, <DateTime>, and <Location>. These are called the element's children.

An element can also contain other paired delimiters that mark up some enclosed text to be treated in some special way. The special delimiter sequences can:

- allow for embedded comments (<!– this example is Figure 2-2 in the Document Engineering book –>),
- suppress the interpretation of markup characters (<![CDATA <Event type="Lecture">]]>) so that delimiters can be treated as text content, or
- pass processing instructions to an application (<?xml-stylesheet type="text/xsl" href="calendar.xsl" ?>).

The close tag that follows all the element's children consists of the "<" bracket and a slash (/) followed by the element's name and the ">" bracket. If an element has no children, it is known as empty and the close tag can be omitted if a special syntax is used for the open tag (e.g. <Title/>).

The top-level element in a document is called the document element or root element; it contains or encloses all the other elements, which can be nested as deep as necessary to represent a semantic or structural hierarchy.

The earliest versions of HTML had about a dozen tags, mostly structural ones for describing parts of a document, and most of the earliest browsers had fixed or hard-wired display rules that determined the arrangement of the text, font, size, and everything else.

2.1.1 THE BROWSER WAR

Unfortunately HTML didn't stay this simple for very long. After the Mosaic browser introduced the Web to the masses in 1993, people wanted more control over the appearance and behavior of web pages. This led to the browser wars of the mid-1990s as Netscape and Microsoft added proprietary tags and scripting languages to HTML that worked only in their browsers.[3] The elegant and easily understood idea of fixed mapping between a limited markup vocabulary and display couldn't survive this transformation of the Web into a competitive battlefield.

The idea of a standard and simple HTML vocabulary didn't survive the browser wars

Simple browser displays with default formatting wouldn't enable businesses to create websites whose appearance could differentiate themselves and their products. But until the creation of the World Wide Web Consortium (W3C) in 1995, there was no control over the evolution of HTML and other technical standards for the Web. Browser vendors complied with customer demand and devised tags that enabled rich graphical sites with precise control of text display, blinking text, and spinning corporate logos.[4]

In 1997, the first W3C version of the Cascading Style Sheet[5] (CSS) recommendation emerged, which deprecated the formatting excesses of the proprietary HTML dialects and encouraged more systematic and reusable formatting by using rules that assigned sets of formatting properties to HTML element types.

2.1.2 FROM THE WEB FOR EYES TO THE WEB FOR COMPUTERS

A more fundamental problem with HTML emerged as the Web was transformed into a platform for commerce. Doing business on the Web requires more than just a highly branded website with attractive product catalogs. Businesses need to have both the "Web for eyes" that draws customers to their sites and a "Web for computers" that can encode product information, orders, invoices, payments, and other business documents in ways that can be processed by business applications. For this latter task HTML was fundamentally inappropriate.

Some of HTML's limitations for business applications were inevitable given a tag set heavy on headings, lists, and links. There were no tags for marking up information as product names, item numbers, prices, quantities, and so on to give it a business meaning.

HTML has no tags for marking up business meaning

Clever programmers tried to work around this limited markup vocabulary with code that used whatever markup was available to extract the business information from web pages. For example, a program might rely on the fact that in some web catalog the first item in a list was a product name, the second its item number, and the third the retail price. But programs like these are tedious to write and difficult to maintain; if the layout of the catalog changed, for example, what the program thought was the price of a pair of shoes might actually be the item number.

But the problem for business posed by HTML isn't just how to work around an inadequate set of element types. Using the Web as a business platform radically changes the problem to be solved by the markup language from presentational formatting to semantic modeling, that is, describing business entities and processes in ways that can be understood by business applications. No single vocabulary—HTML or otherwise—can ever be complete enough to describe information with enough semantic precision for all such applications.

No single vocabulary can have enough semantic precision for all applications

2.2 XML'S BIG IDEAS

What the world needed was a new approach to using tags to mark up documents. Instead of a fixed set of element types, we needed way to define whatever set of element types was required for the business application that would use them. We needed an extensible markup language.

There are five big ideas relating to XML that we'll introduce in the following sections:

- XML is extensible: it enables the creation of new sets of tags for domain-specific content.
- XML encodes content as well as presentation formatting; content and its presentation are kept separate.
- XML schemas define models of document types.
- XML schemas enable XML document instances to be validated.

- XML is often produced by converting non-XML information; and XML documents are often transformed to meet the requirements of specific implementations.

2.3 CREATION OF NEW SETS OF TAGS FOR DOMAIN-SPECIFIC CONTENT

Figure 2-2 shows a simple XML document in which the text content is nearly identical to that of the HTML document in Figure 2-1.

```
<?xml version="1.0" encoding="UTF-8"?>
<?xml-stylesheet type="text/xsl" href="calendar.xsl" ?>
<Calendar>
    <Organization>Center for Document Engineering</Organization>
    <TimePeriod>January 2004</TimePeriod>
    <Events>
    <Event type="Lecture">
            <Title>Delivering on the Promise of XML</Title>
            <Description>Eve Maler will introduce the <Keyword>Universal Business
Language (UBL)</Keyword> and the <Keyword>Security Assertion Markup Language
(SAML)</Keyword> and discuss their XML design features that maximize the sharing of
semantics and processing even when the core vocabularies are
customized.</Description>
            <Speaker>
                <Name>Eve Maler</Name>
                <Affiliation>Sun Microsystems</Affiliation>
            </Speaker>
            <DateTime>Monday, January 12 4:00-5:00 PM</DateTime>
            <Location>South Hall 202</Location>
    </Event>
    <Event type="Workshop">
            <Title>Adobe's XML Architecture</Title>
            <Description>Adobe's XML architecture combines the <Keyword>Portable
            Document Format (PDF)</Keyword> with XML to combine user data and its
            visual presentation and data into a common framework.
            </Description>
```

```
            <Speaker>
                <Name>Charles Myers</Name>
                <Affiliation>Adobe Systems</Affiliation>
            </Speaker>
            <DateTime>Thursday, January 22 1:00-3:00 PM</DateTime>
            <Location>South Hall 110</Location>
    </Event>
    </Events>
</Calendar>
```

Figure 2-2 Simple XML Document

At first glance, this XML document doesn't look that different from the HTML one. Both XML and HTML use the same markup syntax, except for the declaration at the start of the XML document that announces that it should be treated as XML and the processing instruction that specifies a stylesheet.

The XML specification is more precise about syntax than HTML is, but most of the differences between HTML and XML enforce the best practices in HTML anyway, such as case-sensitive names and including close tags even when they can be inferred by the presence of the next open tag (HTML allows them to be omitted; see the <li> items in Figure 2-1a). So it isn't syntax that distinguishes HTML and XML.

What matters is that a document that starts with an <html> tag has a fixed set of tags that it might contain. In contrast, XML is extensible: there is essentially no limit to the element types an XML document can contain, and the elements are often named to suggest the meaning of the content. In Figure 2-2 the first open tag is <Calendar>, and in the container formed by this tag and its associated close tag of </Calendar> we can see elements for <Organization>, <TimePeriod>, and <Event>. Inside each event element we see the specific types of content that define an event. Software that displays calendars or searches for events can easily extract the information it needs.

But the difference between HTML and XML isn't just that the former has a fixed set of presentational structure and formatting tags while the latter allows an unlimited set of content-oriented ones. The difference is that HTML is a specific language, a fixed set of element types plus the grammar or rules that govern where in a document each type of element can occur.

XML defines the rules by which specific markup languages are created

XML, on the other hand, is a metalanguage. It defines the rules by which specific XML markup languages are created but says nothing about what element types they use. These specific XML languages are also called XML vocabularies or XML applications.[6] For example, XHTML is an XML vocabulary that recasts HTML in XML syntax to make it more modular and to more rigorously separate content and presentation. And UBL, the Universal Business Language, is an XML vocabulary for business documents.

So while the XML document in Figure 2-2 might be an instance of an XML-defined markup language for describing event calendars, other types of documents like a Shakespeare play or a purchase order would be encoded using completely different sets of elements. Some element types, of course, like <Title>, <Name>, and <Location> are useful in many different types of documents, not just in event calendars.

This last observation has two crucial implications. If common elements are reused, then XML documents can contain element types from more than one XML vocabulary. But a tag name like <Title> might be part of a vocabulary for books, a deed of ownership, or honorifics for a person, so we need some syntactic mechanism for distinguishing vocabularies from each other. We'll defer this problem until Section 2.5.4 when we discuss XML schemas.

2.4 SEPARATION OF CONTENT AND PRESENTATION

Every document—whether it is an event calendar, purchase order, Shakespearean play, chemistry text, or tax form—contains a variety of types of meaningful information. When we use XML tags to encode this meaning, we can label parts of the document to distinguish different types of content: <Speaker>, <Name>, <Address>, <Personae>, <Scene>, <Speech>, <Molecule>, <Income>, and so forth. These are purely conceptual distinctions, and these bits of content don't have any inherent formatting or presentation associated with them.

It is only when XML documents are printed, displayed, spoken, or otherwise rendered to communicate with people that formatting or presentational information, such as page numbers, type fonts and sizes, color, indentation, column organization, underlining, pitch, and intonation, needs to be added. These presentational devices can assist in understanding the content but generally don't carry much content-specific meaning.

Of course there are important conventions and correlations between presentation and meaning: large type implies more importance than small type, red may signal a warning, line breaks in poems support meter, and so on. We celebrate graphic designers, artists, and book designers when they exploit or violate these conventions in clever ways. But most presentational decisions are more arbitrary. For example, the typeface in which this book is printed has little or no effect on its meaning. We will discuss these issues in more detail in Chapter 12, "Analyzing Document Components."

Sometimes content and presentation are bound together or confounded, often implicitly, as with HTML or with word processors that use style sheets or formatting templates to apply formatting to otherwise unlabeled information components. Cascading style sheets have reduced the implicitness and ad hoc-ery of HTML formatting, but they weren't designed to separate content and presentation. They were just a way to regain some of the core simplicity of HTML by delegating more sophisticated format control to a separate style processor in the browser.[7]

In XML the separation of content and presentation is inherent and desirable

In XML the separation of content and presentation is inherent and desirable. If an XML document can contain any type of element it needs to describe its content, there is no way that a browser can know in advance what it means or how to display it. Most web browsers render an XML document with indentation that corresponds to the hierarchical structure created by its tags, but this display might not be optimal or even appropriate for the semantics embodied in the content. It is almost always necessary to apply to the XML document a transformation or stylesheet that creates HTML or some other presentation-oriented vocabulary to the XML information. Sometimes a stylesheet is then also applied to the transformed HTML to optimize its presentation.

The extra step needed to display an XML document isn't a bug, but a feature. It makes a requirement out of what should be a good habit to practice in any case, that of paying explicit attention to the relationship between content and presentation. It emphasizes the idea that XML elements should be used to encode conceptual distinctions in a presentation-independent manner to enable the reuse and repurposing of information for different contexts or implementations.

Even if an XML document contains elements with the same name as HTML ones that browsers readily display, like <h1> or <p> or <li>, they don't get displayed because no presentation is ever assigned by default. XML elements contain content, pure and simple. So it is misleading and pointless to use element names that assume otherwise.

XML's separation of content and presentation also reinforces and rewards specialization in skills between information modeling and user interface or graphic design. User interface and graphic design skills are useful in Document Engineering, but good information modeling skills are essential.

2.5 DEFINITION OF DOCUMENT TYPES

Documents are ubiquitous. All documents share the idea that they are purposeful representations and organizations of information, but they exhibit great variety. On any given day we encounter dozens of different types of documents.[8] We might start the day with a morning newspaper, go on to deal with reports, emails, catalogs, reference books, calendars, or lectures, and end up with a restaurant menu, murder mystery, TV program guide, or MP3 playlist.

It is easy to distinguish a dictionary from an invoice, a newspaper from a novel, or a restaurant menu from a collection of poems, because each document follows a characteristic structural pattern to arrange types of content unlikely to be found in the other. Because these types of document are so different, even a simple list of the varieties of content in each document would accurately classify any given instance of the document.

This intuitive notion of models of different types of documents is very useful. It explains why we have had standard business forms for centuries, style guides for authors, national and international standards for electronic business messages, templates in word processors and spreadsheets, and various other ways of describing expectations about content and its arrangement in documents.

2.5.1 DOCUMENTS AS IMPLEMENTATION MODELS

In the domain of Document Engineering, we need to define models of different types of documents in a rigorous and unambiguous way so that we can automate their process or exchange within or between applications. We also want to use their formal definitions to generate and drive some of the software needed to process the documents. Implementations or instances of these document models enable software to locate and extract the information needed to connect related document exchanges that combine to form supply chains, auctions, marketplaces, and other business patterns.

XML was designed to give the intuitive idea of a document model a more physical, formal foundation.[9] XML gives us syntactic mechanisms that capture the semantic distinctions between documents in terms of the sets of elements and attributes used to encode their content and the rules that govern their occurrence and organization. Two semantically related document models like purchase order and invoice may share elements from a common library or subset, but they are distinguished by elements that occur only in one of them or that have different possible values in each. So we use different vocabularies to mark up the content of purchase orders and of invoices.

XML can realize document models suitable for implementation in applications

XML's ease of use, its expressive power, and its processability have made it attractive for Document Engineering because it can realize document models suitable for implementation in applications.[10] But what really matters is the quality of the analysis and design that gets represented in conceptual models before we encode them in XML vocabularies. XML is a convenient syntax for encoding the models, but XML per se doesn't help us create good models, and many people have found it a convenient syntax for creating poor ones. We'll return to this problem of the quality of document models in Chapter 6, and starting in Chapter 7 we'll introduce the methods and technologies of Document Engineering to explain how to create good ones.

2.5.2 XML SCHEMAS

The formal description of a document model in XML goes by various names, but it is most useful for our introduction here to call it the XML schema. Simply put, an XML schema defines the possible types of content in a document and the rules that govern the structure and values of that content.

Every XML schema contains definitions of element types. But as we've pointed out, because many types of elements occur in more than one type of document (<Title>, <Name>, <Date>, and so on), a list of legal element types is often not sufficient to distinguish different types of documents. Furthermore, even though the name of an element type can suggest what it means, it is not self-describing.[11] An XML schema also specifies the attributes that can be associated with elements, but they're not self-describing either. So if the full meaning of an element isn't conveyed by its name, where is it conveyed?

The meaning of elements is represented in an XML schema through the constraints or rules that govern the structural arrangement of elements and the values that elements and attributes can have. We call these constraints business rules.

The term, business rule, like model and pattern and other fundamental concepts of Document Engineering, has numerous incompatible or overloaded definitions.[12] Everyone agrees that a business rule expresses a constraint about some aspect of the data or processes used by a business. Furthermore, everyone agrees that it is desirable to represent rules independently from the generic aspects of applications instead of scattering them into multiple layers of application software. But there is little agreement about how to classify business rules and how to translate them from expressions of requirements into implemented systems. We'll present a classification scheme for business rules in Chapter 8, and we'll stress the roles they play in developing an adequate conceptual model of the documents and process in some specified business context. For now we'll focus on the kinds of business rules that can be represented in XML schemas.

The kinds of rules expressed in XML element definitions include containment relationships ("a dictionary entry consists of a word, a pronunciation, and a definition"); sequence and cardinality relationships ("the abstract must be followed by one or more chapters and possibly one or more appendixes"), choices ("the location must be a street address or a pair of latitude and longitude coordinates"), and recursion ("the bill of materials is a list of parts, each of which may consist of a list of parts"). Of course, these kinds of rules are not mutually exclusive; we can represent a containment rule that defines a legal sequence of elements, each of which consists of a choice, one option of which is recursive.

There is often a gap between the conceptual model and what can be described in XML

The document model of a purchase order might include business rules like "the quantity ordered must be an integer less than 1,000," "the unit price must be expressed as a number with two decimal digits," or the "the country code must be one of those contained in ISO 3166." It would be highly desirable to encode these rules in the XML schema that implements the model of a purchase order as constraints on the values of elements or attributes. But as we'll see in the next section, there is often a gap between the conceptual document model and what can be described in XML.

2.5.3 SCHEMA LANGUAGES

There are currently several XML schema languages that differ substantially in how completely they can express the business rules that underlie a document's model. Which schema language to use is influenced by where the document lies on the Document Type Spectrum (see Figure 1-3), because that determines what aspects of the model are most important to express (see SIDEBAR).

Understanding XML Schemas by Analogy

To explain XML schemas it may help to make the analogy to relational database schemas, which describe the database content in terms of possible field values, relationships between fields in tables, and constraints between tables. An XML schema could describe the semantics of a class of documents so that different types of content can be identified and extracted as if they were in a document database. An XML schema can ensure that information exported from a database or other application is assembled as a valid document.

Likewise, we can make an analogy between XML schemas and class definitions in a modern programming language. A class is a template that specifies the meaning of the variables used by an object in terms of their data types or possible values, and classes can be related to each other by association, specialization or generalization. An XML schema might specify the required data types for document content, and might also express relationships between types of document content. This equivalence enables XML schemas to be treated just like classes to guide the creation of objects, a process usually called data binding. This view of XML schemas is appropriate for transactional documents and also very useful when describing web forms and other information-intensive user interfaces.

Finally, we can say that an XML schema defines a vocabulary for a document model expressed with a formal grammar. A grammar for any language is a system consisting of a finite set of tokens and a finite set of rewrite rules that generate all the valid sequences or sentences of those tokens. For an XML schema the tokens are the elements and attributes and the sentences are the document instances. This linguistic perspective on XML schemas fits very well for narrative documents and less well for transactional ones.

The first XML schema language was Document Type Definition (DTD), a legacy of XML's SGML heritage. Because of SGML's origins in technical publishing, DTDs were designed to represent the structural properties of documents, but they treat most data as just text and can't represent meaningful information models.

DTDs have a very simple and compact syntax, but this syntax is not itself XML. DTDs are sufficient for describing models of narrative document types like newspapers, dictionaries, and reports, whose content is primarily text and intended for use by people. DTDs can also easily express mixed content models in which character data can contain "in-line" elements, a very common requirement in narrative documents. For example, a product description is text that can contain glossary terms, company names, or URLs, all of which would be tagged as elements mixed in with the text of the product description.

But as we move on the Document Type Spectrum toward the transactional or data-centric document types that are primarily used by business applications, structural description alone captures fewer of the most important aspects of the document's content. For example, constraints on data values are crucial.

For transactional document types the most useful schema language is the one recommended by the W3C called XSD or XML Schema (with a capital S). XML Schema was developed to meet a much broader and more computer-oriented set of requirements than DTDs were. XML Schema documents are encoded using XML syntax and overcome most of the limitations of DTDs. The XML Schema language includes all the basic data types common in programming languages and databases (string, Boolean, integer, floating point, and so on), as well as mechanisms for deriving new data types. For example, an XML Schema schema can define a Student as a specialization of a Person type with additional required elements, or an alphanumeric PartNumber as a string whose values are restricted using regular expressions.

An extremely important facility in XML Schema is its support for namespaces, a mechanism for distinguishing XML vocabularies so that a schema can reuse definitions while avoiding conflicts between elements with the same name that mean different things (as we suggested at the end of Section 2.3, <Title> might be part of a vocabulary for books, legal documents, or honorifics for a person). A prefix associated with each namespace can be attached to elements in document instances, so that <book:Title>, <legal:Title>, and <honorific:Title> aren't confused. Using a namespace to identify the additional elements needed to customize a standard vocabulary maintains the integrity of the base vocabulary.

Needless to say, the greater expressiveness and extensibility of XSD comes with substantially more complexity, as we can see in Figures 2-3a and 2-3b, which compare a DTD and XSD for the same document model, that of a simple calendar like the example in Figure 2-2.

```
<?xml version="1.0" encoding="UTF-8"?>
<!-- DTD for simple calendar -->
<!-- calendar metadata -->

<!ELEMENT Calendar (Organization, TimePeriod, Events)>
<!ELEMENT Organization (#PCDATA)>
<!ELEMENT TimePeriod (#PCDATA)>

<!-- a calendar is a list of events -->
<!ELEMENT Events (Event+)>

<!-- definition of each event, optional Event Type attribute -->
<!ELEMENT Event (Title, Description?, Speaker?, DateTime, Location)>
<!ATTLIST Event
    type (Lecture | Workshop) #IMPLIED>

<!ELEMENT Title (#PCDATA)>

<!-- mixed content definition to allow for keywords in Description -->
<!ELEMENT Description (#PCDATA | Keyword)*>

<!ELEMENT Keyword (#PCDATA)>
<!ELEMENT Speaker (Name, Affiliation)>
<!ELEMENT Name (#PCDATA)>
<!ELEMENT Affiliation (#PCDATA)>
<!ELEMENT DateTime (#PCDATA)>
<!ELEMENT Location (#PCDATA)>
```

Figure 2-3a. DTD for a Simple Calendar

The DTD for a simple calendar is very compact because of the use of of +, ?, and * to represent occurrence constraints. Commas separate the members of a sequence, and the vertical bar distinguishes choices. Every element has a declared data type of "PCDATA" (parsed character data), which means a string of text in DTD.

In contrast, the XSD for the simple calendar in Figure 2-3b is much more verbose than the DTD. Occurrence constraints, sequences, and choices are all expressed explicitly. It is easy to get lost in embedded definitions.[14] But the syntax is XML.

```
<?xml version="1.0" encoding="UTF-8"?>
<xs:schema xmlns:xs="http://www.w3.org/2001/XMLSchema"
elementFormDefault="qualified">
<!-- XSD Schema for Calendar -->
<xs:element name="Calendar">
<xs:complexType>
 <xs:sequence>
   <xs:element name="Organization" type="xs:string"/>
   <xs:element name="TimePeriod" type="xs:string"/>
<!-- Definition of Event as Sequence of Other Elements -->
   <xs:element name="Events">
   <xs:complexType>
      <xs:sequence>
        <xs:element name="Event" maxOccurs="unbounded">
        <xs:complexType>
           <xs:sequence>
             <xs:element name="Title" type="xs:string"/>
             <xs:element name="Description" minOccurs="0">
               <xs:complexType mixed="true">
                 <xs:choice minOccurs="0" <MaxOccurs="unbounded">
               <xs:element name="Keyword" type="xs:string"/>
                 </xs:choice>
               </xs:complexType>
               </xs:element>
              <xs:element name="Speaker" minOccurs="0">
           <xs:complexType>
            <xs:sequence>
              <xs:element name="Name" type="xs:string"/>
              <xs:element name="Affiliation" type="xs:string"/>
           </xs:sequence>
               </xs:complexType>
               </xs:element>
              <xs:element name="DateTime" type="xs:string"/>
```

```
            <xs:element name="Location" type="xs:string"/>
        </xs:sequence>
    <xs:attribute name="type">
    <xs:simpleType>
        <xs:restriction base="xs:NMTOKEN">
        <xs:enumeration value="Lecture"/>
        <xs:enumeration value="Workshop"/>
        </xs:restriction>
    </xs:simpleType>
    </xs:attribute>
  </xs:complexType>
  </xs:element>
  </xs:sequence>
</xs:complexType>
</xs:element>
</xs:sequence>
</xs:complexType>
</xs:element>
</xs:schema>
```

Figure 2-3b. XML Schema for a Simple Calendar

2.5.4 RULES THAT SCHEMA LANGUAGES CAN'T REPRESENT

Every XML schema language makes tradeoffs that determine the range of document models it can realize, the ease with it defines them, and how readily it can reuse a model or parts of models in more than one schema. For example, even though XML Schema is a powerful schema language, it isn't capable of expressing dependency constraints on element content ("the start time for a calendar event must be earlier than the end time" or "if the total is greater than $1,000 the purchase order requires an authorization code"), even though these may be important rules for the context of use.

Every XML schema language makes tradeoffs

Rules that concern multiple values in a document are easy to express using XML constraint based languages such as Schematron.[15] This uses the XPath language for describing parts of XML documents to make Boolean assertions based on their content. But the tradeoff here is that this approach makes Schematron incapable of representing structural rules except in very tedious ways.

Another grammar based schema language called RELAX NG[16] is widely regarded by experts as more elegant and simpler than XML Schema, but with about the same expressive power. However, because it wasn't developed by the W3C, RELAX NG isn't as widely supported by vendors of XML software.

Obviously no schema language is perfect at encoding all models in XML. But that's probably a good thing, because it reinforces our message that analysis and modeling skills are more fundamental to Document Engineering than XML is.

2.6 VALIDATION

An XML schema communicates the model of a document type to people or applications that need to create or receive document instances. In this sense the XML schema is a contract that defines the rules that any documents must follow. Validation is the process of testing whether an XML document follows the rules defined in an associated schema. A document that follows or satisfies the schema is said to be valid.

For XML documents described by simple DTDs the schema can be carried along with the document content in its prolog, but it is far more common for an XML document to refer to an external schema. This indirect binding is more efficient and flexible than including the schema in the document, because it allows a single schema definition to be reused by all documents of the same type. And of course, if two parties in an ongoing business relationship are exchanging documents with each other, they've already come to terms about the schemas that define what they send and receive. Once the business process is established, there is no need to send schemas with the documents.

A person who understands XML schemas and syntax can examine an XML instance document and validate by eye. But validation is most often carried out by a validating parser embedded in an XML-aware text editor, application server, integration tool, or other software that processes XML. In an XML-aware text editor, an XML schema can speed the creation of documents by inserting required tags and by dynamically controlling the structure of menus or selectors to ensure that only valid documents are created.

A much weaker criterion of quality checking for XML documents is called well-formedness and requires that the XML document meets some minimal syntactic constraints, such as having exactly one root element and having matching start and end tags that don't overlap. An XML document that isn't even well-formed will be rejected by an XML parser and not passed on for further processing.

Even an XML document that is well-formed but that fails some constraint defined in its associated schema might still be acceptable. For example, it would be a good business practice to try to process a purchase order from a potential customer even if it omitted the required postal code in the shipping address.

A document without a schema is just a bag of tags

On the other hand, a well-formed but schema-less document is little more than a bag of tags whose meanings are undefined. It makes little business sense to invent a set of tags and not bother to formally define them with a schema, and it would be risky to attempt to process such documents. Suppose a document from a potential customer begins with a <PurchaseOrder> tag, but other tags inside it contain instructions to empty out a firm's bank account or crash its systems. If that document claimed to conform to the firm's schema for purchase orders we'd be able to tell that it didn't.

Nevertheless, because of the unavoidable limitations in every XML schema language, it is impossible to capture every rule and requirement of a conceptual document model. So even a strong claim that a document is valid should always be understood to mean "with respect to the class of constraints that the schema language being used is capable of encoding." Knowing that a piece of data is in its expected location and of the required data type doesn't mean that it is correct.

Ultimately how much validation is necessary in any situation is a separate question from how much validation power is inherent in the schema language. What matters the most is having a common intention between the producer and consumer of an XML document. Imagine an XML document used by a single software program for the sole purpose of saving its private data. If the file is saved correctly, the information will be valid when that software next uses it. Validation is hardly necessary. At the other extreme, suppose an XML document arrives from a company halfway around the world with which a firm has no prior business relationship. Validation against its assigned schema is irrelevant. The firm would be wise to validate the document against expected data requirements before letting it enter their business application. This is especially important in situations where accepting the document creates a legally-binding commitment between the sender and recipient of the document.

2.7 CONVERSION AND TRANSFORMATION

XML is often produced by converting non-XML information, and XML documents are often transformed to meet the requirements of other contexts or implementations. Conversion to XML and transformation from XML might seem like two views of the same activity, but while related they differ in many respects so we'll discuss them separately. The issues and problems that arise in conversion and transformation are also shaped by where the source and target documents lie on the Document Type Spectrum (see Figure 1-3); the greater semantic precision in transactional documents makes them easier to convert to or transform, regardless of the source or target syntax.

2.7.1 CONVERSION TO XML

A common reason for converting information to XML is to facilitate a single-source publishing strategy in which content is created once and then reused many times. Reuse can involve the same content included in all the instances of a document, as might be the case for a copyright notice, standard terms and conditions, or similar boilerplate text. A variant of single-source publishing is syndication, in which a single source of content is simultaneously published or distributed for reuse in other contexts. Many websites and web publishers convert syndicated news, blogs, or other time-sensitive content to an XML vocabulary called the RDF Site Summary (RSS).

A different perspective on reuse involves extracting or formatting the same piece of content in many different ways to create different documents. This form of reuse is often called repurposing. An example would be using some of the same information in a system's product documentation, a troubleshooting guide, and training materials.

Another important reason for converting information to XML is to extract information from a database, ERP system, or legacy application primarily used inside an enterprise to enable Internet-based transactions with customers or business partners. A similar type of conversion takes place in many EDI implementations, where business-to-business document exchanges in supply chains move to XML to make the content easier to process.[17]

The conversion of information to XML can be completely automated if the information source is well structured with explicit semantics and the structure and semantics are rigorously described with a schema. This description fits databases and some of the file formats used by ERP systems and other enterprise applications. This doesn't mean that mapping between the non-XML format and the target XML document type is automatic. Only that once it is in place, we can create software that converts one into the other.

The benefits of converting to XML are more compelling when information is encoded in less structured or semantically expressive formats such as ASCII, RTF, UN/EDIFACT, ANSI ASC X12, or HTML that don't embody XML's big ideas. But it's a lot of work to design an appropriate XML vocabulary and then apply markup correctly to the content.

If authors follow structure and style standards when they create office documents or web pages, some of the conversion effort can be automated by exploiting the implicit relationships between formatting styles or HTML tags and the target XML vocabulary. But few authors have this much discipline, so conversion usually requires expensive and tedious work by people who understand the content to supply the missing meaning.

The process of adding value to information by converting it to XML is often called up translation to express the work it takes to give XML the informational equivalent of potential energy. Once information is in XML syntax its greater potential energy makes it easy and straightforward to create any other format, so naturally the transformation from XML to a non-XML format is often called down translation. These relationships between XML and other formats are illustrated in Figure 2-4.

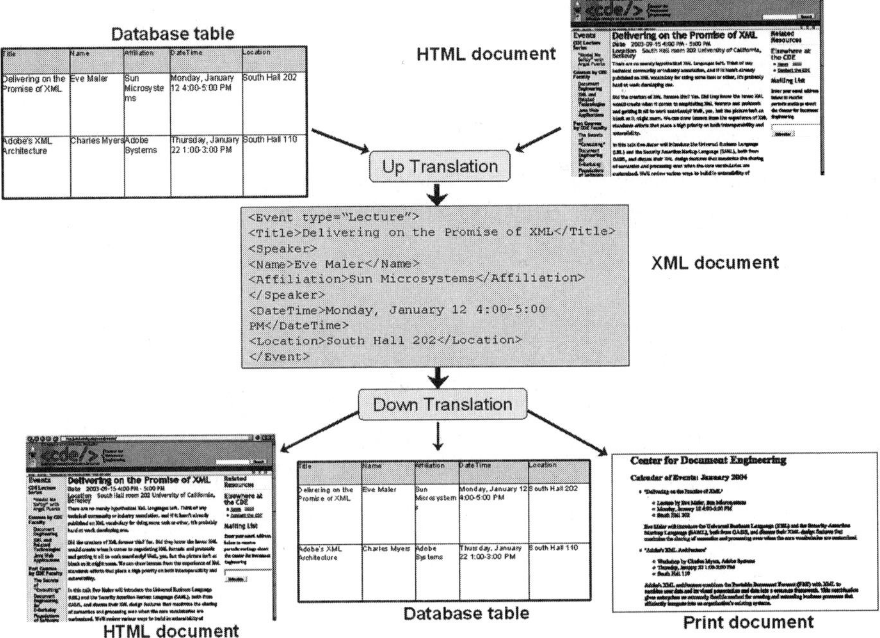

Figure 2-4. Up- and Down-Translation with XML

A corollary here is that if we anticipate that information we are about to create will someday need to be represented in XML, it is more cost-effective to create and manage it as XML and then down-translate to whatever other formats we need in the short term.

2.7.2 TRANSFORMATION FROM XML

XML schemas and documents are often transformed to meet the requirements of other contexts or implementations. Transforming an XML document involves selecting, reordering, or restructuring its content. Transforming an XML document so that it conforms to a different XML schema is often followed by down-translation to a non-XML format, for example by EDI gateway applications.

Transformation reuses or amortizes the investment made to encode information in XML in the first place. Put another way, when we create XML schemas and documents, we should design them expecting to transform them to preserve and extend their value.

As we said earlier, with XML the separation of content and presentation is both inherent and desirable. Thus it is often necessary to transform or down-translate XML to HTML so that it can be viewed in a web browser. The process of applying a presentation to an XML document is sometimes called styling but it is more useful to conceive of applying a style as two separate processes of transformation and formatting. This way of thinking lines up conceptually with two complementary W3C Recommendations: XSLT, the Extensible Stylesheet Language for Transformation, and XSL FO, the Extensible Stylesheet Language Formatting Objects.

XSLT is an XML-aware functional programming language that operates on logical "node sets" derived from the element and attribute structure of XML documents. XSLT has the usual constructs for logical flow of control like conditional, loops, and switches. What makes it most useful for transforming XML are its XPath facilities for expressing and matching patterns in the logical XML structures so that arbitrary trees or subtrees can be selected and rearranged. This is the approach used by the Schematron schema language.

XSL FO, often a target vocabulary of an XSLT transform, is designed for typesetting-quality control of printed XML output. An XSLT transform from XML to HTML can be as simple as a set of rules that assign an HTML tag to each XML element type, defaulting all presentation control to the browser. An XSLT transformation like this can be used to enforce presentation standards for all instances of a document. Figure 2-5 shows a simple XSLT program that transforms the XML calendar instance in Figure 2-2 to HTML to reproduce the appearance of the HTML calendar shown in Figure 2-1b. The processing instruction in the second line of the Figure 2-2 instance associates the XSLT program (calling it "calendar.xsl") with the instance.

```
<?xml version="1.0"?>
<xsl:stylesheet version="1.0" xmlns:xsl="http://www.w3.org/1999/XSL/Transform">
<xsl:template match="Calendar">
    <html>
    <head>
        <title><xsl:value-of select="/Calendar/Organization"/><xsl:text>
</xsl:text><xsl:value-of select="/Calendar/TimePeriod"/><xsl:text>
</xsl:text>Calendar</title>
    </head>
    <body>
        <h1><xsl:value-of select="/Calendar/Organization"/></h1>
        <h2>Calendar of Events: <xsl:value-of select="/Calendar/TimePeriod"/></h2>
        <xsl:apply-templates select="Events"/>
    </body>
    </html>
</xsl:template>
<xsl:template match="Events">
    <xsl:for-each select="Event">
        <ul>
            <li>"<xsl:value-of select="Title"/>"</li>
            <br/><br/>
            <ul>
                <li><xsl:value-of select="@type"/> by <xsl:value-of
select="Speaker/Name"/>, <xsl:value-of select="Speaker/Affiliation"/></li>
                <li><xsl:value-of select="DateTime"/></li>
                <li><xsl:value-of select="Location"/></li>
            </ul>
            <br/><xsl:apply-templates select="Description"/>
        </ul>
    </xsl:for-each>
</xsl:template>
```

```
<xsl:template match="Description">
    <xsl:apply-templates/>
</xsl:template>
<xsl:template match="Keyword">
    <b><xsl:apply-templates/></b>
</xsl:template>
</xsl:stylesheet>
```

Figure 2-5. XSLT Transformation Program

Transforming XML to HTML can be a highly sophisticated process. For example, a set of XML transforms can create a website of highly interlinked HTML files and by making multiple passes through the input documents can extract titles and headings to create tables of contents and navigation aids. These ancillary structures can be regenerated automatically whenever the XML content changes, and cascading style sheets can be switched in and out for precise control of site appearance.

Transforming XML to HTML is often just a small part of a single-source publishing strategy in which XML content is transformed for a variety of output devices or channels such as PDAs, wireless phones, text-to-speech synthesizers, Braille devices, and of course, printers. This form of transformation for reuse in different devices or media is often called repackaging. In this case a given XML document instance may have different XSLT transforms applied to it in different implementations.

XML may also be transformed to send information back into a database, ERP system, legacy application, or EDI exchange. Chapter 6 discusses how transforming XML documents from one schema to another, or extracting and combining information from one or more documents to create an instance that conforms to another schema, are essential techniques for making information interoperable.

2.7.3 WHERE TO TRANSFORM

XML is now used everywhere in distributed computing architectures. It can be the native format in an XML database or created by conversion from a non-XML database, ERP application, legacy system, or EDI data source. XML can be sent anywhere inside or outside the enterprise to expose information or functionality or to create an extended enterprise like the virtual drop shipment bookstore hypothesized in Chapter 1. Since many web browsers contain XML parsers and support XSLT, XML can go all the way to the end user's client. Figure 2-6 illustrates this "XML everywhere" phenomenon.

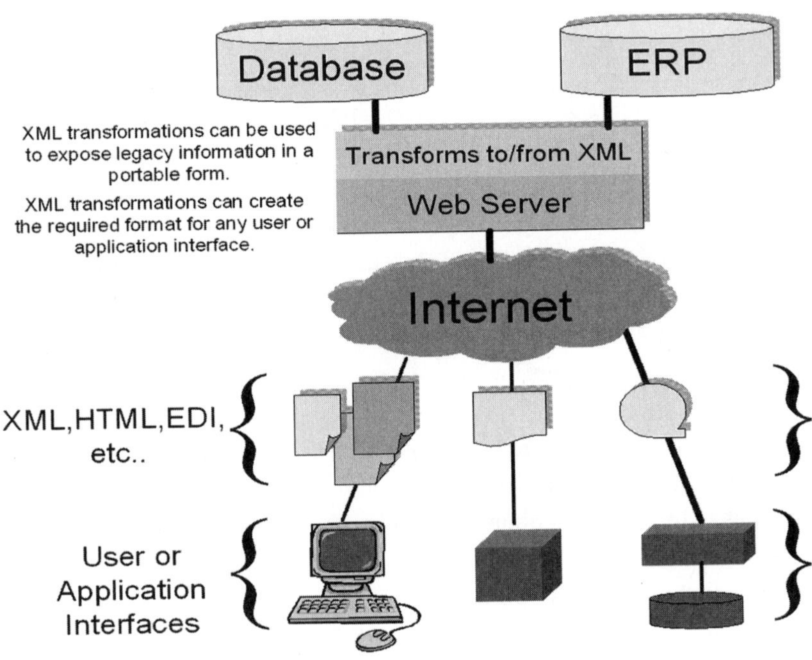

Figure 2-6. XML Everywhere in a Generic System Architecture

XML is now everywhere in distributed computing architectures

But XML is often not sent all the way through a distributed application. Instead it is sometimes transformed to HTML or to non-XML formats before it gets to the browser or the legacy application. But, given XML's flexibility, portability, and processability, why would anyone down-translate to a less expressive and computable format? Sometimes decisions about where to transform are based on technical capabilities. It might be easier, in terms of the tools and people available to do it, to transform XML to another format on one side of a document exchange rather than another.

Or the decision might be based on efficiency considerations. A business may implement all the transformations needed to support its supply chain or trading partners at a single gateway or hub. This consolidates all of the know-how, required technology, and support personnel in one place and allows all the external enterprises to continue using their legacy technology to produce and consume the documents they exchange with the hub enterprise. Documents are also likely to be smaller when they are optimized for a specific device or application.

The decision about where to transform is a business one

Ultimately the decision about where to transform is a business one. Exchanging an XML document and the schema that governs it reveals a great deal of information about how an enterprise organizes its information and conducts its business processes. The information model in a schema might include principles of product classification, manufacturing tolerances, schedule flexibility, pricing algorithms, capacity allocation, and other valuable proprietary information.

We may want to exchange this information with a trusted business partner for mutual benefit, or we may choose to send a substantially down-translated instance that conveys a much simpler view of the business. We might even create customized transformations of our information whose richness depends on how much someone is willing to pay for it.

2.8 KEY POINTS IN CHAPTER TWO

- Using the Web as a business platform changes the problem from presentational formatting to semantic modeling.
- HTML has limited use for business applications because it has no tags for marking up information to give it business meaning.
- XML has rapidly become the preferred format for representing physical models of documents and business processes.
- XML is a metalanguage for markup, and markup languages can be created for very specific document models.
- With XML, the separation of content and presentation is inherent and desirable.
- XML schemas define the rules that govern the arrangement and values of a document's content.
- An XML document without a schema is little more than a bag of tags whose meanings are undefined.
- There is often a gap between the conceptual model of a document and what can be described in an XML schema.
- XML is now everywhere in distributed computing architectures.
- The decision about where to transform documents is a business one.

3 Models, Patterns, and Reuse

3.0 INTRODUCTION

The hypothetical GMBooks.com virtual bookstore in Chapter 1 illustrates two important themes of Document Engineering, the idea of document exchange and the reuse of patterns of document exchange to implement or adapt a business model. In Chapter 4, "Describing What Businesses Do," we begin to make a systematic survey of the kinds of models and patterns that are reused in Document Engineering. Just like every other engineering discipline, Document Engineering emphasizes the reuse of existing specifications or standards that work. Doing so reduces costs and risks while increasing the reliability and interoperability of the deployed solution.

Document Engineering emphasizes the reuse of existing specifications or standards

We'll begin this chapter with our own definitions of model, pattern, and other words that are important in Document Engineering but are overused because they are important to lots of other domains as well. In spite of their overuse, we need these terms to describe what businesses do from a variety of perspectives.

We follow the classical modeling approach in distinguishing three levels of abstraction. The least abstract models, called external models, describe specific implementations of business documents, processes, or other artifacts. Physical models are more general because they describe a set or class of instances, but they still capture the technology in which the instances were implemented. Conceptual models remove the implementation technology to emphasize the concepts and meanings that define some class of instances.

We can also distinguish what businesses do according to the depth or granularity with which we describe each model. From the organizational or business-to-business perspective, most models are coarse with just the important roles and relationships visible. At the process level, more details of the context of use are visible, and we begin to see the documents that are exchanged to carry out each process. The information level is the most granular perspective, and we can see specific information components within the documents.

These two dimensions of model abstraction and model granularity let us define a model matrix that shows in a single diagram the relationships among business model, business process, and business information models at both conceptual, physical, and implementation levels. This gives us a framework for discussing the most important and reusable patterns and for explaining how the most granular patterns for business information and business processes are composed and choreographed to create more complex patterns of greater scope.

3.1 MODELS

The business, organizational, and technological structures and relationships within and between enterprises can be extremely complex, which is why we need models to describe them. Models are simplified descriptions of a subject that remove some of its complexity to emphasize certain features or characteristics and deemphasize others.

Models are simplified descriptions of a subject

Of course there are always differences between the subject being modeled and the model, or else the model serves no purpose. Thus much of the skill of modeling involves knowing what to ignore—if you look at every single tree you never see the forest.

When there is a problem to be solved within a subject, analysts study the subject and ask experts questions about it. The information they gather is embodied in models that record and communicate the issues and constraints of the subject. These models help the analysts, domain experts, and designers understand the existing situation and devise appropriate changes.

In Document Engineering we develop models that emphasize document requirements and patterns of information exchange. We use these models to analyze, communicate, and design the formal definitions of business processes and the documents that are exchanged to carry them out.

In Document Engineering we develop models that emphasize document requirements and patterns of information exchange

We can express a model with many different notations, each of which is effective for some purpose or audience. Simple line and box drawings on whiteboards or the back of an envelope can depict the most important constructs in a model and their relationships to each other. At other times more verbose and narrative descriptions or expressions in formal language may be necessary to represent the important details of a model.

In this book we depict our models in various ways, often using some of the conventional notations of the Unified Modeling Language (UML).[1] But using the UML is not in itself modeling. Nor do you need to use the UML to do Document Engineering. We can use any modeling notation. What matters is that the notation must capture the necessary metadata needed to define the requirements of the context of use. In this text we will use the UML to describe business processes, collaborations and transactions with UML Activity and Sequence Diagrams (Chapters 9 and 10) and document components and structures using UML Class Diagrams (Chapters 13 and 14).

3.2 ADAPTING THE CLASSICAL MODELING APPROACH TO DOCUMENTS

The approach and terminology we use for modeling in Document Engineering is a document-centric adaptation of the classical three-level modeling approaches and architecture[2] depicted in Figure 3-1. This approach distinguishes between external representations that describe specific things, artifacts, or instances in the world, physical (or internal) views that present different models of instances in some technology, and conceptual views or models that abstract those descriptions from any particular implementation.

Whenever we analyze documents we can't avoid dealing with the processes that create and use them, but it is easier to introduce Document Engineering concepts and methods if we discuss documents and processes separately whenever we can. So we will also be analyzing business processes and creating models that describe them, but for the remainder of section 3.2 we will focus on document models and defer business process models until section 3.3.2.

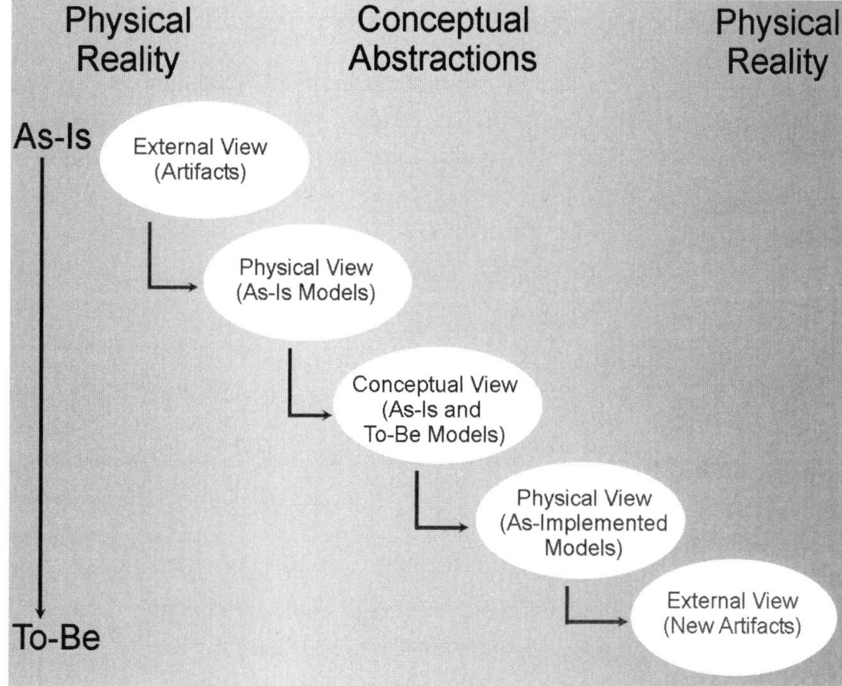

Figure 3-1. The Classical Modeling Approach

The first phase of applying the classical modeling approach to documents is to find and analyze real-world artifacts and represent the results in a model that describes their physical implementation. We then analyze these artifacts to create what are often called the As-Is models.

For business processes, the As-Is models are transformed into To-Be business process models by selecting and adapting patterns appropriate for the required context of use.

For documents we call the As-Is model a document component model and the To-Be models are called document assembly models.

Finally we bring the conceptual view back to a physical view by expressing it in technology appropriate for the contexts in which it will be used. These new document implementation models are the As-Implemented models.

3.2.1 EXTERNAL VIEWS: INSTANCES OF DOCUMENT IMPLEMENTATIONS

When documents exist in printed or tangible form, like Halfat's tax receipt on a pottery fragment (see Chapter 1), it is easy to think of them as artifacts in the world that could be described by external models. But what is most important about a document is the information or intangible content it contains, so the document should be considered an external model of the thing it describes. This is especially true in the domain of Document Engineering where our emphasis is on the documents exchanged by business processes. We deal with inventory reports, not the actual goods stored in a warehouse, for example. Or purchase orders rather than the specific goods being ordered.

A document can be considered an external model of the thing it describes

If we are designing a new business process and no documents currently exist, we must identify information and process requirements by talking to people, sources that are even less directly coupled to the things in the world than documents are. So rather than treat descriptions of specific things in the world (or other information sources like printed or web forms) as models, we will treat them as the primary instances or artifacts that we analyze to create models. For example, Figure 3-2 is an XML document instance, which we'll refer to as Book.xml in the sections that follow. Figure 3-2 is not the book, "Moby Dick" by Herman Melville; it is an external view of it.

```
<?xml version="1.0" encoding="UTF-8"?>
<Book>
    <Title>Moby Dick</Title>
    <Author>Herman Melville</Author>
    <ISBN>0804900337</ISBN>
     <Publisher>Airmont</Publisher>
 </Book>
```

Figure 3-2. XML Document Instance (Book.xml)

3.2.2 PHYSICAL VIEWS: DOCUMENT IMPLEMENTATION MODELS (OR SCHEMAS)

After we analyze a number of document instances like Book.xml, we can represent our results in a model that describes them (the As-Implemented model in the classical approach, or a document implementation model or schema in Document Engineering).

In Chapter 2 we described the role of XML schemas in representing a document type as some bounded set of possible or desired XML documents. Figures 3-3a and 3-3b are XML schemas that validate Book.xml and other XML instances of the Book document type. The first is expressed as a DTD and the second is expressed using XML Schema.

```
<?xml version="1.0" encoding="UTF-8"?>
<!ELEMENT Book (Title, Author, ISBN, Publisher)>
<!ELEMENT Title (#PCDATA)>
<!ELEMENT Author (#PCDATA)>
<!ELEMENT ISBN (#PCDATA)>
<!ELEMENT Publisher (#PCDATA)>
```

Figure 3-3a. Book.dtd

```
<?xml version="1.0" encoding="UTF-8"?>
<xs:schema xmlns:xs="http://www.w3.org/2001/XMLSchema"
elementFormDefault="qualified">
    <xs:element name="Book">
        <xs:complexType>
            <xs:sequence>
                <xs:element name="Title" type="xs:string"/>
                <xs:element name="Author" type="xs:string"/>
                <xs:element name="ISBN" type="xs:string"/>
                <xs:element name="Publisher" type="xs:string"/>
            </xs:sequence>
        </xs:complexType>
    </xs:element>
</xs:schema>
```

Figure 3-3b. Book.xsd

Figure 3-3. XML Schemas for Instances Like Book.xml

Document implementation models such as XML schemas can be very narrow, describing only the exact set of instances that were analyzed, or they can be more general, describing a wider variety of instances that are similar, but not identical, to those that were analyzed. In either case, the more instances we consider when we analyze a document implementation model, the more likely we are to identify and capture the set of rules that govern the possible instances of the document being modeled.

But document implementation models—defined as expressions of structure and integrity constraints on some set of information—are not limited to schemas for XML documents or even to markup languages. They can be expressed using many formal languages, including ISO 9735 for EDI and SQL/DDL for relational databases. There are also less formal ways of expressing As-Implementation models, such as the message implementation guides in narrative form that are often used to explain the structures of EDI documents. Figure 3-4 is a document implementation model that describes a database table in which to store information about book instances.

```
Create Table Book
{
Identifier CHAR(14) PRIMARY KEY,
BookTitle CHAR(50),
AuthorName CHAR(50),
Publisher     CHAR(20)
}
```

Figure 3-4. Database Schema for Instances Like Book.xml

As these three examples show, document implementation models are tightly bound to the technology of implementation, using constructs like XML elements or database fields so that computer programs can interpret the model. But this tight binding can prevent us from thinking beyond the specific implementation, especially if the models were created to describe or validate only a limited set of samples.

For example, if we study the specific documents used by a business process and discover they have a variety of implementations, each with their own schema definition or notation, how can we compare them? Book.dtd, Book.xsd, and the Book database schema are expressed in widely different syntaxes that constrain our ability to understand the common requirements of a "book" in our business applications.

Implementation models limit design and reuse capabilities

Document implementation models also limit design and reuse capabilities. If a bookstore wants to share information between its database and documents, as it does when responding to a customer query, neither the database schema nor the document schema is sufficient. We need to understand the relationship between them, which might be expressed as the mapping of one model to the other. But this is often not straightforward. In our examples here, we might not know that PCDATA and string are synonyms and we can't be sure that the <ISBN> element in Book.xsd plays the same role as Identifier in the Book database schema.

Document implementation models only tell us how their components are expressed in a particular technology. To understand how they relate to each other we also need to know what the components mean; that is, we need to understand their concepts.

3.2.3 CONCEPTUAL VIEWS: DOCUMENT COMPONENT AND ASSEMBLY MODELS

We can best describe the semantics of documents using models of the concepts they contain. This conceptual view lets us distinguish one class of document from another. Conceptual views are independent of the physical implementation and so are not tied to any particular technology.

Prose definitions are often adequate conceptual models for classifying documents. For example, we might say that a typical dictionary is organized as a set of word entries, each of which consists of a main word, a pronunciation guide, and one or more definitions or senses. The entry may also have a derivation showing its roots in some classical language, other forms of the word, a list of synonyms or antonyms, quotations, or an illustration.

Likewise, we might say that a typical invoice contains information about goods or services provided by the seller and the amount and date of expected payment. It may also describe methods of delivery or other terms governing the transactions that occur. Dates, amounts, and account codes are among the kinds of content in invoices for which expected values or ranges of values can be precisely specified.

But similar types of content occur in many documents, and the distinctions between these can be subtle, especially when there is overlap in information and structural patterns. Precisely what is it that differentiates a catalog from a brochure, a newspaper from a magazine, a dictionary from an encyclopedia, a calendar from a schedule, or a purchase order from an invoice? Obviously there are distinctions between them, or we wouldn't have different words to describe them and we couldn't reliably classify them as one type of document or another. But how can we identify and communicate what distinguishes them?

In Document Engineering we introduce two types of conceptual models for documents that are more formal and precise than prose definitions. The first is the document component model, which describes the complete set of information components in a domain,[3] including their structure and relationships. A document component model portrays the network of associations between the components. So rather than describing a single type of document, it implicitly describes many different types of documents. Such a conceptual model of information about books is shown in Figure 3-5 using the notation of a UML class diagram.

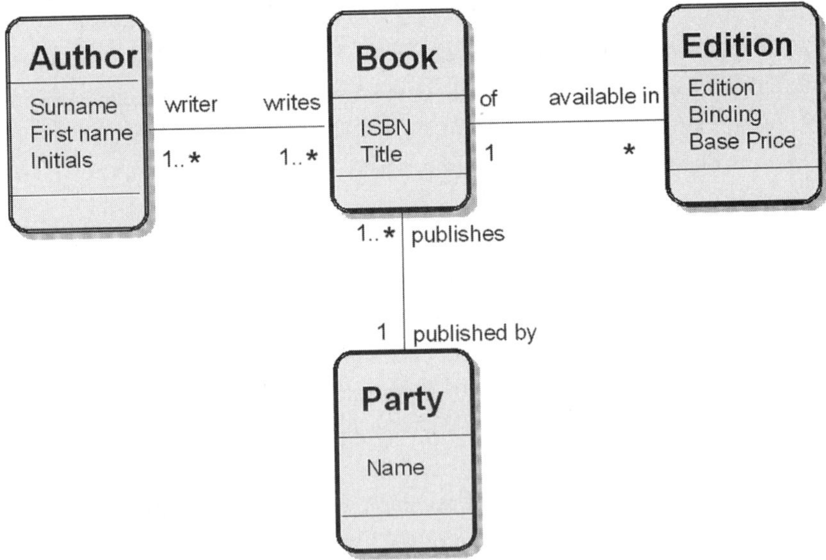

Figure 3-5. Class Diagram for Document Component Model of "Book"

A document component model also captures important rules about the relationships between classes. For example, a publisher can be considered a reuse of the object class called party with a special association to book that we label as "publishes" in Figure 3-5. So the publisher is modeled as the "published by" party. However, an author is not a reuse of party because the former has attributes that do not apply to the latter.

The model in Figure 3-5 also depicts the business rule that an author can write more than one book and that books can have more than one author. It also tells us that even if the book has more than one edition, it has only one ISBN.

A document component model describes the complete set of semantic components in a domain

The Book conceptual model could be implemented as an XML schema, database table, EDI message definition, or paper form. Each of these can represent concepts like author and title even though the implementation models may vary. But there is a crucial activity we must carry out before we can model documents.

We must follow a path through the network of associations represented in a document component model, selecting a subset or arrangement of components to meet the information requirements of our specific context. This assembly describes the way in which the selected components are assembled into hierarchical structures.

A document assembly model describes the way in which required components are assembled into a hierarchical structure

Document assembly models are best visualized as tree diagrams of hierarchical structures. For example, from the document component model in Figure 3-5, we could construct three different document assembly models by traversing the associations using different paths. The resulting hierarchical document models would organize the same components into different structures to impose different interpretations or contexts that emphasize the book, the author, or the publisher. Three such document assembly models are shown in Figure 3-6.

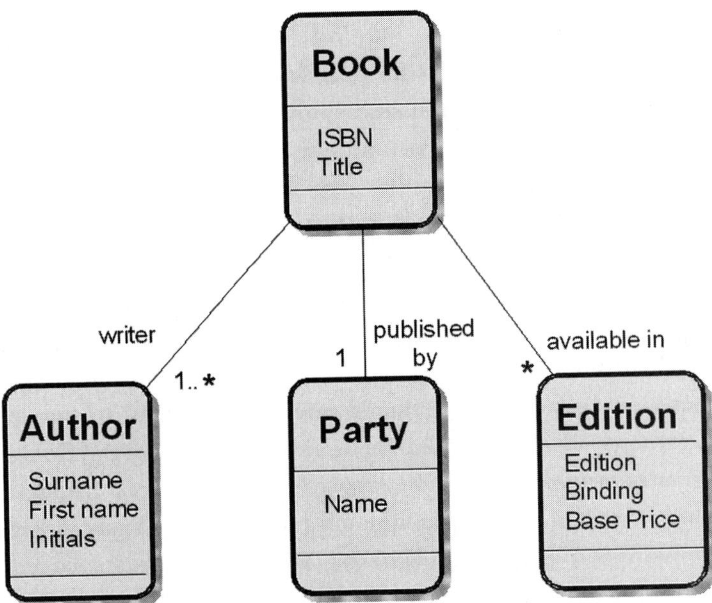

3-6a. Document Assembly Model for Book Context

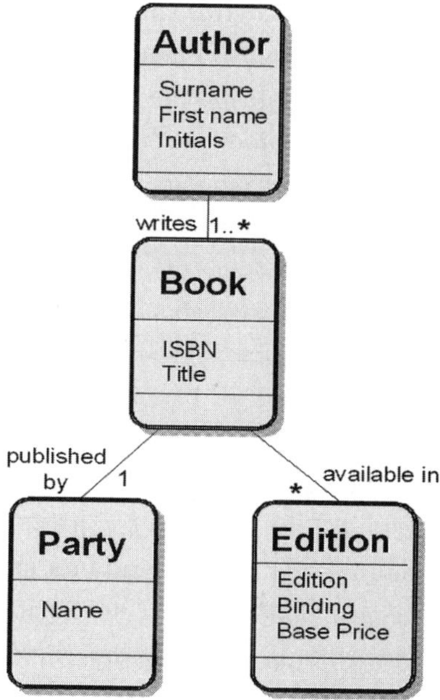

3-6b. Document Assembly Model for Author Context

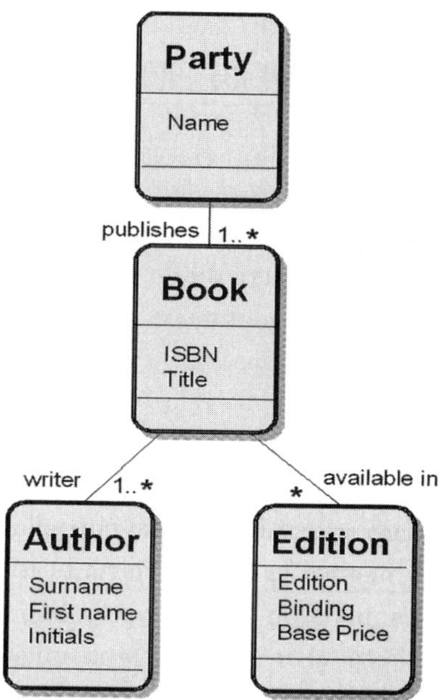

3-6c. Document Assembly Model for Publisher Context

Figure 3-6. Alternative Document Assembly Models

Conceptual views of models like those shown in figures 3-5 and 3-6 are a better way to represent and communicate the results of analysis and design than the physical views in figures 3-3 and 3-4 because they are not constrained by any specific implementation. This technology independence also makes them easier to manipulate or revise. Similarly, at the conceptual level it is easier to generalize a model to make it describe a larger set of possible or desired artifacts than the ones we happened to observe when we first analyzed an implementation model. It is also easier to specialize at the conceptual level, for example, by deriving a related model that incorporates additional characteristics or relationships; in this case, we could express a conceptual model for chemistry books based on the model for a book.

When technologies change, the optimal implementation model will also change even though the underlying conceptual models don't

When technologies change, the optimal implementation model will also change even though the underlying conceptual models don't. A fascinating example goes back 10,000 years to the last part of the Stone Age, when farmers in the Near East began to use clay pegs or tokens to keep track of farm products, often storing them in hollow clay balls.[4] The Neolithic accountants later realized that instead of enclosing the tokens inside a clay ball, they could simply make marks in the clay to represent the one-to-one correspondence between the clay tokens and the goods, ultimately leading to the invention of Cuneiform writing in the fourth millennium BCE. Today we use more modern technologies for tracking inventory, but the underlying conceptual model of counting remains essentially the same. We'll further discuss the role of technology in the relationship between conceptual and physical models in Section 4.4 and Chapter 5.

3.3 THE MODEL MATRIX

Later in this book we will discuss in more detail how to understand documents by creating physical and conceptual document models. We will also apply similar approaches to analyzing contexts and creating models for business processes, and other kinds of reusable patterns.

These two dimensions of model abstraction and model granularity form a matrix for organizing the analysis and modeling approaches in Document Engineering,[5] as shown in Figure 3-7.

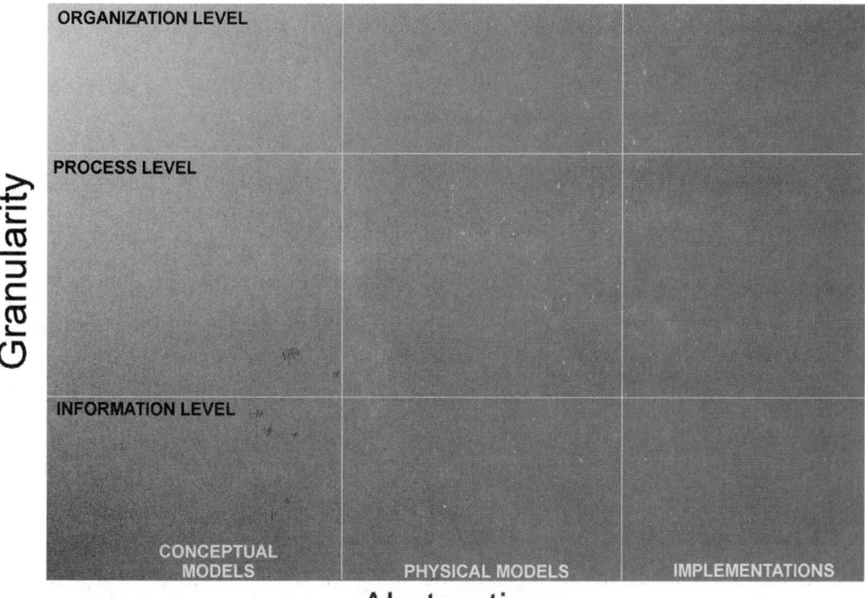

Figure 3-7. The Model Matrix

Let's begin by describing the matrix dimensions. From left to right is the abstraction dimension. The most abstract or context-free conceptual models are arranged on the left. Moving to the right implies more physical models, and finally specific implementations of actual documents or processes are the rightmost external models.

The two dimensions of model abstraction and granularity form the Document Engineering Model Matrix

From top to bottom is the dimension of model granularity, on which we can depict the amount of detail with which we describe the business relationships in each model. From the organizational or business-to-business perspective, models show only the most important roles and relationships. At the process level more details about the relationship are visible, and we begin to see the documents that are exchanged to carry out each process. The information level is the most granular perspective, and we can see specific information components within the document models.

3.3.1 METADATA AND METAMODELS

Metadata might be the hardest term to define in the field of Document Engineering because its usual definition of "data about data" isn't much of a starting point. We are using the prefix meta to convey concern with the concepts and results of the discipline named in the suffix.[6] For example, a metalanguage is a language or system of symbols used to discuss another language or system, and a metatheory is a formal system that describes the structure of some other system. So metadata consists of data structures used to discuss other data structures.

Metadata augments the values of information (or data) with additional properties that explain its meaning, organization, and other characteristics of interest in our models. What constitutes metadata is relative. Data may be metadata depending on your perspective. For example, statistics are data to some people and metadata to others.

What constitutes metadata is relative

In Document Engineering we use various pieces of metadata in our models so that we can define richer models and also compare and align different types of models. Remember, we're not talking about the content of the models; we're talking about the constructs by which the model content is organized or structured.

In XML the metadata are things like elements and attributes. In SQL the metadata includes tables and columns, and in the UML metadata includes features like classes, associations, and attributes.

To help us use metadata, we need a model, which we call the metamodel. A metamodel is a higher perspective of a model, used to describe the type of information in a model. For example, if we were to define a model of a document, the document model's metamodel might specify that the content of a document can be described using separate data objects, each of which has properties such as cardinality, definitions, conditional rules, and sets of legitimate values.[7] For example, the metamodel for Book.xsd is the specification for W3C Schema (XML Schema), which explains how schemas are constructed. By explaining what metadata is required and how they relate to each other, metamodels enable us to build consistent and robust models.

While the overall purpose of metadata may be similar in various types of models, because of their terminology, syntaxes, or different notations, it isn't always easy to recognize the correspondences. For example, is an XML element equivalent to an SQL table? What is the relationship between elements and classes? Metamodels are also useful if we want to exchange or compare these different models. If two models share the same metamodel, it is easier to compare and align the two.

A common metamodel helps align different models

With physical views of models, comparing metamodels is more obvious. Two XML Schemas are easier to compare than an XML Schema and an XML DTD, or any XML schema and a database schema.

But models of conceptual views also have metadata and metamodels to describe them. For example, the ebXML Core Component Technical Specification[8] defines a metamodel for defining conceptual information models for document components. This means that even though there are many different types of document components, they can all be described using a common conceptual framework.

3.3.2 METAMODELS FOR PROCESSES

Metamodels for business processes are especially important in Document Engineering because processes are inherently more abstract than documents, which readily exist as highly tangible implementations with a conventional notion of a document as a container or message with information components. In contrast, business processes can be described at many levels, and the lack of a predictable amount of detail for their constituents would make it less likely that any two process models could be meaningfully compared.

Business processes are inherently more abstract than documents

To deal with this fundamental modeling challenge, metamodels for describing business processes have evolved that distinguish multiple levels of abstraction along with the semantic properties that are necessary to define each level. We prefer the ebXML Business Process metamodel, which specifies three levels of abstraction: processes are defined in terms of collaborations, which are in turn described using transactions.[9] In addition, the ebXML Business Process Specification Schema[10] (BPSS) is designed to express a rich repertoire of patterns in a standard way, making it much easier to understand and compare business processes. We use this metamodel for describing processes in Chapter 9, "Analyzing Business Processes," and Chapter 10, "Designing Business Processes with Patterns."

3.4 PATTERNS

Patterns are models that are sufficiently general, adaptable, and worthy of imitation that we can reuse them. A pattern must be general enough to apply to a meaningfully large set of possible implementations or contexts. It must be adaptable because the implementations or contexts to which it might apply will differ in details. And it must be worthy, that is the implementations or contexts to which the pattern might apply should benefit from following it. Of course, patterns are an important idea in many fields.

Patterns are models that are sufficiently general, adaptable, and worthy of imitation that we can reuse them

For example, the system of government called a parliament is a pattern used by numerous countries and states. In a parliamentary system, people democratically elect others to represent their interests, and the government is headed by a member of the political party with a majority of the elected representatives.

The parliament model is an abstract, conceptual pattern because a country that adopts this model does not adopt any specific politicians and bureaucrats, just the pattern describing the ways in which its elected representatives are organized to govern. For a country to adopt a physical pattern for "parliament" it would have to invade another country and occupy its government buildings or kidnap its politicians (not that such events have never happened).

When patterns are implemented, they are often adjusted or customized to suit their particular context. Thus the parliamentary systems of government in the United Kingdom, Australia, and Japan are not identical, but they have many common features because each follows the same basic pattern.

Patterns are useful in every activity, from constructing houses to building software applications[11] to describing human behavior. Using patterns saves effort and yields more consistent, compatible, and successful designs. Indeed, sometimes a pattern is so consistently adopted it becomes an official or de facto standard (see Section 5.7, "From Proprietary to Standard Models.")

Using patterns saves effort and yields more consistent, compatible, and successful designs

Document Engineering is mostly concerned with patterns of information exchange within and between enterprises and the patterns of components in the documents being exchanged. But is it also useful to take even broader perspectives on what businesses do and the relationships between them because patterns at higher levels of abstraction set the context for more granular ones in which documents are specified.

3.4.1 PATTERNS IN BUSINESS

Businesses exhibit a remarkable variety of behavior. Every business is different because they have different owners, employees, managers, and customers and because they operate in different industry, geopolitical, and regulatory contexts. The diversity of businesses can be seen easily in the yellow pages of a telephone directory or, more systematically, in the business classification codes designed to facilitate uniform collection and analysis of data about businesses. Examples of these formal categorizations include the 6-digit North American Industry Classification System (NAICS)[12] code and the UN/SPSC[13] coding system for products.

But just as they exhibit great variety, businesses also exhibit great regularity in what they do and how they do it. At first glance, there doesn't seem to be much in common between "Computer Systems Design Services" (NAICS code 541512) and "Potato Farming" (NAICS code 111211) or "Bare Printed Circuit Board Manufacturing" (NAICS code 334412). But this diversity in classification belies the fact that most businesses do many things in similar ways.

Businesses exhibit both great variety and great regularity in what they do and how they do it

We call something a business or enterprise because it demonstrates some purposeful and organized activity to provide products or services, usually with a profit motive. But beyond this we can also agree that computer systems designers, potato farmers, and circuit board manufacturers all need to rent or buy, furnish, and insure their business locations, hire employees, procure and pay for supplies, market and sell their goods and services, fulfill orders, issue invoices, finance their operations, provide customer service, and so on.

Indeed, the fact that we have words like procure, pay, order, and invoice to describe common business processes and documents in an industry-neutral way confirms that there are general patterns in how business gets done.

3.4.2 WHY BUSINESSES FOLLOW PATTERNS

Businesses in different industries also adopt patterns specific to their activities for a number of reasons:

- They may be affected by common laws or regulations. Local or national governments might require businesses to obtain permits, to ensure that their products and services meet health or safety standards, to pay taxes, and so on.

- They may follow similar trade practices and be affected by the same microeconomic factors, such as common suppliers or customers and similar opportunities or threats related to the introduction of new technologies or methods.

- They may be affected by common external forces imposed by the overall economic and financial environment such as tax laws and interest rates, levels of employment and education, and consumer confidence and other macroeconomic factors.

- They want to minimize their costs, such as hiring and training workers.

All of these influences encourage the adoption and use of patterns. Yet businesses don't follow patterns just because they are forced to do so by external influences. "Good business practice" is a dominant pattern and businesses also consciously strive to become more efficient and effective at what they do. Obvious examples of intentional patterns in business are those followed by franchises, where every business uses the same detailed operating methods and technology to get the benefits of aggregated purchasing, mass advertising, and data mining of composite transaction information to identify sales trends.

Businesses also need to operate in ways that are intelligible and acceptable to their trading partners or customers or else explain why they don't. Running a retail business according to the usual patterns and practices makes it easier for suppliers and customers to interact with it. A retailer that accepts only cash and doesn't allow purchases to be returned will probably have to post warning signs at its checkout counter or website equivalent and will certainly have difficulty competing with more customer-friendly firms.

Reusing well-understood patterns makes businesses easier to start, manage, and improve. Adopting common patterns can reduce development and maintenance costs, improve performance, and enhance relationships with suppliers and customers. A business can more easily learn from others in its industry if it contributes to and follows industry best practices or reference models. The more systematic the practices in an industry, the more a business benefits from following them because of the network effects of standardization.

So businesses must balance two conflicting goals: to differentiate itself from its competitors and to run their business according to principles and methods used throughout their industry. Of course a business might decide not to follow the standard patterns in its industry. Perhaps it has the market dominance to impose its will on suppliers or customers or it hopes to create a competitive breakthrough by using a radically different technology or process. If it succeeds, the business will be creating a new pattern that others will soon try to adopt.

A business must balance how to differentiate itself and how to run according to industry practice

But for every business that invents a truly new business model or process there are many more who aspire only to get better at doing the things they are already doing. They do this by recognizing and adopting good business patterns.

3.4.3 FINDING PATTERNS IN THE MODEL MATRIX

Generic or abstract conceptual patterns become more specific or concrete by adding context. We will define what we mean by context more completely in Chapters 7 and 8. For now it is sufficient to say that contextualization means moving from left to right in the Model Matrix. Similarly, moving up the granularity axis in the Model Matrix gives a coarser granularity that can suggest patterns disguised by the details, encouraging new innovations.

So it follows that the best place to find reusable patterns in our models will be where they are generalized enough to be applicable across different implementation technologies but have enough context to be meaningful. And at the same time they must give a comprehensive view that is not so detailed it limits adaptations.

To find useful patterns we navigate along the abstraction and granularity dimensions of the Model Matrix to confirm our analysis and understanding of the context of use. We can present this metaphor graphically in Figure 3-8 using a "Pattern Compass." We'll more fully develop these ideas in Chapter 10, "Designing Business Processes with Patterns."

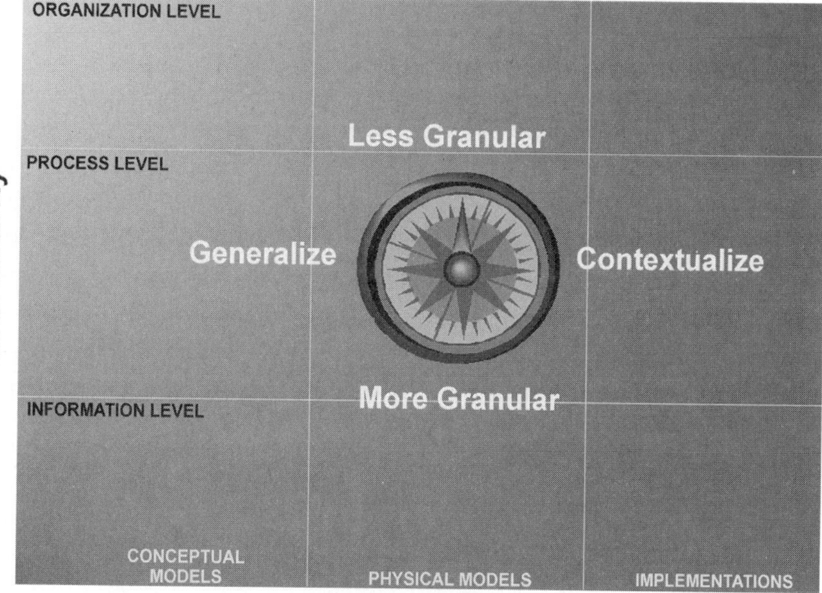

Figure 3-8. The Pattern Compass in the Model Matrix

The organization of patterns and models in the Model Matrix makes them easier to learn and reuse. As we examine other business relationships, processes and information from a Document Engineering perspective, the Model Matrix can provide a convenient framework.

Generic conceptual patterns become more specific by adding context

3.4.4 USING THE MODEL MATRIX AS A FRAMEWORK

A complete understanding of an enterprise's business relationships, the processes that carry them out, and information exchanged by those processes requires compatible and interconnected models of all three. This understanding is achieved when the strategic concerns embodied in organizational patterns that describe what a business wants to do can be linked by process patterns to information models that describe how to do it. In graphical terms, this convergence takes place when organizational and information models "meet in the middle" of the Model Matrix in process models.

So another use of the Model Matrix is as a roadmap for the analysis and design activities and methods that get us to its middle. Here the systematic differences in abstraction and granularity of these kinds of models in the matrix suggest that different kinds of modeling approaches are needed to create them.

A business analyst, document analyst, data analyst, and a task analyst will create different models

Different models emerge from the skills and tools of the business analyst, document analyst, data analyst, and task analyst. Each of these approaches looks at documents and processes differently, and while each of them is highly effective in some areas, they all have blind spots where their methods do not work well. We can overlay these different modeling perspectives on the Model Matrix in Figure 3-9.

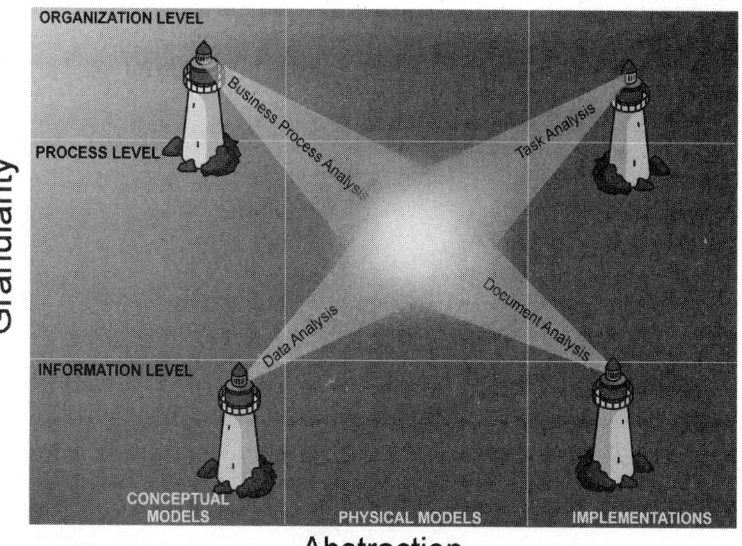

Figure 3-9. Converging Modeling Approaches in the Model Matrix

This depiction shows business process analysis focusing on the top left corner of the Model Matrix. This captures the conventional practice of process analysis in following a top-down approach to progressively refine abstract descriptions of what a business does. In contrast, document analysis techniques emphasize the study of instances of document artifacts, which are found in the lower right corner of the Model Matrix. Likewise, data analysis focuses on logical models of objects and associations, and task analysis focuses on the specific steps and information that users need to carry out a task. In Chapter 7 we introduce the Document Engineering Approach as a set of activities that follow a path through the Model Matrix, employing each of these modeling approaches in turn to yield models that "meet in the middle."

3.4.5 PROCESSES AND DOCUMENTS: YIN AND YANG

Another important idea embodied in the Model Matrix is the essential and inescapable relationship between models of processes and models of documents. At the center of the matrix, where processes are described as transactions and document exchanges, processes and documents are two perspectives of the same thing. Are processes just combinations of document exchanges, or are documents just the payload patterns in processes? The answer is yes to both questions. Business processes and documents are the yin and yang of Document Engineering.

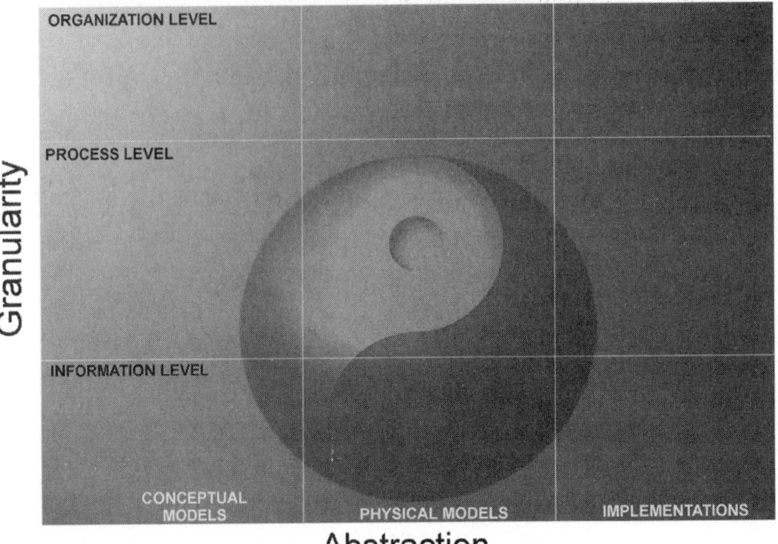

Figure 3-10. The Yin and Yang of Document Engineering

These central concepts of Chinese philosophy might seem out of place here, but they express perfectly the complementary and opposing relationships between business processes and documents. Processes produce and consume documents, which are a static snapshot or the tangible result of the process activity. Process descriptions emphasize business concerns and determine whether ways of doing business are compatible. Document descriptions emphasize semantic concerns and determine whether business systems are compatible. We can separate processes and documents in our analysis, discussion, and models, but in the end they are always interconnected because both business and semantic compatibility are necessary.

There are complementary and opposing relationships between processes and documents

In practical terms this means that models for processes and documents need to be developed with the same care and to compatible levels of detail. And, it explains why we need a Document Engineering approach that exploits complementary modeling approaches.

3.5 KEY POINTS IN CHAPTER THREE

- Document Engineering emphasizes the reuse of existing specifications or standards.
- Models are simplified descriptions of a subject.
- In Document Engineering we develop models that emphasize document requirements and patterns of information exchange.
- A document can be considered an external model of the thing it describes.
- Implementation models limit design and reuse capabilities.
- A document component model describes the complete set of semantic components in a domain.
- A document assembly model describes the way in which required components are assembled into a hierarchical structure.
- When technologies change, the optimal implementation model will also change even though the underlying conceptual models don't.
- The two dimensions of model abstraction and granularity form the Document Engineering Model Matrix.
- What constitutes metadata is relative.
- A common metamodel helps align different models.
- Business processes are inherently more abstract than documents.

- Patterns are models that are sufficiently general, adaptable, and worthy of imitation that we can reuse them.
- Using patterns saves effort and yields more consistent, compatible, and successful designs.
- Businesses exhibit both great variety and great regularity in what they do and how they do it.
- A business must balance how to differentiate itself and how to run according to industry practice.
- Generic conceptual patterns become more specific by adding context.
- A business analyst, document analyst, data analyst, and a task analyst will create different models.
- There are complementary and opposing relationships between processes and documents.

4

Describing What Businesses Do and How They Do It

4.0 INTRODUCTION

Readers who came to Chapter 2, "XML Foundations," knowing something about XML may have gained new insights and ways to apply that knowledge through our Document Engineering perspective. Likewise, readers with business backgrounds will be familiar with some of the material in this chapter but should benefit from seeing it from a Document Engineering perspective.

In Chapter 3 we deliberately used a general notion of business pattern because we wanted to emphasize the great extent to which businesses carry out their activities in regular and systematic ways. Now that we've made that basic point we will get more precise.

Historians, sociologists, business theorists and institutional economists have developed a rich set of taxonomies for discussing variations in business organization and models.[1] This deep body of work has shaped our thinking, but we won't explicitly revisit much of it in this chapter. Instead, we will take a less formal and more pragmatic approach, adapting some of the categories and concepts as we discuss business models that use document exchanges and service oriented architectures. So while some of the topics we'll discuss in this chapter will be familiar to anyone who has studied organizational design, supply chain management, or information technology management, the overall framework provided by Document Engineering is a new one.

We introduced this new perspective in Chapter 3 when we proposed the Model Matrix as a framework for understanding the relationship between organizational, process, and information models, which vary on a dimension of granularity. In this chapter we will take a more detailed look at each of these model layers to understand the orthogonal distinction between conceptual models and physical ones. We will then be ready to learn how to develop compatible and interconnected models from all three layers that describe both what the business wants to do and how it can do it.

We begin with models of how businesses organize their activities. Business models or business reference models are abstract descriptions of what businesses do. We will describe patterns like supply chains and marketplaces that capture complex sets of relationships within and between enterprises.

At the more granular view of business processes, business process models take a view that emphasizes the activities that create business value without focusing on the information exchanges that underlie them.

Only at the most granular level of business information models do we find patterns that reveal documents and their components. These are commonly found in their physical form as XML schema libraries or EDI message standards.

We will introduce these different model perspectives using the distinction between physical and conceptual views we discussed in Chapter 3. Although the contrast isn't always perfect, one can describe most aspects of what a business does do in either way; for example, in highly physical terms of management reporting structures or facility locations or in highly conceptual terms such as whether it seeks efficiency through functional or cross-functional organization. Likewise, the information exchanged between organizations or systems can be described in physical terms by XML schemas or EDI implementation guidelines (that is, as document implementation models), or in conceptual terms by UML class diagrams[2] (as document component and document assembly models).

Even business processes, which may seem inherently abstract for processes that are information-intensive or computational, can be described from both physical and conceptual perspectives. It is certainly true that in contrast to observable processes like manufacturing, packaging, and transport of tangible goods, many business processes like accounting, scheduling, and payment are almost invisible. But even intangible or information-intensive processes need instructions about how they are carried out, and the documents that are the inputs and outputs of these processes also provide physical views of how the process works.

After a business has designed its organizational, process, and information models, many technology and architectural choices remain about how to implement them. And just like those models, the technology and architecture of a business can be described in physical or conceptual terms. Physical descriptions depict the specific computers, operating systems, and software applications that the business uses. In contrast, conceptual and technology-neutral descriptions emphasize functional and topological characteristics, such as whether the solution embodies a service oriented architecture and treats business functions as reusable components.

4.1 VIEWS OF BUSINESS ORGANIZATION

One approach to describing a business is in terms of the organization, management, or control of its activities. These descriptions can explain the organization of a single firm or the organizational relationships between multiple firms.

4.1.1 PHYSICAL VIEWS OF BUSINESS ORGANIZATION

The most visible and tangible view of businesses are based on physical implementations. They describe how the business works.

4.1.1.1 Organization Charts and Facilities Maps

A common physical view of business organization is the organization chart. Organization charts exhibit characteristic structural patterns that portray the arrangement of management and operational responsibilities within the firm and usually include specific people and their associated roles or titles. These patterns are explained in textbooks on organizational design or behavior and in a more mundane way are built into enterprise definition tables in Human Resources and Enterprise Resource Planning applications and into templates for drawing programs like Visio, SmartDraw, or Powerpoint.

Organization charts and facilities maps are physical models of a business

The organizational chart for a business often closely mirrors the facilities map, another common physical model of business organization that shows the locations of offices, factories, distribution points, training centers, or other facilities.

The organizational chart for an enterprise is a highly specific and rich model of how it does business. For example, IBM uses its organizational charts as the core of a dynamic information resource called BluePeople.[3] Starting with a name or email address, BluePeople makes explicit the network of links to coworkers, projects, publications, and other information to provide context for the name or address.

4.1.1.2 Supply Chains

A firm's supply chain is the network of relationships, communication patterns, and distribution capabilities that provide raw materials, components, products, or services to a firm so that it can make what it sells and deliver what it sells to its customers. Because the pattern of a supply chain is a highly abstract one that can be adapted to model any situation in which a product or service is created by bringing together different parts, it is an important part of the Document Engineering pattern repertoire.

Nevertheless, supply chains are often described in highly concrete or physical terms with details about assembly lines, warehouses, factories, and stores full of raw materials, partly finished or finished products, along with the equipment or modes of transport by which materials and products move between them. Likewise, because the perspective of a supply chain follows a product's flow from raw material to consumption, a helpful analogy is to the basin or drainage area for a large river: "A supply chain is much like a river system with raw materials at the headwaters and customers at the delta, with products floating down the river toward the customers."[4]

A simplistic depiction of a global supply chain model is shown in Figure 4-1.

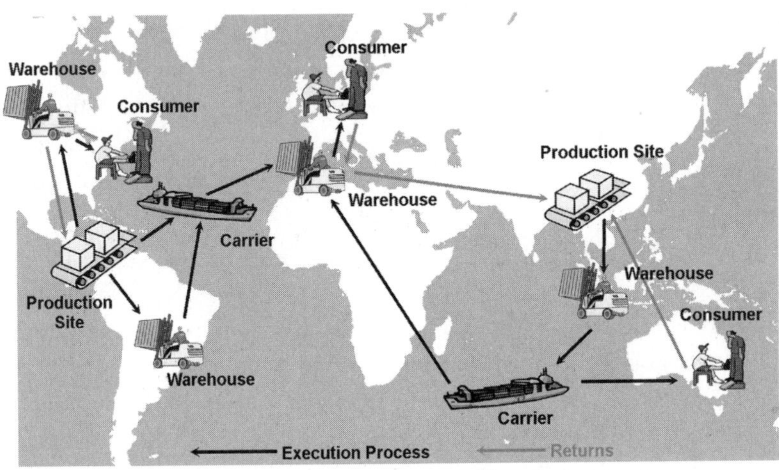

Figure 4-1. A Global Supply Chain Model

4.1.1.3 Distribution Channels

Getting finished goods to the purchaser is called distribution or fulfillment. And as with supply chains, distribution channels are often described in highly physical terms that detail the locations of warehouses or retail stores and the specific modes of transport between them.

The simplest distribution pattern is direct distribution, in which a company sells a product directly to the companies or consumers who buy it. However, most companies use an indirect strategy, selling their products through distributors, resellers, and retail outlets to increase their ability to reach customers. These distribution partners are called intermediaries or channels for the manufacturer; they may be organized according to sales territories, geographical regions, or customer segments. The Internet enabled many firms to shift from indirect to direct distribution, and this disintermediation—literally, cutting out the middleman—allowed them to increase their margins and learn more about their customers. A company can be tempted to sell the same products directly and through channels, but this can lead to channel conflict and alienate distributors.

Like supply chains, distribution channels are a generalized pattern. Applying the pattern involves choosing the roles and locations of intermediaries and balancing the benefits of a larger network against the costs and delays of exchanging information within it.

4.1.1.4 Marketplaces, Exchanges, and Auctions

There are few business patterns that suggest more concrete and stereotyped depictions than marketplaces, exchanges, and auctions. We can all imagine and hear the crowded old town marketplace, the controlled frenzy of the stock exchange trading floor, and the insistent staccato of the auctioneer urging the bidders on.

These patterns have much in common, organizing their participants in characteristic ways to enable familiar business models. All embody the core ideas that bringing together a critical mass of buyers and sellers makes it easier to match them up and creates shared efficiencies and benefits that won't arise in interactions between a single buyer and a single seller. By eliminating the need for participants to be in the same physical location, the Internet allows more of them to take part, yielding much better matching between buyers and sellers. Consider that at any given time millions of items are offered on eBay in a set of categories nearly as broad as the web itself.

The differences between marketplaces, exchanges, and auctions are subtle. While almost any type of products might be offered for sale in a marketplace, an exchange is a type of marketplace for intangible goods like financial securities where price is the essential attribute. An auction is a method for establishing prices when market mechanisms don't work well, usually when goods are scarce for one reason or another.

Supply chains, distribution channels, markets and auctions are general business patterns that can be applied in novel contexts

Like supply chains and distribution channels, markets and auctions are very general patterns that can be applied in novel contexts. For example, an Internet marketplace called getloaded.com matches freight loads and trucks with excess capacity, attacking the costly problem of deadheading when a truck returns without a backload on its return trip from delivering goods.

4.1.2 CONCEPTUAL VIEWS OF BUSINESS ORGANIZATION

Physical views of business organizations are useful depictions of how they operate. In contrast, a conceptual perspective on how a business is organized explains why it exists and the kinds of activities it engages in to stay in business. In its most abstract, conceptual form, the "why" of a business is often simply called its business model.

A business model is concerned with the nature and pattern of exchanges of one form of value for another

At the heart of every enterprise are trades or deals of some kind, exchanges of one form of value for another. A business model is concerned with the nature and pattern of these deals between businesses and their partners that ultimately yield the products or services it offers to its customers. A company's business model also addresses the roles played by other firms that work with and around it, such as suppliers, customers, stakeholders, intermediaries such as brokers, distributors, and agencies, and service providers of one sort or another. Viewed from the perspective of the enterprise at their intersection or common focus, this collection of parties and their organization is called the business ecosystem.[5]

Acronymology in Patterns of Business Organization

A very coarse level of describing patterns of business organization in a conceptual way emerged in the mid 1990s as a set of three-character acronyms beginning with B2B and B2C and still growing.

B2B, for business to business, was the first of these patterns and it is mentioned in millions of websites and domain names. It was used to describe business relationships in pre-Internet days, often in discussions of EDI document exchanges. For example, an industrial chemicals firm whose products are offered only to other businesses would be following the B2B pattern.

B2C, for business to consumer, emerged as a category label for Internet retail sites to contrast them with B2B ones. The number of B2C sites exploded with the popularity of the Web, and it is certainly a more visible category than B2B. Nevertheless, even if the breaking of the Internet bubble hadn't caused a great many B2C sites to disappear, B2C as a sector would still be dwarfed in economic scale by B2B, since all B2C transactions depend on numerous B2B ones (recall our discussion in Chapter 1 of the B2B Drop Shipment pattern that underlies the Internet bookstore).

More recent variants of the B2B and B2C categories distinguish those that involve governments. B2G, for business to government, seems slightly more common than G2B, for government to business, but both have been showing steady growth as governments at both municipal and national levels introduce Web initiatives of various kinds. G2C, for government to citizen, is the dominant variant. None of these acronyms appears to stand a chance against the term e-government, even though a list of the "24 priority e-government initiatives" in the United States sorts them into citizen and business categories.[6]

Many colleges and universities offer e-learning courses on the Internet directly to consumers but haven't adopted the B2C category, perhaps because they aren't for-profit businesses. Nor have they invented another acronym, although E2C, or education to consumer might fit. However, the for profit, distance- or lifelong-learning firms seem eager to embrace both the B2C and B2B labels.[7]

C2C, for consumer to consumer, had a brief appearance on the acronym stage to describe the organization of business relationships facilitated by auction sites like eBay, but this term didn't seem to reach critical mass. In any case, Internet-facilitated business relationships between individuals are now almost universally described as P2P, for peer to peer. This acronym is likely to have a long life because of its notoriety in file-sharing applications.

4.1.2.1 Supply Chains

Supply chains, especially those for heavy manufacturing industries like aerospace and automotive, are highly visible and physical. But when we want to design and analyze supply chains, it is less important to think in terms of buildings, vehicles, and pallets of goods and instead think from a more conceptual perspective.

Document Engineering treats supply chains as information flows

A conceptual view of a supply chain must deal with complex dependencies between the allocation of materials, production, and distribution responsibilities, the number and location of suppliers and distributors, the amount and location of material and product inventories, and the logistics of getting everything to its desired location at the right time.[8] Most of this multidimensional design problem must be solved before applying Document Engineering.

Document Engineering thinks of supply chains in terms of the information flows that accompany the movement of materials and goods; creating an abstract view of the physical events that trigger document exchanges and the reciprocal events resulting from those exchanges.

4.1.2.2 Marketplaces, Exchanges, and Auctions

A conceptual view of marketplaces, exchanges, and auctions defines them in terms of their participants and the services that they provide to each other. There needs to be a least one special participant who performs the role of the market operator. The operator, sometimes called the host or market maker, must have the credibility or market power to attract the buyers and sellers and establish the governing rules. These rules define the terms and conditions for participation, the specifications for the information that participants will exchange, and the processes or services in which the exchanges will take place. The operator must provide a trusted environment, both in terms of technology considerations like security and reliability and in the business sense of trust about privacy and the honoring of commercial obligations.

A minimal marketplace or auction offers the "commodity" services related to buying and selling, but what attracts and keeps participants are other value-added services that create richer relationships between buyers and sellers and induce buyers to return. The services that are most useful depend on the industry, geography, and other characteristics of the context in which the marketplace or auction pattern is being adopted.[9]

By eliminating any need for physical presence the Internet has increased the feasibility and conceptual variety of business models

Auctions have been around since ancient times, but by eliminating any need for physical presence the Internet has increased the feasibility and conceptual variety of auctions. The many different types or patterns of auctions are distinguished by the extent of information exchange among the participants, and by the rules that govern the timing of offers, the selection of the winning offer, and the price the buyer pays.[10]

4.1.3 CONCEPTUAL VIEWS OF BUSINESS RELATIONSHIPS

In the previous section we examined the organization of firms in supply chains, marketplaces, and other business ecosystems using a conceptual perspective that emphasized their functional roles. A complementary perspective looks at the nature of the relationships among the firms, particularly the relative power and capabilities of the parties.

Establishing a business relationship incurs the costs of finding a potential partner, qualifying it and its products or services, and determining whether its business processes and documents are compatible with ours. But compatibility is not an all-or-nothing issue. We need to assess whether the costs of closing the interoperability gap are worth it, and then we must decide how this effort is to be allocated between the parties in the relationship.

System architectures and technologies influence the cost of setting up business relationships

The system architectures and information systems employed by each party strongly influence the cost of setting up a business relationship. Service oriented architectures and web services promise ease and flexibility in exchanging documents to carry out business processes with new partners. But parties with legacy systems and integration technologies must abandon or adapt them to take advantage of these more loosely coupled approaches. Reluctance to incur these transitional costs has helped mainframe computers and EDI maintain an important role in many businesses even though their recurring costs can exceed those of newer technologies.

Some document exchanges enact public processes between two organizations, while others perform private processes between different groups within one organization. We often have to manage both kinds of relationships, but they involve different considerations and require different approaches.

Vertically integrated organizations may require that parts or services be procured from internal suppliers even if their quality or pricing is not competitive with the open market. These non economic business relationships are also common in government organizations, universities, and other enterprises where commercial market forces are often deliberately constrained. Such organizations might employ cost recovery or charge back models for internal transactions, which create disincentives for automation and improved productivity. And just as no one is surprised when new government facilities are located in the districts of powerful legislators, political considerations often come into play when business service roles are allocated within an enterprise.

The maintenance or recurring costs of managing a business relationship are different from the startup costs

The maintenance or recurring costs of managing a business relationship are different from the startup costs. Recurring transaction costs are minimized to the degree that the parties established full business and systems interoperability when they created their relationship. Nevertheless, each party may face continual pressure to change its processes or documents to suit other relationships or technology opportunities, and some effort is required to maintain existing relationships when this happens.

4.1.3.1 Asymmetric Relationships

A topical joke about business relationships that might not seem so funny to those involved goes like this:

What's the second worst business decision that a supplier can make? Making a deal with Wal-Mart.

What's the worst business decision it can make? Not making one.

This scenario is an extreme case because Wal-Mart is currently one of the world's largest companies and the dominant retailer of groceries and general consumer goods.[11] Wal-Mart is unparalleled in its ability to dictate the terms of supplier relationships. With a relentless focus on bringing the lowest possible prices to its customers, Wal-Mart holds down the prices it pays its suppliers. So while having a dominant customer such as Wal-Mart may expand a supplier's sales, it can simultaneously shrink profits unless the supplier can run every aspect of its businesses more efficiently. Such a relationship may distort the supplier's product mix, undermine its brands, and drive it to relocate manufacturing jobs to countries with lower wages.

In other business environments, often where there is a monopoly or an oligopoly, suppliers rather than buyers might control these asymmetric relationships. We can view government regulatory agencies, such as customs, building, or taxation authorities as asymmetric suppliers of clearances, permits, and assessments. In an academic context, we could consider the power of tenured university professors to dictate the specifications and terms under which their products are offered to students as an asymmetric relationship with the university that employs them.

An increasingly common business process that embodies asymmetric relationships between buyers and suppliers is the reverse auction, in which sellers bid against each other to meet a single buyer's specifications. Reverse auctions have been touted as a silver bullet of e-Business that can cut procurement costs by as much as 20 percent, particularly in high-value component assembly industries such as auto manufacturing. However, critics of reverse auctions say that they are toxic for buyer-supplier relationships because they inhibit future collaboration between them.[12]

Asymmetric relationships need not result in costly concessions from one party

But asymmetric relationships need not result in one side extracting profit-killing or costly concessions from the other. The dominant party in an asymmetric relationship can always choose not to exert their dominance, either because of its kinder and gentler corporate or social values or because it recognizes that long-term benefits can accrue from collaboration even in conditions that are supposedly hostile to it.[13]

4.1.3.2 Modes of Exchange

The mode of exchange in a business relationship can be defined as the set of standard procedures, common practices, communication patterns, and norms governing routine behavior in the relationship between a supplier and its customer. This is a much broader definition of what's exchanged than simply the exchange of money that many economists focus on. The mode of exchange also governs the extent of exchange of information and know-how, the level of trust, and norms of reciprocity or fairness in the relationship.[14]

Exit and voice modes of exchange are opposite dimensions of commitment to suppliers and the extent of coordination or collaboration with them. In the exit mode, there is little commitment and often little coordination, and problems with a supplier generally cause the buyer to replace the supplier.

By contrast, with a voice mode of exchange, there is both substantial commitment and communication between the buyer and supplier. So they can resolve problems through collaboration, which creates opportunities to improve processes and designs.

The same information exchange technologies that make it easier to select or change suppliers when relationships are managed in exit mode can enable close collaboration with them when they are managed in voice mode.[15]

But neither the products nor the technology used completely determine buyer-supplier relationships because different modes of exchange can exist in the same industry. The clearest example is the contrasting historical patterns and business philosophies of the Japanese and U.S. automobile industry.[16]

Japanese buyers such as Toyota has been profitable for decades while practicing a voice mode strategy of providing capital and technical assistance to suppliers. Over time this enables suppliers to take on more engineering responsibilities, including "black box" development, in which the supplier builds components with only limited specifications from the buyer.[17]

Black box development demonstrates that closer collaboration doesn't always mean that more information is exchanged between business partners. Long-term partners don't need to be as explicit in communication because they share tacit knowledge and context. This enables the parties to rely on increased information density rather than increased volume or speed as a way of improving productivity.

Information density also results from the use of patterns or reference models. When Intel tells its suppliers that it expects them to conduct business with it using RosettaNet PIPs 3A4, 3A7, 3B2, and 3C6, the seemingly unintelligible statement conveys hundreds of pages of technical specifications that define the context of use.[18]

Closer collaboration doesn't always mean more information exchange

By contrast, U.S. automakers have historically taken exit mode positions with suppliers (including employees), and adverse effects have accumulated over time. Adversarial and stalemated relationships have caused strong labor unions to prevent employers from replacing unproductive workers and have discouraged workers from suggesting or adopting technologies or processes that would increase their own productivity and the financial viability of their employer. Sometimes employees even cause work slowdowns by carefully obeying all the explicit rules and instructions governing their jobs while not doing things that they know would increase productivity.

The commitment and coordination dimensions that underlie contrasting modes of exchange also illuminate other types of problematic relationships. "High commitment with low coordination" aptly describes parties within a vertically integrated enterprise or in sectors not subject to economic market forces who are compelled to work with each other even if they might prefer other partners.

4.1.3.3 Trading Communities

The stability of business relationships ultimately reflects the extent to which the parties trust each other and share some long-term interests. Establishing and maintaining this trust is often the motivation for trading communities. A trading community encompasses the set of firms that fill the roles in business patterns like supply chains, distribution networks, and marketplaces. This collective identity helps them focus on achieving mutual business benefits.

Establishing and maintaining trust is the motivation for trading communities

A central activity of trading communities is reducing both the initial and recurring costs of conducting business relationships. This often requires that all companies use the same (or interoperable) technology and information models for integration and document exchange. It also involves establishing the terms and conditions under which business gets carried out and the mechanisms, legal and otherwise, that enforce them. The definition and management of the technology and business practices of the community are often called the community governance.

The typical goals of a trading community are clearly expressed in the August 2000 press release announcing the creation of the Global Trading Web Association, a trading community of B2B marketplaces that at the time were all using the XML-based marketplace platform developed by Commerce One.[19]

Defining the terms and conditions in a trading community is often a highly contentious and political activity that involves negotiation, compromise, and sensitivity to existing and potential asymmetries in relationships. Not surprisingly, many successful trading communities revolve around a dominant hub enterprise that has the power to influence or dictate technology, terms, and standards.

Many successful trading communities revolve around a dominant hub enterprise

Large telecommunications, software, or professional services firms can create a community around their customer bases. For example, IBM targets the banking, financial services, industrial and manufacturing, and insurance industries through its Web Services Industry Councils, which are "chartered to accelerate time to business value of web services implementations by addressing industry-specific problems and grow the adoption of web services solutions in the respective industries."[20]

On the other hand, instead of using technology requirements or trade relationships to limit membership, sometimes a community will do the opposite, broadening its membership to increase transaction volumes and industry influence by eliminating the requirement that all members use the same technology. In late 2002 the Global Trading Web Association recast itself as the Open Network for Commerce Exchange (ONCE) to emphasize that its members need not use the same marketplace platform.[21]

4.1.3.4 Facilitators, Industry Associations, and Communities of Practice

A trading community or group of complementary business service providers sometimes evolves into a facilitator. The most common type of facilitator is an industry group, trade association, or chamber of commerce created to set industry standards or policies and otherwise promote the interests of its members. These organizations operate outside of traditional business relationships, and their membership typically includes manufacturers, distributors, customers, service providers, brokers, and other entities that are part of an industry ecosystem or geographical business region. They provide a broad and commercially neutral perspective in which firms can cooperate to set standards or policies, often relying on explicit exemptions from the antitrust regulations that would otherwise treat cooperation between businesses as anticompetitive activity. In some countries, these sorts of competitive conflicts are alleviated because the primary trade facilitation organization is a government agency.

Industry groups also initiate projects to develop or improve new business services and the documents they require. For example in the UK, SITPRO is a trade facilitation body dedicated to simplifying the international trading process such as by creating the Aligned Export Documents.[22] In Australia the Tradegate organization was founded to bring together the different regulatory and commercial organizations involved in the trade and transport supply chain to develop a common strategy for the document exchanges required by port operators, shippers, forwarders, and other service providers on the waterfront.[23] Similar initiatives exist in nearly every other international trading community and in many large business ecosystems.[24]

Industry groups often initiate projects to develop or improve new business services and the documents they require

In some cases facilitators have taken on the role of a standards body or are active participants in standards setting activities. For example, the EAN/UCC[25] has developed standards for bar codes and the assignment of company prefixes in the retail goods supply chain. The Electronics Industry Data Exchange (EIDX) organization established the RosettaNet Consortium.[26] UN/CEFACT[27] has long directed work to develop EDI standards. And, the Supply-Chain Council,[28] which developed the Supply-Chain Operations Reference model (SCOR), is also a facilitator organization.

Community of practice is a recent label that describes a facilitator organization composed of individual practitioners who "share a concern or a passion for something they do and who interact regularly to learn how to do it better."[29] The term is broader than the more familiar user group and emphasizes activities for systematizing, storing, and sharing knowledge and best practices. There are scores of user groups and communities of practice focused on XML, vocabulary development and other dimensions of document interoperability.[30]

A variation on the ideas of the industry group, trade association or community of practice is the business alliance, typically a group of companies with the common goal of challenging or defending against the dominant firm or firms in their industry. These business alliances sometimes adopt common technology to eliminate one source of competition among the community members and focus on the rivalry with the dominant outsiders. An example is the Liberty Alliance, whose charter expresses the goal of "developing an open standard for federated network identity that supports all current and emerging network devices," but whose implicit purpose is to provide an alternative to Microsoft's Passport mechanism for managing identity information.[31] So while an alliance may profess the goal of creating a level playing field for its members, it often does so by creating specifications or policies that discriminate against companies who didn't join it or who were not invited to do so.

4.2 VIEWS OF BUSINESS PROCESSES

We've talked about "business process" for three chapters without a precise definition because it is such a common phrase. It is obvious that functional business areas like engineering, manufacturing, and sales carry out systematic activities that are somehow interconnected, and we need a notion of business process to describe how this works. So we'll define business process as a chain of related activities or events that take specified inputs, add value to the inputs, and yield a specific service or product that can be the input to another business process. The chain of business processes is maintained by the flow of information between them as the output of one process becomes the input to the next.

Business process models are the bridge between organizational models and business documents

Business process models are central to Document Engineering because they are the bridge between higher-level strategic expressions of what businesses do represented in organizational models and the lower-level operational concerns reflected in document and information models.

4.2.1 PHYSICAL VIEWS OF BUSINESS PROCESSES

Physical views of business processes describe the way in which specific business activities are implemented by a firm. Most firms have a vast variety of policies and procedures governing how they hire, pay, train, evaluate, and terminate employees, how they approve, budget, staff, review, and learn from projects, how they conceive, design, manufacture, document, test, market, and sell products, how they procure needed goods and services and operate and maintain equipment, how they deal with business partners and customers, how they account for income and expenses and meet government reporting requirements—the list goes on and on.[32] All of these are physical views of business process models.

Some of these policies and procedures exist as documents on employee's desks and office shelves or on the company intranet. Others are embodied as business rules in software applications that range from electronic mail and spreadsheets to enterprise content management and ERP systems.

As we discussed in section 3.4.2, "Why Businesses Follow Patterns," many business processes are dictated by laws, regulations, and standards. These may sometimes function as conceptual models that govern or guide many aspects of individual and corporate behavior and business processes. But sometimes they are highly prescriptive, specifying how things can and cannot be done, possibly even dictating the technology and manner of solution implementation. Prescriptive models of this sort are implemented using mundane document templates or software applications that create customized employee handbooks, procedure guides, and contracts.

4.2.2 CONCEPTUAL VIEWS OF BUSINESS PROCESSES

A company's business model shows the logical relationship between the functional areas in the enterprise. However, the granularity of functional areas often provides too coarse a perspective for analyzing what an enterprise does, what it needs to do better, and what it can do without. It is helpful to further decompose functional business areas into subareas and more specific business processes.

4.2.2.1 Business Reference Models

Because they are more stable descriptions of what an enterprise does, the highest level functional areas are categories for organizing models at lower levels, and the resulting hierarchy of business processes is sometimes called a business reference model. An important business reference model is the recently developed Federal Enterprise Architecture of the U.S. government,[33] which could be considered a pattern for other governments around the world.

A reference model consolidates the best practices of many companies

Business reference models exist in many industries and are most often created by industry associations or by consulting firms that have extensive industry experience. Almost by definition a single firm can't create a business reference model because a good reference model consolidates and abstracts from benchmarking or best practices analyses of many companies in the industry.

4.2.2.2 Supply Chain Reference Model

Many of the patterns in supply chain models can be seen in the Supply Chain Operations Reference Model (SCOR), a reference model developed by an industry group called the Supply Chain Council.[34] SCOR provides standard patterns for describing supply chains in terms of five basic processes: plan, source, make, deliver, and return.

These patterns are organized as conceptual models whose two lower levels of detail refine the basic five processes to describe supply chain models for different industries and partner relationships. Figure 4-2 shows the top level view of the SCOR supply chain pattern.

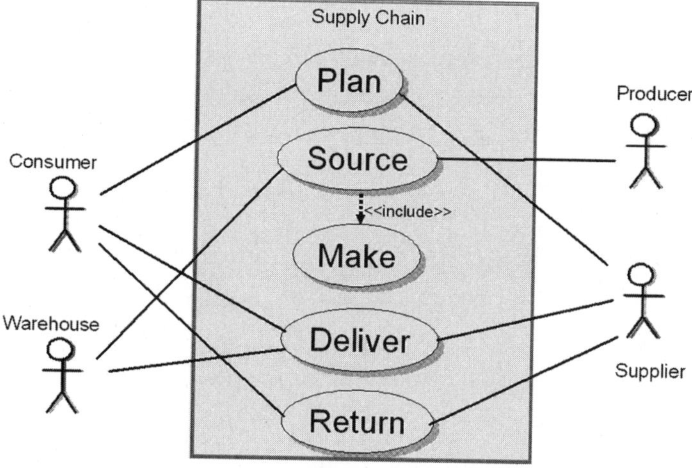

Figure 4-2. The SCOR Supply Chain Pattern

4.2.2.3 RosettaNet

The RosettaNet Consortium has developed standard specifications for processes in the global supply chain for the electronic components and IT industries. Approximately 100 detailed process models called partner interface processes (PIPs)[35] are organized hierarchically by clusters and segments. The first PIPs that most firms implement are those in the Order Management cluster, which contains segments for Quote and Order Entry, Transportation and Distribution, Returns and Finance, and Product Configuration. The fourteen 14 PIPs in Quote and Order Entry, like PIP 3A4 for Request Purchase Order, define both the document implementation models (as XML schemas) and the collaboration of document exchanges between trading partners.

The implementation focus of PIPs means that they provide physical views of business processes that we might have discussed in section 4.2.1. But in other respects the RosettaNet specifications represent a more conceptual view of business processes. In particular, the hierarchical arrangement of PIPs into clusters and segments provides a useful vocabulary for analyzing supply chains at different levels of abstraction. In addition, the PIPs were developed using a common metamodel shared by all the PIPs. This facilitates its generalization to other industries. We will demonstrate the reuse of RosettaNet PIPs as business process patterns in Chapter 10.

The Secret of RosettaNet's Success

RosettaNet, founded in 1998, is a consortium of major information technology, electronic components, semiconductor manufacturing, telecommunications, and logistics companies that is creating and implementing business process patterns. RosettaNet began with the IT supply chain and has sought to expand its membership and scope to extend the coverage of its patterns beyond its current vertical market. RosettaNet stands apart from many communities of practice efforts in its member commitment to implementing these common patterns. Maybe this follows from RosettaNet's steep annual dues—$50,000 in 2004—which means that participation is a high-level strategic decision.

But participation in RosettaNet may be worth it. Intel, one of the founding members of the consortium, reported that more than 10 percent of its supplier and customer transactions in 2002 were based on RosettaNet, a total of about $5 billion. Intel is using RosettaNet standards to work with more than 100 trading partners in more than 20 countries and is counting on RosettaNet to reach the aggressive goal of becoming a 100 percent e-corporation.[36]

4.2.2.4 Information Supply Chains

The flow of materials and goods in a supply chain or distribution channel has always been accompanied by the flow of information about it. When we unpack a box of something we've ordered, we often find that it contains a shipping label with our name and address, a packing slip or manifest that itemizes the contents, assembly or operating instructions, a payment receipt, an invoice, and other types of documents. But information about the processes is increasingly becoming separated from the physical flow of materials and goods, at which point it can be thought of in conceptual terms as an information chain, information value chain, or information supply chain.[37]

Information about the business processes is distinct from the physical flow of materials and goods

An information supply chain specifies who exchanges information, what information they exchange, and the frequency with which they exchange it. The documents exchanged package the content of these information flows. And, while communication and information technology is what makes the information flows possible, the technology itself is less important than the abstract perspective of the patterns of document exchanges and processes.

The information flow of a supply chain differs in three critical ways from the physical supply chain:

- Information can flow qualitatively faster than materials and goods, which might spend weeks in trucks, trains, or shipping containers moving around the world.

- Information may flow in the opposite direction of the materials and goods, moving from customers and retailers back toward distributors, manufacturers, and their suppliers.

- Information can go many places at once so that supply chain participants can know about inventories, locations, sales, and so on without having to witness them.

These three characteristics of the information chain make it an essential adjunct to the physical supply chain and the key to keeping a business competitive and responsive to rapidly changing markets and customer requirements.

4.2.2.5 Demand Chains

When information flows in the opposite direction of the materials and goods, moving from customers and retailers back toward distributors, manufacturers, and their suppliers, the flow is sometimes called the demand chain. This backward (or feedback) flow of information isn't a new thing, but near real-time information about inventories and sales is profoundly more valuable than monthly reports. For example, websites allow a firm to capture implicit or explicit demand information from customers around the clock.

If retailers provide inventory information to suppliers, the suppliers can take responsibility for resupplying inventory and keeping the retailer's shelves stocked. In this vendor managed inventory (VMI) pattern, the supplier ships replacement goods directly to the retail store to keep inventories at agreed levels.

VMI is often the first stage of greater collaboration because its benefits reinforce information sharing between retailers and their suppliers.[38] If retailers are willing to share additional information, such as point of sale transaction data and customer information from loyalty programs, the suppliers and retailers can collaborate on business planning, sales forecasting, evaluations of pricing and promotions, and other opportunities for continuous improvement in their joint processes. This more comprehensive pattern is called collaborative forecasting, planning, and replenishment (CPFR).[39]

VMI and CPFR patterns can be generalized to other information chain situations involving the delivery of services rather than goods for sale. An example is Otis Elevator's Remote Elevator Monitoring system, which monitors numerous elevator functions and initiates orders for service calls or maintenance parts. Remote monitoring of equipment, machinery, or facilities can be thought of as vendor-managed or outsourced asset management.[40]

4.2.2.6 Document Automation and Straight Through Processing

So far we have presented views of business organization and processes that mostly involve the movement of tangible things or information about the movement of tangible things. But a great deal of what businesses do involves even more abstract activities that can be described in terms of the movement of information, and sometimes the activities are so abstract that the only tangible things involved are artifacts that record the information. These kinds of business processes follow the related patterns of document automation and straight through processing (STP).

Every significant business manages its money, files tax returns, and submits financial reports to various government agencies, often for multiple jurisdictions. In industries like healthcare, insurance, banking, real estate, financial services, and securities, the high business value activities centers around document processing for transactions. Many of these industries use some notion of a financial value chain as an analogue to the supply chain in industries with more tangible products.

Many of the information-intensive activities in these industries were once carried out using paper documents that moved from one organization or firm to another, with the documents growing through the incremental addition of evidence, approvals, reconciliations, and other information. Today businesses often make it a goal to use the Internet to capture and exchange documents from the moment they are created to the time they have served their purpose to complete, settle, or reconcile a transaction.

The exact definition of this end-to-end goal differs from industry to industry but is most often called straight through processing. Such initiatives began in the securities industry[41] and document automation initiatives in insurance, real estate, and human resources have all adopted the STP label. For example, even though it isn't described as STP, an effort underway at the Florida State Senate to automate the end-to-end lifecycle of laws from their origins as draft bills all the way through their publication as printed and web documents certainly fits the definition.[42]

Straight Through Processes vary greatly in how completely they can be automated. Those that require clerical functions of data entry, verification and calculation can often be totally automated. The business rules that need to be enforced can easily be encoded in XML schemas, spreadsheets, or in application logic. At the other extreme, those at the other end of the continuum that require expert analysis, tacit knowledge, and the interpretation of business policy with respect to competitors or customers can only be partially automated.

Indeed, the extent of automation in the latter context can sometimes be little more than more efficiently getting the computerized information fodder of the task to the knowledge worker who actually performs it. Nevertheless, even this limited degree of document automation can significantly improve productivity by more fairly distributing the workload in a group of such workers.

Document automation and STP efforts don't simply replace the physical workflow of paper documents with the logical flow of computerized ones. The electronic documents might all be stored in a centralized and shared document management system, which eliminates the need for documents to move from place to place or from system to system. Instead, all of the processing or approval transactions take place using a shared repository, with logical workflow and access privileges ensuring that the appropriate people interact with the documents at the desired time. The U.S. Army, which handles an estimated 15 million copies annually of 100,000 different forms, hopes to save $1.3 billion a year by implementing a centralized forms content management system.[43]

Many STP efforts in the US are now being driven by the Sarbanes-Oxley Act of 2002,[44] enacted to curb corrupt business activities and fraudulent accounting practices like those of Enron and WorldCom. Sarbanes-Oxley requires businesses to implement adequate internal control structures and procedures and attest to their effectiveness. Informal or manual procedures don't enable sufficient auditing and tracing of information about where money came from, where it went, and why it went there.

Sarbanes-Oxley has inspired numerous efforts to create standard conceptual models for the information needed to conduct effective audits.[45] These models describe the relationships among business organization, processes, accounts, control procedures, types of risk, and so on. The overriding goal is to enable better electronic discovery and management of the documents needed by the audit and by the assurance reports. Sarbanes-Oxley is also driving increased spending on the enabling technologies of document and records management, business process automation, and security.[46]

While not every document automation or STP effort is the same, they share some key characteristics or subgoals that define the pattern:

- They emphasize more efficient creation of the initial document or docu-ments through the use of templates for different document types or guided assembly of a custom document from components.

- They seek to minimize manual intervention as the documents flow from process to process by transforming information for reuse in different contexts and by using business rules to automate routing, access control, and exception handling.

- They seek not just to automate existing processes, which would be akin to creating roads by paving cow paths, but to refine or reengineer them, possibly by adopting industry best practices or reference models.

- They view documents as dynamic rather than static, automatically prop-agating changed information into the processing pipeline so that it is current and available when needed.

- They take an end-to-end perspective that maximizes reuse and minimizes redundancy by extracting any sharable models or rules and making them available from a single logical repository.

- They emphasize standards for information and process models because those standards facilitate the other five subgoals.

The standards efforts in each industry have generally been led by industry associations or by firms that hope to prosper by offering the key services in the STP pipeline to firms who don't want to perform them. Notable exceptions are efforts in Denmark and Norway, where the strongest mandates and standards for document automation are coming from the government.[47]

4.3 VIEWS OF BUSINESS INFORMATION

Views of business information are extremely important. We know them as the definitions of business documents and their components that are exchanged between different organizations or enterprises (or, more precisely, between their information systems or services).

4.3.1 PHYSICAL VIEWS OF BUSINESS INFORMATION

Physical views of documents have a long history of defining the interface a business presents to the world. Standard printed forms to initiate or record transactions, taxes, and other business activities have existed for centuries. By the mid-19th century, accounting practices and associated documents like balance sheets, statements of accounts, and business registrations were standard enough for the British government to mandate annual audits.[48]

4.3.1.1 Electronic Data Interchange

Efforts to standardize electronic documents began more than 40 years ago in the trucking industry, spread to the banking, grocery, and retail sectors, and ultimately led in the 1980s to ongoing national and international standards activities for electronic data interchange (EDI).

Efforts to standardize electronic documents began more than 40 years ago

EDI was developed to automate the exchange of structured information in transactional documents such as orders, invoices, and payments between business applications. Initially these exchanges took place over dedicated leased telephone lines or over private networks in a batch store-and-forward fashion. By the 1980s, EDI had penetrated a variety of industries, especially automotive, aerospace, transportation, manufacturing, and retail, where relatively small numbers of firms are the dominant buyers from a large number of suppliers. The ANSI ASC X12 U.S. standards and the Guidelines for Trade Data Interchange (GTDI) European standards began to emerge at this time, followed shortly by the ISO 9735 (UN/EDIFACT) standard developed by the United Nations to consolidate numerous national EDI standards.[49]

In theory, the EDI standards for documents and the business processes they support should be good starting points for relationships between trading partners. But EDI has fallen short of this promise. The competing X12 and EDIFACT standards are somewhat incompatible, and both syntaxes are brittle and encourage practices such as the overloading of meanings into opaque code lists. Furthermore, because the EDI standards process is formal and tedious, it takes a long time to create new standard documents, and the resulting standards are often a bloated laundry list of requirements in which almost everything is optional. None of this encourages the interoperable exchange of information.

In practice the EDI standards are never used in standard ways

So in practice the EDI standards are never used in standard ways. The dominant trading partner typically selects a small subset of the information components from the standard document and imposes ad hoc implementation guidelines on the organizations who do business with it. For example, the EDI requirements imposed by Kroger,[50] a very large U.S. supermarket chain, specify extensive adaptations of the standard EDI documents to which its suppliers must conform. It is easy to understand how this subtractive customization approach makes EDI integration expensive for businesses that must adhere to the document formats imposed by each dominant trading partner they serve.

Despite these many limitations EDI remains an important technology. For firms in established business relationships that have made substantial investments to make EDI work, the sense is "if it ain't broke, don't fix it." EDI is not the technology of choice when setting up new document exchanges with business partners, especially when new documents must be developed for new business processes. But like mainframes and fax machines, EDI can still claim "I'm Not Dead Yet."[51]

4.3.1.2 XMLification

When XML emerged in the late 1990s as the preferred syntax for describing document formats, the EDI standards began to "XMLify," and scores of XML business vocabularies emerged.[52] As with early efforts in EDI, most of the latter were developed in specific vertical industries by trade associations or industry consortia to reduce the development and integration costs for small and medium-sized enterprises that could not afford to invest in EDI solutions.

New XML specifications often reinvent definitions of common information components

But while each new XML specification for a particular industry was a step forward for that industry, they have proliferated definitions of information components that cut across different industries. Each vocabulary reinvented descriptions of businesses and individuals, measurements, date and time, location, country codes, currencies, business classification codes, and basic business documents like catalogs, purchase orders, and invoices. As is often the case with new technologies, it was two steps forward and one step back.

The earliest effort to attack the problem of semantic overlap among XML vocabularies for business applications was the XML Common Business Library, whose first version was released in 1997. XCBL was a freely distributed set of XML business documents and a set of reusable components common to many business processes. XCBL, like many models of business information, is tied to specific technologies or syntaxes such as XML schemas. We call them document implementation models. This means that they are typically published as libraries of XML schemas with the expectation that they will be reused at this physical level. The underlying concepts and meanings encoded in the vocabularies are only implicit or, at best, incompletely documented.

Because of the physical level of the models, syntax differences like those between X12 and UN/EDIFACT with EDI, or between either of these and an XML vocabulary, can get in the way of doing electronic business, even if the concepts underlying the documents being exchanged are compatible. Communication usually requires a knowledgeable person to manually create a semantic map between corresponding syntactic components in the pair of models. This has given rise to a category of integration technology that attempts to reuse these semantic maps.[53]

The reason physical level mapping is difficult is that it requires a common abstract view that defines the concepts involved rather than the implementation technology. So we need conceptual counterparts to our various physical models (see Section 4.3.2).

4.3.1.3 Information Aggregations

Information aggregations occur where documents or data from numerous sources are brought together to create a consolidated information resource that is more valuable than the sum of the sources. In business informatics this composite resource is typically called a data warehouse or data mart. Another common composite pattern is a multivendor catalog that includes product information from many manufacturers or suppliers. More examples can be seen in documents such as daily shipping schedules and stock market trading tables.

Composite information sources can be created by extracting and transforming the original information and are usually built during "off hours" to minimize the impact on production systems, but as businesses become more global it is always "on hours" somewhere. So the challenge facing the enterprise to keep the composite repository accurate becomes more difficult as the source information becomes more volatile.

An alternative approach is to create a virtual repository or virtual catalog in which the metadata from each source is aggregated into the composite resource, not the content itself. This composite metadata enables the content information to be referenced from its source and dynamically transformed to the target implementation model when the information is requested.[54]

Another information composition pattern is syndication, the consolidation and distribution of information products. This is widespread in traditional publishing with information like news events, articles, and editorial cartoons collated into a stream of syndicated content in which items can be selected, routed, and managed using common metadata for each piece of content.

4.3.2 CONCEPTUAL VIEWS OF BUSINESS INFORMATION

We noted in Section 4.3.1 that implementation models of business information have a long history and are quite common. In contrast, models that embody a more abstract, conceptual view are a more recent development.

This is hardly surprising. Conceptual views are intellectually more challenging to develop and not as immediately beneficial as physical ones. Even though models based on conceptual views pay off over time in greater robustness and adaptability, the investment it takes to develop an understanding of the concepts in a domain is often seen as delaying the real work of implementation.

Conceptual views are more challenging to develop than physical ones

A notable attempt to develop conceptual models of business information is David Hay's "Data Model Patterns," whose subtitle "Conventions of Thought" emphasizes the abstractness and implementation-independence of good models. Hay's models cover the basic subject areas of people and organizations, products and inventory, procedures and activities, and accounting. A similar book that organizes conceptual models by industry is Len Silverston's "Data Model Resource Book."[55]

The ebXML initiative, launched in 1999 as a joint venture of EDI and XML standards organizations, was the first serious attempt to create conceptual views of business information components that could be used for document implementation models in any syntax. The resulting document content would be interoperable because of these common semantic foundations, called core components.[56] Unfortunately, the ebXML effort was not entirely successful at delivering on its promise to create a library of core components, but more because of organizational and political squabbling between the standards groups than for technical problems it couldn't overcome.

Nevertheless, ebXML paved the way for the Universal Business Language effort, which seems to be succeeding in its goal of creating a standard XML vocabulary for business that is based on a conceptual document component model.

The Universal Business Language

The Universal Business Language (UBL) effort began in late 2001 with the extremely ambitious goals of building on the idea of ebXML core components, synthesizing the leading XML and EDI vocabularies for business, and creating standard business documents that would be nonproprietary and royalty free. In effect, it is attempting to provide the equivalent of HTML for business document exchanges. It took over two years, but UBL met these goals with the release of version 1 of the UBL library in May 2004.

The UBL Library consists of various document implementation models defined using reusable XML Schema types. These are based on the UBL document component model for common business components like Party, Address, and Item. These components are reused in assembly models for basic procurement documents, including Order, Order Response, Order Change, Order Cancellation, Despatch Advice, Receipt Advice, and Invoice—with many more documents on the way.

A formal set of rules can be applied to transform these document assembly models into document implementation models. In UBL, this means encoding them using XML Schema. The UBL Naming and Design Rules define best practices for transforming the assembly model into the implementation model. These rules specify the use of elements and attributes, naming conventions, namespaces, modularity, versioning, and other considerations about how best to exploit XML Schema. These rules have been embedded into various computer applications that automate the generation of UBL XML Schemas.

For UBL to succeed as a standard global document format, it must deal with the challenge that most companies are part of numerous supply chains or trading partner relationships that require slightly different documents. It is simply impossible to create semantic components and documents that will work in all situations without customization. Instead, UBL aims to make 80 percent of the library directly useful as is, with the remainder requiring some customization. Making most of the library generic invokes the corollary to the 80/20 rule that the remaining 20 percent customization causes 80 percent of the complexity. For this reason, the UBL initiative is now developing a context methodology to support controlled customization of a document implementation model. Other areas of customization include localization of UBL into different business regions and languages such as Chinese, Japanese, Spanish, and Korean. This last issue suggests yet another challenge for UBL—the need to fit in with other XML business information and messaging standards. UBL recognizes that no one vocabulary can express all the relevant semantics for business. So UBL has based its models on the ebXML core components metamodel, making it easier to align conceptually with vocabularies also based on that metamodel.

UBL has attracted worldwide interest from industry associations and governments and is on track to be both an OASIS standard and an international standard for trade through ISO Technical Committee 154.[57]

4.4 VIEWS OF BUSINESS ARCHITECTURE

Another important way to describe businesses is in terms of the information technology or systems they use. This method is especially common for businesses to which the Internet is strategic or essential; recall how popular the term e-Business was a few years ago. Firms like Amazon, eBay, or Google, none of whom could exist without the Internet, often tout their technology innovations.

Organizations can't have a business relationship if they can't efficiently share information

When different organizations within an enterprise or different firms want to do business with each other, they would prefer not to have to know anything about the systems or technologies each uses to carry out their respective activities. Nevertheless, they can't have a business relationship if they can't efficiently share information, so someone always needs to be concerned with how the business systems fit together. We call this the business architecture - an abstract specification of a business that describes its components and their relationships with each other, using hierarchical and compositional structures to define component boundaries.

4.4.1 PHYSICAL VIEWS OF BUSINESS ARCHITECTURE

A description of a system and its components as a physical model is called a systems architecture. A systems architecture describes a business in terms of its computing platforms, operating systems, databases, and software applications.

4.4.1.1 Technology Platforms and Infrastructure

Sometimes we characterize the systems architecture of an enterprise in terms of its dominant software architectures or technology suppliers; this is often called its platform. We contrast Microsoft or SAP shops with J2EE or Linux or PeopleSoft ones. As XML takes hold as an implementation technology for document-intensive and Internet-based business systems, XML-centric system architectures have evolved to promote what works best in their design and implementation.[58]

Companies that have implemented ERP systems often have a similar technology-centered perspective on how they are organized. Their systems connect manufacturing control, production planning, inventory, procurement, finance, and human resources systems through a single database, or through a set of linked databases using middleware of some kind. The common data and associations among applications have been described as the "enterprise nervous system."[59]

Physical system architectures are often depicted using deployment diagrams that show the key information repositories (like databases), computing resources (server farms), and dedicated communications links and networks needed to move data and documents around. These models are often closely related to or overlaid on facilities plans like those described in Section 4.1.1.1. The locations of company headquarters, data warehouses, call centers, and other computing or communications convergence points can be represented in a systems architecture diagram to create an organizational technology "wiring diagram" for the business.

4.4.1.2 Integration Architecture and Patterns

An important corollary to the systems architecture, which shows the interconnections between software systems or applications, is the architecture by which this integration is achieved. Integration is defined as the controlled sharing of data and business processes between any connected applications or data sources.[60]

Integration is the controlled sharing of data and business processes between any connected applications or data sources

The number of potential integration points multiplies with the number of architectural components on each side; simply put, if each side followed the classic three-tier architecture with data-application-presentation layers, there would be nine possible categories of integration techniques. The specific techniques for getting information from one system or application to another also vary immensely to deal with numerous generations of software architectures.

Integration approaches that depend on implementation details or other characteristics at the physical level are said to be tightly coupled. At one extreme are "screen scraping" or database extraction approaches that extract data from legacy mainframe databases that were not designed to share information, techniques that require detailed analysis of the screen layout or internal record and table structures. More modern applications are often integrated within an enterprise through a shared data store or warehouse, or by synchronously invoking application program interfaces (APIs). Application layer to application layer coupling through application program interfaces is typically used when the interconnected systems must exchange data at high transaction rates.

Tight coupling is used to exchange data at high transaction rates

Too often, however, the APIs may be very fine grained while carving up the application functionality in incompatible ways. Exchanging information using APIs in this situation requires many small method invocations that extract and set only one or two data values at a time, making the process cumbersome and brittle with all the liabilities of tight coupling and few of the benefits.

Loose coupling is necessary for integration across enterprise boundaries because interfaces might change

Tightly-coupled approaches generally aren't suitable for integration across enterprise boundaries because of the likelihood of uncontrolled or unexpected changes to interfaces. Instead, cross-enterprise integration approaches try to avoid relying on implementation details, making them more loosely coupled. In effect loose coupling techniques, which we discuss further in the next two sections, raise the level of abstraction of the integration problem.

4.4.1.3 Web Services

Web services have emerged in the last few years as an important physical architectural idea especially for business-to-business relationships where looser coupling through document exchange is required or desirable (see Section 1.3.3).

Because almost anything can be turned into a service by wrapping it in XML document interfaces, there has been enormous hype about web services. A typical claim is "What the Web did for program-to-user interactions, web services are poised to do for program-to-program interactions."[61] Some disappointment may set in when we realize that the essence of web services is a few simple specifications for using XML messaging for application integration.

We can explain the concepts embodied by the primary web services specifications with a simple analogy of sending a fax. If we don't already know the party to whom we should send the fax requesting the service we want, we need a business directory in which we can find their details. First, we need a service description that tells us their fax number. Then we need to know what kind of business message to send, and what kind of response to expect. Finally we need to know how to address the cover page and how to attach the content to it.

More formally, a web service is defined as a platform-independent implementation of functionality that conforms to published specifications for the XML documents it sends and receives as its public interfaces (for example, the Web Service Description Language or the ebXML CPPP), the messaging protocol used to send and receive XML documents through those interfaces (for example, SOAP or ebMS), and a searchable directory of services (for example, a UDDI or an ebXML Registry). Since these specifications have been proposed, many so-called "standards" have proliferated for other components implied by a completely service oriented architecture but none of the basic ideas have substantially changed.[62]

Web services enable a more loosely-coupled integration approach than previous integration technologies

Because they can wrap a hodgepodge of legacy technologies and hide proprietary data models and protocols with XML document interfaces, web services provide a layer of abstraction and enable a more loosely coupled integration approach than previous integration technologies. However, this doesn't entirely solve the integration problem. Security, reliable delivery, performance, scalability, and other critical issues for deploying enterprise-level web services aren't completely handled by current specifications and vendors.

But there is a more fundamental reason why web services alone don't solve the integration problem. While a web service's technical specifications dictate how to reveal the interfaces and message definitions for the XML documents that it sends and receives, they say nothing about the conceptual design of those services and their enabling documents. They tell us how to package information into documents and where to put them, but they don't tell us what any of it means.

4.4.2 CONCEPTUAL VIEWS OF BUSINESS ARCHITECTURE

In contrast to physical systems architectures, the architecture of a business can be described in more abstract terms, sometimes called a logical architecture. A logical architecture doesn't concern itself with specific implementation technologies but instead emphasizes topological or structural relationships between the functional components of business systems. Vendor and technology-neutral concepts like N-tier, middleware, gateways, and service networks are used in logical architectures to describe the conceptual arrangement of computing and communications resources.

A logical architecture can portray the boundaries or interconnections among business systems and represent the extent to which systems are centralized or distributed within an enterprise. Architectural patterns reflect different requirements for system communication or integration. An architectural description can reveal the extent and direction of information exchanged between systems. It can also identify systems that are isolated islands or silos of functionality because they can't easily exchange information with other ones.

IBM's patterns for e-Business[63] are a rich source of conceptual models of business architectures. The IBM patterns grew out of an internal IBM effort to systematize the best practices of its consulting division and identify feasible architectures for large-scale e-business applications.

At the top of the conceptual model hierarchy are what IBM calls the Business Patterns, which describe at the most conceptual level the ways in which users and businesses interact with information. There are four Business Patterns: Self-Service (also known as "user-to-business" or B2C), Collaboration (also known as "user-to-user" or C2C), Information Aggregation (also known as "user-to-data"), and Extended Enterprise (also known as "business-to-business" or B2B). These basic Business Patterns can be combined to create more complex patterns. One example is the "e-marketplace" pattern, which enables buyers and sellers to trade goods and services on a public website by combining the Self-Service and Information Aggregation patterns.

Similar conceptual patterns have been proposed by Weill and Vitale.[64] They describe eight atomic business patterns, each of which describes a distinct but irreducible business function, such as Content Provider, Direct to Consumer, and Intermediary. According to this approach, businesses compound the atomic patterns into more sophisticated business architectures.

Many of these business architecture patterns rely heavily on documents as user or service interfaces, but the patterns have never before been organized in a way that makes this explicit. In Chapter 15 we introduce our own framework, which emphasizes document interfaces, exchanges, and the management of information exchanges and the models they require.

4.4.2.1 Conceptual Views of Integration Architecture

It is preferable for many of the participants in a business relationship to take a technology-independent and conceptual view of the integration architecture and focus on the more abstract goal of interoperability.

Interoperability is a more abstract goal than integration

Interoperability means that the recipient can extract the required information from the sender's document even if the sender's implementation is not immediately compatible with the recipient's business systems. This might require some reverse engineering of the underlying conceptual model from the physical model in which the sender's information is encoded. Then the recipient must establish that the extracted conceptual model is what it needs to carry out the intended process. If this is established, transforming a different implementation to an encoding from which the needed information can be extracted is a necessary, but often trivial thing to do.

In Chapter 6, "When Models Don't Match: The Interoperability Challenge" we describe a range of examples that illustrate interoperability problems.

While it is easy to understand why interoperability challenges can arise when systems from different technology generations must be integrated, technology is neither the primary cause of this incompatibility nor the primary means of eliminating it. The best way to facilitate interoperability is often for the participants in the exchange to jointly define a conceptual model for the shared information, or for both of them to adopt the same industry standard. This approach allows them to use the same information model without any constraints on their implementation of it.

The best way to facilitate interoperability is for the participants to share the same conceptual model

There is no precise point when reducing the assumptions and dependencies between the participants turns the physical view required by a tightly coupled relationship into the more conceptual one implied by a loosely coupled relationship.[65] But a loosely coupled approach generally means that information is exchanged asynchronously rather than synchronously, and in larger, document-sized chunks governed by an explicit schema or model (as it would be by an industry standard) rather than as fine-grained information pieces whose semantic definition is implicit only in the integration code.

The benefits of a loosely coupled approach mean that for the interorganizational and interenterprise applications that are at the core of Document Engineering, the most practical integration architecture is often messaging. Applications communicate by sending messages to a channel that ensures the reliable asynchronous delivery to the recipient while vastly reducing how much the sender and recipient must know about each other's technology.[66] Messaging systems or messaging-oriented middleware must still be configured to fit the addressing, packaging, security, and delivery requirements of each situation, but bringing all these concerns together substantially reduces the complexity of the integration challenge.

4.4.2.2 Service Oriented Architectures

Web services allow a business to take a more abstract view of implementation and integration, and it is reasonable to deploy them in an incremental, point-to-point, and bottom-up manner to integrate systems two at a time. However, an even more abstract view of services in a business architecture is the top-down and strategic one that considers everything a business does as (potentially) realized by business service components that are combined and recombined as needed. This perspective defines a service oriented architecture or SOA.

An SOA imposes a very abstract perspective on supply chains, marketplaces, drop shipment, and other processes because it deemphasizes technology and platform considerations and views them all as combinations of services. The emergence of SOA as an industry buzzword in recent years has been accompanied by other new terms like enterprise ecosystem, enterprise service bus, and business service network that likewise imply more generic approaches for enabling the interconnection of business services.[67]

For example, a service oriented view of marketplaces defines them entirely in terms of their participants and the set of services that they offer each other. (see Section 4.1.2.3). The Drop Shipment pattern followed by our hypothetical GMBooks.com bookstore (see Section 1.1) could be realized using an SOA that combines component business services like the Amazon.com catalog,[68] UPS package delivery and tracking functions, and Visa payment processing. All of these are available as document-based web services for integration into other business systems.

Furthermore, an SOA perspective highlights the principles of discovery and transparent substitutability of service providers because their roles and functional responsibilities are strictly defined by the documents that they produce and consume when providing a service. This is elegantly demonstrated by a Silicon Valley firm called Talaris, which hosts a procurement application for employee business services like travel, package shipping, conferencing, mobile communications, ground transportation, and other services consumed directly by end users. The Talaris application is built natively using web services and SOA principles, enabling it to describe each class of end user services abstractly in an XML vocabulary called the Services Business Language (SBL).[69] Each SBL document harmonizes the APIs or functionality from multiple providers of the same service into a single interface. Each service provider receives exactly the same service request, and suppliers can be added or dropped without any changes to the SBL or the user experience.

An essential and emergent benefit of an SOA is that once some application functionality is re-packaged as a service, new composite applications can be developed by combining them. Furthermore, because of the abstraction provided by document interfaces and the web services standards, composite applications can be created with vastly less effort than required by tightly coupled integration approaches. Another firm called Above All Software[70] has developed visual tools that enable non-programmers like business analysts to create user interfaces that unify the inputs and outputs to separate services. For example, a web service that looks up customer details in a customer database can be combined with one that knows about orders in an ERP system, creating a combined service that locates the current orders for any specified customer.

Applied to the GMBooks.com user interface, this composite services architectural approach means that the Amazon catalog could be transparently replaced by one from Barnes and Noble, UPS by FedEx, and Visa by American Express. Figure 4-3 illustrates the idea of composite services with transparent substitution of service providers.

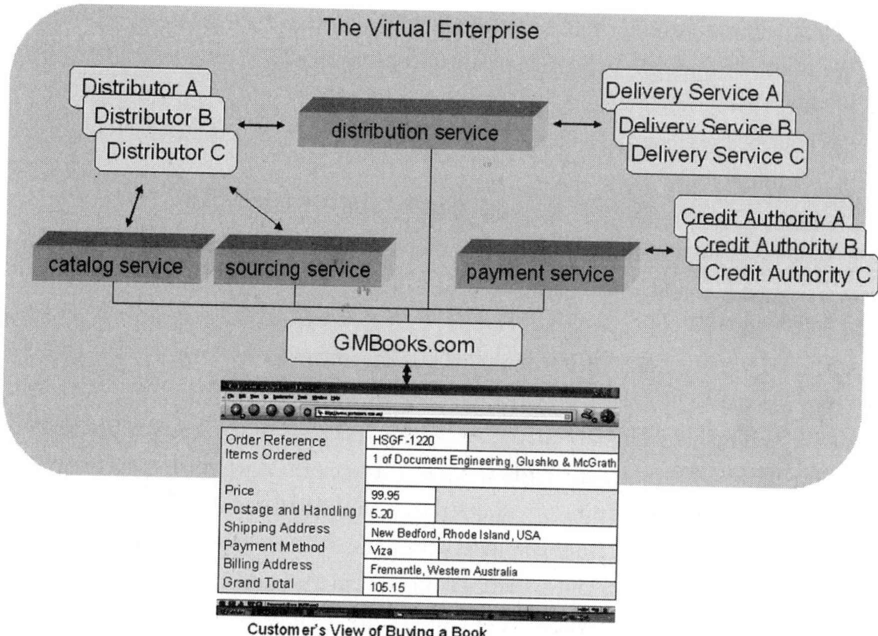

Figure 4-3. Composite Services and Transparent Substitution

And when General Motors transforms the different APIs for the inventory systems in each of their 80 factories into web services using the same interfaces, this lets the firm abstract what's going on in each factory.[71] Any web services enabled application can then get inventory information from any factory whenever it's needed even if the underlying inventory application is changed.

Service oriented architecture is a design philosophy; web services are a set of standards and techniques

The examples of services we've described in this section illustrate the contrast between SOA as a business design philosophy and web services as a set of standards and techniques for platform-independent integration. A SOA perspective drives a business to ask strategic questions like these as it systematically structures its business capabilities as self-contained resources or processes:

- What patterns of service combination are required to meet our business objectives?

- How can we design what each service does so that as a set they will be sufficient and flexible enough as business conditions change?

- Which of these services can we "carve out" of existing applications by changing their implementations or APIs?

- Which services should we build ourselves, and which should we obtain from others?

- Should we offer any of our services to other firms?

Because it makes decisions about the design of services depending on business considerations, an SOA approach tends to yield services that are more process oriented and that provide coarser units of functionality with greater business value than the services that emerge from the more technical perspective of web services. This is not to denigrate useful web services such as those that provide current weather conditions, that decode a coded value (for example, "What country has 'IS' as its ISO 3166 code?"), or that return the author and title of a book given its ISBN.

But the functionality of these bottom-up and more opportunistically provided web services is relatively small, low impact, and not likely to create compelling or competitive advantages for their providers or users. The web services that are more likely to do so are those that produce and consume entire business documents like catalogs, orders, invoices, and payments.

4.5 KEY POINTS IN CHAPTER FOUR

- Organization charts and facilities maps are physical models of a business.
- Supply chains, distribution channels, markets and auctions are general business patterns that can be applied in novel contexts.
- A business model is concerned with the nature and pattern of exchanges of one form of value for another.
- Document Engineering treats supply chains as information flows.
- By eliminating any need for physical presence the Internet has increased the feasibility and conceptual variety of business models.
- System architectures and technologies influence the cost of setting up business relationships.
- The maintenance or recurring costs of managing a business relationship are different from the startup costs.
- Asymmetric relationships need not result in costly concessions from one party.
- Exit and voice modes are opposites on dimensions of commitment to suppliers and the extent of coordination or collaboration with them.
- Closer collaboration doesn't always mean more information exchange.
- Establishing and maintaining trust is the motivation for trading communities.
- Many successful trading communities revolve around a dominant hub enterprise.

- Industry groups often initiate projects to develop or improve new business services and the documents they require.
- Business process models are the bridge between organizational models and business documents.
- A reference model consolidates the best practices of many companies.
- Information about the business processes is distinct from the physical flow of materials and goods.
- Efforts to standardize electronic documents began more than 40 years ago.
- In practice the EDI standards are never used in standard ways.
- New XML specifications often reinvent definitions of common information components.
- Conceptual views are more challenging to develop than physical ones.
- Organizations can't have a business relationship if they can't efficiently share information.
- Integration is the controlled sharing of data and business processes between any connected applications or data sources.
- Tight coupling is used to exchange data at high transaction rates.
- Loose coupling is necessary for integration across enterprise boundaries because their interfaces are nonpartisan.
- Web services enable a more loosely coupled integration approach than previous integration technologies.

- Interoperability is a more abstract goal than integration.

- The best way to facilitate interoperability is for the participants to share the same conceptual model.

- Service oriented architecture is a design philosophy; web services are a set of standards and techniques.

5 How Models and Patterns Evolve

5.0 INTRODUCTION

In Chapter 4 we looked at organizational, process, information, and architectural models and patterns from a mostly taxonomic or static perspective. It is certainly easier to describe them if we treat them as fixed and unchanging, but they are not. Indeed, it is probably more accurate to assume that these models and patterns are always changing, because the business and technology context in which enterprises operate today is increasingly dynamic.[1] A model or pattern that once made a business successful may be inadequate in the face of new global competition or disruptive technologies.

Models and patterns are always changing

We don't need to retell the story of how new telecommunications and information technologies—effectively free bandwidth, almost unlimited computing power, and the Internet—have transformed entire industries and scientific disciplines. These interrelated technologies are intrinsic to the idea of document exchange as the building block for new business models and processes, and it is easy to understand how they have enabled more frequent information exchanges, more granular information exchanges, and information exchanges with more partners.

We will describe some examples of these kinds of changes in document exchange patterns in the context of broader themes about changes in organizational, process, architectural, and information models. We hinted at some of these earlier, but this more systematic presentation will reinforce them. We will also emphasize the contrast between conceptual and physical models along the way.

As this chapter sharpens our awareness of the coevolution of business and technology, it will also show how we can use the new concepts and vocabulary of Document Engineering to understand and profit from it.

5.1 THE COEVOLUTION OF TECHNOLOGY AND BUSINESS MODELS

Technology is usually viewed in a push mode—"we can now do X; how does that affect what we should do?" Using technology as a way to make things "faster, better, cheaper" can mean a new physical model that implements an existing conceptual one. Electronic mail has largely supplanted business mail delivery by the postal service, but many of the messages delivered by electronic mail are little changed from the days of paper letters and envelopes. On the other hand, technology can also create entirely new conceptual models, as the Internet has done by enabling even the smallest business to maintain a global presence around the clock. Often the innovations driven by technology involve process and organizational models that define new kinds of business and work and new ways of managing those who do it.

It is also important to recognize that new technologies often emerge in a pull mode, in which a new idea inspires or even specifies the invention of the enabling technology—"If we want to do X, what technology would we need to do it?" In 1961 President Kennedy made sending a man to the moon a US priority that led to numerous important technology breakthroughs.[2] Wal-Mart's "man on the moon" goal of completely traceable goods led it to mandate that its suppliers identify shipments with Radio Frequency Identification (RFID) tags. This will force RFID chip makers to innovate in design and manufacturing to achieve the enabling quantity and price levels.[3]

Technology and businesses coevolve

Of course, push and pull changes occur at the same time, and it is now in vogue to view technology and business as continuously coevolving. The technological innovations resulting from the Wal-Mart RFID mandate may ultimately change business models and processes in areas far from retail, including building and facility access control, medical supply and specimen protection, branded goods replication prevention, library and rental goods management, baggage handling, and stolen item recovery.

But another implication of the coevolution of technology and business is that it is not enough for a new technology just to do something that was previously impossible. A potentially disruptive technology can sometimes have little impact if it doesn't fit into an existing model or pattern, which can mean that those responsible for the innovation get little or no benefit from it. Compatibility concerns with legacy technologies or proprietary software and data formats may preclude or slow the adoption of better ones. Likewise, existing business models, preexisting relationships, regulations, personnel skills, and cultural norms may constrain the full realization of new technologies.

This need for new technologies to fit into existing patterns was evident in the late 1990s when new Internet technologies first enabled Internet marketplaces (see Section 5.5). Because of the natural analog between the physical model of telecommunications connectivity and the conceptual vision of plug and play marketplaces, many of the first Internet marketplaces were geographically defined ones operated by large telephone companies. These large firms, especially the national monopolies that exist in many countries, have relationships with every significant business in their area and experience with the technical and conceptual infrastructure for routing electronic messages, billing, and network-to-network interconnection.

Similarly, most of the successful industry-specific Internet marketplaces had the critical role of the market operator filled by a large enterprise whose existing supply chains and business relationships would benefit from a move to the Internet. For these firms, the marketplace platform is a convenient place for hosting application services, such as supply chain management, collaborative design, and other services that inherently require the efficient exchange of information among a set of existing business partners.

In contrast, most unsuccessful B2B start-up firms were industry-specific and were unable to establish enough new relationships to create liquidity.

5.2 FROM HIERARCHICAL TO NETWORK MODELS

For most of the 19th and 20th centuries, advances in communications and information processing technologies enabled the growth of huge vertically integrated and hierarchically organized industrial firms. Business historian Alfred Chandler has documented the rise of the "visible hand" of management in coordinating resources within the large-scale U.S. corporation.[4] Economist Oliver Williamson, building on Ronald Coase's framework of transaction costs, explained the shift away from the invisible hand of the market as a rational response to the uncertainty, complexity, and risk in contracting.[5] Hierarchical coordination minimized transaction costs by eliminating problems of imperfect and asymmetric information in the most efficient way. By the 1980s the large corporation was seen as an inevitable and permanent feature of the modern economic landscape.

The focus on reducing costs of internal contracting inspired many document automation efforts of the 1960s and 1970s when the naïve goal of a paperless office reached its zenith. Manual processes with documents are inherently slow and error prone, especially when interrelated documents contain redundant information collected again and again and retyped each time. Large enterprises typically took what seemed to be the most sensible and lowest risk approach to document automation, doing it incrementally, one application at a time. This tactic created islands of automation with gaps that would ultimately have to be bridged by ad hoc point-to-point connections between electronic documents in proprietary formats.

The impact of technology on the structure of firms and marketplaces has radically increased in the last two decades. New technologies like the personal computer, email, instant messaging, web browsers, and web services have "turned Coase on his head" by dramatically reducing external search, communication, coordination, and monitoring costs. The underlying principles have not changed, but factors that are relatively minor in the industrial economy turn out to be critical in the information economy. Most importantly, the textbook assumptions of constant fixed costs and zero marginal costs are actually true for information goods.[6]

Factors that are relatively minor in the industrial economy are critical in the information economy

These information-improving technologies and their impact on cost structures have been associated with a rapid shift away from the vertically integrated corporation with its managerial hierarchies. Scholars have noted both the rise of vertical specialization and an explosion of nonmarket, nonfirm mechanisms of coordination, often called network forms, characterized by long-term collaboration and high degrees of information exchange. As firms rely more on external suppliers and outsource nonstrategic services, hierarchical enterprises are replaced by networks of smaller, more specialized cooperating firms.[7]

Competition is now more appropriately viewed as between entire value chains rather than between firms. This puts a premium on the ability to communicate and coordinate rapidly with suppliers, distributors, or service providers to respond to changes in demand, competitive threats, natural or man-made disasters, or other important business events. And as business models become more demand and event driven, the greater this premium becomes.

Competition is now between entire value chains rather than between firms

The need for greater responsiveness has both organizational and architectural dimensions, both within firms and between them. One that was painfully apparent to existing firms during the late 1990s rush of startup web businesses was that being large and having an extensive network of factories, distribution centers, and retail outlets could be a liability rather than an asset. These investments often limited a firm's flexibility in trying new business models to respond to web competition. The explosive growth of Amazon.com and similar firms with no physical retail presence came at the expense of bookstores that couldn't or wouldn't abandon theirs.[8] While there is no denying that cost considerations alone play a major role in a company's decisions to divest facilities or outsource services, the increased flexibility enabled by these changes is important too.

Another aspect of the shift away from hierarchical organization is a direct result of competition with the new Internet retailers. Firms that exist primarily in cyberspace can readily collect much more explicit and implicit demand information (for example, from browser logs) than firms whose customers primarily interact with them in physical retail outlets. To combat this inherent disadvantage, the latter firms need to analyze and aggregate every bit of demand information and share it immediately with any part of the firm that can benefit from it. Of course, redistributing this information is of little value unless the responsibility and authority to act on it is also delegated, which requires a change in management mindset. The firm still needs a central strategic direction, but if enough information and context is shared to its end points, it can make local decisions in strategically consistent ways. This is the business analog to the bumper sticker admonition to "Think globally, act locally."

The trend toward network organization of business functions is also being manifested in a shift from inwardly focused document automation efforts toward straight through processing initiatives (see Section 4.2.2.6). Increased transaction volumes, global competition, rising customer expectations, new regulatory and reporting mandates, and other forces require businesses to further speed the processing of documents, not just internally but with their business partners. Attacking each automation problem separately results in redundant technology, information, and relationships, an approach that is neither efficient nor scalable. Instead, businesses are increasingly facing these challenges collaboratively, often by working together to create common patterns for business processes and document exchanges.

These patterns are a key enabler of architecture changes that restructure the information collection, aggregation, and redistribution in the enterprise and its ecosystem. Many businesses have adopted marketplace platforms or hubs that businesses or service providers can connect to instead of having to make numerous separate point-to-point connections with each other. The hub routes documents or events to avoid the delays in a linear information supply chain, where speed is constrained by the slowest link.

Virtual enterprises are created by electronically connecting business processes from multiple firms

The goal of creating marketplaces or virtual enterprises by electronically connecting business processes from multiple firms arose in the late 1980s. But the EDI links (see Section 4.4.1.1) that were the dominant mechanisms for business-to-business integration were too brittle and costly to bring together enough trading partners to achieve critical marketplace mass. Likewise, tightly coupled, enterprise application integration technologies (such as CORBA[9]) initially proposed for business-to-business integration simply weren't capable of making it happen, because they depend on unchanging application interfaces.

By the late 1990s, however, Internet marketplaces were being created by the hundreds —maybe even thousands—because lower-cost, more scalable web technologies gave substance to the idea "connect once and transact anywhere." The web offered even small firms the chance to conduct business globally with a large set of possible suppliers or customers.[10]

Finding the optimal balance between hierarchical and network organization is a challenging theoretical problem of enormous practical importance. It is made even more difficult because informal or face-to-face communication can improve some business activities even when they are supported by formal and automated information exchanges. The best solution for organizing the communication links within and between enterprises appears to be multiscale networks that combine hierarchical and peer-to-peer connections.[11] So even though firms can presumably relocate most of their activities anywhere in the world because of the sophistication of technologies for information exchange, companies continue to cluster in certain locations like Silicon Valley or Bangalore.[12]

5.3 INFORMATION ABOUT GOODS BECOMES A GOOD

Before the invention of the telegraph, a business could obtain a competitive advantage by moving goods more efficiently, but information about goods could not move any faster than the things themselves. That's why Antonio, in Shakepeare's "The Merchant of Venice," laments that "Thou know'st that all my fortunes are at sea" and has to borrow money from Shylock. Until his ships return intact he has no way of knowing whether he is rich or poor. But once a separate flow of information was possible, it became important in its own right, and moving information more efficiently became the basis for many new industries and business models. Today "replacing inventory with information" is almost a cliché and the top priority of many businesses,[13] including our hypothetical GMBooks.com which, like other firms using the Drop Shipment pattern, takes orders for goods that it never owns.

For example, improving information flow to attack inventory problems (having too much or too little) is a critical goal for the automobile industry, which has long been burdened by supply chain inefficiencies. Automakers recognize the business benefit of better customer and supplier relationships that would result from more comprehensive and timely information sharing among manufacturers, suppliers, and dealers. As a result there are numerous information supply chain initiatives throughout the automobile industry,[14] many center on an Internet business-to-business exchange called Covisint. At a presentation about Covisint a few years ago, the abstract goal of rapid end-to-end information flow was imaginatively defined as "when someone walks into a dealership and orders a car with leather seats, somewhere a cow will start screaming."

There is no time to lose in these efforts, because consumers are rapidly becoming less patient as they recognize the obvious benefits of more attention to information flow in the businesses they buy from.

Once inventory and information are equivalent, the boundary between the physical and virtual worlds becomes blurred

Once information about the locations and movement of goods is sufficiently available to make inventory and information equivalent, the boundary between the physical and virtual worlds becomes increasingly blurred. The Internet enables people to send email messages or download from websites anywhere in the world in just seconds, qualitatively raising their expectations for speed and responsiveness in the physical world. For example, we have observed people who ordered goods on the Internet attempting to pick them up at the retail store nearest their home or to return to the same local store unwanted goods delivered after an online purchase. They can't believe it when they are told this isn't yet possible. Both are desirable business processes, but one can't trivialize the effort to integrate the applications and systems that would have to exchange order and inventory documents to bridge the virtual and actual worlds (see Section 4.4.1.2) and realize the conceptual business service so easily imagined by the consumer.

The trend to make information about the locations or quantities of goods an independent source of value is being amplified by a steady stream of new "push" technologies. The mundane bar code, introduced in the 1970s to speed checkout in supermarkets, is now ubiquitous for tracking components on assembly lines, packages, luggage, library books, rental cars, and just about anything else of value that moves. RFID chips, essentially enhanced bar codes with built-in transponders, enable the integration of scanning capabilities into store shelves, loading docks, doorways, parking lots, toll booths, and other locations, enabling even greater automation in tracking, along with the spectre of privacy abuses.[15] An even more exotic technology bundles a battery and satellite transponder into a book-sized box that can be attached to a cargo container and report on its location, content, and condition from anywhere, even the middle of the ocean.[16]

New services are arising from the aggregation of information about business transactions

Important categories of new information goods and services are arising in the aggregation or consolidation of information about business transactions and from the experience gained in carrying them out. For example, shipping companies like UPS and FedEx can create information about cargo space availability by summarizing booking transactions. They capitalize on the expertise they developed over decades in package delivery by taking on logistics, distribution, customs brokerage, and international trade services responsibilities for other organizations.[17]

5.4 NEW BUSINESS MODELS FOR INFORMATION GOODS

A related theme to the emergence of information about goods as a distinct source of value is the trend toward business models for information goods that exploit their intangibility. The Internet has vastly increased the viability of direct sales as a distribution strategy on the web for information goods like news, music, movies, and software that can be delivered in digital formats. In the simplest implementation of this idea, the distribution channel is reduced to a web address and the computer to which the material is downloaded.

The Internet has vastly increased the viability of direct sales for information goods

Of course, some of the business models for digital distribution of information goods, like unfettered peer-to-peer music sharing and "discount" downloaded software, are illegal, and a cause of great dismay in the music and software industries and their traditional intermediaries like music stores. This isn't the right place, even if we had the expertise, to pontificate about legal issues. But it is appropriate to observe that new information technologies have always challenged existing business models and that incumbents are often misguided, inept, hypocritical, or downright reactionary in their response.[18]

Two especially significant patterns are evolving for the creation and distribution of information goods and software: the open access movement in scholarly and scientific publishing that seeks lawful free access to online publications[19] and the trend toward software as a service. Both of these patterns are disrupting, and likely to ultimately replace traditional sales and distribution models, and both will require

Document Engineering efforts to develop standards for document and transaction models. Otherwise we are likely to see a proliferation of incompatible platform and format offerings from incumbent publishers and vendors seeking to extend their business models beyond their natural lives, increasing the transition costs to the new patterns for everyone.

The "software as a service" trend is particularly important to businesses. A significant proportion of enterprise software is being transformed from an installed product to a service hosted by an application service provider. Treating software as a service, with the customer paying on a subscription or per use basis to access some functionality using Internet protocols (either programmatically or via a web browser), can substantially reduce acquisition costs and improve return on investment for the customer. At the same time, this approach can reduce support and maintenance efforts for the vendor.

5.5 FROM FORECAST OR SCHEDULE-DRIVEN TO DEMAND OR EVENT-DRIVEN MODELS

Faster collection and distribution of information is also driving a shift from business models that are driven by forecasts and schedules to those that are driven by demand and actual events. Haeckel describes this transformation as moving from "make and sell" to "sense and respond," creating an "adaptive enterprise." Others describe it as greater "responsiveness," "resilience," and creating a "variable business model."[20]

The key to efficiency is not moving things faster according to plans but moving things smarter according to actual demand

Companies traditionally built products that they hoped customers would buy. They used historical data and market trends to forecast customer demand and then carefully managed the execution of their plans. But no forecast can ever be as accurate as actual sales and demand information. As new technologies enable demand information to be captured more quickly, the key to supply chain and distribution efficiency is not moving things faster according to plans but moving things smarter according to actual demand. With better information about actual demand manufacturers can increase or decrease orders from suppliers, speed up shipments by changing the mode of transport (from cargo ship to air, for example), or reroute shipments to destinations with increased demand.

Technologies that speed the flow of information up the demand chain are enabling new business patterns. One that is simple in concept but complex in execution is make-to-order, which is best explained by contrasting it with the two other categories of the Make process in the SCOR reference model: make-to-stock and engineer-to-order.[21]

Most products, especially consumer goods, are made and then sold. This is called make-to-stock in SCOR and is also known as mass production. A manufacturer following the make-to-stock pattern estimates how many products to make and balances the inventory risk of making too few and missing potential sales against making too many and having to sell at a discount, at a loss, or not at all.

At the other extreme, some products are always designed and manufactured to meet unique customer requirements according to a pattern that SCOR calls engineer-to-order. Instead of viewing its business as selling products, an engineer-to-order firm is more likely to think of what it does as contract manufacturing, where each customer's work involves significant design engineering and customization.

Make-to-order fits in between these two patterns. Like engineer-to-order, in make-to-order the product is manufactured to meet requirements for a specific customer, so there is no risk of making a product that no one wants. But the product is built by assembling or configuring make-to-stock components to complete a partially built standard platform or chassis. This hybrid approach, also called mass customization, gives customers what they want within a constrained set of possibilities determined by the modularity of the components, inventory, manufacturing processes, opportunity for higher margin, qualification of the buyer, and other factors.[22]

Depending on the extent to which the customer's order is actively shaped by interactive selling techniques for demand chain management, it might be more appropriate to call this pattern "make-what-we-want-you-to-order." For example, shaping demand with applications that guide the customer to choose personal computer configurations that optimize its inventory and margins has made Dell Inc. the textbook case study for this pattern.[23]

Demand chain patterns like make-to-order, VMI, and CFPR (see Section 4.2.2.5) are revolutionizing retail industries and obliterating traditional business models. The advantages of making only those products that customers have already bought are obvious, but equally obvious are the pressures these demand-driven business models place on acting quickly in response to that demand. The trends will accelerate as more batch EDI implementations are superseded by Internet XML ones, enabling almost real-time information integration into ERP systems.[24]

It was real-time information about movie rentals that enabled the Blockbuster chain to make a fundamental change in its business model allowing it to guarantee that popular movies would be available.[25] Blockbuster used to buy a limited number of copies from the producer and rent them to customers, which meant that the most desired movies were likely to be unavailable when they were most in demand. By installing a network of cash registers to track exactly when each movie was rented and providing this information to the movie producers, Blockbuster could negotiate a revenue-sharing model in which they got many copies cheaply with the agreement that part of the rental fee went to the producer.

Omniscience about supply chains will be limited by privacy concerns and by the complexity of handling torrents of data

We've mentioned several new technologies that enable information to be captured more efficiently when a transaction or other significant event takes place. Some people predict that RFID and GPS, coupled with the IPv6 protocol that enables one million billion unique Internet addresses, will create an "Internet of things."[26] Many of these things will be continually reporting their identity and location as they cross loading docks, toll booths, or other sensor locations. The omniscience of manufacturers and vendors about everything in their supply chains will be limited not by the quality of the information but by privacy concerns and the sheer technological complexity of handling the torrent of data.

5.6 FROM TIGHTLY COUPLED TO LOOSELY COUPLED MODELS

We contrasted tightly coupled and loosely coupled integration approaches in Section 4.4, but it is useful to recast this theme in a broader business model context. The evolution toward demand and event-driven models, and from hierarchical to network models, has corresponding implications for the architectures of business-to-business integration. Larry Downes describes this as the shift from "vertical integration to virtual integration."[27]

When efficiency was a dominant priority for companies, one way to achieve it was to be cautious in establishing relationships with other firms as suppliers and business partners. Major suppliers were selected very carefully, but once selected were likely to remain in that relationship for a long time. EDI (Section 4.3.1.1) was often used to implement the information exchanges called for by this type of business relationship.

In the early 1990s, before the ubiquity of the Internet, even a modest EDI implementation typically cost tens of thousands of dollars. The majority of this cost was (and always will be) in the integration on the participant's internal processes. This was because even though the conceptual model of document exchange viewed EDI implementations as loosely coupled, in reality they were not. Since they were expensive and would be amortized over a high-value, long-term relationship, they were always optimized for each relationship. As a result, the dominant partner in the relationship typically imposed a document implementation model that was advantageous for itself but that the other partner could not reuse in other relationships. This created a lock-in situation for both sides, limiting their flexibility and responsiveness with each other and in the way they did business generally.

EDI's life has been prolonged by adapting it to take advantage of the lower cost structure of the Internet. Internet EDI puts an EDI payload inside a messaging envelope and uses HTTP or SMTP protocols, while Web EDI uses web forms that create or format EDI syntax. Both approaches reduce the entry costs for small suppliers in a way that is essentially transparent to the big trading partner. For example, Wal-Mart has mandated that its suppliers adopt Internet EDI.[28]

More flexible business models complement the loosely coupled architecture of the Internet

The trends toward more flexible document exchange simply could not have happened without the loosely coupled architecture of the Internet. When a business publishes a web page it enables a minimal loosely coupled relationship with anyone who can launch a browser and read the page. The person reading the page doesn't even need to own the computer. There is a perhaps apocryphal story about a lawn maintenance company that was hired by the County of Los Angeles to mow the lawns of public buildings. Orders originated in an automated procurement application and were routed by a marketplace platform to the maintenance company's "supplier mailbox," where they were picked up each morning when an employee logged in using a personal computer at the public library. None of this was visible to the buyer requesting the lawn mowing service.

Loose coupling—in particular using XML documents to define interfaces—allows for the transparent scalability of business process automation as browser-based tasks are incrementally upgraded to application mediated ones.[29] A supplier with a small product catalog and a few sales a day can use a web browser to receive orders and send acknowledgments until increased transaction volume justifies integration with ERP or database applications. Likewise, a buyer who buys only a few items at a time can rely on a browser to send orders and receive acknowledgments, integrating with purchasing or accounting systems only when scale justifies it. In each case, since the same documents are being sent and received, the changes to the implementation are invisible.

5.7 FROM PROPRIETARY TO STANDARD MODELS

Because the Internet exists in a diverse technology context, its fundamental formats and protocols are freely implementable standards. As a result, much of the software that operates the Internet and Internet applications is also freely available on open source or similar licenses. These two factors, and the opportunity for network effects in the unbounded world of the Internet, have created an unstoppable trend away from proprietary models and toward standard ones.

We described many standards at all four levels of business description we covered in Chapter 4: organization, process, information, and architecture. But while standard is an important word in Document Engineering it is somewhat difficult to define. A purist might propose a definition that requires a standard to be a "freely implementable specification developed by consensus among the important stakeholders in some domain, working in a framework that encourages open participation provided by an organization chartered to create standards."[30]

Most of the EDI standards satisfy this definition, but few of the other things we've called standards in this chapter completely conform to it. Most of them, including SCOR, RosettaNet, and the web services standards, were created by ad hoc organizations, consortia, or company coalitions whose common business interests motivated their efforts. Even XML is not called a "standard" by the W3C, the organization that developed and maintains its specification; it is officially a "recommendation."[31]

Nevertheless, it isn't what we call them that really matters. What matters is the undeniable trend toward specifications that businesses can willingly choose to adopt and that are not controlled by a single firm. A firm's flexibility to engage in a network of loosely coupled relationships is increased each time it follows a standard at any level, and standards have become central to business strategy and technology decisions. For example, the largest suppliers in the automobile industry are increasingly choosing their own suppliers based on their capabilities to use the Internet to speed the information supply chain, and conformance to standard information and process patterns is a significant part of these capabilities.[32]

The standards required for loosely coupled relationships have become central to business strategy and technology decisions

Of course, operating systems and most office applications still remain proprietary under the control of Microsoft, which shows no sign of abandoning its disciplined approach of exploiting and extending its desktop monopoly. But even Microsoft is more receptive to the idea of standards than it used to be, especially in the area of web services, and part of its strategy is to advance its interests by submitting its own technical specifications as a starting point for standards work. In any case, the Internet example has made businesses vastly more receptive to standard, nonproprietary architectures and models. In almost every industry, firms that strongly compete on most issues are coming together to develop XML vocabularies that standardize the semantics of their business transactions.

5.8 TOWARD MODELS WITH REUSABLE COMPONENTS

The themes and trends we've described in this chapter about how models evolve all converge in a final theme: Models are increasingly being composed of reusable components. Organizational, process, architecture, and information models are being composed from smaller and more common building blocks, providing more reusable, flexible, and robust results.

Models are increasingly being composed of reusable components

We have observed that information about goods has become a kind of good, often creating new business models in the process and encouraging the creation of standards. Models that involve information about goods can now use common identifiers for business and product categories. For example, standards for product identification enable retailers in the grocery, apparel, office supply, and other industries to use UCCnet as a single reliable source for the latest product information from all their suppliers.[33] Similar standards tailored for RFID technologies will facilitate the incorporation of RFID data streams and services into event-driven business processes.

The evolution from hierarchical to network models also encourages more componentization and reuse of models because document exchanges need to be more explicit and standard when intraenterprise relationships are replaced by interenterprise ones. Inside any large, hierarchically organized enterprise, business activities and information exchange with other parts of the enterprise might seem loosely coupled. In fact, there is a constant stream of informal information exchange about company missions, goals, and projects, along with other dependencies introduced by common budget cycles, technology standards, reporting requirements, technologies, and so on. This shared context enables the business to function even though the interfaces between organizations and their respective roles are not entirely clear, but it creates tighter coupling than is desirable in exchanges with parties outside the enterprise. When those take place, there is no shared context unless it is explicitly provided, and it is necessary to agree on how to package the information and the context necessary for understanding it. These agreements are easier to describe and implement when they are composed of common reusable components.

Agreements on information and context are easier to describe and implement using common components

We can see in the evolution from software as a product to software as a service an increasing abstraction in describing what businesses do as the idea of service oriented architecture (SOA) takes hold. Deriving business models from components defined using technology-independent web services is perfectly consistent with the open and heterogeneous technology environment of the Internet. "Plug and play business" is not just a marketing slogan anymore; it is becoming an accurate description for models of many kinds.

Statistical Data and Metadata Exchange (SDMX)

Nearly all of these themes about how models and patterns evolve are illustrated by the Statistical Data and Metadata Exchange (SDMX) initiative.

SDMX is an ambitious effort, jointly backed by seven major international organizations: the Bank for International Settlements (BIS), the European Central Bank (ECB), the Statistical Office of the European Communities (Eurostat), the International Monetary Fund (IMF), the Organisation for Economic Cooperation and Development (OECD), the United Nations and the World Bank. The initiative is focused on business practices in the field of statistical information that allow more efficient processes for exchange and sharing of data and related metadata.

The overall goal is to foster standards to improve the availability and quality of statistics (e.g., timeliness, accessibility, interpretability) used at the national and international level for analyses and decision making around the world. This will require finding ways to minimize duplication of effort and taking full advantage of the Internet, XML and web services.

National and international statistical information flows can be viewed as a pyramid that starts at the transaction level (e.g., buying and selling of goods and services, borrowing and lending). On top of this level are information aggregations for national, regional and international agencies. These data are exchanged between organizations and also published at various levels of the pyramid on websites, in print, and as part of electronic data feeds.

Over time, a variety of manual and automated processes with differing formats has emerged, some involving highly complex and costly collection and distribution efforts that can be subject to error and delay. Many of these information exchanges rely on tightly coupled, point-to-point EDI messages using variants of a UN/EDIFACT standard called GESMES (Generic Statistical Message).

SDMX is developing a common vocabulary of key metadata items that describe statistical concepts and methodologies used by statisticians in the collection, processing and dissemination of statistical data. Standards for describing statistical data in XML and UN/EDIFACT formats based on a common conceptual model should enable it to be used as needed directly from SDMX-conformant sources, thereby reducing delays, redundant processes and incompatibilities. The metadata descriptions of each data source can be stored in an Internet-accessible registry, facilitating discovery and navigation of available data and metadata.

SDMX standards will turn hierarchically organized and schedule driven processes into a network of demand driven ones. Instead of submitting reports on a schedule, data providers will publish their data whenever it is available, inform others about this via registry services, and recipients will extract it on demand to create new information products. The associated metadata will enable better understanding about what actually was released and how it might be used and transformed.

Version 1.0 of the SDMX standards, covering the information model and data formats, was released in September 2004. Continuing SDMX efforts will cover a standard architecture (involving web services and registry services) as well as further advances with respect to their metadata.[34]

5.9 KEY POINTS IN CHAPTER FIVE

- Models and patterns are always changing.
- Technology and businesses coevolve.
- Factors that are relatively minor in the industrial economy are critical in the information economy.
- More flexible business models require the loosely coupled architecture of the Internet.
- Virtual enterprises are created by electronically connecting business processes from multiple firms.
- Competition is now between entire value chains rather than between firms.
- The Internet has vastly increased the viability of direct sales for information goods.
- Once inventory and information are equivalent, the boundary between the physical and virtual worlds becomes blurred.
- New services are arising from the aggregation of information about business transactions.
- The key to efficiency is not moving things faster according to plans but moving things smarter according to actual demand.
- Omniscience about supply chains will be limited by privacy concerns and by the complexity of handling torrents of data.

- Models are increasingly being composed of reusable components.
- Agreements on information and context are easier to describe and implement using common components.
- More flexible business models complement the loosely coupled architecture of the Internet.
- The standards required for loosely coupled relationships have become central to business strategy and technology decisions.

6

When Models Don't Match: The Interoperability Challenge

6.0 INTRODUCTION

Web services and other technologies for service oriented architectures promise a future in which businesses will be able to discover each other, exchange electronic documents, and conduct transactions with or without prior agreement. This is the vision of extended or "virtual" enterprises composed from a variety of business services, including many provided by small and medium-sized enterprises or those from developing countries who were previously excluded from automated business relationships due to cost or technical barriers. New and more cost-effective and capable technologies will enable a seamless or "plug-and-play" business Internet in which loosely coupled document exchanges are the foundation for flexible, adaptive, and on-demand business models.

But not quite yet.

The most basic requirement for two businesses to conduct business is that their business systems interoperate

The most basic requirement for two businesses to conduct business is that their business systems interoperate. Interoperability doesn't require that two systems be identical in design or implementation, only that they can exchange information and use the information they exchange. Interoperability requires that the information being exchanged is conceptually equivalent; once this equivalence is established, transforming different implementations to a common exchange format is a necessary but often trivial thing to do. Interoperability is an easy goal to express but hard to achieve, especially if you want to avoid the overhead of expensive customized or hand-crafted integration solutions.

In this chapter we will explain why interoperability is a challenging goal by studying the types of conflicts that can arise when two enterprises try to exchange information. Of course, before enterprises can exchange information they must also understand and agree on the appropriateness of the exchange and on their respective responsibilities, roles, and commercial processes in the exchange. We'll return to these contextual issues in Chapter 8, but for now let's assume two enterprises have come to these agreements and are beginning to exchange information.

The information exchanged might not match because of syntactic or encoding conflicts, because of structural or assembly conflicts, or because of conflicts in meaning or semantics. Some of these conflicts can be remedied or worked around, but others reflect basic incompatibilities in how the businesses understand their information and prevent interoperability from being achieved.

We can identify four different ways in which exchanges of information can be misunderstood. These are based on various combinations of content, syntax, structure, and semantic conflicts that can occur in any single document exchange. These categories are best explained by the following examples. As a simple case Figure 6-1 describes the ways in which we might communicate a value of 100 U.S. dollars:

Differences in Content:
- option a. **<A>USD 100</A>**
- option b. **<A>One Hundred US Dollars</A>**
- option c. **<A>$US100</A>**

Differences in Encoding:
- option a. **<Amount>USD 100</Amount>**
- option b. **USD,100**
- option c. **CUR:USD|AMT:100**

Differences in Structure:
- option a. **<Amount>USD 100</Amount>**
- option b. **<Currency>USD</Currency><Amount>100</Amount>**
- option c. **<Amount>100<Currency>USD</Currency></Amount>**

Differences in Semantics:
- option a. **<Amount>USD 100</Amount>**
- option b. **<PreTaxAmount>USD90</PreTaxAmount><Tax>USD10</Tax>**
- option c. **<Price>USD 100</Price>**

Figure 6-1. Four Ways to Misunderstand a Document Component

Each of these categories contains alternative ways to express the value of 100 U.S. dollars; the options in each case illustrate the meaning of the category. In most cases what is expressed might mean something to a person, but that's not what is at issue here. What matters is whether a business system can understand these different expressions to mean the same thing.

To better understand the conflict categories we will work backward from the physical to the conceptual view of our document models. We start with the information value itself, the content carried in a document instance. Every information component in the document follows some form of constraints on its possible values that defines its data type. For example, a value might be alphabetic text, integers, decimal, a specific pattern like those for dates and times, or one of a set of possible values, such as a coded list of countries or airports. The business system of the party receiving the document must know how to interpret these values, and it uses the explicit or implicit information about data types to do that.

In the first category of examples, the recipient's business system is more likely to be able to process "USD 100" than "One Hundred US Dollars" because the former follows a more prescribed data format than the latter, which appears to be informal words of text. We call this a problem in content.

We next consider the language used to describe the information. When two businesses make different choices in the implementation phase of their project, they might introduce conflicts in encoding.

XML, EDI, and structured text offer different languages for implementing document components. So we need to understand how these different implementation models influence interoperability.

We then need to recognize that similar syntax does not guarantee equivalent document or component structures. For example, all the components may be present but not in the expected arrangement. These are called structural conflicts.

Finally we need to examine the most serious conflicts, the ones that occur when component models diverge semantically because they are not defining the same things in the same context. These may reflect different requirements or choices made in the earliest phases of analysis and modeling.

We began this book with a comparison between buying a book in a bookstore and buying one online at GMBooks.com. Now let's imagine that GMBooks.com wants to accept electronic orders from affiliated booksellers that come via documents rather than from people browsing its website.[1]

6.1 THE INTEROPERABILITY CHALLENGE

Making this happen seems simple: GMBooks.com publishes its requirements for the information that electronic orders must contain and the protocols it uses to receive messages.

Some of its partners can easily program or configure their business systems to send electronic orders that conform to the GMBooks.com specification. But others might not be able or willing to do so, and those are the situations that we'll discuss in this chapter.

Figure 6-2 illustrates this idea using the document exchanges among the various participants in the GMBooks.com virtual enterprise. The <BuyersID> in the message sent by the Affiliate Bookseller identifies the buyer, but when this information about the buyer appears in the Purchase Order, Shipping Note, and Transaction Advice documents it has a different meaning, name, or data format. These different documents must work together to carry out the drop shipment process using the overlapping information that flows between them, but unless these differences are resolved, the messages can't interoperate.

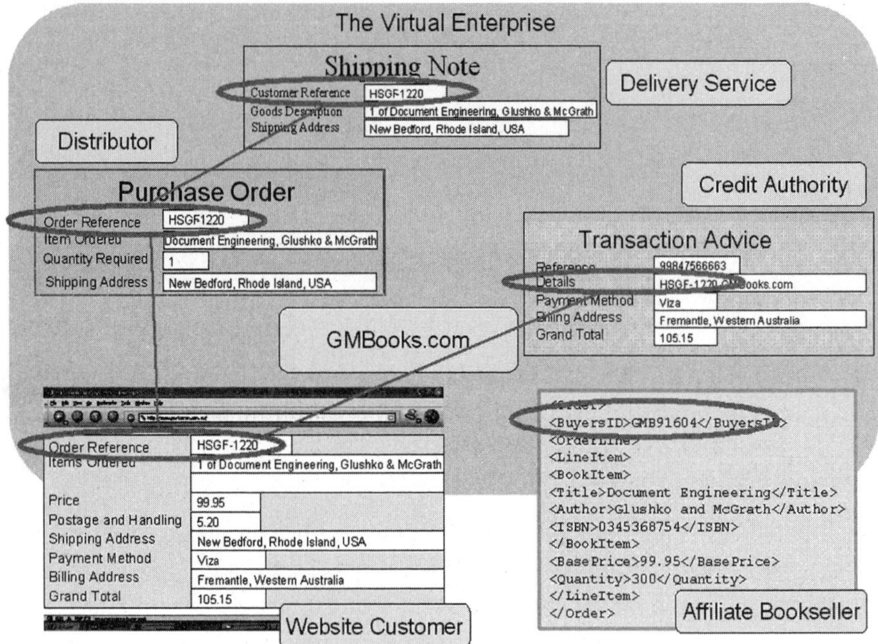

Figure 6-2. The Interoperability Challenge

6.1.1 THE INTEROPERABILITY TARGET

Let us assume that the information GMBooks.com needs for its order system is sensible, the buyer's name and address along with details about the ordered books. The conceptual model for the required order is shown in Figure 6-3 as a class diagram.

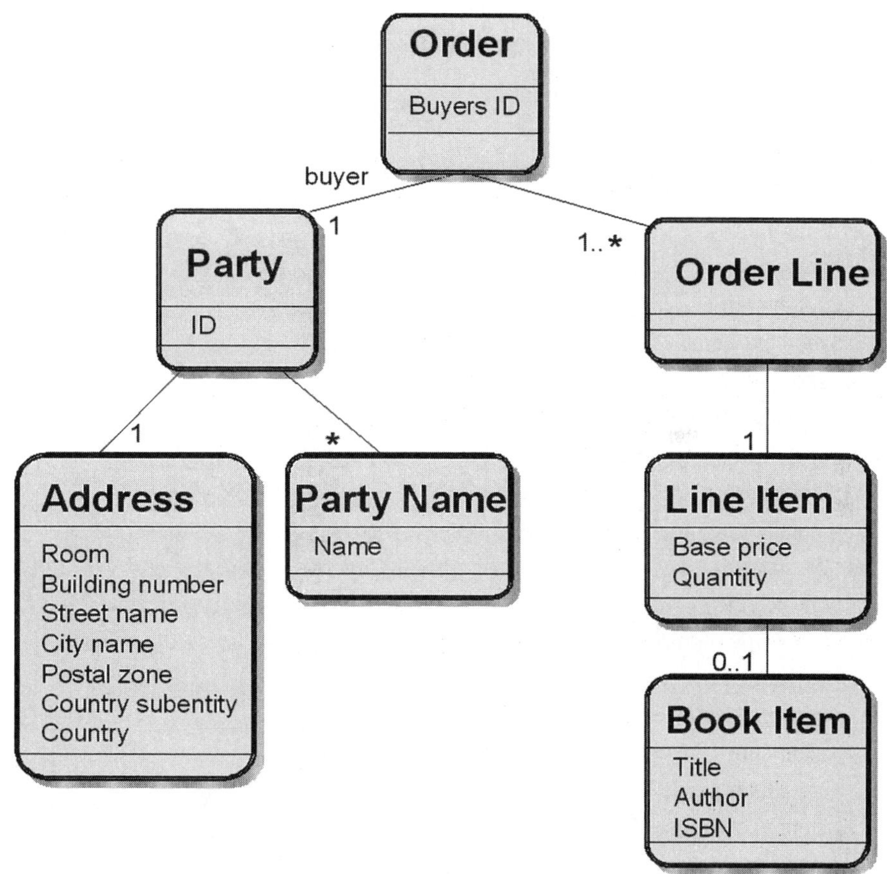

Figure 6-3. Conceptual Model for Orders

GMBooks.com may publish its specification for accepting electronic orders as the document implementation model expressed by the XML schema in Figure 6-4.[2]

```
<?xml version="1.0" encoding="UTF-8"?>
<xs:schema xmlns:xs="http://www.w3.org/2001/XMLSchema"
elementFormDefault="qualified">
 <xs:element name="Order" type="OrderType"/>
 <xs:complexType name="OrderType">
   <xs:sequence>
       <xs:element name="BuyersID" type="xs:string"/>
```

```
      <xs:element name="BuyerParty" type="PartyType"/>
      <xs:element name="OrderLine" type="OrderLineType"
       MaxOccurs="unbounded"/>
    </xs:sequence>
</xs:complexType>
<xs:complexType name="PartyType">
    <xs:sequence>
      <xs:element name="ID" type="xs:string"/>
      <xs:element name="PartyName" type="PartyNameType"/>
      <xs:element name="Address" type="AddressType"/>
    </xs:sequence>
</xs:complexType>
<xs:complexType name="PartyNameType">
    <xs:sequence>
      <xs:element name="Name" type="xs:string" minOccurs="0"/>
    </xs:sequence>
</xs:complexType>
<xs:complexType name="AddressType">
    <xs:sequence>
      <xs:element name="Room" type="xs:string"/>
      <xs:element name="BuildingNumber" type="xs:string"/>
      <xs:element name="StreetName" type="xs:string"/>
      <xs:element name="CityName" type="xs:string"/>
      <xs:element name="PostalZone" type="xs:string"/>
      <xs:element name="CountrySubentity" type="xs:string"/>
      <xs:element name="Country" type="xs:string"/>
    </xs:sequence>
</xs:complexType>
<xs:complexType name="OrderLineType">
    <xs:sequence>
      <xs:element name="LineItem" type="LineItemType"/>
    </xs:sequence>
</xs:complexType>
<xs:complexType name="LineItemType">
    <xs:sequence>
      <xs:element name="BookItem" type="BookItemType"/>
      <xs:element name="BasePrice" type="xs:decimal"/>
```

```
      <xs:element name="Quantity" type="xs:int"/>
    </xs:sequence>
  </xs:complexType>
  <xs:complexType name="BookItemType">
     <xs:sequence>
        <xs:element name="Title" type="xs:string"/>
        <xs:element name="Author" type="xs:string"/>
        <xs:element name="ISBN" type="xs:string"/>
     </xs:sequence>
  </xs:complexType>
</xs:schema>
```

Figure 6-4. Document Implementation Model (XML Schema) for Orders

A typical instance of an order that conforms to this schema might look like Figure 6-5.

```
<?xml version="1.0" encoding="UTF-8"?>
<Order>
     <BuyersID>GMB91604</BuyersID>
     <BuyerParty>
          <ID>KEEN</ID>
          <PartyName>
               <Name>Maynard James Keenan</Name>
          </PartyName>
          <Address>
               <Room>505</Room>
               <BuildingNumber>11271</BuildingNumber>
               <StreetName>Ventura Blvd.</StreetName>
               <CityName>Studio City</CityName>
               <PostalZone>91604</PostalZone>
               <CountrySubentity>California</CountrySubentity>
               <Country>USA</Country>
          </Address>
     </BuyerParty>
     <OrderLine>
          <LineItem>
               <BookItem>
```

```
                <Title>Document Engineering</Title>
                <Author>Glushko and McGrath</Author>
                <ISBN>0262072610</ISBN>
            </BookItem>
            <BasePrice>99.95</BasePrice>
            <Quantity>300</Quantity>
        </LineItem>
</OrderLine>
</Order>
```

Figure 6-5. Instance of an Order Document

6.1.2 RECOGNIZING EQUIVALENCE

We might assume that any affiliate would be able to send this simple document. But experience has taught us that this is not the case. Variations in strategies, technology platforms, legacy applications, business processes, and terminology make it difficult or impossible for some firms to satisfy the requirements.

Variations in strategies, technology platforms, legacy applications, business processes, and terminology make it difficult to use compatible documents

If GMBooks.com were the dominant bookseller on the Web, it might try to compel its affiliates to comply with its process and information requirements as a condition of doing business, but this strategy is rarely successful because it does not encourage loyalty. In most cases, GMBooks.com would adopt the practical approach of trying to accept orders in whatever form they are sent. In this situation, GMBooks.com needs to assess whether it can extract the information it needs from what it receives. So the challenge GMBooks.com faces when it reviews order documents is determining whether they conform to their information requirements; that is, to recognize equivalence.

Initially GMBooks.com might test every incoming order document against its schema in Figure 6-4 and simply reject any order that isn't well-formed XML or a valid instance of their document schema (see Section 2.6). But this assessment is more difficult than it might seem. If an incoming invalid message contains elements or attributes whose names match those that are expected, it would be tempting to extract them and rearrange them to conform to the target schema. However, the same names don't necessarily imply that the meanings are the same. Or the names might not match but the underlying concepts might be identical. To establish semantic equivalence, we need to compare conceptual representations and determine whether the different physical models (such as schemas) relate to the required conceptual ones.

Unfortunately most documents don't arrive with an associated conceptual representation that unambiguously defines the meaning encoded in the physical model. We need to apply Document Engineering techniques to determine whether the required information can be extracted and transformed from the incoming message.

In this case, we might think, "What's so hard to understand about names, addresses, and books?" We hope the examples in this chapter will explain that things are not always as obvious as they seem. In Chapters 11 and 12, "Analyzing Documents" and "Analyzing Document Components," we will introduce some techniques for encouraging semantic clarity in conceptual models.

6.2 CONTENT CONFLICTS

Certain conflicts can arise if two business systems use different data types for the content of the same component. Take, for instance, the following snippet of an order in Figure 6-6:

```
<LineItem>
    <BookItem>
        <Title>Document Engineering</Title>
        <Author>Glushko and McGrath</Author>
        <ISBN>0262072610</ISBN>
    </BookItem>
    <BasePrice>$99.95</BasePrice>
    <Quantity>300</Quantity>
</LineItem>
```

Figure 6-6. Order Fragment with Base Price Content Conflict

In this order example the base price for the book contains a $ symbol. This creates a data type conflict in the content of the component. In Figure 6-4 we can see that GMBooks.com has defined BasePrice in its XML schema as a decimal (meaning a positive or negative number with a decimal point) and this does not allow a currency code or symbol.[3] The $ symbol in the base price value sent by the affiliate may cause it to be rejected by the GMBooks.com order system, even though the meaning, structure, and syntax of the value provided by the affiliate are correct. The content value provided does not satisfy the possible character set specified in the GMBooks.com definition.

Content conflicts occur when two parties use different sets of values for the same components

Content conflicts often happen when the possible values for instances of a component must be conformant to a specified pattern or to a set of otherwise arbitrary codes or identifiers. The latter are commonplace in business documents where using a fixed set of possible values allows for precise identification. For example, many enterprises use an identification scheme for countries, usually the ISO 3166-1 alpha-2 codes that have values like US for United States of America and CN for China. When possible values are taken from external standards agencies, such as the ISO, they are called external codes to emphasize that they are not under the enterprise's control.

Precise identification by each side of an exchange using some set of legal values isn't sufficient in itself. The trading parties need to agree on the set of values or the patterns that define acceptable values.

```
<Address>
    <Room>505</Room>
    <BuildingNumber>11271</BuildingNumber>
    <StreetName>Ventura Blvd.</StreetName>
    <CityName>Studio City</CityName>
    <PostalZone>91604-3136</PostalZone>
    <CountrySubentity>California</CountrySubentity>
    <Country>USA</Country>
</Address>
```

Figure 6-7. Order Fragment with Postal Zone Content Conflict

In Figure 6-7 the GMBooks.com affiliate provides a value for the postal zone using the U.S. Postal Services nine-digit Zip+4 coding scheme. However the example we saw in Figure 6-5 uses the less specific five-digit Zip code. Both of these external coding schemes are acceptable to postal services, but the former may be a content conflict for GMBooks.com.

At other times possible values are internally defined by a single enterprise for its own use. Some examples of internal sets of possible values can be seen in our GMBooks.com document models (Figures 6-3 and 6-4). First, a BuyerPartyID, the value that uniquely identifies each buyer, would probably be assigned by GMBooks.com to each customer when the parties establish a business arrangement. Secondly, a BuyersID may be issued by affiliates to identify their orders. The rules or sets of the values for each of these will be controlled by the originating party.

Content conflicts occur when two parties use the same sets of values for different components

These internal sets of values can often be the cause of content conflicts because both parties may be using the same or overlapping sets for different components. We further discuss the analysis and encoding of sets of possible values in Section 12.1.8.

6.3 ENCODING CONFLICTS

A more obvious way in which information exchanges can conflict is at the level of encoding—that is, the language chosen for implementing the exchange or the way information is represented by the language's syntax.

6.3.1 LANGUAGE CONFLICTS

The most apparent differences in encoding occur when two different languages are chosen. For example, Figure 6-8 denotes an order document using the UN/EDIFACT (ISO 9735) standard.

```
UNH+0GMB91604004600001+ORDERS:1:911:UN+362910 04061815???:15'
BGM+120+362910+9'
DTM+4:040618:101'
NAD+BY+KEEN::91++MAYNARD JAMES KEENAN'
NAD+VN+GMBOOKS.COM::92++GM BOOKS LTD'
UNS+D'
LIN+1'
PIA+1+0262072610:IS'
IMD+F+2+:::DOCUMENT ENGINEERING BY GLUSHKO AND MCGRATH'
QTY+21:300.0000:EA'
PRI+CON:99.95'
UNS+S'
CNT+2:2'
UNT+23+000091604004600001'
```

Figure 6-8. Order Encoded in UN/EDIFACT

Clearly this is not immediately compatible with the order example in Figure 6-4. But as UN/EDIFACT is the only internationally recognized standard for electronic order documents, the affiliate might be annoyed to be told by GMBooks.com that it is using an unacceptable format.

There is also a popular EDI language developed by the American National Standards Institute known as ANSI ASC X12. During the 1990s this standard was increasingly adopted by U.S. publishers and booksellers and built into their order processing systems. In such cases an affiliate's order document might look like that in Figure 6-9.

```
ST*850*000820
BEG*00*SA*820**040605
N1*ST*KEEN*92*GMB91604
PO1*1*1*EA***EN*0262072610
PID*F****Document Engineering GLUSHKO MCGRATH
PO4**300*EA
CTT*2
SE*56*000820
```

Figure 6-9. Order Encoded in ANSI ASC X12

About 20 years before the development of standard EDI languages in the 1980s, the Book Industry Study Group developed a format known as BISAC for ordering books. Many small and medium-sized booksellers might still use specialized sales management software that can produce only BISAC formatted orders. In such cases the order document might look like Figure 6-10.

```
00000018800868 GMB91604 946305INTERNET.BSC F039000178
1000002820 8800868 9230178 040605000000Y 000000001N00020000000
4000003820 Y0000000002620726100000300000000000000000000000041000000
4200004820 Document Engineering GLUSHKO and McGRATH
5000037820 000020000000001700000000029
900003800000000001700001000000000290000100001000000000000170000100000000000000
```

Figure 6-10. Order Encoded in BISAC

We can also imagine a small and technologically unsophisticated affiliate bookseller who keeps records in a spreadsheet. An XML application interface might seem daunting to this partner, and the only way they can export and import orders is in comma-separated files. In such cases the order document might look like Figure 6-11.

```
KEEN91604,Dr.,Maynard,James,Keenan,11271 Ventura Blvd. #505,Studio
City,California,91604
Document Engineering,Glushko & McGrath,0262072610,99.95,300
```

Figure 6-11. Order Encoded in Comma-separated Syntax

A comparison of the documents in Figures 6-8 to 6-11 with the conceptual model of the order depicted in Figure 6-3 reveals that each is based on similar concepts and each appears to convey information suitable for GMBooks.com requirements.

However, the components of all of them require mapping or transforming into their GMBooks.com counterpart. For example, we would need to know that in the UN/EDIFACT order, NAD+BY+ indicates the GMBooks.com Order/Buyer/ID, or that for any rows starting with the code number 42 in the BISAC document, columns 21 to 50 contain the OrderLine/LineItem/BookItem/Title.

A one-to-one mapping of document components is not always achievable

As you can imagine from the above examples, one-to-one mapping is not always achievable. Numerous mapping or translation tools exist to convert EDI and other formats to XML (and vice versa), but most of them work near the surface of the message to relate parts of one message to the other and don't provide much support for understanding or reusing the models below the surface.[4]

6.3.2 GRAMMATICAL CONFLICTS

Even if both parties encode their models using the same language, differences in applying the grammar of the language can prevent their documents from interoperating.

Many XML encoding conflicts result from different uses of the element and attribute constructs.[5] For example, GMBooks.com might have an affiliate whose order system generates XML instances that look like Figure 6-12.

```
<BuyerParty ID="KEEN" Name="Maynard James Keenan" Room="505"
BuildingNumber="11271" StreetName="Ventura Blvd." City="Studio City"
State="California" PostalCode="91604">
    <Item Title="Document Engineering" Author="Glushko & McGrath"
ISBN="0262072610" BasePrice="99.95" Quantity="300"/>
```

Figure 6-12. Order Encoded Using XML "Attribute-Value" Style

In contrast to the XML document that GMBooks.com expects, this partner's XML instance encodes almost everything as attributes to minimize the size of the document. The GMBooks.com order system will not immediately be able to accept this instance. However, a comparison of the XML document in Figure 6-12 with the conceptual model of the order depicted in Figure 6-3 reveals that the conceptual models are essentially the same. Only the XML naming and design rules are different.

As a result, these sorts of encoding conflicts between XML documents are quite easy to resolve using XSLT and XPath (Section 2.7.2).

Encoding conflicts can be resolved if the underlying semantics and structures are compatible

Encoding conflicts are generally resolvable if the underlying semantics and structures are compatible because encoding a conceptual model as a physical one is the last phase before implementation (see Figure 3-1). If two parties have been creating models for the same business context, they will have similar conceptual models and assemblies of structures, any different choices at the encoding phase should be easy to diagnose and reconcile. We revisit issues of encoding rules in Chapters 7 and 15.

6.4 STRUCTURAL CONFLICTS

Another category of conflicts arises when the models of documents or their components have different structures. Even when both parties use the same encoding rules, structural conflicts can cause interoperability problems.

6.4.1 DOCUMENT ASSEMBLY CONFLICTS

In the GMBooks.com business process, an affiliate might model customer information and order information the same way that GMBooks.com does but might produce two documents like those in figures 6-13a and 6-13b.

```
<?xml version="1.0" encoding="UTF-8"?>
    <BuyerParty>
        <ID>KEEN</ID>
        <PartyName>
            <Name>Maynard James Keenan</Name>
        </PartyName>
        <Address>
            <Room>505</Room>
            <BuildingNumber>11271</BuildingNumber>
            <StreetName>Ventura Blvd.</StreetName>
            <CityName>Studio City</CityName>
            <PostalZone>91604</PostalZone>
            <CountrySubentity>California</CountrySubentity>
            <Country>USA</Country>
        </Address>
    </BuyerParty>
```

Figure 6-13a. Buyer Information Document

```
<?xml version="1.0" encoding="UTF-8"?>
<Order>
    <BuyersID>GMB91604</BuyersID>
    <BuyerParty>
        <ID>KEEN</ID>
    </BuyerParty>
    <OrderLine>
        <LineItem>
            <BookItem>
                <Title>Document Engineering</Title>
```

```
                <Author>Glushko & McGrath</Author>
                <ISBN>0262072610</ISBN>
            </BookItem>
            <BasePrice>99.95</BasePrice>
            <Quantity>300</Quantity>
        </LineItem>
    </OrderLine>
</Order>
```

Figure 6-13b. Order Information Document

Because the document instances can be linked by the Buyer's ID number, these two documents can easily be merged to create the order needed by GMBooks.com, and because each document conforms to the expected structure for its part, no additional transformation is required.

6.4.2 COMPONENT ASSEMBLY CONFLICTS

A more serious problem occurs when the two parties have assembled components into structures in incompatible ways. This may happen when they view some of the components in a different context. For example, GMBooks.com might have an affiliate who consolidates orders for smaller retailers and submits one order on behalf of several buyers. This business model naturally results in an item-centric view of the information rather than the customer-centric view expected by GMBooks.com. Such an item-centric order might look like Figure 6-14.

```
<?xml version="1.0" encoding="UTF-8"?>
<Order>
    <OrderLine>
        <LineItem>
            <BookItem>
                <Title>Document Engineering</Title>
                <Author>Glushko & McGrath</Author>
                <ISBN>0262072610</ISBN>
            </BookItem>
```

```
            <BasePrice>99.95</BasePrice>
            <Quantity>300</Quantity>
        </LineItem>
        <BuyersID>91604</BuyersID>
        <BuyerParty>
            <ID>KEEN</ID>
            <PartyName>
                <Name>Maynard James Keenan</Name>
            </PartyName>
            <Address>
                <Room>505</Room>
                <BuildingNumber>11271</BuildingNumber>
                <StreetName>Ventura Blvd.</StreetName>
                <CityName>Studio City</CityName>
                <PostalZone>91604</PostalZone>
                <CountrySubentity>California</CountrySubentity>
                <Country>USA</Country>
            </Address>
        </BuyerParty>
    </OrderLine>
</Order>
```

Figure 6-14. Item-Centric Order Document

Even though they have the same models for names, addresses, and other components in isolation, the differences in how they are put together results in different hierarchies and different documents.

More significantly, the position of components in the hierarchy affects their meaning. For example, the component BuyersID in Figure 6-14 is not necessarily the same component used in the schema in Figure 6-4. We cannot ascertain whether it means the identifier used by the buyer for the item or for the whole order.

In another example we could consider two types of event calendars: One is date-centric, listing for each date the events that take place; another, which might be more appropriate when most dates don't have events scheduled, is event-centric, listing events and for each the date or dates on which they take place. In the former type of event calendar, every scheduled occurrence of an event is explicit. In the latter type, it would be reasonable to specify a start date and end date for events that span multiple dates, making the list of occurrences implicit.

In this situation it might be technically possible to transform event-centric calendars into date-centric calendars by interpolating the implicit occurrence of dates in the former, and most of the time the transformation would be semantically correct. But in some cases the transformation might require other information, like whether the event is something that takes place only during weekdays and whether holidays are excluded, information that is explicit in the date-centric calendar.[6] We will expand on this event calendar modeling project as our case study in Chapters 8 through 15.

The earlier in the modeling process that two parties make different decisions, the greater the possibilities for their models to be incompatible

Such assembly conflicts represent a more serious set of interoperability problems than the simpler encoding conflicts, because assembly occurs before encoding in the modeling process. Put another way, the earlier in the modeling process that two parties make different decisions, the greater the possibilities for their models to be incompatible.

6.4.3 COMPONENT GRANULARITY CONFLICTS

We might also encounter conflicts that derive from identifying components in different levels of detail—these are issues about the granularity of structure in a component. These kinds of interoperability challenges are illustrated in the order fragments shown in figures 6-15a and 6-15b.

```
<BuyerParty>
    <ID>KEEN</ID>
    <PartyName>
        <Name>Maynard James Keenan</Name>
    </PartyName>
    <Address>
        <StreetAddress>11271 Ventura Blvd. #505</StreetAddress>
        <City>Studio City 91604</City>
        <CountrySubentity>California</CountrySubentity>
        <Country>USA</Country>
    </Address>
</BuyerParty>
```

Figure 6-15a. BuyerParty Fragment with Underspecified Granularity

```
<BuyerParty>
    <ID>KEEN</ID>
    <PartyName>
        <FamilyName>Keenan</FamilyName>
        <MiddleName>James</MiddleName>
        <FirstName>Maynard</FirstName>
    </PartyName>
    <Address>
        <Room>505</Room>
        <BuildingNumber>11271</BuildingNumber>
        <StreetName>Ventura Blvd.</StreetName>
        <CityName>Studio City</CityName>
        <PostalZone>91604</PostalZone>
        <CountrySubentity>California</CountrySubentity>
        <Country>USA</Country>
    </Address>
</BuyerParty>
```

Figure 6-15b. BuyerParty Fragment with Overspecified Granularity

In Figure 6-15a, the information components for Room, BuildingNumber, and StreetName from the GMBooks.com conceptual model have been combined into a StreetAddress component.

In Figure 6-15b, the components that make up the Name of the Party in the GMBooks.com model have been more precisely expressed as separate components for FamilyName, MiddleName, and FirstName.

These granularity differences result in one-way interoperability; a more granular model can be transformed into a less granular model, but not vice versa. A transformation could be written that would take the values of Room, BuildingNumber, and StreetName from Figure 6-15b and combine them into StreetAddress to produce the desired instance. But we would not reliably be able to decompose the StreetAddress from Figure 6-15a into the Room, BuildingNumber, and StreetName components required for the GMBooks.com target document.[7]

A more granular model can be transformed into a less granular model, but not vice versa

We won't belabor this argument by showing that the granularity transformation challenge is equally severe when it comes to personal names, dates, telephone numbers and many common document components. We can all imagine how scrambled computer-addressed mail might be for Dr. Jean-Pierre Paul van Gogh-Shakespeare III, Esq.

We will explain our approach for aggregating components and creating document assembly models from a component model in Chapters 12, 13, and 14.

6.5 SEMANTIC CONFLICTS

By far the most complex issues affecting interoperability in document exchange are the result of semantic conflicts. Even if we resolve the encoding and structural conflicts, we have a long way to go to ensure meaningful communication of information.

Even if we resolve the encoding and structural conflicts, we have a long way to go to ensure meaningful communication of information

6.5.1 FUNCTIONAL DEPENDENCY CONFLICTS

Suppose an affiliate of GMBooks.com submits the order shown in Figure 6-16.

```
<OrderLine>
        <LineItem>
            <BookItem>
                <ISBN>0262072610</ISBN>
                <BasePrice>99.95</BasePrice>
            </BookItem>
            <Quantity>300</Quantity>
        </LineItem>
</OrderLine>
```

Figure 6-16. Fragment of an Order Document Lacking Book Titles and Authors

This fragment of an order document omits the book title and author from the item information.

We need to consider why the order might have been designed in such a way. We begin by referring to the GMBooks.com conceptual model for the LineItem in Figure 6-3, which consists of five information components. The modelers at GMBooks.com apparently concluded that title, author, and ISBN (the elements contained in BookItem) are a group of information components that together logically describe a book. We say they are functionally dependent.

By comparison, the components known as BasePrice and Quantity only modify the properties of a book when it appears on a line item within an order. Each order may have a different quantity or price for a book so they are not functionally dependent on the book itself.

However, the designers of the affiliate's documents appear to have decided that there will only be a single price for a book and this information component logically belongs to a BookItem.

Having different views of the dependency relationships mean business rules and semantics are interpreted differently

This is a design conflict based on different views of the dependency relationships between the information components. The business rules and therefore the semantics are interpreted differently. The two parties use different models for how information components associate with each other. In these situations, the resulting documents may be incompatible. We will explore the formation of assemblies of components based on their dependencies in Chapter 13.

6.5.2 VOCABULARY CONFLICTS

When we looked at encoding conflicts in Section 6.3, we discussed the language and grammar of the implementation. But when we talk about semantics we need to examine the vocabulary. We use this vocabulary to convey the semantics of components, including the names we give them. And the way we implement these names also involves syntax considerations, such as with naming tags in XML documents.

XML Tag Names

When encoding document models, the creators of an XML vocabulary sometimes seek to avoid problems and disputes by automatically generating tag names that have no equivalent in any natural language. For example, one proposal to create XML versions of the standard UN/EDIFACT messages suggested five-letter "UN-XML" tags like <HFKDR>, <BBBTS>, and <RTFDS>8 whose meaning would be specified by the mapping of the tag to items in the standard UN/EDIFACT data dictionary.

To some extent, we applaud the use of arbitrary tag names because it further rebuts the notion that XML is somehow "self-describing" and that schemas are optional (see Section 2.5.3). And we appreciate the desire to avoid bias. But we are convinced that generating meaningless tag names is a bad idea. It would be better to start with names that help business analysts, programmers, and other users of the vocabulary to do their jobs. It's easy enough to then transform the names for anyone who doesn't like them or who needs a different set.

Choosing the terms used for naming is often a difficult and contentious activity. Everyone naturally wants to create names in his or her native language, but even in the same language or family of dialects, the same concepts have multiple words or even different spellings for the same word (consider, for example, the bewildering differences among the numerous varieties of English). Even when describing exactly the same document component, chances are very good that two developers or two teams of data modelers will choose different names for it.[9] In Section 7.5.2 we'll mention two possible solutions: controlled vocabularies, a closed set of defining terms, and formal ontologies, which define the meaning of terms using a formal or logic-based language.

Two modelers will often choose different names for the same component

Given this difficulty, GMBooks.com might encounter an affiliate with the instance in Figure 6-17 that has the correct conceptual model but not the expected tag names:

```
<Customer>
    <Number>KEEN</Number>
    <Name>
        <BusinessName>Maynard James Keenan</BusinessName>
    </Name>
    <Location>
        <Unit>505</Unit>
        <StreetNumber>11271</StreetNumber>
        <Street>Ventura Blvd.</Street>
        <City>Studio City</City>
        <ZipCode>91604</ZipCode>
        <State>California</State>
```

```
        <Country>USA</Country>
    </Location>
</Customer>
```

Figure 6-17. Buyer Party with Different Tag Names

This also applies when using different languages. For example, GMBooks.com might receive an order with components such as those in Figure 6-18 from a French affiliate.

```
<Acheteur>
    <ID>KEEN</ID>
    <Nom>
        <NomCommercial>Maynard James Keenan</NomCommercial>
    </Nom>
    <Addresse>
        <Appartment>505</Appartment>
        <Bâtiment>11271</Bâtiment>
        <Rue>Ventura Blvd.</Rue>
        <Ville>Studio City</Ville>
        <CodePostal>91604</CodePostal>
        <Etat>California</Etat>
        <Pays>USA</Pays>
    </Addresse>
</Acheteur>
```

Figure 6-18. Buyer Party with Tag Names in French

Both these document's components conform to the conceptual model in Figure 6-3 and only the names are different. In other words, Buyer Party, Customer, and Acheteur all refer to the same concept, that is, the party purchasing the goods.

XML is not self-describing

This reemphasizes that XML is not self-describing and confirms that the names we assign to tags are only a small part of defining the meaning of the information they contain.

But even if two separate modelers are unlikely to employ an identical set of component names, each single modeling effort should have a system for keeping names logical and consistent. Guidelines for naming conventions are discussed further in Sections 7.6.2 and 12.1.11.

The names of components are only a small part of their semantic definition

6.5.3 CONTEXTUAL CONFLICTS

Imagine that when GMBooks.com developed their order system, they were taking orders only from the North America. Later they decided to branch out into international orders, and they received an order from Japan. Part of this order is shown in Figure 6-19:

```
<Buyer>
    <ID>KEEN91604</ID>
    <FullName>
        <Title>Dr.</Title>
        <FirstName>Maynard</FirstName>
        <MiddleName>James</MiddleName>
        <LastName>Keenan</LastName>
    </FullName>
    <Address>
        <PostalCode>170-3293</PostalCode>
        <Prefecture>Tokyo</Prefecture>
        <Ward>Chuo</Ward>
        <Subarea>Ginza</Subarea>
        <SubareaNumber>5</SubareaNumber>
        <BlockNumber>2</BlockNumber>
        <HouseNumber>1</HouseNumber>
    </Address>
</Buyer>
```

Figure 6-19. Order Fragment with Incompatible Postal Address

This is a perfectly reasonable postal address model in Japan, but it is conceptually incompatible with the postal address model expected by GMBooks.com. In Japan, streets are not all named and addresses are designated by ever-smaller subdivisions of a city. There is simply no way to transform a Japanese address into the desired instance. If GMBooks.com wants to fulfill this order and do business with Japanese customers, it needs to redesign its system to handle Japanese orders. This requires a separate model for Japanese addresses or changes to the existing model to accommodate it. The semantic conflict here resulted from a limited understanding of what constituted an address. The sample of documents or information sources that were analyzed to produce the original address model was too narrow. Perhaps GMBooks.com looked only at examples of American and Canadian addresses or decided that Japanese orders were unlikely. On the other hand, the affiliate in Japan was basing its model on a sample of addresses that seemed representative to it. Both parties thought they were designing for the same business context of online bookselling, but they chose only local sources to obtain their information requirements.

Different document samples can lead to incompatible models

The decision about what information sources to analyze when developing a model—the inventory and sampling phase—occurs early in the modeling process. So if different parties begin with different samples, their context of use can diverge at a very early stage and chances are that the resulting models will be incompatible. We discuss the techniques for collecting the inventory of sources and choosing an appropriate sample in Section 7.5 and Chapter 11. The inventory will include information sources that are not in the form of traditional documents, such as databases, spreadsheets, web pages, and the people who create and use them.

Finally, an even more extreme case of incompatibility can be seen in the order snippet in Figure 6-20:

```
<BuyerParty>
    <ID>KEEN</ID>
    <PartyName>
        <Name>Maynard James Keenan</Name>
    </PartyName>
    <Address>
        <Latitude direction="N">37.871</Latitude>
        <Longitude direction="W">-122.271</Longitude>
    </Address>
</BuyerParty>
```

Figure 6-20. Order Fragment with an Address That Isn't Postal

This (admittedly a bit contrived) document fragment might result if someone wanted to order books to be delivered to an offshore oil platform in the Yellow Sea.[10] But in this case, the location designation is not a postal address in any sense. As a set of coordinates, it is wholly outside the context of the Address model designed by GMBooks.com. This is a case of semantic mismatch. While GMBooks.com defined Address in their model to accommodate locations recognizable to postal services, this example concerns locations in a different context. As such, the meaning of the two component models differs, and no interoperability can really be expected.

Semantic conflicts should be resolved when the context of use is being defined

This is a difficult conflict to resolve, and it can be dealt with only at the very first step in the modeling process when the context is being defined. In Section 7.3, we explore in more detail the activities involved in determining the modeling context, including the identification of patterns, requirements, and business processes that must be supported.

6.6 MOTIVATING THE DOCUMENT ENGINEERING APPROACH

Interoperability is a desirable goal but not one that is easily achieved. Using what may have seemed at the outset to be a simple order document, we have identified a range of potential conflicts when two parties conceptualize, organize, or implement their models of names, addresses, and books differently. Some types of conflicts are minor and can be easily resolved, while others require case-by-case analysis or may be impossible to resolve (See SIDEBAR).

Many of the claims about web services and a "plug-and-play" business are exaggerated and naïve

The variety of ways in which two models might not match should make it obvious that many of the claims about web services and a seamless or "plug-and-play" business Internet are exaggerated and naïve. Likewise, even though extraction, mapping, and transformation technology continues to improve, fixing problems when two models don't match is likely to remain a labor-intensive activity.

Automatic Resolution of Interoperability Conflicts

Applications can be written to have very precise expectations about the input they receive and to reject any input that doesn't conform. This is generally a bad approach from both technical and business standpoints. While it is good for an application to be conservative in what it sends, it should try to be liberal in what it accepts and be programmed with the philosophy that unexpected inputs may represent new requirements that it should be able to handle.

Nevertheless, being open and extensible for new input requirements doesn't mean that the application should automatically try to accept nonconforming messages. As we've seen in this chapter, a mismatch in physical implementations may or may not imply a mismatch in conceptual models, and most of the time it takes a person rather than a program to decide. Automated programs can propose classifications or diagnoses of the nonconforming messages, but ultimately the decision about whether to accept a message and try to make use of its contents should be made by someone who understands interoperability from a broad business and technical perspective in the specific context in which the message is received.

Once we understand the meaning of the input, some kinds of conflicts are relatively superficial, and we can write general-purpose data extraction and transformation programs to resolve them. From then on any messages with those conflicts can be automatically processed. Other kinds of conflicts are deeper, and while we might be able to work around them with custom programming, we need to be concerned that the differences in conceptual models might cause problems elsewhere in our business systems.

But it is worthwhile studying how things can go wrong only if we use what we learn to make things go right. Each way in which documents can fail to interoperate—each problem or conflict we encounter—can be turned around to motivate a Document Engineering activity to remedy or prevent such problems. Modeling is difficult, but we can and should study good modelers and good models to learn skills and principles to use when we do it. This makes a good model a significant intellectual achievement that deserves to be reused. Starting with Chapter 7, we introduce a Document Engineering approach that emphasizes careful modeling and the reuse of models whenever possible.

6.7 KEY POINTS IN CHAPTER SIX

- The most basic requirement for two businesses to conduct business is that their business systems interoperate.
- Many of the claims about web services and a "plug-and-play" business are exaggerated.
- Variations in strategies, technology platforms, legacy applications, business processes, and terminology make it difficult to use compatible documents.
- The earlier in the modeling process that two parties make different decisions, the greater the possibilities for their models to be incompatible.
- If projects begin with different samples, their models can diverge and the resulting models will be incompatible.
- A one-to-one mapping of document components is not always achievable.
- Content conflicts occur when two parties use different sets of values for the same components.
- Content conflicts also occur when two parties use the same sets of values for different components.
- Encoding conflicts can be resolved if the underlying semantics and structures are compatible.
- A more granular model can be transformed into a less granular model, but not vice versa.

- Even if we resolve the encoding and structural conflicts, we have a long way to go to ensure meaningful communication of information.
- Semantic conflicts should be resolved when the context of use is being defined.
- Having different views of dependency relationships creates different contexts of use.
- Two modelers will often choose different names for the same component.
- The names we assign to components are only a small part of defining their meaning.

THE DOCUMENT ENGINEERING APPROACH

7

The Document Engineering Approach

7.0 INTRODUCTION

The engineering in Document Engineering implies a systematic application of intellectual and technical knowledge to create tangible end products with economic or social value.

The essence of Document Engineering is a set of analysis and design techniques that yield robust and reusable models of documents and their roles in business processes. The discipline of an engineering approach ensures that these models are complete, useful, and reliable when realized as the data format for integration or as the interface and process specification in document-centric or service oriented applications. The practicality of an engineering approach and a heavy reliance on design and implementation patterns ensures that the models can be developed and deployed at acceptable cost in a reasonable time.

In this chapter we'll introduce a complete overview of the phases involved in Document Engineering. In Chapters 8-15 we'll discuss each phase and its constituent activities in detail, using experiences from a real-world case study that typifies the struggles of enterprises with incompatible models and applications.

7.1 AN APPROACH, NOT A METHODOLOGY

Our goal here is not to define a formal methodology. We aim more modestly to present a coherent and pragmatic approach for modeling documents and services that provide solutions that are practical and effective.

Document Engineering is a coherent and pragmatic approach for modeling documents and services that provide solutions that are practical and effective

Three key factors shape the concepts and methods we present as the Document Engineering Approach:

1. *End-to-end scope.* We must be able to describe the information content and processes in a document exchange, identify the context of use and its relevant requirements and constraints, analyze and design a solution, and then implement and deploy that solution. Furthermore, we must expect that the requirements and constraints will change, so our solution must be evolvable. It would be pointless to develop a solution that can't be adapted to changing environments, no matter how theoretically elegant or powerful it might be.

2. *The breadth of documents that we must be able to analyze, design, and implement.* In Chapter 1 we introduced the Document Type Spectrum that spans from narrative, publication-style documents to transactional, data-intensive ones. These contrasting types of documents have traditionally been analyzed and designed using substantially different approaches, which we unify by emphasizing what they have in common.

3. *The requirement that document exchanges must be implementable in a loosely coupled, technology-independent manner.* It is a fundamental principle of distributed and service oriented architectures that the relationships between organizations or service providers must be adaptable and flexible because only the document interfaces are visible. It is neither necessary nor desirable for each party to know anything about the implementation on the other side of the exchange.

What each side needs to know can be completely captured using two types of modeling artifacts, models of the documents exchanged and models of the business processes, collaborations, and transactions. The latter form the context and specify the patterns and sequencing for the exchanges.

These three factors of scope, breadth of document types, and loose coupling, provide an approach that is flexible and heuristic. We present the tasks of Document Engineering in sequential phases, but within and between each phase, activities often overlap or repeat, and not every activity is required in every effort. However, presenting them in a typical progression makes them easier to introduce and better motivates the modeling artifacts that organize and visualize the most important results of each activity.

7.1.1 MODELING METHODOLOGIES

Modeling is inherently difficult. Modeling documents and the processes that use them is harder still because they can be both informal and abstract, giving us little to grab onto when we start. There is no single correct way to create these models, and many different methodologies have been proposed. They share the common goals of defining the rules and requirements of the context of use and communicating this understanding in one or more modeling artifacts.

There is no single correct way to create document and process models

Every modeling methodology proposes a set of modeling activities. They may differ in the order in which the activities are carried out or how prescriptive they are about the activities and descriptions of their results.

How the models are described reflects the metamodel adopted by the methodology (see Section 3.3.1). Metamodels define the kinds of information that models contain, so more prescriptive metamodels increase the consistency among models, which in turn more easily exposes patterns within collections of models. Common metamodels also provide a useful basis for libraries of reusable patterns because the models they contain can be interpreted by anyone or any application that understands the metamodel.

For example, the UN/CEFACT Modeling Methodology (UMM)[1] proposed a metamodel that specifies a set of progressively more detailed views of business processes, refining a high-level, goal-oriented view of the specific transactions in which documents are exchanged. Similarly, the RosettaNet initiative has defined a metamodel for describing supply chain processes called the Partner Interface Process (PIP).[2] The UMM and RosettaNet metamodels were used as the foundation for the ebXML Business Process Specification Schema (BPSS), which has strongly influenced how we think about business collaborations that use web services.[3]

We use aspects of these metamodels in Document Engineering, but we aren't prescriptive about it. We advocate a less prescriptive and more pragmatic modeling approach to be consistent with the loosely coupled architecture of the Internet on which we expect that most of the models developed using Document Engineering will be deployed. Indeed, we are somewhat reluctant to use the term methodology when describing Document Engineering. We prefer to call Document Engineering an approach that can be followed to exploit the potential of extended enterprises, service oriented architectures, and web services that embody the principle of loose coupling through document exchanges.

This approach embodies the principle of loose coupling through document exchanges

When the participants in a business relationship can be on opposite sites of the globe, it is impossible for one side to impose a modeling methodology on another or audit the techniques the other uses to build a model. Once the model is defined and communicated, the process taken to develop it is invisible. So the methodologies each enterprise or organization uses to design its business processes and their associated documents should be as loosely coupled as the document exchanges. If only the document interfaces are visible, there is no justification for imposing a prescriptive modeling and design methodology. All that matters is whether the parties can produce and consume the expected documents or models appropriately.

Once the model is defined and communicated, the process taken to develop it is invisible

As web services and service oriented architectures become more ubiquitous, businesses will expect reductions in the costs to evolve and operate new business models and the implementation technologies. This implies a pragmatic approach to modeling: one that is efficient, does not require nonessential activities to achieve the desired result, and, most importantly, actively strives to build on previous efforts.

7.2 THE DOCUMENT ENGINEERING APPROACH

In Chapter 3 we introduced the Model Matrix (Figure 3-7) to depict the relationship between the different kinds of models enterprises use to arrange their activities. The models we organize in the upper left corner of the matrix are broad in scope and abstract in perspective. As we move to the right and down in the matrix, models become narrower in scope and more concretely tied to technology and implementation. We are now ready to introduce the Document Engineering approach as a set of activities to create and reuse these models.

7.2.1 UNIFIED APPROACH TO MODELING

Document Engineering relies on the skills and tools of business process, document, data, and task analysts. One of the innovations of Document Engineering is to exploit these different techniques for reaching the same goal. That goal is developing models that are abstract enough to be reused as patterns but concrete enough to be implemented. Figure 7-1 graphically depicts this common goal as reaching the middle of the Model Matrix from different starting points.

Document Engineering exploits different analysis techniques for reaching the same goal

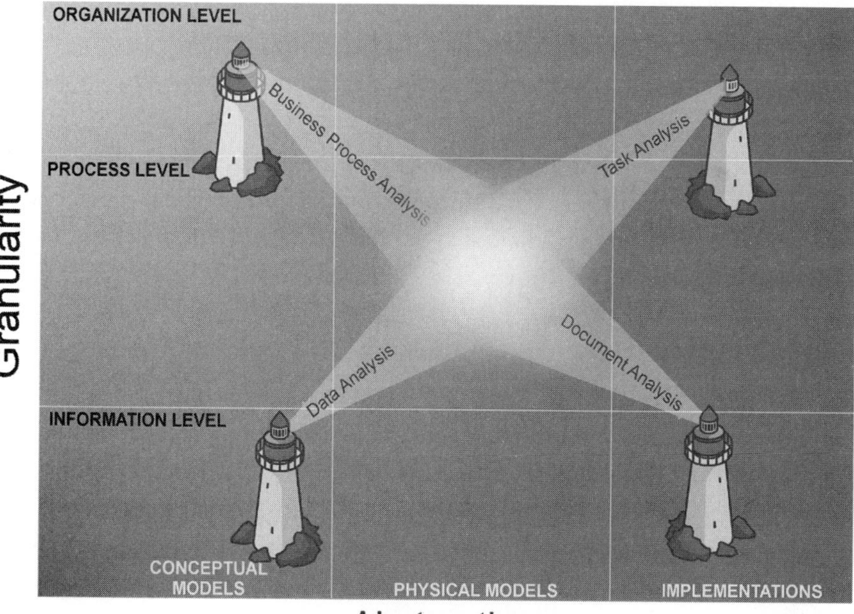

Figure 7-1. Analysis Perspectives Used in Document Engineering

Business analysis typically starts with abstract views of business models and processes, which are organized in the upper left corner. This high-level analysis establishes the context for understanding the semantics of the information in the other sections of the matrix.

Task analysis (or user analysis) is the observation of people performing the tasks or use cases when the application or system must support human interfaces and not just other applications. Task analysis identifies the specific steps and information that people need to carry out a task, so it is based on implementation artifacts and activities, which are represented on the right side of the matrix. Task analysis and document analysis are closely related; document analysis reveals candidate information components and task analysis reveals rules about their intent and usage. Task analysis is especially important when few documents or information sources exist, because human problems or errors can suggest that important information is missing.

Document analysis tends to start from analysis of document instances. We show this on the lower right side. These techniques extract or disentangle the presentational, structural, and content components of documents or other information sources.

Data analysis (or object analysis[4]) techniques often start from a conceptual perspective about a domain and yield an abstract view of the information components revealed by document analysis. So this approach is represented as starting from the lower left corner of the Model Matrix.

Modeling methodologies are a means to a desired end—the set of modeling artifacts produced by the analysis and modeling effort. These artifacts include documents, their models, and libraries of reusable patterns used in models. We advocate a stronger focus on these artifacts than on the means for creating them. We call this an artifact focused view of modeling.

7.2.2 ARTIFACT FOCUSED VIEW OF MODELING

The artifact focused view of modeling concentrates on producing modeling artifacts and on reusing existing modeling artifacts when they fit. We'll explain this approach by using an analogy with the income tax systems that operate in most countries.

A formalized methodology is equivalent to the entire tax code. Because the tax code has to be comprehensive, it is generally too complex for people other than tax attorneys and accountants to use. So the taxation authority provides forms that assist taxpayers by organizing the information they need to provide to comply with the tax code rules. These forms are themselves supported by booklets (or guidelines) that provide instructions for filling them out. Finally, software vendors have developed applications (such as TurboTax) that guide taxpayers through the process of filling out electronic forms and perhaps even submitting them over the Internet.

When most people pay their taxes, they focus on the tax forms because these are the artifacts required by the taxation authority. They may consult the guidelines or even the tax code, but only on an ad hoc basis. They certainly don't start by reading the tax code and all the guidelines from beginning to end. Likewise, the taxation authority doesn't care about the process the taxpayer or accountant followed to fill out the forms; only the numbers matter.

We are proposing the same approach in Document Engineering. We provide lots of guidance and explanation to help create models of documents and processes, but we emphasize the models. By focusing on the artifacts rather than the methodology by which they are created, we give the document engineer more flexibility in capturing relevant data or metadata about documents and processes whenever they arise. This is also a key benefit of most tax software applications, which allow the various subparts and forms to be filled out in almost any order, pulling the information together at the end to calculate any required payments or refunds.

7.2.3 THE MODELING PHASES, TASKS, AND ARTIFACTS

Figure 7-2 depicts the Document Engineering approach as a path through the Model Matrix to carry out a set of analysis, assembly, and implementation tasks. We show this path as being equally wide as it winds its way through the phases of Document Engineering, but in practice different phases may get more or less emphasis, depending on the management and strategy decisions that shape the project. Top-down or strategic efforts to align business organization and technology cut a broad swath through the top of the Model Matrix. These efforts create models that are very abstract or very generalized, partitioning activity into large, goal-oriented chunks to provide a big picture view of the context of use.

In contrast, bottom-up and more document-driven projects emphasize the path through the lower half of the model matrix. These efforts may yield a large number of models for transactional processes, often refined by the specific types of document they produce or consume.

But high-level, goal-oriented models lack the detail needed for implementing and integrating the applications built to achieve them, and low-level models of documents and information components by themselves don't provide much help in aligning high-level business goals with technology choices and implementation decisions. That's why it is worthwhile to follow the entire path through the matrix. Developing a variety of models of varying emphasis and granularity ensures that any new models we create for business processes and documents are complete, consistent, robust, and deployable in applications that meet actual business requirements.

Following the complete path also helps to overcome the fundamental modeling challenge of achieving a consistent level of abstraction so that patterns and models from different perspectives can fit together. There is a large granularity gap between business models and document models. Our path through the Model Matrix yields successively more granular models that bridge the gap.

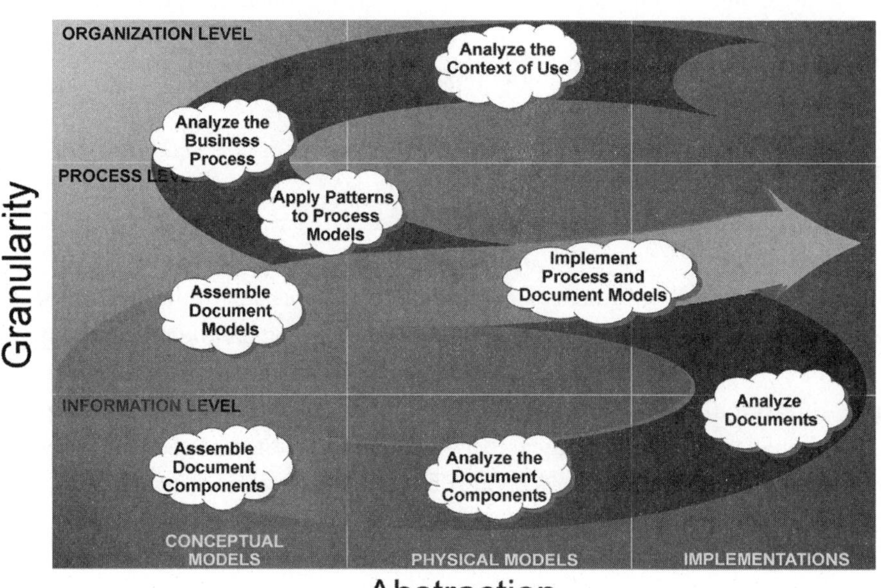

Figure 7-2. Phases of the Document Engineering Approach

On the top row we begin with high-level, organizational analysis to understand the main business activities and the people and organizations that participate in them. This strategic perspective is an essential foundation for developing a service oriented architecture or carrying out mergers or acquisitions. For example, when HP and Compaq merged, teams of executives and business analysts spent months analyzing how each enterprise did business to decide what practices, divisions, products, and people should be retained. Models at this level, called the business domain view in ebXML, describe the broad context of use for the documents and processes we will define at more granular levels.

What we call context is the collective sum of the requirements for our project. So the first phase of Document Engineering, "Analyzing the Context of Use," involves identifying strategic business objectives in terms of business model requirements and the rules they must satisfy.

Understanding the business process is important for expressing the context of use. In business process analysis we often contrast the way things are with how we would like them to be. After we describe an As-Is model, we can improve its processes by applying existing patterns or we can invent completely new ones.

We create these process As-Is models in the "Analyze the Business Process" phase.

As we saw in Chapter 4, much of what businesses do can be described using a small repertoire of business patterns. For example, we might decide that our context of use fits the Procurement pattern, and that its processes and information exchanges describe the transactions and documents required. Or we may best describe our model as an incremental information trail in which documents are created, consumed, added to, and subtracted from as they are passed along from one process to the next.

Choosing and instantiating appropriate patterns for business processes entails adopting a predefined context of use. Using a business process pattern also suggests the relevant users and other stakeholders from whom we can obtain or confirm requirements.

Choosing a pattern for a business process entails adopting a predefined context of use

So designing business processes can be best described as "Applying Patterns to Process Models."

Describing the actual documents needed by a business model starts to take place during the "Analyze Documents" phase.[5]

The To-Be process model identifies the roles that documents will play. Document analysis exposes the specific business rules that govern the instance, structure, presentation, syntax, and semantics of the information contained in the documents.

We analyze existing document models (such as XML schemas) as well as any implementation guidelines and standards, sample document instances, web pages, and other information sources to harvest all potentially meaningful information components and the constraints that govern their values, arrangement, and use. Of course we can't ignore the people who create, review, approve, query, or do other things with these documents. In particular, in domains or new business models where few documents exist, what we can learn from people is critical because we can derive information and document requirements from their goals and tasks. In many situations existing documents are extremely valuable proxies for, or confirmations of, what people tell us.

The "Analyze Document Components" phase starts with the harvesting task. This identifies the individual components contained in each of the selected documents or information sources. Part of this rationalization involves choosing meaningful names for these components. But naming is inherently a contentious and iterative task, so the names are tentative at this point.

In "Assemble Document Components" we assemble sets of these information components into meaningful structures to create a coherent conceptual view we call the document component model. We advocate doing this by using data analysis techniques that normalize the components into structures based on their functional dependency.

We then turn from analysis to design as we start to create models for each type of documents required, based on the components, structures, and associations in our document component model. We call these new models document assembly models. In the "Assemble Document Models" task we apply the rules for assembling the information components necessary for each different type of document required for the given context of use.

Effective design involves the analysis, reuse, and creation of patterns

Effective design of processes and documents requires us to recognize when a pattern can be reused, when a new pattern should be created, and what distinguishes one pattern from another. So any conceptual document assembly models and process models we develop can reuse the patterns from a variety of internal and external sources.

7.2.4 IMPLEMENTING MODELS IN APPLICATIONS

These conceptual models represent substantial investments in understanding sets of business rules and capturing contextual requirements. In the implementation tasks, we create modeling artifacts to define and drive applications. We can use these in an explicit way to implement a solution in an automated or semiautomated manner, what we call a model based application. In other words, we exploit the conceptual models to bridge the gap between knowing what to do and actually doing it.

We exploit conceptual models to bridge the gap between knowing what to do and actually doing it

Model based applications are often implemented using software whose generic functionality is made context-specific by configuring or extending it to use the context-dependent information and behavior specified in the model. The first step in achieving this is to realize the conceptual models in a suitable language.

For documents we call the realized artifact the document implementation model. Document implementation models realized in markup languages are more commonly known as schemas, as we saw with XML in Chapter 2. For example, when XML is used to encode document implementation models, many aspects of the integrity of a document's information components, as well as the business rules applied to the data, can be derived from the XML schemas.

Is Document Engineering Compatible with User-Centered Interface Design?

The Document Engineering approach for design and implementation of user interfaces might at first seem incompatible with the conventional user-centered or usability engineering approach to interface design. The latter approaches rely heavily on iterative prototyping and evaluation with an outside-in perspective in which document and process models are less explicitly considered. In contrast, the model-based approach of Document Engineering is more inside out, is especially appropriate for designing systems rather than user interfaces, and defers user interface design until the models are mostly complete.

Nevertheless, we think that Document Engineering is both compatible with and complementary to usability engineering, especially for applications enabled by web services and document exchanges. We certainly aren't claiming that document implementation models can directly determine every aspect of user interface design. But models can:

- Define the information that needs to be presented in user interfaces.

- Serve as hypotheses or checklists to help user interface designers determine the optimal presentation and interaction structure for applications used by people.

- Generate prototype interfaces.

- Enforce rules or best practices about user interface design along the way.

Likewise, functions that control the transaction workflow or application logic can often be derived by analogy from models of business process. What is important is that these models remain loosely coupled with the user interface design. Further transformations that apply presentation rules to document instances can also be implemented to meet formatting or other rendering requirements for different classes of uses or devices.

For models of business processes, realization involves adopting a suitable metamodel (such as the ebXML BPSS) to encode the specific rules and the requirements for our given context of use. This means that the modeling artifact itself is encoded as a document instance. We call this realized artifact the business process implementation model. For example, RosettaNet PIPs are examples of business process implementation models encoded in XML. Web services and service oriented architectures can be implemented in this model based way when the document and process models they use are designed to separate generic and context-dependent functionality.

7.3 ANALYZING THE CONTEXT OF USE

The universe of discourse for any business or Document Engineering project is potentially a vastly complex set of processes and information components. We cannot hope to analyze its entirety. By necessity we must define a subset of the most important components and processes. This isn't always easy because, to misquote John Donne, "No document is an Island, entire of itself."[7]

A typical large organization or firm might use dozens of different types of documents with complex organizational and process interdependencies. For example, information on an order document can be connected in some way to account ledgers, sales reports, catalogs, production schedules, advertisements, user manuals, and numerous other documents. Furthermore, the relationships among these different types of documents vary for different information components. A Product Description may relate to catalogs and advertisements, but Buyer Party would relate to sales reports and accounts ledgers. It is not hard to see how the scope expands very quickly, and we must explicitly identify what is in and out of scope to make sense of any of it.

7.3.1 REQUIREMENTS

Identifying requirements in the initial stages of a project reduces the likelihood that you'll have to throw away or rework the analysis, design, and implementation phases that follow. But too often people view technology adoption as a requirement rather than requiring a business need to justify the adoption of technology. A focus on new technology and new ways of doing things often suppresses consideration of important legacy technology or existing business processes. The collapse of the dot-com bubble should have taught us lessons about putting technology before business considerations and ignoring the core requirement of making enough money, but if we're not careful we'll forget it all in the next waves of hype about web services, RFID, ubiquitous computing, and whatever comes next.

Requirements are constraints on possible solutions that must be satisfied for the solution to be acceptable

Requirements are constraints on possible solutions that must be satisfied for the solution to be acceptable. They are most often expressed as functional descriptions (or rules) of what the solution must do. But they can also include performance characteristics, quality attributes, or conformance to regulations or standards. In other words, requirements are the way we express the context of our document exchanges. Of course, rules and requirements will continue to emerge throughout the project, but identifying as many requirements as we can is a pretty good starting point. Identifying and categorizing requirements are the main topics in Chapter 8, "Analyzing the Context of Use."

Many of these requirements will be expressed as rules about the content, structure, and presentation of documents and their components. We use these to identify and design new types of documents. Other requirements will be expressed as usage rules or policies about access to information or control of its processing. We use these to formalize the definitions of the context in which the documents are used.

Collecting requirements and rules is a heuristic and iterative exercise

Collecting these requirements and rules is a heuristic and iterative exercise that requires us to take the complementary perspectives of the archaeologist and the anthropologist. Like the archaeologist, we search for artifacts and try to interpret them even though the organizations or people who created them might be extinct and no longer available to help. We might discover legacy formats and paper documents whose processes have been frozen in time. But these artifacts might refer or link to other artifacts, and slowly we begin to understand them. And like the anthropologist, we locate people who work with the artifacts, and they may refer or link us to other people, who help us find more artifacts and people.

Sometimes requirements don't emerge until after the first version of a solution is implemented. If we anticipate this and implement the application in a loosely coupled and model based manner, we can view new requirements as good news rather than bad news.

Business analysis and task analysis techniques such as user interviews and questionnaires can tell us how people think they use information and documents. But because people sometimes tell us what they think we want them to tell us, we can't always take what they say at face value. That's why the best way to gather requirements is to balance the artifact-driven work of the archaeologist with the perspective of an anthropologist studying people and phenomena in their natural surroundings.[8] We must observe and listen carefully to learn about what processes and documents exist, where they can be found, how they are used, how useful they are, and the rules that govern their use. But we must be on the lookout for errors and inconsistencies in what we hear and discover and sometimes let the documents speak for themselves. In this book we represent the models we develop during these activities in artifacts such as UML use case diagrams and descriptive worksheets.

7.3.2 PATTERNS OF CONTEXT

In Chapter 3 we defined patterns as models that are sufficiently general, adaptable, and worthy of imitation that we can use them over and over. We also described how businesses follow patterns because of common requirements for their specific processes, geography, products, legal environment, business models, and so on. So we can see each combination of these factors as a common pattern of requirements.

We use the context of use to organize and analyze requirements and rules

Consideration of the generic procurement pattern of one buyer and one seller will ultimately be situated in a richer context that specifies the industries in which the procurement takes place, goods being procured, locations of the buyer and seller, regulations or laws governing the activity, and so on. These dimensions of context are a common way of classifying patterns of business rules and requirements. In other words, we use our appreciation of the overall context of use to organize and analyze the requirements and rules that will drive our design of processes and their documents.

7.3.3 SCOPE OF CONTEXT

To understand the scope of the processes in our business model, we need to recognize dependency relationships among business processes. Dependency describes the impact that a change to one object has on another object. We say that if a change to A inherently changes B, then B is dependent on A.

Many businesses processes are completely independent. For example, hiring a new employee doesn't affect the product catalog, but adding a new product to the manufacturing schedule may change the catalog, and changes to the catalog may change the structure of sales orders. So we could say that while hiring is independent of marketing and sales, marketing and sales are dependent on manufacturing.

The organizational charts and policy or procedure manuals we discussed in Chapter 4 are examples of documents that can suggest dependencies within an enterprise. But often these are descriptions of what the dependencies are supposed to be rather than what the people or systems actually do.

The more legitimate dependencies we encounter in our project, the more patterns for reuse we will find, but at the cost of greater complexity. So we should aim for a scope that includes enough dependencies to ensure that the context is realistic, but not so many we cannot comprehend the interactions among them. Understanding the patterns involved can help us with this. For example, suppose we identify a pattern that describes the business processes that interests us. When applied in a specific industry, with specific firms, in a geopolitical environment, and so on, the pattern is inevitably customized to meet the requirements of a more concrete situation. Seeing how a pattern has been adapted for different contexts of use can help us understand potential dependencies.

7.4 ANALYZING BUSINESS PROCESSES

We define a business process as a chain of related activities or events that take specified inputs, add value to them, and yield a specific service or product that can be the input to another business process.

Some business processes are conducted entirely within a firm and are called internal, enterprise, or private business processes. In contrast, external, collaborative, or public business processes are carried out between two or more business parties. The Document Engineering approach applies to both kinds of processes but is especially useful for the latter, where different implementation technologies mandate the loosely coupled architecture of document exchange.

Of course, private business processes and public ones overlap because they must connect if a firm is to do business with any other party; the business exists to exploit the results of its private business processes in its public ones. This intrinsic connection between the private and public processes establishes a dependency between them.

Businesses exist to exploit the results of their private processes in their public ones

But it can be difficult for processes to span the boundary between two firms, because of the inherent flexibility in how abstractly processes are described. Two businesses might use different levels of abstraction or granularity to describe the processes they need to connect, making their process descriptions incompatible. Chapter 9 explains two ways in which we can avoid this problem:

- Use the concepts and components provided by a business reference model, whose hierarchical organization of processes has been rigorously designed to reinforce granularity.

- Express all process models at the granularity where we can identify the documents that they produce and consume.

Chapter 9 also introduces the modeling artifacts we typically produce during the Business Process Analysis phase. These include worksheets that help us organize the information we learn about processes and UML activity diagrams, UML sequence diagrams, and other forms of flowcharts that record the processes once we understand them. These diagrams depict the structure of collaboration and interaction between the people and services implied by the pattern. These models also begin to express our understanding of both the transaction semantics and the required contingencies between each document exchange.

7.5 DESIGNING BUSINESS PROCESSES

The relationship between public and private processes is complicated by the tension every business faces in balancing the benefits of designing documents to accomplish its private processes in an optimal way with the need for its processes and documents to be understood by other businesses. This tension induces businesses to reuse existing models for processes and documents whenever possible and encourages them to design new models that encourage reuse by others, even if doing so results in a less-than-perfect solution for its internal needs. This is why the task of designing new business processes often involves more adopting and adapting of patterns than invention of something new. Much of business process design is actually more like reusing existing business patterns. This is the perspective we take in Chapter 10, "Designing Business Processes with Patterns."

This tension between public and private processes induces businesses to reuse existing models

As we saw in Chapter 3, when identifying reusable patterns it is desirable to describe the models in conceptual rather than physical terms. Business process libraries are a useful repertoire of business process patterns precisely because they do not dictate specific technologies for implementation.

Even if a business process pattern is only a partial fit to a particular context, it can still provide useful insights for identifying further requirements. For example, some aspects of the procurement pattern are the same whether one is buying steel, paper clips, or university courses.

7.6 ANALYZING DOCUMENTS

The objective of document analysis is to create a conceptual model that encompasses all the information requirements within the required context of use. We start this phase by determining what documents and information sources we need to analyze. This is the primary topic of Chapter 11, "Analyzing Documents."

7.6.1 CREATE THE DOCUMENT INVENTORY

A document inventory is the collection of documents and related artifacts we analyze. The inventory lists the sources we identify along with metadata about their purposes, origins, and other attributes that will help us select a subset to analyze in detail.

The richer the document inventory, the more effective any analysis will be

Because the inventory exposes both information components and related business rules, the richer this inventory, the more effective any analysis will be. So we need to take a broader view that goes beyond traditional printed-paper documents and their electronic analogs.

In fact, much of what we need to analyze may not be in a traditional document form; much of it may look more like sets of data. So we stretch the meaning of document to include information in databases, spreadsheets, and accounting systems, as well as catalogs, brochures, schedules and calendars, word processing files, and web pages.

And not all information requirements are necessarily recorded in documents themselves. There may be useful metadata about documents and their components in the form of document definitions, data models and schemas. Additional metadata can be found in style guides, industry standards for the domain, application interfaces, and artifacts from previous studies and analyses.

Last but not least, the inventory should include any undocumented information from the people involved in the exchange of documents. The people who create and use the tangible parts of the document inventory can tell us what to look for and where to find it. They also have much tacit knowledge that they subconsciously understand and apply, and we can encourage them to make it explicit by engaging them in conversation, or we can learn it implicitly by observing them at work. We'll need their help to understand the documents and information sources we find. And before we're through, we'll want them to review the proposed models and their embodiment in applications.

7.6.2 SAMPLE THE DOCUMENT INVENTORY

It is unlikely that we'll be able to analyze everything in the inventory in detail, so we need to take a representative sample. Determining what sources are representative is another iterative task, because we won't know the size and variability of the inventory until we've collected it. The people who provide the documents might be able to help, but they often have a limited or inaccurate understanding of business processes and documents other than their own.

Not everything in the inventory is equally valuable. We may also want to emphasize or give more weight to documents that are especially important or authoritative, but we won't always know this at first either. For example, a document implementation model in the form of a schema or its proxy (such as a data entry form) may give more and better information about requirements and constraints on components than an individual document instance can. However, a set of several sample document instances may prove more suitable for identifying additional business rules.

In general, the more document instances we consider when we do our analysis, the more precisely we can recognize the business rules that express requirements. Obviously, if the instances are homogeneous we need fewer of them than if they are not. This means there is a law of diminishing returns that decides when we have seen enough instances; as long as new instances expose new rules, we're probably not done.

7.7 ANALYZING DOCUMENT COMPONENTS

After we select a representative sample from our document inventory, the next activity is to isolate any semantic components they contain. We call this harvesting the components. This phase is discussed in detail in Chapter 12, "Analyzing Document Components."

7.7.1 HARVEST THE COMPONENTS

There are two distinct tasks involved in harvesting: separating the underlying meaning from presentational components and disaggregating existing structures. We can illustrate both tasks with some examples.

In Chapter 6 we described some of the interoperability challenges that GMBooks.com faces if organizations can order books either by filling out a form or by having an application order them using electronic documents (see Figure 6-2). These two different physical representations of orders must both contain the same content components or they won't be acceptable to GMBooks.com. They both have content components such as the publisher supplying the books, the book titles and authors, the quantity ordered, details of the party making the order, the address to which the books are to be delivered, the instrument or mechanism by which the affiliate proposes to pay GMBooks.com, and so on. However, how these components appear can be radically different.

Separating meaning from presentation involves recognizing the stylistic conventions or presentation components being applied to information in its various formats. For example, the affiliate ordering books by fax might create the order using a word processor, sort the books by publisher, and center and underline the publisher's name before each set of books. Another affiliate might send an electronic order for the same books using a procurement application that intermixes books from different publishers with no additional formatting. The books being ordered are identical, but the documents differ in the presentations assigned to their components.

In addition, the two orders may be arranged in different structural components. Some of these may be groups or composites of components to facilitate tasks like data entry or display. These presentational structures are usually required by people because business applications don't care. For example, the components in an order may be organized into separate structures such as the order header, details, and summary, or in sections relevant to different parties or types of information. One set of components may be arranged in a structure labeled Delivery Address, another labeled Billing Address, and a third labeled For Office Use Only.

Presentation components like boxes, rules, shading, indentation, and other formatting devices can be used to reinforce these presentational structures.

Presentational structures are often the most salient patterns in narrative documents

Presentational structures are often the most salient patterns in narrative documents because their individual content components are not explicitly distinguished; occcasional exceptions when content components like Note, Warning, or Code Sample label parts of narrative documents prove the rule. It is more likely that narrative documents use structural terms like Chapter or Section as the primary organizational mechanism. Others use hierarchical numbering schemes that are correlated with presentational components like type face or size to reinforce the structural distinctions, as we do in this book.[9]

Identifying presentation components and presentational structures enables us to determine whether these stylistic characteristics are necessary to understand the information contained in the document. Differences in appearance of the two physical implementations may or may not affect the semantic equivalence of the information they convey.

As we analyze these components, we try to replace any required presentational components with content components. We also try to disaggregate any presentational structures into their atomic information components, because that is the granularity necessary to identify their meaning and also to find reusable components.

While we treat presentation components and presentational structures as cues or clues for locating content components, that doesn't mean we can discard them once we've located the content. There are often fidelity and integrity requirements for information components that we need to record as rules in our models. For example, we might have a presentation integrity requirement for preserving the original appearance of a document when it is reimplemented using different technology, such as when publishing printed articles on the Web. Similarly, we can use the presentational structures in which we find components as design hypotheses about how to organize information into the most effective user interfaces for applications that display or collect information.

7.7.2 NAME THE CONTENT COMPONENTS

As we harvest candidate content components we give them names to distinguish them and suggest their meaning. These component names need to be unambiguous within their context of use.

Sometimes unambiguous names aren't difficult to create, especially for transactional documents where each field on a form may already have a label. But in more narrative types of documents, where fewer components are explicitly distinguished, much of the time we have to use less obvious starting points. In addition, existing names probably won't be consistent, so we should develop or adopt rules to make names precise and unique.

How rigorous we need to be with naming components depends on the size of the document inventory and the complexity of the project. At a minimum, we should maintain a component name dictionary, a list of the terms used in the names of components along with their definitions. In a more complex environment, we might find it necessary to use a controlled vocabulary or a formal ontology to improve the quality and consistency of component names.

Naming components is a contentious, iterative and ongoing activity

Naming is a contentious, iterative and ongoing activity throughout our analysis. As we identify candidate components, we should not be surprised if new components suggest changes to names already assigned. We should also not be surprised when user testing reveals that names that seemed perfectly sensible to us don't make sense to the people who have to use them.

The primary modeling artifact from the analysis of information components is a Table of Candidate Content Components. This aligns the components harvested from all the information sources so that we can identify synonyms, homonyms, and semantic overlaps.

7.7.3 CONSOLIDATE THE CANDIDATE COMPONENTS

At this stage in our analysis we consider all the components as candidates, because we don't know if they are to be part of the final model or not. The way we confirm this is to establish their individuality by identifying what makes them separate components.

In other words, we need to merge any synonyms (components with different names and the same meaning) by selecting a single term to replace the different ones. And we need to split the different senses of homonyms (components with the same name but different meanings) by assigning more distinctive names to each one.

This consolidation activity merges the separate sets of candidate components we created from each source during the harvesting activity into a master or combined set. The modeling artifact we produce is called a Consolidated Table of Content Components.

7.8 ASSEMBLING DOCUMENT COMPONENTS

The result of the consolidation activity is a set of semantically unique components. The first step in creating models of documents from this set is to establish the required structures and identify any associations between them. This is the subject of Chapter 13, "Assembling Document Components."

Put simply, we want to organize the set of content components we've created into structures like Address or Item that can be reused as building blocks in the more complex structures we know as documents.

But how many structures should we create for our content components? The optimal structures may not be obvious. If we don't create any, we have unlimited flexibility in how we can assemble the individual components into documents. However, this flexibility would be inefficient and prevent us from recognizing patterns suitable for reuse because we would not be building in any of the lower-level dependency rules like those between the components aggregated into structures like Address or Item.

At the other extreme, we could create a few rather large or coarse aggregates like a Catalog Entry or an Order Details structure. It would be straightforward to reuse components of this size because most documents wouldn't need many of them. But there would likely be substantial redundancy between each different implementation, leading to possible confusion in their meaning.

7.8.1 FORMALIZE THE COMPONENT MODEL

If we treat this problem of assembling components as an informal one and apply intuitive and heuristic techniques, it may be possible to come up with a set of structural components that let us build models of the documents we need. In fact, we've used the example of Address and Item precisely because it is the kind of obvious and intuitive composite that would emerge from even an informal design approach.

When we have a very small set of candidate components in a controlled environment of limited scope, an informal assembly approach may be sufficient. But in most contexts an informal approach that creates structures because they seem reasonable isn't likely to yield an optimal solution. Nor is it likely that any related projects would get the same or even compatible results.

More predictable results come from following more rigorous techniques for refining content components into aggregate structures.

More rigorous techniques for assembling structural components produce more predictable results

We advocate an approach based on the concept of functional dependency. We first introduced the concept of dependency when we discussed analyzing context earlier in this chapter. Functional dependency is the principle behind a set of data analysis techniques collectively called normalization. These techniques are widely used by database designers to yield relational models that minimize redundancy and maintain information integrity.[10] We have adapted these techniques to produce models of document components.

We call this modeling artifact a document component model but it may be more familiar to data analysts as a domain model.

This model presents an overall conceptual view of the all the information components required for a given context of use. It is convenient to represent this model as a UML class diagram. From this set of associated structural components we can assemble all our new document models that may span the transactional and narrative ends of the Document Type Spectrum.

7.8.2 ASSOCIATIONS BETWEEN STRUCTURES

The document component model that emerges from our analysis does not describe a single document. Rather it defines a network of all potential document structures that might be required within our context of use.

For example, if our context of use involved procurement, we might identify structural components such as Order, Buyer Party, and Invoice. Each of these may have associations with the others. An Order may be placed by a Buyer Party, a Buyer Party may receive an Invoice, and an Invoice may reference an Order. These rules describe a networked set of associations with no defined start and end points. Their document component model would describe all these possible associations.[11]

We design specific models of documents by organizing their structural components into what we call document assembly models. In effect, when we create a document assembly model we are defining a specific path through this network of associations. This creates what data analysts may call a view. Which paths (or views) we choose for a specific type of document is an issue of design rather than analysis—and we're not quite there yet.

7.8.3 REFINE THE COMPONENT NAMES

During the consolidation phase we gave tentative names to candidate components. An important checkpoint at the end of the analysis tasks is to refine these names.

For example, now that we have organized content components into structures, the qualified names we may have assigned to eliminate ambiguity might now be redundant. Do we need to call the component Order Reference if it is part of the Order structure? Will Reference be an adequate name?

7.9 ASSEMBLING DOCUMENT MODELS

A document component model is the capstone of the analysis work we carried out. It represents the As-Is model of things as they are. But our true goal is to find a way to make things better, and to do that we need to design new, To-Be documents. This is the subject of Chapter 14, "Assembling Document Models."

In fact, it is often when we create a document component model that we start to formulate what that better way may be. Experience tells us that the analysis involved in creating a document component model gives us a deeper appreciation of the rules and requirements of the context of use. Answering the questions arising from this analysis leads to the possibility of improvement in design. Indeed, at several points during analysis our inner voice has probably cried out, "There must be a better way."

One of the first considerations in designing documents is that they have always been (and presumably always will be) hierarchical in their structure. Whether they are encoded on clay tablets or in electronic characters, a document can be seen as a set of nested structure of components. This is why models of documents are often expressed as inverted tree diagrams because such a hierarchy is the best way to represent them.

However, the document component model produced by our analysis represents a network, not a hierarchy. It cannot define a document tree because it has no definite roots, branches, or leaves.

Consider the component model of the procurement scenario we described earlier. If an Order may be placed by a Buyer Party, a Buyer Party may receive an Invoice, and an Invoice may reference an Order, it is unclear whether the Order structure would be a root, branch, or leaf in a document hierarchy. This is because the context of use for the Order structure is not fully defined in the document component model.

Network models such as document component models (or domain views) are useful for information storage because they are versatile and reusable for many purposes. They encompass a broad context of use. But they aren't so good for information exchange.

When it comes to exchanging information, we need to enforce a precise context of use that only a hierarachical structure describes. Put another way, Document Engineering extends conventional data modeling or database design practice by also defining the models needed when applications or databases exchange information.

Document Engineering extends conventional data modeling by also defining the models needed to exchange information

To create a suitable hierarchical model of a document we first select the structural component required as the root of the hierarchy. We call this the entry point. Then we add the required roles and associations as dictated by the business rules and requirements of the document's context of use. We refer to this task as assembling a document model.

For example in the Order, Buyer Party, and Invoice scenario, the document assembly model for an Order document may implement the rule that "an Order requires a Buyer Party." The document assembly model for a Sales Report might use another rule that "a Buyer Party may have one or more Invoices covering one or more Orders." And the document assembly model for an Invoice may contain the rule "an Invoice for a Buyer Party may relate to one or more Orders." In each case the assembly of components is driven by rules based on the specific context of use. This example highlights the fact that certain components may be reused when creating different document assembly models for different contexts.

7.10 IMPLEMENTING MODELS

Any To-Be models for new processes or documents are purely theoretical unless we represent them in a physical form so that they can be used in applications.

So the final phase in the Document Engineering approach is to use our conceptual models for some practical effect. Specifically this means using our document models for defining business interfaces and validating documents, and using our process models in model based applications that control business services.

Business applications exist to enforce some set of rules or constraints about information or process

The reason business applications exist is to enforce some set of rules or constraints about information or process. So any application can be thought of as a software artifact that presents, collects, and manipulates information according to these rules.[12]

The fact that our models represent the rules and requirements of a context of use means that any software application that satisfies those requirements should be able to rely on these models to determine their behavior. In doing so, the rules about information and process captured by the models remain explicit or externalized from the software that enforces them. This implementation is preferable to any that has these rules buried in the application logic where they are not easily examined or modified.

To realize model based applications we need to create physical, computable artifacts from our models. While none of the analysis and design methods we've discussed so far have anything inherently to do with XML (or any other syntax), the best available way to realize physical models from our conceptual ones is to encode them in an XML schema language.

These activities are discussed in Chapter 15, "Implementing Models in Applications."

7.10.1 ENCODING DOCUMENT IMPLEMENTATION MODELS

Document assembly models are realized by encoding them as what we call document implementation models.

This is actually the inverse of the harvesting task in which we took document artifacts and removed their implementation features to yield the underlying meaning. Now we can apply new implementation features in a more consistent and formal way.

With XML encoding we can choose from any of several different XML schema languages we discussed in Chapter 2. Each offers different tradeoffs in simplicity, expressive power, and maintainability.

Along with the decision about XML schema languages comes the potential to reuse patterns from existing XML vocabularies. Some XML vocabularies (such as UBL) provide re-usable definitions for common components such as Item, Party, Code, Address, Amount, and Location. These are usually published as physical models or schemas using one language as their authoritative format.

The implementation language influences the potential to reuse existing patterns

Choice of schema language alone is not sufficient to encode a document implementation model. Regardless of the language chosen, it is also necessary to develop or adopt grammatical rules that govern the techniques for encoding that language.

Business service interfaces can then define and validate document exchanges against these schemas and process the content as required.

7.10.2 ENCODING BUSINESS PROCESS IMPLEMENTATION MODELS

Business process implementation models encode the To-Be process, collaboration, and transaction models we defined together with any patterns we have adopted or adapted for our new designs. As we noted in Chapter 3, there are many metamodels for defining business processes, so we need to select a metamodel appropriate for our implementation model.

Because XML permits extensible vocabularies, it is increasingly common to find business process metamodels expressed as XML schemas (such as the ebXML BPSS or

BPEL). These encode implementation models as instances of XML documents based on the schemas their metamodels describe.

Business service interfaces can then interpret these documents to guide the processing of the documents they receive

7.11 SUMMARY OF MODELING PHASES AND ARTIFACTS

Figure 7-3 summarizes the modeling artifacts that are developed by following the Document Engineering approach. These artifacts are designed to ensure an effective and sufficient transition of information between the various phases.

Phase	Artifact
Analyzing the Context	UML use case diagrams
Analyzing/Designing Business Processes	Business Domain View Worksheet UML use case diagrams
Analyzing/Designing Business Collaborations	Business Process Area Worksheet UML activity diagrams
Analyzing/Designing Business Transactions	Business Transaction View Worksheet UML sequence diagrams
Applying Patterns to Business Processes	Document checklist
Analyzing Documents	Document inventory
Analyzing Document Components	Consolidated table of content components
Assembling Document Components	UML class diagram
Assembling Document Models	UML class diagram or spreadsheet assembly model
Implementing Model Based Applications	XML schema for document models XML instance for process models

Figure 7-3 Summary of Modeling Phases and Artifacts

7.12 KEY POINTS IN CHAPTER SEVEN

- Document Engineering is a coherent and pragmatic approach for modeling documents and services that provide solutions that are practical and effective.
- There is no single correct way to create document and process models.
- This approach embodies the principle of loose coupling through document exchanges.
- Document Engineering exploits different analysis techniques for reaching the same goal.
- Choosing a pattern for a business process entails adopting a predefined context of use.
- Effective design involves the analysis, reuse, and creation of patterns.
- We exploit conceptual models to bridge the gap between knowing what to do and actually doing it.
- Requirements are constraints on possible solutions that must be satisfied for the solution to be considered acceptable.
- Collecting requirements and rules is a heuristic and iterative exercise.
- We use the context of use to organize and analyze requirements and rules.
- Businesses exist to exploit the results of their private processes in their public ones.

- This tension between public and private processes induces businesses to reuse existing models.
- The richer the document inventory, the more effective any analysis will be.
- Presentational structures are often the most salient patterns in narrative documents.
- Naming components is a contentious, iterative and ongoing activity.
- More rigorous techniques for assembling structural components produce more predictable results.
- Document Engineering extends conventional data modeling by also defining the models needed to exchange information.
- Business applications exist to enforce some set of rules or constraints about information or process.
- The implementation language influences the potential to reuse existing patterns.

8 Analyzing the Context of Use

8.0 INTRODUCTION

During the first phase of a Document Engineering effort, we identify the context of the business problem and the requirements that must be satisfied by the documents and business processes in its solution. Understanding the problem in terms of a pattern like those discussed in Chapter 4 is desirable because it often helps us reuse all or part of an existing solution. In particular, a pattern can suggest which types of documents we'll need to find or design, in which business processes we are likely to deploy them, and the relevant users and other stakeholders from whom we can obtain requirements and with whom we can test our proposed solution. The chosen pattern brings with it a set of requirements, rules, and constraints that we can verify and extend in subsequent analysis and design.

As we saw in the Model Matrix (Figure 3-7), patterns we might reuse range from abstract or generic to very specific. Conceptual business patterns like supply chain or document automation are widely applicable but don't convey many specific requirements, whereas more specific patterns like collaborative, planning, forecasting, and replenishment (CPFR) or straight-through processing (STP) embody rich patterns of requirements that relate to specific business processes, industries, types of products, and so on. Adding requirements to an abstract pattern customizes it to suit our context of use.

Before we go any further, we must make it clear that when we talk about requirements in Document Engineering, we are focusing on the requirements that must be satisfied by models of documents and business processes and by their computer-processable implementations (most often using XML). Of course not all the requirements will emerge at the beginning, and a more complete understanding of the context of use will develop as we go through our analysis. In addition, there will be requirements for the software applications that will use or enforce the document and process models, but these are outside of the scope of Document Engineering. We don't minimize the importance of identifying and satisfying these software requirements, but we don't have anything special to say about those activities.

The requirements for the documents and processes must be precise and verifiable to be useful. This means we need to express them as rules (or constraints). We also find it helpful to distinguish different types of rules. Some types of rules define the meaning of information components, their possible values, and their presentation. Other types of rules govern the combination and assembly of individual information components into reusable aggregates and documents. Still other types determine the processing of information components and documents, including the roles and policies that control what processes or people can access or change information.

When these rules are expressed in models we can use them to define and drive the business services using them. We can then share models with other organizations and enterprises and promote interoperability by ensuring that we understand each other's contexts.

Beginning with this chapter, we will detail the typical phases and activities of the Document Engineering approach, using as a case study the Event Calendar Network Project at the University of California, Berkeley.

CAL

Introducing the Event Calendar Network Project

In Chapters 8 through 14, we'll illuminate many of the concepts used in the Document Engineering approach, using a project known as the Berkeley Event Calendar Network.[1] This project makes a good case study because it deals with a familiar domain, illustrates many common business processes, and is relatively small and self-contained. It also involves a variety of different documents that span the Document Type Spectrum from highly designed graphical publications to transactional data content.

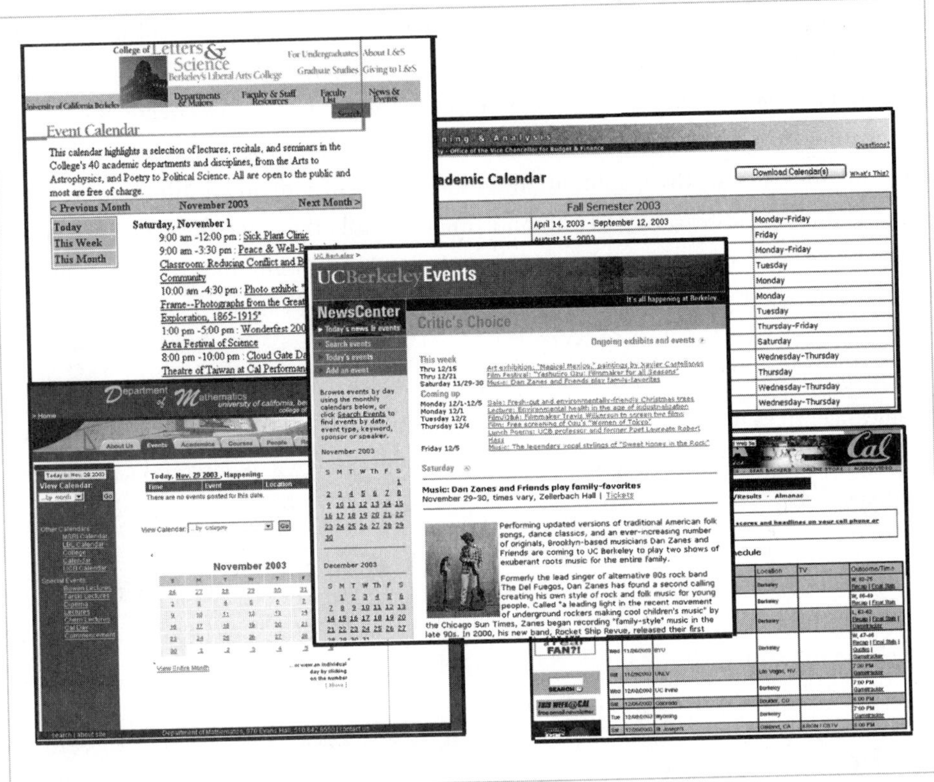

Figure 8-1. Sample Documents from the Event Calendar Network Project

The Event Calendar Network project was initiated at UC Berkeley to improve the creation and reuse of information about events taking place on campus. At Berkeley, academic units and organizations use a variety of calendars, schedules, and lists of events, and there are scores of different calendars on the Berkeley.edu domain. Each calendar has its own way of describing events, uses different forms for submitting them, and follows different rules governing content, structure, and presentation. Because some events and calendars are of interest to overlapping audiences, many of the events are appropriate for multiple calendars. However, incompatible information models prevent the automated exchange of event information between calendars, so each event must be manually submitted to each calendar.

Despite its university setting, this situation is typical of problems that occur in every large organization with time sheets, expense reimbursement, registration, and other administrative documents. It also represents many business-to-business interactions with incompatible catalogs, product descriptions, and trading terms and conditions.

Just before this book went to press, a group called the Calendar and Scheduling Consortium announced plans to encourage vendors to adopt standard calendar and schedule models so that their applications could share information.[2]

8.1 UNDERSTANDING DOCUMENT AND PROCESS REQUIREMENTS

Document and process requirements are constraints that must be satisfied for a Document Engineering solution to be considered acceptable. Identifying the correct requirements early in a project makes it less likely that we will have to throw away or rework the analysis, design, or implementation activities. But how do we identify good requirements? There are three basic guidelines:

- Requirements are most often functional: descriptions of what the solution must or must not do or prevent or enable someone to do. Good requirement rules are expressed using verbs and conditions such as "may," "must," and "must not."

- While requirements can be quantitative or qualitative, they should always be verifiable. For example, it is not much good to define a requirement like "the document model must be robust," or "the process model must follow relevant standards," if we have no way of measuring document robustness or determining what process standards are relevant.

- Finally, requirements should not dictate how the solution is to be achieved. That is the responsibility of design.

Requirements should not dictate how the solution is to be achieved

8.1.1 STRATEGIC AND TACTICAL REQUIREMENTS

The Document Engineering approach is suitable for a diverse range of projects. Some projects are tactical or narrow in scope, like deploying a simple web service, automating an existing workflow process involving a business or administrative form, or aggregating a few information sources of the same type. Others are strategic and broad in scope, like the design of an end-to-end information supply chain or the development of service oriented architectures.

Whether a project is more tactical or strategic defines what is or is not possible, how much work it will take, the scale or scope of technology needed to implement a solution, and the likelihood that the project will succeed. It also affects the scope of the requirements gathering process.

A tactical effort, like exposing some existing business functionality as a web service or straight-through processing for a printed form, may appear to have a relatively small number of requirements to consider. It is tempting in these cases just to "get on with it" by creating an XML schema directly from an API or the labeled data entry fields and begin working on the software that will handle document instances, especially if the system is chartered as a proof-of-concept or prototype. Rigorous requirements, conceptual models that capture them, and other intermediate artifacts called for in a Document Engineering approach can seem superfluous.

Even in a tactical project it is important to identify requirements in a disciplined way

Yet even in an apparently tactical project it is important to make the effort to identify document and process requirements in a disciplined way. In particular, it is critical to determine whether what starts off as a tactical effort is likely to stay that way or may be incrementally burdened with additional strategic requirements. Making it clear what is out of scope at the onset of a tactical project can prevent creeping featurism, which undermines whatever elegance and maintainability the initial design might have.[3]

For example, as businesses increasingly turn to the Internet, a challenging situation often arises when an application meant for internal use only is suddenly expected to operate across organizational or enterprise boundaries or to comply with external standards. Too narrow a view of the initial requirements might make it difficult to function in such broader contexts. We saw this in one of the interoperability scenarios in Chapter 6, with orders from Japan arriving at a bookstore application designed only for U.S. postal addresses. Meeting new requirements will be impossible if the internal system began as a prototype that was gradually hacked into the "real" system, because its informal requirements will be deeply embedded in its programming code.

In contrast, an application designed to be based on an explicit model would be much more able to replace a system that meets internal requirements with one that meets external ones. The extra effort in understanding current and potential requirements and implementing them in a more formal way can prevent cost and schedule overruns, customer support and retention problems, and operational inefficiencies.

The stakes are too high in strategic projects to proceed without a requirements phase

The stakes are simply too high in strategic projects to proceed without a requirements phase, because a failure can severely hamper the company's ability to carry out its business strategy, cause substantial financial losses, and even cause it to go out of business. In strategic projects like the introduction of ERP or integration with numerous supply chain partners, no one would proceed without a careful effort to identify the document and process requirements. In fact, large companies or organizations often identify and validate their requirements by conducting a contract definition phase or issuing a request for information (RFI) document in which they engage multiple companies or consultants to define the required context of use and come up with some preliminary solution or design concepts.

Nevertheless, because the number of requirements to consider may be almost impossibly large in strategic projects, a different kind of scoping challenge arises. Because the problem being defined might be too large to take on all at once, it is necessary to conduct it in phases. But we can understand how to safely break up a complex problem into simpler parts only if we understand how the parts fit together. So it is essential to understand the dependencies between requirements to identify phases with minimal overlap.

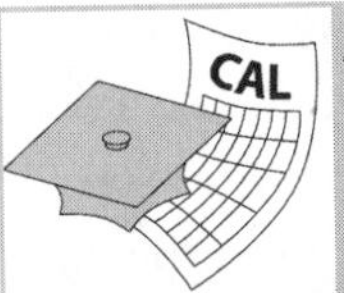

At UC Berkeley, calendar events are similar in many ways to announcements, policies, procedures, and other types of content that are distributed on a regular basis to the campus community. It might have been possible to scope the Event Calendar Network project more broadly to address this general publishing or syndication problem. However, the IT culture at Berkeley is very decentralized, almost by conscious analogy to the autonomy of academic departments, and relatively few enterprise projects are attempted. So the Event Calendar Network team explicitly ruled out designing a general-purpose content distribution system and focused narrowly on the requirements of the calendar domain.

8.1.2 SOURCES OF REQUIREMENTS

The initial motivation for a Document Engineering project can come from almost anywhere—a management task force, an assessment conducted by an external consultant, or a suggestion by a clerk or machine operator to improve a process they struggle with every day. But we can identify some common sources of requirements.

There is no sharp line dividing requirements analysis and document analysis

It is tautological for us to say that many of the requirements in document-intensive projects are contained in existing documents, and there is no sharp line dividing "requirements analysis," in which we get requirements from people, and "document analysis," in which we obtain them from documents. But it is easier to explain the latter if we begin by discussing the former, treating them as separate activities, so we defer the special issues and steps for getting requirements and rules from specific documents to Chapters 11 and 12.

Users, operators, customers, clients, and experts in the domains within the scope of our project will all have useful things to say about what processes an application should or should not carry out and the information they require. Marketing and sales people, because of their relationships with customers and competitors, can also provide essential requirements. Product managers are especially good people to interview about requirements because their job is to assemble and balance the often-conflicting perspectives from customers, marketing, and engineering. The executive project sponsor or whoever is funding the effort might not provide technical requirements but will certainly have requirements for an acceptable solution.

Of course, we cannot assume that these people know each other, talk to each other, or even agree with each other. Deciding in advance whose requirements take priority helps resolve conflicts when they arise and helps maintain consistency in designs.

In some start-up situations the problem calls for a truly new system and there will not be any current users from whom to obtain requirements. Nevertheless, we can and should identify intended users and make specific hypotheses about their characteristics, preferences, and capabilities that would determine requirements. Inventing a few of these concrete personas or roles can help prevent assumptions about a single typical user who doesn't actually exist.[4]

There are also some less reliable sources of requirements. Software designers and developers often think they are user surrogates, but this is almost never true even if they were once part of the user population. Managers of the users are not good user surrogates, either. People who manage users often think they can speak for them. Who else understands the big picture that the mere users may not grasp? But managers might not know the real problems users face, especially if there are disincentives for revealing those problems. A worker is not likely to tell his boss that he makes errors, lacks essential information, or simply can't understand the forms he is asked to fill out, even if it is not his fault.

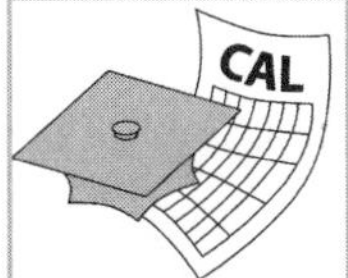

Event calendars at UC Berkeley are used by students, staff, faculty, alumni, and the general public. But because the viability of a calendar network depends on a critical mass of calendars sharing events through a central repository, the calendar administrators were treated as the most important sources of requirements. The Event Calendar Network team set out to define requirements that would meet or exceed the current needs of existing calendars to make it worthwhile for calendar administrators to adopt the new system.

8.1.3 GENERIC REQUIREMENTS

Some requirements apply to almost every Document Engineering situation and might seem obvious. But requirements that are so fundamental that everyone assumes them are precisely those that should be made explicit, because of their importance.

Requirements that are so fundamental that everyone assumes them are precisely those that should be made explicit

We've compiled a list of some of the generic requirements for Document Engineering efforts:

- *Automated information capture.* Eliminate manual entry (or reentry) of information when documents are created, reusing as much as possible from other documents or sources.

- *Straight-through processing.* Minimize the need for any human intervention as a document flows through some specified processes.

- *Timeliness.* Make information available to those who need it when it is needed and when promised, and update it promptly when it changes.

- *Accuracy.* Ensure that every piece of information in a document is correct.

- *Completeness.* Ensure that a document contains all the information it should or that its recipient (person or application) expects.

- *Automated validation.* Provide a schema or specification that enables information to be validated.

- *Interoperability.* Enable information to be used "as is" or via automated transformation by systems or applications other than the one that created it.

- *Standards compliance.* Conform to regulations or standards for information accessibility, availability, security, and privacy.

- *Customizability.* Facilitate the internationalization, localization, extension, and restriction of information.

- *Usability.* Present information in a format or medium that is easy to use and understand by its intended users.

- *Identifiability.* Ensure that the design or appearance of a document signals that it comes from our organization or company; also called branding of the information.

Not all of these requirements apply to every project, and they can be somewhat incompatible with each other. For example, efforts to ensure that a document is accurate and complete can undermine its timeliness, just as emphasizing timely publication might jeopardize accuracy and completeness. The generic requirements that focus on document processing by applications or machines can sometimes conflict with those that emphasize document use by people.

Requirements can be incompatible with each other

Because of these inevitable tradeoffs, it is essential that we understand the perspectives and priorities of the different stakeholders in our project, because they can disagree substantially. Marketing, technical writing, and web design personnel can sometimes be adamant about identifiability and the importance of high production values in documents and user interfaces, but once basic usability is achieved, customers usually care much more about information accuracy and timeliness.

We once saw an engineer almost start a fistfight with a graphic designer when the former learned that the latter had rounded some data values to create a more aesthetic layout with columns of equal width. The engineer said something like "the company has spent millions of dollars getting the product to meet a competitive benchmark and your stupid desire to line up the decimal points just threw it away."

8.2 CONTEXT AND REQUIREMENTS

The generic requirements listed in the previous section are a convenient checklist when starting a Document Engineering project. But we don't want a generic solution; we want one that fits the specific situation we face. On the other hand, while the specific situation may be a new one for our organization or company, much of what businesses do can be described using a small set of reusable patterns. We have described organizational, architectural, process, and information patterns. But an even more general way to think of them is as predictable combinations or clusters of requirements. That is, as patterns of context.

Organizational, architectural, process, and information patterns are clusters of requirements

So we could say that the context of a Document Engineering effort is composed of a set of requirements made up of two parts: a part that is specified by contextual patterns, and a part that reflects specific rules that customize or refine these patterns. This situation is just another instance of the Pareto 80/20 principle; in this case it means that we can obtain most of our requirements fairly easily if we can identify one or more appropriate patterns, but identifying the remaining small proportion of our requirements will take most of our effort.

Most requirements can be identified by using patterns, but identifying the rest will take more effort

Figure 8-2 illustrates this idea about patterns as reusable combinations of requirements. The context of use for Context C is covered by a common context pattern defined by Requirement 4, a shared contextual pattern with Context B as defined by Requirement 5 and its own specific Requirement 6.

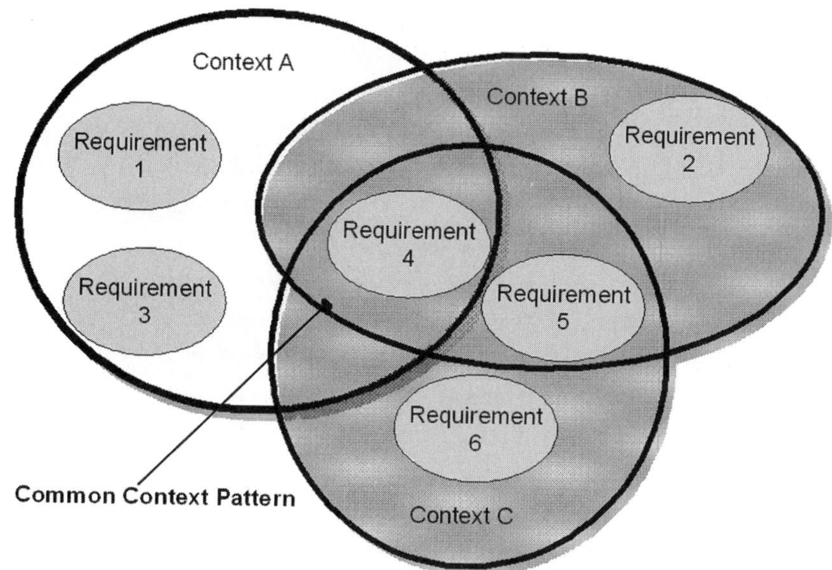

Figure 8-2. Patterns as Reusable Combinations of Requirements

To put this into practice, let's consider a generic procurement context that involves a buyer party, a seller party and perhaps a carrier party (to ship the goods). Figure 8-3 depicts this procurement process pattern as a use case diagram.

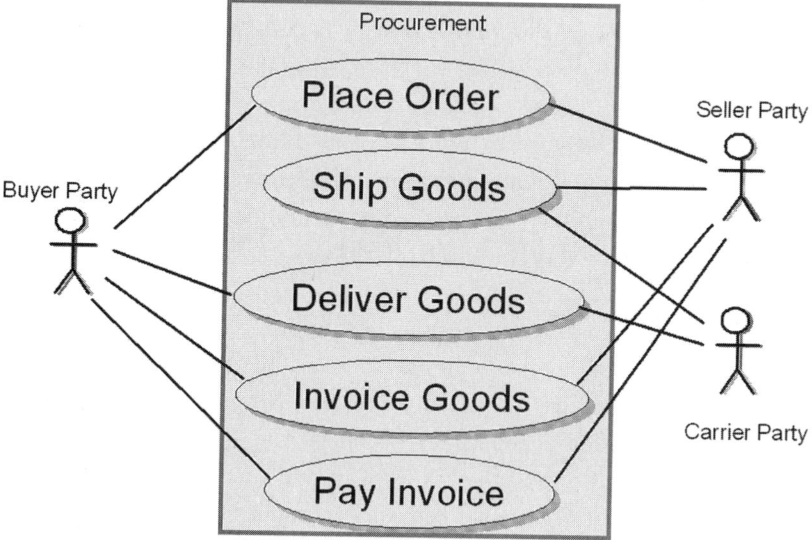

Figure 8-3. The Procurement Pattern

This generic pattern includes the business processes and roles for the participating businesses. The complete pattern would also include a set of documents, but these are not shown.

Adding requirements to an abstract pattern customizes it to suit our context of use

In an actual procurement implementation the requirements provided by this pattern will need to be augmented. For example, the processes used to order fuel from Japan will need to follow additional rules. These may differ slightly from the process of dealing with ordering fuel from Norway, and differ significantly from the processes needed to order tickets for events on the Berkeley Events Calendar. Yet these are all variations of the procurement pattern.

We can apply the notion of context dimensions to organize and analyze these different environments so that we can more easily reuse their sets of requirements and rules that will drive our designs.

The notion of context dimensions helps us more easily reuse sets of requirements

The most serious attempt to describe contexts for this purpose was that of the ebXML project,[5] which proposed eight dimensions suitable for describing business-to-business global trade. These were Business Process, Product Classification, Industry Classification, Geopolitical, Official Constraints, Business Process Role, Supporting Role and System Capabilities. Using these dimensions to describe a specific context or project domain requires some way to uniquely identify points on each one, sometimes called context drivers (see SIDEBAR).

Not all of the ebXML context dimensions are appropriate in other application domains, but numerous other taxonomies are potentially useful for defining context drivers. For example, when we discussed patterns in business in Section 3.3.1, we mentioned two classification schemas for products, the North American Industry Classification System (NAICS) and the UN/SPSC product and services coding system. To distinguish geographical or regional contexts we might use the ISO 3166 country codes and for more localized contexts (at least in the United States) we could use the FIPS codes or Standard Metropolitan Statistical Areas from the U.S. Census Bureau.[6]

There are also many classification schemes for business models and business organization contexts, such as those proposed by Afuah and Tucci, Timmers, and others.[7]

Context in ebXML

The ebXML project proposed eight context dimensions. These can be envisioned as defining a multidimensional "8-space" or coordinate classification system in which millions of different contexts would be distinguished by their values on each dimension.

We can best explain this idea with an example. Consider an export broker buying aircraft fuel in Japan for shipment to Korea. The documents required in this situation would need information appropriate for contexts such as:[8]

- Business Process = Procurement
- Product Classification = Aircraft Fuel
- Industry Classification = Petrochemicals
- Geopolitical = Japan
- Official Constraints = Export
- Business Process Role = Buyer
- Business Supporting Role = Intermediary

Each of these values would have associated with it sets of rules that satisfy the requirements for that context dimension, and taken together they would form the set of requirements for the unique situation defined by all eight dimensions. The ebXML architecture further envisions a repository in which these sets of rules are stored and from which they can be retrieved to assemble the document definition needed for any context.[9]

While the ebXML context dimensions are helpful in describing typical requirement patterns, we aren't convinced that many contexts in the real world can be distinguished this neatly. For example, contexts are sometimes dependent on each other in complex combinations. Using the example in the sidebar, we may discover that some petrochemical industry requirements or constraints are not applicable in Japan. What if the buyer is also an exporter? Which context takes precedence? Maybe there are requirements that apply only when exporting to Korea, or only to petrochemical exports to Korea.

So while it is important to have some way of organizing requirements for documents and processes that helps us understand their constraints and dependencies, the exact scheme we use isn't critical. We prefer to take a more heuristic and informal approach to show how context dimensions can aid in understanding patterns of requirements without requiring their rigorous and perhaps overly simplistic, formal classification.

Informal context dimensions can aid in understanding patterns of requirements

Suppose we refine the generic procurement pattern in Figure 8-3 to locate the seller party in another country. We have now created an imported goods procurement context. The use case diagram for this more specific context is shown in Figure 8-4.

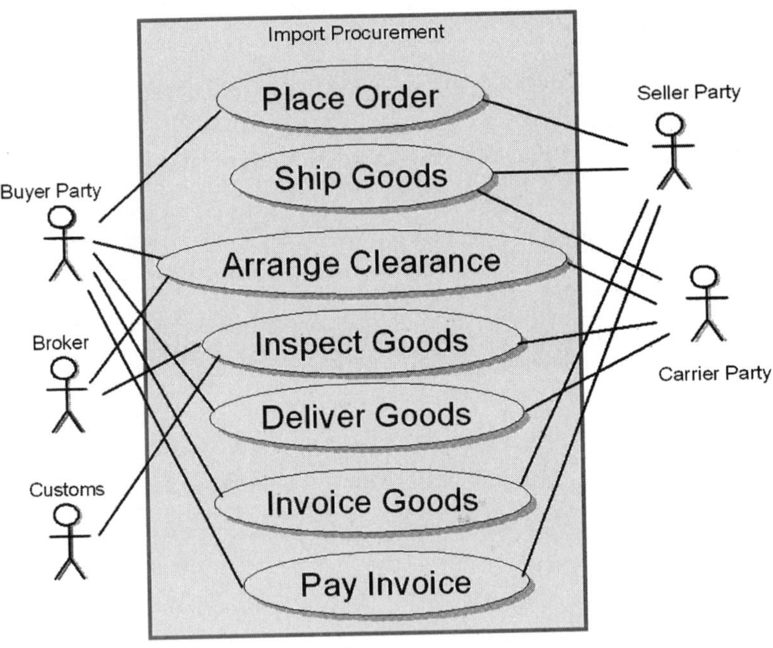

Figure 8-4. The Imported Goods Procurement Pattern

Comparing these two models reveals some additional requirements for the imported goods context. Two new roles of broker and customs are involved because they are dependent on the seller party. In other words, if the seller party is not in the same country as the buyer party, we need additional roles in our process.

In addition to these two new roles, there are also additional transactions and related documents that are dependent on this new context. We now need to arrange customs clearance and have the goods inspected. All these new roles, transactions, and documents are dependent on the primary roles, transactions, and documents. The context of use establishes the dependencies of the business process and exposes the underlying reusable patterns.

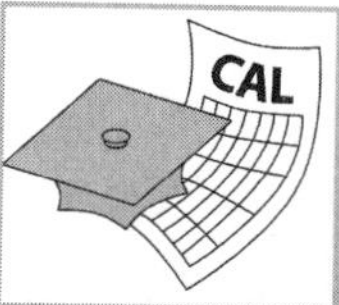

It seems easy to describe the Berkeley Event Calendar Network project on some of the ebXML context dimensions, such as:

- Industry Classification = Public University
- Geopolitical = California USA
- Official Constraints = Mandates of open disclosure and free access

These dimensions and values suggest many of the important requirements for the solution and help to control the scope. But the dimension of Product Classification doesn't offer us any insights about our domain of Calendar Events.

It is also not obvious how to categorize this business process, because both supply chain and content syndication patterns might be appropriate. In Chapter 10 we'll consider the implications of using either of these two process patterns for our case study.

8.3 EXPRESSING REQUIREMENTS AS RULES

Whether they come from people, documents, or patterns, we must carefully record the requirements we identify as we analyze our context. Some analysts advocate using formal logic languages to enable precise expression of requirements, while others advocate using more natural languages.[10] Because we will ultimately encode most of the requirements in conceptual models of documents and processes and then in XML, we don't feel a need to be prescriptive about their format in this initial phase. We will use a semiformal style of recording requirements as rules.

Requirements are more useful when expressed as rules

However, we do propose some rigor in categorizing the requirements we identify because it helps ensure that we have a comprehensive set of them. In the following sections we will discuss seven types of requirements that can apply to documents and processes:[11]

- *Usage* requirements define the policies or privileges that govern user access to information or applications.

- *Structural* requirements define co-occurrence or aggregation relationships between components.

- *Semantic* requirements define the meanings of components by specifying properties, dependencies, or roles as generalizations or specializations of other components.

- *Process* requirements define actions to be applied whenever a given condition or set of information is encountered.

- *Syntactic* requirements concern the form in which documents or processes are encoded in a physical or implementation model.

- *Presentational* requirements govern the appearance or rendering of information components.

- *Instance* requirements establish rules or constraints about the values of information components.

These classifications are also compatible with the framework embodied in the Model Matrix. The first three apply at the conceptual end, the next three at the physical column, while instance rules apply to the implementations themselves. This is shown in Figure 8-5.

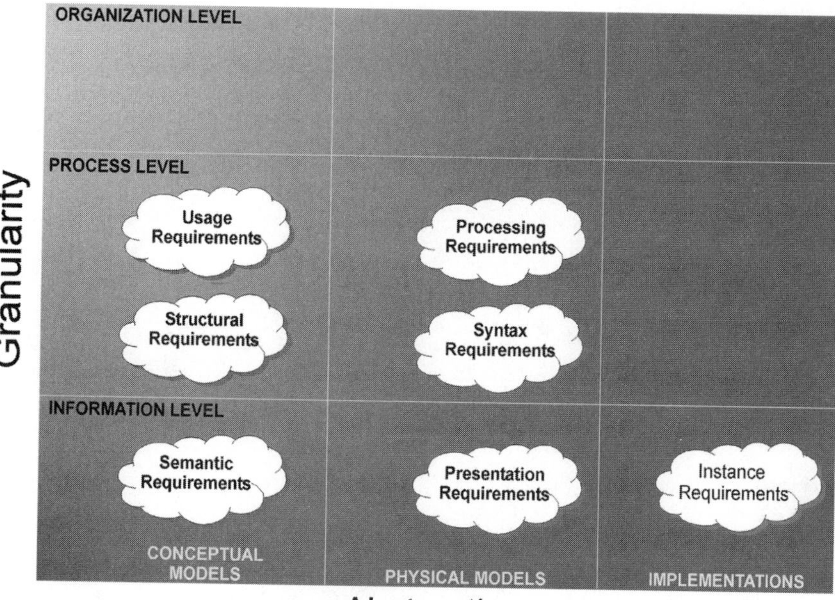

Figure 8-5. Modeling Matrix showing Requirement Classifications

We should not look for or expect to find requirements in exactly these categories, but we can use them as convenient bins to hold the rules for the requirements that may arise from an interview, document, or some other information source.

8.3.1 USAGE REQUIREMENTS

Usage requirements define the policies or privileges that govern user access to information or applications. Access policy is often governed by roles within an organization, with each category of users having different privileges for viewing or changing information, sometimes at the granularity of a single component.

Role-based access control requirements are usage rules that require organizational roles or responsibilities to be represented in a model that drives an application.[12]

Externalizing these rules is essential to enable an organization to change policies if needed without reimplementing the applications to which they apply. Examples of role-based access control requirements would be "An employee's salary can be viewed by a Manager but can only be changed by the Human Resources Department."

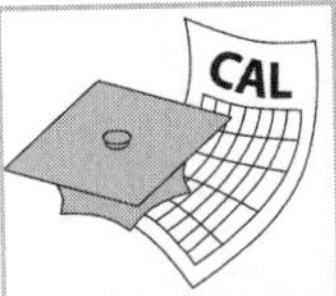

Usage requirements in the Berkeley Event Calendar Network project include controls on who can submit information to calendars. For example, there is a rule that states "Events can be submitted to the central calendar only by a campus-recognized department, unit, organization, or registered student group."

8.3.2 STRUCTURAL REQUIREMENTS

Structural requirements define co-occurrence or aggregation relationships between components. Their rules determine the assembly of components into documents.

Structural rules determine the assembly of components into documents

For example, in the context of a repair manual one requirement might be, "it is good practice to include a warning along with any procedure that might be dangerous to the person doing it." Likewise, following the adage that a picture is worth a thousand words, there might be a rule to "include one or more illustration or diagram that portrays the arrangement or assembly of parts in the device or machine to which the dangerous procedure applies." Yet another structural rule might state that "a caption is required for each illustration."

In a procurement context, we might have a rule such as "every order must have an order number, a buyer, and an issue date." This defines the required aggregation of components. Other structural rules, such as "an order must have at least one order line," establish both required roles and number of occurrences in the associations between structures.

Structural rules can identify sets of components that are naturally related to each other. A common example would be those that apply to both an order and an order change document. There may be a rule that the structure of these two documents must be identical.

Structural integrity is a requirement for consistent assembly of structures in physical or implementation models, such as requiring identical page boundaries for the electronic and printed versions of documents. Structural integrity is a common requirement when a document exists concurrently in multiple formats, especially when content revisions are highly localized (as in loose-leaf publications with placeholder pages that say "this page intentionally left blank").

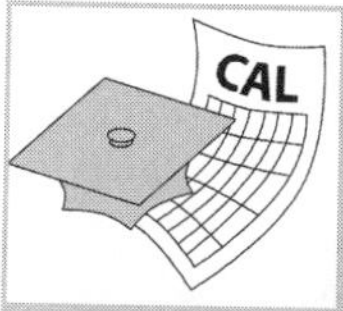

With Event Calendars, some of the requirements were expressed in rules such as:

- "An Event may or may not have a Location."
- "A Location is of interest only if there is an Event there."
- "An Event may have a Start Date and either a Duration Period or an End Date."

We will say more about structural rules when we look at disaggregating structures in Chapter 12 and assembling new structures in Chapter 13.

8.3.3 SEMANTIC REQUIREMENTS

As we saw in Chapter 6, the most important requirement in achieving interoperability in a document-centric application is agreement on the meaning of components. Semantic requirements define these meanings.

The most important requirement in achieving interoperability is semantic agreement

Rules for meanings can be discovered in dictionaries of terms, controlled vocabularies, thesauri, or formal ontologies and are the foundation of any document component model because they must be satisfied by every document instance. For example, "an order number is an identifier that is unique to the buyer" establishes properties for the component referred to as Order Number.

Another type of semantic rule establishes a pattern or generalization for a component. For example, "a buyer is a specific type of party."

Semantic rules may also expose dependencies, such as "the price of an item can vary depending on the buyer."

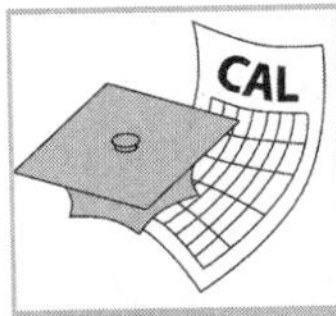

In the Berkeley Event Calendar Network, some of the semantic requirements were given in rules such as:

- "An Event is something that takes place."
- "An Event is identified by its Title."
- "Only approved Events can be in the University Calendar."

We will say more about semantic rules when we look at building a document component model in Chapter 13.

8.3.4 PRESENTATION REQUIREMENTS

Presentation requirements govern the appearance or rendering of an information component. Their rules are more common in documents from the publication or narrative end of the Document Type Spectrum because they sometimes have usability or aesthetic implications, which are important to people. For example, "an item description must be on the same page as the product's image," might be a presentation rule for a product catalog.

Presentation rules are more common in publication-type documents because their rules are important to people

Gathering these requirements for technical publications, reports, policies, procedures, reference books, and other nontransactional documents can be difficult. The associations between these components reflect only general principles or best practices in document markup. Sometimes the rules are specified in style guides, rules, or templates that guide authors when they create instances of these documents.

Presentation integrity is a particularly stringent requirement, often mandated by legislation or contracts, to reproduce a document exactly as it appeared in its original presentation. We see this with International Letters of Credit and Bills of Lading, where we can readily imagine a bank or customs inspector carefully comparing computer-generated and original printed documents. So it is not uncommon in international trading contexts to have rules such as "a Bill of Lading must conform to the UN Layout Key."[13]

An important presentation requirement that emerged in the Berkeley Event Calendar Network project was the need to generate customized calendars from events in a central repository that reproduced the appearance of existing calendars. Many departments and other campus organizations strive to maintain a distinct visual "brand" for their websites, and an integrated calendar driven by the central repository must be stylistically consistent with its host site.

8.3.5 SYNTACTIC REQUIREMENTS

Syntactic requirements concern the language in which documents or processes are encoded for implementation. We saw in Chapter 6 that even documents that conform to the same conceptual model can differ substantially if they don't use the same encoding syntax or follow the same encoding rules.

In most current Document Engineering efforts, the preferred syntactic requirement is to use XML for implementation. An additional syntactic requirement to use a particular XML vocabulary might also inherit some semantic, content, and structural requirements.

8.3.6 PROCESS REQUIREMENTS

Process requirements define actions to be applied whenever a given condition or set of information is encountered. The rules for process requirements are sometimes called behavioral or procedural rules. So when an ordered item is out of stock, for example, a process requirement could be that a customer back order request is created. An example of a process requirement that constrains the scope of the transactions involved is "the procurement process covers all the transactions involved from the requesting of goods until the charging for those goods." The process rule that defines an explicit transaction would be something like "the seller may respond to an order with an order response."

Process rules provide the bridge between documents identified in a business transaction and the components needed by those documents.

Process rules can also provide the bridge between documents identified in business transactions and the components needed by those documents. For example, the rule "details of goods that are receipted must be acknowledged" implies that any acknowledgment document must contain details of the goods involved.

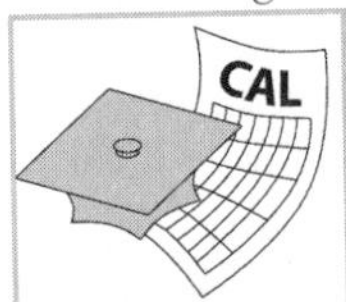

In the Berkeley Event Calendar Network project one of the business processes involves parties submitting information about an event to the Public Affairs Department for publication in the central calendar. One of the requirements of this process was given by the rule "an Acknowledgment Receipt is given to the Event Owner for every Event submitted."

8.3.7 INSTANCE REQUIREMENTS

Instance requirements establish rules or constraints about the values of information components. In contrast with the other types of requirements, instance requirements apply to the document instances rather than to the models. A document model might follow all semantic, presentation, structure, syntax, and processing rules, but any given instance of the document might fail to satisfy the instance rules.

A document model might follow all semantic, presentation, structure, syntax and processing rules but the document itself might fail to satisfy instance rules

Two examples of instance rules that constrain value include "the total value of a single order cannot exceed US$1 million," and "descriptive text must not exceed 80 characters." Another example, where the value of a component is constrained to a fixed set of values, is "the currency code should be expressed using ISO 4217 codes."

Rules for the values of one component can also be dependent on the value of others, such as "the issue date must be earlier than the delivery date." There are also complex combinations of instance rules, such as "extended price is quantity multiplied by price." This rule not only makes the value of "extended price" dependent on two other components but also describes the semantics of the component itself. So this is an instance rule that also contains a semantic one.

Referential integrity is a special instance requirement to keep dependent information synchronized throughout a document. For example, "all cross references must refer to valid section identifiers," or "the number of items on an order must agree with the stated total."

Content integrity is another special requirement that seeks to preserve the content (but not necessarily the presentation) of the original document. This requirement is especially important in transactional documents that are data-intensive, where it is essential that values in documents need to be precise and fixed so that every document that uses them can use them in exactly the same way. Content integrity is usually a default requirement, but we include it here because we want to contrast it with the other kinds of integrity requirements that are not usually imposed by default.

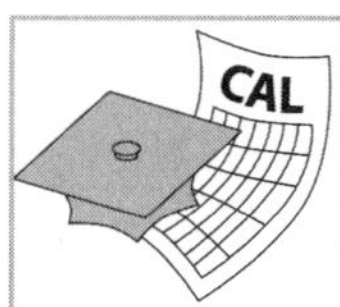

In the Event Calendar Network project, one of the content requirements was given by the rule "The End Date of an Event must be the same or later than the Start Date."

8.4 RULE TYPES AND CONTEXT DIMENSIONS

It is often difficult to decide when the activity of identifying requirements is finished. It can be hard to defend limits on a project's scope and there is always another person or document to interrogate for potentially important requirements. One method we have used to determine a stopping point for this process is to arrange the requirements we've identified according to the rule types and the context dimensions to assess how much of the universe we've covered.

We can arrange the requirements according to their types and context to assess how much of the universe we've covered

We don't believe strongly enough in the ebXML context dimensions to suggest that we cannot stop before we find 56 categories of requirements (7 rule types in each of 8 context dimensions) or anything nearly that prescriptive. But it is enlightening to apply whatever model of the context we use to organize and analyze the requirements and rules that will drive our design of processes and their documents.

So let us return to the example from earlier in this chapter of an export broker buying aircraft fuel in Japan for shipment to Korea. Some of the business rules in this situation could be applied to the ebXML context dimensions as shown in Table 8-1.

Context Dimension	Type of Rule	Example
Business Process = Procurement	Semantic Process	Every offer must have a unique identification. Every offer must have an acceptance transaction.
Product Classification = Aircraft Fuel	Structural	An item is identified by both quality and a batch number.
Industry Classification = Petrochemical	Structural	Hazardous regulations may apply that involve supplementary information components.
Geopolitical Environment = Japanese	Semantic Instance	Parties are identified using Japanese business registration identifiers. Japanese business registration identifiers must be valid.
Official Constraints	Process Presentation	Certificate of Origin must be supplied on delivery. Bill of Lading must conform to the UN Layout Key.
Business Process Role = Buyer	Process	Specify party to organize delivery.
Business Supporting Role = Intermediary	Process	Separate Offer and Acceptance transactions are reflected from the ultimate Buyer to the ultimate Seller.

Table 8-1. Examples of Rules Expressing Requirements of Context

The set of rules shown in Table 8-1 is obviously incomplete and perhaps even a little simplistic. But we hope it demonstrates the value of a systematic approach for collecting and organizing the initial requirements for a Document Engineering project.

As we progress through our Document Engineering approach, our analysis will expose more requirements and rules. We will exploit these when we come to design documents to better satisfy our context of use.

8.5 KEY POINTS IN CHAPTER EIGHT

- There is no sharp line dividing requirements analysis and document analysis.
- The stakes are too high in strategic projects to proceed without a requirements phase.
- Even in a tactical project it is important to identify requirements in a disciplined way.
- Requirements that are so fundamental that everyone assumes them are precisely those that should be made explicit.
- Requirements are more useful when expressed as rules.
- Requirements can be incompatible with each other.
- Organizational, architectural, process, and information patterns are clusters of requirements.
- Most requirements can be identified by using patterns, but identifying the rest will take more effort.
- Adding requirements to an abstract pattern customizes it to suit our context of use.
- The most important requirement in achieving interoperability is semantic agreement.
- Structural rules determine the assembly of components into documents.

- Presentational rules are more common in narrative or publication documents because their rules are important to people.

- Process rules provide the bridge between documents identified in a business transaction and the components needed by those documents.

- Even if a document model follows all semantic, presentation, structure, syntax, and processing rules, the document itself might fail to satisfy instance rules.

- We can arrange the requirements according to their types and context to assess how much of the universe we've covered.

9 Analyzing Business Processes

9.0 INTRODUCTION

In Chapter 8 we introduced the notion of context as predictable combinations or clusters of requirements, and we looked at various context dimensions sometimes used to organize them. The context dimensions included aspects such as Product Classification, Industry Classification, Geopolitical, Official Constraints, System Capabilities, and Business Process Roles.

It should be evident that the business process has an important place in understanding the context of use. We emphasize processes because unlike other context dimensions, we often have the freedom to refine or reengineer them to create new processes. We can't easily change the country we're in, its regulatory environment, or the industry conventions or practices that strongly shape how business gets done (the latter are sometimes called the implied terms and conditions of an industry or business relationship).[1] But we can change many of the processes we carry out. So while it makes no sense to talk about the As-Is and the To-Be geography, in analyzing business processes we often contrast the way things are with how we would like them to be. After we describe the As-Is model, we can improve its processes by applying existing patterns or best practices (see Chapter 10), or we can invent completely new ones.

This flexibility is greater for processes that are completely internal to an enterprise than for those that involve other enterprises. But the promise of service oriented architectures implemented using loosely coupled document exchanges is that as long as the interface doesn't change, the processes that create and consume the documents can.

Internal processes can change but the external business interface should not

This flexibility has both positive and negative aspects. It is desirable because it allows us to satisfy the specific requirements of our situation. But it is undesirable because it introduces ambiguity in our definitions and descriptions of the processes. This can make it difficult to align our processes with those of other businessess with which we want to do business, because different businesses may exploit the flexibility in incompatible ways. Without a sufficient amount of detail, it is unlikely that any two process models can be meaningfully compared. For example, a business whose process models are very high-level and abstract can't easily respond to a buyer asking, "Will you accept my UBL purchase order?"

So the lesson of this chapter is how to describe processes in unambiguous and compatible ways. We advocate the metamodel proposed in the ebXML Business Process Specification, which specifies three levels of abstraction: processes, which are defined in terms of collaborations, which are in turn described using transactions.[2] The patterns at the higher levels help us identify appropriate patterns for reuse at the lowest level, where transactions and documents are visible together and most easily implemented.

Furthermore, when we describe processes in terms of document exchanges, we can more easily align and interconnect processes from different organizations or businesses to enable patterns such as straight through processing, supply chains, or virtual enterprises. The documents are the interfaces to these loosely coupled business processes, and they can easily be realized in highly tangible ways according to the conventional notion of a document as a container or message with information components.

Business process models will contain some information components and document models will contain some processing rules

The complementary nature of processes and documents is another reason for emphasizing process analysis in Document Engineering. In Section 3.4.5 we called this the yin and yang of Document Engineering. That description is perhaps a bit fanciful, but it is undeniable that documents and processes have an inseparable and complementary relationship. Documents contain the information that represents requests to and responses from a business process, and business processes produce and consume documents. Business process models will contain some information components and document models will contain some processing rules. We cannot know the true meaning of the information exchanged in documents unless we understand the processes involved.

9.1 THE LEVELS OF ABSTRACTION CHALLENGE

Consider the question, "What are you doing now?" We can answer this question at many levels of abstraction. We might say:

- "I'm living in Berkeley and taking courses at the University."
- "I'm studying Document Engineering."
- "I'm reading section 9.1."

All these answers may be true, but they may not be equally useful or informative to the questioner. How we answer the question depends on how much context we share with the person asking the question. What do they already know about us and what we are doing? Did we last talk to them 10 minutes or 10 years ago? If we have a common context, it makes sense to answer the question with a very specific answer. If we don't, a general or more abstract answer is more appropriate.

This simple example illustrates a fundamental challenge when we analyze anything. Some things have a conventional level of description, and some levels may seem more intuitive or natural than others, but there are almost always alternatives to any description.

Business processes can be described at many levels of abstraction

Business processes are particularly subject to this description ambiguity. Often we can't directly observe the processes we want to analyze. We can see them more easily when they deal with tangible or physical objects, but many business processes involve intangible goods or only information about goods. Modeling business processes is also difficult because the key involvement of people and organizations, as opposed to mechanical or physical factors, can result in models that have idiosyncratic or unexpected characteristics.

We will attack the level of abstraction problem by systematically decomposing our process descriptions into a three-level hierarchy. We will use business reference models as a guide because their hierarchical organization of processes has been designed to reinforce different levels of granularity. We will use metamodels for process descriptions at each level that provide us with standard metadata for defining what the processes mean and how they are carried out.

9.2 ANALYZING BUSINESS ORGANIZATION

We analyze a business to create a common understanding of how it works and the domain in which it operates. The level at which we start our analysis, and the amount of detail in the resulting analysis, depends on where our emphasis lies on the continuum from strategic initiatives to merely tactical projects.

We'll present a modeling approach in this chapter that starts with the most abstract perspective and works its way down to progressively more granular models. Some business organizational patterns are described using the B2C, B2B, and the other acronyms we discussed in Section 4.1.2 that characterize business relationships by their commerciography.[3] Even these extremely coarse patterns raise predictable issues and challenges about producer-consumer relationships, legacy technology, competition, governance, and regulations.

When we look inside a business, we might be tempted to rely on its organizational model as an analogy to its process model. But from a business process perspective, the functional business areas of any organization, such as manufacturing, engineering, marketing, sales, finance, and human resources, are purely logical entities that exist to carry out a company's business model. There is no necessary relationship between business process patterns, an enterprise's management structure, and the support for carrying out the processes in facilities, technology, and systems.

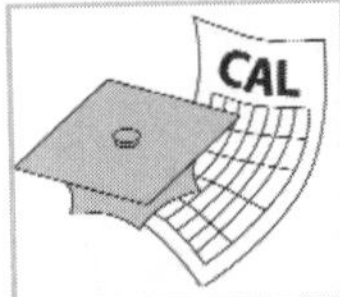

UC Berkeley's organizational model is appropriately complex for an enterprise with thousands of employees. Its organization charts depict an enterprise headed by a CEO called the Chancellor, with dozens of staff and academic units arranged in a multi-level hierarchy of departments and schools, each with an executive manager called the Department Head or Dean. But these organization charts don't capture the unique character of a university, where the principle of academic freedom is fundamental, with each professor and researcher free to pursue the work that most interests him or her. This autonomy in academic affairs has a parallel manifestation in the operational side of the university, and there is substantially less top-down management than in a commercial corporation of similar size. What this means for the Event Calendar Network project is that there are no enterprise standards or procedures for event calendars and that any organizational unit is free to create its own calendar.

There are no necessary relationships between business processes, management structure and facilities, technology, and systems

This is a subtle but important point. The fact that an enterprise performs a purchasing process does not imply that it has a purchasing organization, or that it uses a purchasing application. And even a phrase like Enterprise Resource Planning (ERP)—which usually suggests an application from SAP, Oracle, or PeopleSoft—can be used in a purely functional or conceptual way to describe a business that has standardized on data models to create a synchronized and consistent view of the business's processes. Most ERP systems use a shared information store to ensure that purchasing, inventory, and accounting functions are tightly coupled so they can yield an accurate and consistent view of an enterprise's processes, orders, and accounts. But a business might achieve the same view by exchanging information between separate purchasing, inventory, and accounting applications. In this latter sense, we can describe the business as "doing ERP processes" even though it doesn't have a conventional ERP system.

Of course, an enterprise's business processes, its organization, and the information technology it uses can reinforce or constrain each other. For example, a functionally organized business is very hierarchical and usually reflects a bureaucratic management philosophy that believes in centralized authority and direction. Strategy and plans are developed, goals and directives are issued, and then each part of the company follows the plans to achieve the strategy.

The model of business organization shapes the need to exchange information or coordinate across organizational boundaries. For example, functional organization enables an enterprise to focus on efficiency within each business unit and can minimize exchanges and interactions with other organizations to carry out its core business processes; a purchasing department can focus on purchasing and a finance department can focus on invoicing and accounting. But these functional units would still need to share information to reconcile orders and invoices.

The model of business organization shapes the need to exchange information across organizational boundaries

The nature of interorganizational information exchange (or the lack of it) reflects an assumption behind functional organization that the business environment in which the business operates is relatively stable and that operational efficiency is the key to its success. Such a business might have carefully documented processes and be relentlessly focused on both following them and improving them.

But a business can't be good at everything; one business may view operational efficiency as its key to success, while another may strive for product innovation, and another may aim for unsurpassed customer satisfaction.[4]

A focus on satisfying customers is often the motivation for a cross-functional organization in which some of the core business activities are duplicated across product lines, customer segments, or geographies. A cross-functional organization requires more coordination and information exchange between business units, but this overhead can yield substantial benefits if it is used to create a more responsive and value-focused business. Such businesses are likely to tolerate less rigorously specified processes, and some might even encourage employees to ignore them if they get in the way of satisfying customers.

Few companies need to develop all functional business areas to the same extent, because the relative emphasis and resources they require depends on their role in the enterprise value chain. A successful business focuses on the activities that are essential to its definition of success and doesn't squander attention and resources on those that are not.[5]

This idea of core competency is the essence of a high-level description of a business. A model of a business at this very high level helps us understand it independently of its current or future technology. It is a strategic view that can identify some of the gaps, inefficiencies, overlaps, and opportunities in what the business currently does or does not do. At this level of modeling, the view of a business is highly qualitative and usually recorded in narrative form, perhaps with some accompanying diagrams like organization charts.

9.3 ANALYZING BUSINESS PROCESSES

Our ultimate goal when we model business processes is to describe what the business does in a hierarchy of detail from a high level down to the level where documents and specific information components in document exchanges are visible. But when we analyze processes, the information we discover will come from many sources and at many levels of abstraction and granularity.

It helps ensure consistency and completeness if we try to answer the same questions for each process we encounter. If our goals are strategic, we will be taking a top-down approach and interviewing senior executives or managers with a big picture view of an enterprise. This method tends to yield processes that are very abstract or very generic, partitioning activity into large, goal-oriented chunks. Questions whose answers describe processes at this level are

- What is the name of the process?
- What are the goals or purposes of the process?
- What industries, functional areas, or organizations are involved in the process?
- Who are the stakeholders or participants in the process?
- Are there any problems with the current process?
- How could the process be improved?

Asking questions and recording their answers in a disciplined way rapidly creates a web of related information about interconnected processes from which we can develop models. We will get more useful information if we ask our questions and record the answers using the standard vocabulary and definitions for the concepts and processes within the domain we're working in, if such a business reference model exists (see Section 9.3.2).

There is no single correct way to model business processes

But the simple truth is that there is no single correct way to model business processes and no set of questions that will magically lead to the models. For example, if we ask these same questions of less senior people in the organization, or ask people who have an operational focus or role, the analysis will take on a more bottom-up and more technology-driven character. This will yield a greater number of transactional details, often identified by the specific documents they produce or consume. This view is necessary for implementing and integrating the applications that will carry out the processes, but the processes will be at a vastly different level of abstraction and granularity than those identified by top-down or strategic approaches.

To truly understand a business process we need information from both the top-down and bottom-up points of view. Informants higher in the organizational hierarchy with a strategic focus are less likely to know process details or problems. But they might advocate and clearly articulate an end-to-end, customer-oriented philosophy that describes the process in an idealized form. Conversely, the salespeople, customer service representatives, order processors, shipping clerks and others who actually carry out the processes will be experts about the processes, their associated documents, and problems or exception cases they encounter. But they rarely recognize the conflicts in priorities between functional departments that undermine the company's overall success at satisfying customers.[6]

In any case, using only abstract organizational-level and concrete transactional-level models leaves a gap in the middle, and we can't connect business issues to technology concerns unless we can cross it.

9.3.1 BUSINESS PROCESSES, COLLABORATIONS, AND TRANSACTIONS

There seems to be an emerging agreement that to bridge the level of abstraction gap there needs to be a third level of granularity in process models that fits in between the process and transactional levels. We use the three-level terminology from the ebXML business process metamodel in which a process is composed of a set of related business collaborations, which in turn describe the sequence and transitions between business transactions. Each of these levels represents a different view of the enterprise; the process view, sometimes called the business domain view (BDV) describes the processes most broadly. Models of collaborations create a perspective known as a business requirements view (BRV). The finer granularity of the transactional perspective is sometimes known as a business transaction view (BTV).[7]

This hierarchical or compositional relationship between business processes, collaborations, and transactions is shown in Figure 9-1.

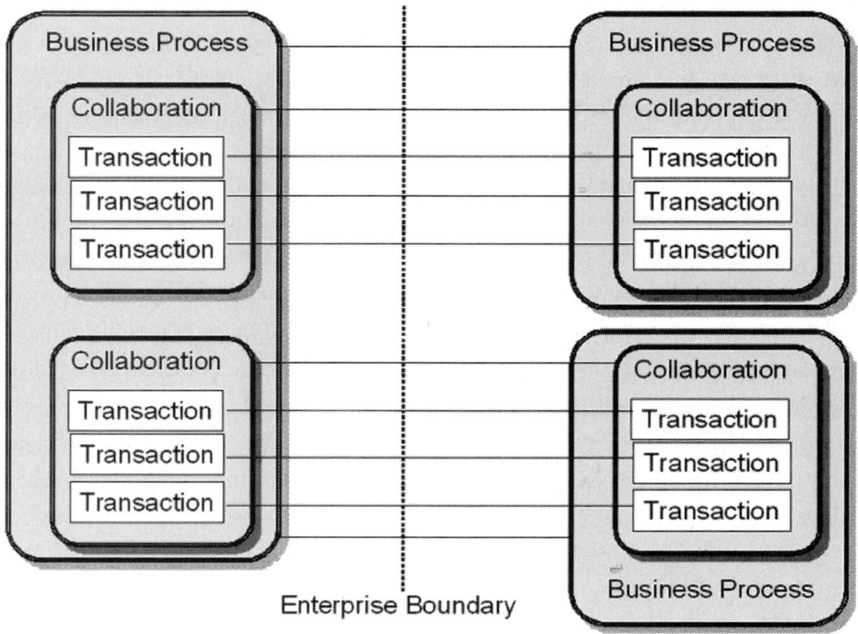

Figure 9-1. Business Process, Collaborations, and Transactions Conceptual View

Within each level of granularity we need to synchronize the various processes and collaborations as well as the transactions that implement them. Another significant requirement implied in Figure 9-1 is that one organization's business processes may need to synchronize with more than one external process, some of which may be undertaken by different organizations. For example, what a buyer sees as a single process for procurement may include one set of collaborations involving the seller supplying the products and a separate collaboration involving the carrier who delivers them.

Business processes are synchronized by loosely coupled information exchanges using documents

This synchronization of processes within and between enterprises requires information exchanges of some kind. As businesses adopt web services or service oriented architectures, interenterprise exchanges have increasingly become loosely coupled document exchanges. Many of the intraenterprise exchanges have also become loosely coupled, but a wider range of integration architectures and patterns are feasible when the information doesn't cross an enterprise boundary.

And of course, business processes do not operate in isolation. They form part of the overall business activity that defines the existence of the organization. So if we redraw the Figure 9-1 depiction to include the entire business organization, we see that there are both private (within the organization) and public (extending outside the organization) processes to synchronize. Figure 9-2 illustrates this conceptual view of an enterprise with connections between each level of process granularity.

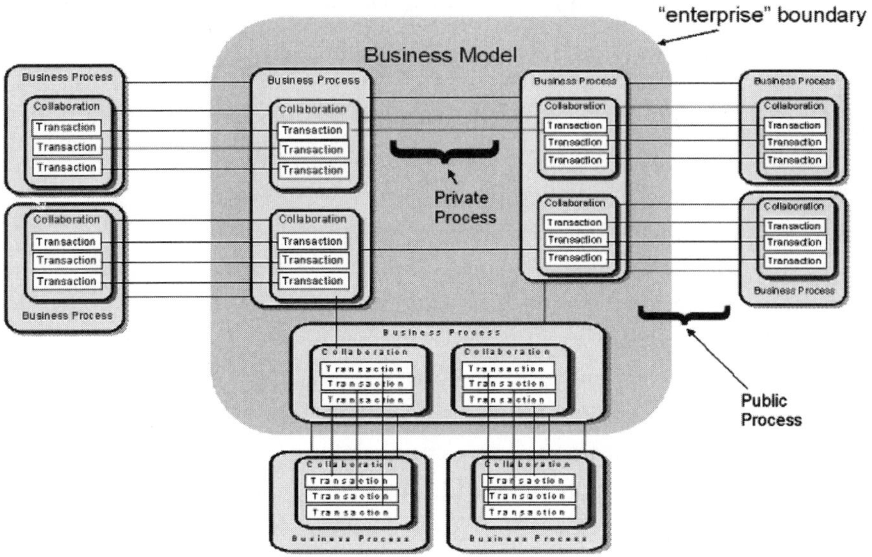

Figure 9-2. A Business Model Conceptual View

We've used the phrase enterprise boundary because it is often used to distinguish between processes that can be controlled and those that can't. But the same distinction can apply to the interaction between the head office of a single large business and other divisions or subsidiaries that have the autonomy to operate in ways that best fit their environments. Domain of control or service domain are more general phrases that fit both the within-enterprise and between-enterprise situations.

9.3.2 BUSINESS REFERENCE MODELS

A business reference model captures the consolidated wisdom about how to think about and carry out the most important or frequent business processes. It standardizes the vocabulary and definitions for processes within a particular industry or domain. These standards enable unambiguous communication between participants and facilitate the measurement, management, and improvement of their processes. For example, SCOR is an influential reference model for describing supply chains.

A reference model can be the default To-Be model for a business

Because it embodies the best practices in an industry, a reference model is the default To-Be model for a business. So a reference model focuses a business modeling effort on identifying the gap between the As-Is and the reference model and determining whether it is possible to close it.

Many reference models organize processes using a three-level hierarchy, which supports our argument that a third level is needed to bridge the abstraction gap between processes and transactions. Reference models are highly reusable precisely because of the significant care taken in their development to create a hierarchical framework in which the process descriptions at each level are consistent in abstraction and detail. If a reference model exists in an industry, it would be foolish not to use it because such models consolidate a great deal of domain knowledge. Nevertheless, many businesses fail to take advantage of them.[8]

We expect the Federal Enterprise Architecture of the U.S. government to become an extremely influential reference model for the many e-government initiatives now underway throughout the world.

Federal Enterprise Architecture

The U.S. government consists of a bewildering number of departments, agencies, programs, and other organizational entities that do not interoperate well because of legacy technology, processes, policies, and politics. Consider the challenge of creating the Department of Homeland Security from 22 different agencies, with 22 different personnel systems, 7 payroll systems, and more than 170,000 employees.[9] At least 11 of these agencies have some responsibility for border security.

The Federal Enterprise Architecture is an extremely ambitious and important effort to improve how the U.S. government does business by taking a cross-agency perspective on products, services, and processes and recommending XML and web services throughout. The FEA Business Reference Model (BRM) is one of several interrelated reference models.

The BRM organizes what the government does in four business areas: Services for Citizens, Mode of Delivery, Support Delivery of Services, and Management of Government Resources. In turn, these four areas contain 39 lines of business, 19 of which are in Services for Citizens and are called external. The rest are the internal ones that support the external ones. The lowest level in the BRM hierarchy is that of subfunctions, of which there are 153. For example, the Community and Social Services line of business contains subfunctions for Homeownership Promotion, Community and Regional Development, Social Services, and Postal Services.

By describing the U.S. government in terms of business areas and activities instead of according to the agencies, bureaus, and offices that provide them, the FEA BRM will identify and reduce redundant capabilities, activities, and infrastructure. It is hoped that this will facilitate standardization of data models and business processes and encourage shared technology investments. But because it will improve the delivery of products and services to the government's customers, the ultimate beneficiaries of the FEA BRM will be any business or person who interacts with the U.S. government.

9.3.3 BUSINESS PROCESS MODELING ARTIFACTS

We've stated numerous times and in numerous ways that it is the model that matters, not the notation or set of specific artifacts in which it is represented. We might draw a diagram by hand on a piece of paper, use a general-purpose graphical design application, or a UML or XML-based modeling tool. But if we haven't done the hard work to develop a good model, no depiction can make it valuable.

The information needed to create a model comes from many sources and emerges over time. We have found it useful to organize what we learn in a set of worksheets whose fields provide a checklist for capturing both descriptive information and the metadata needed by more formal notations.[10] Figure 9-3 is a business domain view worksheet, the first of several business process modeling worksheets that we introduce in this chapter. This worksheet records our initial high-level observations about the Event Calendar Network project.

BUSINESS DOMAIN VIEW WORKSHEET	
Worksheet ID	UCBCalendar-BDV-1.0
Business Domain Model Name	Event Calendar Network
Industry Segment	Public University
Relevant Standards or Reference Models	SKICal[11]
Domain Scope	Describe upcoming events and publish them on one or more calendars.
Business Justification	Improve efficiency in producing calendars and publicizing events. Enrich the academic, cultural, and social experiences of members of the university community.

Figure 9-3. Business Domain View Worksheet for the Berkeley Event Calendar Network Project

A more formal modeling artifact for process models is a UML use case diagram (Figure 9-4a). It is relatively straightforward to derive a use case diagram from information collected in a business process area worksheet (Figure 9-4b) or a business process use case worksheet (Figure 9-4c). These capture the progressively refined answers to the questions about the process that we posed at the beginning of section 9.3. Naming each process by following a verb-noun pattern ("Submit Event," "Review Event") with optional adjectives makes the analysis and its recording more consistent.

CAL

The primary goal for our Berkeley Event Calendar project was to create a service that could describe events taking place on campus.

From this we identified the two major activities as maintaining information about events and creating calendar documents that describe these events.

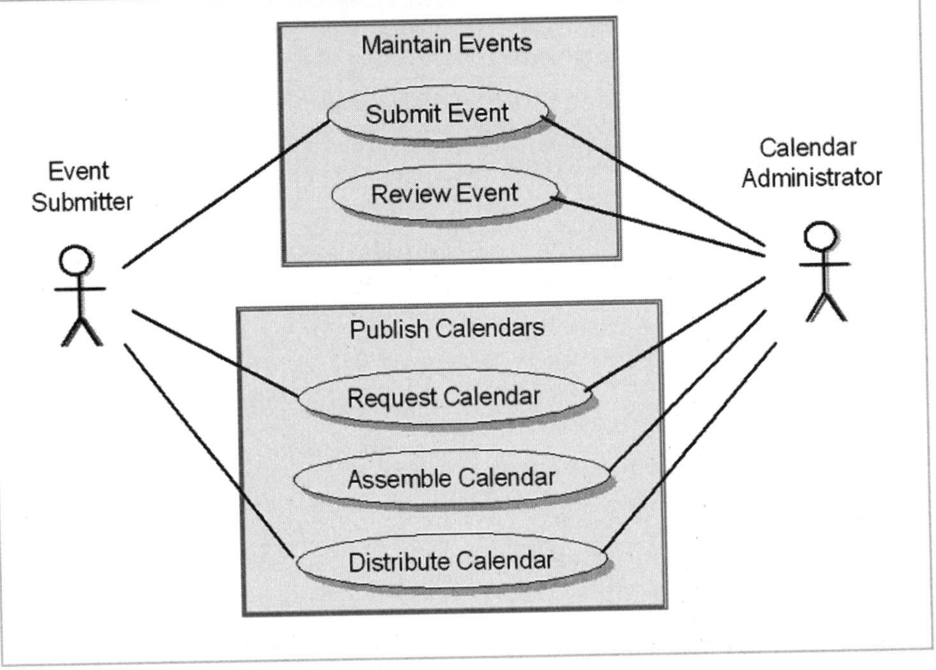

Maintain Events
Submit Event
Review Event
Event Submitter
Calendar Administrator
Publish Calendars
Request Calendar
Assemble Calendar
Distribute Calendar

Figure 9-4a. Business Process Model of the Event Calendar project

We can represent these business processes using the use case diagram in Figure 9-4a. The diagram portrays most of the information in the business process area worksheet (Figure 9-4b) and business process use case worksheet (Figure 9-4c).

BUSINESS PROCESS AREA WORKSHEET	
Worksheet ID	UCBCalendar-BPA-1.0
Business Area Name	Central calendar
Description	Parties submit event information to Public Affairs Department for publication in university calendar.
Scope	Decentralized culture of university rules out a general-purpose content distribution system; focus on semantics and processes of event calendars.
Stakeholders	Primary: event submitters, calendar administrators. Secondary: students, staff, faculty, public.
Process Areas and Business Processes	Maintain events: • Submit event • Review event Publish calendars: • Request calendar • Assemble calendar • Distribute calendar
Process Goals	Efficient event submission. Secure and reliable event maintenance. Prompt publication to interested parties and relevant calendars.
Constraints	Need a common model of "event." Calendar administrators must be able to approve events before publication.

Figure 9-4b. Business Process Area Worksheet for the Event Calendar Project.

BUSINESS PROCESS USE CASE WORKSHEET	
Worksheet ID	UCBCalendar-BPA-MaintainEvents-1.0
Business Process Use Case Name	Maintain Events
Description	Events submitted to main calendar are first reviewed by calendar administrator. Submitter is informed of approval or rejection. Approved events are entered into the central calendar. Changes to approved events may be updated in the central calendar.
Actors	Event submitter, main calendar administrator.
Preconditions	Event submitter must be authorized individual or organization.
Begins When	Event submitter fills out "submit event" form.
Ends When	Expired or cancelled events are deleted from the central calendar.
Constraints	Event submitter must be notified of acceptance or rejection within reasonable time (TBD).
Exceptions	Event rejected.
Postconditions	Event published in main calendar.

Figure 9-4c. Business Process Use Case Worksheet for the Event Calendar Project.

Worksheets and UML diagrams of various types are complementary representations of models that are highly useful for people. However, neither format is directly able to drive or be interpreted by an application, so a more computer-processable format is ultimately necessary. In a web service application, for example, the model's final implementation is likely to be in XML.

Application interfaces require a computer-processable model format

Automating the link between a model and its implementation empowers the business analyst, but it is also valuable to follow the linkages in the opposite direction so that developers (or other applications) can understand the business processes that software is carrying out. This end-to-end traceability from implementations to the original business requirement and vice versa is very difficult to achieve because it requires a huge amount of discipline to ensure that every modeling artifact can be related to those that precede and follow it.

High-level process level models are unlikely to be directly executable because of the abstraction gap between them and the specific transactions that ultimately carry them out. But they can be indirectly connected by links between process, collaboration, and transaction models. So even if we don't expect to realize complete traceability, the goal is worth keeping in mind.

Making the effort to maintain accurate modeling artifacts is essential when the work crosses enterprise or organizational boundaries. Detailed worksheets and diagrams can be critical mechanisms for communicating requirements in strategic projects of broad scope where a large team of designers and developers must work together.

Accurate modeling artifacts are essential when the work crosses enterprise or organizational boundaries

But ultimately, it is the end result that matters, not the intermediate modeling artifacts. In tactical projects of narrow scope, a small team might prefer more agile modeling[12] approaches that emphasize rapid and iterative design cycles and that de-emphasize efforts to create and maintain the linkages between various models. Even then, there is a fine line between investing too much in modeling artifacts and not investing enough to make them useful, and each project needs to find an appropriate balance.

9.4 ANALYZING BUSINESS TRANSACTIONS

The business transaction level of granularity in business process analysis is the easiest to recognize because it is where we find the documents that are exchanged. We define a business transaction as describing the exchange of documents and business signals in a trading or commercial relationship between two parties. A transaction implements a binary relationship between two parties, one playing the requesting role and the other the responding role. There will always be a requesting document, and transactions may also involve one or more responding documents.

More questions must be answered to analyze processes at the transactional level. These include:

- When does the transaction take place?
- What transactions precede and follow the transaction?
- What information is needed to start the transaction?
- What information is produced by the transaction?
- What can go wrong?

It is worth noting that business transactions and database transactions both have at their core the notion of an indivisible unit of work, but they are distinct concepts.

Business Transactions and Database Transactions

The classical definition of a database transaction is a group of statements or instructions to a database whose changes can be made permanent or undone only as a single unit. A reliable database guarantees the four so-called ACID properties about transactions —Atomicity, Consistency, Isolation, and Durability—and can do so without any additional human intervention.

Database transactions also provide a simple model of success or failure: a transaction either commits (all its actions happen) or it aborts (all its pending actions are undone). A database transaction can be rolled back in the same unit with which it was committed to undo all of its effects and return the database to a prior state. It does this by locking the resources used before the transaction begins.

In contrast, business transactions cannot be rolled back. However, any obligations established by a successful transaction can sometimes be undone by a compensating transaction.

This fundamental difference between the classical database transaction and business transactions is mostly a result of differences in time scales. The time scale for a database transaction is measured in fractions of a second. But many types of business applications involve transactions that take place over a longer period of time (from seconds to days, weeks, or longer) often interspersed with other transactions. Database theory and design has been evolving to deal with these long-running transactions[13] that cannot reliably lock the resources they need, making it impossible to roll back to a previous state.

Database applications involving long-running transactions usually involve users in creating the actions that are part of the transaction, and the actions are based on the results of earlier actions or workflows.

9.4.1 DESCRIBING TRANSACTIONS

Figure 9-5 depicts a purchasing or procurement process called Buy a Book, in which the buyer or customer buys a book from a seller, in this case GMBooks.com. The process consists of several transactions whose relationships are shown using the UML sequence diagram notation. This type of diagram is a convenient artifact for describing transactions because it emphasizes the temporal ordering of the information exchanges (see SIDEBAR).

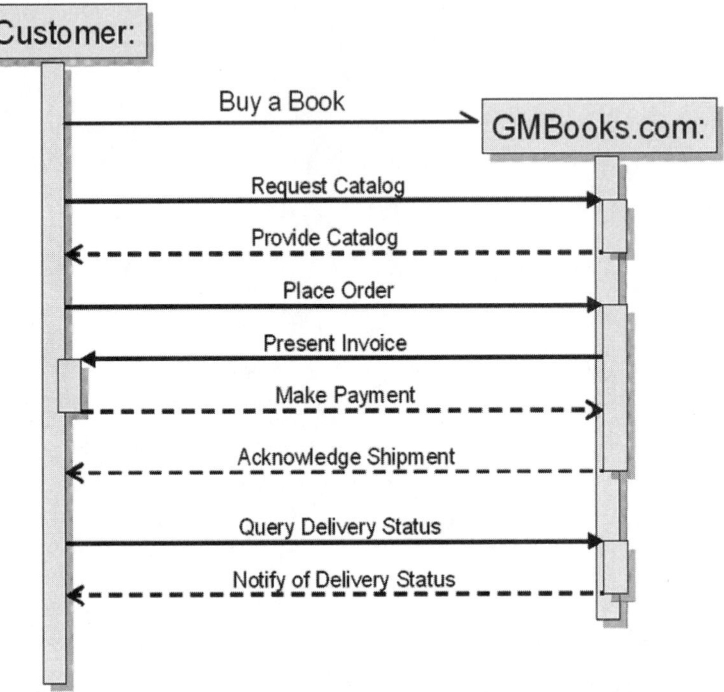

Figure 9-5. A Transactional Model of the Buy a Book Process with GMBooks.com.

UML Notations for Sequence Diagrams

We use the UML Sequence Diagram for representing the sequence of messages sent between participants in transactions. Descending from each participant (Customer and GMBooks.com in Figure 9-5) is a lifeline or timeline that implies the enduring existence of the participants before and after their interactions take place. The arrows between the lifelines represent the messages exchanged by the participants.

Many of the arrows terminate on rectangles superimposed on the lifeline that are called activations. These show the duration of the process that takes place in response to the message. The three types of messages are simple (represented by a simple arrowhead), synchronous (shown by a full triangular arrowhead), and asynchronous (shown using half a simple arrowhead). An optional message exchange is shown as a broken line.

9.4.2 DOCUMENTS IN TRANSACTIONS

Because transactions involve documents, their names often include or suggest the documents that are involved. From Figure 9-5 we see that the document we typically call a catalog is delivered to the customer when it is requested from GMBooks.com. The customer then sends an order to GMBooks.com to request the purchase of a book. GMBooks.com then either accepts or rejects the offer. After the customer sends a payment, GMBooks.com arranges for the book to be shipped and informs the customer. The customer might track the shipment by sending a delivery query.

We may not all be familiar with all of the names for these different types of documents. The names attached to specific types of documents are not always the best indicators of their purpose, because it is not the name of a document that defines its use. What defines a document is its role in a business transaction, because that determines the meaning of the document's content and how it should be processed.

It is not the name of a document that defines its use, but its role in a business transaction

For example, in some procurement processes, the seller responds to a buyer's offer with an order acknowledgment document. But in the book-buying process shown in Figure 9-5, this order acceptance is implicit when the seller presents an invoice to the buyer. In other procurement processes there may not be explicit payment documents because payment is not initiated until the buyer sends a goods receipt.

This sometimes unclear relationship between conventional document names and function is evident in situations such as ordering space for shipping freight, where the document used to place the offer is known as a booking—even though it performs the same role as the document we know as an order. And of course there are numerous examples of synonyms for most common business documents, such as invoice or statement and dispatch advice, delivery docket, or shipping note.

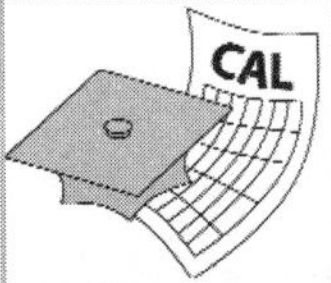

In the Event Calendar project, we refined our process model by recognizing that in addition to the UC Berkeley Events calendar, many academic departments maintain their own separate calendars (or lists of events) that might be relevant to students, faculty, or alumni from that department. Administrative and nonacademic areas also maintain calendars (such as the schedule of classes, calendar of key dates for admissions and registration, academic calendar, sporting events).

To get more publicity for their events, the administrators of these calendars also enter information about events they are holding into the UC Berkeley Events calendar.

The UML sequence diagram in Figure 9-6a describes the transactions required for submitting a new event. This diagram consolidates the information from three business transaction view worksheets, one for each of the three binary relationships between the event submitter, the local calendar administrator, and the central calendar administrator. One of these worksheets is shown in Figure 9-6b.

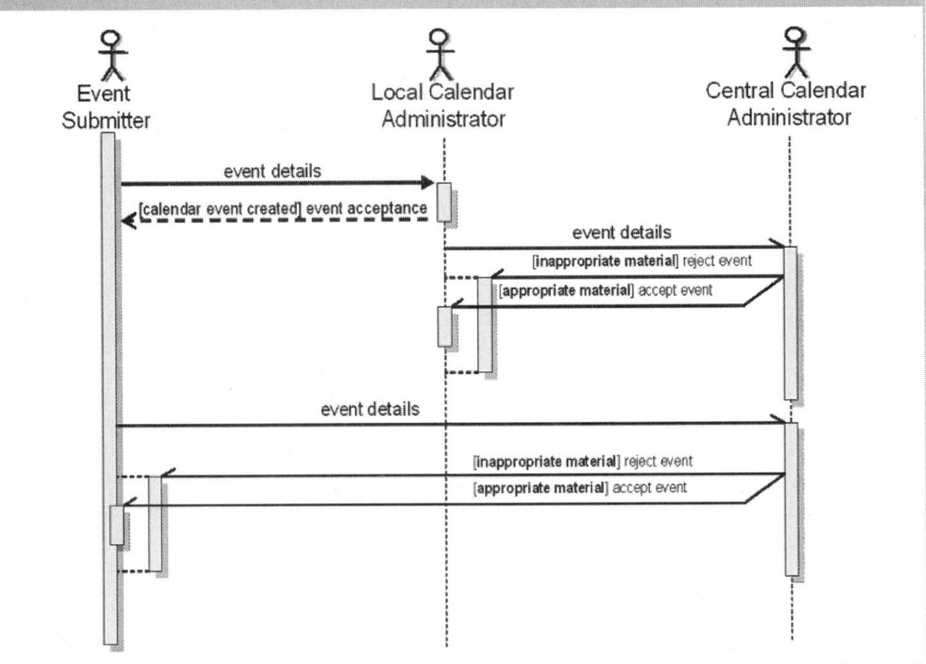

Figure 9-6a. The Submit Event Business Transactions

From this model we start to see the requirements for information components such as Event Details, Event Acceptance and Event Rejection. Further analysis exposed additional components such as Event Identification (to establish whether it was actually a new event), Calendar Identification (to determine the correct calendar) and their related business rules.

BUSINESS TRANSACTION VIEW WORKSHEET	
Worksheet ID	UCBCalendar-BTV-SubmitLocalEventToMain-1.0
Business Transaction Name	Submit Local Event to Main Calendar
Description	Submission of event from local calendar to main calendar for publication and further distribution.
Transaction Pattern	Offer-Acceptance
Initiating Partner Type	Local calendar administrator
Responding Partner Type	Central calendar administrator
Preconditions	Event accepted for local calendar
Begins When	Local calendar administrator fills out "submit event" form.
Ends When	Central calendar administrator sends "accept event" or "reject event" message.
Exceptions	Events can be rejected as inappropriate for central calendar.
Constraints	Submitted event should be acknowledged on receipt. Acceptance or rejection should be determined within 24 hours of submission.
Postconditions	Local event republished on central calendar.

Figure 9-6b. Business Transaction View Worksheet from Event Calendar Network Project

9.5 BUSINESS SIGNALS: RECEIPTS AND CONFIRMATIONS

Figure 9-5 is not a complete picture of the information exchanges between the buyer and seller. It shows the business documents exchanged by the parties, but omits the business signals used by applications to inform the other side of certain types of events. The signals are not in themselves business documents, but they provide useful feedback to the sending side when the receiving side can't respond to a business document immediately because additional processing or decision making is necessary.

Business signals and some types of business documents function as business acknowledgments. These acknowledgments are sent in addition to any messages associated with the lower-level physical protocol layers that move information between the two parties. These lower layers are not visible and are mostly irrelevant to the perspective taken by Document Engineering in analyzing business processes.

Business Process Protocols

Protocols specify the rules that allow different parties to communicate with or transfer information to each other. Multiple protocols can be required to describe different aspects or layers of the same communication. The protocols that govern the exchange of information between businesses span the entire protocol "stack" from those involving physical devices and data connections to the behaviors and obligations required by business relationships.

The guiding principle for good communication systems is that the entity responsible for a given protocol should respond only to events or messages from its counterpart in the same layer at the other end of the communication. For example, an email server can signal receipt of a message from another email server, but it cannot respond to messages from higher-layer applications like procurement systems that might be using email to convey purchase orders. There is no way for the email server to know anything about inventory information, contractual relationships, and other factors that determine whether the order should be accepted.

Likewise, a higher-layer protocol program sometimes cannot respond to its counterpart on the other side of the business process because of communication failures at lower layers. A procurement system might not receive the seller's message that an order was accepted because it was not delivered by one of the email servers involved. It would be wrong for the procurement system to conclude that its offer had been rejected. It needs a message from the seller's order management system, which is at the same layer in the protocol stack.

The lowest-level business signal that might be required in a business transaction model is a receipt.[14] This signal informs the sender that its business document has been received by the appropriate business application. It signals that the message containing the business document is (or isn't, in the case of a negative receipt) structurally and syntactically correct. This is like signing for a package from a delivery service; it communicates only that the package arrived and that it looked OK from the outside.

It may also be useful or required in a business transaction for the recipient to send a confirmation. This business signal informs the sender that the business document is valid (or invalid) according to the recipient's business rules. This indicates that the recipient understands the document and is willing to process it because it contains enough of the required information. It does not mean that the recipient accepts the offer conveyed by the sender's document. In the delivered package analogy, this confirmation is equivalent to opening the package and confirming that it contains all the items listed on the packing slip. Confirmation signals are often used in transactions involving legal requirements, money, uncertainty, or competing proposals.

A confirmation might contain significant business information from the document being acknowledged, making it a substantive confirmation. Confirmations of this type might include the entire contents of the received document. Alternatively, the confirmation is nonsubstantive if it contains only an identifier for the received document. A nonsubstantive negative confirmation is an error message informing the sender that the document did not have valid syntax or content, perhaps with some limited explanation for its rejection.

Finally, when the recipient decides to accept or reject the offer made by the sender, it sends a business document with the response.

These three levels of acknowledgments are superimposing, meaning that sending a response business document implies confirmation and receipt of the received document. Likewise, sending a confirmation implies the receipt. The business document is the most important acknowledgment because it enables the business process to advance to the next step. But the lower-level signals can be important as well because they inform the participants of events that keep transactions and collaborations synchronized or on track, and it is a good practice to employ them when implementing business processes.

Signals keep transactions and collaborations synchronized

For example, a negative confirmation signal that an order isn't valid could be sent not just to the sender but also to another process or person on the recipient's side. Using the signal in this way to reroute the order is in effect promoting the signal to a higher level in the business protocol. The relationships between the three types of acknowledgments are shown in Figure 9-7.

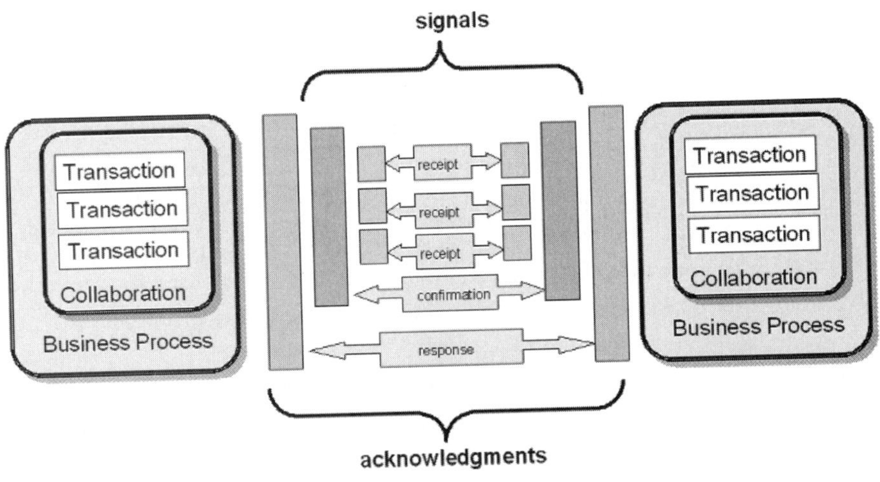

Figure 9-7. The Three Types of Business Acknowledgments

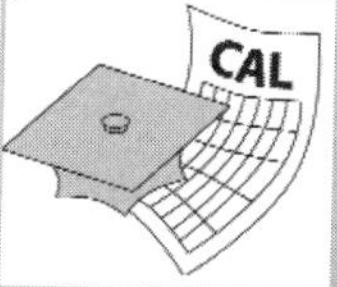

In the Event Calendar project, we identified a rule that an email confirmation is required for each event that has been successfully submitted. This should include an identifying reference for the submitted event. This business rule identifies a requirement not only for a receipt signal but also for a transactional component.

9.6 TRANSACTION PATTERNS

Business signals help to interrelate the different parts of a business transaction, and are an essential part of what the transaction means. The presence or absence of signals also influences which of the six patterns defined in the ebXML Business Process Specification[15] is being followed by a particular transaction.

The transaction patterns differ in whether the two parties have a preexisting relationship and the extent of their business obligations or commitments to each other. These obligations can change as a business process takes place, and the change is often the intent or result of a transaction.

Where possible, we will explain the transaction patterns using the Buy a Book process illustrated in Figure 9-5.

9.6.1 OFFER AND ACCEPTANCE

Many business transactions are variations of an Offer and Acceptance pattern (Figure 9-8), also called the Commercial Transaction pattern. One party sends an offer and exposes itself to the imposition of legal liability by another in doing so. Because of this legal exposure, it can be important to the offerer to know the status of the offer, so the recipient might respond with a receipt when the offer arrives and with a confirmation when it is determined to be a valid offer.

As they have commercial obligations, the offer and the acceptance are both nonrepudiable, meaning that both parties must authorize and guarantee their roles in the transaction, perhaps by providing a verified or notarized signature (digital or otherwise) but most often by commercial trust.

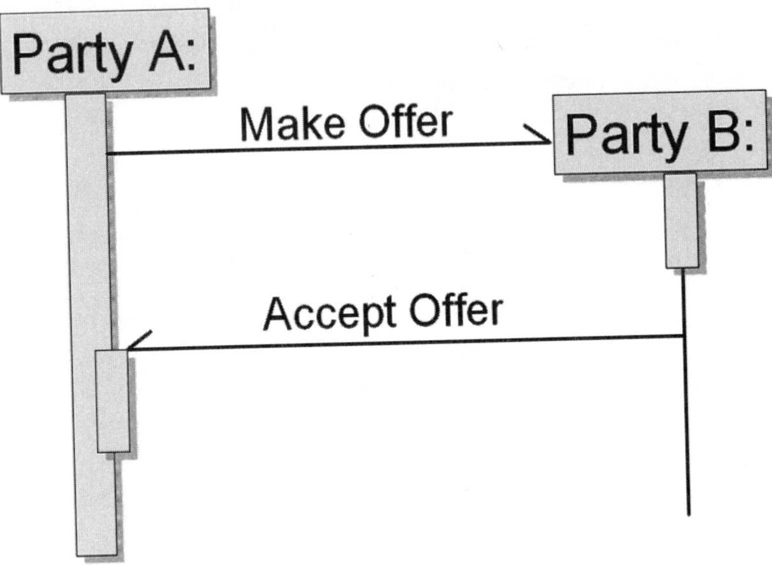

Figure 9-8. The Offer and Acceptance Transaction Pattern

A common example of this transaction pattern is that of placing an order. In fact, this offer and acceptance pattern provides the basis for the United Nations Convention on Contracts for the International Sale of Goods,[16] which is about as standardized as a transaction pattern can be. Placing an order with GMBooks.com, as shown in Figure 9-5, is an instance of this pattern.

9.6.2 REQUEST AND RESPONSE

Another transaction pattern is Request and Response (Figure 9-9). This pattern is used in transaction models when one party makes a request for information and the responding party has to apply some business logic before responding. The response might depend on the identity of the party making the query—for example, when we check an account balance with a creditor. Or maybe the response needs to be dynamically generated—for example, when we enquire about stock availability of an item.

In this pattern, no binding obligations are created for the responding party. In the GMBooks.com scenario, Request Catalog would be an example of the Request and Response pattern, if the catalog were tailored for each customer.

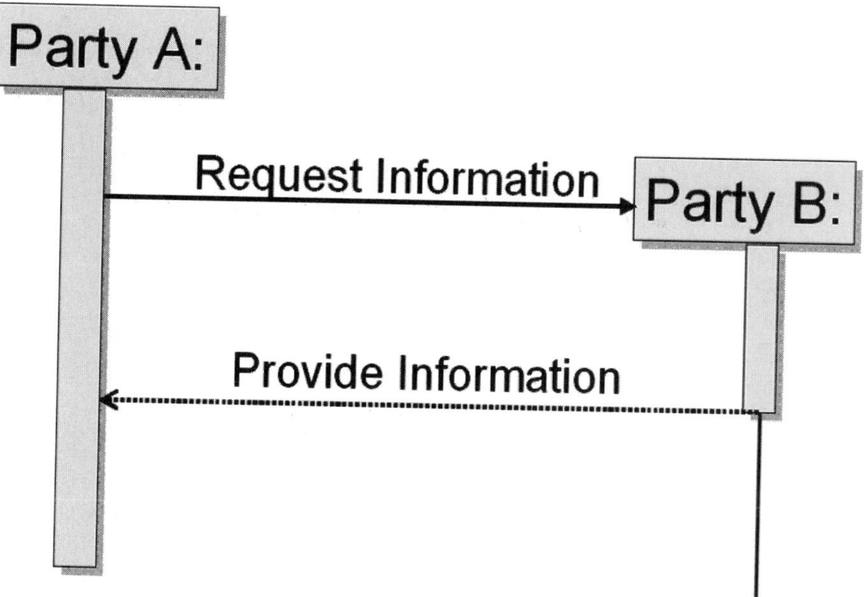

Figure 9-9. The Request and Response Transaction Pattern

9.6.3 REQUEST AND CONFIRM

If a request for information assumes a previously established contract or obligation, the transaction pattern is known as Request and Confirm (Figure 9-10). In this pattern, one party requests confirmation or status information from another, for example, as a Request Order Status transaction. In the GMBooks.com example the Query Delivery Status transaction is an instance of this pattern.

This pattern may also require some form of nonrepudiation on the responder's part.

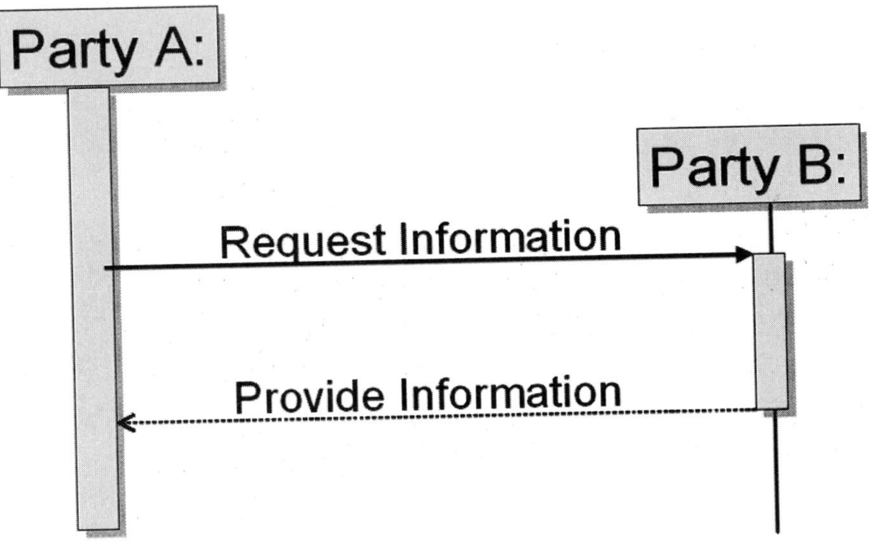

Figure 9-10. The Request and Confirm Transaction Pattern

9.6.4 QUERY AND RESPONSE

In contrast to Request and Response and Request and Confirm, with a Query and Response (Figure 9-11) transaction pattern, the response provided doesn't depend on an established business relationship. This pattern is an appropriate model when the information being sought is static or slow changing so that it doesn't depend on the identity of the party initiating the transaction.

In the GMBooks.com scenario, Request Catalog and its response would be an example of the "query and response" pattern if the catalog were static and every customer received the same one.

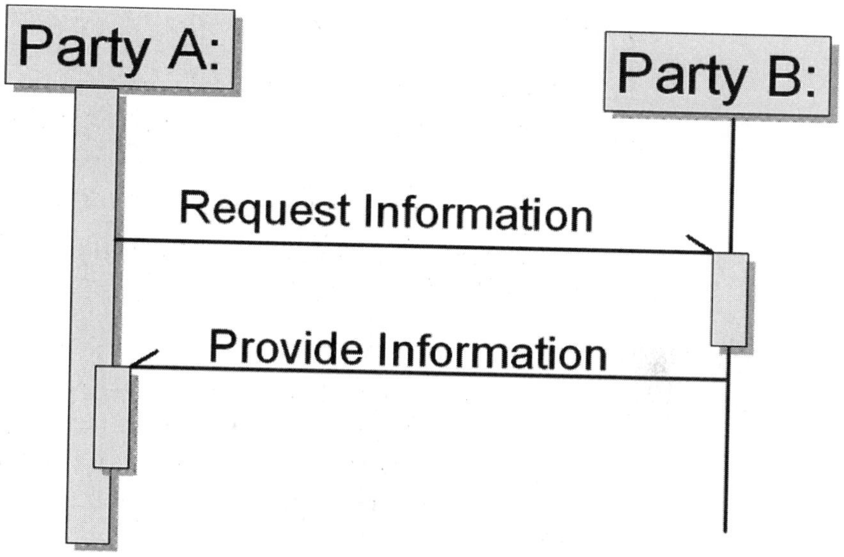

Figure 9-11. The Query and Response Transaction Pattern

9.6.5 NOTIFICATION

Some transaction patterns do not require any responding document because they are inherently about unilateral distribution of information rather than bilateral exchange. The most common of these is the Notification pattern (Figure 9-12). In this pattern, one party informs the other about the status of an existing business relationship or obligation.

While there may be nonrepudiation requirements for the sender, the recipient isn't required to send a formal acceptance document. However, it is not uncommon to send an acknowledgment that the message was received.

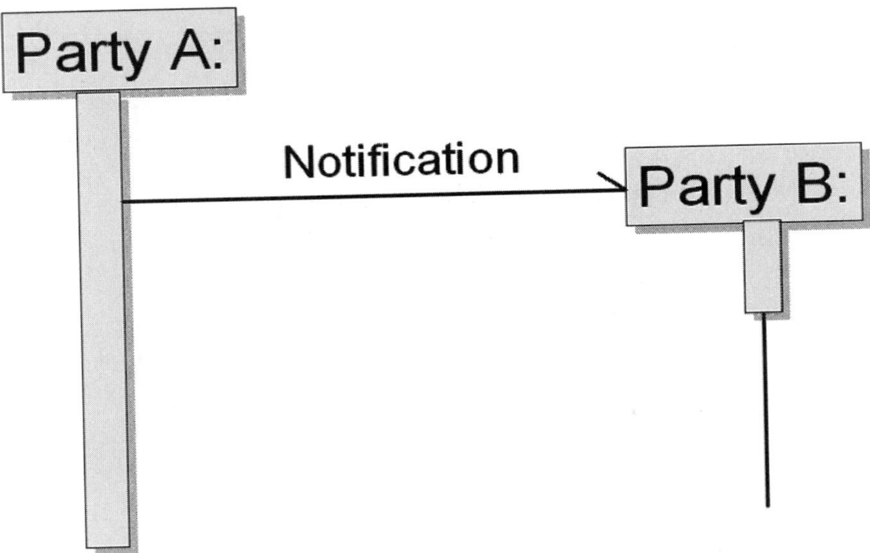

Figure 9-12. The Notification Transaction Pattern

If GMBooks.com notifies the customer when the book is shipped from the distributor, that would be an instance of the Notification pattern.

9.6.6 INFORMATION DISTRIBUTION

The final transaction pattern in the ebXML taxonomy is called Information Distribution (Figure 9-13). This is also a one-way transaction, often used for syndicated information exchange. It is similar to Query and Response but doesn't require a responding business document because the relationship between the sender and receiver is informal rather than contractual.

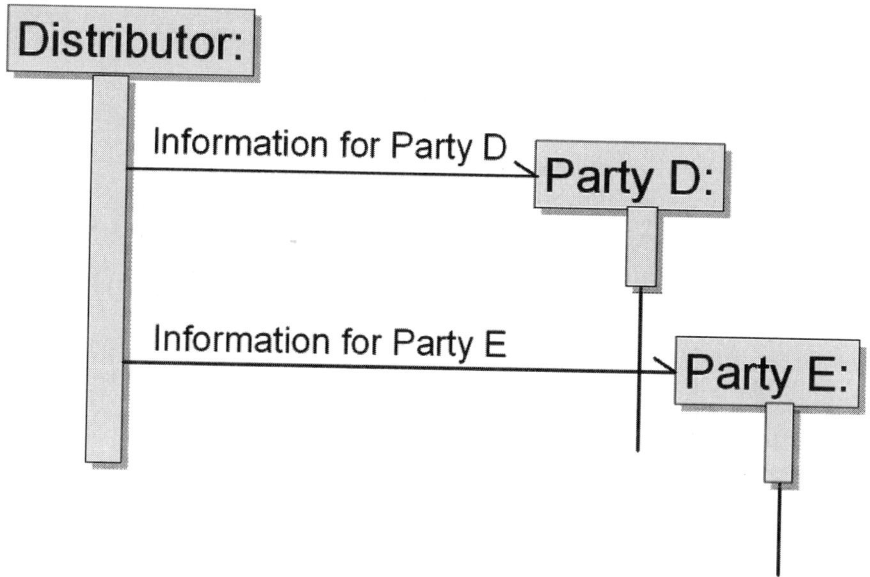

Figure 9-13. The Information Distribution Transaction Pattern

So, if GMbooks.com wanted to send out promotional material or catalogs to potential customers, they would probably adapt an Information Distribution pattern.

9.7 ANALYZING BUSINESS COLLABORATIONS

In Figure 9-1 we illustrated the idea that the collaboration level in process models could group related transactions among two or more parties to provide an intermediate level of description between processes and transactions. The rationale for a collaboration level is easy to see in Figure 9-5, where the process of buying a book proceeds over an extended time period. It would be useful to organize the transactions into sets where there is a close relationship in purpose or time because then they can be reused. Ordering, tracking, and fulfillment might be thought of as reusable phases of a procurement process, each comprised of characteristics sets or sequences of transactions.

When transactions are grouped in sets where there is a close relationship in purpose or time they can be reused

We define a business collaboration as a set of transactions with meaningful and necessary semantic or temporal overlap with each other. Put another way, a collaboration is a set of transactions that have more overlapping context with each other than with other parts of the business process that contains them all. The overlap must be have business significance. For example, they must have parties in common. Similarly, the overlap must be necessary. That is, the parties must need to know about each other's transactions with a third party for those transactions to be viewed as collaborative.[17] This "need to know" principle keeps collaboration models at a manageable size.

As an example of a business collaboration we may find that the carrier who delivers the books does not need to know about GMBooks.com's Request for Service or Contract Formation collaborations with the customer. Likewise, the customer doesn't need to know about the Book Shipment transaction between GMBooks.com and the carrier. However, all three parties need to know about the delivery of the book.

Knowing about a collaboration doesn't imply anything about which party initiates or controls it. We can differentiate a collaboration controlled or initiated by a single party (an orchestration) from those that are mutually controlled (a choreography), but this distinction is primarily important in implementation and doesn't determine which transactions it contains.

The business rules associated with transactions identify common dependencies that form collaborations

The business rules associated with each transaction, such as the preconditions, postconditions, and triggering events can identify relationships and dependencies between the transactions in a collaboration. For example, the business rule that "Goods must be delivered within 48 hours of receiving the order" creates a collaboration by connecting an order transaction to those related to fulfillment.

Figure 9-14 applies these guidelines for identifying collaborations in the buying a book scenario of Figure 9-5.

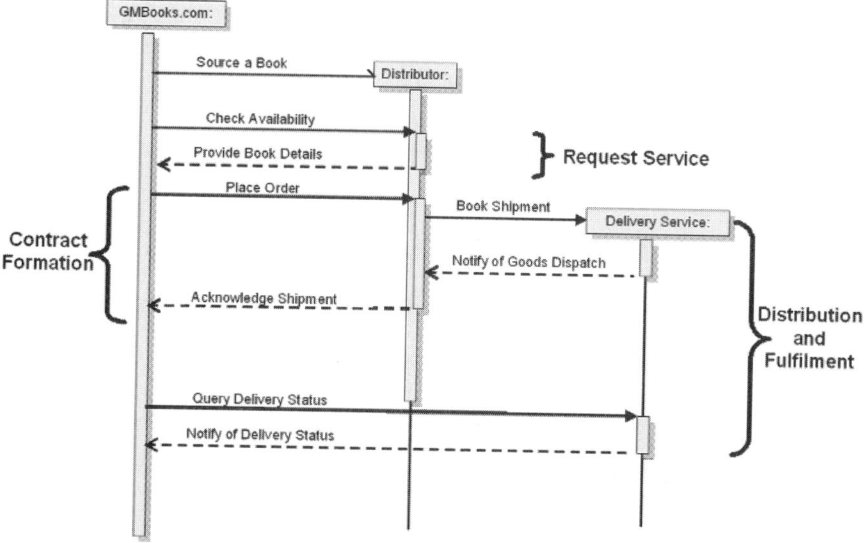

Figure 9-14. Collaborations in the GMBooks.com Scenario

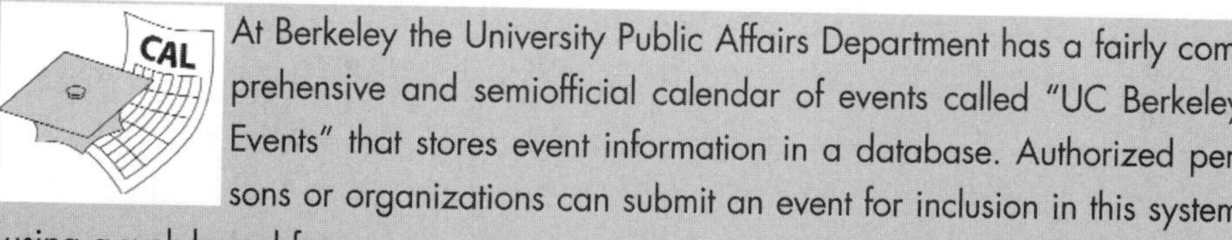

At Berkeley the University Public Affairs Department has a fairly comprehensive and semiofficial calendar of events called "UC Berkeley Events" that stores event information in a database. Authorized persons or organizations can submit an event for inclusion in this system using a web-based form.

Figure 9-15 depicts the collaboration required for submitting a new event to the calendar using a UML activity diagram.

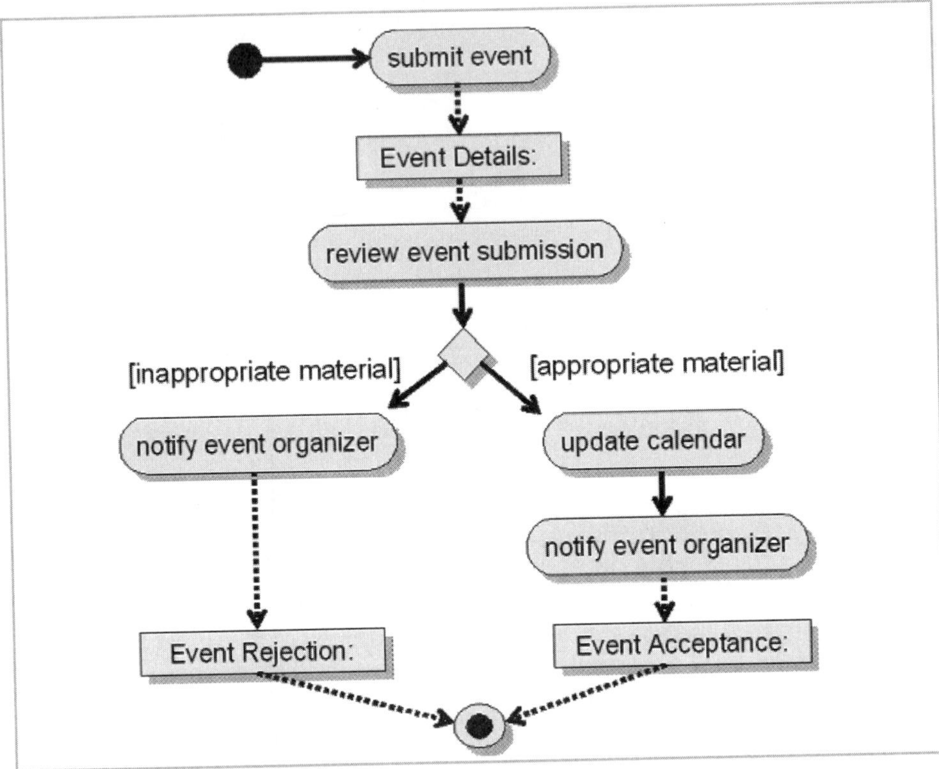

Figure 9-15. The Submit Event Business Collaboration

The collaboration begins with submission of an event and ends with either rejection or acceptance. Within this collaboration, we see transactions for exchanging event details, rejection notifications, and acceptance notifications.

9.8 COLLABORATION PATTERNS

It's not surprising that collaborations also form patterns. As we did with business processes and transaction patterns, we can list some of the more common ones as examples.

9.8.1 CONTRACT FORMATION

The Offer and Acceptance transaction pattern (section 9.6.1) is simplest case of a collaboration pattern called Contract Formation. The full contract formation pattern extends back in time from the offer to include transactions that seek information needed to make one or more nonbinding proposals. It also generalizes the offer and acceptance transaction to include negotiations and counteroffers. The contract is formed when a binding offer is responded to by a binding acceptance.

The pattern is well documented in the ebXML e-Commerce Patterns Technical Report[18] from which Figure 9-16 is taken.

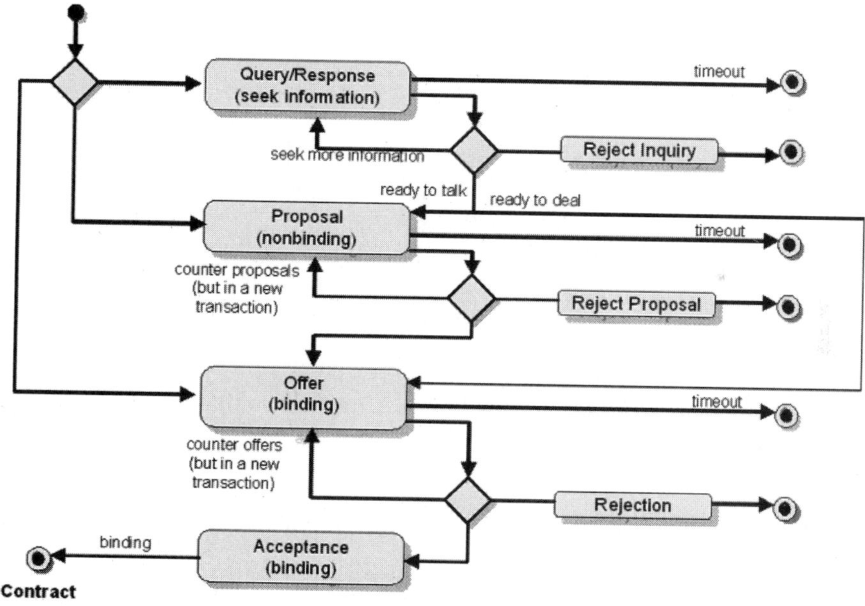

Figure 9-16. A Contract Formation Collaboration Pattern

The contract formation collaboration is often part of the procurement and auction processes. It is also a component in other collaboration patterns, such as the Sourcing and Escalating Commitment patterns we describe next.

9.8.2 SOURCING

A more complex contract formation pattern is Sourcing, the critical business process of selecting suppliers of goods or services. Sourcing can require extensive and iterative information exchange between buyers and suppliers before the buyer places an order.

The buyer might first publish a Request for Information (RFI) or a Request for Quote (RFQ) to identify qualified suppliers. The Contract Formation pattern might be invoked in negotiations to determine whether a supplier is allowed to bid. Then, before responding with a quote, a supplier might ask the buyer to explain some aspect of the requirements or might suggest why some requirement is impossible to satisfy. This might result in a revised RFQ from the buyer and might also require the contract formation collaboration to create it.

9.8.3 ESCALATING COMMITMENT

If a contract negotiation ends successfully, it may trigger another contract negotiation with progressively stronger obligations to create a collaboration pattern called Escalating Commitment. We see this with business processes used in supply chains, where businesses negotiate an intention to supply goods and then increase the commitment as time progresses. This allows for scheduled manufacturing, warehousing, and subsequent shipment of goods.

9.8.4 MATERIALS MANAGEMENT AND DISTRIBUTION AND FULFILLMENT

The Materials Management collaboration pattern brings together all the planning, scheduling, and inventory control transactions that enable a manufacturer to ensure that the things it buys get to specified places at specified times in specified quantities. The contractual relationship between the buyer and supplier will specify the content, sequencing, and acknowledgment of Planning Schedules (or Forecasts),

Shipping Schedules, Shipping Notices (or Despatch Advice) and other documents they will exchange.

The Distribution and Fulfillment collaboration pattern is the mirror image to materials management. It includes the transactions needed to get goods from a manufacturer to its customers. Distributors, resellers, and retail outlets are usually involved as intermediaries to multiply the manufacturer's reach. Delivery service providers of various types will have separate collaborations with these entities in the delivery chain.

9.8.5 RECONCILIATION

The Reconciliation collaboration pattern brings together information from related transactions to ensure a single consolidated and accurate view. When we balance our checkbooks, we are reconciling our information about our transactions with the bank's information about them, being careful to consider transactions that we've initiated that do not yet appear on the bank's statement.

Many business processes involve regularly scheduled activities of aggregation, comparison, and exception handling to reconcile the work carried out by different organizations or applications. Nearly every business needs to reconcile its order with delivered goods with payments.

Reconciliation is critically important in information-intensive industries like health care, insurance, banking, real estate, financial services, and securities, where the goal of straight-through processing can't be achieved without reliably reconciled transactions and accounts. Reconciliation is also essential in synchronizing the flows of information and goods to ensure that cargo manifests accurately describe the goods being transported and that all are accounted for when they arrive.

9.8.6 INCREMENTAL INFORMATION TRAIL

A final example of a collaboration pattern is known as an Incremental Information Trail.[19] In this collaboration, a document in an information chain process is amended in a series of transactions involving different participants. Each may add additional information to the document at each stage in the process.

Incremental information trails are particularly relevant to the domestic and international transport community, where details of goods in transit must pass between a variety of documents such as orders, bookings, shipping advices, forwarding instructions, customs declarations, ship's manifests, delivery notes, and payments. But incremental information trails also occur in other business processes, such the criminal justice information chain where police, prosecutors, courts, and correctional services each receive case information collected and generated in prior steps and add to the documents they create.

In fact, any document workflow process could be considered an instance of this collaboration pattern. The simplest possible variant is a Document Approval collaboration, where the information added to the original document might be nothing more than the signature (perhaps with comments) of the reviewer.

9.9 KEY POINTS IN CHAPTER NINE

- Internal processes that create and consume documents can change but the external business interface should not.
- Business process models will contain some information components and document models will contain some processing rules.
- Business processes can be described at many levels of abstraction.
- There are no necessary relationships between business processes, management structure and facilities, technology, and systems.
- The model of business organization shapes the need to exchange information across organizational boundaries.
- A reference model can be the default To-Be model for a business.
- There is no single correct way to model business processes.
- Application interfaces require a computer-processable model format.
- Accurate modeling artifacts are essential when the work crosses enter prise or organizational boundaries.
- It is not the name of a document that defines its use, but its role in a business transaction.
- Business processes are synchronized by loosely coupled information exchanges using documents.
- Signals are used to keep transactions synchronized.

- When transactions are groups in sets where there is a close relationship in purpose or time they can be reused.

- The business rules associated with transactions identify common dependencies that form collaborations.

10

Designing Business Processes With Patterns

10.0 INTRODUCTION

Patterns are models that are sufficiently general, adaptable, and worthy of imitation that we can reuse them. They are an essential theme in Document Engineering; we began Chapter 1 with GMBooks.com and the drop shipment pattern, in Chapter 4 we presented a repertoire of organizational, process, information, and architecture patterns, and in Chapter 5 we explained how those patterns mutually evolve with technology. In Chapter 9 we introduced transaction and collaboration patterns in the framework of a three-level metamodel for describing processes. In Chapters 12-14, we will discuss patterns in document and document component models.

We devote this chapter to specific techniques for applying and adapting patterns to business process designs because the choice of process pattern strongly influences what information is required and how that information is packaged and exchanged as documents.

10.1 WHY WE USE PATTERNS IN PROCESS MODELS

In Section 3.4.2 we discussed why businesses follow patterns. Now we will take a closer look at the benefits of using patterns for our process models:

- *Simplify work.* Patterns provide the immediate benefit of reduced design and integration efforts and the longer-term benefit of greater consistency and standardization.

- *Encourage best practices.* We call something a pattern because it captures typical or preferred ways of doing things, making it worthy of imitation. As such, patterns are always candidates for To-Be models.

- *Assist in analysis.* A process pattern brings with it a set of roles, requirements and rules. For example, the drop shipment pattern includes roles for the retailer, the inventory distributor, the shipper, and the payment authority. The pattern may also suggest the types of firms that can perform one or more of these roles and the types of users and other stakeholders with whom we can verify the requirements in our context. Patterns also give us insights that we can't see in instances; for example, generalized patterns let us recognize that both automobile and computer makers are adopting similar component assembly and make-to-order processes.

- *Expose inefficiencies.* In a typical instantiation of the drop shipment pattern, the distributor simultaneously sends shipment information to both the customer and to the retailer (so that the latter can handle customer queries). In contrast, we might find in an As-Is model that the distributor sends shipment information to the seller, who then forwards it to the customer. Comparing the As-Is model to the pattern suggests an inefficiency that might be removed in an improved To-Be model.[1]

- *Remove redundancies.* For example, we might learn in an As-Is model that both the seller and the distributor are sending shipment information to the buyer. The pattern helps us identify and remove the redundant information exchange.

- *Consolidate interfaces.* Using a common pattern allows different contexts of use to share a common interface. Using a single integration point to support all of the information exchanges can substantially reduce implementation and maintenance costs. For example, a buyer can use a common interface for both direct and indirect procurement processes.

- *Encourage modularity and transparent substitution.* When patterns are organized for reuse, they are more easily adopted, and the network effects yield even greater benefits to those who follow them. The standardization and generalization that comes from using patterns over time encourages more modular perspectives and architectures for roles and processes and further reduces implementation and maintenance costs. For example, it becomes easier to replace one service with another to meet quality of service or cost goals and facilitates the outsourcing of internal functions to external services.

These benefits help explain why designing business processes more often involves applying and adapting patterns than inventing new ones.

Designing business processes more often involves applying and adapting patterns than inventing new ones

10.2 HOW WE USE PATTERNS IN PROCESS MODELS

To design new business process models we want to identify patterns that best satisfy the requirements of our context of use. If a business process pattern is an excellent fit to a set of requirements we can use it without change. Then we simply follow the pattern exactly to design our To-Be Model, just as we might make a pizza by following a recipe exactly. In recent years many merchants have followed the drop shipment pattern exactly, playing the role of the retailer with other enterprises serving as inventory distributor, shipper, and payment authority.[2]

Even when a standard pattern isn't the best match to our requirements, we might consider changing some of those requirements and adapting to the pattern. Otherwise, the advantage we might gain by changing the pattern to better satisfy internal needs might be outweighed by new costs imposed on customers, external partners and services that can no longer use the standard pattern in dealing with us. If the process isn't one where innovation can yield competitive advantage, standard processes win the cost-benefit analysis over customized ones. Business strategist Geoffrey Moore puts it succinctly: "Differentiation that does not drive customer preference is a liability."[3]

But sometimes we do need to adapt a pattern and make changes to fit the specific requirements of our context of use. This is analogous to how we adapt a pizza recipe when we substitute different cheeses or toppings for those it specifies.

Sometimes our adaptations are successful enough to be imitated as patterns in their own right

Sometimes adaptations are successful enough to be imitated as patterns in their own right. The Hawaiian Pizza, created by substituting the Polynesian ingredients of ham and pineapple for more traditional ones, has become popular enough to become part of the pizza pattern library. In contrast, the much rarer Indonesian Pizza adaptation that uses soy sauce, cane sugar, peanuts, and chili has not been followed enough to warrant calling it a pizza pattern.[4]

We don't need to invoke any mechanisms of natural selection or evolutionary advantage to appreciate the reasons and benefits for patterns to take hold. Is it better to drive on the right side or the left side of the road? We won't argue either way; the right-side or left-side pattern becomes worthy of imitation in some jurisdictions just because people have agreed to it.

10.3 PATTERNS AND THE MODEL MATRIX

In Chapter 4 we discussed a range of patterns at different modeling levels to give you some familiarity with the more common patterns at each level from the new perspective of Document Engineering. Our survey was by no means exhaustive, especially at the process level, where there are several much more comprehensive collections of business process patterns and business reference models.[5]

But our survey was sufficient to show that what distinguishes Document Engineering is its systematic approach for discovering and formalizing the relationships between the patterns and artifacts at the organizational and business process levels and those of documents and their information components. This connects the strategic perspective of what to do with the implementation perspective of how to do it.

We can use the dimensional framework of the Model Matrix depicted in Figure 7-2 to demonstrate how different kinds of patterns relate to each other.

We begin with a discussion of how we can use both the abstraction and granularity axes in the Model Matrix to find candidate patterns for our required (To-Be) models. Then we will discuss how to choose the most appropriate patterns and adapt them if necessary.

The most abstract patterns of business organization describe business roles and functions from a context-free, generic perspective. These are depicted on the top left side of the Matrix. Patterns of this type would include Manufacturing, Transporting, Selling, and so on, with no specification of the industry or type of product or service involved.

As we move to the right, we add context to these abstract patterns to describe a narrower set of situations. For example, in Figure 10-1 we depict a Computer Manufacturer pattern as a specialization of the manufacturing pattern in the information technology industry. When we reach the top right side of the Matrix we encounter specific firms that follow the pattern as customized to meet all the business rules of a particular enterprise or ecosystem; in Figure 10-1 we use Dell as an implementation of the Computer Manufacturer pattern.

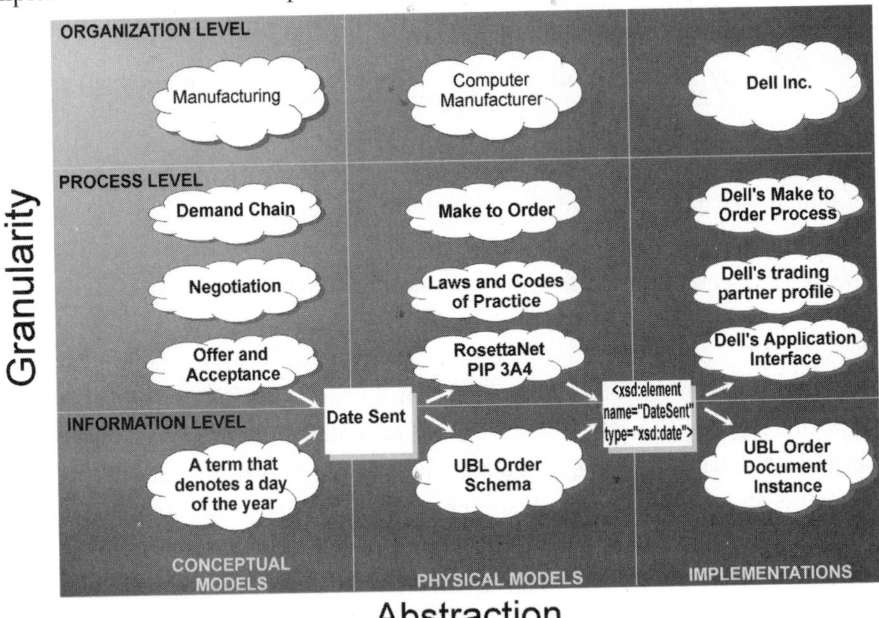

Figure 10-1. Reusing Patterns in the Model Matrix

A similar progression from generalized patterns to contextualized implementations is represented at the process layer in the Model Matrix. We've depicted three rows in the process model layer to remind us of the three layers of the Chapter 9 metamodel for processes, which treats processes as consisting of collaborations, which in turn consist of transactions.

At the coarsest process granularity are the business process patterns, such as Demand Chain, Information Aggregation, Procurement, or Auction. We described these (and others) in Chapter 4.

As we move to the right, we contextualize the Demand Chain process pattern to distinguish the Make-to-Order pattern for products manufactured from components. These patterns can be further contextualized to describe the specific operational processes and business rules used when Dell applies the Make-to-Order pattern for personal computers in its relationships with its suppliers of disk drives, microchips, and other components.

Collaborations offer a level of granularity between business processes and the transactions that implement them. In Figure 10-1, collaboration patterns that are used in the Demand Chain pattern such as Negotiation are contextualized as industry codes of practice and contract laws. These in turn, may be implemented as the specific terms and conditions expressed in trading terms used by Dell.

Transactional patterns provide the finest level of granularity in the process layer. On the conceptual side we find general transaction patterns like Offer-Acceptance or Query-Response. As we move to the right we find these patterns applied in a more specialized purchasing and order management context. For example, the RosettaNet PIPs would fit here, once we've specified the context of the electronics and information technology product Demand Chain using a Make-to-Order pattern. Companies like Dell then build interfaces to their supply chain using these transactional patterns as specifications.

Along the bottom row of the Model Matrix we can see the same progressive contexualization of abstract patterns for information components that we saw for processes in the rows above it.

Collaboration and transactional patterns require certain key information components. For example, we know that the Demand Chain/Negotiation/Offer and Acceptance process pattern requires a component for the date (or time) an offer is sent. On the conceptual side we might use a generic definition of a component pattern known as Date. This may be further qualified as Date Sent to define its use as the sending date. As we move to the right in this row this pattern might be reused in the more specific context of a physical model, perhaps as the element DateSent in a UBL Order schema. We would then see implementations of these components as the value of the date the actual offer was sent.

10.4 IDENTIFYING CANDIDATE DESIGN PATTERNS

When we use the idea of the Model Matrix to identify suitable patterns for our design, we are simply moving along the abstraction and granularity dimensions to confirm our analysis and understanding of the context of use.

We are not the first to recognize how compelling these dimensions are for navigating between different types of models. Our approach adapts and extends ideas that are embodied in the MIT Process Handbook (see SIDEBAR). Our innovation is to incorporate the lowest level of patterns for documents and information components using the same two dimensions. So we call our navigation mechanism the "Pattern Compass" in contrast to the "Process Compass" in the MIT framework.

Figure 10-2 illustrates this idea of navigation in the Model Matrix to identify and evaluate candidate patterns.

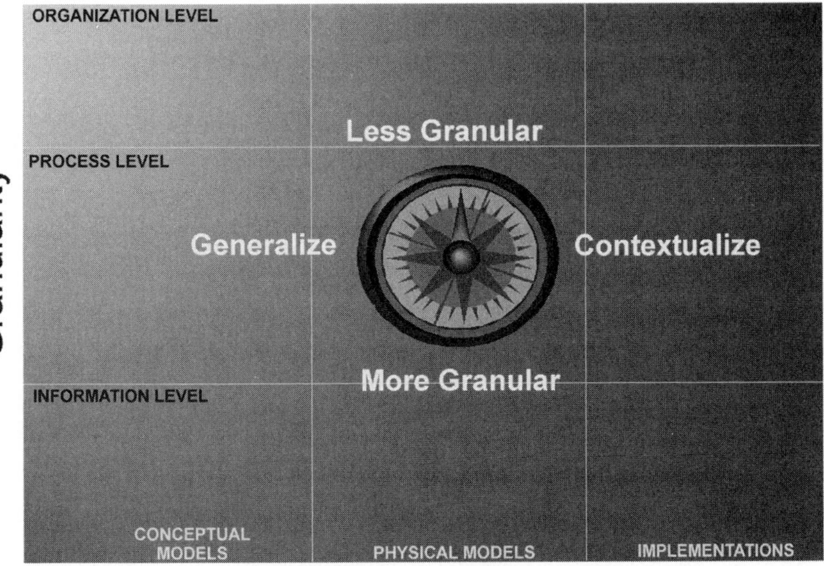

Figure 10-2. The Pattern Compass in the Model Matrix

- Movement from left to right is in the Contextualize direction. As we illustrated when we explained Figure 10-1, this makes patterns more specific (or specialized) for a particular context.

- Movement in the reverse direction from right to left follows the Generalize direction to select patterns that are more abstract.

- Movement from top to bottom on the Granularity dimension increases the granularity of the pattern. As we move in this direction we take a close up perspective on a pattern to see details that aren't visible at the higher levels; we might call this looking at the trees instead of the forest. This means we see the processes in organizational patterns and the document exchanges and information components that aren't visible in process patterns.

- Movement in the reverse direction from bottom to top on the Granularity dimension reduces the granularity of the pattern. We progressively hide the lower level details to create a coarser, big picture view of the pattern; now we're looking at the forest instead of the trees.

MIT Process Handbook

The MIT Process Handbook contains thousands of process descriptions and case studies and is a unique resource for process analysis and redesign. It has three important characteristics: it is comprehensive, easy to use, and based on the formal analysis of businesses using a consistent theoretical base.

The project's repository goes beyond traditional process databases and pattern libraries by explicitly storing the abstraction and compositional relationships among the process patterns. Explicit representation of these two dimensions enables the navigation metaphor to be implemented in the user interface to the pattern repository as a "process compass." In addition, users can annotate existing patterns or create new ones that they can link into the appropriate locations in the logical grid.

The network of associations between processes enables a great deal of information to be automatically inherited from more abstract patterns. It also makes it possible to generate alternatives for how a given process could be performed.[6]

Rather than create our own physical repository to support the Model Matrix, we hope to someday add these lowest level patterns for documents and information components to the MIT one. A repository that contained patterns at all three levels would be significantly more useful than two separate ones.

The business process models we developed in Chapter 9 usually describe current (As-Is) business processes, together with their collaborations and transactions. When our process analysis is grounded in existing implementations, this means that we will be starting the design phase on the right side of the Model Matrix. As we create To-Be models, we will be taking a more conceptual and general, and less granular, perspective on processes and moving left and up in the Model Matrix.

In contrast, if we are designing a business process where there is no existing implementation, or if we are developing a standard pattern or reference model for an industry association or standards activity, we might start with a more abstract pattern. Then we work our way to the right in the Model Matrix as we systematize the roles and rules needed for these more specific contexts.

10.4.1 GENERALIZING PATTERNS

We generalize patterns by relaxing or eliminating requirements in our context of use and assessing the resulting effects and dependencies. We might vary the product, the industry, geography, regulations, or other context dimensions and determine if we can ignore them without consequence. A pattern also becomes more general if we discard or choose not to implement rules or properties that govern the state or behavior of the transactions and collaborations in the pattern (we'll discuss these in Section 10.7.2). And, because our process models are conceptual and not bound to any specific implementation technology, we can generalize patterns from widely different contexts.

We generalize patterns by relaxing or eliminating requirements in our context of use and assessing the resulting effects and dependencies

Figure 10-3 illustrates the idea of generalizing patterns with a depiction of some of the contents in a hypothetical repository of process patterns. A bookstore might use the most specific relevant pattern, the one labeled Sell Books. But we could generalize this pattern into selling tangible products other than books, or further generalize it to include sales of intangible products like information or digital entertainment.

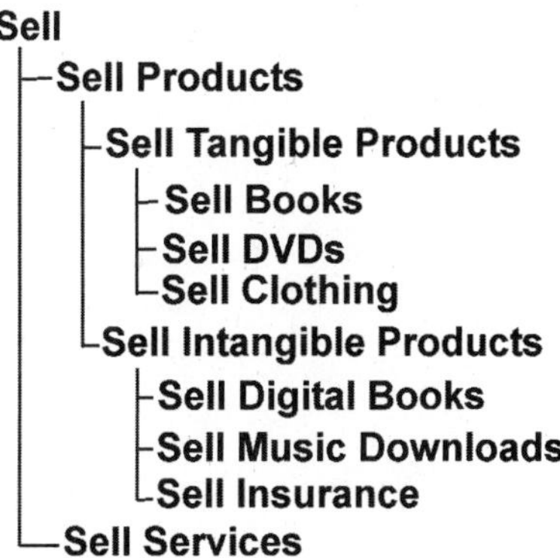

Figure 10-3. Generalization in a Process Pattern Repository

Their reduced contextual constraints means that generalized patterns can also be used to consolidate disparate processes. For example, a department store or supermarket would probably want to avoid distinct processes for sales and inventory control for each type of product. So they generalize their patterns wherever possible. Processes for some categories of goods, such as perishable ones, might be specializations of the general sales and inventory patterns. But even they would be governed by more general patterns. For example, processes for selling perishable goods are driven by expiration date, whether the goods are cut flowers or airline tickets.

We need to emphasize that when we're discussing how to generalize patterns as part of process design we are still at the conceptual level. The bookstore, department store or supermarket in our examples are generalizing their business models; that is, how they think about the businesses they are in and the processes they carry out. In reality, a store's ability to generalize its implementation of these models will be constrained by the application software used to run the business (as well as by the software used by its business partners). Using ready-made software tailored for a specific industry can be the most efficient way to set up a business but also makes it difficult to scale it up or expand it beyond its original business model. That's why it is so critical to think about processes before choosing the technologies for implementing them.

Generalizing the Business Pattern of Colocation

We can demonstrate the idea of generalizing a business pattern by examining the instances of business models involving colocation. Consider:

- A bank inside a supermarket
- A post office inside a supermarket
- A photo processing service inside a supermarket.

These three examples suggest a pattern that we might call Colocation of Complementary Product or Service for Supermarket Customers.

Once we've described it in this more general way, we can readily apply this pattern to recognize other ways in which an errand or quick business interaction could be made more efficient by co location of a business service in a supermarket. Dry cleaning and shoe repair businesses are appropriate candidates because of their quick transactions; dentists and auto body shops aren't because their transactions are neither short nor complementary.

We might try to further generalize the pattern by relaxing the supermarket requirement and making it Colocation of Complementary Businesses. We can use this more abstract pattern to generate additional ideas for new business combinations; one that is already well established is the large bookstore that contains a coffee shop franchise.

10.4.2 VARYING THE GRANULARITY OF PATTERNS

The granularity of an As-Is process model is shaped by the sources of information about processes and whether the analysis was more top-down or bottom-up. Top-down analysis yields large, goal-oriented processes; bottom-up analysis produces a more detailed, transactional view. Both views of processes can be correct, but process models are most useful when they contain at least a little of both perspectives.

The granularity of an As-Is process model is shaped by the sources of information about processes and whether the analysis was more top-down or bottom-up

Moving down on the Granularity dimension in the Model Matrix increases the granularity of a process model and suggests documents and information components that we need to find or design in the document and component analysis phases of Document Engineering. We will describe this activity in Section 10.7.

Moving up on the Granularity dimension decreases the granularity of a process model to create a broader view that hides details. Describing processes at a higher level makes it easier to make models more rational or consistent because the equivalences among instances are no longer obscured by specific low-level details. Coarser or less granular models also suggest patterns that encourage new specializations.

Coarser grained models suggest patterns that encourage new specializations

Returning to our pizza analogy, we notice that following an extremely detailed recipe with precise descriptions of processes and ingredients (like those at the bottom of Figure 10-4) ensures that the pizzas come out exactly the same every time. But a less detailed recipe that consists of only the midlevel steps would make it easier to recognize possibilities for reuse and adaptation of other patterns. This coarser view might inspire the realization that making pizza has much in common with making bread. From such insights emerge new models like focaccia, the Italian bread-pizza hybrid.

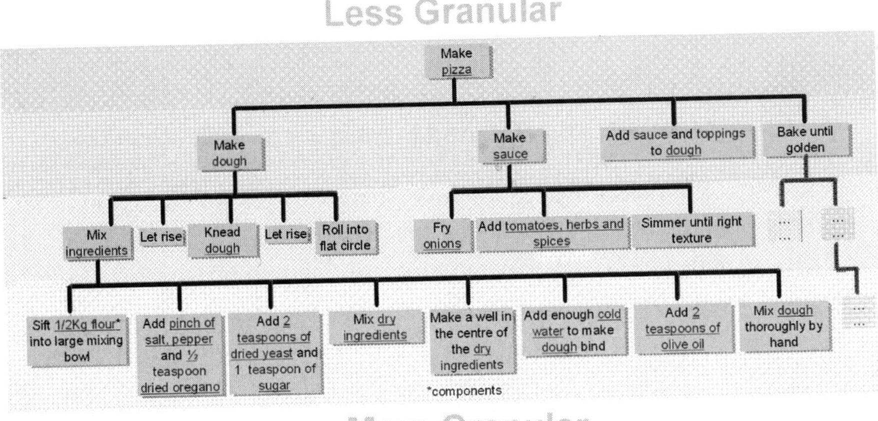

Figure 10-4. Different Granularity in Pizza Recipes

Process libraries like the MIT Process Handbook or the RosettaNet Partner Interface Processes (PIPs) are organized hierarchically to encourage process analysts to vary their perspectives on processes until they find a level of granularity that works for them. The RosettaNet process library is especially useful because its three-level hierarchy of process clusters, segments, and PIPs reinforces the three-level metamodel of processes, collaborations, and transactions.[7] This consistency makes RosettaNet a helpful guide for both novice and experienced analysts, and we have adapted the PIPs as patterns in domains far from the information technology supply chain for which they were originally designed. In Figure 10-5 we show a subset of the library that includes some of the order and inventory management patterns we often use as examples in this book.

The RosettaNet Three Level Process Hierarchy (partial)		
Clusters	**Segments**	**Partner Interface Processes (PIPs)**
1 Partner Product & Service Review		
2 Product Information		
3 Order Management	3A Quote & Order Entry	3A1 Request Quote
		3A2 Request Price & Availability
		3A3 Request Shopping Cart Transfer
		3A4 Request Purchase Order
		3A5 Query Order Status
		3A6 Distribute Order Status
		3A7 Notify of Purchase Order Update
		3A8 Request Purchase Order Change
		3A9 Request Purchase Order Cancellation
		3A10 Notify of Quote Acknowledgment
		3A11 Notify of Authorization to Build
		3A12 Notify of Authorization to Ship
		3A13 Notify of Purchase Order Information
		3A14 Distribute Planned Order
	3B Transportation & Distribution	
	3C Returns & Finance	
	3D Product Configuration	
4 Inventory Management	4A Collaborative Forecasting	
	4B Inventory Allocation	
	4C Inventory Reporting	
	4D Inventory Replenishment	
	4E Sales Reporting	
	4F Price Protection	
5 Marketing Information Management		
6 Service & Support		
7 Manufacturing		

Figure 10-5. The RosettaNet Business Process Hierarchy

10.4.3 COMBINING PATTERNS

We also can create composite processes by combining separate ones. Consider the processes that are carried out to make arrangements for a business trip. A traveler might need an airplane ticket, a rental car, a hotel room, and a restaurant reservation near the hotel. These four procurement processes involve different business service providers and might be conducted separately, but this is highly inefficient because they have overlapping information requirements and dependencies. It would be desirable for the processes to be combined as a composite service in which the overlapping information about time, location, and price is collected just once (perhaps in a single web form). The composite service handles all the interactions and dependencies among the four processes in a way that is invisible to the traveler or the process that invoked the service.

We can create composite process models by combining separate ones

The composite service is not a generalized travel process; it simply carries out the original four processes for making airplane, rental car, hotel, and restaurant reservations. But it has a single interface and is invoked with just one document or web form.

Composite processes can be faster, cheaper, and more reliable than separate ones and can even be reused. But there are some significant challenges in creating composites. Unlike the composite travel service example, in which the composite is a single interface to multiple services but doesn't change any of them, many composite processes require changes or agreements about the separate processes from which they are composed.

For example, the Single Administrative Document (SAD) for cross-border European trading replaced numerous documents for customs declarations and transport procedures. Harmonizing and simplifying the information contained in the SAD required governments, shippers and transport companies to combine their processes into a single process, changing the timing and responsibility for information exchanges among them.[8]

A second and more abstract challenge in creating composite services is that the separate processes must have enough overlap in their goals and requirements to justify bringing them together. Some amount of contextual overlap is essential, but there must also be some business necessity for the combination, and both are difficult to specify.

Separate processes must have enough overlap in their goals and requirements to justify putting them together

For example, referring back to the business colocation pattern from the sidebarearlier, unless the businesses that colocate have some overlapping customers, processes, and business goals, nothing is gained by their colocation. That is why some shopping malls thrive while others fail.

The Science of Business Combination

What exactly has to be "in common" for combinations of business processes or services to be successful? Why it makes sense to bring together some sets of processes but not others is one of the emerging research questions for Document Engineering.[9]

We hinted at this problem in our discussion of Service Oriented Architectures in Chapter 4, because it limits the "plug and play" vision of virtual enterprises in which new businesses are created by combining component services. It doesn't seem efficient to attack the problem with brute-force methods like those used by Thomas Edison, who tried thousands of materials for light bulb filaments until he identified the most appropriate combination.[10]

A more deterministic and theoretical approach would require a metamodel for describing services that captures many more aspects of their information and process semantics. Such metamodels will undoubtedly be layered to correspond to the abstraction and granularity dimensions we use to organize patterns and will also exploit the metadata that specifies the contexts in which the patterns are appropriate.

There are some glimmers of this idea in version 3 of the UDDI specification, which allows for arbitrarily complex and extensible service descriptions.[11] But until service providers fully use these enhancements little automated service discovery is feasible. Nevertheless, we can imagine a virtual business builder that interrogates registries of richly described business services, computes some metric of semantic distance to find service combinations with the necessary amount of complementary overlap and then proposes new kinds of virtual enterprises that exploit undiscovered business opportunities by applying patterns to new domains.

10.4.4 USING IMPLEMENTATIONS AS PATTERNS

Sometimes we want to replicate a process exactly as it has been implemented in another instance. This usually means that the target context of use is effectively identical to an existing one. In this case, we apply the physical model that describes the implementation of the process to be copied, rather than a conceptual model. So the target process uses the same implementation technology and duplicates the specific values currently filling the roles and activities in the source process.

Using implementations as patterns is the principle behind franchising and is manifested in the identical appearance and operation of the stores in hamburger, coffee, pizza, and other retail chains. Each outlet is essentially a clone, with rigorously specified and enforced facility designs and processes to ensure a predictable customer experience and minimize the business risk to the franchisee.

But exact replication of a process can be a denial that patterns often must evolve over time in response to changes in the technology and business context in which enterprises exist (see Chapter 5).

Exact replication of a process can be a denial that patterns will and must evolve over time

Doing things the way they have always been done can give enterprises too narrow a view of why they are in business and institutionalize practices that might have become inefficient or uncompetitive. In the 19th century, railroad companies viewed their business model as running railroads, and they failed to adapt to new technologies for transportation and communication. More recently we've seen a similar myopia in the music industry, whose fixation on maintaining tight control over the distribution of records, tapes, and compact discs made them late to exploit digital distribution processes. And even the local pizza parlor that reliably produces the exact same excellent pizza will eventually find that its customers want to try something different.

It is easier to copy than to innovate because it isn't necessary to understand underlying motivations and conceptual models

Exact copying of a business pattern can make it less necessary to understand underlying requirements and conceptual models. This can be a costly shortcut, however, because if this knowledge is lost then so too is the chance to improve the process at a later time. So while making an exact electronic copy of a printed form may reduce the initial effort to automate paper-based document processes (see Section 4.2.2.6), not analyzing the process and context carefully when new technology and processes are introduced will over time create an increasing burden of processes and documents that contain unnecessary steps and data requirements. These process rituals and document relics persist because no one understands them well enough to redesign them.

Process Rituals and Document Relics

A ritual is a customary activity or series of actions performed in a given context. Sometimes there is no apparent reason or purpose for the activity, or the original justification has been lost. Rituals are often associated with relics, carefully preserved artifacts from the past.

A famous example of a process ritual is the cargo cult. During and immediately following the Second World War, groups of indigenous peoples in New Guinea fabricated all the surface manifestations of an airport, from cleared jungle runways to wooden headsets with bamboo "antennas." They were following the processes they had seen performed by military personnel when ordering a drop of cargo. But the airplanes and the goods never arrived.[12]

Most of us have encountered situations in which a paper document and the processes that it participates in have been frozen in time across numerous changes in document and workflow technology. The cause in most cases appears to be a shortsighted desire to simplify a document automation effort by exactly preserving printed forms and manual processes. But now no one knows why the forms look the way they do or why the process involves as many approval steps as it does.

For example in the Course Approval System at the University of California, Berkeley, many aspects of the original printed Course Approval Form have survived for decades in computer systems despite having little or no contemporary value. One such relic on the current form is a data item for the Short Title of the course, a shortened form of the complete course title needed in the 1980s when course registration used 80-column computer punch cards. The form also contains a list of course format codes that includes some types of courses not taught for decades with codes that are meaningless. Finally, the form contains data entry fields for tracking the state of the approval process that would be unnecessary if the process were effectively automated.

What this means is that even when a business copies a pattern exactly it is best to be equally meticulous at extracting and preserving the contextual understanding it contains so that it can improve the processes if necessary. This is the approach Intel takes when it uses the slogan of "Copy Exactly" as it copies everything about the plant where a new microprocessor was developed to the facilities where it will be manufactured: "everything at the development plant – the process flow, equipment set, suppliers, plumbing, manufacturing clean room, and training methodologies - is selected to meet high volume needs, recorded, and then copied exactly to the high-volume plant."[13] Intel credits this strategy with substantially increasing quality and reducing time to market.

But Intel follows equally disciplined methods for updating technologies and processes in its network of identical manufacturing plants. Any changes must be implemented in parallel everywhere with continuous information sharing between the installations to ensure that they remain the same in every respect.

And while it is possible for Intel to continuously improve its internal processes even while exactly copying them, a firm may not be able to change its processes after they are implemented because of their connections to external processes that it can't control. The benefits from improving processes must always be weighed against the cost of changing them, and when others must pay some of the costs it may be difficult to persuade them to change.

10.5 CHOOSING APPROPRIATE PATTERNS

The inherent flexibility in our description of processes, the diversity of the sources of information about them, and the varying levels of abstraction of the information we gather make it inevitable that many different patterns will seem appropriate.

This is often desirable because evaluating a variety of potential process patterns can encourage innovation. Choosing the most appropriate pattern means selecting the one that best satisfies the requirements of the context of use. We evaluate pattern alternatives by instantiating the roles and testing the rules of the pattern using the requirements we identified during process analysis.

Evaluating a variety of potential process patterns encourages innovation

Selecting the most appropriate pattern can thus be somewhat subjective, and the choice might be based on which pattern provides the most insight about the target context. One pattern may describe the existing processes (the As-Is model) better than another, but another might more clearly illustrate the changes that would make the processes more robust or effective (the To-Be model).

10.5.1 VALIDATING REQUIREMENTS VS. DISCOVERING THEM

The benefits of applying broadly relevant, generalized patterns must be balanced against those that arise when an existing pattern closely fits a well-defined context. For example, a highly abstract and general pattern, such as the one for procurement in Figure 8-3, describes many situations but lacks the precision to satisfy all the business rules of complex contexts. If our context were "German automaker buying from a US supplier of industrial chemicals," it would be better to start with a more specialized pattern that is already tailored to the target requirements. It is easier to validate the requirements of a specific pattern than to discover and formalize those needed to contextualize a general one. It is also easier to assess the comparative costs and benefits for the parties involved in the more detailed context assumed by a specific pattern.

10.5.2 REINFORCING CONTEXTS WITH PATTERNS

But in addition to satisfying contextual requirements, using a pattern also reinforces an interpretation of the context by emphasizing some requirements and business rules more than others.

Using a pattern reinforces an interpretation of the context by emphasizing some requirements more than others

For example, earlier we described Dell as a computer manufacturer because we wanted to highlight its Make-to-Order manufacturing pattern and focus on its relationships with organizations in its supply chain. But if we wanted to emphasize Dell's direct sales model, we would apply a pattern with a set of requirements and business rules associated with direct distribution.

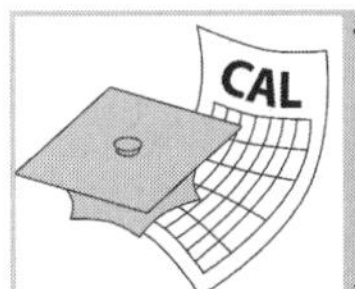

The Berkeley Event Calendar processes could be described using a syndication pattern, which emphasizes content or catalog management and distribution processes, or using a supply chain pattern, which highlights production, scheduling, and inventory management processes. Abstracting the business process this way allows us to consider business process libraries (such as the RosettaNet PIPs) for potentially re-usable collaboration patterns.

Figure 10-6 shows the reuse of a syndication pattern (based on the RosettaNet Distribute Product Catalog Information pattern - PIP2A1). In this scenario, the collaboration of Publish Calendar is based on a calendar being treated as a syndicated product. The suppliers/providers of calendar products/events wish to get them to buyers/public who can easily find the products/events they want to purchase/attend. As an optional feature of this pattern, a notification message advises buyers/public of new products/events.

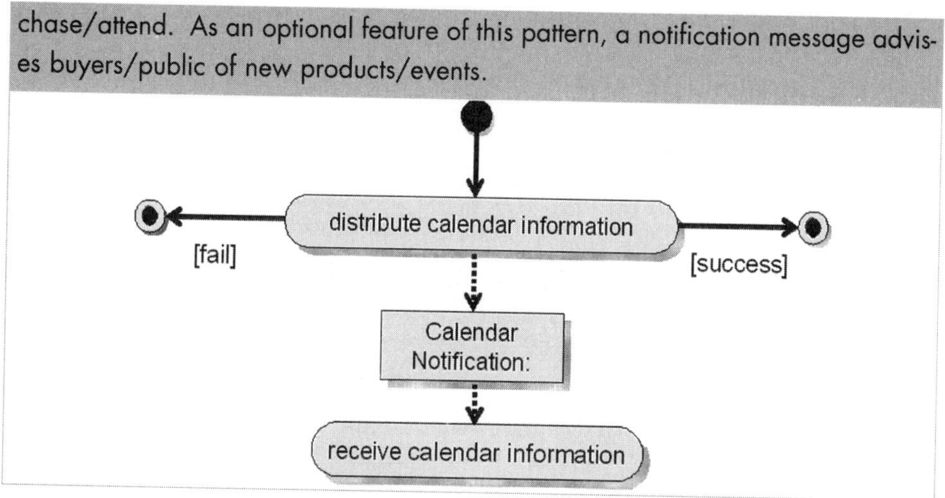

Figure 10-6 Publish Event using a Syndication Pattern

But we can also view this collaboration as a reuse of a supply chain pattern (for example, the RosettaNet pattern for Distribute Inventory Report – PIP4C1). Here the scenario is based on treating the events that form a calendar as inventory.

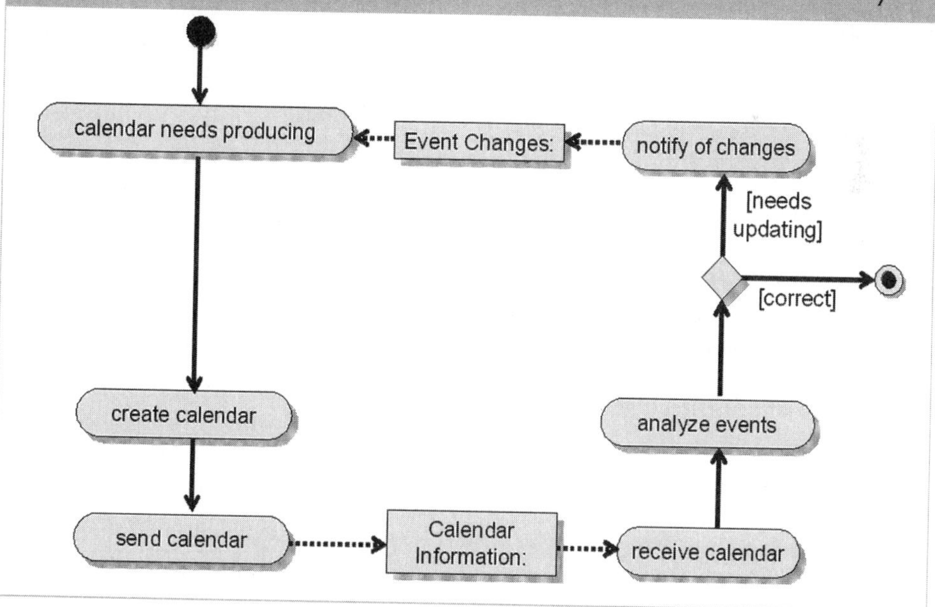

Figure 10-7 Publish Event using a Supply Chain Pattern

In the pattern shown in Figure 10-7, producers/providers of inventory/calendars want to keep their inventory/calendars up to date and remove expired stock/events.

Naturally there will be customization differences between these patterns. For many kinds of goods, expired goods aren't desirable so they get removed from the inventory report. Expired events, on the other hand, help people understand the nature of events likely to appear on a calendar so they should not be removed; expiration is implied by their date being in the past.

The choice between syndication and supply chain patterns here is important, because it highlights different factors and concerns in the context of use. The supply chain pattern seems a better fit because it calls attention to the critical mass problem: without a steady stream of events from different sources, there would be no benefit of shared content.

10.5.3 APPLYING PATTERNS TO ACHIEVE INSIGHT

Sometimes we can get new insights about a business problem or inefficiency by trying to apply a pattern to a context substantially different from its usual ones. The pattern will probably not fit the target context well enough to be used as the To-Be model, but this design exercise is a way of thinking that forces us to take a fresh and almost metaphorical look at the roles and rules that the pattern entails.

We can get new insights about a business problem or inefficiency when we apply a pattern to a substantially different context

Suppose we apply the general patterns of component-based manufacturing and supply chains to the university, treating it as a factory from which students buy their degrees. This isn't an entirely new metaphor; schools with low academic standards are sometimes derogatorily described as "diploma mills." We can apply the Supply Chain Operations Reference (SCOR) pattern (Figure 4-2) to the university by treating it as the manufacturer that drives the supply chain. This makes the university course catalog a multivendor catalog (Section 4.3.1.3) that aggregates the products offered by the competing suppliers, the various schools or academic departments. The students are the buyers who hope to obtain a valuable degree by paying the university to enforce graduation requirements, which are analogous in the supply chain to the bill of materials for each manufactured product. Finally, selecting courses and registering for classes each term are analogous specializations of the sourcing and ordering transactions in the procurement process.

Why do some courses and majors always have wait lists while others fail to meet their enrollment targets? Interpreting the supply chain pattern in the university context gives us some insight about these typical mismatches between supply and demand that plague students and university officials. SCOR tells us that every supply chain should have a rigorous planning phase with binding commitments where possible between buyers and suppliers to make demand predictable. But most universities don't control their supply chains with this degree of sophistication, and most lack any equivalents to supply chain processes and documents like Forecasts, Inventory Reports, and Commitment to Supply, whose use might reduce these typical problems.[14]

Of course, factors like faculty tenure limit the application of these control mechanisms in the university supply chain, and applying that pattern disregards the essential role of the university as a research institution. So when we gave students at UC Berkeley the assignment to apply the Make-to-Order pattern (used so successfully by Dell Computer as a computer manufacturer) to the university's operations, many of them initially resisted the extent of commercialization implied by viewing themselves as product consumers and their professors as product suppliers. Later, though, after applying the commercial patterns to a new domain and thinking about the implications, most students appreciated that a "Dell-iversity" might offer them more course choices and personalized majors.

10.6 ADAPTING PATTERNS

Even if a process pattern fits the target context requirements in most respects, it might need to be adapted to improve efficiency, reduce costs, or satisfy other business goals.

Even if a process pattern mostly fits the target context requirements, it might need to be adapted

For example, for products that are highly configurable with components that suffer from rapid obsolescence, it is advantageous to adapt the drop shipment pattern so that a distributor, instead of shipping finished goods from inventory, performs some final assembly to customize the inventoried goods. This modified pattern, called channel assembly, was introduced in the late 1990s by indirect retailers of personal computers to enable them to compete better with direct retailers like Dell.[15]

Adapting a pattern may involve consolidating roles. For example, the drop shipment pattern distinguishes the roles of the distributor and shipper but does not require that they be carried out by different enterprises. So for products like spare parts for which timely delivery to the customer is essential, pre-positioning the inventory to delivery service distribution hubs near customers can dramatically reduce delivery times while reducing transportation costs. This colocation of the distributor and shipper roles is sometimes called field stocking and is one of many logistics services offered by UPS.[16]

There is no sharp line at which changes to an existing pattern are substantial enough to consider the adapted pattern a newly invented one. Business process patterns are certainly evolutionary, but the family boundaries are blurred.

Business process patterns are evolutionary, but the family boundaries are blurred

Channel assembly can be considered a minor adaptation of drop shipment because the basic role of the distributor does not change when it takes on some assembly responsibilities. But field stocking is a somewhat more substantial adaptation because it eliminates one of the roles through consolidation.

Another adaptation of drop shipment called hosted drop shipment also changes the basic pattern in a radical way. As used by Amazon.com, this pattern nearly eliminates the traditional role of the retailer. The Amazon Merchant Platform, which uses software Amazon developed for its own book-selling business, enables Amazon to carry out the catalog management, shopping cart, and personalization services for the retailer. This makes the actual retailer almost completely virtual because it does little more than decide what products to sell and the distributors from which to drop ship them. The retailer follows this pattern by uploading its product information to Amazon.com as XML documents using web services.[17]

10.7 INSTANTIATING PATTERNS TO CREATE NEW MODELS

After a process pattern is identified, selected and adapted it must then be instantiated for the specific context of use. To do this we begin by designating the actors, organizations, or enterprises that will carry out the generic roles and activities defined in the pattern. Then we must configure the collaboration and transaction properties that implement business rules like quality of service levels or other guarantees about how the process behaves.

10.7.1 INSTANTIATING ROLES

When we instantiate roles in a pattern we need to consider the existing technology environments, organizational and business relationships, as well as any competition, trust or antitrust concerns. For example, are some enterprises XML-capable while others only support EDI? Is there a market operator who is a neutral participant or is there a dominant buyer or seller? What preexisting relationships or agreements must be preserved or strengthened? We may need to apply some bias when we assign roles to accommodate factors like these.

In Chapter 1 we introduced GMBooks.com as an instantiation of the drop shipment pattern, which includes four primary roles for the retailer, the distributor, the delivery service provider, and the credit authority. GMBooks.com, like many Internet startups, might have instantiated the drop shipment pattern in a bottom-up way, trying to copy successful Internet-only firms like Amazon.com as implementation patterns.

But it would have been better for GMBooks.com to take a more strategic and top-down route to choosing the pattern. Starting with the intention of opening a bookstore, GMBooks.com might have considered traditional retailing with a physical bookstore and inventory, a hybrid model of a store with an Internet presence, and the

Internet-only business. The latter approach with more systematic analysis of a range of patterns would have given GMBooks.com better insights about the advantages and disadvantages of using drop shipment or one of its adaptations as a process pattern.

When we instantiate the marketplace pattern, we need to specify the market operator, market participants, and service providers. The market participants are often the suppliers and distributors in the supply chain centered on a dominant enterprise that also operates the marketplace. The services that are most useful depend on the industry, geography, and other characteristics of the context in which the pattern is being adopted.

10.7.2 CONFIGURING COLLABORATION AND TRANSACTION PROPERTIES

The level of granularity below the business process patterns goes from business collaborations down to transaction patterns.

In Section 9.6 we described the six transaction patterns that come from ebXML: Offer and Acceptance, Request and Response, Request and Confirm, Query and Response, Notification, and Information Distribution. The contrasts between these patterns reflect whether the two parties already have a business relationship, which affects their obligations to each other and the need for acknowledgments.

But in any contextualized implementation of these patterns, we often need to make finer distinctions. Because of varying business rules and technology capabilities, the same transaction pattern can work differently within a particular collaboration for specific trading communities, supply chains, or marketplaces.

Even the routine collaboration of order management that combines the order process for a buyer with the sales process for the seller has dozens of permutations depending on the responses, changes, and cancellations allowed.[18] For example, some buyers would want to receive an explicit acknowledgement for every order; some sellers may only want to send acknowledgements for orders that cannot be fully filled. If they want to do business with each other, one or both must compromise.

An order-driven demand chain must necessarily operate faster than a forecast-driven supply chain. This speedup typically derives in part from faster information flow enabled by improved information technology, but also from the commitment of the participating businesses to work faster and respond more rapidly to requests or information from each other.

These different kinds of contextual configurations are enabled by properties (or metadata) that further define the rules of collaborations and transactions to tell the participating businesses precisely what to expect from each other. These are called collaboration or transaction properties.

Each transaction or collaboration pattern has a characteristic profile of properties

Each transaction or collaboration pattern has a characteristic profile of collaboration properties. Sometimes these profiles are set by a market operator or industry consortium to guarantee acceptable service levels for all participants in some specified context or trading community. These profiles are represented in a trading partner agreement or Service Level Agreement (SLA) between the collaborating parties that specifies their roles and mutual obligations with respect to reliability, performance, security, problem resolution, and a host of other dimensions that define their relationship in objective terms.

A large enterprise is likely to have different agreements for the same process conducted with business partners of varying capabilities. For example, some small or technologically unsophisticated partners might use email or web forms, and they can't respond as quickly or handle the same transaction volumes as those using fully automated document exchanges or web services.

10.7.2.1 Time-based Properties

The lifespan of business collaborations and their transactions can range from seconds to days, weeks, or longer. For very short transactions that involve little processing or decision making such as verifying a credit card or checking inventory, the response can come quickly.

For long running business transactions, however, it may take some time for the recipient of a business document to determine how to respond to it. During that time, the process that initiated the transaction might not be able to do anything. So it is good practice to send business signals (Section 9.5) when the document has been received or when it is validated so the sender knows that the recipient's processing has begun. When the recipient must send receipt and confirmation signals is specified by the Time to Acknowledge Receipt and the Time to Acknowledge Acceptance properties, respectively.

A more important time-based property is the Time to Respond (or time to perform). This is the time in which a recipient of a document must respond with the next document in the business transaction. For example, this property might specify how long a supplier can take to decide whether to accept a purchase order.

Because every delay with a supplier ripples through the chain to lower tiers that contain that supplier's suppliers, well-managed supply chains impose and measure tight performance requirements with time-based transaction properties. The RosettaNet specification for the Request Purchase Order PIP 3A4 sets Time to Acknowledge Receipt at 2 hours and Time to Respond at 24 hours.[19] Dell's legendary efficiency in building computers to order requires almost ruthless performance standards for its suppliers, who must respond to component orders so efficiently that they never have more than two hours worth of inventory in a Dell manufacturing plant.[20]

10.7.2.2 Other Properties

Three other properties might need to be configured to meet the contextual requirements of transaction or collaboration patterns:

- *Authorization Required.* The partner role sending the message must sign the document and the recipient must validate the signature and the role associated with the signature.

- *Non-Repudiation of Origin and Content.* The sender must store the business document in its original form for a mutually agreed duration; the nonrepudiation process includes validating the identity of the sender and the integrity of the content.

- *Non-Repudiation of Receipt.* The sender of the receipt must store the Acknowledgement Receipt for the mutually agreed time period; the nonrepudiation process includes validating the identity of the sender and the integrity of the content.

These properties are especially important in contexts involving high-value transactions or actions that are expensive or impossible to undo.

10.8 USING PATTERNS TO SUGGEST INFORMATION COMPONENTS AND DOCUMENTS

Every business collaboration and its transactions has requirements for the information components they produce and consume. Business analysts sometimes refer to these components as the business entities or business objects of the business process. The complete models for these information components and for the document into which they are assembled emerge only with careful analysis of existing documents, other information sources, and business rules. But some of the information components and documents will be suggested by process patterns.

10.8.1 KEY INFORMATION COMPONENTS

Most business processes will have multiple instances of the same unit of work being carried on at the same time. For example, in the procurement process a supplier will exchange documents with many buyers and vice versa. The process thus needs information to distinguish the participants in these parallel and interleaved business transactions and to identify the document instances associated with each of them. Furthermore, many business collaborations consist of a chain or choreography of documents that are interrelated because each contains information that flows from one document and process to another. We can consider this as a kind of memory of the collaboration.

There may also be a requirement to reconcile the information on a series of business documents, such as Order with Invoice, Statement with Remittance Advice, Dispatch with Receipt or Claim with Payment documents.

So every process model needs information components that link threads of related document instances within the process. We could describe these as the component patterns within processes, but that's a bit confusing. Instead we will call them the key information components.

Every process model needs information components that link threads of related document instances within the process

Key information components include, but are not limited to, the following types:

- Identifiers for the transactions or the documents within them. These might be business-based like Purchase Order Number, Order Reference, and Invoice Numbers, or application-based, like time stamps or message identifiers.

- Identifiers for the participants in the process. These might be instantiated as Social Security numbers, employee IDs, business registration numbers, D-U-N-S numbers, or other unique or contextually unique values.

- Identifiers for the product or service that is mentioned in the transaction so that authoritative information about it can be retrieved from any process that involves it (pricing, ordering, invoicing, shipping, etc.). A unique Global Trade Item Number (GTIN) can be obtained from an international "article numbering" organization. A similar goal motivates the Unique Consignment Reference number (UCR) proposed by the World Customs Organization[22] to access information about goods shipped in international trade.

- Integration or interoperability information, such as values or codes used by processing applications or ERP systems.

We inevitably discover key information components when we ask about business transactions (see Section 9.4), and standards like the RosettaNet PIPs document the information components that are generally required to implement the transaction.

However, the generic recommendations in the standard PIPs may be superseded by trading partner agreements or implementation guidelines for more specific contexts.[23]

In the Event Calendar, a component known as Submission Identification is used to distinguish submission transactions. Components for Authorized Party and Event Identification are used to identify event submissions as they move through the business processes.

10.8.2 THE DOCUMENT CHECKLIST

In addition to identifying key information components, business process analysis typically yields the names of actual or potential documents produced or required by transactions. This in an inevitable result of what we called the Yin and Yang of processes and documents, since at the transactional level they are essentially the dynamic and static views of the same thing (Section 3.4.5). Our As-Is process models or the To-Be models captured in process patterns often name the transactions with Verb-Noun pairs like Request Catalog or Make Payment, where each Noun is a placeholder for the document payload of the Verb process (see Figure 9-5 for an example).

Business process analysis typically yields the names of actual or potential documents

These document placeholders, along with the key information components, create the link between process modeling and document modeling in the Document Engineering approach. If we use a process pattern as our To-Be model, we move on to document and information analysis with a template or checklist to assist us in finding or designing the documents needed to implement the process. The process pattern may help us discover that some documents and information components in our As-Is model are either unnecessary or missing, and so we can improve our processes if we remove or provide them. This is the kind of insight we had when we applied the supply chain pattern to the university context in Section 10.5.3.

Let's revisit the Buy a Book process used by GMBooks.com, whose transactional patterns are shown in Figure 9-5 and whose collaborations are depicted in Figure 9-14.

We can transform these models into a Document Checklist to guide us in identifying the types of document we will need to implement this process. Figure 10-8 is an example of this modeling artifact. Its portrayal of the model shows the transaction patterns and their key information components as rows and the collaboration patterns as columns. We can then easily visualize where the documents are required.

	Procurement Process Pattern				
	Collaborations	**Request Service**	**Contract Formation**	**Payment**	**Distribution and Fulfilment**
Function	**Key Information Components**				
Request details of item(s)	Product Identifier, Customer Identifier	X			
Provide ordering details	Product Description	X			
Request item(s)	Product Identifier, Customer Identifier, Quantity		X		
Acknowledge commitment to fulfill request	Order Identification, Status		X		
Request delivery of item(s)	Product Identifier, Customer Identifier, Destination, Quantity				X
Confirm sending of item(s)	Product Identifier, Customer Identifier, Destination, Quantity, Shipment Identifier, Date				X
Confirm delivery of item(s)	Product Identifier, Customer Identifier, Destination, Quantity, Shipment Identifier, Date				X
Enquire about status of item(s)	Shipment Identifier, Status	X			X
Advise on status of item(s)	Shipment Identifier, Status	X			X
Notify of required payment	Product Identifier, Customer Identifier, Quantity, Amount			X	
Request funds transfer	Invoice Identifier, Customer Identifier, Amount			X	
Acknowledge funds transfer	Invoice Identifier, Customer Identifier, Amount, Status			X	

Figure 10-8. A Procurement Process Document Checklist

In this checklist, the key information components will occur in more than one type of document. To put it another way, if a component appears in only one type of document, it is either not a key component or a document type is missing from the model.

Of course, such checklists are just guides, and not all implementations will follow it exactly. But as we move on to the document and information component modeling phases, it gives us a useful point to start joining the models of process requirements with the models of information requirements.

10.9 KEY POINTS IN CHAPTER TEN

- Designing business processes more often involves applying and adapting patterns than inventing new ones.
- Sometimes our adaptations are successful enough to be imitated as pat-terns in their own right.
- We generalize patterns by relaxing or eliminating requirements in our context of use and assessing the resulting effects and dependencies that result.
- The granularity of an As-Is process model is shaped by the sources of information about processes and whether the analysis was more top-down or bottom-up.
- Coarser grained models suggest patterns that encourage new specializations.
- We can create composite process models by combining separate ones.
- Separate processes must have enough overlap in their goals and requirements to justify putting them together.
- Exact replication of a process can be a denial that patterns will and must evolve over time.
- It is easier to copy than to innovate because it isn't necessary to understand underlying motivations and conceptual models.
- Evaluating a variety of potential process patterns encourages innovation.

- Using a pattern reinforces an interpretation of the context by emphasizing some requirements more than others.
- We can get new insights about a business problem or inefficiency when we apply a pattern to a substantially different context.
- Even if a process pattern mostly fits the target context requirements, it will probably need to be adapted.
- Business process patterns are evolutionary, but the family boundaries are blurred.
- Each transaction or collaboration pattern has a characteristic profile of properties.
- Every process model needs information components that link threads of related document instances within the process.
- Business process analysis typically yields the names of actual or potential documents.

11 Analyzing Documents

11.0 INTRODUCTION

The ultimate goal of our document analysis is to create a conceptual model that encompasses all the information components for any documents required by the context of use. We refer to this domain view as a document component model. But we have some work to do to get there.

In Chapter 8 we discussed how analyzing requirements and rules for documents and business processes helps us establish the context for a Document Engineering effort. Starting in Chapter 9 we used these rules to identify the information exchanges that are required to carry out the processes of the desired business model. In Chapter 10 we then created a checklist of potential documents and their key components based on the business process model.

But as yet these document exchanges are still fairly coarse or unrefined as the payload of transactions. Most of the information components in the documents remain to be specified. In this chapter we will discuss the first phase of this work, identifying documents that will focus our further analysis. The modeling artifact that will emerge from this phase is a document inventory that lists the sources we identify along with metadata about their purposes, origins, and other attributes that will help us select a subset to analyze in detail.

In Chapter 12 we will take the document inventory and extract or harvest the information components potentially useful in our context. To ensure that the meaning of these components isn't biased by their manifestation in some specific physical implementation we also separate them from any specific presentations and structures in which we find them. In Chapter 13 we will aggregate or reassemble these semantic components into a document component model that satisfies the rules and requirements of our context of use.

11.1 WHAT ARE DOCUMENTS?

Documents exist because a self-contained package of related information is a good fit for the manner in which people and businesses interact with each other. Some types of common business documents like catalogs, orders, invoices, receipts, and double-entry ledgers have existed for centuries. In each case the type of document has evolved as an aggregation of information that suits the context of use and accommodates the cost of producing and processing the documents and the predictability or stability of their contents over time.

Of course, as new technologies emerged, the implementations of these documents changed. But the underlying concept of a document has been surprisingly stable. From clay tablets to parchment, paper, and then electronic bits, a tax receipt, for example, is still a document that records a transaction between one party and some entity with the authority to collect taxes from it.

The concept of a document has been surprisingly stable

New document types are often invented to support new processes and applications enabled by new technologies, and sometimes one type of document replaces another when a business process changes to take advantage of the new possibilities. For example, improved global communications and transport logistics have replaced negotiable Bills of Lading with Waybill documents. Similarly, reengineered supply chain processes are making Invoice documents unnecessary. Most noticeably, we have seen many new types of documents develop as paper-based publications go on the Web and become more dynamic and interactive.

On a personal level, we are receiving and writing fewer checks as electronic funds transfers and online banking take hold. We've also seen the emergence of new types of documents for our personalized and information collections like MP3 playlists and instant messaging buddy lists.

11.2 CREATING THE INVENTORY

Whether documents are traditional or brand new, we need to identify and understand them because they are the most visible parts of the processes that people and businesses carry out.

Our first task is to identify any relevant documents and information sources that will form the basis of our document inventory. For example, when GMBooks.com implements its drop shipment business model it might populate a checklist like that in Figure 11-1.

		GMBooks.com Procurement Process				
		Collaborations	Request Service	Contract Formation	Payment	Distribution and Fulfilment
Transaction	Function	Key Information Components				
Request Catalog	Request details of item(s)	Book Identifier, Customer Identifier	Book Query			
Provide Catalog	Provide ordering details	Book Description	Catalog Query Response			
Place Order	Request item(s)	Book Identifier, Customer Identifier, Quantity		Purchase Order		
Acknowledge Order	Acknowledge commitment to fulfill request	Order Identification, Status		Shopping Cart		
Book Shipment	Request delivery of item(s)	Book Identifier, Customer Identifier, Destination, Quantity				Shipping Note
Notify of Goods Dispatch	Confirm sending of item(s)	Book Identifier, Customer Identifier, Destination, Quantity, Shipment Identifier, Date		Acknowledge Shipment		Dispatch Advice
Notify of Goods Received	Confirm delivery of item(s)	Book Identifier, Customer Identifier, Destination, Quantity, Shipment Identifier, Date				Receipt Advice
Query Delivery Status	Enquire about status of item(s)	Shipment Identifier, Status	Status Query			Shipment Query
Notify of Delivery Status	Advise on status of item(s)	Shipment Identifier, Status	Status Response			Shipment Report
Present Invoice	Notify of required payment	Book Identifier, Customer Identifier, Quantity, Amount			Shopping Cart Total	
Make Payment	Request funds transfer	Invoice Identifier, Customer Identifier, Amount			Transaction Advice	
Confirm Payment	Acknowledge funds transfer	Invoice Identifier, Customer Identifier, Amount, Status			Remittance Advice	

Figure 11-1. The GMBooks.com Document Inventory Matrix

If we contrast this with the checklist in Figure 10-5 (which was derived from the standard procurement pattern) we can see that this implementation uses an additional type of document for acknowledging the shipment of goods. There is also a document known as Shopping Cart that acknowledges orders and notifies the buyer about the required payment.

While business process models and patterns can indicate likely documents, creating an accurate inventory requires more subtle analysis

What this tells us is that while business process models and patterns can indicate likely documents, creating an accurate document inventory requires more subtle analysis. In particular we have to face two kinds of challenges:

- We need to keep an open mind about what a document is and be patient in finding them, because much of what we need to analyze may not be in a traditional document form.

- We need to overcome organizational barriers that can prevent us from locating candidate information sources.

11.2.1 DOCUMENT ARCHAEOLOGY AND ANTHROPOLOGY

Much of what we need to analyze may not look very much like a document. Much of it looks more like data or software—things like sets of database tables, spreadsheets, accounting systems, printed or web forms, and descriptions of application program interfaces (including the code that implements them). There may also be metadata about documents in the form of written or formal specifications of schema, style guides, or standard document models or pattern libraries.

Last but not least, there could be unwritten or tacit information available only from the people involved in the creation, exchange, and use of the documents.

Our goal is to identify all the potentially relevant sources of components within our context of use, but this is inherently an iterative task. We locate documents, which may refer or link to other documents, and we locate people who work with the documents, who may refer to other documents or people.

Identifying all the sources of components is an iterative task

We must balance the complementary perspectives of the archaeologist and the anthropologist as we discover and interpret the information sources. The archaeologist struggles to interpret document artifacts, legacy data sources or forms and their associated business processes that were created by organizations or people who are no longer there to help. The anthropologist studies people and phenomena in their natural surroundings with an open, nonjudgmental mind. We can use interviews or questionnaires to find out how people think they use documents and information, but sometimes they tell us the conventional wisdom, their organizational policy, or whatever they think we want to hear. And even when they think they are telling us the truth, they may be wrong. That's when the archaeologist's perspective takes over and lets the information artifacts speak for themselves.

The anthropologist's perspective frees us from assuming that the methods or strategies that people use for organizing and storing documents are entirely rational, because they certainly aren't. People differ substantially in how they use information and documents, even in the same organization. A classic 1983 study by Malone[1] contrasted the strategies and methods of "filers" and "pilers." Filers maintain clean desktops and systematically organize their papers, while pilers have messy work areas and make few attempts at organization. Malone's work suggests that it would be useful to seek out an organization's filers to help identify the types of documents that are important to its functions and processes.

But more recent studies[2] of how people manage their personal document archives lead to the counterintuitive suggestion that pilers may be better informants in the document inventory activity. Filers are often inexperienced workers who are unsure of a document's relevance and file many documents without reading them, often rationalizing that they are deferring judgments about value but in fact never revisiting the documents. In contrast, many pilers are experienced workers who can readily identify what is worth keeping and know which colleagues or organizational repositories maintain the most authoritative or comprehensive document collections. We hesitate to suggest that we begin our document inventory with the person who has the most interesting looking piles of documents, but this is probably a better strategy than starting at random.

The document anthropologist also does not assume that the names given to documents fit the people, tasks, and organizations in which we locate them. Sometimes documents have names that might once have been accurate or appropriate but no longer reflect their current value to the work of the organization. Thinking in terms of requirements and function and observing what people do is more likely to lead to the appropriate documents and to a correct assessment of their value.

Thinking in terms of what people do is more likely to lead to the appropriate documents

For example, a shipping clerk's responsibility is not to fill out shipping forms but to get stuff from one place to another. An equipment operator or factory mechanic's job is not to read operations and maintenance manuals but to keep the machines and equipment running. They might be getting their jobs done even though they aren't completing or consulting the nominally relevant documents. We might find that handwritten job aids, cheat sheets, sticky notes attached to computer monitors or equipment, and other unofficial documents are more useful and essential. Sometimes documents whose names suggest they are essential to initiating a process are created afterward simply to ensure compliance with an outdated audit process.

Finally, when we ask people to provide samples of relevant documents, they may give us what is readily available to them or what they can afford to do without. Maybe they don't understand why we want them, and they aren't predisposed to be helpful (they might think our goal is to automate a business process that will eliminate or de-skill their job). An incomplete or biased document inventory won't yield the complete set of information components we're trying to discover; it is like trying to determine what library books are most important by studying what's on the shelves even though many of the most important books are those that are checked out. Occasionally we have to ask people to provide us with documents a second time, after we've gotten them to trust us.

11.2.2 UNDERSTANDING THE ORGANIZATION

One of the most helpful documents to locate when beginning a document inventory is the organization chart. It can suggest the functions and business processes conducted by different parts of the enterprise, identify the people most likely to know about them, and help us maintain the critical boundary between what is in and out of scope.

An organizational model provides clues about the patterns of information exchange we are likely to find

A firm's organizational model also provides strong clues about the patterns of public and private document exchanges we are likely to find. Functionally organized firms, which have separately managed departments or divisions for product management, engineering, human resources, sales, and so on, minimize the need to exchange information or coordinate across organizational boundaries to get work done. In such firms each document or information source is likely to have a single origin and the requirements for it are more likely to be consistent and clearly identifiable.

In a cross-functional organization, some of the core business activities are duplicated across product lines, customer segments, or geographies. For example, General Motors has divisions for Cadillac, Oldsmobile, Saturn, and so on, and the University of California has separately run campuses in Berkeley, Los Angeles, San Diego, and other locations. A cross-functional organization requires more coordination and information exchange between business units. In addition, the redundancy inherent in this organizational model means that there will be many sources for the same types of document and some ambiguity about its definition and requirements.

Unfortunately we can't always take the organization chart at face value. It is tempting to assume that job titles and formal organizational structure reflect what people actually do. But these can be misleading, and a document anthropologist treats them cautiously. Sometimes the organization chart hasn't kept up with the ongoing activities of promotions, reassignments, organizational mergers and divisions that take place in any large enterprise. Sometimes people treat the organization chart as a convenient fiction about how work is carried out and deliberately work around the official accounting and responsibility structures in the firm. The latter situation is especially common when the organizational model reflects an inefficient topology or architecture imposed by legacy systems.

11.2.3 GENERIC INVENTORY PROCEDURES AND QUESTIONS

On large projects where the inventory spans many organizations, it can be helpful to have a team of analysts tracking down documents and information sources. This ensures that the inventory defines a reasonably stable snapshot of the information requirements. Another benefit is that a team can often make better judgments about what to collect and what to analyze in detail than a single person can.

Of course, if more than one person is assembling the document inventory, other challenges can arise. The same document might have different names in different parts of the firm, or different documents might go by the same name. This problem often arises in very large or multinational enterprises where geographical, political, or cultural differences in laws or local customs can affect business practices and the terminology they use. For example, most economies have different names for the documents that deal with retirement investment savings, superannuation, pension plans, and savings bonds. They use a range of terms to define practices, such as paid time off from work, which might be called a holiday, a vacation, or paid leave.

In large inventory efforts it is essential that everyone follow the same procedures and collect sufficient metadata about each potential information source to resolve these sorts of issues. The information collected must be consistent or we can't make the right decisions about what sources to analyze in detail.

We've developed a set of standard questions that will help capture some of the most important information about the documents in use.

For documents received by an organization, we can ask the following questions:

- What is the official name of the document? Does it also have other informal or unofficial names?
- From whom (or in what process) do you receive the document?
- Why do you receive it?
- What are you expected to do with it?
- How often do you receive it?
- What events trigger the sender's actions?
- Does the document contain all the information you need for the process for which the document is received?
- Does the document contain information that is unnecessary for the process?
- What do you do with the document after your process has been carried out?
- To whom (or to which organization) do you send it?

And for documents sent by the organization, we ask:

- What is the official name of the document? Does it also have other informal or unofficial names?
- To whom (or what process) do you send the document?
- Why do you send it?
- What do you expect the recipient to do with it?
- How often do you send it?
- What events trigger your actions?
- Does the document need to conform to any standards for content, structure, or presentation?
- What does the recipient do with the document after their process has been carried out?

As we follow our anthropological approach to understand the connections between documents and people, we should constantly remind ourselves of the requirements and business rules we've identified for our overall effort. Our ultimate goal is to design new documents and processes that enhance the efficiency and effectiveness of people and organizations in a particular context, so we need to make sure that our inventory includes everything that will contribute to that goal.

Our ultimate goal is designs that enhance the efficiency and effectiveness of organizations in a particular context

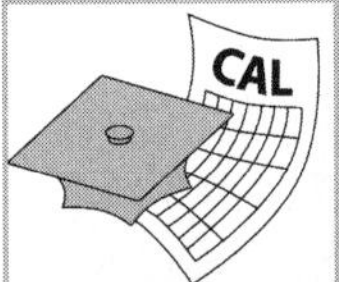

For the Berkeley Event Calendar project, the inventory identified scores of calendars and associated forms for describing calendar events within the Berkeley.edu domain. These calendars included those published for academic departments, sports schedules, music concerts, exhibitions, course timetables and capital works schedules. As such, the majority of the documents were toward the narrative end of the Document Type Spectrum, rich with presentational features. However, some of these calendars were supported by more transactional types of documents such as data entry forms. The variety of the calendars is indicated in Figure 11-2.

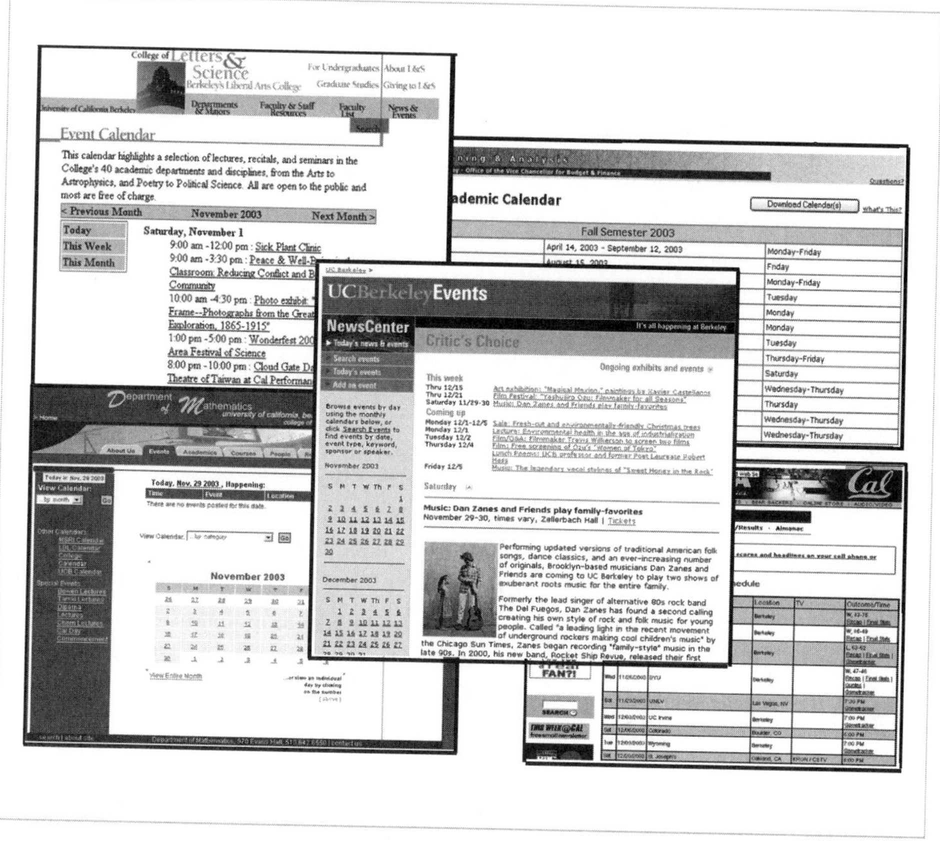

Figure 11-2. Some of the Calendars in the Berkeley.edu Domain

The inventory also included the work of the IETF iCalendar project (a standard specification for the exchange of calendar information) and the supplementary Structured Knowledge Initiative (SKICal) that contextualized iCalendar for public events (concerts, sports competitions, conferences, and so on).

In addition, the inventory included interviews of the many people who publish calendars or support the software applications used by them.

11.3 SAMPLING THE INVENTORY

It is unlikely that we'll be able to analyze everything in the document inventory in detail, so we may need to create a smaller sample. Some of the criteria for this sample are relatively objective and reflect characteristics of the documents and information sources. Others are more subjective and reflect organizational, political, or strategic considerations.

11.3.1 SAMPLING BASED ON DOCUMENT CHARACTERISTICS

A useful factor to employ when deciding what documents to analyze is where they fall along the Document Type Spectrum (Figure 1-2). Documents that are more transactional will probably have more clearly defined components than narrative documents. Consider how easy it is to formally identify the individual components of a transactional form (with labels or markup tags that identify the type of content they contain) and how hard it is for a search engine to decide what a narrative web page is about.[3]

CAL

If we compare the University of California's official online calendar in Figure 11-3 and the Add Event form for it in Figure 11-4.

Identifying the components of an event in the online calendar (Figure 11-3), which is primarily a narrative type of document, is harder than recognizing them in an event transaction form (Figure 11-4).

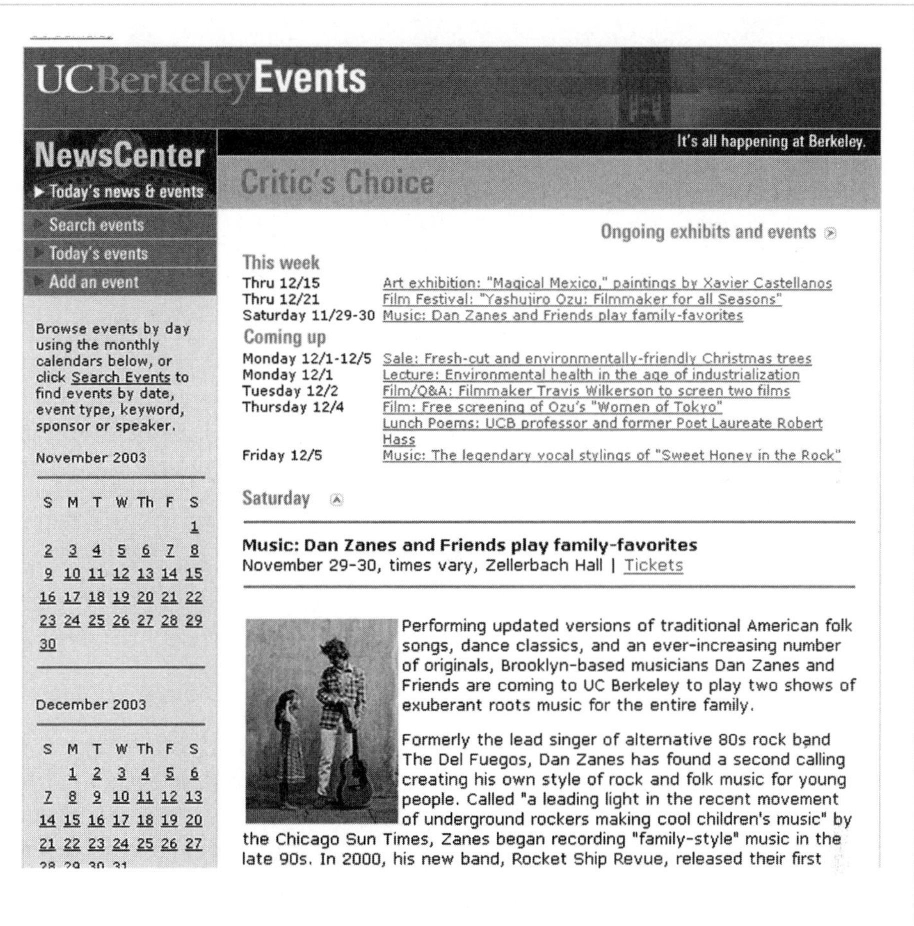
UCBerkeleyEvents
NewsCenter
▶ Today's news & events
Search events
Today's events
Add an event
It's all happening at Berkeley.
Critic's Choice
Ongoing exhibits and events
This week
Thru 12/15 Art exhibition: "Magical Mexico," paintings by Xavier Castellanos
Thru 12/21 Film Festival: "Yashujiro Ozu: Filmmaker for all Seasons"
Saturday 11/29-30 Music: Dan Zanes and Friends play family-favorites
Coming up
Monday 12/1-12/5 Sale: Fresh-cut and environmentally-friendly Christmas trees
Monday 12/1 Lecture: Environmental health in the age of industrialization
Tuesday 12/2 Film/Q&A: Filmmaker Travis Wilkerson to screen two films
Thursday 12/4 Film: Free screening of Ozu's "Women of Tokyo"
Lunch Poems: UCB professor and former Poet Laureate Robert Hass
Friday 12/5 Music: The legendary vocal stylings of "Sweet Honey in the Rock"
Browse events by day using the monthly calendars below, or click Search Events to find events by date, event type, keyword, sponsor or speaker.
November 2003
S M T W Th F S
1
2 3 4 5 6 7 8
9 10 11 12 13 14 15
16 17 18 19 20 21 22
23 24 25 26 27 28 29
30
December 2003
S M T W Th F S
1 2 3 4 5 6
7 8 9 10 11 12 13
14 15 16 17 18 19 20
21 22 23 24 25 26 27
Saturday
Music: Dan Zanes and Friends play family-favorites
November 29-30, times vary, Zellerbach Hall | Tickets
Performing updated versions of traditional American folk songs, dance classics, and an ever-increasing number of originals, Brooklyn-based musicians Dan Zanes and Friends are coming to UC Berkeley to play two shows of exuberant roots music for the entire family.
Formerly the lead singer of alternative 80s rock band The Del Fuegos, Dan Zanes has found a second calling creating his own style of rock and folk music for young people. Called "a leading light in the recent movement of underground rockers making cool children's music" by the Chicago Sun Times, Zanes began recording "family-style" music in the late 90s. In 2000, his new band, Rocket Ship Revue, released their first

Figure 11-3. The University of California's Official Online Calendar

Refresh
NewsCenter
▶ Today's news & events
Calendar home
Search events
Today's events
Add an event

It's all happening at Berkeley.

Add an Event

Adding Event #1

After completing this form, you will have a chance to review your submission before it is listed in the online calendar and submitted to Berkeleyan.

After you submit an event, this screen will appear again, allowing you to post additional events. When you have no more events to submit, click the button below or here.

To make changes to an event that has already been submitted, e-mail that information to the calendar editor.

Required fields are marked with a *

*Date: [ ] to [ ]
e.g. 1/27/98
Put end date in second box if event continues over consecutive days.

*Title of Event: [ ]
125 Character limit

*Time: [ ] or [ ]
e.g. 9:00 am, 12:00 pm, or 3:30 pm
If more than one start time applies, enter those times in the second box.

Speaker: [ ]

Affiliation: [ ]
Title, department, institution

Location of Event: [ ]
Include specific address

Browse events by day using the monthly calendars below, or click "Search Events" to find events by date, event type, keyword, sponsor or speaker.

November 2003

S	M	T	W	Th	F	S
						1
2	3	4	5	6	7	8
9	10	11	12	13	14	15
16	17	18	19	20	21	22
23	24	25	26	27	28	29
30						

December 2003

S	M	T	W	Th	F	S
	1	2	3	4	5	6
7	8	9	10	11	12	13
14	15	16	17	18	19	20
21	22	23	24	25	26	27
28	29	30	31			

Figure 11-4. The Add an Event Form for the University of California's Official Online Calendar

For example, how can we identify the type of an event in Figure 11-3? Does the presence of a photograph as part of a calendar description imply that the event is a photography exhibition? Or is it a photo of the speaker in a lecture, or of an actor in a stage performance? We might not be able to tell.

In contrast, in the transactional Add an Event form in Figure 11-4, we easily see a defined set of possible values, information we can only infer from the calendar with our human interpretive skills.

This suggests that it is a good tactic to begin the sample with the transactional documents. We can use the information components we identify in these as clues to locate the components in more narrative documents.

Another consideration is the frequency of different types of document and the variety of instances within them. We can generally best identify business rules, constraints, and patterns when we see a range of representative instances. We must study the documents that are the most important to the organization, but raw frequency is only partly reliable as a guide.

Once again, our method is shaped by the Document Type Spectrum. We don't need to study many instances of transactional documents, even if they occur by the hundreds or thousands, because their content and structure is homogeneous and they're all essentially the same. For example, if we were conducting a document inventory for GMBooks.com, we'd certainly find lots of purchase orders, but we don't need to analyze many of them to harvest the components needed to describe them. There are often fewer instances of narrative documents like reports or technical publications, but their content and structure is more heterogeneous, and we might need to analyze more of them to understand the underlying requirements.

But this application of the Document Type Spectrum is modified by the context of our Document Engineering efforts. It is true that we don't need much analysis to determine that there is little regularity in content and structure if we compare two documents on the narrative end of the spectrum like Moby Dick and the Bible.[4] And it is easy to see common patterns if we compare a purchase order for a copy of Moby Dick and a purchase order for a copy of the Bible.[5] So, if our context of use is buying and selling books, we don't need to analyze many books or purchase orders to harvest the components needed to describe them. If, on the other hand, our context is publishing book reviews, we will need to analyze many more books than purchase orders to identify the appropriate components.

Less analysis is possible when the set of documents is very small and heterogeneous or when the tasks that users carry out are diverse or hard to specify. This is especially true when the document is unique or so important that we know it by name, like the Magna Carta, Declaration of Independence, or Gettysburg Address. While these could be analyzed as instances of document types for contract, formal announcement, and commemorative speech, respectively, what makes these document instances distinctive cannot be captured in a schema and cannot easily be reused in new documents. And how useful would it be to itemize the information components that form the Declaration of Independence?

In general, as the variation among the instances of a given type of published document increases and their number decreases, analyzing documents becomes more descriptive than prescriptive, and its purpose shifts toward identifying the markup for text encoding that captures the specific and idiosyncratic character of each instance.

Where rules are fewer, we need to analyze fewer components

This emphasizes that what we need to analyze is based on the requirements of our context of use. Where rules are fewer, we need to analyze fewer components. And because narrative style documents typically have fewer rules, they will also have fewer components. This is why we should expect to have many rules about the processes, content, structure, and semantics of a purchase order for a book but far fewer rules about the content of the book itself.

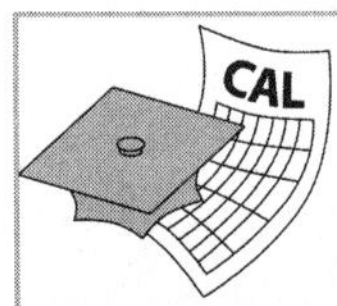

In the Berkeley Event Calendar inventory sample, the majority of the documents were narrative types, rich with presentational features. We found fewer transactional types of documents, which were used primarily for creating and managing events in the most important calendars.

This reflected the less formal business processes for small calendars. When a calendar didn't contain many events, the "create new event" process was less rigorous and events were often submitted in email or phone messages to the person in charge of the calendar.

We should also include in our analysis samples of any specific document instances that expose special rules or requirements. For example, if a wholesale procurement process may also occasionally permit direct retail purchases, the sample must also contain some of these different types of order documents.

Of course we want to analyze any documents that are especially important or authoritative, but we won't always know what these are at first. We should not assume that a document is significant because it has an important sounding title or classification or that it is unimportant because it has a mundane one. Sometimes extremely important or sensitive documents are given ordinary or uninteresting names to discourage people from reading them.[6] On the other hand, a document with a name like Style Guide or Standard is almost certainly important, but before assuming that it is a definitive specification, we should assess whether the instance documents actually conform to these rules.

This isn't always easy; if we simply ask people whether they follow the guide or standard, their answer is predictable. Once again we need to take the anthropologist's perspective and observe how people use the documents in their environment. A style guide or glossary stacked in a pile of unopened books has much less value to us than one sitting on someone's desk with coffee stains on it.

The hierarchical organization of the university into undergraduate and graduate divisions, and into schools with academic departments, makes some calendars more important than others and helps define the sets from which to sample. The functional organization of the university designates some calendars as official or authoritative and others as less so. These considerations helped winnow the complete list of calendars to 23 that merited careful analysis.

11.3.2 SAMPLING BASED ON OTHER CONSIDERATIONS

It is essential that the sample of documents and information sources that we select for careful analysis is representative of the inventory and sufficient to yield the requirements needed by the context. But even if creating the right sample to meet these goals is the highest priority, sometimes we must consider other factors when we define the sample.

Any document that is handled by more than a few departments or organizations is probably important enough to analyze carefully. But it may be necessary to include some types of documents in our sample that aren't as pervasive in the enterprise if they are created or used by people or organizations who can influence the overall success of our Document Engineering effort. It would be difficult to explain to an executive champion or project sponsor that the documents from his or her organization are not important enough or different enough to provide new requirements; it's better to analyze a few redundant documents and talk about them in our project status report than to explain why we rejected them. Likewise, our sample might include documents provided by CTOs, architects, or other influential technical people even if we have located them through other means.

We can easily rationalize the extra effort of including a few extra documents by reminding ourselves that the boundary between what is in and what is out of scope is always fuzzy and we can never create the optimally efficient or informative sample. Furthermore, the real value of the inventory doesn't emerge until we analyze it, the subject of the next chapter.

11.4 KEY POINTS IN CHAPTER ELEVEN

- The concept of a document has been surprisingly stable.
- While business process models and patterns can indicate likely documents, creating an accurate inventory requires more subtle analysis.
- Identifying all the sources of components is an iterative task.
- Thinking in terms of what people do is more likely to lead to the appropriate documents.
- Our ultimate goal is designs that enhance the efficiency and effectiveness of organizations in a particular context.
- Where rules are fewer, we need to analyze fewer components.

12

Analyzing Document Components

12.0 INTRODUCTION

So far in our Document Engineering approach we have identified requirements, rules, business processes, collaborations, transactions, and the document inventory for our context of use. A successful document inventory yields a variety of documents and information sources. Our next task is to look inside each of them to understand its components.

Our ability to understand the common semantics embodied in the inventory can be constrained by differences in how the documents or information sources are presented. To identify the concepts and meanings for our components, we need to see past these differences. Extracting the underlying semantic components from their physical implementations is called harvesting the inventory.

12.1 HARVESTING COMPONENTS

Each of the documents and information sources that we've selected from the inventory will yield a set of candidate components. We call them candidates because we don't yet know how useful they will be or whether they'll be part of the final document component model.

We aren't prescriptive at this stage about how much additional information or metadata should be collected about each candidate component, but it will include at least its name and description and any business rules. In addition, we can use the answers to the generic questions of Section 11.2.3 about the who, what, why, when, and where of each document in the inventory to help us understand their components.

The Modeling Artifacts for Harvesting Components

As a modeling artifact for organizing information about harvested components, we have found it useful to build a harvest table for each information source we analyze. Each row of this table begins with the name of the candidate component, either the one it already has when we harvest it or the one we invent for it. The other columns contain a description of the component and any constraints or rules we discover about it from interviews or observations.

In Section 12.2.1 we'll go through a detailed example showing how to merge the separate harvest tables into a single consolidated table of candidate components.

The most useful rules are instance rules that constrain possible values and semantic rules that describe dependencies between components.

As we'll see in the following sections, more rules and metadata will emerge during the analysis. And sometimes after we've analyzed a few sources we'll have a feel for how much metadata we need to record to distinguish one candidate component from another. We might even need to conduct additional interviews or meetings with the people who provided documents or materials for the inventory.

Of course, if the components we harvest don't have obvious labels or names associated with them, we may have to invent them. We will revisit component names at various points, so any names we come up with at this stage are tentative. Nevertheless, it is helpful to start constructing a separate dictionary list of the words used when composing names because this will make our component names more consistent. This may sound rather simplistic, but we'll introduce more formal approaches for naming components later in this chapter.

Documents from all parts of the Document Type Spectrum contain components but those we find on the narrative end tend to be presentational and at the transactional end more content based. In the center we find structural components that may be required for presentational or semantic requirements. Figure 12-1 annotates the Document Type Spectrum we introduced in Figure 1-2 to depict these systematic differences.

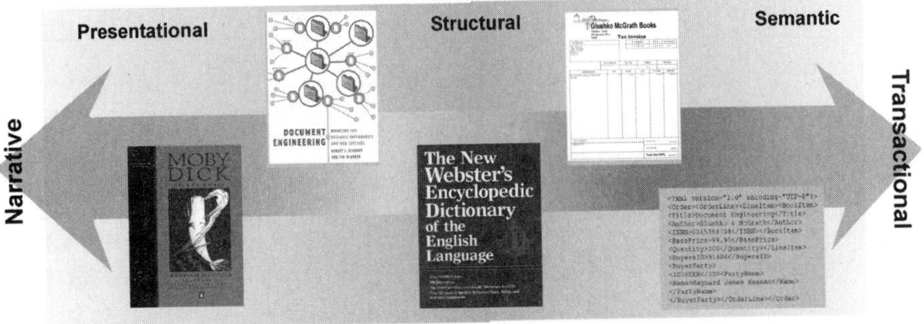

Figure 12-1. Components on the Document Type Spectrum

Put another way, it is the mix of the three varieties of components that determines where a document fits along the spectrum.

12.1.1 FINDING COMPONENTS IN TRANSACTIONAL DOCUMENTS

The easiest components to find are those in transactional documents. Here candidate components typically appear as labeled data entry fields in forms or are explicitly marked up or delimited in some stream of data.

Components are easier to find in transactional documents

A useful guide for transactional documents is that any piece of information that has a unique label or identifier is a candidate component. Another less precise but useful guideline is that a candidate component can be any piece of information that is self-contained and comprehensible in its own right.

Common sources of information components are implementation models or schemas for transactional documents and forms (which are usually straightforward transformations of these models). It is also useful to study the source code of any relevant applications that process documents. These may contain both business rules and hidden components disguised as data variables. Application or markup code often describes a component more precisely than the labels that appear in a user interface.

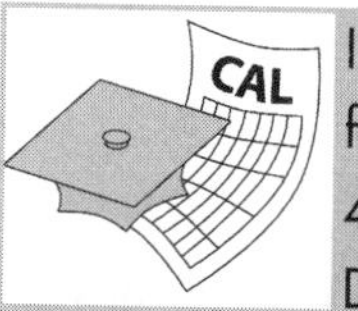

In the Event Calendar project, the inventory included the web form for adding new events to the official university calendar (Figure 10-4). The entry form contains labeled components for entering the Date, Title of Event, Time, Speaker, Affiliation, and other event information. The HTML code for the form reveals additional information about these components. Some simplified excerpts from the HTML are shown in Figure 12-2.

```
<b>Date: </b><input type="TEXT" name="AddStDate" size="8" value="">
to<input type="TEXT" name="AddEnDate" size="8" value="">
<i>e.g. 1/27/98</i>

<b>Title of Event: </b><input type="TEXT" name="AddTitle" value="" size="45"
maxlength="125">

<b>Time: </b><input type="TEXT" name="AddTime1" value="" size="8" maxlength="8">
or<input type="TEXT" name="AddTimex" value="" size="35" maxlength="255">

<b>Speaker: </b><input type="TEXT" name="AddSpeaker" value="" size="25"
maxlength="50">

<b>Affiliation: </b><input type="TEXT" name="AddSpeakerA" value="" size="25"
maxlength="100">
```

Figure 12-2. HTML Excerpts from the Add Event Form for the University of California's Official Online Calendar

The first extract from the HTML creates the bold "Date" and "to" labels on the form and names the components that captures the Date values as "AddStDate" and "AddEnDate." The example date (1/27/98) suggests that the format for the date is MM/DD/YY, but the HTML code can only enforce the weaker format for the input as a text field of 8 characters.

We see similar presentation and instance rules in the HTML that collects the Title of Event, Speaker, and Affiliation. In these cases we can also see other rules specified in the code but not explicit on the entry form, such as the minimum and maximum lengths for the text inputs.

Application code and its data variables often enforce semantic rules that are not exposed in the interface. However, in other cases, the code may mislead us into identifying false components and incorrect rules.

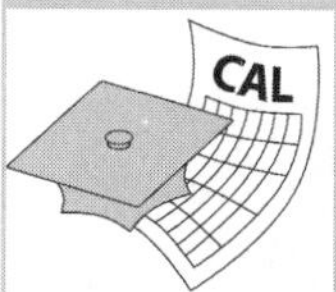

Figure 12-2 reveals two components, AddTime1 (8 characters) and AddTimex (up to 255 characters). We could be deceived into believing these are two separate components because of their different format specifications, but in fact they are both the time of the event; the second option is used for specifying event recurrences that can't be described compactly. In this case, the fact that they are joined by the label "or" on the form is a clue that they share the same semantic rules—they are synonyms with different presentational rules.

12.1.2 FINDING COMPONENTS IN NARRATIVE DOCUMENTS

In contrast to transactional documents, documents on the narrative side of the Document Type Spectrum are likely to have fewer, harder-to-identify candidate components. These documents generally have fewer processing requirements and therefore fewer rules about specific components. And with fewer rules, we need fewer components because we don't need to distinguish them.

Narrative documents have fewer components because we don't need to distinguish them

This is true, almost by definition, for documents that are entirely narrative because they tell a story whose themes, characters, and plot develop gradually. While it is possible to label sections or chapters of the text with titles or assign index terms to them, it just isn't useful to treat those parts as specialized types of content on that basis.

Narrative documents can hide or obscure candidate components in paragraphs or other blocks of text. Document analysts refer to these as mixed content components because they are mixed into surrounding text that may be more generic. A common form of mixed content is an otherwise unstructured text paragraph that contains emphasized words, glossary terms, references to tables or figures, citations to supporting documents, or links to footnotes or endnotes (these are often called inline components).

We should be on the lookout for components in mixed content where latent content could be made more explicit. For example, a Product Description might contain trademarks, company names, measurements, or other technical specifications, all of which could be considered as candidate components even though they might not be currently identified as such in the document. The significance of these components depends on having rules that require their use. For example, if we don't need to know about trademarks, we need not consider this a candidate component.

As we move from the narrative end of the document type spectrum toward regions with hybrid document types such as reference books, product documentation and operating or assembly instructions, components are more readily identified. Sometimes the components are explicitly labeled, such as Note, Warning, or Instructions, but most of the time they aren't. But we can often recognize components such as Question, Answer, Code Example, Illustration, Caption, Map, and Portrait. There are more presentational rules about these components so they occur more predictably and have a more consistent appearance when they do.

It is useful to examine source documents as well as published ones

As with transactional documents, it is often useful with narrative publications to examine the source document (that is, the digital version or markup language) as well as the published or formatted document. The former may contain statements that tell something about the components and the information model involved in the latter's creation. How useful this will actually be depends on how well the author separated the semantic and presentational rules. For example, in some word-processed documents the style tags are indicators of components, but their value depends on the discipline with which the author applied them. Text with a "normal" tag and formatting overlaid on an ad hoc basis reveals less about components than text with a rich repertoire of named styles consistently applied. Similarly, markup languages that focus on presentation, such as Postscript and HTML, are often less useful because their markup follows few or no semantic or instance rules.

The preferred case is an XML (or SGML) document accompanied by its schema, because a schema is a formal specification of the implementation model. However, even though schemas make components easier to harvest, there is no guarantee that the model they implement is semantically precise enough or appropriate for our required context.

12.1.3 FINDING STRUCTURES FOR COMPONENTS

All types of documents contain structures that group their components. These can be either presentational or semantic, but we are most concerned with the semantic ones.

Structures can be presentational but we are most concerned with semantic ones

Presentational structures are more common in published documents. Components such as Page, Header, or Details are presentational structures. They are generally used as printing conventions or as aids to formatting.

Semantic structures are more evident in transactional documents. Because of their formal and precise definitions, we generally find semantic structures implemented as containers for components. In more narrative types of documents, cross-references, footnotes, and hypertext links and anchors are the most typical mechanisms for implementing semantic structures.

Any semantic structures we discover are candidate components in their own right. They are the subject of business rules, such as rules about their existence (or number). As such they should be entered in our harvest table.

12.1.4 FINDING SEMANTIC CONTENT IN PRESENTATION COMPONENTS

A well-designed narrative document will employ layout, typographic, or other presentational devices to indicate the boundaries of information components. But the rules used to separate content and presentation can be complex, subtle, or even misleading.

For example, the cover and title page of this book contain the text string "Robert J. Glushko and Tim McGrath." A human reader has no trouble realizing that there are two coauthors whose names have been combined in a single presentational structure that masks the semantic distinction that there are two names, not one. If we need to be able to identify other texts by the individual authors, we must recognize these as two instances of the same Author component.

In a similar way, if we consider the multiple lines often used for addresses on forms, how can we be sure that the first line is conventionally used for Number and Street, the second for City, State/Province, and Postal Code, and the last line for Country? What if we have a requirement to analyze this information by region or city? To make these semantic distinctions, we must separate semantic structures from presentational ones.

We must recognize any content components that are implied by presentation rules

Separating semantic meaning from its presentation means we must recognize any information components that are implied by presentation rules. This task is partly intuitive and experimental, but the existence of books on graphic design or illustration proves that techniques do exist.[1] We'll describe the most common of these here.

In Figure 12-3 we can see that the UC Berkeley Academic Calendar uses bold capitals to distinguish the beginning and end of a semester and italics to indicate university holidays. Ordinary events use neither bold nor italics.

Office of Planning & Analysis
University of California, Berkeley - Office of the Vice Chancellor for Budget & Finance
Questions?

UC Berkeley Academic Calendar

Download Calendar(s) What's This?

Fall Semester 2003		
TeleBEARS	April 14, 2003 - September 12, 2003	Monday-Friday
Fee Payment Due	August 15, 2003	Friday
Welcome Week	August 18, 2003 - August 22, 2003	Monday-Friday
FALL SEMESTER BEGINS	August 19, 2003	Tuesday
Instruction Begins	August 25, 2003	Monday
Labor Day Holiday	September 1, 2003	Monday
Veterans Day Holiday	November 11, 2003	Tuesday
Thanksgiving Holiday	November 27, 2003 - November 28, 2003	Thursday-Friday
Instruction Ends	December 6, 2003	Saturday
Final Examinations	December 10, 2003 - December 18, 2003	Wednesday-Thursday
FALL SEMESTER ENDS	December 18, 2003	Thursday
Winter Holiday	December 24, 2003 - December 25, 2003	Wednesday-Thursday
New Year's Holiday	December 31, 2003 - January 1, 2004	Wednesday-Thursday

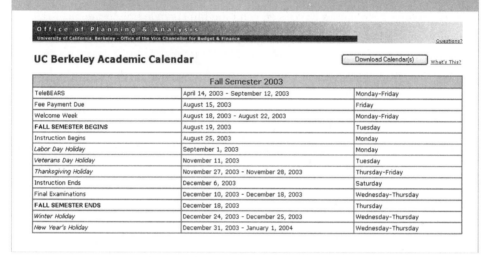

Figure 12-3. A sample of the Berkeley Official Academic Calendar.

This tells us that events may need to be distinguished by their status within the school term. If there is a requirement for this information, we need an additional component, perhaps called Term Status to capture this rule.

One of the most useful techniques for finding meaningful content in published documents is to examine the stylistic conventions they use. Rules, boxes, and white space create visible boundaries that identify different types of content by separating them from each other. Changes in layout patterns can also indicate component boundaries.

For example, indentation reliably suggests that the author intends a structural division, and the extent of indentation and the amount of following white space indicates the relationships between the components on each side of the division. Similarly, a switch from justified to ragged margins almost always indicates a change in component content (look at any newspaper or magazine and compare editorial to advertising copy). And line breaks in the middle of sentences may indicate that the content is poetry or song lyrics.

Even the typography used can provide important clues for identifying semantically meaningful components. Large type signifies more importance than small type, red may signal a warning, and italics identify special words. Footnotes are formatted with smaller type than the main text to suggest that they contain information for specialists or the curious. Program or schema code examples or tabular data often use Courier or other monospace fonts to achieve regular alignment. On web pages, underlining frequently denotes hypertext links, and the link color may indicate whether it has been followed recently.

In the presentation of this book we use numerous formatting conventions to indicate a change in the type of narrative content. "Pull quotes" are extracted from the text and surrounded with space to emphasize important ideas. The case study examples and secondary topics we call "sidebars"[2] are distinguished with graphically distinct backgrounds. Superscript numbers refer to endnotes that provide clarifying details or references that might be distracting if they appeared in the running text.

Documents frequently use the subtle presentational convention of association by proximity. This means meaningful associations between components are implied by placing them near each other. For example, publishers of catalogs commonly arrange pages so that add-on or complementary items appear near the product that supports them. The semantic association between these components is driven by the business requirement to use suggestive buying tactics. There are specialized terms for identifying the components distinguished by proximity association rules: an Illustration is a graphical or figural component that supports a textual one, a Caption is a textual component that supports in the other direction, a Callout is a textual label for some important part of an Illustration, and so on.

If we analyze the UC Berkeley Events calendar in Figure 7-3, we can see both an image and a narrative description in the lower right area of the page. Our perceptual experience teaches us that this component relates to the event identified immediately above it. But this is not formally stated. It could just as easily be a description of some other event or general information about the page itself. The physical proximity gives us a clue that an identified event may have a narrative description and image associated with it.

In this case, we might want to capture this implicit association by distinguishing these components as Event Narrative and Event Image.

We can personally experience the power of presentation components by trying to read a newspaper in an alphabet or language we don't understand. Even though we can't understand the words, we can tell the importance of stories and associated images by the conventional presentational components alone.

Another presentation component that may imply semantic content is the order or sequence of information presented in lists. We probably realize that our personal shopping would be more efficient if the sequence of items on our shopping list corresponded to the arrangement of goods in the grocery store. In warehousing and product distribution, this may be expressed as a formal business rule that the sequence of items on incoming orders should reflect the arrangement or location of products in the store; this is sometimes called a picking list. So in this context of use we may find hidden or latent semantically meaningful content in the list order. To enable this rule we would need to introduce a candidate component, perhaps called Stock Pulling Sequence.

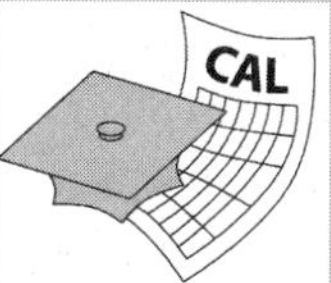

The web page in Figure 12-4 comes from the Event Calendar for the School of Letters and Science at UC Berkeley. If we examine the order of events within days, we see that they are listed in chronological order. But it is not enough to harvest the component for Start Time and End Time of the Event, we must also know the Date that contains it.

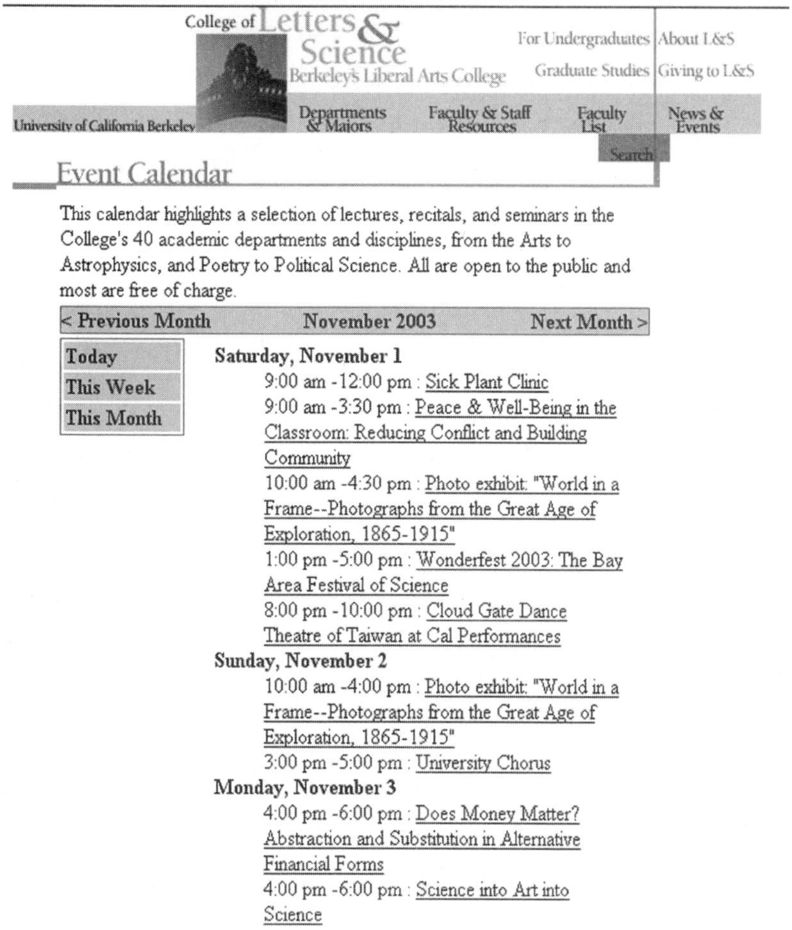

College of Letters & Science
Berkeley's Liberal Arts College

For Undergraduates | About L&S
Graduate Studies | Giving to L&S

University of California Berkeley

Departments & Majors | Faculty & Staff Resources | Faculty List | News & Events

Search

Event Calendar

This calendar highlights a selection of lectures, recitals, and seminars in the College's 40 academic departments and disciplines, from the Arts to Astrophysics, and Poetry to Political Science. All are open to the public and most are free of charge.

< Previous Month | November 2003 | Next Month >

Today
This Week
This Month

Saturday, November 1

9:00 am -12:00 pm : Sick Plant Clinic
9:00 am -3:30 pm : Peace & Well-Being in the Classroom: Reducing Conflict and Building Community
10:00 am -4:30 pm : Photo exhibit: "World in a Frame--Photographs from the Great Age of Exploration, 1865-1915"
1:00 pm -5:00 pm : Wonderfest 2003: The Bay Area Festival of Science
8:00 pm -10:00 pm : Cloud Gate Dance Theatre of Taiwan at Cal Performances

Sunday, November 2

10:00 am -4:00 pm : Photo exhibit: "World in a Frame--Photographs from the Great Age of Exploration, 1865-1915"
3:00 pm -5:00 pm : University Chorus

Monday, November 3

4:00 pm -6:00 pm : Does Money Matter? Abstraction and Substitution in Alternative Financial Forms
4:00 pm -6:00 pm : Science into Art into Science

Figure 12-4. Event Calendar for the School of Letters and Science at the University of California, Berkeley.

Of course, not all presentational conventions will have semantic meaning. In fact, many presentational decisions are more arbitrary. For example, the type face in which this book is printed doesn't affect its meaning.

However, the type face for a wedding invitation conveys a lot of meaning about the event's formality and dress code. And some documents use a complex variety of type fonts, sizes, and text attributes simply because the author is infatuated with them. We've all probably wasted time tweaking the appearance of a document in a word processor without conveying any more meaning to the reader.

12.1.5 FINDING MEANINGFUL CONTENT IN STRUCTURAL COMPONENTS

Like careful analysis of presentation components, careful analysis of existing structural components can yield implicit meaningful information. Indeed, structure is an essential aid to understanding the semantics of components. We certainly hope that the structural organization of this book into numbered chapters, sections, subsections, and sub-subsections helps in understanding what a specific part of the book is about. At the very least, it should convey the information that Section 12.1.5 is more strongly related to 12.1.6 than it is to 2.2.1.

Structure is essential to understanding semantics

Structures can be either presentational or semantic. Presentational structures like tables of contents, running heads, and page footers are created to display structures to human beings. In contrast, semantic structures indicate distinctions between different types of content. In narrative publications we see these as presentational devices such as boxes and tables. In more transactional documents these are seen as the containers that aggregate components.

But structures should never be taken at face value. We should not presume that any of the structures we find when we harvest from the document inventory are optimal or even desirable. We must first confirm their suitability for our requirements.

We've all struggled with poorly designed forms in which the fields and their groupings do not fit our understanding of the content. And we've all read technical manuals or textbooks where critical explanations that would be have been useful in introductory chapters don't appear until near the end. To avoid this kind of difficulty we must first disaggregate structures to establish the individual identity of its content components.

For example, because a section of a form is labeled Applicant and contains data fields for Street, City, and Country, we should not presume the components we find in this structure are suitable for our requirements. To confirm their suitability, it is better to harvest Street, City, and Country as individual information content components and discard their existing structure. If Applicant is the appropriate aggregate structure for these semantic components, it will reemerge when we build our document component model.

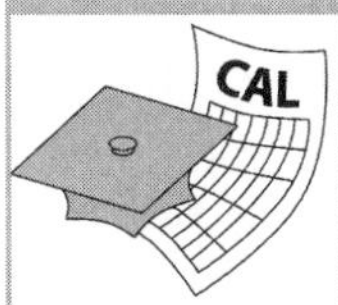

In the Add Event form in Figure 7-4, the candidate components Date, Title of Event, Time, Speaker and Affiliation appear together. But this does not mean that they are all logically part of the structure called Event.

As we saw with presentation components, structures can also defy or hide content definition—especially when the separation of structure and presentation is incomplete or inconsistent. For example, consider the text in Figure 12-5, an extract from a technical standards document, MIL-STD 1472D.[3]

5.4.2.2 Continuous adjustment rotary controls.

5.4.2.2.1 Knobs.

5.4.2.2.1.1 Use. Knobs should be used when low forces or precise adjustments of a continuous variable are required. A moving knob with fixed scale is preferred over a moving scale with fixed index for most tasks. If positions of single revolution controls must be distinguished, a pointer or marker should be available on the knob.

5.4.2.2.1.2 Dimensions, torque and separation. The dimensions of knobs shall be within the limits specified in Figure 12. Within these ranges, knob size is relatively unimportant, provided the resistance is low and the knob can be easily grasped and manipulated. When panel space is extremely limited knobs should approximate the minimum values and should have resistance as low as possible without permitting the setting to be changed by vibration or merely touching the control. Resistance and separation between adjacent edges of knobs shall conform to Figure 12.

5.4.2.2.1.3 Knob style. Unless otherwise specified by the procuring activity, control knob style shall conform to MIL-STD-13412.

5.4.2.2.2 Ganged control knobs.

Figure 12-5. Text Extract from MIL-STD 1472D.

Every heading and text paragraph in MIL-STD 1472D begins with a numeric identifier that follows a deep hierarchy. But while it is tempting to see this as a semantic structure, there is actually less significance to this than the numbering scheme suggests. The arrangement of Knobs and Ganged Control Knobs as children of Continuous Adjustment Rotary Controls suggests they are both to be treated as subtypes of the latter. But couldn't Ganged Control Knobs just as easily be treated as a subtype of Knobs? Given the differences (and inconsistency) in the substructures below Knobs and Ganged Control Knobs, it is unlikely that the structural hierarchy is a reliable indicator of content components here.

This example shows that the "unique label or identifier" rule that usually works for transactional documents can break down for more narrative types of documents. Laws, regulations, standards, or specifications often give every paragraph a unique number or identifier, but this rarely indicates that each paragraph contains a different type of content. In this case the identifier is satisfying a presentational rule, not a semantic one.

That presentational structure isn't a perfectly reliable indicator of semantics shouldn't surprise us, but it helps to reinforce the idea that at this stage in our analysis, our goal is to capture the individual components, not their structures. Semantically meaningful structures based on their dependencies will emerge during the building of our document component model.

Disaggregating structures may mean reviewing the names given to components. Sometimes we need to ensure the uniqueness of the name given to the individual components. We can do this by qualifying the name with a term that reflects its original structure.

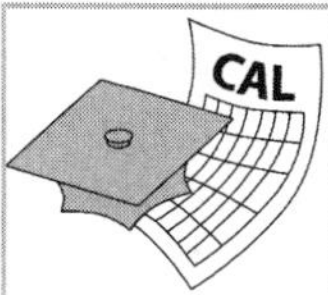

In the Add Event form in Figure 7-4, we recognize that both Date and Time Period apply to Event in this context. We can record this observation by qualifying their names as Event Date and Event Time.

However, despite sharing a common qualifying term, each of these components is still independent. At this stage, we should not assume they are all part of the same structure.

12.1.6 THE TROUBLE WITH TABLES

Tables often form an important part of the document inventory because they can convey implicit semantics as both presentation and structural components. Tables present information by structuring a set of components to emphasize the intersection or relationships between different values. The manner in which combinations of components interact is often explicitly described in the headings for rows and columns or in formatting conventions like boxes and line rules. However, tables can fuse presentational and semantic structures in ways that require, and sometimes defy, careful analysis.

The presentational and semantic structures in tables require careful analysis

Most tables follow regular matrix patterns in which the presentational components and structures are consistent with or reinforce the semantic structures of the content contained in the cells. This applies to the extent that the mere existence or nonexistence of values within the cells can have significance. For example, a table in an online catalog for a clothing store might have row and column headings for Size and Color with the cell at their intersection containing the product number of the item with that combination of size and color. If there is no product number, it means the item is not available in this combination. In our analysis we would need to capture these implied rules with a candidate component, perhaps called Availability.

It would be extremely fortunate if the implementation models for the tables in our analysis captured the rich semantics conveyed by table formatting. For example, if we harvested a database or document schema with components about size, color, and availability explicitly encoded, it could easily be transformed into the table described in the previous paragraph. Different stylesheets or tabular presentations could then arrange the information in various ways to emphasize different characteristics or combinations of the set of products.

Unfortunately the predictable geometry for organizing tables has encouraged many authors to represent them in specific presentational structures rather than as a set of interrelated semantic structures. That is, the table content is described in terms of the physical or presentational features (rows, columns, widths, spans, etc.) required by a particular rectangular formatting of the information as a table. This geometric encoding is used in HTML web pages and is encouraged by most authoring tools for creating tables. Semantics are left behind and must be extracted with great care from row and column headings, comments, or supporting documentation.[4]

The contrast between the semantic and presentational encodings is shown in Figure 12-6:

```
<Shirt>                    <TR>
<Size>L</Size>             <TD>L</TD>
<Color>Red</Color>         <TD>Red</TD>
</Shirt>                   </TR>
```

Figure 12-6: Semantic vs. Presentational Encoding in a Table

Presentational sophistication means that some tables, such as the periodic table or astrological charts, can't be represented using regular table matrices because they merge content, structure, and presentation in ways that are highly conventional or regular but not a matrix (see Figures 12-7a and 12-7b). At the same time, web designers and web publishing vendors have learned so well to abuse the HTML table tag set to enforce rectangular formatting that most of the information marked up using HTML <TABLE> has nothing to do with tables at all.[5]

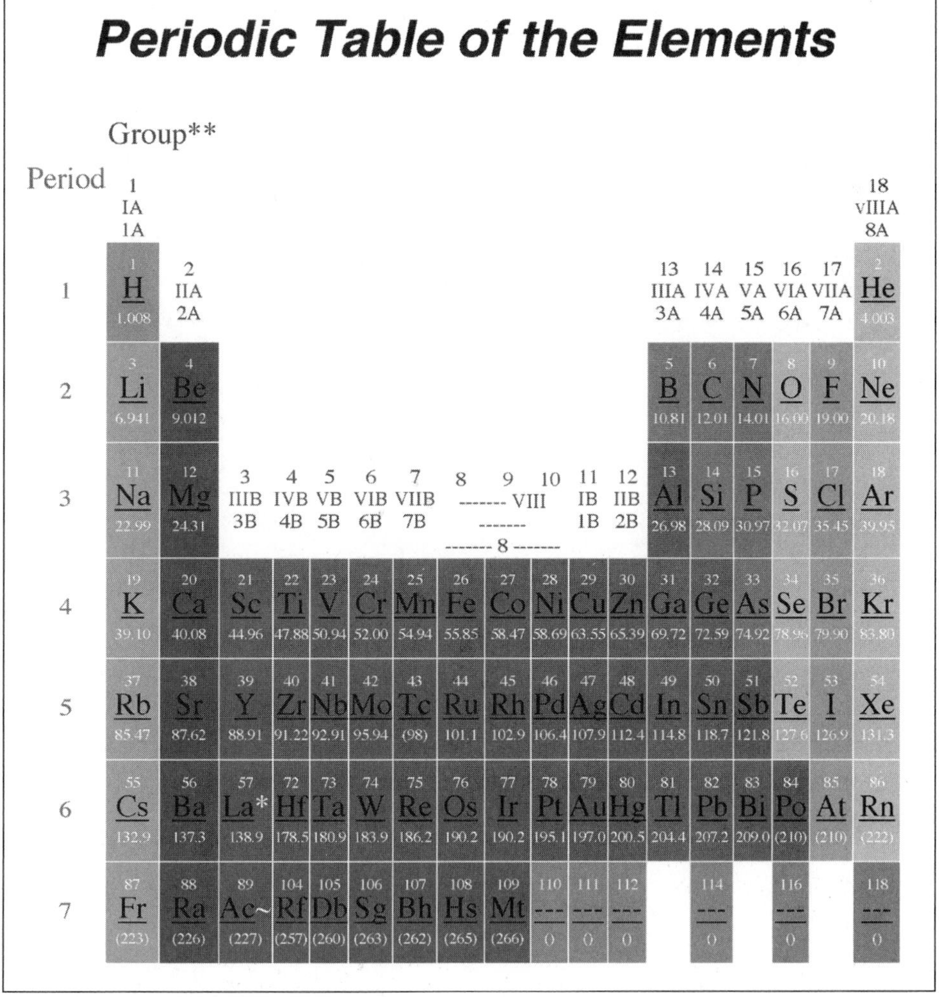

Figure 12-7a. Tables with Regular but Nonrectangular Structures: Periodic Table

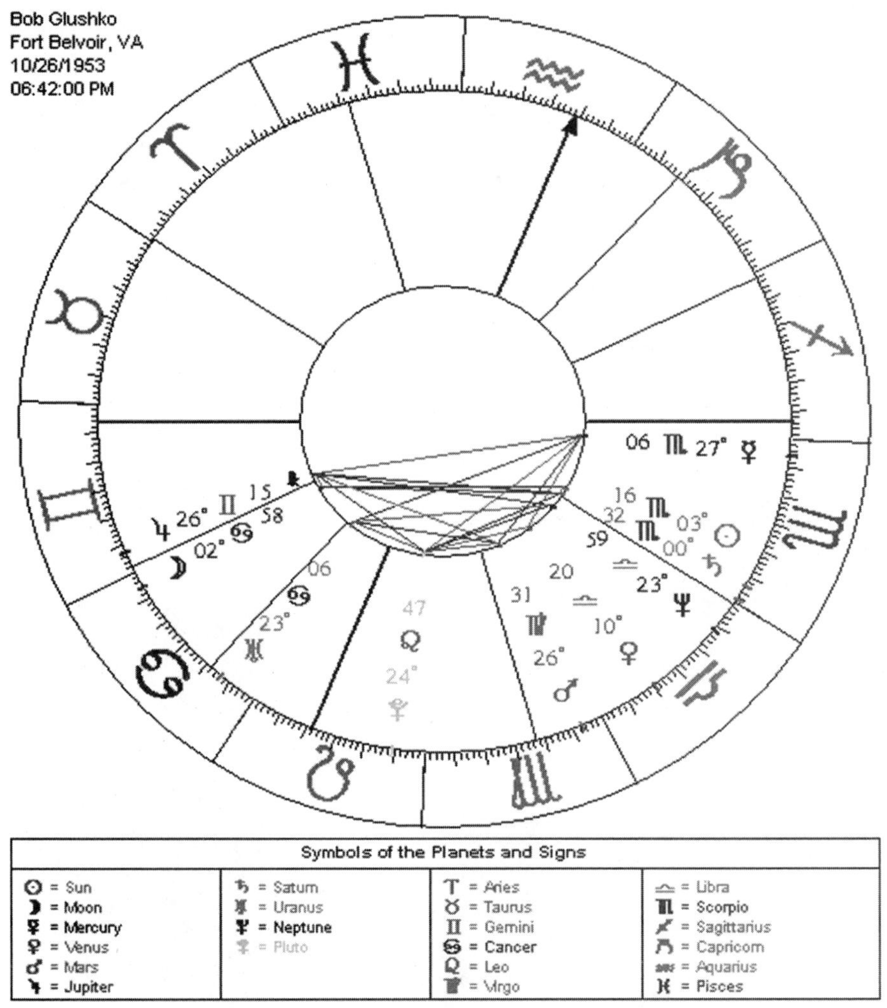

Figure 12-7b. Tables with Regular but Nonrectangular Structures: Astrological Chart.

12.1.7 PRESERVING PRESENTATION COMPONENTS

Before we move away from the presentation components, we should remind ourselves that the purpose of these components is to define rules for the appearance of a document instance. Having a formal description of these rules can be useful for establishing and communicating a common understanding of the information model between stakeholders.

In particular, the degree of care or precision with which we need to record presentation rules will be based on the requirements for presentation integrity. We must ensure that we capture enough rules to relate structural and presentation components to the content whenever these will be needed.

When we identify requirements for presentational structures such as tables of contents, lists of tables, or other structural entry points, we should recognize the derivation rules that are used to generate them. They are called derivative because if we preserve the rules used to generate these artifacts, we don't need to treat them as candidate components in their own right.

12.1.8 ANALYZING SETS OF POSSIBLE VALUES

Another key task when harvesting candidate components is to capture any instance rules relating to constraints on the values the component can assume.

Some components have an unlimited set of possible values. For example, a Book Title can be almost any construction of one or more words that need not even be grammatical, such as "Moby Dick." Also, a Product Name may consist of (or contain) newly invented words, like "iPod" or "Furby." The only reliable test of validity might be someone saying "this is the name of a book/product." So, while there are some instance rules that constrain each of these components, they are so weak that they are hardly worth noting.

However, many other components can take on only a limited set of possible values. Often these sets of possible values enforce interoperability. So it is extremely important to identify them during the analysis phase. In effect, these are patterns in the values that components can take on. It is common to call some of these reusable content patterns "code sets," but in the next section we will give a more precise definition of what we mean by codes.

Many components have patterns for their possible values

There are some important differences in the types of sets of possible values for components. The broadest set of values possible would be those dictated by an agreed representation or language. For example, Quantity must be an integer, or Product Description must be in English. But there are more specific constraints that can be applied.

For some components like Day of Week, the set of possible values is conventional and fixed—within an agreed representation. And even when they are arbitrary, sets of possible values can still be fixed when they span the complete semantic range on some domain, as values of "AM" or "PM" do for Period of Day, "Off" or "On" for Power Status, and as "Credit" and "Debit" do for Account Transaction Function.

But many other components (even the ones we think of as codes or identifiers) actually have lists of possible values that are dynamic rather than fixed because the range is theoretically unlimited or effectively so.

A common example is seen in the values a manufacturer uses to identify its product range. These sets of values may be internally determined by the specific implementation of a business process (such as the Manufacturer's Product Code). The values aren't fixed because products are continually added or discontinued.

Internally governed value sets like Manufacturer's Product Code contrast with sets whose values are determined by standards organizations or some other external body (such as the product barcodes maintained by the EAN/UCC organization). When using standardized patterns for the values of a component, there is greater potential for alignment and interoperability between different implementations. This is another reason why we must strive to identify these rules and components wherever possible.

Standardizing Sets of Values

By definition adopting a common set of values for a component means standardizing on a fixed pattern. Consequently, any unilateral changes to a value set will affect interoperability. But in many cases identifying and maintaining standard sets of values can be problematic:

- Very few sets of values remain static. New countries and currencies emerge, laws change, new business practices develop—so their sets of values are dynamic.

- The choices within a set of values may be too comprehensive. For example, we might want to constrain a component to only a few of the 180 or so international currencies.

- The set may be too small. Perhaps, for example, the type of manufactured goods involved in our business process does not fall within a category of the UN/SPSC code set.

This means we can have requirements for different business rules that customize sets of values. And this, in turn, creates governance and housekeeping issues about the maintenance of these values.

In practice, the solution often results in each implementation mapping between values—both of which are volatile and each of which might have been customized further. Sometimes, what seemed like a good idea in theory develops into a best-fit compromise in practice.

In certain circumstances, it is possible to specify the rules that form the set of legal values using expressions or formulas (also known as facets). For example, an Australian postcode is defined by the pattern expression XNNN, where X is a digit between 1 and 6 (representing the state or territory) and N is a digit between 0 and 9. We also see expression patterns in the 16 numeric digits used on most credit cards. The first six of these identify the issuing financial institution, and the last is often used as a checksum based on the previous 15.

In most of these cases the set of possible valid values for the expression is likely to be much greater than the set of values actually used. So compliance with the pattern is a necessary but not sufficient test that the value is not just legal but is actually the intended value.

Compliance with a pattern is not a sufficient test that the value was the intended one

There are many situations where analyzing sets of possible values and identifying candidate components go hand in hand. For example, suppose we harvested a component that can take on values such as "camel," "pipeline," "railroad," "pneumatic tube," and "bicycle." These values appear to have nothing in common, so what might the meaning of this component be? If we determine that they are all means of carrying things, we might propose a candidate component called Means of Transport. But for our context of use it probably isn't useful to create a component whose next two values might be "pack mule" and "space shuttle." Its generalized definition suggests that the context of use is too broad. It would be better to narrow down the context to a more concrete concept with a more uniform set of possible values. So for Means of Transport it might be better to qualify the possible values into smaller sets for differing contexts, such as Freight Means of Transport or Personal Means of Transport.

This approach isn't just a matter of personal preference. Research in cognitive psychology and psycholinguistics[6] suggests that some levels of abstraction in categories are more basic or psychologically natural than others. For example, a pet cat could be considered an animal, a mammal, a cat, or an American Shorthair, but we are most likely to talk and think about him as a cat (how odd it sounds to say "Let the mammal [or American Shorthair] out"). It is at this level of generalization that the similarity among the possible values seems to be the most useful and that people can make the most accurate classifications. Components that are too generalized also pose a level of abstraction problem; abstract terms can apply to a huge range of objects and categories. So while a cat may be both a mammal and an American Shorthair, if we categorize it using the abstract category of animal we can't as easily talk about what makes it a cat.

The level of abstraction for a component can also cause difficulty when it is defined using a supplementary qualifying value rather than a qualified name. We often see this in harvested components with names ending in the word "type." In these components the true semantics are disguised or dispersed by generalization.

For example, suppose we have a candidate component called Address whose context is qualified by the value of a component called Address Type. Address Type might have possible values like "Ship From," "Deliver To," and "Postal."

While this seems to be a reasonable method for specifying the different contexts for an address, it simply defers any semantic resolution from the model stage where the component is defined to the document instances where the qualification is represented. And if there is no shared pattern for these qualified values, their meanings can easily overlap. For example, is the "Deliver To" Address the same as the "Postal" Address when we post a shipment? This type of ambiguity makes the task of interpreting the true meaning very complex.

There can also be side effects when the value of a qualifying component affects the meaning of a dependent component. For example, the type of address may affect the valid means of transport used for delivering to that address. We suggest that "pack mule" is not a viable value for Means of Transport when the Address Type is "website" (although this would depend on connection speeds).

Dispersing or obscuring the semantics of a component by using qualifying values for similar components is widespread in traditional EDI systems and in early XML business vocabularies that copied the EDI approach. The components resulting from this approach are often difficult to analyze, even by those who created them, because they have complex and brittle meanings. The net effect is that we can have two implementations of the same document model that aren't interoperable because they encode different meanings. In fact, if we were to extend this idea we could express any document model by two components – one to hold the content and the other to qualify its meaning. At best we get tightly coupled applications and plenty of work for consultants determining how to map the qualifying terms from one vocabulary to the other.

We maintain it is better to qualify components directly by capturing the differences in contexts as separate components in our model. Using the Address example above, we would propose separate components for Shipping Address, Delivery Address, Postal Address, and so on. These can all reuse a common pattern for addresses, and their qualifying names become part of the common model understandable by all interfaces that require it.

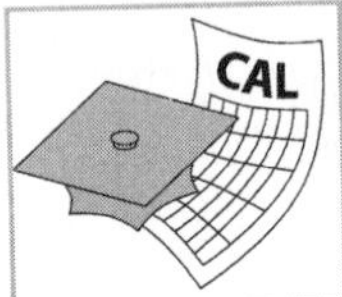

In the Event Calendar project, the Add New Event form defines a set of possible values for Event Type. The values are shown in the HTML fragment shown in Figure 12-8.

```
<SELECT NAME="AddType" SIZE="1">
<OPTION VALUE=" SELECTED>--All Types--
<OPTION>Academic Calendar
<OPTION>Conference/Symposium
<OPTION>Course
<OPTION>Exhibit
<OPTION>Film
<OPTION>Lecture
<OPTION>Performing Arts
<OPTION>Performing Arts - Dance
<OPTION>Performing Arts - Music
<OPTION>Performing Arts - Theater
<OPTION>Seminar
<OPTION>Special Event/Other
<OPTION>Sport
<OPTION>Workshop
</SELECT>
```

Figure 12-8. Values for Event Type in Add Event Form for UC Berkeley Calendar

This list actually defines the various contexts of use for an Event—that is, the ways an Event can be qualified for more precise meaning.

But some dependency rules can't be implemented using this component. For example, if the Event Type is "Seminar" it will require a Speaker, if it is "Sport," it may involve one or more Results, and so on.

We can also foresee problems with forcing a choice among semantically overlapping qualifiers like the different values for a Performing Arts event. We have no way to describe an event as Workshop at a Conference. So we could end up with documents that describe the same Event in different ways.

In our Event Calendar analysis we decided to define Seminar Event, Sporting Event, Performing Arts Event, and so on as separate components.

Not all sets of values will turn out to be useful patterns. Some sets may contain apparently arbitrary or unrelated values, forming distorted combinations of a component's meaning, as we saw with our Means of Transport example. Another example is the standard set of values for Item Characteristics (element 7011) from UN/EDIFACT.[7] This set contains "Size System," "Color" and "Quantity," which seems appropriate, but also "Weather Data," "Primary Grape," and "Music Style." Rather than collect all these diverse item characteristics in a single component, we would recommend these be defined using separate components for Wine Item Characteristic, Meteorological Item Characteristic, Recording Media Item Characteristic, and so on.

12.1.9 CODE SETS

Code sets are a specialized implementation of constrained sets of values. What denotes sets of possible values as codes is that they establish their meaning by reference to other values, often by abbreviations. Semantically, they convey intension by extension (see SIDEBAR).

Code sets are constrained sets of values that convey intension by extension

It is important to harvest and analyze code sets whenever we discover them because, as with other forms of constrained sets of values, their use indicates and reinforces rules and constraints for standardization that our models need to represent. Adopting common codes promotes consistency and removes ambiguity in the meaning of components.

Intension and Extension

Research in philosophy and cognitive psychology has long considered how people understand words and concepts. Some of it directly applies to how we develop and represent information components.

According to Gottlob Frege (1841-1925), we study the "intensions" of words by asking about the key features or attributes that people use to categorize things. We then apply these to their "extensions," the set of things that are members of the category. Put another way, Frege's theory of meaning is that we understand words or concepts in terms of the things in the world they describe.

For example, we know that the currency code of "USD" means U.S. dollars because we understand the concept (intension) of currency code in terms of its extension in ISO 4217, which enumerates all the valid codes.

But Ludwig Wittgenstein (1889-1951) rebutted Frege with the argument that most words and concepts lack fixed or enumerable extensions. There may be defining features that are true of typical instances, but sometimes features that people consider part of a concept's definition may not apply to all the instances. For example, not all birds fly, so how can we categorize a bird? Different instances may vary substantially in how typical or representative they are of the category even though they share all the essential features (both cricket and lotto are games, but as Wittgenstein pointed out, game is defined only by "family resemblances" among the instances). Even when characteristics can be identified, they change in different contexts and over time, so Wittgenstein concludes that "meaning is use."

The impact of this for Document Engineers is that some components can't be precisely defined in terms of features or attributes or in terms of the possible values they can take on. This isn't merely a bit of language philosophy. It means that while concepts like "currency code" are Fregan and can be reduced to context-free enumerations (for example, ISO 4217), most concepts are Wittgensteinian and defy simple definitions. In other words, there are no ISO codes for most of the objects or concepts we deal with.

So we can't define money the way we define currency codes. Money means "dollars" to some of us, "Deutschmarks" (and now "Euros") to Germans, colored plastic chips in casinos, or anything else that people are willing to accept as a medium of economic value. Money means different things to economists than to anthropologists or historians.

Of course, this doesn't mean we can't use money as an information component, but it warns us that it will be more precise if we specify that money can be understood as a currency code together with an amount.

When words can't be looked up to find their possible values, we have to understand intensions by using other intensions—looking at the definitions and relating them to each other.

This makes us appreciate the importance of the names we give to components, a topic we will consider in detail later in this chapter. It also supports the value of having a controlled vocabulary that precisely defines all the terms used in component names or an ontology that defines the shared meaning of terms along with their associations.

Code values themselves are symbolic representations for other values. While they are often abbreviations (initialisms, acronyms, or apocopations)[8] they can also be purely arbitrary values. This is especially common in international code sets. For example, the UN/EDIFACT Message Function Code (element 1225) uses the code value sets "1", "2" and "3" for the extension values of "Cancellation," "Replacement," and "Deletion." The ISO also provides an alternative numeric set of values to avoid language dependencies or biases, so a currency code of either "CNY" or "156" identifies the Chinese Yuan Renminbi.

The arbitrariness of such code values is exemplified by one of our favorite (though possibly apocryphal) stories that explains why all the air and sea port codes in Canada start with the letter "Y" (like "YYZ" for Toronto and "YUL" for Montreal) instead of using more memorable codes like "SFO" for San Francisco or "SYD" for Sydney. According to the story, the Canadians failed to attend the standards meeting at which the codes were assigned so they were given all the Ys, which no one else wanted.

12.1.10 IDENTIFIERS

Components whose values uniquely identify specific objects are another form of constrained set of values. For example, the values allowed for a Social Security Number in the United States are limited to the set of issued numbers. We call these components identifiers.

What differentiates identifiers from code sets is that they don't have to establish their meaning by reference to other values. They need not have an extension value.

What differentiates identifiers from code sets is that they need not have an extension value

It is common practice to use codes as identifiers but it does not make sense to use identifiers as codes.

12.1.11 NAMING COMPONENTS

Good naming rules are as important in Document Engineering as they are in any form of modeling. Meaningful names not only promote a common understanding and thus improve interoperability, they also aid in the analysis and design of reusable document components.

Meaningful component names promote a common understanding and encourage the use of reusable components

One of the means of dealing with ambiguity and variations of names is to formalize the language used. This formalization may vary from a common dictionary of terms to a specified ontology.

What is the word for...?

There are progressively more rigorous ways to explain what the terms we use mean.

A dictionary of terms is simply a set of allowed words. Its function is to constrain the set of words used in naming components. Typically this is an unbounded set, in the sense that new words can be added once they are used to name new components.

A controlled vocabulary is a fixed or closed dictionary. All components must be named using the same set of terms. The rationale for a controlled vocabulary is that to be learnable and useful the set of terms used to name components must be significantly smaller than the set of things being described. This is the challenge faced in any indexing or classification activity.

The most rigorous way to explain meaning is by using a formal ontology. This defines the agreed meaning of terms using a formal or logic-based language, so that all the relationships among the various terms are expressed in a consistent and precise fashion. In some ontologies, the set of relationships between the terms is itself a controlled vocabulary; for example, all topic maps express knowledge about a domain using topics, relationships, and occurrences, with the domain-specific semantics represented by names and types applied to each.

Formal ontologies range from simple ad hoc organizational schemes (like the categories used by Yahoo or eBay) to much richer and more formal mechanisms for assigning metadata and classifications to terms (like the progressively more sophisticated schemes for resource description emerging from the World Wide Web Consortium to support the vision of a semantic web).[9]

Not only is it never too early to apply good naming rules for components, it is a task that is refined throughout the Document Engineering phases. As the true meaning of each component expose itself via business rules, sets of values, associations with other components and reuse of patterns, we need to ensure that their names reflect their context of use as well as possible.

A common case of this is with the use of qualifying adjectives to nouns. For example, the business term shipping container may mean a cardboard box to a stationery storeowner, but to a freight forwarder it means a sea container—a steel box that can be 40 feet long. The results of any business transaction between these two parties could be interesting![10] However, the term is not a homonym. Both interpretations have the same general definition: "a container used to transport goods." But the specific context of use is missing from the name. Good names distinguish the context in which they are used. Names such as palletized shipping container or maritime shipping container qualify the objects for their more specialized contexts.

Qualified names specialize the context of use

Qualified names specialize general terms to convey the context in which a component is being used. For example, Party is a broad term that has many meanings. But in the context of the procurement business process, we would take the meaning of Party to be "a group acting on one side of an agreement." We can further specialize the term by qualifying it with the party's role in the business process by naming it Buyer Party. As with other components, the names of associations between components can be used as qualifiers to give specialized contextual meaning. For example, in narrative report documents we might have two contrasting associations, one called See Also for supporting arguments and another called But See Also for disconfirming ones. Or as we saw in Chapter 3 we might describe a publisher as the Publishing Party.

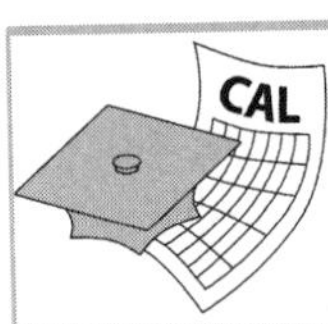

The Event Calendar project found it useful to establish a controlled vocabulary of terms that could be used in names and other semantic descriptions. Figure 12-9 is a sample of this vocabulary.

Word	Definition
Additional	further or added
Address	A. A description of the location of a person or organization, as written or printed on mail as directions for delivery: wrote down the address on the envelope. B. The location at which a particular organization or person may be found or reached: went to her address but no one was home.
Admission	The price required or paid for entering; an entrance fee.
Affiliation	To associate (oneself) as a subordinate, subsidiary, employee, or member.
Amount	a quantity of money
Area	A division of experience, activity, or knowledge; a field: studies in the area of finance; a job in the health-care area.
Associated	To connect or join together; combine.
Association	The act of associating or the state of being associated.
Audience	The part of the general public interested in a source of information or entertainment
Building	A structure that has a roof and walls and stands more or less permanently in one place
Cancelled	adj : (of events) no longer planned or scheduled
Charge	The price asked for something
Contact	N: a person who is in a position to give you special assistance; V: to communicate with
Date	Time stated in terms of the day, month, and year.

Figure 12-9. Sample Vocabulary for the Event Calendar Project

It is both practical and legitimate for a component to have different names in different artifacts of the modeling process. Each modeling artifact is targeted for a specific audience or purpose. For example, business models need common business names, document component models need formal business terms, and document implementation models (like XML schemas) need tag names. It is neither necessary nor desirable to have artificially terse program names for business users or descriptive language terms for tag names. What we need are clear rules for formulation and transformation of these names.

A component might have different names in different artifacts of the modeling process

In the Event Calendar project, the component called Affiliation in the conceptual models might be known as SpeakerAffiliation in the physical schema. And (as we saw in Figure 12-1) it may be called AddSpeakerA in any stylesheet or transformation application.

The typical names given to information components may be semantically misleading. For example, Product Number may not be a number, and could be better named a Product Identifier. A Product Name may be more like a narrative description including codes, sizes, quantities, and weights (that may require decomposition into individual components). And a Postal Code or Zipcode may not be a code (that is, a reference to another set of values) and should perhaps be called Postal Zone.

Throughout our approach we iteratively refine the names of components and get more precise about the rules for creating them.

12.2 CONSOLIDATING COMPONENTS

After we have harvested and disaggregated candidate components from our sampled document inventory, we need to ensure that every component is semantically distinct. That is, we want to have only one name for each component. This means we must merge synonyms (candidate components with different names but the same meaning) and rename homonyms (candidate components with the same names but different meanings). Our resulting modeling artifact will be a consolidated table of content components.

12.2.1 CREATING A CONSOLIDATED TABLE OF CONTENT COMPONENTS

We can best explain the task of creating a consolidated table of content components with a simple example using our Event Calendar project.

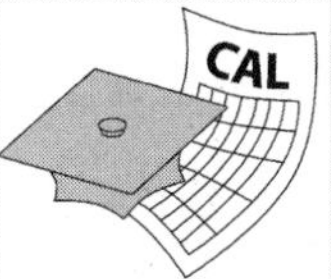

Let's suppose we have analyzed three information sources and arranged the candidate components from each of them in separate harvest tables as in Figure 12-10. (For simplicity we haven't shown any of the columns containing metadata or rules we collected to help us understand the meaning of each component).

SOURCE 1 HARVEST TABLE	
NAME	SEMANTIC DESCRIPTION
Title	The title of the event
Start Date	The date of the event, or the first date of a recurring event
End Date	The last date of the event
Location	The location of the event

SOURCE 2 HARVEST TABLE	
NAME	SEMANTIC DESCRIPTION
Title	The title of the event
Venue	The location of the event
Speaker	Name(s) of the person(s) speaking at the event
Description	The description of the event

SOURCE 3 HARVEST TABLE	
NAME	SEMANTIC DESCRIPTION
Title	The title of the speaker
Location	The location of the event
Speaker	Name(s) of the person(s) speaking at the event
Description	The description of the event

Figure 12-10 Candidate Components from Three Information Sources

We can begin consolidation with the candidate components from any of the information sources, but we recommend using the most authoritative source or the one that yielded the most components.

In our example we will use Source 1 as the table into which we merge the candidates from the other information sources.

The consolidation activity starts with a table whose dimensions are N x 3: N rows, one for each candidate component, and 3 columns, one for the component's name, the second for its description, and the third for the source from which it was harvested.

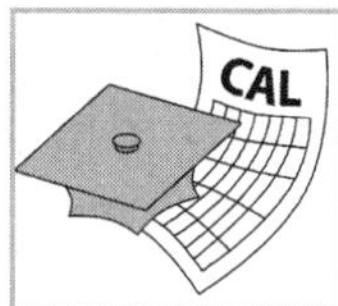

Because we are starting with Source 1 the consolidated table looks like Figure 12-11.

CONSOLIDATED TABLE OF CONTENT COMPONENTS		
Name	Semantic Description	Source 1
Title	The title of the event	X
Start Date	The date of the event, or the first date of a recurring event	X
End Date	The last date of the event	X
Location	The location of the event	X

Figure 12-11. Initial Consolidated Table of Content Components

Then consider each of the other information sources analyzed. Each new source adds a column to the consolidated table and any component that isn't already in the table adds a row. The consolidated table thus grows in both dimensions.

With Source 2 we add a column to the consolidated table where we will record the results of our analysis of that harvest table. The first candidate component, Title, is already in the table so we put a check mark in that row. We determine that Venue is a synonym of Location, already in the table, so we put a check mark in the row for Location and note that Source 2 had contained Venue, a synonym. The last two candidate components, Speaker and Description, are not already in the table, so we add new rows and make check marks in the column for Source 2.

CONSOLIDATED TABLE OF CONTENT COMPONENTS			
Name	Semantic Description	Source 1	Source 2
Title	The title of the event	X	X
Start Date	The date of the event, or the first date of a recurring event	X	
End Date	The last date of the event	X	
Location	The location of the event	X	X (merged with synonym Venue)
Speaker	Name(s) of the person(s) speaking at the event		X
Description	The description of the event		X

Figure 12-12. Intermediary Consolidated Table of Components

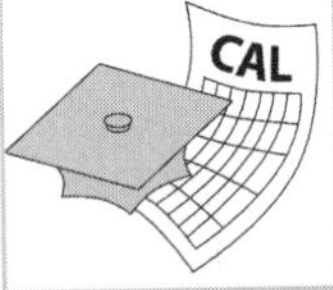

When we analyze the candidate components in Source 3, we determine that even though Title has the same name as a component already in the table, the Title in Source 3 is a homonym that means something different (the title of the speaker not the event). So we invent the new component name Speaker Title and make a check mark in that row for Source 3, noting that we had originally harvested it with the unqualified name of Title. When we're finished with our analysis of Source 3, the consolidated table looks like Figure 12-13.

CONSOLIDATED TABLE OF CONTENT COMPONENTS				
Name	Semantic Description	Source 1	Source 2	Source 3
Title	The title of the event	X	X	
Start Date	The date of the event, or the first date of a recurring event	X		
End Date	The last date of the event	X		
Location	The location of the event	X	X (merged with synonym Venue)	X
Speaker	Name(s) of the person(s) speaking at the event		X	X
Description	The description of the event		X	X
Speaker Title	The title of the speaker			X (renamed homonym Title)

Figure 12-13. Completed Consolidated Table of Content Components

Of course, things are never as simple in reality as they are in examples. Sometimes it will be difficult to decide whether a candidate component duplicates one already in the consolidated table. To improve semantic understanding, we should confirm any business rules that apply to harvested components, especially those that constrain its possible values or dependencies on other components. And we also should expect heated discussions and debates as components are added to the consolidated list.

Even if we're conducting a document analysis in our own organization or company, it is helpful to view the work as a consulting engagement. Our foremost consulting task is to help document creators and users reach a consensus understanding about the content components in their domain. The secondary task is to systematize this understanding into models.

Document analysis is a consulting engagement to help document creators and users reach a consensus understanding about the content components in their domain

12.2.2 ENSURING SEMANTIC UNIQUENESS

If we sort the rows of the consolidate table according to the number of sources in which candidate components appear, we'll discover those that are common to most or all of them. This suggests either that these components are at the core of the meaning of the analysis domain or that there is a lack of semantic precision in which a single name is assigned too broadly to different concepts.

The latter reflects the presence of homonyms. For example, a component called Item Identifier that appears in many documents may mean a physical product in some (for example, serial number of its manufacture), a type of product in others (such as its catalog number), and the specific requisition of a product in still others (as in a line item on an order).

A good way to distinguish homonyms is to add a context qualifier to the name

A good way to distinguish homonyms is to add a context qualifier to create more precise names. We might distinguish among the three types of Item Identifiers by naming them Specific Item Identifier, Catalog Item Identifier, and Line Item Identifier.

Using this naming rule to distinguish reuse of a component is something we tend to do naturally with things like dates (such as Deliver by Date) and codes (such as Replacement Product Code). We did this with the Title homonym in the consolidation example (Figure 12-13), when we renamed Title as Speaker Title—we could also have made the other Title into Event Title.

Conversely, once we sort the rows of the consolidated table, any components that appear in only a few sources are either components that contain more context-dependent semantics or are synonyms for other candidates with different names. In the former case, it is important to identify the contexts in which related sets of these components come and go. In the latter case, we can rename the synonym and merge two components into one.

But before congratulating ourselves for clever consolidation, we should ensure that these are true synonyms. They may be similar but not identical terms with meaningful semantic distinctions.

Shoehorning a component's definition to fit a different model is also risky when reusing standards or existing libraries of components. We should try not to subconsciously bend one component's meaning to fit another's definition. For example, it has been common practice in UN/EDIFACT implementations to use the component known as Size to include all measures, such as mass and dimension. So the weight of an object is described by a component called Size specified in kilograms and its length described by a component, also called Size, specified in meters. It would be better practice to name the components Mass and Dimension or even more specifically as Weight and Length. If we wanted to show the reuse of a common component (Size) we should qualify the reuse by calling the components Mass Size and Dimension Size. All of these options are more appropriate than trying to use a once-size-fits-all component.

Shoehorning a component's meaning to reuse a pattern is risky

Having expressed some caution about merging synonyms, we need to point out that there are situations where, even if two terms are not true synonyms, we might want to make them so to minimize overlap. While we can be descriptive and say "these two terms mean slightly different things," a good analyst asks "is this slight difference intentional or unintentional? And even if it is intentional, is it necessary? Do the business rules for our documents require us to enforce a semantic separation?"

In the consolidated table of content components for the Event Calendar project Public Contact Information was found in only one information source. This component was then modeled as a reuse of Contact Information in the context of being provided to the general public.

One possible merger of components to remove a synonym was the recognition of Venue as a synonym for Location. But the Location of an Event is not synonymous with Building Number or Room Number even though these are often used as values for Location. Some Locations were broadcast addresses, such as a URL for a webcast. These nuances precluded the use of standard library patterns for Location in our model.

Another potential pair of synonyms was Start Date (in 15 harvests) and Commencement (in only 1). But Commencement may take on values such as "second semester"—which is clearly not a meaningful Start Date. Further analysis revealed that Commencement may be related to Start Date, but it has additional properties, such as an association with Related Events. These different properties mean that they are not true synonyms.

At the end of the component analysis, the Event Calendar project identified more than 300 candidate components. The list included many obvious ones such as Event Description, Location, and Speaker but also more specialized components such as Admission Charge, Public Contact Information, and Work of Art Image.

Some of these candidate components are shown in Figure 12-14.

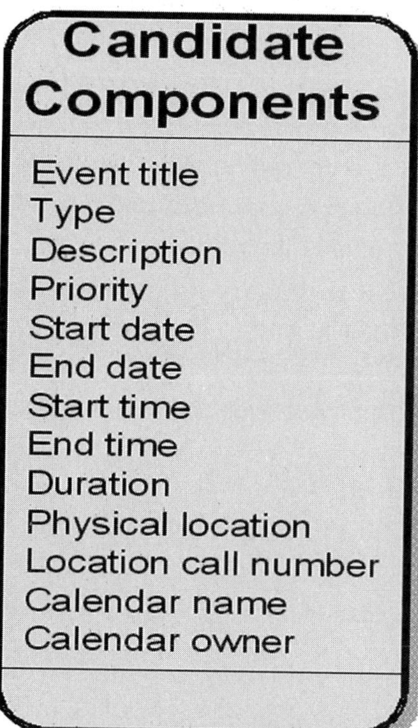

Candidate Components
Event title
Type
Description
Priority
Start date
End date
Start time
End time
Duration
Physical location
Location call number
Calendar name
Calendar owner

Figure 12-14. Some of the Candidate Components for Event Calendars

Having harvested and consolidated a list of components, we can take our consolidated table of candidate components and construct a conceptual model of the components by assembling them into a document component model. This is the subject of our next chapter.

12.3 KEY POINTS IN CHAPTER TWELVE

- Document analysis is a consulting engagement to help document creators and users reach a consensus understanding about the information components in their domain.
- Components are easier to find in transactional documents.
- Narrative documents have fewer components because we don't need to distinguish them.
- It is useful to examine source documents as well as published ones.
- Structures can be presentational but we are most concerned with semantic ones.
- We must recognize any content components that are implied by presentation rules.
- Structure is essential to understanding semantics.
- The presentational and semantic structures in tables require careful analysis.
- Many components have patterns for their possible values.
- Compliance with a pattern is not a sufficient test that the value was the intended one.
- Code sets are constrained sets of values that convey intension by extension.
- What differentiates identifiers from code sets is that they need not have an extension value.

- Meaningful component names promote a common understanding and encourage the use of reusable components.
- Qualified names specialize the context of use.
- A component might have different names in different artifacts in the modeling process.
- A good way to distinguish homonyms is to add a context qualifier to the name.
- Shoehorning a component's meaning to reuse a pattern is risky.

13

Assembling Document Components

13.0 INTRODUCTION

In Chapter 12 we described the harvesting and consolidation tasks of document component analysis. On completing these activities, we should have identified a consolidated set of candidate components that have three critical properties:

- The names of the components are distinct, because any synonyms now have the same name and any homonyms now have different ones.

- The components carry no presentational information, because we have identified and removed any styling or rendering.

- They are individual content components, because we have disaggregated the structures in which they were located to the level of granularity required by the context of use.

These candidate components are a set of meaningful building blocks that can be used to assemble semantically richer structures and models of documents.

The basic model of a document consists of two types of components, the content components that contain discrete information values and the structural components that are aggregations of the content ones. On this basis, a document model can be described as a top-level structural component that assembles the set of components needed to carry out a self-contained exchange of information.

Defining this document model is a two-stage process. First, we must assemble our components into structural building blocks composed of dependant components. These structural components also associate with other structural components in various roles. This creates a generalized view of the domain or context of use sometimes known as a Domain Model but which we prefer to call a document component model.

We then use this component model to assemble the components into one or more document assembly models. Each document assembly model takes a different view of the document component model by following the relationships between components that enforce the interpretation required for its more specialized context of use.

In this Chapter we will discuss the first of these tasks, how to assemble structural components that offer the most effective (if not optimal) re-usable components.

Then in Chapter 14, we will look at the design choices to be made when using this component model to create document assembly models for each type of document required.

13.1 ASSOCIATIONS BETWEEN COMPONENTS

After completing the consolidation activity we should have an understanding of the meaning of each content component in isolation. But we don't yet have a complete understanding of them in a specific context of use.

Many requirement rules concern dependencies and relationships between components

Many of the requirement rules identified when we analyzed the context of use concern dependencies and relationships between components. For example, we might identify pairs of components such as Caption and Illustration, or Name and Address. The relationships between the members of each pair are essential to understanding the meaning of both components. For example, there may be a rule that states that a Caption and Illustration go together to define a Figure, or a rule that a Name and Address go together to create a Contact. And we also need to recognize that "going together" means different things in the association between Caption and Illustration than it does between Name and Address. We might say that a Caption describes an Illustration, whereas a Name is located at an Address.

In terms of a building block analogy, some of the smaller blocks like Caption or Name always (or almost always) participate as part of larger structures like Figure and Contact, so these bigger blocks are necessary to make reuse more efficient and consistent.

13.2 DOCUMENT COMPONENT MODELS

The ultimate objective of information analysis in Document Engineering is to create a generalized, conceptual model capable of expressing the business rules for all types of documents required within the context of use. We call this artifact a document component model.

A document component model should define all the necessary components to maximize reuse and minimize redundancy when designing new document models. In fact, document designers have always pursued these twin goals of minimal redundancy and maximal reuse because they apply to models across the entire Document Type Spectrum.[1]

Document designers pursue the twin goals of minimal redundancy and maximal reuse

How rigorously we can define a document component model depends on the number and precision of the business rules it needs to satisfy. But there are some simple principles.

A small set of loose rules indicate a context of use that can be satisfied by a simple document component model, while more precise rules demand more sophistication in the model.

Business rules and the components that emerge from transactional documents tend to be more content oriented. This means the components for these contexts lend themselves to precise definition in terms of data types, possible values, and occurrence restrictions. In contrast, the rules emerging from contexts dominated by narrative documents are more qualitative and less precise. So the components that emerge from their analysis tend to be larger, have a more generalized meaning, and are less suited for or subject to absolute instance or structural rules.

But before proceeding we should mention the modeling artifacts we will be using for these tasks. We could continue to represent our model in descriptive or tabular form as we did in Chapter 12. But we prefer a graphical notation for describing component models to ensure more clarity and rigor in representing the relationships among components.

Notations for Describing Models

Conceptual models such as document component and document assembly models are often depicted using graphical notations because most of us can more easily comprehend structural patterns and associations in graphical depictions. Graphical representation lets us apply perceptual as well as cognitive analysis and helps improve our designs by making it easier to identify missing or redundant information.

One of the most effective ways to describe document models is by using a data modeling notation such as Entity Attribute Relationship (EAR) diagrams or the Class Diagrams provided by the Unified Modeling Language (UML).

Not surprisingly, EAR (sometimes just called ER) diagrams define Entities (what we call structures) of Attributes (content components), and their Relationships (associations). These are particularly suited to document component models because they provide all the necessary constructs for the models and no more. However, their intrinsic relational network format is less suited for describing document assembly models.

The UML Class Diagrams are similar to EAR diagrams, but use Object Classes (structures), Attributes (content), and Associations (associations). As we noted earlier, the UML is increasingly popular for Document Engineering because of its rich metamodel for describing both information and processes.

13.2.1 RULES IN NARRATIVE DOCUMENT CONTEXTS

As we discussed in Chapter 12, within transactional types of documents, content components hold individual pieces of information. But in contexts with more narrative types of documents such as technical publications, reports, policies, procedures, and reference books, the content components tend to be in coarser blocks of text without much regular internal structure. Even in these components the rules we discover may concern the relationships among components and reflect principles or best practices in document design. These are often specified in style guides, rules, or templates that guide authors when they create these types of documents.

For example, the style guide for equipment Operator Instructions might include a rule that requires a warning for any procedure that might be dangerous to the person doing it. Likewise, following the adage that a picture is worth a thousand words, there may also be a requirement to include one or more illustrations or diagrams that portray the arrangement or assembly of parts in the device or machine for which the dangerous procedure applies. This would in turn imply the requirement for a caption for each illustration or diagram.

Note that these rules are primarily structural in character, specifying relationships about the occurrence or co-occurrence of components. The style guide is unlikely to specify the exact wording of the warning text, the number of steps in the procedure, the number of illustrations, the choice of illustrations, or other rules that concern the content of the components. These decisions are left up to the author of the content. It requires skill and judgment to write the warning and procedure, to design and draw the appropriate illustrations, and to write concise captions that convey the necessary information without the text that the illustration supposedly makes extraneous.[2]

In the Event Calendar project we analyzed the narrative style document known as the UC Berkeley Events directory. The example in Figure 13-1 shows the types of content we might expect in this document.

Saturday

Music: Dan Zanes and Friends play family-favorites
November 29-30, times vary, Zellerbach Hall | Tickets

Performing updated versions of traditional American folk songs, dance classics, and an ever-increasing number of originals, Brooklyn-based musicians Dan Zanes and Friends are coming to UC Berkeley to play two shows of exuberant roots music for the entire family.

Formerly the lead singer of alternative 80s rock band The Del Fuegos, Dan Zanes has found a second calling creating his own style of rock and folk music for young people. Called "a leading light in the recent movement of underground rockers making cool children's music" by the Chicago Sun Times, Zanes began recording "family-style" music in the late 90s. In 2000, his new band, Rocket Ship Revue, released their first

Figure 13-1. a Narrative Event Calendar

We determined that this narrative event document has a component that describes some form of classification, in this case "Music," and a title, "Dan Zanes and Friends play family favorites."

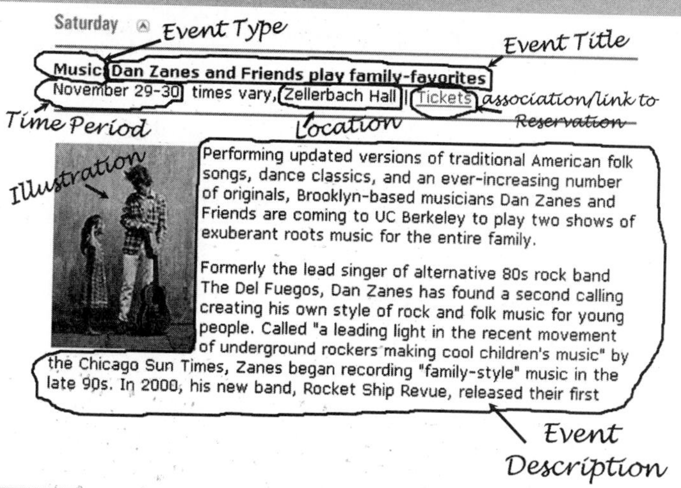
Saturday
Event Type
Event Title
Music
Dan Zanes and Friends play family-favorites
November 29-30
times vary,
Zellerbach Hall
Tickets
association/link to Reservation
Time Period
Location
Illustration
Performing updated versions of traditional American folk songs, dance classics, and an ever-increasing number of originals, Brooklyn-based musicians Dan Zanes and Friends are coming to UC Berkeley to play two shows of exuberant roots music for the entire family.
Formerly the lead singer of alternative 80s rock band The Del Fuegos, Dan Zanes has found a second calling creating his own style of rock and folk music for young people. Called "a leading light in the recent movement of underground rockers making cool children's music" by the Chicago Sun Times, Zanes began recording "family-style" music in the late 90s. In 2000, his new band, Rocket Ship Revue, released their first
Event Description

Figure 13-2. Analysis of a Narrative Event Calendar

Further analysis revealed that Time Period and Location were also separate components and that the document had an association through a hypertext link to reservation information. But the main body of the document was mixed content that described the event including some embedded illustrations.

From this we established some basic rules: that Description may contain one or more Illustrations, an Event may be linked to Reservation information, and that Time Period can have narrative content.

Narrative documents might conform to structural rules, but their content is inherently heterogeneous

Indeed, it is often because of the obvious need to leave decisions about content up to the author in some contexts that narrative documents are employed rather than transactional ones. Instances of narrative documents like repair procedures, policies, or textbooks might conform to structural rules, but their content is inherently heterogeneous and the semantic relationships among their content components can be only weakly specified. We can't easily reduce the process of creating them to "filling out a form" in which every instance has exactly the same components in precise and fixed relationships.

This doesn't mean that anything goes in narrative components. But the regularity and consistency between their content largely depends on the discipline of the author to follow a consistent policy or style guide.

13.2.2 RULES IN TRANSACTIONAL CONTEXTS

The context of use for transactional documents typically yields a comparatively larger number of similar document instances.

Because these documents are often produced and processed by automated business systems, the relationships among their components need to be precise and fixed so that every application that needs them will understand them in exactly the same way. This is why the semantic and structural rules concerning components such as Price and Quantity used for Orders, Invoices, or Receipts need to be unambiguous and unchanging.

13.3 METHODS FOR AGGREGATING COMPONENTS

The differences between transactional and narrative style documents and the nature of the business rules that apply to them influence the approach to creating document component models. In particular, they may determine the extent to which we can employ formal and rigorous techniques to decide which candidate components go together to create aggregate or composite structural components.

The weak semantic constraints in narrative components often don't provide unambiguous justification for deciding what components go together. But this doesn't mean we have no way of advancing the goals of increased regularity and minimal redundancy in our component models. We can use our judgment as designers to enforce stronger and clearer constraints in models. We can also eliminate choices that could lead to inconsistencies or interoperability problems.

For example, if analysis for the As-Is model reveals that not all of assembly instructions contain illustrations, we could establish a requirement to make them mandatory in our To-Be model so that they always go together. Similarly, as we discussed in Section 12.2.2, when our component harvest yields a set with nuanced distinctions, we might decide that such additional complexity isn't required by our context. So we could merge the separate components into a single one with a slightly broader meaning that can be reused in place of the others.

13.3.1 THE CLASSICAL DOCUMENT ANALYSIS APPROACH

Eve Maler and Jeanne El Andaloussi's "Developing SGML DTDs: From Text to Model to Markup"[3] is the definitive treatise on document analysis with SGML for technical publications and other narrative types of documents. Published in 1995, this book was the first to systematize the evolving best practices for using SGML as an encoding syntax for models of documents.

Maler and El Andaloussi's methodology for identifying and aggregating components proposes a series of iterative steps. These include Identifying Potential Components (similar to what we call harvesting), Classifying Components (part of the activity we call consolidation), and Identifying Block Components (part of what we call assembling structures). The capabilities and constraints on models imposed by SGML permeate each step of the methodology.

This methodology was designed for analyzing and modeling the technical publications and other narrative documents for which SGML was invented. Because the business rules in these contexts tend to be weak and nonspecific, there are limits to the rigor with which components can be grouped into structures. Any document analysis methodology that focuses on narrative contexts inevitably pays more attention to the hierarchical structures in which components are found in existing documents. So instead of yielding an explicit document component model that describes only semantic relationships among the content components, the set of candidate components that emerges is a combination of content and presentational structural ones (such as lists and tables). The relative proportions of each type of component in this mix are hard to predict and heavily influenced by the skill and biases of the document analyst.

In narrative documents weaker semantic and content rules limit the rigor for grouping components into structures

Such a modeling approach can produce good models, but there are no objective criteria for assessing whether a model is optimal. Furthermore, the qualitative and heuristic character of the methodology emphasizes the possibly idiosyncratic stylistic contributions of the document analyst to the models.

Of course, in contexts where there are few strong semantic constraints, we can't fully exploit the power of formal techniques for assembling document components. We may resort to an approach that assembles structures iteratively through a kind of reverse engineering of the documents required or suggested by the context. We call this approach core plus contextualization, which we will describe in Chapter 14. In effect this approach bypasses the formal analysis of component assemblies in favor of direct assembly of document models.

However, the emergence of XML, new schema languages other than DTDs, and the exploding need for models of documents for business processes highlighted the limitations of this document analysis approach. Document Engineering for these contexts required an approach that applies more formal and rigorous modeling techniques.

13.3.2 THE CLASSICAL DATA ANALYSIS APPROACH

The stronger constraints we find in contexts that include transactional documents inspired us to adapt formal techniques from the disciplines of data analysis and database design for assembling content components into their composite structures.

In particular, the principle known as normalization involves a set of techniques for modeling components and structures that minimizes redundancy and supports integrity. These principles were developed as part of Codd's Relational Theory for the design of databases,[4] but we have applied them with good results to the design of models for document components.

13.4 APPLYING NORMALIZATION TO DOCUMENT ENGINEERING

A document component model emerges as a network of structural components through a series of refinements that are collectively called normalization. The final model has many desirable properties:

- It reuses common patterns, and
- It involves minimal redundancy and duplication.

Most importantly, it captures the true semantics of the components within the context of use by embodying any instance, semantic, and structural rules in an unambiguous and formal way.

A document component model embodies instance, semantic, and structural rules in an unambiguous and formal way

Our goal here is not to teach the principles of normalization. There are already many good texts available.[5] Our objective is to demonstrate the practical use of its data analysis techniques to help us develop a document component model.

Logical and Physical Data Models

Data analysts and database designers should be aware that we will not address issues involved with turning logical data models into physical database ones.

Database models require resolution of any many-to-many associations and any duplicate association paths to be removed. But such issues are not relevant in the design of a document component model because we want our logical component model to show all possible associations.

For Document Engineers, the physical data models are the document assembly models.

13.4.1 FUNCTIONAL DEPENDENCY

Functional dependency is the most significant concept in normalization and the one most applicable to Document Engineering. In general terms, dependency describes the impact on one object of change to another. Functional dependency is a specialized form of dependency. It means that if the value of one component changes when the value of another component changes, the former is dependent on the latter. Formally stated this is:

"Given an object X, property A of X is functionally dependent on property B of X, if and only if each A-value in X has associated with it precisely one B-value in X (at any one time)."

This may sound daunting, but it is something we all tend to do intuitively when grouping sets of data. For example, if we recognize that the price per sheet (A) of printer paper (X) reduces if the pack size (B) changes from reams to cartons, this means price per sheet (A) is functionally dependent on pack size (B). The price per sheet (A) is known as the dependent component and the pack size (B) is called the determinant component.

It follows from this that for every value of the determinant component (B) there is only one value for the dependent one (A). In other words, at any one time the pack size for our printer paper has only one price per sheet. This apparently simple statement lies at the heart of assembling structures that are aggregations of dependent components.

In transactional documents we find rich sets of dependency rules that apply to components that deal with organizations, addresses, taxes, payments, deliveries and personal details. Dependency rules may even be explicitly stated in documents such as forms. These may indicate the relationships of components using instructions for their completion. For example, an instruction like "If you are the owner of the vehicle, complete section 17," identifies one part of the form as being owner information and section 17 as being dependent on the status of the applicant.

The principle of functional dependency identifies essential semantic components and reusable patterns

In more narrative types of documents, dependencies among components are often expressed in cross-references, footnotes, and other kinds of links between content. This is especially true in publications like encyclopedias, dictionaries, and scientific and legal literature, where most authors make precise links and clearly express the reasons for making them. Unfortunately, many of the links found on web pages lack this semantic rigor, and there may be little relationship between the components on each end of the link.

Understanding the functional dependencies of components does more than clarify their meaning in the document component model. If done well, these components also provide patterns suitable for reuse.

13.4.2 ESSENTIALITY

Another of the primary objectives when building a document component model is to achieve essentiality. That is, to model only the essential components and nothing else. Having duplicated or redundant components in our model degrades its integrity, introduces ambiguity into their meaning, and creates an unnecessary overhead.

It is important to remember that at this point we are creating a conceptual model of the components required for all the documents in our context of use. While some of these components are likely to be duplicated across (and even within) different document models, they should all share the same component model definition.

For example, in Section 10.8.1 we described key information components that must be contained in different documents to link information within one instance of a business collaboration. Essentiality means that these components should share the same definition in our document component model.

Avoiding the problems of duplication and redundancy is as important to Document Engineers as it is to database designers. Of course, one of the significant differences between information used in documents and in databases is its persistence.

Storing information in a single, common database means the component's values will persist over time. Maintaining integrity of the information is critical to its business purpose, so it's necessary to build essentiality rules into any database model. By contrast, many document exchanges are transitory or impermanent.

So it could be argued that essentiality is less critical in the design of document models. However, the goal to provide clarity of meaning about values found in any component still applies—even if their values do not persist over time. We still need essential components even if we aren't concerned with essential values.

If a repeated component has different values in more than one document or more than one place in a single document, which one do we treat as correct? For example, if an Invoice document contained an Order Reference and each Item on the Invoice also had an Order Reference, can we trust they will not contradict each other?

There is a universal requirement in any document for content integrity and modeling only essential components supports this requirement.

Content integrity of a document means using only essential components

Essentiality also means avoiding modeling components that are derivative, that is, those whose values are derived from the values of other components. For example, an order might contain an Extended Price whose value is computed by multiplying Quantity and Price. We may not want to treat Extended Price as a "first class citizen" in our document component model because if the value for Extended Price did not equal to Quantity times Price, all the values would be suspect.

Derived components also appear in models of narrative documents. Tables of Contents, Permuted Indexes, and Lists of Figures and Tables are all structures that aggregate or extract values from other content in the document. Modeling these as separate components creates integrity problems when we're trying to keep them current and synchronized. In fact, it is better to consider them as presentation components that are generated from the content when needed.

Of course, what is considered essential information comes down to the business rules for the context of use. If organizations exchange only the source components they must use (or at least understand) the same rules for deriving the result from the source.

Striving for essentiality exposes additional rules

An important benefit of striving for essentiality is that we often expose additional rules for the context of use, further enriching the model. For example we might identify a semantic, instance, and processing rule that says Extended Price must always be calculated from Quantity multiplied by Price. The rule supports essentiality. In a similar way, control totals and checksums are not derivative if they are used to validate content integrity because then they have additional rules associated with them.

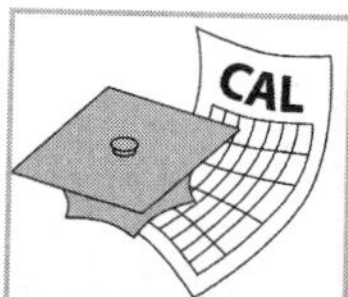

In the Event Calendar project, if we define the Start Time and End Time of an event, do we also need to convey Duration? In other words, is Duration a derived component that we need not include in our model? This questions the semantics of the component called Duration. Does Duration include all time between the Start Time and End Time of an Event? What about breaks? Do we always have an End Time?

In this case we realized that Duration cannot always be derived and must remain a separate component.

13.4.3 THE NORMAL FORMS

The process of normalization progressively refines the relationships between components to satisfy a set of five normal forms.

Normalization starts with models in the first normal form, often abbreviated as 1NF, when every component identified can have only one value. That is, they are atomic within our context of use.

The remaining forms of normalization combine the components into aggregate structures that capture more of their semantic, instance, and structural rules. We might say that normalization identifies meaningful structural components for a component model.

Normalization identifies the associations that guide the assembly of document models

Normalization also identifies how these structural components relate to each other. And it is these relationships or associations that determine how we subsequently assemble our required document models.

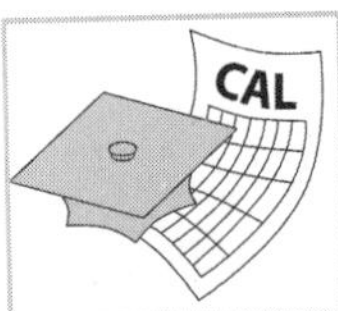

For example, in the Event Calendar project, identifying a structure as an Event and identifying the structure for a Speaker does not tell us which Speakers are talking at which Event or whether an Event can have more than one Speaker. We implement these rules by modeling the association between the two structures.

13.4.4 IDENTIFYING PRIMARY KEYS

The first step in normalizing document components is to nominate something (sometimes called an entity or an object class) that we expect will be a structure in our model.

In the Event Calendar project, we knew that Event was going to be an important part of our model. So we started with a structure called Event.

We then identify the content component from the consolidated list that uniquely identifies a single occurrence of this structure. That is, its value is unique for every occurrence of the structure. This component is known as the structure's primary key. For example, if our chosen structure is an Order, the obvious choice for a primary key component may be the Order Number.

Composite and Surrogate Keys

When trying to uniquely identify a specific instance of a structure, it is possible that no one component will suffice.

For example, an Order Number seems like a good candidate for the primary key of an Order. But from a seller's perspective it may not be adequate. This can happen if there is a processing rule that the buyer issues the Order Number. This means different buyers may use the same identifier, and a seller might receive the same Order Number on different Orders from different buyers.

In this case, only the addition of a component such as Buyer Identifier, combined with the Order Number, will create a unique primary key. This combination of more than one component to uniquely identify a structure is known as a composite key.

There are also situations where not even a composite key can be made unique for every instance of a structure. For example, addresses are very hard to identify uniquely without using all the components in the structure as a composite key. In these cases it is common practice to create a "surrogate" key. Surrogate keys are artificially created purely for the purpose of unique identification. So we might introduce a unique identification number to provide the primary key for an address. In a similar way to how a social security number uniquely identifies a US citizen. The value of the surrogate primary key has no meaning beyond identification.

The choice of what to use is almost arbitrary. We say almost, because there are usually some things that intuitively seem like natural structural components. We apply experience and heuristics to make a meaningful choice. It really won't affect the final outcome, but some choices make the process feel more logical.

Taking the initial structure and its primary key, we then identify components that are functionally dependent on the primary key. We do this by reviewing the structural, semantic, and instance rules already identified. We may also want to pose new questions about business requirements to expose new rules.

Functional dependency is determined by structural, semantic, and instance rules

Functionally dependent components will change value with changes to the value of the primary key component. This means that each value of the determinant primary key component can have only one value for the dependent component.

Normalization rules tell us that any components that are not dependent on the primary key need to be separated into other structures.

In the Event Calendar project, the Event Title component was the primary key of Event—each Event would have an Event Title and every Event Title would uniquely identify an Event. This was a deliberate simplification of the model and meant introducing a new business rule ensuring that only unique event titles were used.

In our set of candidate components, we then determined that Event Type, Description, and Priority were all dependent on the Event Title. Every new Event would have a new Event Title and one set of values each for Event Type, Description, and Priority.

By noting requirement rules and studying sample instances from the calendars, we established that an Event Title might actually be the same for a different Start Date and End Date. For example, an Event like a course at the university may run over different semesters. Therefore, Start Date and End Date cannot be dependent on the Event Title because there can be more than one value for each of them. This means they cannot be functionally dependent on the Event.

So the Start Date and End Date components must be dependent on another structure. In this case we called the structure Time Period. Our analysis also suggested that the Start Time and End Time components belong to this structure as well because they are also functionally dependent on the Time Period.

In fact, all these components form part of the composite primary key of Time Period. If we changed the Start Date, the Start Time, the End Date, or the End Time, we would have changed the Time Period. All four components are needed to uniquely identify a time period.

And, of course, an Event is not changed just because the timing has changed.

Whenever we separate structures, we need to identify any associations that may exist between them. These associations will also have metadata that describes how the structural components associate with each other.

For example, the roles in an association determine the context that applies to each structure when it participates in the association. If an Order structure may have an association with a Party, then in one context Party may take on the role of Buyer Party. There are roles for each end of an association (although some are more meaningful than others). So in another context, Order may take on the role of Current Order.

Both roles in a single association will also have cardinality. A role's cardinality determines how many occurrences there may be for each structural component in an association. We use cardinality to express structural rules in our model. For example, a cardinality of one-to-many Order Lines in an association with Order implements the structural rules, "an Order must have at least one Order Line" and "an Order may have an unlimited number of Order Lines."

Cardinality helps us understand the association between two structures

Sometimes cardinality helps us understand why there is an association between two structural components. For example, if the cardinality of both roles between two structures can only be one to one, then the structures are codependent and should probably be combined into one.

To give roles in associations a name, we typically use a verb to describe its purpose.

With the Event Calendar, we determined that an Event played a role in its association with a Time Period—an Event takes place over a Time Period. In fact, as we saw with the example earlier, an Event may take place over several Time Periods. So the cardinality for an Event's role in this association is zero to many. The zero cardinality makes the association optional—an Event may not yet have any designated Time Period (perhaps the event is still being planned).

With the Time Period's role of this association, it seems reasonable to add that a Time Period can have zero or many Events—there may be several Events happening at any given time, or none at all.

In the Event Calendar model, we chose the name "happens at" for the role taken by an Event in its association with a Time Period. The name came from the observation that an "Event happens during/on/at/over Time Period." For example, "The Dan Zanes and Friends play Family-Favorites concert happens at 8:00 p.m. on November 29."

This association is shown in Figure 13-3.

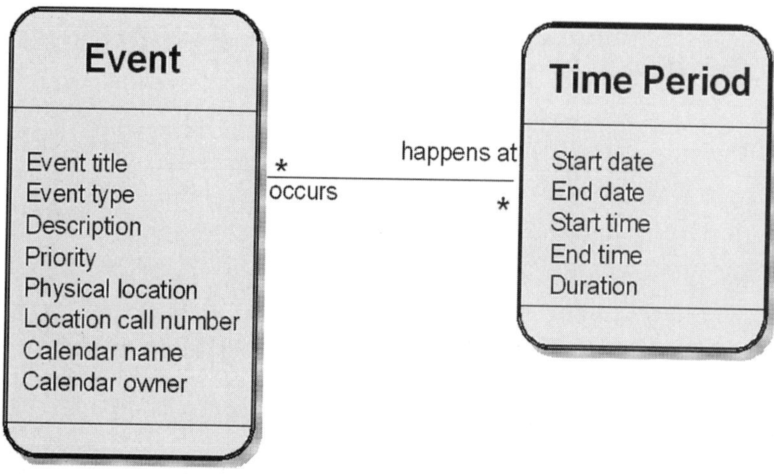

Figure 13-3. Model for the Association between Event and Time Period

In some cases it may be difficult to give meaningful names to the roles in an association. We might have to compromise with a semantically weak name for the role, such as "has a" or "relates to."

But naming roles can be a useful semantic device for describing the context of use. These names become useful qualifiers when we use the roles for assembling document models. As discussed earlier, naming a role in the association between an Order and a Party as Buyer effectively qualifies the role of the Party as the Buyer Party. We can then have another role named Seller and so qualify the Party for a different context.

The naming of roles can be a useful semantic device for qualifying the context of use

In assembling components for the Event Calendar model, we realized that there were two different roles in the associations between an Event and a Sponsor. We named these two different roles "local" (for the organization putting on the event) and "corporate" (for the organization funding the event). These both create an association between an Event and a Sponsor, but their different roles reflect the different contexts required. These different roles and associations are depicted in Figure 13-4.

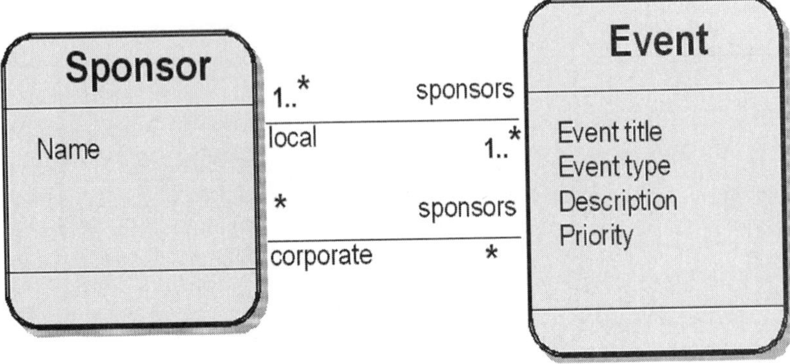

Figure 13-4. The Two Associations between Sponsor and Event

To complete the process of normalization, we continue with this dependency analysis until we have aggregated all components in the consolidated list into appropriate structures.

In our analysis of Event Calendars, we found that neither Physical Location nor Location Call Number appeared to depend on the Event Title. Both depended on where the Event takes place, because an Event may take place in several Locations, either simultaneously (both as a lecture and a Webcast) or sequentially (an exhibition may move to another venue). Once again, these components needed to be separated into another structure we called Location. We then defined the role names and cardinality for the association between the Event structure and the Location structure.

Figure 13-5 depicts the resulting model with separate structures for Event, Location, and Time Period.

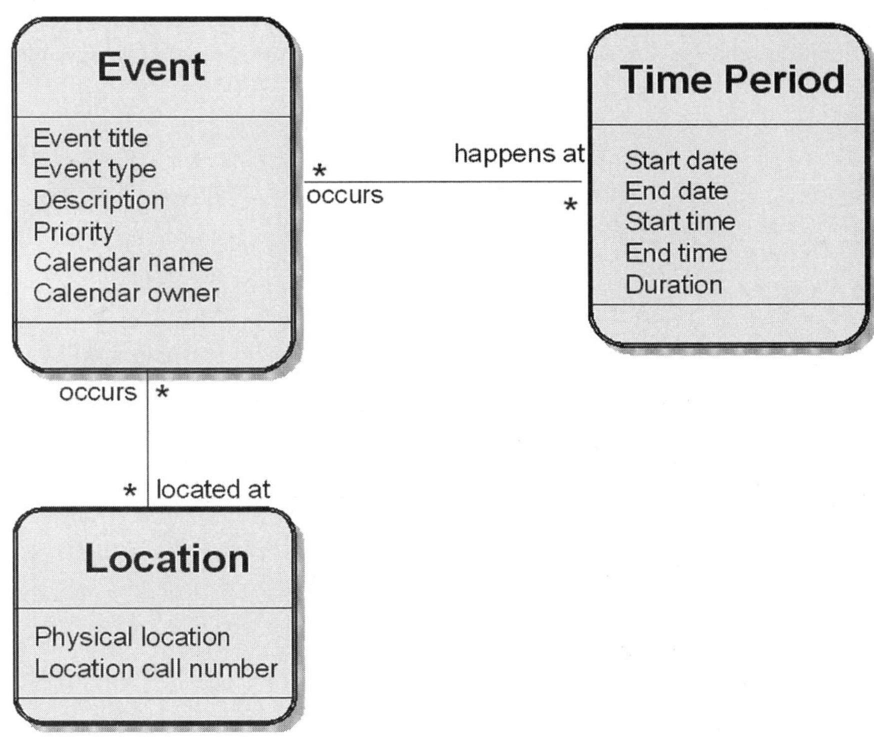

Figure 13-5. Model Showing Event, Time Period, and Location Aggregates

13.4.5 RECURSIVE ASSOCIATIONS

When assembling components into dependent structures, we may find components that appear to be dependent on different occurrences of the same structure. For example, the component Alternative Part Identifier within a Part structure may refer to another instance of a Part structure. In other words, a part may have one primary identifier for itself and several part identifiers for alternative parts. In these cases the component is actually qualifying a role in an association between the structure and other occurrences of itself. We call these recursive associations.

Recursive associations are not uncommon. We see them when packages may be contained within other packages, when transactions may refer to previous transactions, or when an article references another article.

In the Event Calendar, an Event was sometimes part of a group of Events, such as a Seminar series or Sports Carnival. The structural pattern of the group of Events was found to be the same as an individual Event. They both have locations and time periods and so on.

We modeled this association by allowing an Event to be related to another Event using a role that we called Parent as shown in Figure 13-6.

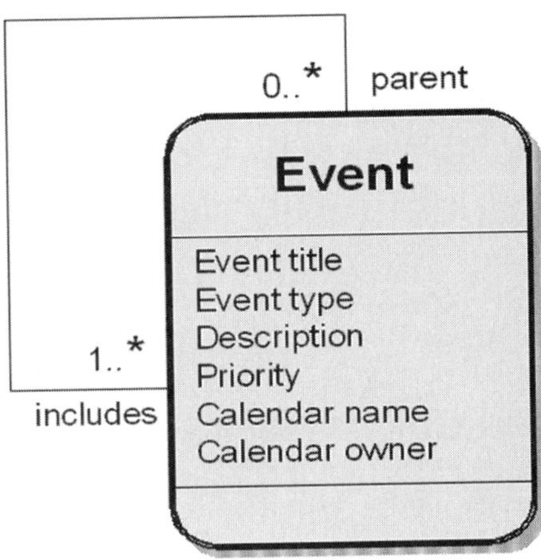

Figure 13-6. Recursive Association for Event

The stage of normalization we have reached is known as the third normal form (3NF). Often this is the point at which database designers stop their analysis and start creating physical models of database tables.

However, 3NF may not describe all the rules we need to define. There are additional normal forms that deal with rules that apply when pairs or sets of components have values that are dependent. These are known as multivalue dependencies.

13.4.6 MULTIVALUE DEPENDENCIES

Identifying any multivalue dependencies allows us to capture more sophisticated structural, semantic, and instance rules in the document component model.

Multivalue dependencies identify more sophisticated structural, semantic, and instance rules

Modeling multivalue dependencies requires a special type of structure, one that has no other purpose but to associate instances of two or more other structural components. This type of virtual structure is sometimes called an intersection entity or an association class because it involves converting what were properties of associations into their own structures. In fact, the names given to these types of structures are often the nouns taken from the roles in the associations they resolve.

Like recursive associations, multivalue dependencies are not uncommon when modeling document components.

They are elusive and subtle but can usually be identified by careful analysis. We can best explain this by using an example from the Event Calendar study.

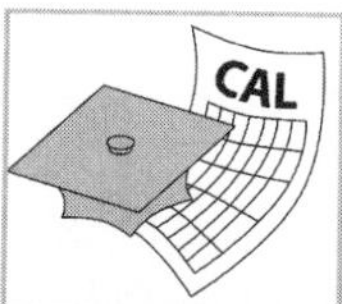

In the Event Calendar model, we realized that an association also exists between Location and Time Period. This did not emerge during our initial modeling, but it appeared when we were reexamining the inventory.

It was clear that every Location may experience several Time Periods—time passes at every place. Also, a Time Period will occur over several Locations—all places experience the same time (at least in our simple universe) regardless of any events.

The diagram in Figure 13-7 shows this new association.

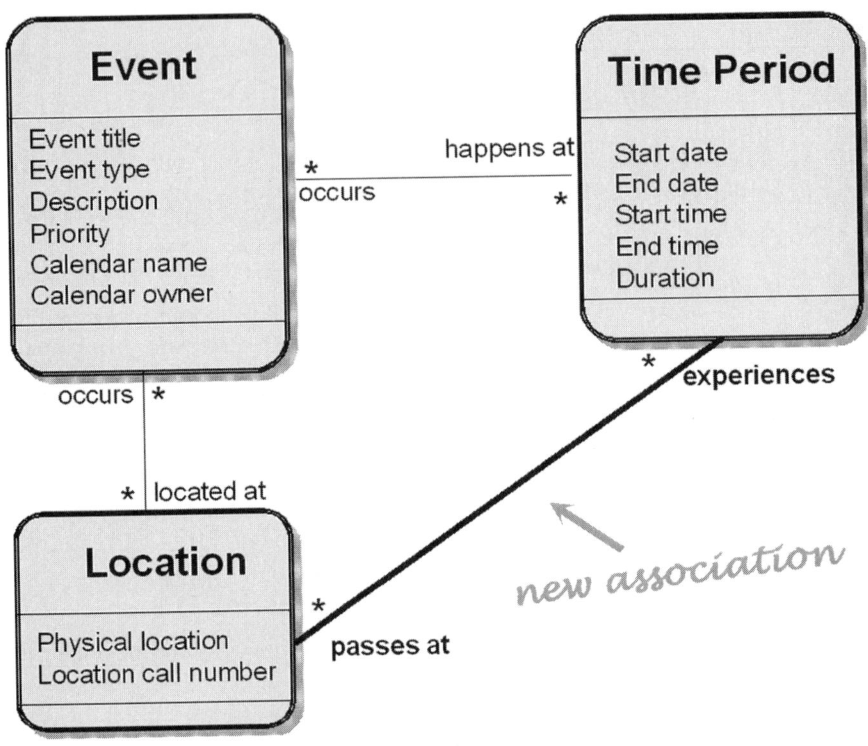

Figure 13-7. Circular Sets of Associations

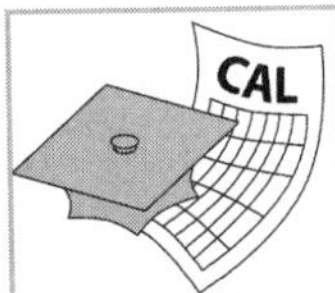

Unfortunately, this new association creates a circular set of associations between Event, Time Period, and Location. This may not be as meaningful as we intended.

Our model can show only how each Event relates to a Time Period, or each Time Period to a Location, or each Location to an Event. What our model can describe is what events are happening at what location, what events occur at what times, and what are times and places. We can describe that "Dan Zanes and Friends play Family Favorites on November 28, 29, and 30" (Event and Time Period). Or we can say that "Dan Zanes and Friends play Family Favorites in the Amphitheater and in Zellerbach Hall" (Event and Location). Or we can say that "the

Amphitheater is in use on November 28 and Zellerbach Hall is in use on November 29 and 30"(Location and Time Period).

But we cannot describe one specific event at one time at one place. For example, "Dan Zanes and Friends play Family Favorites on November 28 in the Amphitheater" and "Dan Zanes and Friends play Family Favorites on November 29 and 30 in Zellerbach Hall" (as can be seen on the UC Berkeley Event Calendar page in Figure 13-1). We cannot define the multivalue dependency that exists between Time, Location, and Event.

To define this in our model we need to associate a specific Time Period with the combination of one Location plus Event set of values—that is, a multivalue set. The model described above does not do this.

A good name for the new structure we create to eliminate this problem might be Occurrence, because it will combine one Event occurring in one Location during one Time Period.

The diagram in Figure 13-8 describes the structure Occurrence, used to resolve the multivalue dependency between Event, Location, and Time Period.

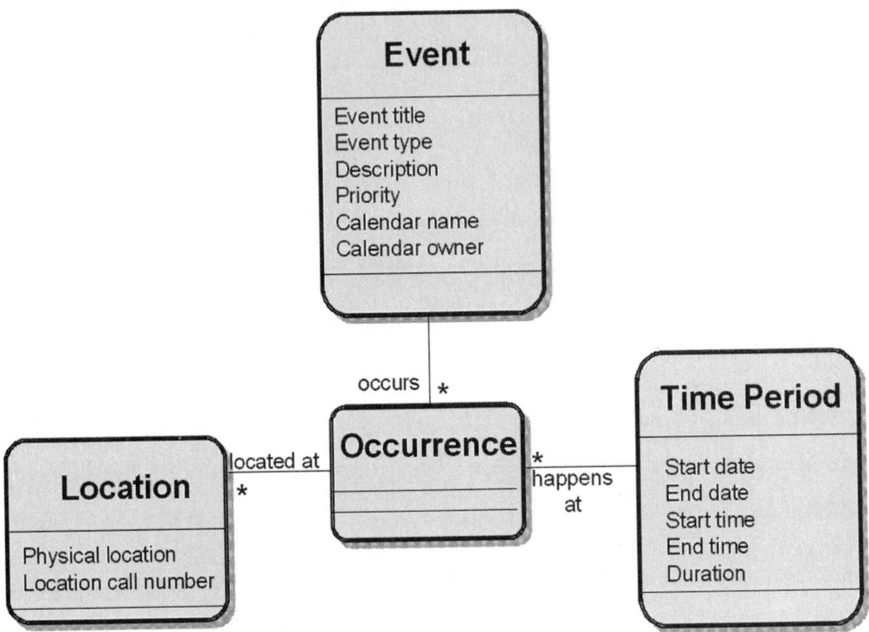

Figure 13-8. Resolving a Multivalue Dependency

13.5 REFINING THE DOCUMENT COMPONENT MODEL

We have just about reached the stage where modeling for analysis gives way to the opportunities for design. But before we complete a document component model, we should consider some refinements.

While the processes of normalization are formally defined, ultimately it is the heuristic interpretation of business requirements and rules that determines how we apply these formalisms and therefore determine the quality of the final component model.

Practical experience tells us that we may need to reverse or relax our interpretation of dependency for the sake of other requirements such as simplicity, interoperability, or efficiency. This may result in a smaller set of somewhat larger components than complete normalization would yield.

Having structures based on dependent components allows us to make conscious rather than ad hoc modeling refinements

But even in these cases, having dependent component structures as a reference allows us to make conscious rather than ad hoc modeling refinements. In other words, while it is not essential to have a perfectly normalized document component model, we should at least understand if and why it is not.

One common refinement is to try to reduce the number of associations in the model. For example, if we determine that actually having multiple instances of a role in an association is rare, even though not impossible, it may be simpler to merge the two structures and accept some potential duplication and therefore redundancy. In effect, we denormalize parts of the model.

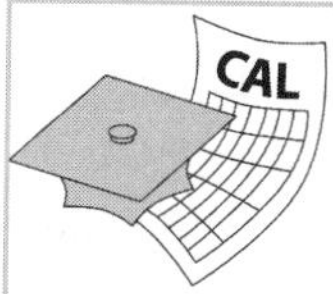

In the document inventory we determined that the Charge Structure of an Event is also dependent on the Time Period and the Location of the Event. For example, matinee performances are cheaper and outdoor concerts may be free.

We decided to simplify these dependencies by deciding that using a different Time Period or Location with a different Charge Structure would constitute a different Event. This simplification may require us to duplicate some event information, but it achieved a simpler model and clarified what we meant by an Event.

13.5.1 REUSING COMPONENT PATTERNS

One of the most important refinements we can make to a document component model is to adopt patterns.

In Chapter 3 we described how patterns are powerful design tools that promote interoperability, provide trading community conformance, and encourage standardization through natural selection. And in Chapter 10 we explained how patterns can be applied to business processes. Now we need to understand how to detect and apply patterns in our document component models.

Patterns exist not only in structural and content components but also in associations. For example, an Address structure may be reused in roles such as Postal Address, Delivery Address, and Pickup Address. These may all use an identical address structure—they are just applied in a different context as suggested by qualifying their names.

Reusable patterns are often found in common components such as Dates, Identifiers, and Measurements. So we can have Birth Date and Start Date, Organization Identifier and Product Identifier, or Gross Weight and Net Weight as reuses of Date, Identifier, and Weight component patterns respectively.

13.5.2 IDENTIFYING COMPONENT PATTERNS

Just as we did when working with business process patterns, we encounter the challenge of finding an appropriate level of abstraction for component patterns.

In Chapter 10 we used the example of recipes for making pizza and contrasted a granular one with many very detailed processes with one that summarized many steps into coarser processes (Figure 10-4). In this analogy the ingredients are the components. And if we compare "add 2 teaspoons of dried yeast" with "make dough," we see that the level of abstraction for the ingredients varies along with the level of abstraction for the processes. Describing the pizza ingredients as "dough," "sauce," and "toppings" generalizes these ingredient components to a level of abstraction where the pizza recipe can be reused in many more contexts.

One way to generalize components is to remove any qualifiers in their names. In effect, this is the opposite of adding context by qualifying names. For example, two components whose names differ only in their qualifiers, like Order Contact and Shipping Contact, suggest a common, decontextualized component called Contact. In this way the generalized Contact component becomes a reusable pattern.

However, qualifiers in component names are not the only clue for finding patterns. We also can identify patterns by noticing different structures with similar content components or structures that inherit, extend, or restrict the number of components for another. This relies on understanding the meaning of a component by its structure rather than name.

For example, if the structure for Contract has some similar content components to a structure called Shipment (such as Start Date, End Date, and Duration) it may be that these share a common pattern. In this case, we may decide that Start Date, End Date, and Duration form a structural pattern called Period. Then the Contract and Shipment structures can both reuse the same pattern.

In the Event Calendar project we saw this situation with the components Contact Name and Email Address. These components appeared (in various guises) within the Contact, Reservation, and Website structures, as shown in Figure 13-9.

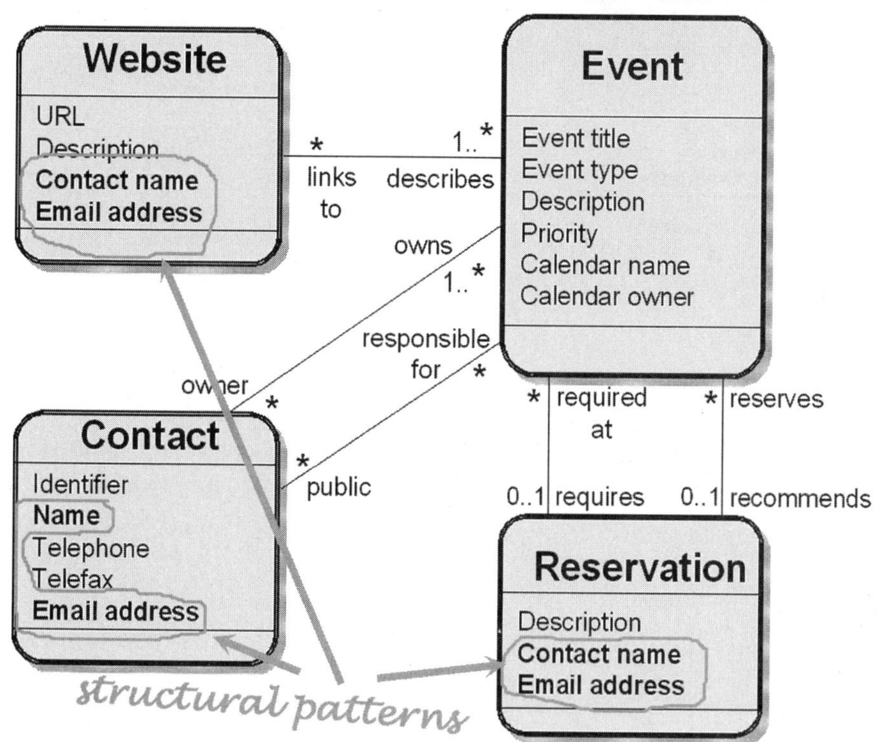

Figure 13-9. Structural Patterns in Website, Contact, and Reservation

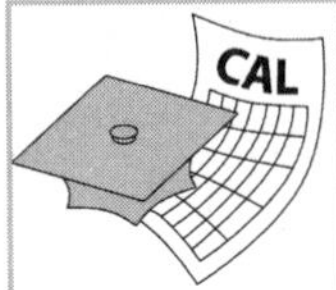

We consolidated these by reusing the Contact structure as a pattern, as shown in Figure 13-10.

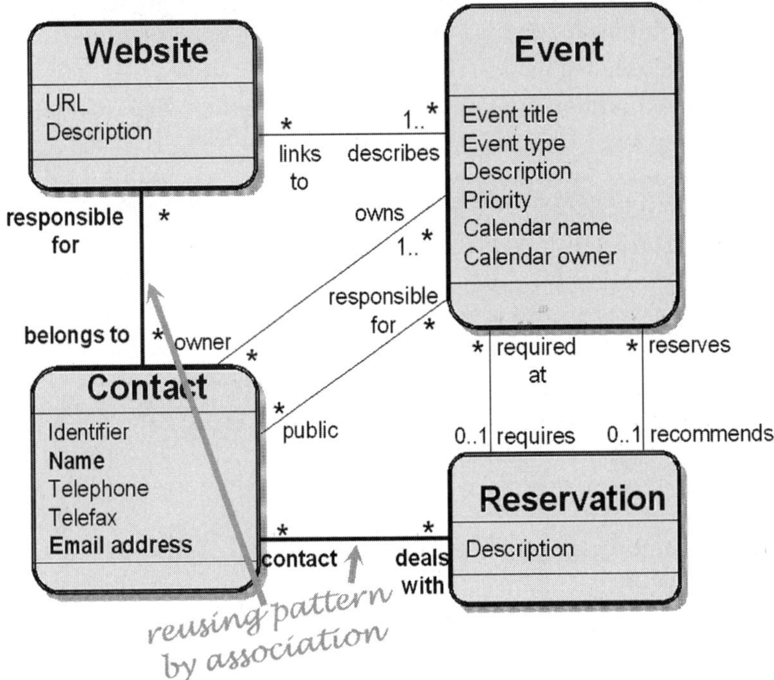

Figure 13-10. Contact Pattern to Consolidate Repeated Structures

In a similar way, structures that have similar sets of associations may indicate a pattern. For example, if the structure for Credit has the same set of associations as those for Debit, it might be sensible to generalize these into a common structure called Transaction.

We refine models to emphasize the way in which structures and their associations support semantics

What many of these refinements are doing is emphasizing the way in which we can use structures and their associations to clarify the context of the components.

13.5.3 APPLYING COMPONENT PATTERNS

Component models are conceptual and not bound to any specific implementation or technology. This means they can adopt patterns from a range of different sources.

First, we can refer back to previous analyses to find reusable patterns.

We may also revisit the original document inventory armed with a greater appreciation of what patterns are useful. These patterns may be hidden within artifacts such as web pages, database schemas, data file structures, and EDI messages. Similarly, the data formats used by any legacy applications may reveal useful patterns pertinent to the context of use.

The work of industry bodies (such as EIDX[6] and SWIFT[7]), national standards initiatives (such as ANSI ASC X12[8]), and international standards initiatives (such as UN/EDIFACT[9] and UBL[10]) are also rich sources of component patterns.

We identify patterns by looking past any implementation to the underlying conceptual model

The key to using these as patterns is to look past the jargon, implementation technology, or syntax to the underlying conceptual model and see if any common conceptual patterns exist. For example, there are at least a dozen organizations currently trying to define a common XML schema for an address structure.[11] Each is working in a different geographical, political, or industry context, but beneath them all are useful conceptual patterns that could be incorporated into specialized components for a specific context.

In the Berkeley Event Calendar, we considered that the Organization of a Sponsor might be the same type of thing as the Affiliation of a Speaker (Figure 13-11).

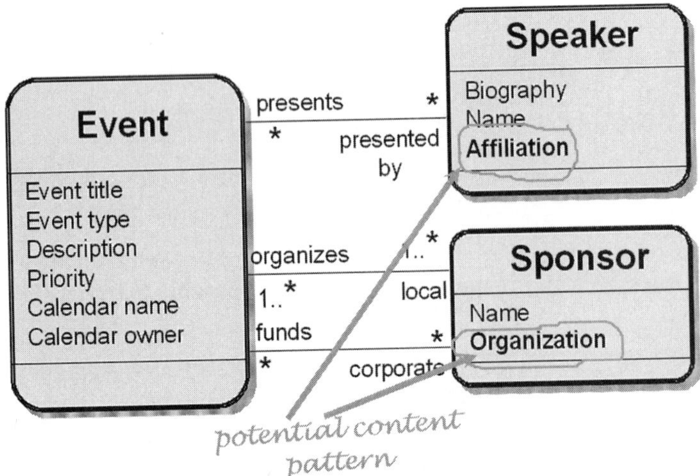

Figure 13-11. Speaker and Sponsor Potential Content Pattern

We then determined that they could both be described as a Party (Figure 13-12).

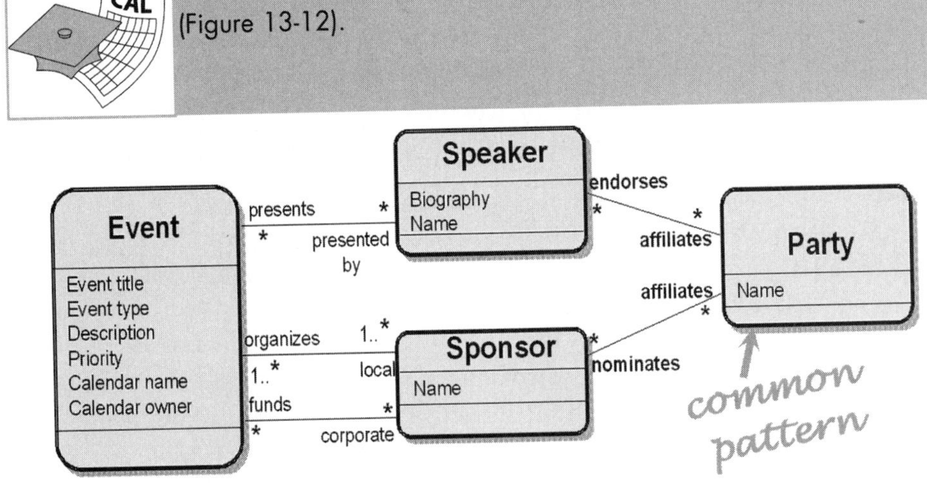

Figure 13-12. Speaker and Sponsor reuse Party Pattern

Then we recognized that the structure for Party and Contact could both reuse patterns from the UBL Library

Furthermore, within the UBL Party structure, there was already an existing association with Contact. This is shown in Figure 13-13.

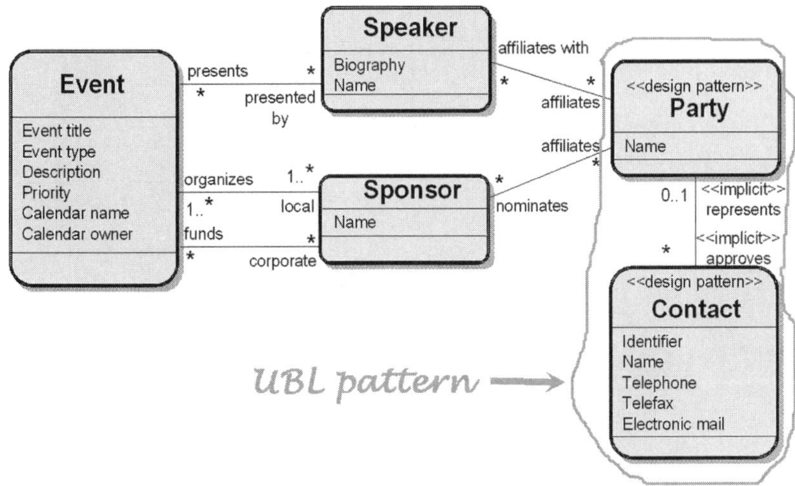

Figure 13-13. Speaker and Sponsor reuse UBL Party and Contact Pattern

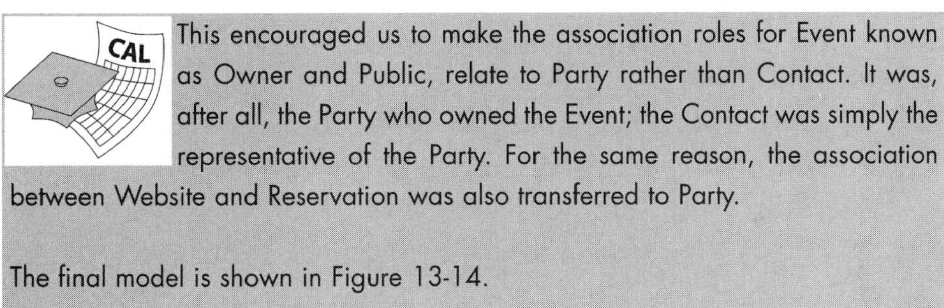

This encouraged us to make the association roles for Event known as Owner and Public, relate to Party rather than Contact. It was, after all, the Party who owned the Event; the Contact was simply the representative of the Party. For the same reason, the association between Website and Reservation was also transferred to Party.

The final model is shown in Figure 13-14.

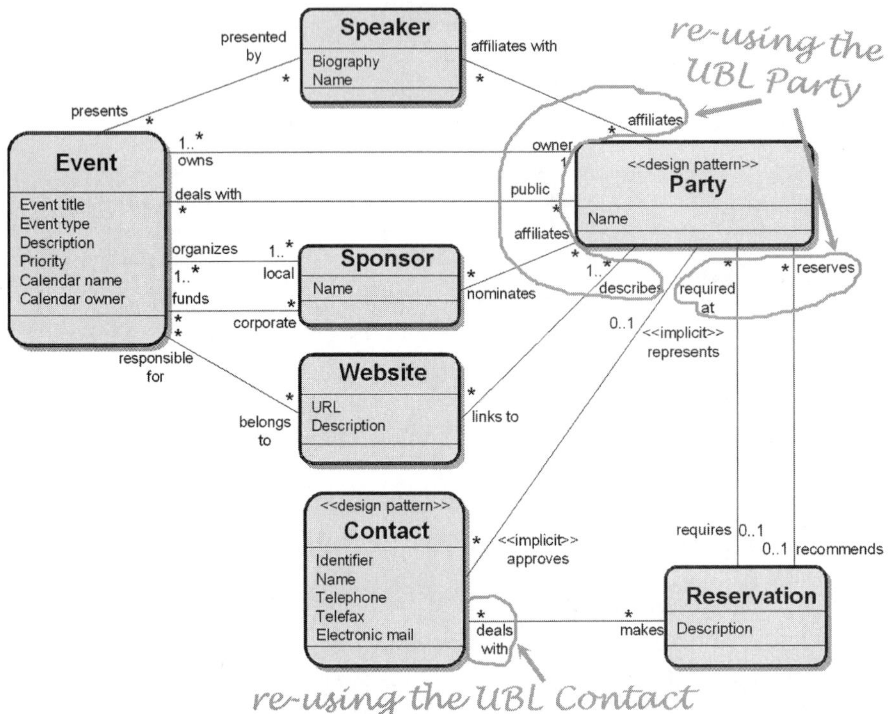

Figure 13-14. Speaker, Sponsor, and Event reuse UBL Party and Contact Pattern

By reusing these standardized external patterns, we not only improved the quality of the Event Calendar model but also provided the potential to share information about parties and contacts with other business processes that have adopted the UBL component library.

13.5.4 REFINING THE NAMES FOR COMPONENTS

At this stage it is worthwhile reviewing the names given to components. The modeling we have applied should have given them meaningful structures, and it is useful to have this reflected in their names. As we have mentioned before, using good naming rules not only promotes consistency; it also encourages the reuse of common patterns.

Using good naming rules promotes consistency and encourages the reuse of common patterns

Because they are now contained in aggregated structures, some components may now have unnecessarily qualified names.

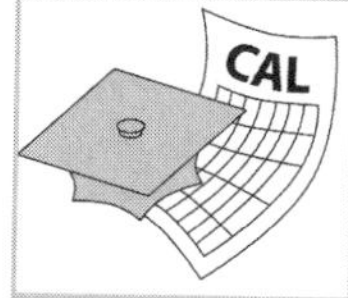

In the Event structure we no longer needed to call the component Event Title or Event Description because their occurrence within an Event component explains their context of use.

Other components may benefit from additional qualification. For example, qualifying the name of an association by its role helps to clarify the context of its use.

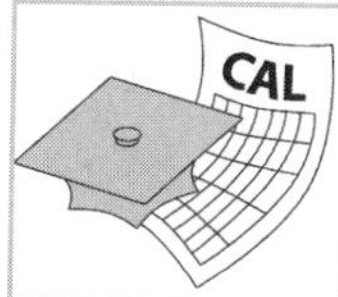

In the Event Calendar we have qualified names such as Local Sponsor and Corporate Sponsor for an Event. The qualifier reflects the role required within this association.

A framework for this type of naming refinement is the ISO 11179 naming rules used for the specification of ebXML Core Components.

ebXML Core Component Naming Rules

Because it was designed to support the needs of document designers, the ebXML Core Components Technical Specification[12] (CCTS) provides a useful basis for document component naming rules.

The CCTS refers to generalized information components as core components. When these core components are applied in specific contexts they are known as Business Information Entities (BIEs). For the sake of simplicity we will assume that what we call structural components are Aggregate Business Information Entities (ABIEs) and what we know as content components are called Basic Business Information Entities (BBIEs).

In the specification, each BIE is given a Dictionary Entry Name that is unique across the context of use. This name is based on the principles of ISO 11179, the international standard for the specification and standardization of data elements.[13]

Both these initiatives follow the same principles as Document Engineering—as can be seen in the following table.

ISO 11179	CCTS	Document Engineering
(Object-Oriented Terminology)	**(ebXML Terminology)**	**(Our Terminology)**
Object Class	Association Business Information Entity or ABIE	Structural Components
Property	Basic Business Information Entity or BBIE	Content Component

The ebXML CCTS specifies that we create a Dictionary Entry Name for all structural components (ABIEs) based on the rule:

[Qualifier(s)]_[Structural Component].Details

That is, the name given to each structure (and any qualifiers if they exist) has appended to it the characters ".Details." For example, when the structural component Order is qualified by the term Export, the name is:

Export_Order.Details

Dictionary Entry Names for content components (BBIEs) are formed from the rule:

[Qualifier(s)]_[Structural Component].[Qualifier(s)]_[Content Component].[Qualifier(s)]_[Representation Term]

That is, the name for a content component—and any qualifiers—has a prefix consisting of the name of its structure and with a suffix consisting of its representation term. A representation term is a constrained sets of terms used to describe how the information is to be presented.

For example, the name:

Export_Order.Payment_Currency.ISO4217_Code

tells us that a content component known as Currency within an Order structure is also qualified as being the Payment currency. We also know that this is represented by an ISO 4217 code value (the international set of currency codes, such as "USD" for American Dollars and "CNY" for Chinese Renimbi Yuan).

Because it was designed for use in document definitions, the CCTS also appreciates that structures associate with other structures. It calls these associations Association Business Information Entities (ASBIEs). Their naming rules are also based on ISO 11179, and are formed by the rule:

[Qualifier(s)]_[Structural Component].[Qualifier(s)]_[Association Role Name].
[Qualifier(s)]_[Associated Structural Component]

Thus two different roles in the association between Order and Party may be called:

Export_Order.Buyer.Party
and
Export_Order.Seller.Party

While it may take some effort to follow precise rules for naming components, for a large set of components this investment is justified by the consistency and potential interoperability it brings.

13.6 CHECKING THE QUALITY OF ANALYSIS

There are some final checks to make that ensure we have appropriately assembled structures of components into a robust model.

First, we should make sure there are no similarly qualified components within the same structure. For example, if Country Code and Country Name are both within an Address structure, this suggests a hidden dependency between the Name and Code and Country component. These components appear to share more context with each other than with the remaining components.

One indicator of insufficient structure is the use of counters in repeating component names, such as Contact-1 and Contact-2. This naming scheme indicates the flattening of a natural hierarchy and can be remedied by introduction of a structural container for the repeating components. In this case, it would be called Contact with multiple cardinality role in its association with the original structure.

At the other extreme, a model may have unnecessarily deep hierarchies, which suggests overly zealous application of dependency rules. For example, unless we have business rules that require extremely precise knowledge about time events, the model probably should not have components for Hours, Minutes, and Seconds within Time of Day within Payment Date.

Finally, the presence of presentation components instead of structural ones (such as Order Header rather than an Order structure), indicates that we may have not been rigorous enough when selecting the consolidated list of candidate components.

Once we have normalized, refined, and reviewed the assembly of components into structures, the result is a complete document component model that encapsulates many of the requirement rules for the context of use. This is a view of the entire context domain and not a specific document.

Achieving this complete document component model concludes the analysis phases of Document Engineering. In the next chapter we turn to the design phase as we assemble models for the documents we require.

13.7 KEY POINTS IN CHAPTER THIRTEEN

- Many requirement rules concern dependencies and relationships between components.
- Document designers pursue the twin goals of minimal redundancy and maximal reuse.
- Narrative documents might conform to structural rules, but their content is inherently heterogeneous.
- In narrative documents weaker semantic and content rules limit the rigor for grouping into structures.
- A document component model embodies instance, semantic, and structural rules in an unambiguous and formal way.
- Normalization identifies the associations that determine how we assemble document models.
- Functional dependency is determined by structural, semantic, and instance rules.
- Understanding functional dependencies identifies essential semantic components and reusable patterns.
- Cardinality helps us understand the association between two structures.
- The naming of roles can be a useful semantic device for qualifying the context of use.
- Multivalue dependencies identify more sophisticated structural, semantic, and instance rules.

- Having structures based on dependent components allows us to make conscious rather than ad hoc modeling refinements.

- We refine models to emphasize the way in which structures and their associations support semantics.

- We identify patterns by looking past any implementation to the underlying conceptual model.

- Using good naming rules promotes consistency and encourages the reuse of common patterns.

Assembling Document Models

14.0 INTRODUCTION

A document component model might be the final conceptual modeling artifact if we were designing databases, but we have more work to do if we want to design documents.

The reason we're not done yet is because a document is a self-contained set of information for a specific purpose. So a document that describes a book, tax receipt, customer, purchase order, or flight reservation will organize the information it contains from the perspective of a single transaction or event. A book is published, taxes paid, a customer signed up, a purchase order issued, a flight reservation made. But a document component model is a description of the network of all possible interpretations of the components and their associations. If we want to exchange documents with a specific interpretation we need another kind of model. What we call a document assembly model is such a model.

By document assembly we mean defining a top-level structure and nesting the subsidiary components within a hierarchy to form an inverted tree of components. The challenge with document assembly is to design models that satisfy the requirements and optimize the reuse of common components.

14.1 DOCUMENT AND DATABASE MODELS

Documents have always been based on hierarchical models because the structural nesting in the hierarchy imposes interpretations on the information appropriate for the specific context of use. For example, when <Book> contains <Title> in Figure 3-2 we know that the Title is that of the Book.

Documents have always been based on hierarchical models

In contrast, the purpose of a database is to reliably manage a collection of information —all of the books, tax payments, customers, purchase orders, flight reservations, or whatever—so that the collection can be updated, queried, and reassembled in many different ways without losing any information or creating inconsistencies. The model that describes the organization of the information in the database (the database schema) is primarily designed to ensure the integrity of the stored information during transactions on the database. A database schema describes the model that describes of the documents as a set of interrelated views of its relational tables.[1] Rather than impose only a single interpretation, the database schema is designed to allow a variety of them. That's why the relational model of a Book in Figure 3-5 can provide the three different views shown in Figures 3-6a, b, and c.

Extracting information from a database in response to a query or application request means imposing a hierarchical view consistent with the interpretation required by the context of use. Storing information from a hierarchical document in a database involves breaking it out into a relational model and creating a less contextualized view. Each view serves a different purpose.

14.2 DOCUMENT ASSEMBLY MODELS

Exchanging information requires all parties in the exchange to understand the context for the document's components. Because the network structure of the document component model describes all potential roles and associations it can't guarantee this common interpretation.

Document exchanges require unambiguous clarity in semantic interpretation

When we are dealing with document exchanges, we don't want flexibility, we want unambiguous clarity in semantic interpretation. For example, in the model of a specific type of document we do not want to allow any alternative roles and associations, only those required for the context of that document. Therefore a document assembly model defines one document-specific view of the more complex document component model (see SIDEBAR).

For this reason documents are based on hierarchical models.

A Metaphor for Document Assembly

We could think of the document component model as the road map of a city that depicts the entire network of roads. A particular document assembly model describes a specific route through that network. The rules or restrictions of the precise context, such as origin, destination, mode of transport, and time available determine the most appropriate route (or document assembly).

And of course, several different routes may share common roads and intersections. These are our reusable patterns.

For example, the diagram below depicts a simple document component model containing four structures called A, B, C, and D.

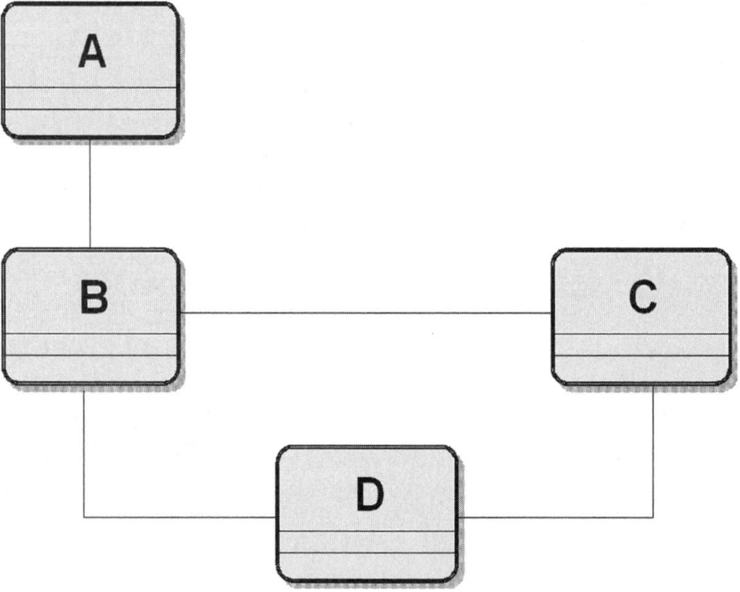

Figure 14-1. A Simple Document Component Model

By following different paths through the associations in this model, we could assemble several different document assembly models, such as those shown in Figure 14-2.

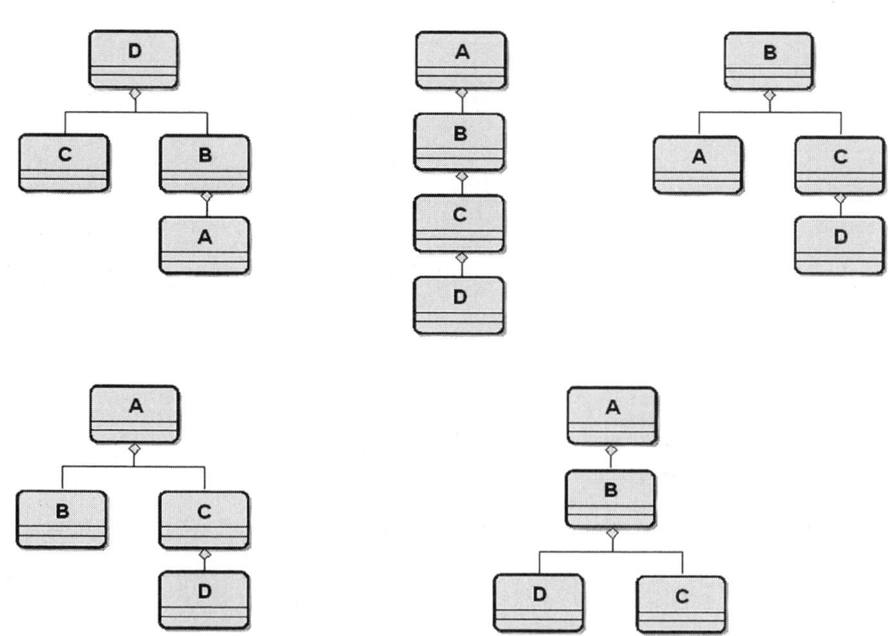

Figure 14-2. Different Assemblies from the Same Document Component Model

Each of the models in Figure 14-2 imposes an unambiguous definition of a document structure. The hierarchy expresses rules about the use of the components. In effect, when we present a hierarchical document assembly model we are saying; "for this document, interpret the information this way." This ability of hierarchical structures to convey semantics makes them natural for documents and the document assembly models that define them.

Only a hierarchical structure can express certain semantics

In the Event Calendar project, the meaning of an Occurrence, Event, Time Period, or Location depends on which roles in associations are used. For example, if we refer to the component model in Figure 13-6, we can see that assembling Occurrence using its role within an Event describes Occurrence as "the Location and Time Period of the Event," as shown in Figure 14-3.

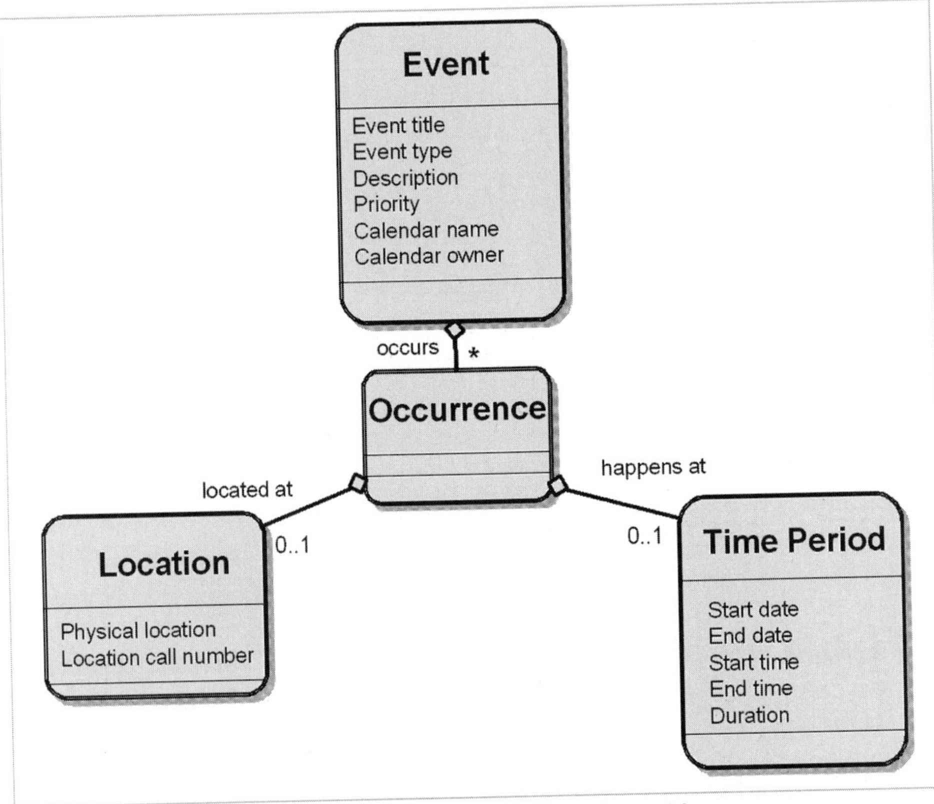

Figure 14-3. Event Document Assembly

However, we can also see in Figure 14-4 that assembling Occurrence from its association with Time Period defines Occurrence as "the Location and Event occurring during the Time Period."

So the meaning of Occurrence depends on its position within the assembly model.

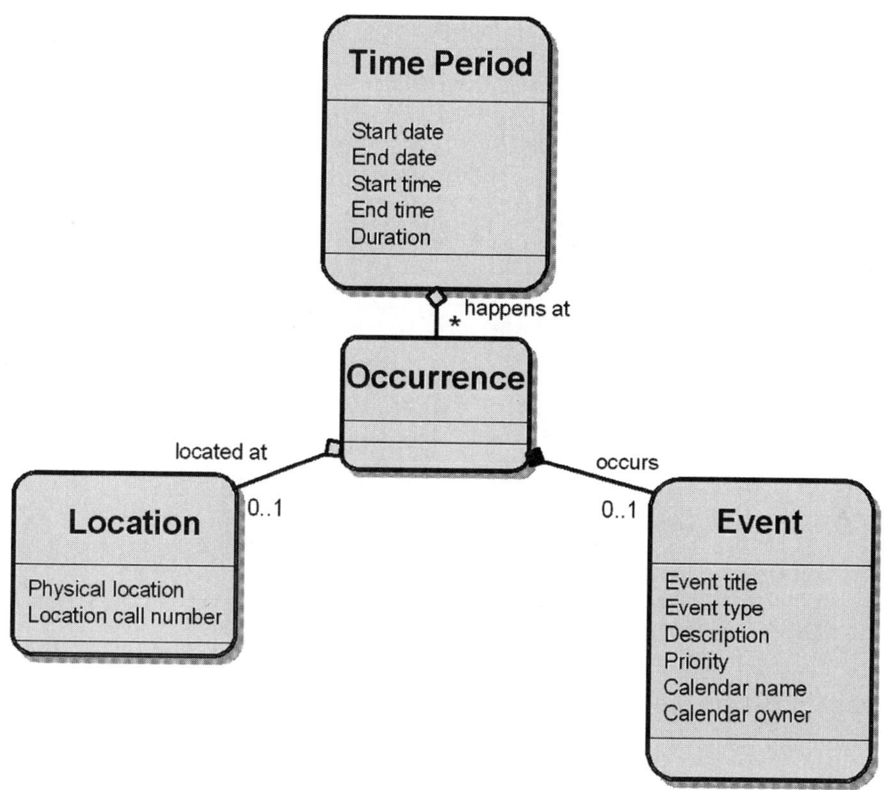

Figure 14-4. Time Period Document Assembly

14.3 REFERENCE MODELS FOR DOCUMENT ASSEMBLY

Document assembly models attempt to capture business rules based on the context for the type of document required. Of course, many of these will be determined by the function the document performs in each business transaction.

Some types of documents, particularly those on the narrative end of the Document Type Spectrum, have such a common assembly model that it is immediately recognizable as a pattern. Maler and El Andaloussi put it this way: ". . . the class of components that represent the upper part of the document type . . . capture the essence of that type, and once they are modeled, they give a characteristic 'shape' to every instance conforming to that model."[2]

As an example, Figure 14-5 is a document assembly model for a typical textbook.

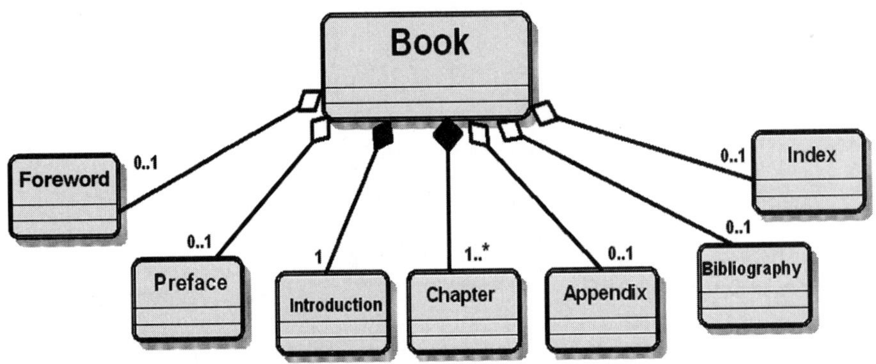

Figure 14-5. A Common Document Assembly Pattern

The assembly patterns for narrative documents might seem different from those for transactional documents such as orders, flight bookings, or calendar event submissions. However, they all follow the same principle that assembly is based on the contextual requirements for a given document. For example, in narrative documents, the requirement for structural integrity is sometimes so common it could almost be considered a reference model.

Some requirements are so common they define a reference model for document assembly

As they assemble their document models, authors and publishers employ these patterns because they recognize that those processing the documents will be familiar with them. In this case, one of the requirements is for a reader to easily navigate the text material. This is the same principle used in printed business documents that may have a heading, details, and summary pattern.

14.4 DESIGNING A DOCUMENT ASSEMBLY MODEL

The previous chapter noted how the fundamental differences between transactional and narrative style documents determine the extent to which we base the assembly on formal representations of business rules.

In narrative documents, weaker semantic and instance rules limit the rigor for grouping components. In these cases we may have to rely on more informal or implied structural components from which to assemble document models.

However, in most cases we should have enough rules to develop a document component model for the components in the target context.

14.4.1 USING BUSINESS RULES TO GUIDE ASSEMBLY

While it is possible to arbitrarily navigate the document component model or even to use no formal rules when assembling structures into documents, there are more rigorous approaches.

When we assemble document models we aim to build in the requirements expressed through any semantic and structural rules. This means any modeling notation used should be capable of describing these types of rules.

Semantic and structural rules determine how we assemble document models

Semantic rules describe the need for and the purpose of the document. For example, "the Testing Manual describes the process of verification" or "a Reverse Purchase Order allows the seller to requisition stock for delivery to the buyer."

These give an overall guide to what components we might expect to find in a document assembly model. Semantic rules may also specify the components required. For example, "A catalog lists the available products."

In some cases semantic rules may describe a choice. For example, "The location must be a street address or a geographic coordinate."

Structural rules are used both to specify the cardinality and sequence of assembling components. These rules can apply both to roles within associations and to content components within structures themselves.

For example, a structural rule for an association is "An order may specify more than one delivery address (or no address at all)." Another example is "In a textbook, the abstract must be followed by one or more chapters and then optionally by one or more appendices." Note that the sequence of assembly being specified in the latter case is also an example of a structural integrity rule (as we noted in Section 8.3.2).

Structural rules may also define the assembly path for recursive associations. They describe the difference between "Each package may contain other packages" and "Each package may be part of a larger package". Or "An article may reference other articles" and "An article may be referenced by other articles." The way the rule is phrased determines which role is required and therefore the direction in which the association is assembled.

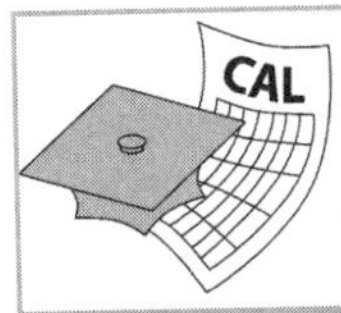

In the Event Calendar project, a semantic rule for a location calendar document could define it as "a document that defines the Events happening in a given Location." And a structural rule might be "If there are any reservation requirements for an Event, they must be included."

So we assembled different recursive roles for an Event for the different types of documents:

- For the document describing a calendar for Events, the association role assembled was that of Subsidiary Event. This gave us the view of a parent Event containing all its subsidiary Events.

Σ • With the Location calendar document, the role chosen was Collective Event— where each Event contained details of its parent Event.

14.4.2 ASSEMBLING ASSOCIATIONS

There is a significant difference in the way document assembly models and database models implement associations between structures.

In document assembly models associations between structures are implied by the hierarchy

In document assembly models, associations are implied by the hierarchy (or in poorly designed schemas by the sequential repetition of components) but database schemas use explicit reference values known as foreign keys to implement their associations.

Foreign Keys

In most database environments, designers implement structural components as relational tables. Relational tables define their associations with other tables by using a special component known as a foreign key. That is, they include the primary key component of one structure (the determinant one) as a foreign component within another (the dependent one)—thereby allowing a link between structures. In fact, we can think of foreign keys as link components—connecting instances of one structure with instances of another by this reference.

For example, referring to Figure 13-12 we can see that the document component model for the Event Calendar project has an association between Event and Speaker. If we were building a database schema, we would resolve the association between Event and Speaker by either adding the primary key component of the Event (the Event Title) to the Speaker structure, or by adding the primary key component of Speaker (perhaps the Speaker Name) to the Event structure.

The decision about which one to use should of course be based on the rules for the context of use.

In the Event Calendar, a conference system might add the primary key component of Event (say the Event Title) to the structure for Speaker. This makes it is easy to find out at which Events a Speaker is presenting. But, for a speaker's itinerary, adding the primary key component of Speaker (say the Speaker Name) to the structure for Event makes more sense.

While foreign keys are essential for database designers, they are not necessary for document designers. Foreign keys in document assembly models would duplicate information and create ambiguity in understanding document components.

14.4.3 CHOOSING THE ENTRY POINT

Each type of document usually requires its own document assembly model. To start creating this model we must choose the structural component that will form the root of the document tree. We can think of this as the entry point into the document component model.

The entry point structure normally has its own content components. For example, an Order may have an Order Identifier, Issue Date, Currency, and so on. It's tempting to think of these as properties of the entire document, but they are not; they are properties of the structural component used as the entry point of our model.

What Is a Business Header?

We sometimes think of business documents as having a common pattern based on a "header" and "details" (and maybe a "summary") structure. This is because we are all familiar with structures such as Order Headers, Invoice Summary, and Line Item Details.

In fact, this is confusing a document's semantic structures and their presentation. For example, a properly designed document assembly model for an Order should have neither "header" nor "details" components because they aren't meaningful or necessary structural components for business interfaces. They are presentational devices.

In fact, the components belonging to the Order's "header" would be either components of the entry point structure (such as an Issue Date) or part of other structures associated with it (as with the Name component of a Buyer Party structure associated with the Order). So defining an additional "header" structure adds nothing to the document assembly model—it is redundant and misleading.

What is worse is that we may feel obliged to make other documents fit this pattern when many clearly do not. For example, in the transport context, a Shipping Waybill document may typically have an identifiable "header," and a set of goods "details" and another set of transport "details." Container Release documents have just "details" with no "header" and Arrival Notices are just "headers" with no "details."

This confusion makes sense when we realize that document "header" and "details" are presentational structure patterns for printed documents. They support the requirement to aid human readability they are not part of the semantics of the document's content and should not be part of the document assembly model.

The situation is further confused because message exchange protocols often use the concept of header and body to enforce distinctions between the contents of the message and its addressing. For example, in SOAP the <Header> contains routing and other information that is needed to deliver the message. This contrasts with the <Body> whose contents should not be available to any party other than the final recipient.

In many cases we can easily identify a structural component as the entry point for each type of document. This is because it is not uncommon to find structural components like Order, Invoice, Insurance Claim, Article, and Calendar in document component models. These are obvious choices as entry points for documents of the same name.

But this is not always true. The business terms used to describe types of document are often ambiguous or synonymous. For example, the same document might be called an Order or Purchase Order and an Invoice could be known as a Statement.

Sometimes none of the terms used for a type of document are recognizable in the document component model. In the transport industry, the types of documents used to describe a shipment of goods may be known as a Waybill, Forwarding Instruction, Shipping Note, or Bill of Lading. These may all share the same common entry point structure, typically known as Consignment, and yet there is no document called Consignment.

The entry point structure does not have to share the same name as the document

So we shouldn't get too fixated on forcing the entry point structure for the document assembly model to share the same name as the common title of the business document.

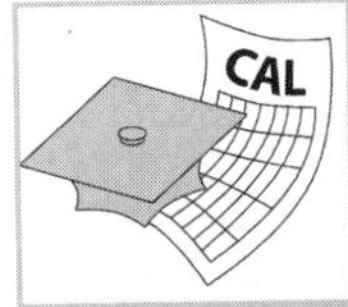

A synonymous document name used in the Event Calendar project was Schedule as an alternative to Calendar. In many cases documents with schedule in their names shared the same information requirements as those called calendar, so they were not considered different types of documents.

If we have done our analysis correctly, the components of the point of entry structure will be based on functional dependency just like the other components in the model. After all, these structures are not special—they are just the point the chose to begin assembling document models.

14.4.4 FOLLOWING THE PATHWAY

Having established the point of entry, we need to make decisions about the inclusion of other structures and their components. These decisions are based on the business rules the roles other structures have in their associations with the entry point structure.

First, the choice of associations available is influenced by the cardinality of the role. If the role is mandatory, the associated structure must be assembled into the model. Optional associations are assembled into the model only if their roles are required by structural or semantic business rules.

For all structures in the assembly model we must also decide which content components are required. Again, we must include any mandatory content components. And once again, the use of optional components is based on the rules for our context of use.

In this way we see how cardinality controls the depth of the hierarchies we create by specifying which structures appear in the document assembly model.

Cardinality controls the depth of the document hierarchy

Cardinality also describes how many instances of each contained structure are permissible. We can further restrict the cardinality of roles or content components, but we can't loosen it. In other words, while we can make optional components mandatory, we cannot make mandatory ones optional. Or we can limit the multiplicity of cardinality but not increase it. So we can limit the number of occurrence to one, where the component model allows multiple. But we cannot allow multiple occurrences if the component model allows only one.

Of course, not all roles in all associations are relevant to each type of document. We must decide whether a role in a particular optional association is required, optional, or prohibited in each assembly. For example, we may wish to assemble an Order document model so that its association with a Payment structure is optional. But in the Invoice document assembly, the association with Payment may be mandatory.

So if a document component model allows one-to-many occurrences of Product in its association with Catalog, we may restrict the maximum number of Products permissible in the document assembly model but we cannot make the role optional. The Catalog must have at least one Product.

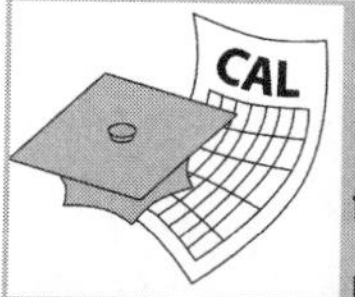

In the document assembly for a calendar based on locations, we have a requirement rule that we only need to know about locations that actually have events happening at them. In this case, the document assembly would make the associated role between Occurrence and Event mandatory. That is, there must be one instance of an Event for each Occurrence (refer to Figure 13-6). Otherwise they are not of interest to us.

So, taking the Calendar structure as our entry point, we created the document assembly model for the Calendar of Events by following its association to Event and nesting the Event structure within the Calendar structure.

As shown in Figure 14-6, from Event we associated its role with an Occurrence and from this to both Location and Time Period, each time nesting the new structure into our growing hierarchy.

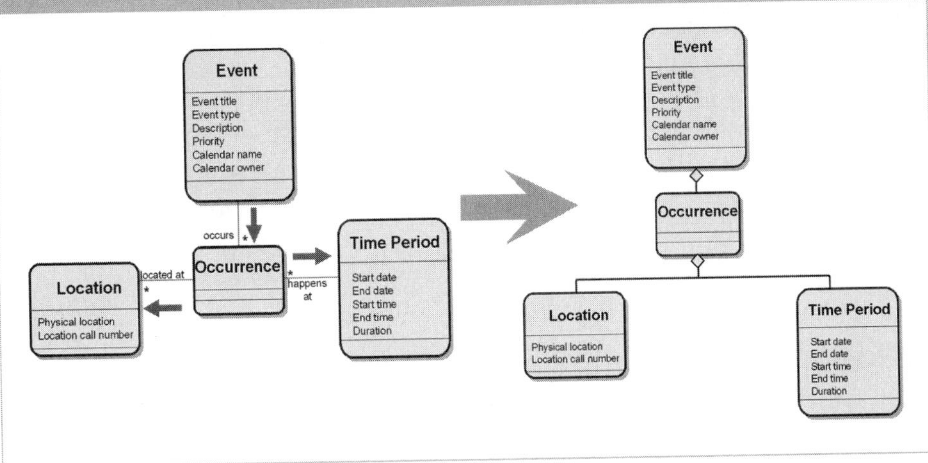

Figure 14-6. Calendar of Events Document Assembly Pathway

At the same hierarchical level as Occurrence we also have associations with Frequency, Participation, Speaker, Local and Corporate Sponsor, Owner and Public Party, Website, Required and Recommended Reservation, and Image. These have been omitted from Figure 14-6 to simplify the diagram.

It is also worth mentioning that in the document assembly for a Sporting Event Calendar, we chose not to include the association role "presented by" for Speaker because it is unnecessary in that more specific context (refer to Figure 13-12).

For other types of document, for example a calendar for a location or a calendar diary based on times, we would use different assembly paths such as those shown in Figure 14-7.

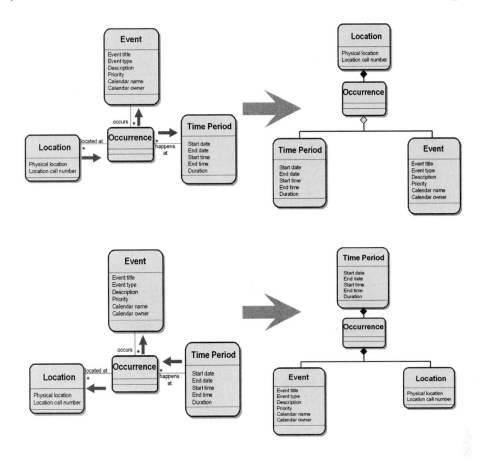

Figure 14-7. Location and Time Period Document Assembly Pathways

The order or sequence in which components are assembled is arbitrary unless they are determined by a requirement for structural integrity.

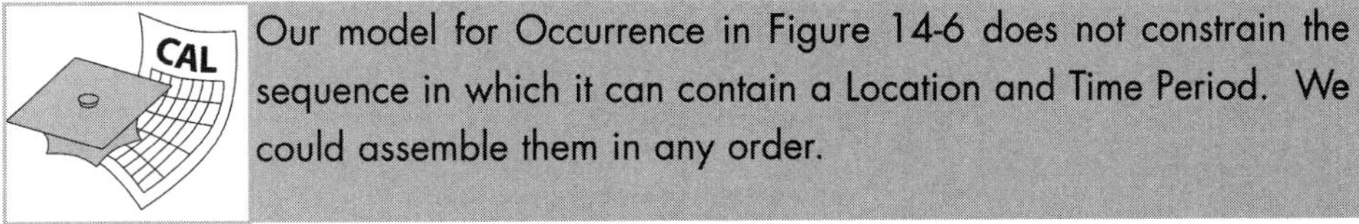

Our model for Occurrence in Figure 14-6 does not constrain the sequence in which it can contain a Location and Time Period. We could assemble them in any order.

When assembling structural components based on their roles in associations there are some general integrity constraints we should comply with:

- Don't backtrack along an association path (use both roles in a single association) because this creates an ambiguous interpretation. It potentially creates an infinite depth of hierarchy where component A can contain B, which can contain A, which can contain B, ad infinitum.

- However, it is possible, and not uncommon, to return to a structure following a different role in the association. Returning to a structure is what we do when we define recursive associations, such as a Package may contain another Package (as noted in Section 12.5.2).

- Assembly pathways may also reuse a structural component again using different roles in different associations.

An example of an assembly with different roles for the same component involves Event, where the Owner of an Event may Sponsor other Events.

Adhering to these constraints and the rules for the context of use, we start from the entry structure and follow the required pathways of associations through the model, assembling the complete document hierarchy.

14.4.5 DESIGNING FOR IMPLEMENTATION

If we know the ultimate implementation language and its encoding rules for our documents, we may chose to define additional metadata. This can facilitate a consistent implementation of the conceptual assembly model into a physical implementation model.

For example, each content component will be represented in its instances using one of the data types supported by the encoding language. We may use additional metadata to specify that the value must be represented as a set of valid numeric or alphanumeric characters, a date value, a Boolean indicator, and so forth. Obviously the actual data types available will vary according to the language involved.

Providing such metadata at this conceptual modeling stage will ensure that when we apply encoding rules we do so consistently for all implementations. And if we provide enough detail we may even be able to automate the implementation by building encoding rules into a program.

The assembly model may also describe rules that cannot be encoded in the implementation language. In particular, we may require conditional logic such as "If the goods are hazardous then these additional components are mandatory." Not many implementation languages support these types of dependency rules and any encoding needs to recognize this. The unimplemented business rules should become part of the supporting documentation of the implementation model.

Providing additional metadata in assembly models can ensure that encoding rules are applied consistently

14.5 DESIGNING FOR REUSE

It is likely that every different business transaction will involve different rules and therefore separate document assembly models for each type of document. Even so, many of these assemblies will share some common structures. In other words they will have patterns of assemblies.

Different assemblies may share common structures or patterns

This idea encourages the use of common patterns or libraries of assembled components.

However, the reuse of component patterns introduces the challenge of customizing these common models to suit the requirements of each specific context of use. There are several approaches to specializing components while maintaining some degree of compliance to the common pattern.

14.5.1 THE CHALLENGE OF CUSTOMIZATION

One approach to the customization problem is called subsetting or subtractive refinement. It is the document design philosophy incorporated in many document standards initiatives, especially those known collectively as EDI.[3]

Subtractive refinement begins by collecting all the components that would be needed by any of the required contexts and creating a single "superassembly" that contains all of them, but in which most of them are optional. This is sometimes called an umbrella model.

For example, we could create a generalized Order document that would contain components needed for orders involving different products, industries, geopolitical areas, and business processes. This generalized pattern will contain overlapping or redundant components contributed by the communities centered in these different contexts. For example a common Address component might contain components for Street Number, Street, and City, as well as components named Address Line-1, Address Line-2, and Address Line-3. These are obviously incompatible models of an Address. But since no one expects to use the complete pattern, this does not appear to be a major problem for each separate implementation.

Unfortunately, it is a serious problem for interoperability.

With this approach, each specific document assembly is created as a subset of the common pattern by stripping away the components that are not needed and specifying the interpretation of the context of the remaining components using a descriptive manual often referred to as a message implementation guide.

Customization by subtraction doesn't work because the overlapping information isn't explicitly identified

Since the components that are not needed were optional in the generalized pattern, each of the contextualized assembly models may still be technically valid with respect to the pattern. However, customization by subtraction doesn't promote interoperability because the overlapping information in different components isn't explicit and requires some additional extraction or mapping to identify it.

So there are situations where one standard EDI Order document may assemble an address as three lines of text and another as Street Number, Street, City and Country as shown in Figure 14-8. Both comply with the standard, but mapping is possible in only one direction, from finer to more coarse definitions.

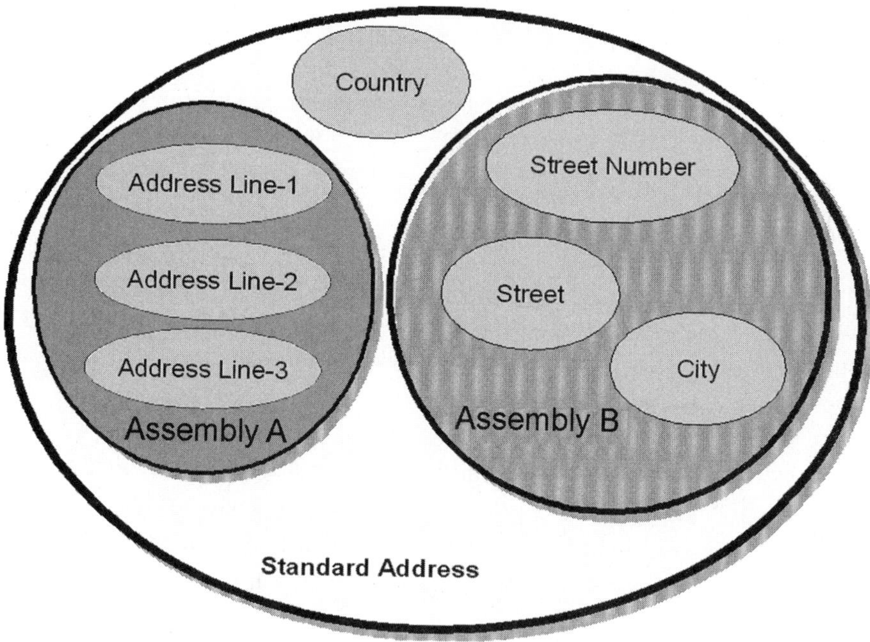

Figure 14-8. Customization by Subtractive Refinement

A more fundamental limitation to this approach is that it requires an ever expanding umbrella model that adds new components when more and more specialized contexts of use are identified. Organizations who manage these patterns as standards are rarely able to move fast enough or be flexible enough to accommodate the inevitable need for this kind of innovation or customization.

14.5.2 CORE PLUS CONTEXTUALIZATION

An alternative and more attractive approach to customization is to organize sets of document assembly components into a core pattern that can be reused by each contextualized document assembly. We refer to this as the core plus contextualization approach. The basic goal is to create a family of related document assembly models that share a common set of structures.

The core patterns are common to all or most of the document models. In contrast, the contextualized structures are used in more specific contexts and assembled with the core ones, alone or in combinations, to create the required document assembly models.

So instead of putting the burden of supporting customization in a central pattern meant to be used by subsetting from the top down, core plus contextualization distributes the responsibility among the implementations that need to be customized and works by assembling from the bottom up.

This doesn't eliminate the role of standard patterns, but it shifts their focus from the nearly impossible challenge of developing standard document models to the more tractable problem of developing a library of standard components to be used in assembling document models for specific contexts. This approach was used for the Universal Business Language initiative, which developed a library of components and produced document models primarily to illustrate the use of those components. (See the sidebar "Universal Business Language" in Section 4.3.2.)

We applied the idea of core plus contextualization in a project at UC Berkeley that analyzed the documents and applications that deal with academic courses.[4] In this project, Course emerged as a core component common to the Course Catalog, the Schedule of Classes, Transcripts, and Graduation Requirements document models. By contrast, Instructor and Semester Offered were contextualized components because they are needed only in some of the assembled document models.

Figures 14-9a and 14-9b depict the reuse of the core Course structural component in two different document assemblies.

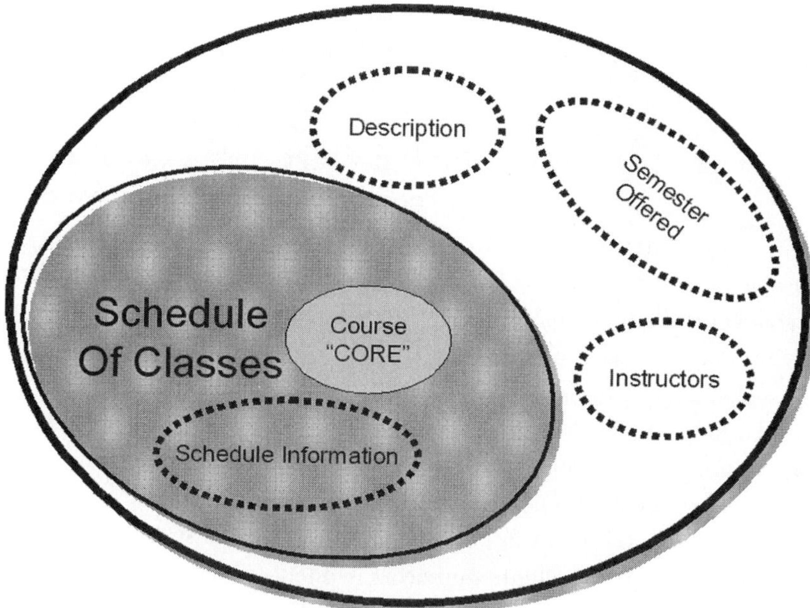

Figure 14-9a. Core plus Contextualization in a Schedule of Classes

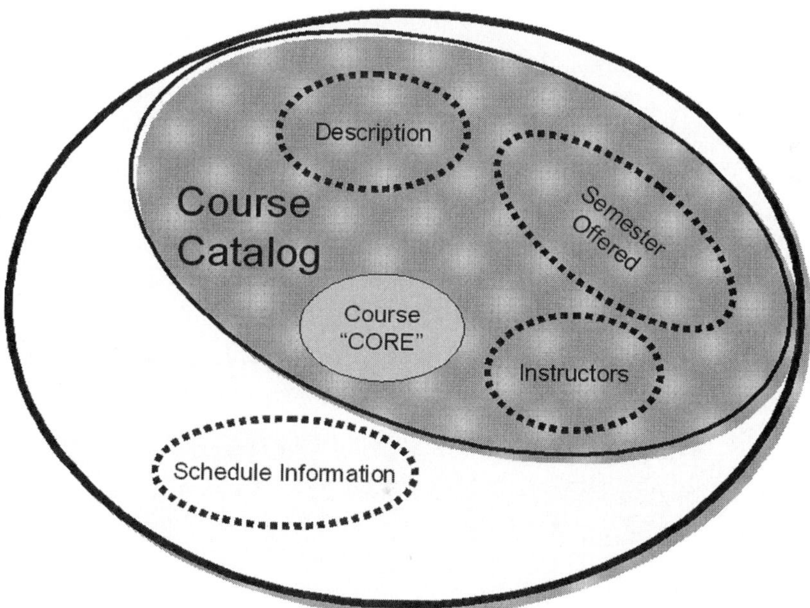

Figure 14-9b. Core plus Contextualization in a Course Catalog

Many contexts require models with more than one core pattern, and the distinction between core and contextualized components is just a matter of the degree of component reuse.

The distinction between core and contextualized components is the degree of reuse

For example, in a manufacturing environment with complex equipment the inventory of documents might include Assembly and Operator Instructions, Troubleshooting Guides, Training Manuals, and Process Control Plans. The components harvested from this document inventory might include Objective, Procedure, Question, Quiz, Answer, Warning, Tool, Part Number, Torque Specification, Figure, Illustration, Caption, Station, Station Number, Effective Date, and many others. Some of these components would be reused in more than one document assembly. And keeping the content of the actual documents up to date, accurate, and consistent requires arranging them in models that facilitate authoring, content management, and document generation processes.[5]

We would begin to apply core plus contextualization here by observing that some of these components are needed in every document assembly. Two obvious core components are those for Figure and Procedure. Components like Station, which might be included only in the Process Control Plans, or Quiz, which is needed only in the Training Manual, are some of the contextualized ones.

Using the core plus contextualization approach makes the adoption of patterns or standards iterative, because the resulting set of core components that emerges at first might seem brittle later. In particular, as the number of related document models being assembled grows, the core tends to get smaller because the models have less in common. Likewise, as more document models are assembled, many of the contextualized structures are likely to be split into smaller ones to provide more flexibility.

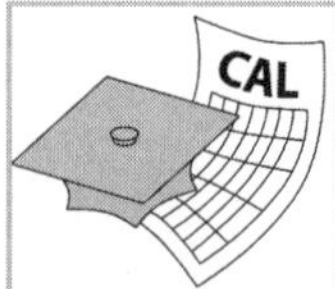

The Event Calendar project identified several reusable components and also adapted patterns from standard libraries such as UBL and SKICal.

From UBL we reused the assembly pattern for Party and from SKICal we used the model for Frequency. We describe the dependencies created by these multiple layers of reuse in Figure 14-10.

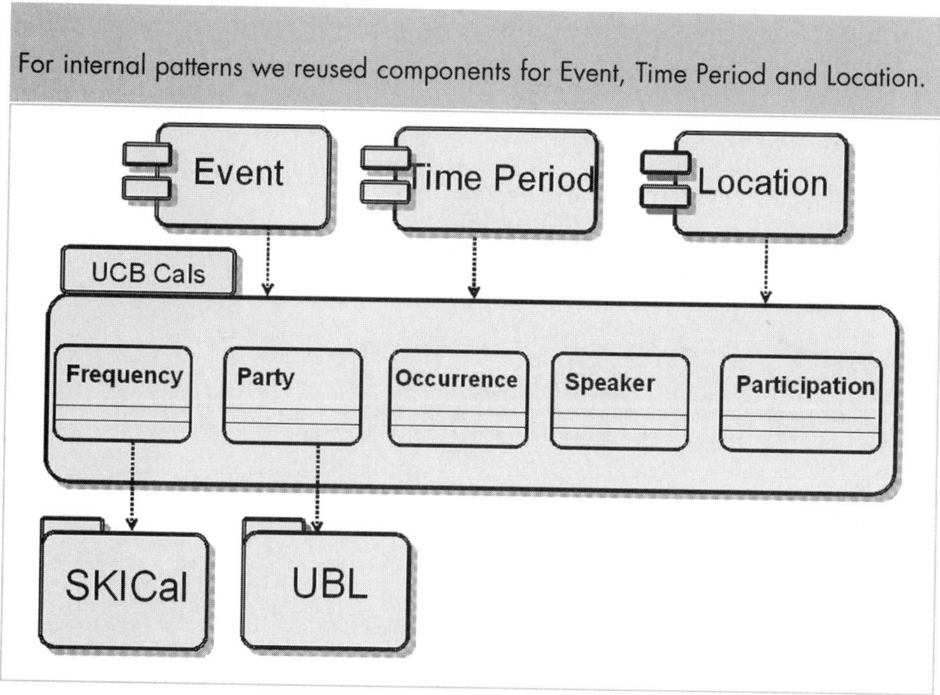

Figure 14-10. Multiple Layers of Component Reuse in Document Assembly Models

14.6 DOCUMENTING THE MODEL

The process of building document assembly models is facilitated by using a formal notation to describe the resulting hierarchy of components. Common notations are UML class diagrams, ELM[6] tree diagrams, or tables. If these notational forms are rich enough in their metadata, often encoding them into a language for implementation (such as XML Schema) can be formalized or even automated using an application program.

Document assembly models described in UML Class Diagrams commonly use aggregations and composite associations. Aggregations (denoted by an open diamond on the parent end of the association) describe an assembly path that is optional. Compositions (denoted by a filled diamond at the parent end of the association) are a specialized form of aggregation where the assembly path is mandatory.

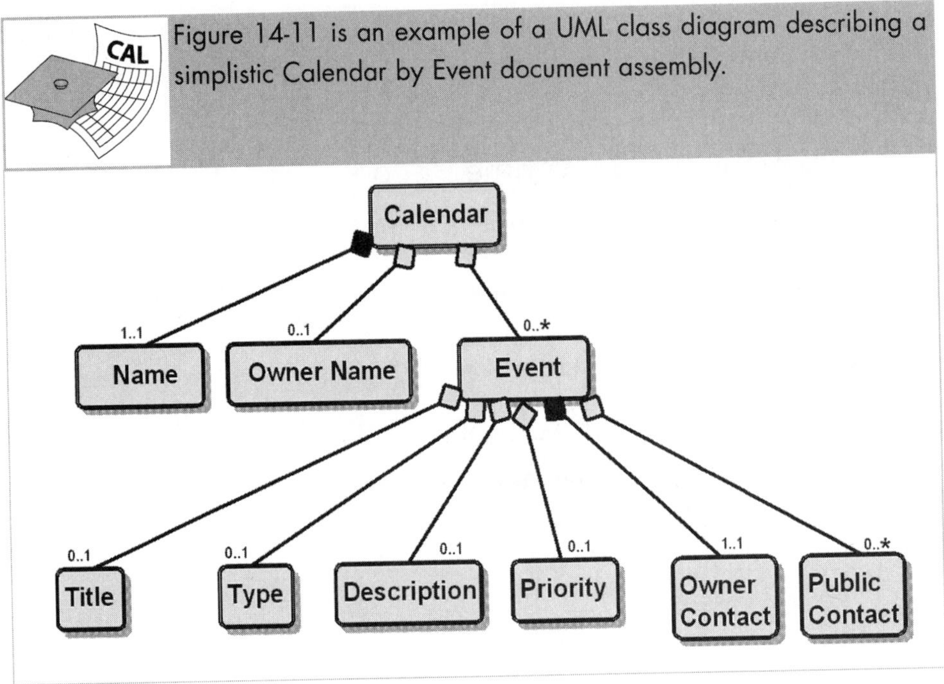

Figure 14-11. Calendar by Event Assembly Model as a UML Class Diagram

ELM diagrams are often used to describe the assembly models of SGML or XML DTD schemas. This notation embodies the principle of preparing for encoding that we discussed in Section 14.4.5 because it uses the SGML occurrence indicators (such as '+','*' and '?') in the assembly model to capture metadata helpful in creating the implementation models as DTD schemas.

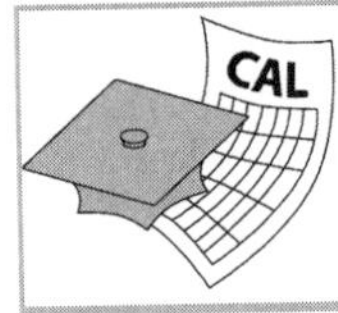

Figure 14-12 is an example of an ELM diagram describing the Calendar by Event document assembly.

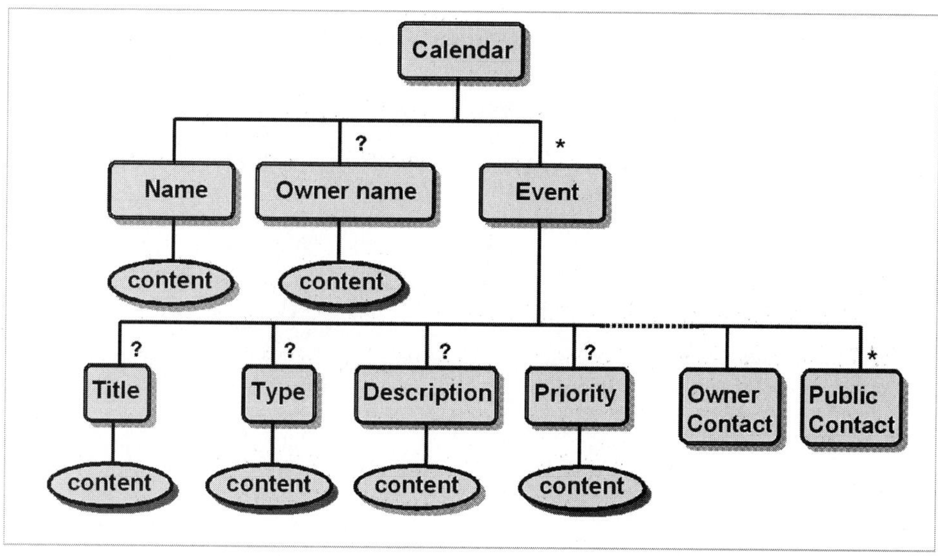

Figure 14-12. Sample of the Event Calendar Assembly Model as an ELM Diagram

However, most graphical notations do not describe all the metadata needed to describe a complete document assembly model. So we will often need to rely on more generalized notations.

Using tables or spreadsheet formats for document assembly models overcomes some of the limitations of graphical representations. The flexibility of a customizable metadata allows for more complete semantic descriptions and customized assembly metamodels. In addition, tables are a more familiar syntax for a nontechnical audience than either the UML or ELM notations. For example, the spreadsheet developed by the UBL project supports both the ISO11179 naming rules and the metamodel of the ebXML Core Components Technical Specification. It also has additional metadata required for implementation in the XML Schema language.

UBL Spreadsheets for Document Assembly

To comply with the ebXML Core Components metamodel, UBL developed a spreadsheet for its document assembly models.

Each column represents the value of a piece of metadata, such as the full ebXML Dictionary Entry Name, Object Class, Property Term, and Representation Term that define the name of the component. In addition, because UBL is an XML implementation, specific XML metadata such as UBL Name (for the XML tag name) are also defined in the assembly model.

Each type of component is distinguished by a different background color. An example is shown in Figure 14-13.

An additional benefit of using the spreadsheet format is that the values for the UBL Name and ebXML Dictionary Entry Name of the components can be calculated by formula. This ensures consistency in applying naming rules.

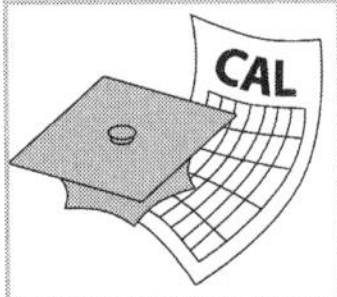

For its document assembly models, the Event Calendar project adapted the spreadsheets used by the UBL project. Figure 14-13 is an extract from this assembly model.

UBL Name	BIE Dictionary Entry Name	Object Class	Property Qualifier	Property Term	Representation Term	Associated Object Class	Occurrence
Calendar	Calendar. Details	Calendar					
Name	Calendar. Name. Text	Calendar		Name	Text		1..1
Owner	Calendar. Owner. Text	Calendar		Owner	Text		0..1
Event	Calendar. Event	Calendar		Event	Event	Event	0..n
Event	Event. Details	Event					
Title	Event. Title. Text	Event		Title	Text		0..1
Type	Event. Type. Text	Event		Type	Text		0..1
Description	Event. Description. Text	Event		Description	Text		0..1
Priority	Event. Priority. Text	Event		Priority	Text		0..1
OwnerContact	Event. Owner_ Contact. Contact	Event	Owner	Contact	Contact	Contact	1..1
PublicContact	Event. Public_ Contact. Contact	Event	Public	Contact	Contact	Contact	0..n

Figure 14-13. Sample of the Event Calendar Assembly Model as a Table

14.7 KEY POINTS IN CHAPTER FOURTEEN

- Documents have always been based on hierarchical models.
- Information exchanges require unambiguous clarity in semantic interpretation.
- Only a hierarchical structure can express certain semantics.
- Some requirements are so common they define a reference model for document assembly.
- Semantic, structural, and instance rules determine how we assemble document models.
- Associations between structures are implied by the hierarchy.
- The entry point structure does not have to share the same name as the document.
- Cardinality controls the depth of the document hierarchy.
- Providing encoding metadata in assembly models will ensure that encoding rules are applied consistently.
- Different assemblies may share common structures or patterns.
- Customization by subtraction doesn't work because the overlapping information isn't explicitly identified.
- The distinction between core and contextualized components is the degree of reuse.

15

Implementing Models In Applications

15.0 INTRODUCTION

We've now described an analysis and design process that yields conceptual models of information components and documents and the processes that use this information or exchange the documents. We are ready to put these models to use, so that our applications or systems meet our business requirements. This generally means we need to develop and deploy one or more document-centric software applications or services.

Document Engineering has nothing inherently to do with XML and we might choose to encode our models in one or more languages. But the good fit between XML models and software enables us to use XML-encoded models to generate code or configure how software works in what are often called model based applications.

The simplest case of a model based application is also the most common, the web browser. For countless information-based activities that have moved to the web, the application does little more than display an HTML document. The web browser allows the user to interact in ways that are determined by the HTML model and the HTTP protocol. The server software that displays and captures the document can be thought of as a platform that runs or interprets the model of the particular document needed by the application.

A well-designed web service is also a model based application. It exposes interfaces as document models and interacts with other applications or services according to a process model. Process models specify the information components produced and used by the service. In most cases, any code that is needed to receive the document and extract the information in its components can be automatically and reliably generated from the models.

More complex enterprise applications that automate business processes involving numerous document exchanges or composite services can also be model based. Their software components can include workflow, process choreography, or integration "engines" that are controlled by business rules from process models.

In this chapter we will introduce a framework for understanding model based applications in Document Engineering. The framework applies to both the narrative and the transactional ends of the Document Type Spectrum, and beginning with simple e-books and e-forms, it describes progressively more complex types of applications, including the evolving visions of web services and other applications with service oriented architectures.

This descriptive framework organizes the specific design issues, types of platforms, and XML and web services standards as they apply to different environments. We hope this approach can help establish a formal ontology and eventually a registry for model based approaches to software development in Document Engineering that might complement broader efforts to develop software engineering patterns.

Of course, not every type of application can be completely implemented from models of documents and processes. Some applications are simply too complex or too new a category for the emergence of software tools and platforms that can explicitly use models. In other cases, the application must support exploratory or unpredictable user interactions that are guided more by the user's system-level conception of how the application works than by the document and process models embodied in the application.

We will only occasionally mention specific software products or vendors and will take a more abstract perspective than software developers may be used to. This lets us frame some of the important innovations in terms of integrating business functionality and services and software support for implementing the models we've developed. We've found that this approach enables people with a business or modeling background to appreciate some important issues about software architecture without having to understand so much technology.

15.1 ENCODING MODELS IN XML

Our conceptual models represent substantial investments in capturing requirements and understanding context, and for some people that knowledge is easiest to understand when it is expressed in a conceptual rather than a technology-dependent way. On the other hand, many software developers are more comfortable when models are expressed in a programming language or data format. In less than a decade XML has become ubiquitous in computing both as a format for encoding information and as a metalanguage for programming and domain-specific modeling languages. Because XML has a syntax that is easily computed with, there are many benefits to encoding these models in XML.

XML is the preferred language for encoding models of documents and of the processes that use them

XML's common use for both information and logic description brings together Document Engineering and software engineering and unifies many of their overlapping concerns. So XML is now the preferred language for encoding models of documents and of the processes that use them in emerging service-oriented architectures and web services.

15.1.1 DOCUMENT MODELS

A primary focus in Document Engineering is on models of documents and the information components they contain. Their document assembly models embody system requirements as rules for semantics, structure, and content in a conceptual form.

Throughout this discussion we are going to assume that we will be encoding document assembly models as XML schemas and will focus on the issues that matter there (see SIDEBAR).

Of course, interoperability or legacy requirements may mandate other document implementations using UN/EDIFACT, ANSI ASC X12, or industry-specific languages. We may even have to encode each document assembly model concurrently as several document implementation models in different languages. For example, the UN/CEFACT group has chosen both UN/EDIFACT (ISO 9735) and XML Schema for their document implementation models.

Selecting a Schema Language

The various XML schema languages differ in expressive capabilities that affect their suitability for encoding document models at different points on the Document Type Spectrum (see Section 2.5.3). For example, models of narrative style documents are often thought to be best encoded using the RELAX NG schema language. RELAX NG schemas are also easy to transform to and from other schema languages. But since schema languages differ in the rules they can represent, not every transformation can be accomplished without loss of information.

However, XML Schema is the schema language endorsed by the W3C, and so is likely to be supported by more XML tools, books, and knowledgeable people. Even so, XML Schema is often criticized for offering too many options for encoding models and for organizing element and type definitions.

It would be wise to adopt a conservative style and not use complex features of a schema language that are hard to understand or may be used incorrectly. Unfortunately there isn't complete consensus about which features are mainstream and which are exotic and should be avoided.

15.1.1.1 Rules For Encoding

Even if there is no agreement on how to best use schema languages to create a document implementation model, there is general agreement that it's essential to adopt encoding rules and follow them consistently.

It's essential to adopt encoding rules and follow them consistently

There may be many different schemas that can validate the same XML documents but vary in their comprehensibility, reusability, compactness, composition, extensibility, and other characteristics. Any set of encoding rules has to find a balance between these often competing goals. Documents may not be directly interoperable unless all participants agree on which encoding rules to follow.

For example, some of the XML Schema encoding decisions to be made include:

- Whether to use only elements, or elements and attributes.
- Naming rules for elements and attributes.
- Which types to declare globally so they can be reused and which to make local.
- When to use type extension and when to use restriction.
- Whether to use abstract types.
- How to make types extensible.
- How to use substitution groups.
- How to use attribute groups.
- How to use enumerations and code lists.
- How to use namespaces.
- How to organize schemas into modules.
- How to name the files containing schemas.
- How to annotate and document schemas.
- Whether to reuse types from existing schemas.

These are important and often contentious questions. But instead of presenting an inadequate review of these encoding questions here, we refer readers to more comprehensive and authoritative resources that focus on them in detail:

- For many years the bible on markup language encoding rules was Maler and El Andaloussi's "Developing SGML DTDs: From Text to Model to Markup," but its emphasis on SGML and narrative document types makes it less applicable to encoding business vocabularies.[1]

- Van der Vlist's "XML Schema," Bean's "XML for Data Architects," and Daum's "Modeling Business Objects with XML Schema" are more recent books that offer prescriptive advice on XML encoding. The last of these takes a highly theoretical point of view informed by the author's perspective as a member of the W3C working group that developed XML Schema.[2]

- "Definitive XML Schema" by Walmsley—another member of the W3C XML Schema working group—contrasts with the last three books in not taking strong positions about encoding rules. Its value is in clearly explaining the encoding alternatives, which is useful given the familiar complaint that XML Schema has too many ways of expressing the same model.[3]

- Orchard and Obasanjo each tackle the difficult issues and encoding rules for schema extensibility and versioning.[4]

- The UBL Naming and Design Rules[5] are a comprehensive set of naming and design rules for encoding document components and assembly models to optimize their reuse and customization in business-to-business vocabularies. These requirements and constraints, and the goal of making UBL an interchange format, precisely tailor these rules for a much narrower context than those targeted by the other XML resources here.

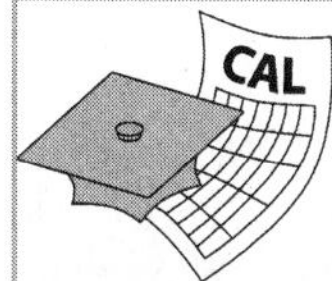

The rules used to encode the Calendar Events schema reflect a desire to create a flexible model that can be customized to almost any domain.[6]

In XML Schema terms, the schema follows the "Garden of Eden" style where all the elements and types are global. Global elements allow for substitution groups, which allow one element to substitute for another. For instance, a Performance Event might have different elements and constraints, but using a substitution group it can be substituted for a generic Event, thus giving the user the ability to add these additional constraints.

Given the sophistication of these issues we suggest that even experts at creating XML schemas should resist the temptation to start from scratch and should instead consider common encoding rules (such as the UBL Naming and Design Rules).

15.1.1.2 Generating Implementation Models

The complexity of XML schema languages makes it challenging to develop or apply a set of encoding rules. So it is appealing to consider automating the process of generating implementation models (the schemas) from conceptual models (see SIDEBAR).

An automated encoding process is faster and more consistent than manually writing schemas and makes them easier to maintain when models change. More importantly, it emphasizes that modeling skill is more essential than schema encoding expertise in developing schemas that meet business requirements.

Modeling skill is more essential than schema encoding expertise when developing schemas

Automated Schema Generation Tools

Many types of software development tools, including XML editors, modeling tools, and databases, contain functions that generate XML schemas.

XML editors generally infer a schema from one or more instances rather than from conceptual models, but many of the encoding rules followed by the instances can be preserved. Furthermore, these functions usually can be configured to follow different rules, most often about the scope of type definitions. The inferred models should be used only as starting points, however, because they obviously can't infer aspects of the model that aren't illustrated by the instances.

Several modeling tools generate XML schemas from conceptual models. David Carlson, the author of "Modeling XML Applications with UML," has also developed an analysis and design tool called hyperModel that maps between the UML metamodel and an XML Schema metamodel so that the modeling artifacts of one can be recreated in the other.[8] So in addition to generating XML schemas from UML models, hyperModel can import XML schemas into UML to create class diagrams that aid in understanding models encoded in XML.

The common requirements for storing XML components in databases or externalizing XML documents from databases have yielded two approaches for encoding relational models as XML schemas: table and object-relational mapping. Table mapping treats rows as XML elements and columns as child elements or XML attributes. This approach is easy to follow, but works only for simple models because it doesn't handle the hierarchical associations between elements. The object-relational approach is more flexible and uses the keys that join relational tables to create the required assembly model as an XML schema.[9]

However, the benefits of an automated approach must be weighed against the limitations or inflexibility of the naming and design rules embedded in the software that generates the schemas. Automated tools might also restrict the ability to include or reuse and customize schema patterns from existing libraries or XML vocabularies.

15.1.1.3 Reusing Document and Component Libraries

Document Engineering projects frequently require the exchange of documents with a partner or trading community using an existing document implementation model or schema library. This is especially common when the library is considered a standard that defines common patterns used by all or most of the document exchanges in an industry.

Some schemas and type libraries are recognized as standards and represent thousands of even tens of thousands of hours of industry expertise, analysis, and design work. For example, the UBL schema library took two years to develop and was partly based on three years of work represented by XCBL, which itself involved a significant effort in extracting semantics from decade-old EDI standards.

During the implementation phase we should review these libraries of physical models carefully to determine whether we can use their schemas for the components that fit our context of use. The more we adopt the common library's implementation components unchanged, the less we'll need to transform any instances.

Reuse standard schema components wherever possible

Even if we have no requirement to use a particular library, we should reuse standard schema components wherever possible and avoid reinventing existing models. This is especially essential for general components like names, codes, identifiers, amounts, dates, and measurements. The most robust and respected set of these components emerged from the ebXML initiative and are provided as core component types in the UBL schema library.

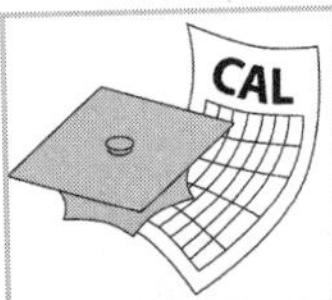

One way to make the Event Calendar implementation models more robust and reusable was to incorporate existing standards. As we described in Chapter 13, we evaluated the UBL conceptual model and adopted some of its components in the assembly model for an Event Calendar.

The implementation models were then able to include the corresponding parts of the UBL schema library. By reusing these physical components, we not only improved the quality of the Event Calendar implementation model but also created the potential to share information with other business processes that also adopt the UBL component library.

The biggest challenge when reusing an existing library is in correctly understanding its context of use

The biggest challenge posed by reusing an existing library is making sure that we understand its context of use correctly. This is not always easy because the library might be published only as XML schemas or other forms of physical implementation models, without the conceptual models that specify their context. This is why these schema artifacts should be one of the informative sources harvested during the document analysis phase, and the analysis techniques in Chapter 12 should abstract the implementation features to get at the underlying rules and requirements.

15.1.1.4 Reuse With Customization

It is conceivable that the common library pattern is a close enough fit to our model that we could adopt it in its entirety and use it both inside our enterprise and outside it in document exchanges with partners. But it is far more likely that we need to enforce business rules that apply only to internal processes, and we might even have different sets of rules that apply to different processes within the enterprise. The best solution is often to adopt the patterns or standard implementation models for document exchanges with external parties while enforcing our customized business rules internally.

One approach is to add assertions or adjunct models that apply additional business rules. For example, Schematron[10] is a popular schema language for adding cross-element validation constraints to a base schema.

Another approach is to use features of the modeling language to extend or restrict the existing rules. For example, XML Schema allows its schemas to be extended or restricted in such a way that the customized schema can validate documents conforming to both the customized and the original pattern's business rules. However, achieving this requires careful consideration and consistent application of the schema derivation mechanisms to ensure that customizations intended to be backward compatible actually are. For this reason, the UBL project organized its type library and developed a customization guideline to encourage best practices for XML Schema customization.[11]

15.1.2 PROCESS MODELS

As we emphasized with document models, it is the conceptual models of processes that capture the rules and requirements of the context of use. Chapters 9 and 10 used a number of different notations and artifacts for developing process models, and it really isn't critical whether we define them using worksheets, hand-drawn box diagrams on a piece of paper, graphical designs in tools like Visio or SmartDraw, or modeling tools such as Rational Rose.

But when we reach the implementation or realization phase, it is highly desirable to express the process model in a computer-processable form or application specific language. Process models encoded in an XML vocabulary can be interpreted either directly or after compilation into code, by workflow systems, process engines, or other software that controls the sequencing and behavior of document exchanges. Software platforms that can enforce an explicit link between the process implementation model and its execution ensure that the process is performed as designed.

For example, when a document is sent, a copy would be saved along with other information that relates it to the process model. As we saw in Section 10.8.1, these key information components are the identifiers for the documents and transaction together with any relevant times or status conditions of the exchange.

When a document is received, the model for the specified transaction, collaboration, or process can be consulted to determine if the document is compliant.

Process models encoded in XML can control the behavior of document exchanges and monitor compliance to rules and agreements

This kind of provable compliance helps businesses satisfy trading partner or service level agreements and is essential for those subject to auditable accounting controls and procedures (such as those required by the Sarbanes-Oxley Act in the United States). Of course, being confident that these processes work the way they should is a good goal even if it's not required by a law or contract.

It is also useful to be able to trace the links between process code and models in the opposite direction so that software developers or other "code readers" can understand the business processes that the code is carrying out.

15.1.2.1 Common Process Metamodels

As we've noted, processes are inherently more abstract than documents, so we find them described using many different conceptual approaches. But if we want to compare or interconnect them, we need to realize process models using a common metamodel.

Several different process metamodels are being developed in the document automation, enterprise integration, and business-to-business contexts most important to Document Engineering. These include:

- Business Process Execution Language (BPEL).
- ebXML Business Process Specification Schema (BPSS).
- OMG Business Process Definition Metamodel (BPDM).
- RosettaNet Implementation Framework (RNIF).[12]

These process metamodels are similar because they all specify the parties involved in the process, the documents or messages they exchange, and the sequencing or choreography of the exchange. They also agree in some respects about how to describe the document payloads. And the typical way to use any of them is with a visual process modeling tool that enables business analysts to design and document their processes without editing or inspecting the XML instance of the model.

Nevertheless, it is remarkable and somewhat disappointing how different these metamodels are in their details. The lack of interoperability between these four metamodels impedes the adoption, exchange, and reuse of business process models.

BPSS and BPDM take a much more abstract and business-level view than RNIF and BPEL, which take a more implementation-level perspective. BPDM, BPSS, and RNIF share properties with the UML metamodel for activity specification, and emphasize externally visible states and state transitions. In contrast, BPEL has mechanisms for sequencing, synchronizing, exception handling, and compensating actions more like those in procedural programming languages.

Perhaps this diversity is not surprising, since the different metamodels have somewhat different goals and have different organizational and intellectual roots. BPSS emerged from the RosettaNet and the ebXML initiatives. BPDM came from another industry consortium with only partial overlap with RosettaNet and ebXML and with a different history in developing integration and process specifications. In contrast, BPEL emerged as the synthesis of proprietary approaches by single vendors to build XML process specification languages executed by their business process platforms. It has a task analysis perspective and assumes particular implementation technologies. BPEL was not submitted to a standards organization for endorsement until after it was essentially complete.

15.1.2.2 BPSS vs. BPEL

Because they are often considered alternatives, the contrasts between BPSS and BPEL are especially noteworthy. Even though BPSS was designed to describe business-to-business processes, it is a generalized metamodel that takes an abstract view of processes involving document exchanges. The BPSS metamodel makes explicit use of transaction patterns (Chapter 9) to encourage reuse of models and uses transaction properties (Chapter 10) to enable fine distinctions between otherwise similar models. Because BPSS takes a more conceptual view of business processes, we use it as the basis for the worksheets in Chapter 9 and prefer it to BPEL, which mixes conceptual description with implementation specifications.

In contrast to BPSS, BPEL describes the request and response process models in web services and doesn't distinguish the variety of types of transactional exchanges required by business-to-business processes. BPEL has constructs for describing processes abstractly, but these are much less widely used than those for describing the processing flow between web services in a directly executable way. For example, BPEL instances expose many physical implementation details like URLs, and use XPATH to locate variables that correlate related documents.

BPSS supports sequencing and synchronization since it supports the expression of UML Activity Diagrams for the choreography of business transactions. But the BPSS does not support exception handling and compensating actions because its designers believe that all exceptions and compensating actions at the collaboration level should be explicitly modeled. This ensures that business partners fully understand the ramifications of late or lost documents and failed transactions. Put another way, in BPSS compensating and exception handling are not needed at the transaction level because they are dealt with at the collaboration level.

Because BPEL's description of a process is more directly executable than a BPSS one, it is easier to implement. However, BPSS is intended to be used with an ebXML Collaboration Protocol Profile and Agreement (CPPA), which provides the necessary implementation specifications. The BPSS and CPPA combination is architecturally superior because it separates the business model from its technical realization. BPEL might be better viewed as a physical interface target for process models created in more conceptual metamodels like BPSS.

15.2 MODEL BASED APPLICATIONS

The reason business applications exist is to enforce some set of rules or constraints about information or processes. Any application can be thought of as a software artifact that presents, collects, and manipulates information according to these rules.[13]

So in the sense that a model represents some understanding of a context and its requirements, any software application that satisfies those requirements is relying on the model to some extent. But it makes a huge difference how the model is used in the implementation.

15.2.1 HOW MODEL BASED APPLICATIONS WORK

In the ideal case, the requirements and rules of the application's context are completely captured in one or more models that are explicitly used in the software that implements them. The model can be used to generate the software, or the model can be interpreted by a generic software platform to configure its behavior, or some combination of code generation and platform configuration may be employed.

15.2.1.1 Generating Software From Models

Techniques for generating software from models have proven successful in the domain of internal business process integration, or enterprise application integration (EAI). In this environment they are typically called model driven architectures (MDAs) and use models represented in UML.

Model Driven Architecture

"Imagine if the construction worker could take his blueprint, crank it through a machine, and have the foundation of the building simply appear."[14]

This vision of a model driven architecture doesn't prescribe the format of the blueprint or how it is cranked through a machine.

In contrast, the model driven architecture (MDA) from the Object Management Group does mandate the high-level architectural specifications for software application interfaces. The MDA models are represented in the conceptual format of the Unified Modeling Language (UML).[15] Numerous software vendors provide tools that use these platform independent models (PIMs) to generate enterprise integration or data warehousing code in various languages. The generated artifacts are known as platform specific models (PSMs). The mappings from conceptual PIMs to physical PSMs follow standard software design patterns to achieve high levels of productivity, interoperability and reliability. Currently the MDA approach is being extended to web services, with service interfaces being treated as PIMs and XML schemas added as alternate PSM targets for MDA code generators.

The approach we call "model based" in Document Engineering shares many high-levels goals with MDAs, but it is not as prescriptive about modeling methodology and tools. In that respect MDAs are a more extensively developed subset of our world-view. Because the linkage between models and code can be tighter in MDAs, the latter can be "driven by" rather than just "based on" the former.

The linkage between models and code is tighter in model driven architectures than in model based ones

When code generation techniques turn XML schemas into logically equivalent representations in software, it is called data binding.[16] This functionality is an essential feature of development environments, databases, application servers, and other platforms where XML meets software. Data binding transforms XML schemas into programming language classes in Java, C#, Python, and so on to guide the creation of objects that convey the document's content. Populating these objects with content is called unmarshalling or deserialization; the inverse process of creating document instances from objects is called marshalling or serialization.

15.2.1.2 Software Platforms That Use Models

With software platform techniques, the model isn't treated as the input to a code generator. Instead, the platform is considered a software "engine" whose metamodel interprets the model to determine how the software behaves. These platforms embody a repeatable approach for solving some class of problems by providing interfaces that get extended or configured by the model. The model remains distinct and inspectable, separate from the generic functionality provided by the platform.

The idea of this platform can best be explained by example. Consider any application that involves a large amount of regularly structured data. The need for reliable persistent storage of this information is a generic concern that has been successfully addressed by the relational data models used by relational database management systems. We can encode the conceptual model of our data requirements as the implementation model called the database schema. The database management system platform uses this schema to configure the database to store information for our application. Packaged relational databases are so commonplace and sophisticated today that few people would ever write a new one. Nobody thinks of a platform that uses one as being "model based," but those are exactly the hallmarks of a ubiquitous platform.

Similarly, any application that collects structured information from a user can rely on an electronic forms platform that is configured for the application by the document schema that describes the model of the input information. We know this platform as a web server.

15.2.1.3 Mapping Between Interfaces

For both code generation and platform approaches, there is a defined link between the models and their target physical interfaces. Sometimes this link is itself expressed as a model, called a mapping, that expresses the relationship between components of the model and software components. The explicit connection means the models provide accurate and complete documentation of the application's design and implementation.

The models should make it easier to understand how and why a model based application works, because the intent should be more visible in the model than it is in code. Any changes in the model or the mapping are easily reflected in regenerated application code or in revised behavior of a software platform. In the latter case, of course, none of the code in the software platform needs to change, only the model that it uses.

15.2.2 WHEN APPLICATIONS AREN'T BASED ON MODELS

Few professional software developers would implement an application without making at least some effort to systematize its requirements in conceptual models. And the typical programmer knows that it is poor practice to "hard code" into an application values for filenames, directory paths, error message text, and other strings that should be externalized for internationalization. But the same programmer may, unfortunately, "hard code" the document and process models or fail to fully represent them in the software that implements them. For example, many applications involving documents flatten their structured and hierarchical model into a set of attribute-value pairs. And in extreme cases the application may describe documents as just blobs of text.

Models are often not fully represented in the software that implements them

Other implementations may fail the key test of separating the content from its presentation. This problem is typical of many web applications built using scripting approaches that mix formatting instructions for content (especially HTML) with procedural scripting. The end result of flattening the model or mixing it in with procedural code is the same; the application's code can't easily recognize the document's semantics.

When applications aren't based on models, all information requirements and processing logic is encoded in the software. This indicates that the linkage between the conceptual interface of the application's requirements and the physical code is informal and fixed. The lack of a formal, direct connection means that if the requirements and the conceptual models change, the application code must be revised by hand recompiled, and redeployed. Over time the code is likely to become unstructured and disconnected from what little of the model it represented.

15.2.3 MODEL BASED APPLICATIONS AS A GOAL

Some requirements, especially those relating to user capabilities and preferences, are inherently difficult to represent in models. Many interactions with a complex application are determined by the user's system-level conception or metaphorical understanding of how it works.[17]

Most system platforms fall between the ideal and worst cases. We must not forget that models are simplified descriptions of a subject that abstract from its complexity to emphasize some features or characteristics and deemphasize others. So no model is likely to encode every rule and requirement for any given context of use. If it did the model would not be a simplification, it would be as complex as the application.

Furthermore, even for rules that are represented in the model, there are limits to what modeling languages can express. The more specialized the application's context of use, the less likely it is that platforms and devices exist that completely support it. So there will inevitably be rules that require coding into applications.

Our goal should be to maximize the extent to which our applications rely on model based rules and minimize its use of programmed ones. The more applications are model based, the more understandable, robust, and maintainable they will be.

15.3 MODEL BASED APPLICATIONS IN DOCUMENT ENGINEERING

We can apply the concepts of model based applications and platforms to Document Engineering wherever an application has distinct interfaces when it is realized in software systems or devices.

We can use document implementation models to define the physical interfaces of applications by describing the information that the application needs to operate and the information that it produces. At the same time, process implementation models can control the application's interactions with other interfaces (both human and application), often on the basis of the information that the application receives. Using these rules, the platform can apply the required interfaces when it processes documents in ways appropriate for different kinds of system, device, or user interfaces.

Many applications that involve documents need to support different physical interfaces. Applications that use documents from the narrative side of the Document Type Spectrum generally have user interfaces, often on multiple devices, while those with transactional documents may have interfaces to other applications or services as well as user interfaces. These requirements imply many-to-many mappings between the input and output interfaces for each application.

Many-to-many mappings can be avoided by mapping all physical interfaces to a common conceptual interface

We can avoid this complexity by introducing a common conceptual interface to which all mappings of physical interfaces resolve. If the mapping between the conceptual interface of the application and its physical interfaces is maintained in a model based platform, we can change the physical interface to the application without manually changing all its mapped physical interfaces. Similarly, we can add new physical interfaces (perhaps for new display or output devices) without changing the conceptual interface.

Most of the remainder of this chapter consists of progressively more complex examples of platforms for model based applications. We start with simple e-form and e-book applications, and proceed to single source publishing and portals, B2B document exchanges, and marketplace hubs and composite service platforms. We end with the visions of the semantic web and semantic web services, where the models describing documents and services continually evolve as they are incrementally annotated or extended by metadata applied by people or computational agents. The set of examples is illustrative and not exhaustive, but its range should demonstrate the value of a model based approach to implementation as the last phase in a Document Engineering project.

15.3.1 E-FORM APPLICATIONS

One of the simplest applications involving documents is one in which a person completes a form to create a valid instance of a document that is saved and forwarded to another user or application for further processing. Usually computer programs can then handle all the normal cases, with only the exceptional cases requiring intervention by people. Often the application is little more than "webifying" a document interface to a legacy printed document or client-server document application.

We can easily imagine applications where form-based information moves within and between organizations for purposes such as filling out purchase orders, submitting a budget or timesheet, seeking reimbursement for expenses, applying for a grant or job, registering for classes or events, filing income taxes, making insurance claims, and so on. We can also imagine the uninspired formulaic names given to these applications—e-order, e-time, e-expense, e-job, e-registration, e-tax, e-insure, and so on—with "e-" followed by either a document name or a process.

Figure 15-1 illustrates the different parts of a simple e-form application. The application directly maps the document's physical interface to that of the required form. All processes and business rules are encoded directly in the e-form application.

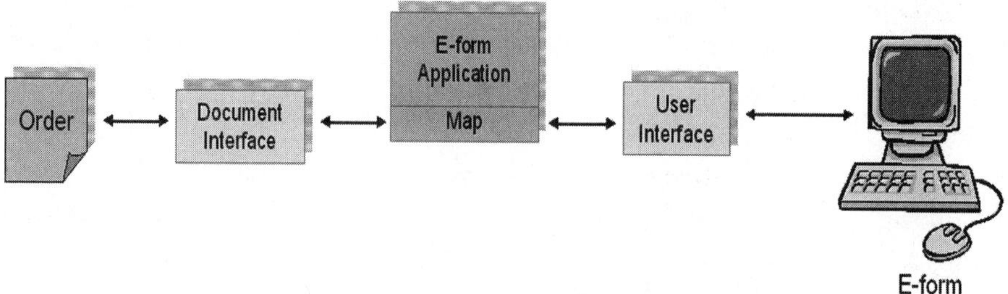

Figure 15-1. An E-Form Application

Let's assume that this application is used to create orders that comply with the UBL Order schema (the document implementation model). So the application supports an Order document interface containing an element called IssueDate. This defines the date (and possibly the time) when the order was issued. In its physical interface, an IssueDate element is encoded as an XML Schema datatype of datetime and would expect values like "2005-02-14T14:00:00".

It wouldn't be difficult for an automated purchasing function in an ERP or legacy system to create an IssueDate in this format, but this date format wouldn't be helpful in the user interface for a person filling out an order e-form. It would be better to collect the date and time of issue as separate components. In addition, the optimal presentations may also differ if the physical interface were for a web form or a portable device such as a handheld PDA or cell phone. But in the architecture shown in Figure 15-1, each of these new interfaces would require a separate and mostly redundant mapping between the physical document interface and the physical user interface.

In contrast, in a model based e-form application, we would introduce a common conceptual interface to which both the physical document interface and the physical form interface are mapped (Figure 15-2).

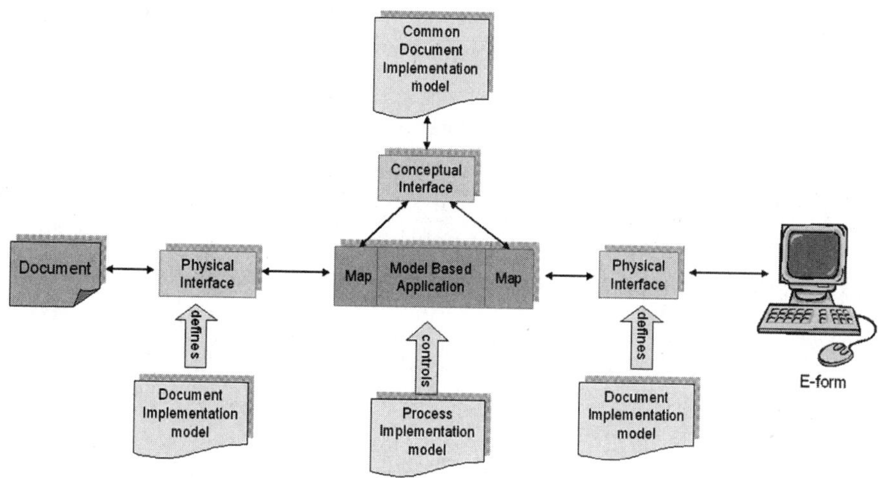

Figure 15-2. An E-Form Model Based Application Platform

In this architecture, both physical interfaces are defined by document implementation models. Using the previous example we could say the document's physical interface is defined by the UBL Order schema and the e-form's interface is defined by the XHTML schema. The common conceptual interface may also be defined using another document implementation model.

Basing the physical user interface needed by a person and the physical document interface used by an application on a common conceptual interface ensures that the documents they process are interoperable. It also enables transparent migration from one interface to the other if changing requirements make this necessary.

Basing the user and application interfaces on a common conceptual interface ensures that the documents they process are interoperable

There may also be procedural rules in the process implementation model. For example, specifying that once an order has been placed, its date of issue cannot be changed. A model based platform can also enforce this rule by making the physical interface for displaying or changing an order different from that for creating one.

Then all of the mappings to physical interfaces that need to follow this rule can be controlled by a single expression of the rule.

Workflow or document automation applications in which a form moves through an organization for approvals or incremental augmentation (see Sections 4.2.2.6 and 9.8.6) can be implemented in a consistent model based way by treating the differences between the successive document implementation models in the "pipeline" as the prescription for the information to be collected from a user or process at that step (Figure 15-3).

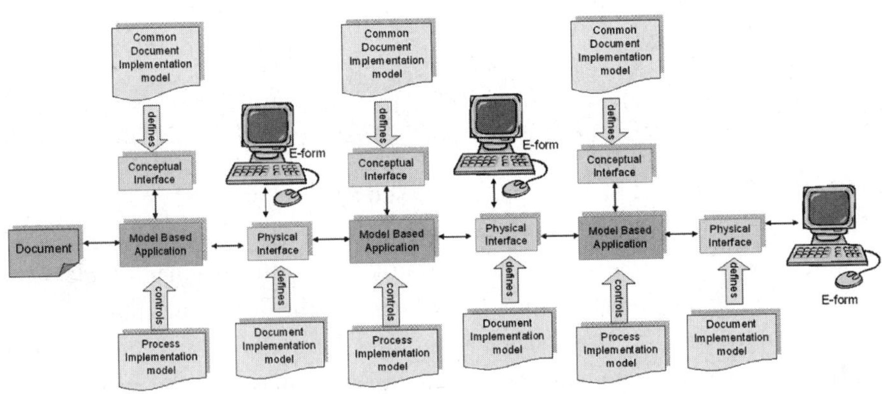

Figure 15-3. A Model Based Document Automation Platform

From HTML to XForms

Many e-form applications are implemented using the web as their platform. The web browser has evolved, not entirely gracefully, from its original ability to display the single hardwired document model of HTML to the ability to render any XML document instance as HTML with an XSLT transform. In effect, the XSLT transform is a preprocessor for the platform, converting the document implementation model into the HTML model interpreted by the platform. Cascading style sheets can provide precise formatting control to the transformed XML.

The facilities in HTML for collecting structured information in forms are very limited. Because the form content isn't distinguished from its presentation and the browser does little data validation, e-form applications using HTML require lots of scripting code that isn't model based.

These limitations are overcome in the W3C XForms Recommendation, which completely separates the conceptual interface of the form (called the abstract interface) from the physical interface (called the concrete interface) and uses XML markup to invoke model based processing of form contents.[18] For example, an XForms user interface model specifies the conceptual interface function of "select one" rather than the physical interface widget of "radio button." This architecture defers the presentation details to the presentation layer, allowing each XForms-capable platform to make its best use of capabilities while preserving as much interoperability of functionality as possible. XHTML 2.0, which specifies full support for XForms, will become an excellent basis for form-based applications when it is fully implemented in browsers.

15.3.1.1 Implementation Models For User Interfaces

More complex applications whose user interfaces need additional functionality that "wraps around" a form are becoming model based with the emergence of XML vocabularies as domain-specific modeling or configuration languages for user interfaces.

For example, the open source Mozilla browser contains a rendering engine called Gecko that uses an XML language called XUL.[19] The elements of the XUL vocabulary include standard user interface components like menus, input controls, dialogs and tree controls, and keyboard shortcuts. Microsoft is adopting a similar approach for future versions of Windows with its own XML vocabulary called XAML,[20] as is Macromedia with an XML vocabulary called MXML that is interpreted by its popular Flash Player.[21]

In addition, Microsoft, Adobe, and some smaller vendors have created proprietary alternatives to XForms in platforms for deploying graphically sophisticated applications that collect and display XML data in forms. All of them give the user interface designer a starting point by using the document implementation model to generate a palette of form elements and data types.

However, because these platforms were mostly designed with a focus on user interface implementation, they tend to have a physical component repertoire that can't directly handle conceptual components that reuse common patterns, require aggregation or disaggregation, or have integrity constraints.[22] In addition, once these tools have imported the required elements from the document implementation model, they no longer enforce most of the rules represented in it, allowing user interface designers to build forms that create invalid and even nonsensical instances.

15.3.1.2 Designing Model Based User Interfaces

Whatever the technologies that are used by these various platforms, they don't eliminate the initial user interface design tasks:

- Determining which components in the document conceptual model will be displayed or collected in the user interface. For example, attributes such as the language code would rarely appear in a user interface.

- Defining the transformation from the document implementation model to specify which user interface component will collect or display each component in the conceptual interface.

- Determining how the rules in the process model will be represented in the task guidance, navigation, screen or window sequencing, error handling, and similar interactive functions of the platform; this is sometimes called the interaction design.

Whatever the technologies that are used by user interface platforms, they don't eliminate the design tasks

Since its emergence as a discipline in the 1980s, user interface design has always had an iterative and heuristic character, informed but not completely governed by objective rules about what made one user interface better than another. So by the early 1990s researchers were hoping that "automatic generation of window and menu layouts from information already present in the application data model can relieve the application designer of unnecessary work while providing an opportunity to automatically apply style rules to the interface design."[23]

But while a substantial body of research in model based user interfaces has identified much knowledge and proposed many mechanisms for automating or improving the efficiency of mapping to the physical interface, little of it has been incorporated into conventional user interface design methods and applied in commercial software tools. Graphical design tools, interface builders, and development environments make it easier to record the mapping between components in the document and process implementation models and those in the physical interface, but the mapping must still be created by some combination of human judgment, creativity, and default rules.

Research in Model Based User Interfaces

Many complementary approaches and techniques for automating the design and implementation of model based user interfaces have been explored in the last decade, including the following:

- User interface design patterns.[24]
- User interface modeling languages and XML vocabularies.[25]
- Tools for generating user interface prototypes from XML specifications.[26]
- Multiple device interfaces and "graceful degradation" rules for generating a set of related user interfaces for devices of different capabilities.[27]
- Automated evaluation of user interface quality.[28]
- Expert systems that advise user interface designers.[29]
- Algorithms for generating graphics from descriptions and automating graphical layout.[30]
- Reverse engineering of website designs.[31]

It is astonishing and disappointing how little impact this work has made in the day-to-day work of user interface design. Some of this is an inevitable result of academic research funding, which invests in finding new results and approaches but doesn't pay for making them robust or scalable. We think there are plenty of lessons in this research that could be applied systematically in contemporary user interface design practice to yield good interfaces with more predictable methods. For example, models can generate user interface prototypes that follow design patterns to more efficiently and systematically sample the overall design space. Usability testing will inevitably refine the interface design, but the model can provide hypotheses or checklists to help user interface designers determine the optimal presentation and interaction structure.

But the good news, especially for XForms and the nonproprietary user interface technologies, is that once a mapping from the document implementation to the platform language is defined, the subsequent process of applying the mapping to the physical interface can usually be substantially automated. This is essential when multiple mappings are necessary to meet presentation requirements for different classes of users or devices.

15.3.1.3 The Future of Model Based User Interfaces

As more applications are built with model based platforms, the models for their interface documents and process choreography will unavoidably become explicit because they are required for web services to work. Many of the tools that create web services are adjuncts or extensions of visual design tools, and they will undoubtedly continue to improve as platforms for implementing model based user interfaces.[32]

In addition, the explosive growth of applications for devices like mobile phones with rapid obsolescence and limited interactive capabilities will inevitably result in condensed user interfaces. These two trends should further encourage model based approaches and greater automation in user interface design and implementation.

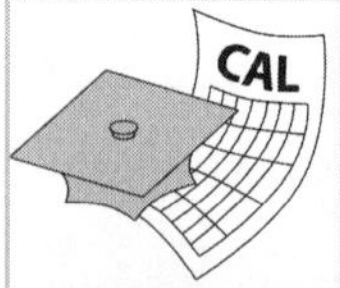

We've extensively described the analysis and design of the Event model in this book, and it is fair to say that the Event Calendar application as a whole is model based.

The system architecture for the UC Berkeley Event Calendar is illustrated in Figure 15-4. The main components include:

• A centralized repository of event information, based on the Event conceptual model

• A Calendar Management model based application that provides two physical interfaces:

One allows users to manage their events in the repository.

One helps users customize a visually compelling, dynamic, web-based calendar.

• A single conceptual interface based on document implementation models of Events for external calendars to send event information to, and extract information from, the central repository.

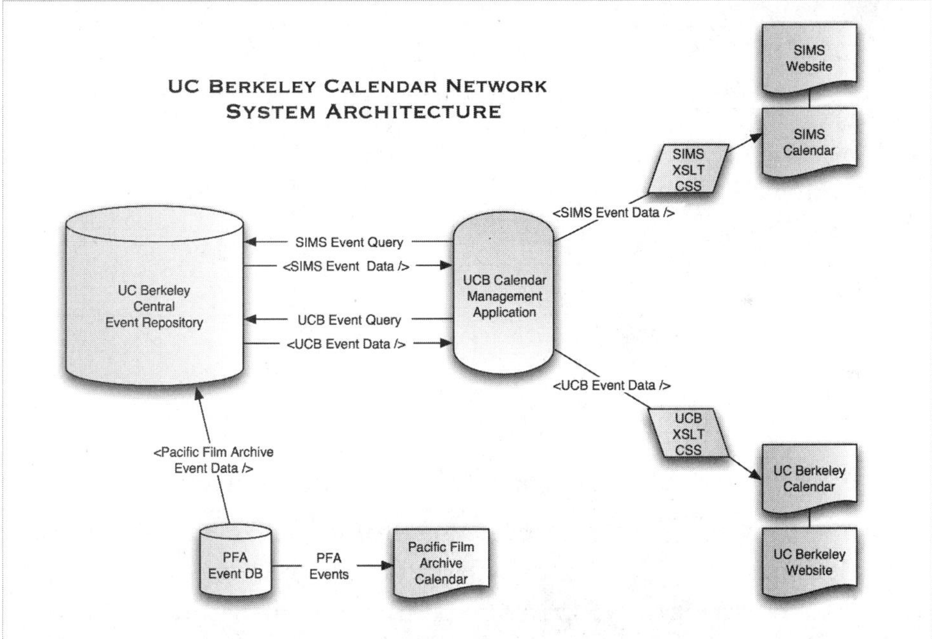

Figure 15-4. UC Berkeley Event Calendar Platform

Other applications and calendar users may access the repository through the Calendar Management application. The interfaces available are either a default calendar, a customized version of the default calendar created by modifying the Cascading Style Sheet (CSS), or a completely new calendar created by modifying the default XSL transform.

Alternatively, web services can be used to send an XML document to the central repository to upload information or request a download of event information, which is returned in an XML document.

In addition, the Add Event function shown in Figure 15-5 closely reflects the Event model and the functional dependency and co-occurrence constraints of the model ensure that components appear grouped in meaningful ways.

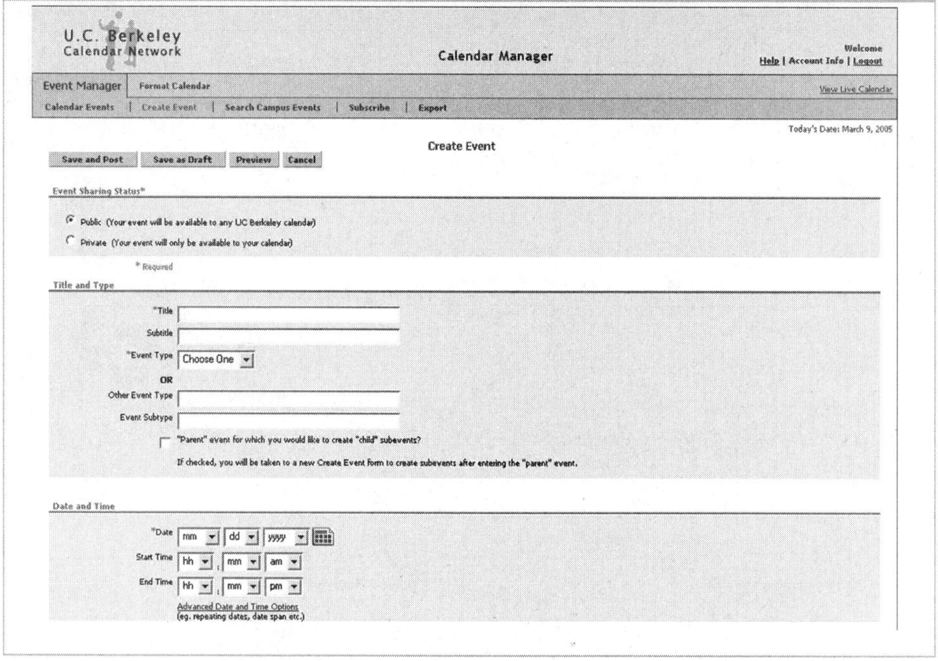

Figure 15-5. Add Event Form in Calendar Management Application

But we hesitate to claim that the Calendar Management application is entirely model based. The focus on supporting calendar owners to encourage them to share events led us to incorporate the Add Event function as part of the more comprehensive Calendar Management application, whose overall complexity exceeds what can currently be described in either a process implementation or document implementation model. Specifically, much of the user interface design of the application emerged through extensive usability testing and heuristic analysis.

15.3.2 E-BOOK APPLICATIONS

On the narrative end of the Document Type Spectrum are e-books or other publishing applications with presentationally structured documents in which users interact with the content by using tables of contents, hypertext links, bookmarks, and navigation aids. An e-book application applies some presentation mapping or rendering to transform the document interface components into the required components for the various presentation devices. For example, the information in all heading components may be aggregated to form a table of contents that is suitably formatted for the various devices.

Some e-book applications present content to look like printed books, with page-oriented layout, running heads, margins in which notes can be added, and other traditional presentation conventions. Other e-books present content in text frames to emphasize hypertext or web navigation by following the explicit or implied links in the content. But almost all e-books contain different stylesheets or transformations that change the selection or arrangement of the content in the document, and some allow the user to select either of these presentation metaphors.

Other typical conceptual components in e-books are outline or summary views of the publication created by a transformation that suppresses information from lower levels in the content hierarchy. Different physical interfaces might select different sets of these conceptual components to support distinct uses of the information. For example, an electronic version of the Oxford English Dictionary might show the complete entry for a word, a short entry that omits etymologies and quotations, or only the word and its quotations.[33]

Figure 15-6 illustrates how a model based e-book platform that uses a common model to describe the document's conceptual interface could meet all these requirements in a consistent and scaleable manner. Functions like aggregation of headings or annotation are defined generically in the conceptual interface. Each document has its components mapped to these concepts and the realization of these functions is determined by another set of models that describe the physical mappings suitable for each physical device on which the e-book is rendered. For example, annotation may be enabled by typing notes on one device and by voice recording on another.

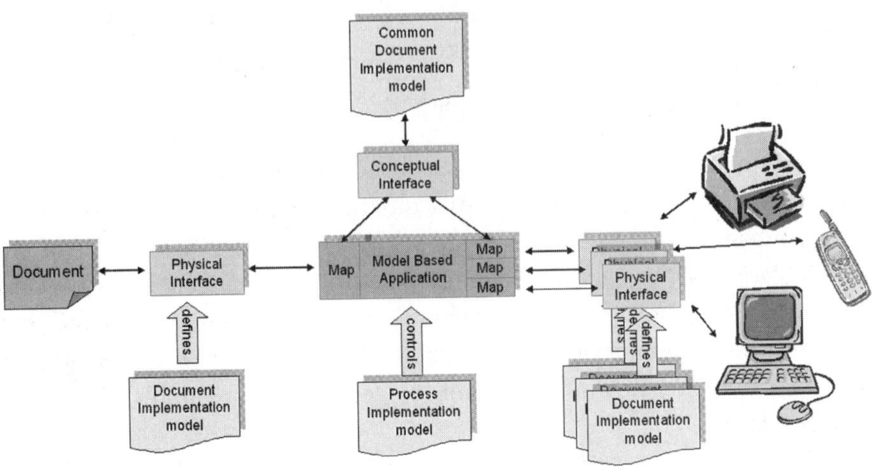

Figure 15-6. A Model Based E-Book Platform

Many mass-marketed e-books use an application called an e-book reader, and some of these implement a standard document interface model called the Open eBook Publication Structure Specification. However, many e-books are still published in proprietary formats to restrict them to a single e-book platform.[34]

At a further level of sophistication, Interactive Electronic Training Manuals (IETMs) are an important category of e-books whose primary purpose is to enhance training, maintenance, and repair activities for complex systems of equipment like those found in military or commercial aircraft. The U.S. Department of Defense defines five classes of IETMs; Class IIIs provide model based functionality like that of most e-books, while the most advanced Class V IETMs combine rule-based expert systems to provide precise procedural guidance with integrated e-form functionality for ordering needed parts or submitting maintenance reports.[35]

15.3.3 SINGLE SOURCE PUBLISHING AND PORTAL APPLICATIONS

Also on the narrative side of the Document Type Spectrum but more complex than e-books are structured publishing applications that involve a number of related document implementation models. What makes these applications model based is that their multiple document models are interrelated by overlapping conceptual components (see Section 10.8.1, "Key Information Components" and Section 12.2, "Consolidating Components").

Because multiple document implementation models come together to define the conceptual interface of these kinds of applications, there are no processes specific to any of the individual document types. The conceptual interface describes the union of all the requirements for the context of use rather than imposing the more specific interpretation of a single document implementation model. The application functionality is created by (or at least describable as) transformations that involve or exploit the network of relationships among the overlapping components.

The conceptual interface for publishing applications and publishing portals describes the requirements for the context of use

Furthermore, because these applications typically involve multiple instances of different documents, the application must ensure persistent storage for the component content. This storage requirement is often addressed by a content management or repository platform that also satisfies the related versioning, configuration management, access control, and security requirements. Important design concerns for applications of this type include the granularity at which the document components are managed and the metadata associated with them that enable the platform to carry out its many functions.

Figure 15-7 illustrates model based, single-source publishing in an engine assembly plant using an example cited in Chapter 14. Assembly and Operator Instructions, Troubleshooting Guides, Training Manuals, and Process Control Plans reuse information components from a content repository by assembling them in different ways.[36]

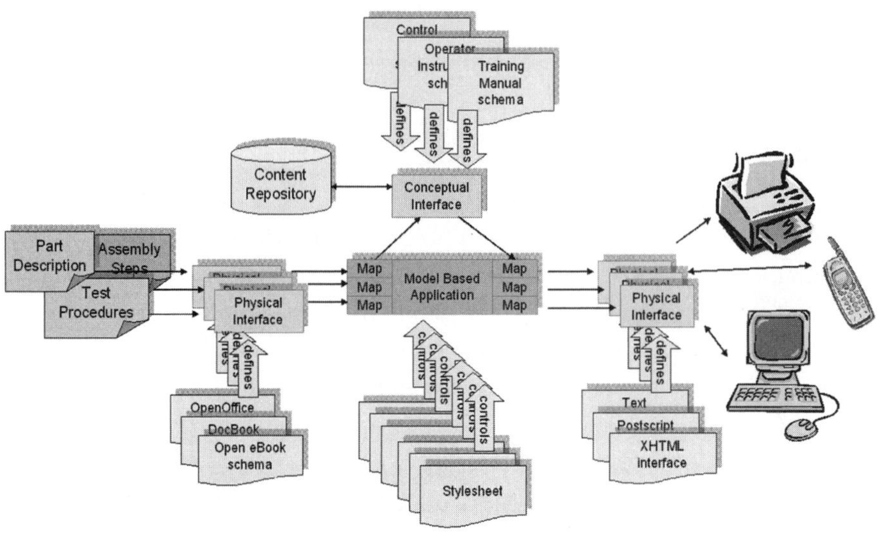

Figure 15-7. Single-Source Model Based Publishing

Instead of directly creating the various types of complete documents, the authors create tool and part descriptions, assembly steps, test procedures, and other reusable content fragments. These are stored in the content repository along with the models that define the assembly of these pieces into the complete documents and the transformations that create different physical views of each type of document. New types of content fragments, new types of document assemblies, and new views for devices or contexts can be introduced as needed.

Of course, the fact that transformations can be programmed to assemble the interconnected components in the application doesn't imply that the content is static. Content components in structured publications can be dynamic information sources, such as news or weather feeds and stock quotes, whose content is continuously updated.

Architecturally related to single-source publishing applications are model based websites or portals where content is woven together by overlapping components from various document implementation models.

The website for the Center for Document Engineering (CDE) at UC Berkeley illustrates this idea. The CDE is one of about 100 "centers" on the UC Berkeley campus, most of which share the same conceptual model of a small academic research unit: a center has information components that describe its mission, people, initiatives, publications, events, news, and resources.

This common conceptual model has been encoded in an application called "Center in a Box," which consists of a set of XML schemas for these common components and associated XSLT transformations that automatically build the CDE website from the XML documents containing the content.[37] The transforms create valid XHTML and other formats, generating appropriate links and user interface components like tables of contents, links, and navigation aids.

For example, a CDE researcher's name might appear as an author in an instance of the Publication schema and as a contact person in an instance of an Initiative schema. Both occurrences would be automatically linked by the transforms to the researcher's minibiography conforming to the Person schema. All of the tedious and error-prone linking of web pages is eliminated, and broken links simply can't exist.

15.3.4 BUSINESS-TO-BUSINESS DOCUMENT EXCHANGES

Most e-form, e-book, and single-source publishing or portal varieties of model based applications share the simplifying principle that they present a single conceptual interface to the people or other applications that use them. This simplification often reflects a single technical and organizational control point where decisions are made about document and process models so that all the participants can agree on their interpretation. But many applications involve document exchanges between applications and organizations that don't have a single control point, and as a result there may be little agreement about their conceptual models or the physical interfaces that they use internally or offer to each other. As we saw in Chapter 6, there are many ways in which two parties can fail to achieve interoperability in their document exchanges.

Many business-to-business applications have been built using point-to-point integration techniques that directly connect the physical interfaces on one side of the document exchange to those on the other (see Section 4.4.1.2). These tightly coupled applications are notoriously hard to maintain.

Many business-to-business applications have been built using tightly coupled interfaces and are hard to maintain

An alternative is to build model based applications that expose conceptual interfaces rather than physical ones. This approach is illustrated in Figure 15-8.

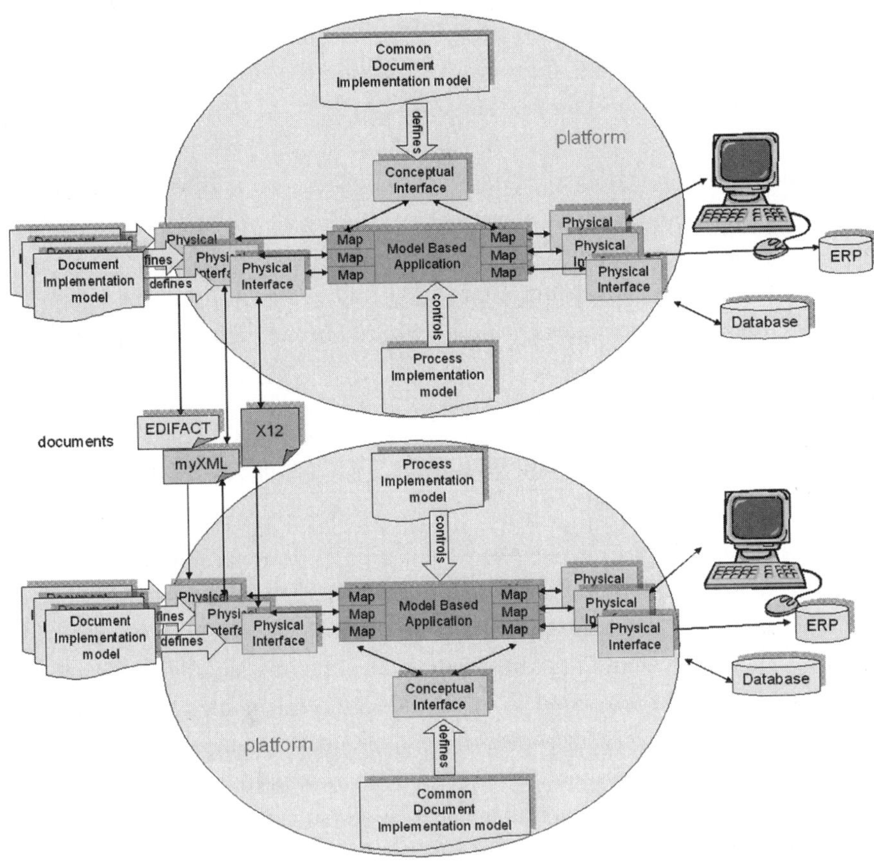

Figure 15-8. Model Based Business-to-Business Applications

Figure 15-8 shows how the tight coupling of physical interfaces can be replaced with the loose coupling of conceptual interfaces. A wide variety of types of software, including integration servers, process control engines, and message-oriented middleware, can provide the platform on which the required mapping and transformation takes place.[38] The physical interfaces to databases, ERP systems, or other internal applications are hidden by their mappings to a common conceptual interface that in turn is revealed to the other side as document implementation models. This means that private rules and requirements can be expressed internally as physical interfaces without sacrificing the ability to interoperate externally.

Model based business-to-business applications expose their physical interfaces as document implementation models and are controlled by process implementation models

Model based business-to-business applications are those in which both parties expose a physical interface as a document implementation model. These are controlled by a process implementation model that also allocates the transformation responsibility. In the generic case shown in Figure 15-8, each side transforms its documents to the interfaces required by the other, but because the physical interfaces are hidden, the transformations are more stable and easier to implement.

15.3.4.1 Connectors and Gateways

Figure 15-8 shows document and process implementation models running on the platform on each side of the business-to-business document exchange. But sometimes the dominant party in an asymmetric business relationship imposes implementation guidelines or contracts that specify the physical interfaces and document implementation model of the documents being exchanged. This transformation is often carried out using connectors or mapping software that uses templates or configurable translations for common physical interfaces to ERP, enterprise database, or messaging software formats.

The subservient party might be required accept documents in whatever form the dominant party wants to use and do the transformation to its own required physical interface. The software component that performs this function is called a gateway.

The most common gateway software in business-to-business applications provides physical interfaces for EDI messages. This can be a difficult technical challenge but may be necessary to do business with a partner whose legacy technology would otherwise prevent it.

15.3.4.2 Orchestration and Choreography

A similar implementation decision concerns the control of document exchanges in the business processes between two parties. The generic illustration in Figure 15-8 implies that each enterprise plays the same role in controlling the flow of documents between them. Instead, these exchanges might be initiated and controlled by the process model of one of the parties, with the second party responding to documents without any knowledge of the controlling model. Alternatively, the document flow could be mutually controlled as both parties follow the same process model. In Section 9.7 we made this distinction between an orchestration, where one side is serving as the conductor, and a choreography, where there is distributed coordination with equivalent responsibility.

In the cases we've discussed so far, the business-to-business document exchanges are controlled by one or both of the parties involved. In the next section we consider another model based platform in which the exchanges are controlled or mediated by a third party.

15.3.5 APPLICATIONS WITH INTERMEDIARY PLATFORMS

In Section 4.1.2.2 we discussed marketplaces, exchanges and auctions as patterns of business organization in which an intermediary, typically called the market operator, defined the terms and conditions under which buyers, sellers, and service providers participated. The role of the intermediary from a business perspective is to support and sustain the relationships among the participants.

When we revisit the intermediary pattern from an implementation perspective, we can identify the capabilities of a model based platform suitable for achieving these business goals. The defining characteristic of an intermediary platform is that it adds another participant to a document exchange process. We can view this role as analogous to a post office that interprets addresses to ensure the appropriate routing of documents, or to a traffic cop at a busy intersection who signals to the participants when it is their turn to go. In either case, because the intermediary separates the process control of document exchanges from the services that produce and consume the documents, it is easier to manage, measure, and change the process flow.

A model based intermediary platform might also function as a gateway to transform the messages it routes into the recipient's physical interface model. If the market operator or the community of practice as a whole establishes patterns (or standards) for document implementation models, gateway transformations at the intermediary platform can drastically simplify the integration problems each participant would face in dealing directly with every other participant.

The intermediary platform might maintain directories or registries that organize information about the participants, the services they provide, and the models that govern their document and process interfaces. Centralizing the storage of this information ensures its integrity, simplifies the task of joining the marketplace or trading community, and makes it easier to discover potential business partners or service providers. Storing schemas, mappings, and transformations in the platform repository encourages their reuse and facilitates standardization, especially when supported by design tools that let implementers use these components in a more graphical and abstract way.

An intermediary platform may also be controlled by process implementation models. This enables process orchestration for business services. For example, the intermediary may generate alerts for timed-out acknowledgments or proactively notify parties of events that will trigger further processes, such as advising importers when ships carrying their goods arrive in port.

Finally, the intermediary platform may maintain a repository of document content, or at least summaries of the content. This might enable the intermediary to add value by providing statistics about transactional activity, maintaining profiles of participants, verifying compliance with terms and conditions, or performing other activities that are appropriate for intermediaries.

Figure 15-9 illustrates a model based intermediary platform.

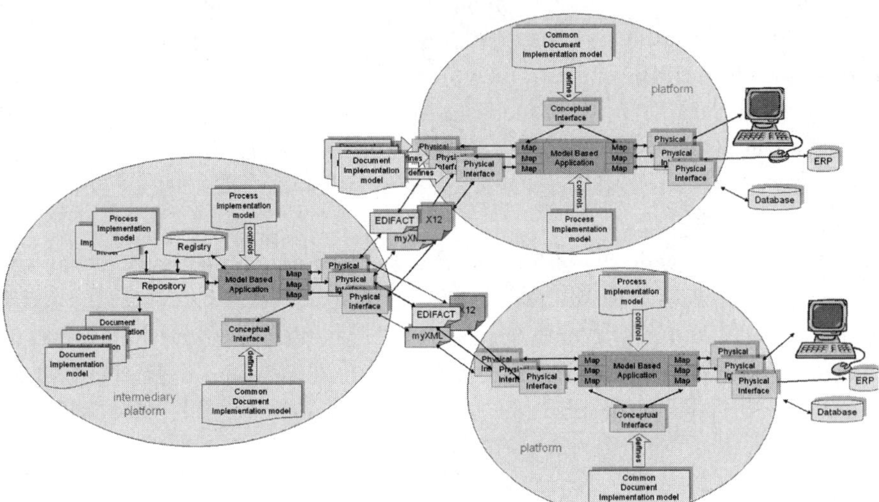

Figure 15-9. Model Based Applications Using an Intermediary Platform

In the late 1990s, when new technologies first enabled Internet marketplaces, many were implemented using intermediary platforms that attempted to provide this complete set of routing, transformation, and registry services. But this makes the marketplace platform an overly complex application. In addition, it is somewhat incompatible with the business reality that most participants in one marketplace need to exchange documents with at least some participants in other marketplaces.

The "heavyweight" intermediary platform is losing weight and functionality

So the "heavyweight" intermediary platform is losing weight and functionality. Its capabilities are more likely to be implemented with a set of independent specialized platforms like message queues, registries, and service management applications. These separate platforms may work together to provide composite services on a virtual platform under the control of a document-driven enterprise service bus.[39]

15.3.6 COMPOSITE SERVICES

Composite services provide a single interface to a set of services linked by overlapping information requirements, business rules, and processes. They are a broad category of model based applications that share aspects of e-forms, single source publishing and portals, and business-to-business and intermediary applications.

Composite services provide a single interface to a set of services linked by overlapping information requirements, business rules, and processes

The simplest variety of composite services combines separate services that are carried out by legacy applications within a single organization. The composite service bridges the gap between two or more transactional applications by merging otherwise redundant data entry and display into a single form. In Section 4.4.2.2 we described a composite web service that combines a query for customer details in a customer database with a query for orders in an ERP system to locate the current orders for any specified customer.

The conceptual interface to the composite service is constructed by merging the document implementation models from the separate services, much as the conceptual model at the heart of a single-source publishing application combines multiple document implementation models. The process implementation model that describes the sequencing and dependencies among the constituent services controls the composite application's interactions with the user and with the services that join to create the single service that the user experiences.

The separate services in a composite might all be performed externally, making the composite service the initiator and controller of a long-running, multistep collaboration. In Section 10.4.3 we described a composite travel service in which a traveler can request an airplane ticket, a rental car, a hotel room, and a reservation at a nearby restaurant by filling out a single web form. The overlapping information about time, location, and price is collected just once.

Model based implementation of a composite service is illustrated in Figures 1-3 and 4-3. These show how the order form for GMBooks.com collects information like the customer's name and address, the title of the book being purchased, and the payment method and then reuses it to satisfy the document interfaces to inventory, shipment, and billing services.

15.3.7 SEMANTIC WEB AND SEMANTIC WEB SERVICE APPLICATIONS

Beginning with e-forms and e-books, the examples of model based applications in this chapter have grown progressively more complex to involve more types of documents, more complex processes, and multiple enterprises or intermediary service providers. Nevertheless, in all the types of applications we've described, the document models, the processes, and the participants' roles are fixed when the application is designed. Even when the models and resources are distributed and controlled by multiple parties, the applications are designed on the assumption that all parties use the same models or agree in advance about the relationship between their internal models and those of the other parties.

But many believe that these assumptions about application design are too constraining.

The semantic web vision promoted by Tim Berners-Lee and others holds that

> "The Web can reach its full potential only if it becomes a place where data can be shared and processed by automated tools as well as by people. For the Web to scale, tomorrow's programs must be able to share and process data even when these programs have been designed totally independently."[40]

We can easily imagine applications that reuse documents and processes in ways not anticipated by their creators

Making the web a globally distributed knowledge base with easily repurposeable services is a compelling goal, and we can easily imagine applications that reuse documents and processes in ways not anticipated by their creators.

The Event Repository in the Event Calendar Network (Figure 15-4) might be used not just by calendars but also by complementary campus applications for selling tickets, facilities management, and scheduling of security personnel. The event repository might even become a general information resource usable through a web service as a component of a travel planning application when customers are interested in trips to the San Francisco Bay Area.

But the vision of the semantic web and semantic web services goes far beyond this straightforward kind of reuse of domain-specific content and business logic, which isn't that different from the reuse enabled by enterprise content repositories, data warehouses, and database management systems. The semantic web's vision assumes that the models that describe documents and processes aren't fixed and that, regardless of the original intent of the author, the meaning of documents or information resources can continually evolve as they are annotated by additional metadata applied by people or computational agents.

The semantic web assumes that the models that describe documents and processes aren't fixed for a single context of use

If the same documents and services can be used by multiple applications and the documents and services they rely on are subject to change, then the applications can't tightly bind to those resources. Instead, the applications might employ dynamic discovery and inferencing to find the most appropriate documents and services at runtime.

The idea of dynamic discovery and reasoning about resources is best illustrated with some hypothetical examples:[41]

- A social activities planner can take a user's preferences for films, restau-rants, and so on to plan activities for an evening. During the service determination/matching process, ratings and review services may also be consulted to find closer matches (for example, consulting reviews and ratings of films and restaurants to find the "best").

- Small, handheld, wireless computing devices need to discover other devices, printers, sensors, and services in a dynamic manner because devices appear and disappear as their owners carry them from one room or building to another. Devices that weren't necessarily designed to work together should be able to discover each others' functionality and take advantage of it.

For applications like these to be implementable, the resources and services must have rich semantic descriptions of their characteristics, capabilities, and invocations and of the policies or conditions governing their use. Because for applications to reason about resources, they have to know what this metadata means. For example, the social activities service must understand that a "best" rating might be a 1 in one source, a 10 in another source, and four stars or smiley face symbols in another. It might also need to realize that some sources are more credible or unbiased than others. Similarly, the ad hoc wireless service network builder doesn't just need to detect other services; it needs to assess their technical and business process compatibility and determine whether their security and payment mechanisms are acceptable.

Anyone who has gotten this far in this book surely knows how hard these tasks would be for people, let alone for applications. For the latter to work, we need standard metamodels for making assertions about documents and processes and relating them to each other. The most commonly used metamodel on the world wide web for these purposes is the Resource Description Framework (RDF),[42] but Topic Maps[43] have similar syntaxes and mechanisms for making inferences through networks of assertions to deduce new knowledge. It may be obvious to us that if "Bob Glushko is the author of the Document Engineering book" and "Tim McGrath is the author of the Document Engineering book," then Bob and Tim are coauthors. But encoding these separate assertions using RDF or Topic Maps would let a computer reach the same conclusion.

In addition, the terms and properties used in the metadata must be grounded in ontologies that formally define them and express constraints about them to prevent incompatible inferences; the Web Ontology Language (OWL) has emerged as the synthesis of several ontology languages.[44] An application can conclude that the statement "Bob Glushko is the creator of the Document Engineering book" means the same as assertion in the previous paragraph only if an ontology formally expresses the equivalence of the "author" and "creator" roles.[45]

The semantic web and semantic web services radically change how applications are designed. When document and process implementation models are no longer fixed, and any person or computational process can assert its own metadata on any document or service, the design challenge for applications is to make sense of this semantic chaos by imposing models that create a consistent interpretation. The application must follow chains of assertions back to a semantic control point in an ontology or schema registry. This may not always be possible, but it does mean that every application in the semantic web is inherently model based.

15.4 IMPLEMENTING MODELS IN APPLICATIONS: THE FUTURE

We hope that these examples of model based applications have demonstrated the value of this way of thinking about implementation using a Document Engineering perspective. Our objective is to encourage the use of patterns in a model based application community like the community that has been created around software design patterns.

Our objective is to encourage the use of patterns in a model based application community

Moreover, defining and separating concerns at the higher level of abstraction of document exchanges should ultimately result in orders of magnitude more reuse of software design patterns. And because these are business level abstractions, the contributors and users of the patterns don't need to be software developers. Business analysts and consultants will then be not only the architects, but also the engineers.

15.5 KEY POINTS IN CHAPTER FIFTEEN

- XML is the preferred syntax for encoding models of documents and of the processes that use them.
- It's essential to adopt encoding rules and follow them consistently.
- Modeling skill is more essential than schema encoding expertise in developing schemas.
- Reuse standard schema components wherever possible.
- The biggest challenge when reusing an existing library is in correctly understanding its context of use.
- Process models encoded in XML can control the behavior of document exchanges and monitor compliance to rules and agreements.
- The linkage between models and code is tighter in model driven architectures than in model based ones.
- Models are often not fully represented in the software that implements them.
- Many-to-many mappings can be avoided by mapping all physical interfaces to a common conceptual interface.
- Basing the user and the application interfaces on a common conceptual interface ensures that the documents they process are interoperable.

- Whatever the technology used by user interface platforms, they don't eliminate the design tasks.
- The conceptual interface describes the requirements for the context of use.
- Many business-to-business applications have been built using tightly coupled interfaces and are hard to maintain.
- Model based business-to-business applications expose their physical interfaces as document implementation models and are controlled by process implementation models.
- The "heavyweight" intermediary platform is losing weight and functionality.
- Composite services provide a single interface to a set of services linked by overlapping information requirements, business rules, and processes.
- We can easily imagine applications that reuse documents and processes in ways not anticipated by their creators.
- The semantic web assumes that the models that describe documents and processes aren't fixed.
- Our objective is to encourage the use of patterns in a model based application community.

16 Management and Strategy

16.0 INTRODUCTION

In 1843, when telegraph technology was only seven years old, an amateur clock maker named Alexander Bain combined a telegraph machine with parts from old clock mechanisms. Bain received a British patent for "improvements in producing and regulating electric currents and improvements in timepieces and in electric printing and signal telegraphs." At the time Bain's invention was called the chemical telegraph, but today we regard it as the first fax machine.[1]

Bain died in obscurity and poverty, and it was 100 years after his death before the fax machine was widely adopted as a business tool. Why wasn't this invention taken up with the telegraph and telephone (an even later invention)?

It would be wrong to imagine a hopeful but naïve Bain trying to send faxes when no one had the capability to receive them. Bain and other early advocates of fax machines implemented the same business model for fax machines that was being used for telegraphs, with fixed office locations for city-to-city transmissions. This deployment architecture allowed fax machines to become an important means for distributing news photographs, but it didn't provide much benefit to businesses. A network pattern, in which every business has its own fax machine, provides far greater benefit, but wasn't possible as long as fax machines were expensive.

The fact that it took 180 years for Bain's innovative technology for document exchange to succeed motivates us to write this final chapter to complete the story of Document Engineering. The dominant theme of this book so far has been how to understand documents and the business processes that use them. In this final chapter we look at the management and strategy concerns that cut across and frame the various phases and tasks in a Document Engineering effort.

While technology considerations are important, it is not the technology that primarily determines whether Document Engineering approaches will be successfully adopted within an enterprise or by two or more firms with business relationships. Other significant factors include the existence of industry standards or reference models, mechanisms that encourage technology adoption, the technological and process maturity of the enterprises, their relative power in their relationships, and the extent to which they have complementary long-term business strategies.

Finally, the project has to make financial sense for the organizations or firms carrying it out because for almost every enterprise, one key measure of business success means making enough money to stay in business.

Putting a chapter on management and strategy concerns at the end of this book doesn't mean that we should defer these concerns until the end of our project. Indeed, we should begin with these issues because they determine the goals and scope of our work, or even whether we should attempt to do it. But many of the concepts and examples in this chapter would be hard to understand if this chapter appeared earlier in the book.

And emphasizing these management and strategy dimensions of Document Engineering in a separate chapter doesn't mean that we've ignored them up to now. For example, when we reviewed the big ideas of XML in Chapter 2, we noted that many apparently technical questions like how much validation to perform or the architectural locus of transformation were better answered by business and relationship factors. This theme, and the related idea that business models and technology continuously co-evolve, became more prominent in Chapters 4 and 5. There we presented a view of business in which patterns for processes and document exchanges function as building blocks both for improving existing business models and inventing new ones. Which pattern fits best is determined by both technical and business factors.

In Chapter 5 we described the co-evolution of technology and business to explain why a potentially disruptive technology can sometimes have little impact if it doesn't fit into an existing model or pattern—or if the original technology proponents fail to identify that a relevant pattern exists.

Our review in Chapter 6 of interoperability challenges showed that mismatches between models in technology or syntax were far less detrimental than those resulting from a lack of shared context and goals between the parties in a business relationship. The importance of these business considerations shows why a purely technical perspective on business informatics, document exchanges, and web services is inadequate.

That's why the Document Engineering approach that we presented in Chapters 7-15 began with the goal of understanding the requirements of the context of use. Defining the context identifies relevant organizational stakeholders and determines whether a more strategic or more tactical perspective is appropriate. Collecting and sampling the document inventory, taking stock of the existing information exchanges, and balancing the concerns of different stakeholders also require both technical and business insights. As we harvest components and develop conceptual models of the rules for our information requirements, we confront issues about the scope of analysis. Again, these are more often influenced by capabilities, management goals, and allocation of resources than by purely technical requirements. Finally, when we are ready to deploy new documents and services, their priority and organization will be influenced by business opportunities, relationships, competition, and strategic considerations that shape the business case.

16.1 ORGANIZATIONAL MATURITY

Throughout this text we have talked about standards and reference models and how they encourage the evolution and adoption of Document Engineering approaches and technologies. But while these are often necessary ingredients for success, they aren't sufficient. Standards and business patterns are of no value unless an enterprise can recognize that they are relevant and can adapt them to close the gap between its current, As-Is models of documents and processes and its desired, To-Be ones. We should not even assume that an enterprise could understand that its current processes and documents might be inefficient or suboptimal and that there is a better way of doing things. Its ability to do this is dependent on its level of organizational maturity or capability.

One aspect of this capability is the pure resources needed: budget, time, technology, and available people.[2] But a more important aspect of capability is the overall readiness of an organization to make a Document Engineering effort successful. Document Engineering is too new a discipline, and service oriented architecture too new as a domain in which to exercise it, for most companies to have any direct experience in doing it or doing things like it. So we won't deal too much with generic resource concerns; instead we will focus on how capability and maturity affect Document Engineering.

16.1.1 MOTIVATING CAPABILITY ASSESSMENT

It can be expensive when a product or a project fails. It may be harmful or even fatal to a business. But while we can measure the performance of an organization after it builds a product or carries out a project, we can't measure performance on something that hasn't been done before. However, we can do a capability assessment to predict the likely success of a project.

A guiding assumption in capability assessment is that the maturity, predictability, and repeatability of the process used will determine the quality of the service produced. How these processes are managed matters just as much as what they are. We have developed a Document Engineering Capability Maturity model to guide this assessment.

A capability assessment can predict the likely success of a project

16.1.2 THE CAPABILITY MATURITY MODEL

In the late 1980s, the Software Engineering Institute at Carnegie-Mellon University developed a Capability Maturity Model for Software that had a profound effect on software engineering practices throughout the world.[3]

The CMM describes the principles and practices underlying software process maturity and is intended to help software developers improve the maturity of their software processes in terms of a 5-level evolutionary path from ad hoc, chaotic processes to mature, disciplined software processes (see SIDEBAR).

For two decades the CMM has been used to assess the capabilities of software firms, and despite being officially retired by the Software Engineering Institute, it is still widely used to make contracting or outsourcing decisions. The most common rating (2004 data) for firms is still only Level 2, meaning that processes are repeatable but not standardized. However, it is encouraging that the average capability rating is steadily improving.[4]

The CMM Levels

The typical characteristics of organizations at each of the 5 CMM levels are:

Level 1. Initial (heroics)

- The software process is ad hoc, and occasionally even chaotic.
- There is no stable environment for development and maintenance.
- Schedules are "backed in" and not based on quality.

Level 2. Repeatable (basic project management)

- Projects start from requirements that are subsequently tracked.
- Processes are established to manage cost, schedule, and functionality.
- Processes include version control, automated builds, and so on.

An effective process is one that is documented, trained, practiced, enforced, and capable of being improved.

Level 3. Defined (process standardization)

- The software process for both management and engineering activities is documented, standardized, and integrated into a standard software process for the organization.
- Typically some group or department is responsible for developing and standardizing processes.
- Training programs ensure that all staff and managers have required knowledge and skills.

Level 4. Quantitative (charts and graphs)

- Detailed measures of the software process and product quality are collected.
- Both the software process and products are quantitatively understood and controlled.

- Capabilities are quantifiable and predictable, with measurable limits and tolerances.
- When problems (variation from prediction) arise, the causes are identified and addressed.

Level 5. Optimizing (continuous process improvement)

- Processes are enabled by quantitative feedback from the process and from piloting innovative ideas and technologies.
- The entire organization is focused on identifying best practices and institutionalizing them.

The idea that organizations can be classified according to their capabilities is a very sensible one, and we've used the CMM philosophy in many projects to assess and manage risk.

16.1.3 THE DOCUMENT ENGINEERING CAPABILITY MATURITY MODEL

The CMM was developed for the domain of software development, but it can also be useful for understanding an organization's problems and prospects in other domains because we always need to understand current capabilities and perspectives to plan improvements. We can't get from here to there unless we know where "here" and "there" are. The challenge lies in the fact that in any business ecosystem different people, even within the same organization, see "here" and "there" differently.

We adapted the concepts of CMM to Document Engineering and found it useful as a diagnostic tool to predict and understand problems and to communicate with high-level executives who don't need to know about the nuts and bolts of their documents and business processes. But they do need to be sure of the effectiveness of their documents and processes that ensure quality and transparency of financial reporting, for example, as required by the U.S. Sarbanes-Oxley mandate[5] (see Section 4.2.2.6).

We've made two important changes to the original CMM approach in adapting it for Document Engineering:

- We don't believe it is useful to force assessments into levels.
- We need to distinguish between technology maturity and process maturity.

16.1.3.1 The Problem With Levels

Levels often encourage an adversarial character to the assessment. People fixate on the levels, and we want them to pay attention to a more nuanced assessment and recommendations. If an organization's documents and processes are too informal or underspecified to enable an effective audit or successful automation effort, it is important to address the specific problems, not the summary evaluation that the organization has reached a particular maturity level.

16.1.3.2 Technology and Process Maturity

Technology maturity and process maturity are separable dimensions; we can have mature capabilities on one and not on the other. Understanding this distinction helps us portray our assessment more accurately and give more precise recommendations about what to do to improve capabilities and therefore the chances for success.

Cultures with mature procedures and processes take a strategic view of their business. They can usually adopt new technologies if they choose to do so. They have the skills and the tools to predict the business value of adopting new technologies and processes and to measure their progress in doing so. Of course, the organization may be disrupted by the new technology, but presumably that's the point, and the organization understands how to systematize the new processes enabled by new technologies.

Organizations with low process maturity often don't recognize the inefficiencies in how they do business and can't adopt technology easily. Even when they recognize problems, they may put up with them because they don't have the confidence in their ability to introduce new processes and technology that would eliminate them.

Organizations with low process maturity can't adopt new technology easily

How a firm handles its procurement is a good indicator of its process and technology maturity. Procurement is a common business process where automation has substantial benefits. Most large enterprises have substantially automated the document exchanges in their supply chains for the direct procurement of the goods and materials that go into the products they make (often with EDI). But many companies, especially those with weak process maturity, have not yet automated their indirect procurement of the goods and services needed to run the business. These include office supplies, travel, maintenance and repairs, package shipment, temporary help, and many other categories with large numbers of low value transactions often initiated by employees other than the purchasing specialists who conduct direct procurement.

It may seem harmless for employees to disregard the company's purchasing processes and buy office supplies during their lunch hour or make airline reservations that maximize their personal frequent flier miles. But the company then pays the retail price rather than a discounted corporate one that might be much less. Automating indirect procurement eliminates this maverick purchasing and lets businesses track and aggregate their purchases to negotiate volume discounts with suppliers. Furthermore, automated systems can encode and enforce corporate policies about preferred providers and spending limits and prove compliance to management and auditors.

Research or advanced technology organizations are chartered to explore new technologies and always have strong technology capabilities. But the people who work in these organizations probably don't have it in their job description or their nature to systematize and measure processes. Firms with high process maturity recognize this gap and institute technology transfer processes to put new technologies into practice. In contrast, firms with low process maturity squander the work of their R&D labs and see it commercialized by competitors or by researchers so disappointed by the firm's inertia that they quit to launch start-ups.

16.1.3.3 The CMM Framework and the Model Matrix

We can use our familiar Model Matrix to understand the application of the Capability Maturity framework to Document Engineering.

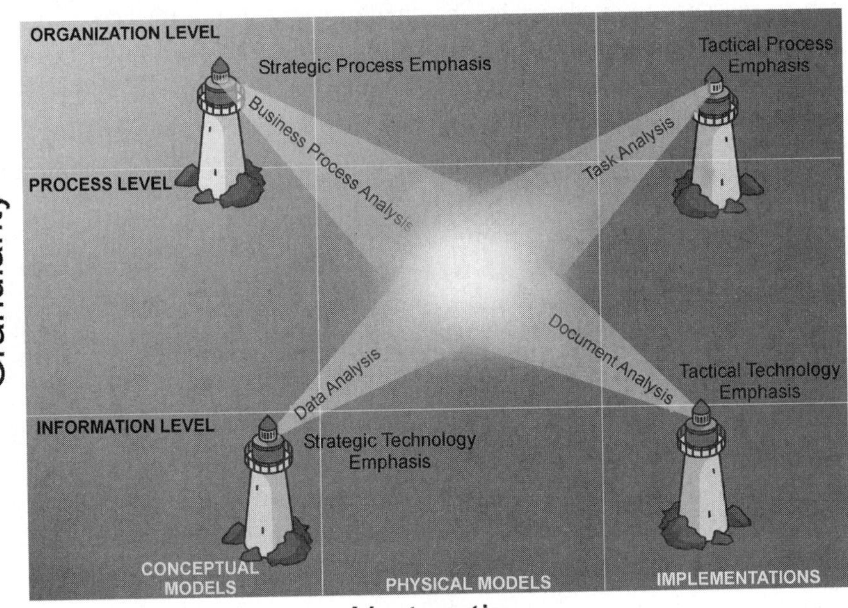

Figure 16-1. Different Maturity Emphases on the Model Matrix

Figure 16-1 reminds us of the different skills sets and perspectives that come together in Document Engineering. It helps us understand how all of them contribute to achieving a complete understanding of an enterprise or organization that spans from its business model to the documents exchanged at the information level to carry it out. But such a complete perspective isn't always possible or necessary. The capability maturity of the organization determines the amount of emphasis each of these perspectives will be given.

Some document automation, user interface, and even EDI projects have the explicit or implied goal of transforming printed documents or forms into electronic versions. If an organization's primary capabilities are in these technology areas, it is not surprising that their modeling activities take a more tactical perspective. They just aren't used to considering the enterprise-level and business process context of their projects. This tactical perspective is also referred to as a bottom-up approach.

The business case for these projects is often a mandate by a dominant business in an asymmetric relationship for its trading partners to automate the exchange of information. Typically they will need to conform to the dominant company's proprietary formats or implementation guidelines.

Here the goal is seen as taking an existing process (often, someone else's) and encoding its rules directly in applications or electronic documents. Thus modeling is often viewed as needing little resources or, in the worst case, as irrelevant.

In contrast, organizations with strong process capabilities usually take a strategic approach that looks at organizational and high-level business concerns between an enterprise and its trading partners. This top-down approach provides a very coarse grained view focusing on business capabilities or competencies.

Process modeling concerns in these kinds of projects include the compatibility of business models, customer and supplier relationships, accounting practices, and acceptable business practices. No one pays much attention to the design of models for documents or their implementation technology as they assume these will become someone else's (tactical) problem.

The Document Engineering modeling approach tries to balance the bottom-up and top-down approaches and depends on both process and technology capabilities. While technology and implementation decisions should always be secondary to business and information requirements, business processes and business documents are complementary and should receive the same level of engineering rigor. They can both be encoded so that computer applications can process them directly. But this requires bridging between the strategic and tactical perspective—what we call meeting in the middle.

Processes and documents are complementary and should be receive the same level of engineering rigor

As we discussed in Chapter 8, whether a project is more tactical or strategic defines what is and is not possible, how much work it will take, the scale or scope of technology, and the resources needed to implement a solution. A service oriented architecture is an example of a strategic platform that, once established, can be used to develop and deploy web services more incrementally as tactical projects.

However, even on tactical efforts there may be numerous conflicting project goals, so we should define them precisely and prioritize them to have a basis for deciding how to proceed when conflicts emerge. In some sense, this means that we have to take at least a somewhat strategic perspective when we carry out tactical projects.

16.1.4 CONDUCTING A CAPABILITY ASSESSMENT

The tasks we collectively called analyzing the context in Chapter 8 often yield an informal sense of the capability maturity of the enterprise we're studying as we initiate a Document Engineering project. But normally we wouldn't describe this work as an assessment unless we ask explicit questions about technology and process maturity in the course of understanding the context.

A strategic, executive-sponsored project is more likely to contain an explicit activity to conduct an assessment, because senior management is more comfortable with bringing in outside consultants to take an objective look at things and is increasingly being required by law to do just that. Middle managers are less likely to be able to do this explicitly, but they can conduct a stealth or implicit assessment so that they can scope the project and manage the risks.

16.1.4.1 Questions That Assess Capability Maturity

We've found that a surprisingly small number of simple questions can tell us a lot about the capabilities that predict success or failure in Document Engineering efforts. The best questions yield unambiguous answers that can be supported by objective evidence. Obtaining evidence for answers is essential because when the assessment is an explicit activity, people often respond with what they think are the right answers even when they don't have the capabilities that the question is trying to evaluate. Good questions cut through what people do or say at the surface to expose deeper values or themes about how focused the firm is on understanding, measuring, and improving what it does to add value to its business and how capable it is of doing so.

Below is a list of some generic questions and some interpretation of possible responses in terms of capability maturity. In an assessment these questions need to be augmented by others that address factors specific to the context of use, but this list should convey the value of asking simple questions to diagnose capability maturity.

- Why is your organization considering this project?

Respondents in an organization with mature process capabilities will justify a project in terms of measurable business value, such as reduced operating costs or delivery times. If the organization also has mature technology capabilities, respondents might emphasize its innovative use of new technologies to achieve these process improvements. In contrast, if an organization has weak process capabilities and a bias toward technology, respondents might mention the goal "to explore new technology" without making an explicit connection to measurable business events.

Respondents in organizations with immature capabilities on both dimensions might describe the project as being imposed on them by upper management or by a dominant business partner and express some concern about their skills to carry it out or describe their efforts in heroic terms.

- What are the procedures for processing documents (in transactional con-texts) or creating publications (in narrative contexts)?

Respondents in an organization with process maturity will describe an explicit and formal step-by-step process generally followed to complete transactions or produce publications, supported by current documentation. The process is completed on time and meets explicit quality criteria. If this organization has commensurate technology maturity, the processes will be automated and enforced by workflow or process management software and the quality criteria might involve validation or conformance to templates or schemas at each step.

Respondents in less mature organizations will describe their processes as less formal, and mention work-arounds and exception-handling activities that occasionally cause delays or lower-quality results. In the least mature organizations respondents might describe informal processes in which external actors or organizations control events; "we sometimes just go with the documents we have when the product is ready to ship or when the customer demands it."

- How are the source files for important documents managed?

Organizations with process maturity have clear policies for document and data retention and might maintain a centralized repository with access and configuration controls. Technologically sophisticated organizations will automate backups and archiving to ensure conformance with these policies.

Less mature organizations delegate the management of documents to the organization or person who creates or processes them. Organizations with the weakest capabilities manage important documents informally or even outsource their storage; respondents might say "A contractor performs our customer support, and we don't know what records are kept."

- What kind of support is there in your organization for reuse of informa-tion that appears in more than one type of document or application?

Organizations with process maturity carefully analyze their information requirements and maintain libraries of reusable models, schemas, or document fragments and have governance policies for controlling versions and maintaining interoperability.[6] The best of them use technology to encourage reuse, promote the idea of model based applications, and develop or follow industry or company standards to facilitate reuse both within the enterprise and with other companies.

Less mature organizations recognize the value of reuse but only encourage it informally. They don't make the investments in modeling, training, or technology necessary to institutionalize the practice. The least mature organizations don't have any cross-document or cross-application initiatives for reuse, and any reuse that happens is informal and ad hoc.

16.1.4.2 Capability Implications for Document Engineering

Conducting a capability assessment and identifying requirements for a context of use (Chapter 8) are closely related activities. Businesses with a process bias may be inclined to support a strategic, top-down business driven analysis and may be more willing to consider process redesign and reengineering. Businesses with a technology bias may favor more tactical, bottom-up approaches such as automating the documents that already exist in printed or legacy formats.

Businesses with good process capabilities are more likely to implement model based applications

Businesses with good process capabilities are more likely to have the discipline needed to implement model based applications. One of the benefits of using models is in reinforcing common patterns or standards, and creating and deploying standards requires a process perspective.

An enterprise that has immature processes and immature technology—running by ad hoc means with trailing edge technology—will undoubtedly resist Document Engineering efforts. They might view enterprise models with defined and measured processes as a threat to their current autonomy and operations. They might not know which applications or organizations would benefit from improvements in document processing or information architecture because they don't have the system inventories, enterprise data dictionaries, or data warehouses that demonstrate a strategic focus on information technology. Their lack of processes for technology adoption might require remedial measures and hand-holding to deploy new models and applications.

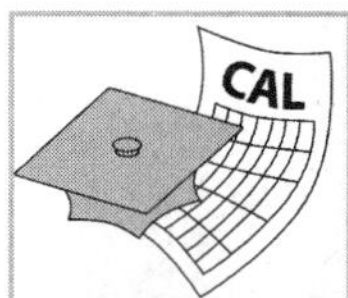

In the Berkeley Event Calendar project, some aspects of the model and solution can be related to maturity considerations for the adopting departments.

The core model was kept small to impose minimal information requirements for describing an event. This meant that even organizations with informal processes and calendars that were not automated, would be able to comply with the event model, encouraging them to contribute their events to the repository. On the other hand, the complete event model was complex enough to meet the needs of even the most technically sophisticated calendars, and the planned web service interfaces will enable them to extract and transform events into their own models.

In addition, the calendar management application was designed to enable departments with little technical sophistication to create highly customized and automated calendars. Departments with somewhat greater technical capabilities can modify the XSLT transforms used by the calendar application to replicate the appearance of their existing HTML-based calendars.

The inventory-gathering activity is also shaped by the capability assessment. A mature organization can readily provide the appropriate information sources for analysis, but an immature organization may lack methods for responding to requests. In such organizations Document Engineers may need to use indirect means to capture requirements and business rules. And if interviews cannot be conducted without causing problems or provoking resistance, they must rely more on artifacts such as existing documents, forms, and program interfaces to determine information requirements.

When working in this kind of organization, we may need multiple stages of inventory gathering because the documents that are offered up first are sometimes the least useful. What makes them readily available is the fact that no one uses them. This is like being in a library where the most interesting books are always checked out. Richer artifacts take more careful analysis to discover.

16.2 BUSINESS OBJECTIVES

Every organization or enterprise, whether it is a commercial firm or a governmental, educational, and non-profit institution, has reasons for its existence. They will have different goals and carry out different activities to achieve them, but they have the common motivation of being successful enough at what they do to be able to continue doing it. So before they undertake Document Engineering, each must make a case for it that identifies the business objectives and the likely return on investment for a project.

An enterprise with immature process capabilities will have a hard time justifying any project, Document Engineering or otherwise, because if its processes aren't systematic and measured it can't estimate the benefits of doing them differently. Nevertheless, the lack of systematic processes for initiating and managing projects causes some immature enterprises to suffer from the opposite problem of undertaking too many projects, some of which are redundant or lack clear business payoffs. In addition, if an enterprise can't or won't consider reducing its workforce because of legal, negotiated, or cultural constraints on staffing levels, it can't easily capture the cost savings of automating manual processes and replacing employees with computers.[7]

In contrast, an enterprise with mature process capabilities understands and controls its business processes, even if they aren't fully automated. It measures its baseline costs and can determine what it needs to do to become more efficient or compete more effectively. It can also measure how close it is to where it wants to be and can modify its plans to deal with unforeseen requirements or events. What focuses all of these capabilities is the business case for the project.

16.2.1 MAKING A BUSINESS CASE

The business case for a tactical Document Engineering project like automating a document-intensive process, making such a process available as a web service, or integrating a document exchange with a business partner can be a straightforward and formulaic cost and benefit calculation:

- Compare the processing cost and time per document in the As-Is and To-Be applications.

- Estimate the value of other benefits that will emerge from the latter.

- Estimate the resources and time required to analyze, design, and imple-ment the latter.

- Calculate when the new application will pay for itself by comparing the recurring benefits against the one-time costs.

- Decide whether the return is worth the investment.

The business case for a tactical project can be a formulaic cost and benefit calculation

This is a minimal approach to justifying the project, but it is pretty easy to do, and making a simplified business case is better than proceeding without one. Much of the time savings in document processing costs alone are sufficient to justify the project. But even in a small tactical project we think it is appropriate to attribute some value to the greater visibility and control that results, and to the improvements in organizational capabilities that will reduce development costs and improve productivity on subsequent projects.[8]

In contrast, even though they can yield substantial benefits, strategic projects are much harder to justify because they involve more complex and intangible factors on both the cost and benefit sides of the equation. For example, establishing a service oriented architecture as a unifying technical and business vision for an enterprise might:

- Involve many organizations and enable them to collaborate more effectively.

- Extend the lifetime and value of legacy systems and information sources.

- Enable the more rapid implementation and deployment of software functionality.

- Inspire new and more adaptable business models with both internal and external partners.

- Improve the usability or quality of the services it provides.

But precisely because of this broad impact, it is difficult to predict exactly which benefits will be the most important, when they will emerge, and which organizations will most effectively capture them. Many of them, like improvements in collaboration or business adaptability, are hard to quantify in monetary terms.

Strategic projects are much harder to justify because they involve more complex and intangible factors

It is tempting to avoid these uncertainties by justifying a strategic initiative on a project-by-project basis, but this weakens the business case because it doesn't account for the enterprise-scale investments in modeling, infrastructure, and organizational alignment whose payoffs emerge over time. Furthermore, a project-by-project focus necessarily distorts long-term goals to fit the shorter-term payoffs of each project.

For example, for a business to transform itself from a forecast-driven, make-to-inventory manufacturer to a demand-driven, make-to-order one, it must improve visibility and speed information flow throughout its supply chain, manufacturing, and inventory management processes. Each of these processes could be improved incrementally, but the new business model requires that all of them be improved with a coherent end-to-end perspective.

Similarly, it is possible to accumulate an enterprise information architecture from separate modeling efforts—but unless some of the modelers maintain an enterprise focus and iteratively evaluate and reconcile the modeling work done separately in projects, the whole will be less than the sum of the parts, with less consistency and reuse than desirable.

There is no perfect solution to the unavoidable tradeoffs between strategic and tactical projects. We recommend the approach advocated by Larry Downes in "The Strategy Machine."[9] Downes recommends creating a strategic project portfolio that includes projects with different time frames and risk profiles. This enables some tangible value to emerge earlier, which can protect the overall initiative from budget cuts or cancellation during economic downturns. Not every project in the portfolio will be successful, but focusing only on narrow tactical projects because they have fewer risks than strategic ones can be costly in lost business opportunities and missed productivity breakthroughs. We acknowledge, however, that effective management of the project portfolio requires mature capabilities for monitoring and measuring the impact of each project, decisively terminating those not likely to succeed, and reallocating resources to those that appear more promising.[10]

16.2.2 A SAMPLE OF PROJECT JUSTIFICATIONS

In the following sections we discuss a variety of justifications for projects in the Document Engineering project portfolio.[11] The list is illustrative, not exhaustive, and we begin with the most obvious reasons for projects—being able to do things cheaper, better, and faster.

16.2.2.1 Reduce the Processing Costs for Goods and Services

Potential cost savings resulting from automating the manual processing of paper documents drove the adoption of electronic data interchange in the 1970s and 1980s. In the late 1980s it was estimated that the cost of processing an average order or invoice document could be reduced by 75 percent if they were exchanged electronically, a saving of US$10 to $15 per document. The automobile industry interpreted this as a saving of $800 per car.[12] However, even with these significant savings, the high costs of developing and operating suitable business interfaces with EDI limited its adoption to enterprises and supply chains with high transaction volumes.

A 2001 estimate of order-processing costs suggested the same 75 percent cost reduction through automation, but the savings were now $83 per document.[13] Furthermore, the cost of document exchange efforts using the Internet and XML can be substantially lower than with traditional EDI. So while EDI remains important to companies with extensive legacy implementations, it is rarely the technology of choice for document exchange projects involving new business processes.[14]

Since most enterprises spend between 50 and 80 percent of their total spending on external goods and services, the estimated 5 to 10 percent that can be saved by automating procurement can save tens of millions of dollars annually for large firms.[15] For the U.S. government, whose US$305.5 billion in purchases of goods and services in 2003 made it the world's largest buyer, even 5 percent cost reductions through the Integration Acquisition Environment initiative would save $15 billion.[16]

In October 2004 Denmark mandated that all firms doing business with the government must send their invoices in the XML format of the Universal Business Language (see Section 4.3.2). For each of the more than 18 million invoices annually, a conservative estimate is that ten minutes of handling time can be saved for a cost savings of €94 million, (more than US$125 million at end of 2004 exchange rates). The Danish government is considering automating its procurement and reconciliation using the UBL purchase order, which would save another €66 million.[17]

As large as these cost savings are, Denmark is a relatively small country and these estimates assume the UBL-ification of only orders and invoices. The average international business transaction can involve up to 40 different types of documents. The preparation and handling of documentation to move goods across borders, and the delays caused by processing all those paper documents, adds an estimated 10 to15 percent to the costs of the goods traded. If cross-border trading were made paperless, savings in trade between the countries in the Asia-Pacific Economic Cooperation region alone could be greater than US$60 billion annually.[18]

These huge estimates of potential cost savings through automating document exchanges are also emerging from banking, securities, insurance, health care, and other document-intensive industries. A 2003 study by Accenture estimated that a single bank with a 5 percent market share would derive between US$200 and $400 million in new revenue and save about $100 million in operating costs by automating all of its information exchanges and transactions that involve financial research.[19]

Huge estimates of potential cost savings are emerging from many document-intensive industries

16.2.2.2 Improve Operational Visibility and Control

Automated processes are more visible and measurable than non-automated ones, and they provide management with information about operations that can be used to further reduce costs and improve efficiency.

Many business problems with supply chains and distribution channels, including excess or insufficient inventory, demand variability, and high transportation costs primarily result from poor visibility and lack of collaboration. Technologies and business processes that speed information flow across the chain or that allow more information to be shared in controlled ways can substantially reduce these problems.

Many business problems result from poor visibility and lack of collaboration

For example, if a manufacturer and its supplier exchanged information about each other's inventory, excess raw materials at the supplier might trigger a collaborating manufacturer to temporarily increase its own production. Likewise, impending shortages of critical components in the manufacturer's inventory might cause the supplier to temporarily increase its own output to ensure that its customer could keep its production lines running.

Better information exchange for collaboration is also essential for satisfying social goals such as product traceability in safety recalls[20] or for infection and contamination control. An exemplary initiative for the latter is the Notifiable Infectious Disease Information Messaging System (NIDIMS), developed in Hong Kong in response to the 2003 SARS outbreak. NIDIMS exchanges information about 28 infectious diseases between the Department of Health and various healthcare providers to increase surveillance with faster response time and fewer errors.[21]

An important component of the benefit from automating document-intensive business processes is the elimination of errors when information flows from one document to another. As we've repeatedly shown, many business processes consist of a chain of related documents with overlapping content components; one estimate is that 75 percent of computer output becomes input to another system. Manually reentering this information is not just costly in time but also prone to error. For some clerical processes up to 30 percent of the effort may involve preparation and correction of information being passed through.[22]

As much as 75 percent of computer output becomes input to another system

Information accuracy also affects cash flow. In 1986 the UK banking industry estimated that 50 percent of international Letters of Credit contain errors that require clerical intervention. The resulting delays resulted in the annual loss of US$100 million in interest on monies deposited.[23] Automating the receiving and payment of invoices enables firms to reconcile orders and payments more quickly, allowing them to use early payment discounts and avoid late payment fees; the estimated savings has been put at 68 percent after five years.[24]

In case anyone thinks these kinds of document exchange problems in supply chains or finance have no relationship to day-to-day experiences, consider the sobering report from the U.S. National Academy of Sciences Institute of Medicine called "To Err Is Human: Building a Safer Health System."[25] This report concludes that thousands of people die each year as a result of adverse drug effects and errors in medication, and 95 percent of the deaths would be avoided if doctors entered prescriptions using automated order entry systems. In one effort to improve the situation, WellPoint Health Networks, a leading health insurance company, is spending US$30 million to give 20 percent of the physicians it serves either a PC or a handheld computer so they can enter computer-readable prescriptions instead of scribbling them by hand.[26]

16.2.2.3 Accelerate Existing Processes or Enable New Ones

Automated processes are also faster. A reduction in sourcing and procurement cycle time can lower inventories and enable firms to make more informed tradeoffs between maintaining inventory and reducing costs through bulk buying.

Faster access to information also enables better resource scheduling. When they are proactively notified of events relating to container and vessel movements, trucking companies can better schedule their vehicles and speed cargo deliveries.[27] The wireless handheld package scanners used by FedEx drivers save ten seconds per package per stop, with estimated savings of at least US$20 million annually.[28]

But while speeding up existing business processes is often an important goal, automation projects primarily provide an opportunity to rethink and redesign them. In fact, making existing processes faster may not be the right strategy. When we introduced the Document Automation and Straight Through Processing patterns in Chapter 4, we cautioned against "paving the cow paths" and suggested that automation projects should consider implementing industry best practices and their enabling standards. So instead of merely accelerating invoice processing, why not notify the supplier when payment is authorized, initiate payment when the goods are scanned at the receiving dock, or adopt some other event-driven process that completely eliminates the need for the supplier to send an invoice document?

Conversely, accelerated cycle times can also enable entirely new business processes. Making it easier to get goods through customs with paperless trade administration has created new cross-border markets for smaller producers of perishable items like fruits, vegetables, and flowers.[29] New online booking services for other kinds of perishable goods and services have been spawned by real-time inventory reporting for airline seats, hotel rooms, restaurant reservations, concert tickets, and so on. For example, if someone procrastinates in making restaurant reservations, they may still get a table at a posh restaurant that usually fills up weeks in advance by searching OpenTable.com.[30]

Accelerated cycle times can create new business processes

We discussed several other new business patterns enabled by electronic information and document automation in Section 5.4, "New Business Models for Information Goods," and Section 5.5, "From Forecast or Schedule-Driven to Demand or Event-Driven Models."

16.2.2.4 Make Publishing Processes Cheaper, Better, and Faster

So far, we've emphasized benefits for the transactional end of the Document Type Spectrum, but we'd be remiss if we didn't briefly mention that much of our discussion in the three previous sections about making processes cheaper, better, and faster also applies to narrative types of documents.

Lynda Brooks reviews three case studies of "applying a media-neutral publishing approach using XML technology" while reengineering traditional publishing processes and reports 25 to 40 percent operating cost savings with the additional benefit of a shorter time to market. Instead of maintaining multiple versions of the same content and incurring redundant production costs, additional revenue results when multiple publications and formats are produced from the same base of structured content.[31]

Multiple publications and formats can be created from the same base of structured content

16.2.2.5 Reduce System Development, Maintenance, and Integration Costs

Just as the reuse of content is the primary basis for benefits in XML-based publishing, the reuse of type and class libraries and software frameworks is the basis for these benefits in contemporary software development practice. These two contexts converge when document and process models are encoded as XML schemas, which can be used just like programming language classes to guide the generation of software. The underlying economic justification is the same—amortizing the development and maintenance costs of the content, software artifact, or schema over multiple uses.

A new principle for reuse that we've introduced in Document Engineering is the emphasis on patterns and artifacts of a wider range of abstraction to include organizational and business process patterns as well as the more fine-grained patterns of documents and information components. We've also strongly emphasized the methods and artifacts needed to facilitate reuse during the analysis and design phases. While we advocate using models when we implement applications, we believe that the careful design of conceptual document and process models yields the biggest payoff. This is especially true in contexts involving information whose useful life is longer than that of the software that produces and consumes it.

Put another way, in software engineering fixing errors in designs is far more cost-effective than fixing them in implementations, and that rule also applies in Document Engineering. In a recent assessment of the benefits of a model based architecture approach using UML and XML models, Martin Soukup reports "projects where the code generation saved person-years of effort, but the modeling errors found during the metamodel analysis phase saved tens of person-years."[32]

The careful development of conceptual document and process models yields the biggest payoff

Every software tool or application vendor makes claims about the productivity and quality benefits provided by their technology. Most of them emphasize how their products employ standards to counter their customers' often-justified fear of being locked into a proprietary approach. But it is hard to differentiate the overlapping vendor categories of integration, collaboration, hub, portal, document management, middleware, enterprise infrastructure, and the new ones invented in each product marketing cycle. So we're not going to repeat any of the specific percentages or return on investments in development, maintenance, and integration costs found in vendor case studies and white papers. The latest numbers can generally be found on the vendors' websites.

Instead, we conclude this section with some caveats about the benefits attributed by vendors to the standards they support, which often differ depending on the business alliances they've made and the industries in which their customers predominate. Not every specification that is called a standard is equally likely to yield benefits.

Traction and sanction are two factors that steer a pattern or specification toward the status we recognize as a standard. Traction generates de facto standards, whose status is determined by adoption and popularity. Sanction creates de jure standards, where status is granted by a recognized authority. Internationally this means bodies such as the Internet Engineering Task Force (IETF), International Electrotechnical Commission (IEC), International Organization for Standards (ISO), or the International Telecommunication Union (ITU).[33] However, there are many industry groups and regional bodies working at a more local level or outside these international bodies, and their credibility as standards-makers varies widely.

So any given pattern or specification, at any moment in time, has some degree of de facto and de jure standardization. Decisions by vendors or enterprises to adopt them are shaped by this mix. Vendors are usually more biased toward adopting de facto standards than de jure ones because of their customer focus, but governments, universities, and other institutions with longer time horizons are more biased toward de jure standards.[34] Intellectual property terms also strongly affect standards adoption. Vendors and for-profit enterprises are more amenable to reasonable and nondiscriminatory (sometimes abbreviated to RAND) licensing terms than governments and open source advocates, for whom royalty-free terms can be essential prerequisites for adoption.[35]

Ross Altman recently proposed a Standards Maturity Model analogous to the Capability Maturity Model that we discussed earlier in this chapter. In his model a Level 5 standard is functionally adequate, a product of a standards body, and ubiquitous in deployed platforms and applications. He cautions, however, that most standards never reach that level of maturity, and rates most web services standards as Level 3, that is, functionally adequate and published by a credible standards body but without much traction.[36]

For most Document Engineering purposes the traction of adoption is more critical than sanction, especially for intraenterprise projects. Sanction is a means of encouraging traction, but a pattern, standard, or specification without industry adoption doesn't offer many benefits.

A pattern, standard, or specification without industry adoption doesn't offer many benefits

16.2.2.6 Enhance Employee and Customer Satisfaction

A final category of benefits that can emerge from Document Engineering projects involves the enhanced quality of the experiences for the employees or customers who interact with the systems or applications that implement new document or process models. The common theme for both employees and customers is the satisfaction that comes from doing higher-value activities instead of the routine or tedious ones that can be automated. It can be hard to put a direct monetary value on this benefit, but creative business cases might attribute reductions in employee turnover or absenteeism and higher customer retention to the increased satisfaction of using well-designed applications.

For example, with electronic documents, bank employees can spend less time checking errors on printed Letters of Credit and accounts payable clerks can spend less time trying to reconcile orders and invoices. Truck drivers or patients can spend less time waiting around. Authors can concentrate on creating and editing content and rely on transformations to provide the various presentations and formats needed for different devices or information products.

We've all experienced the satisfaction of being able to check on the status of our order, payment, delivery, or other transaction with a self-service web application. Being able to go to an Internet café, check a bank account balance, and transfer money into it can save a vacation. But not all self-service applications increase customer satisfaction, as we all know from our own painful encounters with impersonal, hard to use, or unreliable ones.

16.2.3 A SAMPLE OF PROJECT RISKS

We've discussed the most common justifications for projects, so we will now discuss some of the common risks that can affect a project's success.

The biggest risk in a Document Engineering project is attempting one that exceeds the technology or process capabilities. This is why we advocate an explicit or implicit assessment before we start.

The following are some other risks that may have an impact.

16.2.3.1 The Commoditization of Business Relationships

Reducing the initial and recurring transaction costs of business relationships through Document Engineering efforts is one of their most important justifications. But the reduced costs are not always of mutual benefit. The flexible, plug-and-play vision of service oriented architectures can enable a brutal Darwinism in business relationships. Loosely coupled business relationships that are easy to create and inexpensive to maintain with little or no risk of proprietary lock-in are also easy to exploit or terminate.

The same technologies that can facilitate commitment and collaboration in a voice mode relationship can also enable an exit mode one. In the latter, a business can easily switch to alternate suppliers or outsourced service providers. From the perspective of the dominant partner, this is the benefit of transparent substitutability; from the perspective of the dominated one, it is a cost that shows reduced value for loyalty or continuity. The business relationship itself becomes a tradable commodity.

Business relationships can become a tradable commodity

For the dominant enterprise in an ecosystem to make the best use of its own capabilities, it almost has to exercise its market power to secure a larger portion of the value created by its business relationships. Companies have different reward structures for risk taking and innovation, which often amplify the conflicts of interest they always have with each other. For example, the standards to adopt when implementing a collaborative business process is a conflict typically resolved in favor of the most powerful party.

In a paper whose title cleverly asks, "When is Virtual Virtuous?" Chesbrough and Teece summarize the rule of business relationships as follows: "The most successful virtual companies sit at the center of networks that are far from egalitarian."[37] So from the perspective of the less powerful firm in asymmetric business relationships, the result of more efficient document exchanges is not always desirable.

16.2.3.2 Incomplete Automation and Zombies

In ambitious strategic initiatives that span one or more enterprises and that involve many processes and parties, some of the predicted benefits are likely to have an all-or-nothing character emerging only if all of the tactical projects that comprise the initiative are successful. And since large efforts must be carried out incrementally, automating one transaction or collaboration at a time, we must choose where to start.

It is typical to start where the largest incremental benefits can be obtained. In some firms, the process and document exchange project with the highest payoff might be part of order management or payment processing. For a firm acquiring another company, integrating the acquiree's financial systems or product catalogs might add the most value.

In any case, a common risk is that one or more of the tactical projects to automate manual processes or replace expensive or brittle legacy automation technologies may not succeed. It isn't necessarily a failure if a process can't be completely automated; business processes that require expert analysis, tacit knowledge, and the interpretation of business policy can be made more efficient with document automation but a knowledge worker is still needed to perform the process. Nevertheless, a project that achieves partial automation is a failure if full automation is essential to satisfy project requirements—even if they were unreasonable.

Incomplete automation can leave the enterprise with a slow link in its information flow that nullifies most of the investments to improve other processes. The math is simple and brutal: for example, if automation eliminates 99 percent of the time taken to carry out nine of ten interconnected business processes, if the tenth manual task formerly took 10 percent of the total time, it now consumes 92 percent of it, and the end-to-end time is still 11 percent of what it was before automation.

Incomplete automation can leave the enterprise with a slow link in its information flow that nullifies most of the investments to improve other processes

A related bad outcome when a project doesn't succeed in its automation goals is that both the original and the partly automated processes now run in parallel, with duplicate sets of costs and management overheads. The legacy and new systems live in a kind of half-dead state and are sometimes referred to as zombie systems.

A Family of Zombie Projects

What has been described as "possibly the most complex IT-based undertaking attempted in Australia" seems to be the latest in a family of zombie projects. The Export Integration (EXIT) system, developed in phases from the late 1980s to the late 1990s, was an EDI-based automation initiative to enable exporters, freight consolidators and forwarders, and airline and shipping companies to submit electronic documents to the Australian Customs Service (ACS). Unfortunately, only a minority of the intended users opted to use EXIT, and the ACS allowed the others to continue to submit paper forms.

The Australian government tried to kill the zombies by mandating electronic submission and by 2002 expected to replace the EDI-based EXIT with an XML-driven Integrated Cargo System (ICS) that used web forms. But ICS failed to meet its original goals and by late 2003 was a year late and more than AUD$100 million over its budget. Again the Australian government stepped in with legislation that would severely punish the IT vendors if ICS failed to meet a revised "go live" deadline in July 2004.

The Australian government amended the legislation and the "go live" date slipped again to October 2004 after a near-revolt by consultants and integration firms. They complained that the government mandate forced the ICS vendors to ship them code that was "not even worthy of alpha test status."[38]

In late 2004, ICS finally went live. Today the ACS proudly proclaims on its website that ICS is live and that EXIT is no longer available. But on the same page it lists "Communication options for unprepared clients" and acknowledges that "Export goods can be reported to Customs through an export agent, freight forwarder, Customs broker, bureau, or value added network." So while Customs no longer has to handle manual processes, they've just been pushed onto others. The zombie (or son of the zombie) still lives.[39]

Disaster stories for document exchange projects are unfortunately too common. We hope that Document Engineering will help make them rarer.

16.2.3.3 Unusable User Interfaces

Many business processes begin as user interactions with a printed document or web form, followed by automated processes that take place with little human involvement. These user interfaces are the document exchange equivalent of a telecommunication network's "last mile."[40]

Throughout this book we've stressed the benefits of treating all kinds of document-model based interactions in the same way, emphasizing the commonalities between documents as interfaces for people and documents as interfaces to business processes.

It is essential for both user and process interfaces that they convey and capture the right information. But there is one difference that we can't ignore. For user interfaces, usability also matters, adding an additional layer of requirements when we implement models in applications. As we pointed out in Chapter 15, user interfaces can sometimes be completely or partly generated from models. But we must often ensure that we provide an additional level of usability beyond what we can automate. Otherwise, as with incomplete automation, unusable user interfaces become a weak link in our information chain that undermines the benefits we created by automating the interfaces to other processes.

16.2.3.4 Unimplementable Models

There is an essential difference or gap between the real world being modeled and the conceptual domain of the model, or else the model would serve no purpose. Likewise, there is always a gap between a conceptual model and a physical implementation model, because a conceptual model is often most useful when it isn't tied to specific or feasible implementations or technologies. But this means we can sometimes see what the current world looks like and what we would like it to be without being able to see how to get from one to the other. Our model might be unimplementable.

Some models can't be implemented because of technology limitations. History is littered with designs like that of Leonardo Da Vinci's "helical air screw," which accurately embodied the principles of the helicopter in 1483 but couldn't be tested until the early 1900s.[41] A more recent example is the Sydney Opera House, whose award-winning sail-shaped concrete vaults couldn't be built with the engineering technologies existing at the time its design was chosen. As a result, construction times tripled and its costs increased by a factor of 13.[42]

Some models can't be implemented because of technology limitations

16.3 KEY POINTS IN CHAPTER SIXTEEN

- A capability assessment can predict the likely success of a project.
- Organizations with low process maturity can't adopt new technology easily.
- Processes and documents are complementary and should be receive the same level of engineering rigor.
- Businesses with good process capabilities are more likely to implement model based applications.
- The business case for a tactical project can be a formulaic cost and benefit calculation.
- Strategic projects are much harder to justify because they involve more complex and intangible factors.
- Huge estimates of potential cost savings are emerging from many document-intensive industries.
- Many business problems result from poor visibility and lack of collaboration.
- As much as 75 percent of computer output becomes input to another system.
- Accelerated cycle times can create new business processes.
- Multiple publications and formats can be created from the same base of structured content.

- The careful development of conceptual document and process models yields the biggest payoff.

- A pattern or specification without industry adoption doesn't offer many benefits.

- Business relationships can become a tradable commodity.

- Incomplete automation can leave the enterprise with a slow link in its information flow that nullifies most of the investments to improve other processes.

- Some models can't be implemented because of technology limitations.

THE END OF THE BEGINNING

17 Epilogue

17.0 INTRODUCTION

We have reached the end of this book, but we are just at the beginning of Document Engineering. We hope that we have demonstrated why a document-centric analysis and design discipline is needed to exploit the potential of XML, web services, and other technologies and business concepts for information exchange. And we also hope that we have laid down the foundations upon which to build this emerging discipline.

17.1 WHEN DISCIPLINES COLLIDE

We describe Document Engineering as being at the intersection of many different disciplines, primarily information and systems analysis, electronic publishing, business process analysis and business informatics, and user-centered design. When different disciplines and perspectives come together, the outcome is unpredictable. One discipline can become dominant and absorb parts of the others. Or the overlapping pieces can break away and form a new field for a while, but never become more than the sum of its parts and fade away over time. But occasionally a new and important discipline emerges as a synthetic combination. Ecology is an example whose emergence as a discipline is precisely documented; the term was coined in 1866 by German philosopher/biologist Ernst Haeckel. A more recent one is cognitive science, which was created in the late 1970s at the intersection of cognitive psychology, computer science, and linguistics.[1]

Document Engineering is a creative synthesis of other disciplines

We think that Document Engineering is a similarly creative synthesis of other disciplines. It doesn't merely appropriate concepts and methods from other fields. Instead, it unifies and transforms them to create a new way of looking at documents and business processes. It fills in the gaps between the existing perspectives to yield a more comprehensive understanding of how they must fit together. That's why we chose the lighthouse metaphor in Figure 7-1 to suggest that Document Engineering more brightly illuminates the center of the Model Matrix, where documents and processes come together, than any of the other analysis approaches does on its own.

17.2 THE BUSINESS OF DOCUMENT ENGINEERING

We introduced Document Engineering as a set of methods for specifying, designing, and implementing document and process models to satisfy business objectives like those we described in Chapter 16. But we can also look at Document Engineering as a business in its own right.

In mid-2004 IBM announced new software and consulting services intended to help corporate users more efficiently create and deploy service oriented architectures.[2] It is too early to tell how this business model will evolve or how successful it will become. Initial announcements like these often describe offerings that aren't yet fully developed as a way to gain mind share in a new market. But it is illuminating to look at some of the major offerings because to us it seems that IBM is creating a business centered on Document Engineering.

- Assessments for Service-oriented Architectures – aimed at corporate users. "When people start using web services in service oriented architectures, they want an understanding of what their IT infrastructure is ready for."

- Strategy and Planning Services for Service-Oriented Architecture– designed to help users identify the business and technology capabilities needed to take advantage of service oriented computing.

- Component Business Modeling Services – helps users map business processes across industries and break down an individual business into a series of discrete activities. This can "make those processes less redundant by getting rid of the overlap among the different pieces and make sure you have consistency across the business."

The third offering "Component Business Modeling" has been the dominant focus of this book, but first two offerings have been sub-themes throughout and are primary topics of Chapter 16.

17.3 THE SUCCESSFUL DOCUMENT ENGINEER

Since this is the first book that defines Document Engineering as a discipline, before today no one could have started a professional career as a Document Engineer.[3] Practitioners of Document Engineering will most likely come from the other disciplines from which Document Engineering was synthesized. But they might also come from philosophy, cognitive science, literature, or industrial organization. Any discipline that teaches people to think abstractly and reason about information and processes provides a good starting point from which to enter Document Engineering.

Before today no one could have started out as a Document Engineer

The principles of Document Engineering seek to find a balance between technology and business, between process and information, between bottom-up and top-down thinking, and between concepts and implementation. Successful Document Engineers will do the same.

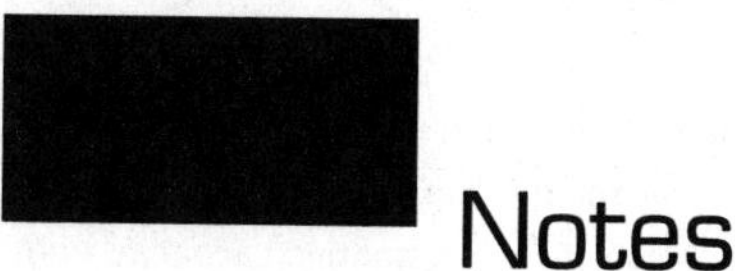

Notes

1

Introduction To Document Engineering

1. Israel Eph'al and Joseph Naveh, ARAMAIC OSTRACA OF THE FOURTH CENTURY B.C. (Magnes, 1996). An ostracon is a fragment of pottery. Halfat's tax receipt is Ostracon #13 in Eph'al & Naveh's book. Such ancient tax receipts are commonly found in Egypt and elsewhere.

2. This validation might have taken place in the "bricks and mortar" bookstore, too, but it is essential in the online store because more stringent regulations apply whenever the merchant doesn't see the actual card. But an even more important point here is that what looks like a single information exchange from either bookstore's perspective is in fact several transactions between the merchant, the merchant's bank, the authorization network, and the bank that issued the customer's credit card.

3. Robert Glushko, Jay Tenenbaum, and Bart Meltzer, "An XML framework for agent-based e-commerce," COMMUNICATIONS OF THE ACM, 42 (1999): pp. 106-115. This paper introduced the idea that XML documents could serve as interfaces to business services that could be combined to form virtual companies. It significantly predates the "web services" announcements.

4. The website at http://www.the-drop-ship-guide.com is a useful guide, written from the perspective that you want to set up an Internet store that uses drop shipment (last visited 18 January 2004).

5. The Federal Enterprise Architecture Program Management Office (FEAPMO) publishes all of its documents at http://www.feapmo.gov (last visited 18 January 2004).

6. Nick Wingfield, "In latest strategy shift Amazon is offering a home to retailers," WALL STREET JOURNAL, 24 September 2003. See also Amazon Web Services at http://www.amazon.com/-gp/browse.html/104-5602037-8299135?node=3435361 (last visited 19 January 2004).

7. NASA, MARS CLIMATE ORBITER MISHAP INVESTIGATION BOARD PHASE I REPORT (10 November 1999): 16. "The MCO Investigation Board has determined that the root cause for the loss of the MCO spacecraft was the failure to use metric units...Specifically, thruster performance data in English units instead of metric units was used in the software application code." Available from ftp://ftp.hq.nasa.gov/pub/pao/reports/1999/MCO_report.pdf (last visited 3 September 2004).

8. The most comprehensive listing of relevant standards is the XML Cover Pages list of "XML Applications and Initiatives" at http://xml.coverpages.org/xmlApplications.html (last visited 19 January 2004).

9. The home page for the UBL initiative is at http://www.oasisopen.org/committees/-tc_home.php?wg_abbrev=ubl (last visited 19 January 2004).

10. A wide range of application development approaches are called model based or model driven, but the latter term is strongly associated with specific technologies and methods proposed by in the Object Management Group's MDA initiative (http://www.omg.org/mda/), so we prefer to use the former term in a more generic sense.

11. We are certainly aware that the Object Management Group's MDA considers UML models the normative representations, playing the same role as XML schemas do for us. For a UML-centric approach, see David Carlson, MODELING XML APPLICATIONS WITH UML (Addison-Wesley, 2001) or Anneke Kleppe, Jos Warmer, and Wim Bast, MDA EXPLAINED (Addison-Wesley, 2003).

12. We use web form generically here to include HTML forms, which have long been the primary user interface for fill-in-the-form services, as well as those based on the W3C XFORMS recommendation or implemented using Adobe Reader, Microsoft InfoPath, or similar software for rich client applications.

13. See the publication Australian Department of Foreign Affairs and Trade, PAPERLESS TRADING: BENEFITS TO APEC (2001),at http://www.dfat.gov.au/publications/paperless/paperless_trading.pdf (last visited 28 December 2004). This lists the most common paper documents required for international trade as: Insurance Certificate, Certificate of Origin, Letter of Credit, Bill of Lading, Waybill, Manifest, Declarations, Sanitary and Phytosanitary Certificates, Payment Order, Remittance Advice, Debit Advice, Customs Clearance, Purchase Order, Invoice, Forwarding Instruction, Stowage Plan/Bay Plan, and Arrival Notice Advice.

14. Heather Kreger, "Web services conceptual architecture," IBM, at http://www-4.ibm.com/software/solutions/webservices/pdf/WSCA.pdf (last visited 23 September 2004).

15. Bart Meltzer, "XML and the network economy," keynote address at CommerceNet Japan XML Conference, Tokyo, June 1998.

16. Although you might conclude from its limited availability, slow response latency, or other similar quality of service measures that a service was being provided by a person rather than by a computer.

17. There are numerous directories of web services. See, for example, the Microsoft UDDI service registry at http://uddi.microsoft.com/ (last visited 3 September 2004) or http://www.xmethods.com/ (last visited 3 September 2004).

18. To IBM, this is business on demand; to HP, it is adaptive; to Microsoft, it is agile. Real-time or event-driven are related terms that aren't as clearly tied to particular companies.

19. The SOAP and WSDL Web Services specifications are maintained by the W3C at http://www.w3.org/TR/soap/ and http://www.w3.org/TR/wsdl. The UDDI specification is at http://www.uddi.org/. Other Web Services specifications are maintained by the Web Services Interoperability Organization at http://www.ws-i.org/ and by OASIS at http://www.oasis-open.org/com-

mittees/tc_cat.php?cat=ws (all last visited 3 September 2004). O'Reilly publishes a wide range of books on web services, which are listed at http://webservices.oreilly.com/ (last visited 3 September 2004).

20. Alorie Gilbert "Wal-Mart project boon for software makers," C/NET News.com, 14 August 2003. at http://news.com.com/2100-1017_3-5064075.html (last visited 10 June 2004).

21. Data analysis is related to object analysis. Object analysis techniques focus on the methods that will operate on or manipulate the information embodied in the object.

22. Utrecht University, Master's Programme in Business Informatics, http://businessinformatics.nl/-index.php?id=1&subid=0

2 XML Foundations

1. XHTML is a modularization of HTML to make it fully XML compliant, so this criticism of HTML doesn't apply to anyone who uses XHTML. But relatively few web pages use XHTML, and most of the Web's HTML isn't even valid with respect to any HTML specification.

2. At UC Berkeley the XML and Document Engineering courses have used Eric Ray, LEARNING XML (O'Reilly, 2003), Elliotte Harold and W.Scott Means, XML IN A NUTSHELL (O'Reilly, 2002), and Priscilla Walmsley, DEFINITIVE XML SCHEMA (Prentice Hall PTR, 2002).

3. Michael Cusamano and David Yoffie, COMPETING ON INTERNET TIME: LESSONS FROM NETSCAPE AND ITS BATTLE WITH MICROSOFT (Free Press, 1999). Microsoft won this first browser war, but a second browser war may now be developing, with the anti-Microsoft forces winning some small battles as a result of the security vulnerabilities in Internet Explorer. See Robert McMillan, "Mozilla Gains on IE," PC WORLD, 9 July 2004, at http://www.pcworld.com/news/article/0,aid,116848,00.asp (last visited 3 September 2004). Unlike the first browser war, in the second one neither side is creating proprietary tags, and indeed, some of the competition rests on which side can claim better compliance with W3C specifications.

4. Even worse was the emergence of a genre of web publishing software that completely inverted the original premise of HTML. Instead of using standard HTML to mark up document structure for display in a simple and predictable way, people could now use powerful graphical layout software to design visually rich and complex web pages. However, this seductively appealing outcome required that "under the hood" the application would create a proprietary HTML dialect that only it could render, often by using <table> tags for most of the content and otherwise abusing the HTML tag repertoire. Users of such software are captives of the vendors, since tools expecting HTML to work the way it was originally intended can't easily maintain HTML created that way.

5. Hakon Lie and Bert Bos, CASCADING STYLE SHEETS: DESIGNING FOR THE WEB (Addison-Wesley, 1997).

6. We think that using application in this sense is confusing because of the more conventional meaning of "a bundle of functionality embodied in software." So we will always use XML language or vocabulary for the former and XML software for the latter.

7. This can be done in strict conformance to standards without sacrificing any of the precise design control that often tempts graphical designers to use proprietary techniques. See the CSS Zen Garden at http://www.csszengarden.com/ (last visited 3 September 2004).

8. For a colloquial list of many dozens of different types of documents, see THE ORIGINAL ROGET'S THESAURUS OF ENGLISH WORDS AND PHRASES (Dell Publishing, 1962), especially Section 520, "Publication," and Section 589, "Book."

9. It would be more accurate to credit XML's parent technology of SGML (Standard Generalized Markup Language) for the idea of formally defined document types. But XML was optimized to be an SGML for the Web, abandoning the most difficult features of SGML that restricted its widespread adoption.

10. Up to now in this chapter we've used documents like newspapers, novels, purchase orders, and invoices to motivate the idea that the expected information content of some class of documents can be described in formal models. But it is equally important to model the business processes that create and consume documents, and we can also use XML to represent the models. It may sound a bit awkward at first to talk about document types for specifying business processes, but from an XML encoding standpoint it simply means that there is a set of tags useful for describing them.

11. Many articles and books about XML say that it is "self-describing," usually to contrast the idea of marked-up content with record-based syntaxes that contain position-sensitive and fixed-length data fields or use delimiters like commas or semicolons to separate variable-length fields. For either of the latter, the meaning of each data element must be defined somewhere else in a catalog or dictionary. But while we agree than an XML element can have a name that suggests the meaning of its content, this doesn't make it self-describing. To be self-describing an XML element would have to simultaneously convey its specific content and all the rules that govern its relationships to other content without any additional information. If elements could do that we wouldn't need schemas or any other documentation.

12. See Section 8.3.

13. As we said in Section 2.5, it is conventional for most web browsers to render an XML document with indentation that corresponds to the hierarchical structure created by its tags. Browsers generally don't do anything at all with DTDs, because they aren't encoded in XML.

14. XSD provides many different (some would say too many) options for organizing the element and type definitions within a schema. The nesting structure determines the scope and reusability of the defi-

nitions. The approach illustrated in Figure 2-3b is called the Russian Doll style because it is strictly nested, with each definition containing those that it uses, making them local and unavailable for reuse outside of that structure. See Eve Maler, "Schema Design Rules for UBL...and Maybe for You," IDEALLINACE XML 2002 CONFERENCE, at http://www.idealliance.org/papers/xml02/dx_xml02/papers/05-01-02/05-01-02.html for discussion of the Russian Doll schema design style and three others called the Venetian Blind, Salami Slice, and Garden of Eden (last visited 10 October 2004).

15. See http://xml.ascc.net/resource/schematron/schematron.html, or Eddie Robertson, "An Introduction to Schematron," XML.COM, 12 November 2003, at http://www.xml.com/-pub/a/2003/11/12/schematron.html (both last visited 3 September 2004).

16. See the RELAX NG website at http://www.relaxng.org/ (last visited 3 September 2004).

17. A very practical guide to EDI-XML integration is Michael Rawlins, USING XML WITH LEGACY BUSINESS APPLICATIONS (Addison-Wesley, 2003).

18. See "XSL Transformations (XSLT)," W3C Recommendation, 16 November 1999, at http://www.w3.org/TR/xslt (last visited 26 September 2004).

19. See W3C, "The Extensible Stylesheet Language Family (XSL)," at http://www.w3.org/Style/XSL/ (last visited 26 September 2004).

3 Models, Patterns, and Reuse

1. Object Management Group, "Introduction to OMG's Unified Modeling Language (UML)," at http://www.omg.org/gettingstarted/what_is_uml.htm (last visited 18 September 2004).

2. "Information processing systems—Concepts and terminology for the conceptual schema and the information base," ISO/TR 9007 (1987).

3. Data analysts may be more familiar with the term Domain Model for what we call a document component model. The terms are almost interchangeable but we wanted to emphasize the document-centric view.

4. Denise Schmandt-Besserat, HOW WRITING CAME ABOUT, (University of Texas Press, 1996). The discovery of non-iconographic counting tokens overturned the conventional view that Cuneiform writing evolved as an abstraction and simplification of pictorial representations.

5. The Model Matrix is itself a conceptual artifact because we haven't yet created a physical knowledge repository organized in this way. But we are inspired to do so by the online MIT Process Handbook, which resembles it in some respects. See Thomas Malone, Kevin Crowston, and George Herman (Editors), ORGANIZING BUSINESS KNOWLEDGE: THE MIT PROCESS HANDBOOK (MIT Press, 2003). An

online version is at http://ccs.mit.edu/ph/. This is an ambitious effort to organize knowledge about business models and business processes. It doesn't take the document / information exchange perspective of the Model Matrix or describe processes at that level of granularity, but it has a huge repertoire of patterns at less granular levels.

6. This is distinct from the use of meta to mean change or alteration (as in metamorphism).

7. The standardization of metadata for information exchange is led by the ISO TC154 Subcommittee 32. See http://metadata-stds.org/, (last visited 18 April 2005).

8. A downloadable version of the ebXML CCTS is available at http://www.oasis-open.org/committees/download.php/4259/CEFACT CCTS Version 2 of 11 August.pdf (last visited 18 April 2005).

9. UN Economic Commission for Europe, UN/CEFACT Modeling Methodology, version 8.1 (CEFACT/TMWG/N090R8.1, 2001.

10. UN/CEFACT ebXML Business Process Specification Schema. Version 1.10. 18 October 2003. By using the BPSS as the conceptual model for business processes we are not really creating a business process model as an XML schema. Since all of our process descriptions follow the same metamodel schema, it would be more correct to say we are creating a Business Process Model Instance. But this sounds a bit unnatural and makes it harder to treat document models and process models as two related views of the same thing, so we will often not tack on "instance" when we talk about business process models.

11. The idea of patterns as standard solutions in software design goes back several decades but is most often associated with the landmark book DESIGN PATTERNS by Erich Gamma, Richard Helm, Ralph Johnson, and John Vlissides (Addison-Wesley, 1995). See also Jonathan Adams, Srinivas Koushik, Guru Vasudeva, and George Galambos. PATTERNS FOR E-BUSINESS: A STRATEGY FOR REUSE (IBM Press, 2001) and Gregor Hoppe and Bobby Wolfe. ENTERPRISE INTEGRATION PATTERNS: DESIGNING, BUILDING, AND DEPLOYING MESSAGING SYSTEMS (Addison-Wesley, 2004).

12. U.S. Census Bureau. NORTH AMERICAN INDUSTRY CLASSIFICATION SYSTEM. See http://www.census.gov/epcd/www/naics.html (last visited 18 April 2005).

13. United Nations Standard Processes and Services Code. See http://www.unspsc.org/ (last visited 18 April 2005).

4 Describing What Businesses Do and How They Do It

1. Some of the classic works here are Alfred D. Chandler, THE VISIBLE HAND: THE MANAGERIAL REVOLUTION IN AMERICAN BUSINESS (Cambridge University Press, 1977), William McKelvey, ORGANIZATIONAL SYSTEMATICS: TAXONOMY, EVOLUTION, CLASSIFICATION (University of California Press, 1982), Oliver Williamson. MARKETS AND HIERARCHIES: ANALYSIS AND ANTITRUST IMPLICATIONS (Free Press, 1975), and Oliver Williamson, THE ECONOMIC INSTITUTIONS OF CAPITALISM (Free Press, 1985). Carl Shapiro and Hal Varian's, INFORMATION RULES: A STRATEGIC GUIDE TO THE NETWORK ECONOMY (Harvard Business School Press), 1999 isn't quite old enough to be a classic but it is on its way.

2. Object-oriented programming techniques usually use UML class diagrams in highly physical ways to describe models that have a one-to-one correspondence to implementing code, but in Document Engineering we use them more conceptually (see Section 3.2).

3. Demo of BluePeople seen in May 2004 at IBM Watson Research Center.

4. Robert Haugen and William E. McCarthy, "REA, a semantic model for Internet supply chain collaboration," at http://jeffsutherland.org/oopsla2000/mccarthy/mccarthy.htm. (last visited 20 October 2004).

5. This use of a word more commonly associated with biology to describe an Internet-based network of a firm's relationships with other entities originated in Jay Tenenbaum, Tripatinder Chowdry, and Kevin Hughes, "Eco System: An Internet Commerce Architecture, " COMPUTER, 30 (5), May 1997, 48-55. Scores of articles on ecosystem topics can be found at Internet newsmagazine LINE56's E-business Ecosystem section at http://www.LINE56.com/articles/ebiz_ecosys_index.asp. (last visited 18 October 2004).

6. Federal Enterprise Architecture Program Office, "24 presidential priority e-gov intitiatives," at http://www.feapmo.gov/resources/24_PPE-Gov_Init_Rev_1.pdf (last visited 14 February 2004).

7. "Education anytime, anywhere. How do you spell B2B and B2C?" at http://www.trendsreport.net/2000/education/3.html (last visited 15 February 2004).

8. This problem is increasingly attacked with linear or constraint-based mathematical programming techniques that evaluate huge numbers of feasible designs for a supply chain network against some objective function like minimizing cost, maximizing customer service levels, or minimizing cycle time. Some of these capabilities are built into the planning and scheduling components of ERP systems. See Jim Shepard and Larry Lapide. "Supply Chain Optimization: Just the Facts." ASCET, Volume 1, 15 April 1999. Available at http://www.ascet.com/documents.asp?d_ID=217# (last visited 20 October 2004).

9. Some generally useful services include those that provide information about potential business partners (like credit or customer satisfaction ratings), that facilitate financial or accounting processes (like tax calculation, payment, factoring), or that ensure the delivery of goods (like escrow, trade facilitation, freight forwarding, and shipment).

10. The most common auction pattern is the forward or English auction typified by eBay, in which one seller offers something to many potential buyers. When information about price is continuously exchanged, the offered price moves up as buyers bid against each other. Another auction pattern involving aggregated buyers is the uniform price or Dutch auction in which multiple identical products are available, and the price moves down until there are enough buyers willing to pay that clearing price. This kind of auction has been used in stock market floats to set an offering price that maximizes the money going to the newly public firm while ensuring that all the new shares are sold. Auction patterns can also involve aggregated sellers, most often in direct procurement where the buyer provides product specifications and the sellers bid against each other in what is called a reverse auction. The price the seller pays goes down as the sellers bid against each other. For a serious discussion of auctions, see Vijay Krishna, AUCTION THEORY (Academic Press, 2002), or Lawrence Ausubel, "Auction theory for the new economy," in Derek Jones (Ed.), NEW ECONOMY HANDBOOK (Academic Press, 2003).

11. Charles Fishman, "The Wal-Mart you don't know," FAST COMPANY, December 2003, at http://www.fastcompany.com/magazine/77/walmart.html (last visited 12 November 2004).

12. Mohanbir Sawney, "Forward thinking about reverse auctions," CIO, 1 June 2003, at http://www.cio.com/archive/060103/gains.html (last visited 12 November 2004).

13. Susan Helper, John Paul MacDuffie, and Charles Sabel, "Pragmatic collaborations: Advancing knowledge while controlling opportunism," INDUSTRIAL AND CORPORATE CHANGE 9 (2000): pp. 443-489.

14. Susan Helper and John Paul MacDuffie, "B2B and modes of exchange: Evolutionary and transformative effects," in Bruce Kogut (ed.), THE GLOBAL INTERNET ECONOMY (MIT Press, 2003), at http://wsomfaculty.cwru.edu/helper/b2bfinal.pdf (last visited 12 November 2004).

15. Helper and McDuffie, ibid., p. 2

16. Takahiro Fujimoto, THE EVOLUTION OF A MANUFACTURING SYSTEM AT TOYOTA (Oxford University Press, 1999), p. 104.

17. Fujimoto, ibid., Chapter 5, "Evolution of the Black Box Parts Supplier System."

18. Intel, Automating through RosettaNet, January 2003, at http://www.intel.com/-techtrends/trends/rosettanet/automating.pdf (last visited 6 January 2005).

19. "The Bylaws signed by these Charter Members create the ability for the Global Trading Web to adopt rules, standards, guidelines and best business practices that will enable and promote the seamless buying and selling of goods and services securely over the Web on a worldwide basis. The Global Trading Web Association will also allow members and their customers to benefit from the expertise, experience and capabilities of other member companies across the globe." From "23 of the World's Leading Companies Join Commerce One in Incorporating the Global Trading Web Association," Commerce One Press Release, 14 August 2000, at http://web.archive.org/-web/20000815093416/www.commerceone.com/news/-us/gtw_association.html (last visited 27 December 2004).

20. IBM Web Services Council, at http://www-306.ibm.com/software/solutions/webservices/council (last visited 28 December 2004).

21. Demir Barlas, "GTWA becomes ONCE," LINE 56, 3 December 2002, athttp://www.LINE56.com/articles/default.asp?NewsID=3980 (last visited 27 December 2004).

22. See http://www.sitpro.org.uk/ (last visited 2 January 2005).

23. Tradegate's foremost role is to facilitate the use of electronic commerce techniques for the exchange of information between customers and their suppliers. It does this by bringing together all the different types of organizations involved in each supply chain so that a common agreed strategy can be developed and implemented using the relevant international standards. See http://www.tradegate.org.au/ (last visited 2 January 2005).

24. UN/CEFACT maintains a list of National Trade Facilitation Contacts at http://www.unece.org/cefact/trafix/bdy_part.htm (last visited 28 December 2004). Among the most advanced efforts to automate the submission and processing of cross-border documentation are those in Southeast Asia in Singapore (Tradenet, http://www.tradenet.gov.sg/trdnet/index_home.jsp), Hong Kong (Tradelink, http://www.tradelink.com.hk/eng/index.html), and Taiwan (Tradevan, http://www.tradevan.com.tw/97English/Index.htm) (all URLs last visited 28 December 2004).

25. EAN/UCC standardizes bar codes, EDI transactions sets, XML schemas, and other supply chain solutions. See http://www.ean-ucc.org/ (last visited 2 January 2005).

26. EIDX is the leading organization in the definition and development of industry standard approaches to enable high-tech enterprises and their business partners to integrate across disparate e-commerce and enterprise application integration technologies. See http://www.rosettanet.org/ (last visited 2 January 2005).

27. UN/CEFACT is a United Nations body that encourages close collaboration between governments and private business to secure interoperability for the exchange of information between the public and private sector. See http://www.unece.org/cefact/ (last visited 2 January 2005).

28. The Supply-Chain Council's membership is primarily practitioners representing a broad cross-section of industries, including manufacturers, services, distributors, and retailers. See http://www.supply-chain.org/public/aboutus.asp (last visited 2 January 2005).
29. Etienne Wegner, COMMUNITIES OF PRACTICE: LEARNING, MEANING, AND IDENTITY (Cambridge University Press, 1998). See also Communities of Practice: A Brief Introduction, at http://www.ewenger.com/theory/index.htm (last visited 28 December 2004).

30. User Groups for XML and Related Structured Information Standards are listed at http://www.xml.org/xml/user_groups.shtml (last visited 28 December 2004). Many of the U.S. government's key XML architects and practitioners have created a community of practice that is described in Brand Niemann, "The Federal CIO Council's semantic interoperability community of practice (SICoP)," IDEALLIANCE XML 2004 CONFERENCE, November 2004, at http://www.idealliance.org/proceedings/xml04/papers/224/bniemann11162004.html (last visited 28 December 2004).

31. See Liberty Alliance Project at http://www.projectliberty.org/ and Microsoft .Net Passport at http://www.passport.net (both last visited 28 December 2004).

32. For example, there are hundreds of administrative policies and procedures at the University of California, Berkeley. One of them guarantees a free reserved parking place for life to any employee who wins a Nobel Prize. See http://campuspol.chance.berkeley.edu/directory.htm (last visited 15 February 2004).

33. Federal Enterprise Architecture Program Management Office. BUSINESS REFERENCE MODEL (BRM) VERSION 2.0. at http://www.feapmo.gov/feaBrm2.asp (last visited 20 October 2004). Denmark has a similar e-government effort underway: see the Openness Initiative at http://www.oio.dk/english (last visited 20 November 2004).

34. The Supply-Chain Council's Supply-Chain Operations Reference Model is described at http://www.supply-chain.org/public/scor.asp. (last visited 20 October 2004).

35. RosettaNet PIP Directory at http://www.rosettanet.org/pips (last visited 20 October 2004).

36. Tom Krazit, "Intel conducts $5b in transactions via RosettaNet," INFO WORLDS, 10 December 2002 at http://archive.infoworld.com/articles/hn/xml/02/12/10/021210hnintelrose.xml?s=IDGNS (last visited 14 February 2004). See also "e-Business at Intel" at https://supplier2.intel.com/B2Bi/ (last visited 14 February 2004).

37. The term "value chain" is usually attributed to Michael E. Porter, COMPETITIVE ADVANTAGE: CREATING AND SUSTAINING SUPERIOR PERFORMANCE (Free Press, 1998). Treating the flow of information in a value chain as an independent source of value is discussed in Chapter 4, "The Information Supply Chain," in Larry Downes, THE STRATEGY MACHINE (Harper-Collins, 2002).

38. Christopher Koch. "It all began with Drayer," CIO, 1 August 2002, at http://www.cio.com/-archive/080102/drayer.html (last visited 20 October 2004). Both parties in a VMI relationship benefit from the increased efficiency of procurement and logistics: the retailer no longer loses sales because goods are out of stock and no longer has to maintain inventory in warehouses, and the supplier can control inventory and transportation costs while providing better service. VMI works best for consumer packaged goods, consumables, and other merchandise that is purchased regularly and in large volumes, such as clothing, cosmetics and groceries.

39. See http://www.cpfr.org (last visited 20 October 2004) for a rich archive of specifications and case studies. See also Dirk Seifert, COLLABORATIVE PLANNING, FORECASTING AND REPLENISHMENT: HOW TO CREATE A SUPPLY CHAIN ADVANTAGE (SAP Press, 2003).

40. "Remote elevator monitoring," at http://www.otis.com/innovationdetail/0,1416,CLI1_IID805-_RES1,00.html (last visited 20 October 2004) and Jay Miller, "Keeping Tabs," MANUFACTURER, May 2003, at http://www.themanufacturer.com/content_detail.html?header=article&contents_id=1236&t-=manufacturer_us#. (last visited 20 October 2004).

41. Much of the work is in response to a mandate by the U.S. Securities and Exchange Commission that firms settle trades in just one day (called T+1, following a T+3 initiative in 1995). Settlement involves getting information from the front office of the selling entity to its back office and then to the back and front office of the buying entity. The goal is to reduce the time to "settle" securities trades to one day after the trade takes place.

42. Jonathan Parsons, "Legislation, deliberation, and documents: XML and the legislative process," IDEALLIANCE XML 2004 CONFERENCE, November 2004, at http://www.idealliance.org/proceedings/xml04/papers/179/XML_and_Legislative_Process.html (last visited 20 November 2004).

43. Eric Auchard, "U.S. Army aims to halt paperwork with IBM system." COMPUTERWORLD, 17 December 2004, at http://www.computerworld.com/printthis/2004/0,4814,98358,00.html (last visited 5 January 2005).

44. See US Securities and Exchange Commission, "Spotlight on Sarbanes-Oxley Rulemaking and Reports" at http://www.sec.gov/spotlight/sarbanes-oxley.htm (last visited 20 October 2004).

45. Nigel King, "Web services to support Sarbanes Oxley activities," IDEALLIANCE XML 2004 CONFERENCE, November 2004, at http://www.idealliance.org/proceedings/xml04/papers/-16/XML2004.html (last visited 20 November 2004).

46. Jim Ericson, "Technology rising for SOX," LINE 56, 23 November 2004, at http://www.LINE56.com/articles/default.asp?ArticleID=6172 (last visited 5 January 2005).

47. Mikkel Brun and Brian Nielsen, "Naming and design rules for e-government - The Danish approach," IDEALLIANCE XML 2003 CONFERENCE, December 2003, at

http://www.idealliance.org/papers/dx_xml03/papers/05-06-04/05-06-04.html (last visited 20 November 2004).

48. Not surprisingly the British Companies Act of 1844, was soon followed by the creation of a slew of accounting firms in London by people whose names were Deloitte, Price, Waterhouse, Coopers, and Peat. Two centuries later these names remain associated with the largest global accounting firms.

49. The US EDI standards are maintained by an ANSI Associated Standards Committee at http://www.x12.org. The international EDI standards are maintained by the United Nations Centre for Trade Facilitation and Electronic Business at http://www.unece.org/cefact/.

50. Kroger, "EDI Programs & Requirements," at http://edi.kroger.com/edi/programs_001.htm (last visited 14 February 2004).

51. John Edwards, "I'm not dead yet," LINE56, May 2001, at http://www.LINE56.com/-articles/default.asp?NewsID=2563 (last visited 14 February 2004).

52. Many XML vocabularies are published at web sites whose domain names are the vocabulary acronym and ".org". For example, http://www.xcbl.org/ (last visited 20 October 2004) is the web site for the XML Common Business Library. Lists of XML vocabularies can be found in the Cover Pages at http://xml.coverpages.org/xmlApplications.html and at http://xml.org. (last visited 20 October 2004).

53. John Edwards, "Doing it with meaning," CIO, 15 August 2002, at http://www.cio.com/-archive/081502/et_article.html (last visited 20 October 2004). For a more theoretical treatment see Joshua Fox, "Know what your schemas mean," IDEALLIANCE XML 2003 CONFERENCE, December 2003, at http://www.idealliance.org/papers/dx_xml03/papers/04-03-04/04-03-04.html (last visited 20 October 2004).

54. See, for example, Narinder Singh, "Unifying heterogeneous information models." COMMUNICATIONS OF THE ACM, 41 (1998): pp. 37-44, or Michael Stonebraker and Joseph Hellerstein, "Content Integration for E-Business," ACM SIGMOD 2001, pp. 552-560.

55. David Hay, DATA MODEL PATTERNS: CONVENTIONS OF THOUGHT (Dorset House, 1996) and Len Silverston, THE DATA MODEL RESOURCE BOOK (John Wiley, 2001).

56. Electronic Business XML at http://ebxml.org/ (last visited 18 April 2005). The original Core Component Dictionary created by the ebXML working group is at http://ebxml.org/specs/ccDICT.pdf (last visited 20 October 2004). The Core Components work is now being carried out under the auspices of UN/CEFACT and a more recent version of the specification is at http://www.unece.org/-cefact/ebxml/CCTS_V2-01_Final.pdf (last visited 20 October 2004).

57. The UBL home page is Organization for the Advancement of Structured Information Standards (OASIS) Universal Business Language at http://www.oasis-open.org/committees/tc_home.php?-wg_abbrev=ubl. (last visited 20 October 2004). See Mark Crawford (Editor), OASIS Universal Business

Language (UBL) Naming and Design Rules, 15 September 2004 at http://www.oasis-open.org/committees/download.php/9236/cd-UBL-NDR-1.0.pdf (last visited 20 October 2004). See also Eve Maler, "Schema design rules for UBL...and maybe for you," IDEALLIANCE XML 2002 CONFERENCE, December 2002,,at http://www.idealliance.org/papers/xml02/dx_xml02/papers/05-01-02/05-01-02.pdf (last visited 20 October 2004). The UBL customization methodology is described by Arofan Gregory and Eduardo Gutentag in "UBL and object-oriented XML: Making type-aware systems work.", IDEALLIANCE XML 2003 CONFERENCE, December 2003 at http://www.idealliance.org/-papers/dx_xml03/papers/04-04-04/04-04-04.html. (last visited 20 October 2004).

58. See, for example, David S. Linthicum, NEXT GENERATION APPLICATION INTEGRATION (Addison-Wesley, 2004), or W. Scott Means, STRATEGIC XML (SAMS, 2002).

59. This phrase originated with the Gartner Group. See Gian Trotta, "Get a grip, with enterprise nervous systems," ebizQ, 23 September 2003, at http://www.ebizq.net/topics/real_time_enterprise/features/2807.html (last visited 20 October 2004).

60. David S. Linthicum, B2B APPLICATION INTEGRATION (Addison-Wesley, 2001).

61. Heather Kreger, "Web services conceptual architecture," IBM, at http://www-4.ibm.com/software/solutions/webservices/pdf/WSCA.pdf, p 6. (last visited 18 April 2005). We single out this author only because her report was one of the first clear explanations of Web Services and undoubtedly encouraged others to adopt a similarly enthusiastic perspective.

62. The idea of using XML specifications for services and the documents they exchanged had emerged a few years earlier in a 1997 proposal titled "XML in Component-Based Commerce" to the U.S. Department of Commerce Advanced Technology Program by several Silicon Valley firms. See Brad Meltzer and Robert Glushko, "XML and electronic commerce: Enabling the network economy," ACM SIGMOD 27 (1998), and Robert J. Glushko, Jay M. Tenenbaum, and Bart Meltzer, "An XML framework for agent-based commerce," COMMUNICATIONS OF THE ACM, 42 (1999): 106-114. This work also inspired a quasi-standards effort called the eCo Framework that in 1998-1999 developed a set of specifications two years before the Web Services "standards stack." See "eCo Architecture for Electronic Commerce Interoperability," at http://www.commerce.net/docs/ecoframework.pdf (last visited 20 October 2004). The ebXML initiative, begun in 1999, had also begun to cover some of the same ground a year before the Web Services specifications emerged. The most important work today on specifications for Web Services is being conduced under the auspices of the Web Services Interoperability Organization at http://www.ws-i.org/ and OASIS at http://www.oasisopen.org/committees/tc_cat.php?cat=ws (both last visited 20 October 2004).

63. Jonathan Adams, Srinivas Koushik, Guru Vasudeva, and George Galambos, PATTERNS FOR E-BUSINESS: A STRATEGY FOR REUSE (IBM Press, 2001). See also IBM Patterns for E-Business at http://www-106.ibm.com/developerworks/patterns/ (last visited 18 April 2005).

64. Peter Weill and Michael R.Vitale, PLACE TO SPACE (Harvard Business School Press, 2001).

65. David Kaye, author of LOOSELY COUPLED: THE MISSING PIECES OF WEB SERVICES (RDS Associates, 2003) at http://www.rds.com/doug/weblogs/webServicesStrategies/2002/11/18.html (last visited 20 October 2004), says "Loose coupling is like pornography. Everyone talks about it, but when challenged, few can tell you what it is."

66. Gregor Hoppe and Bobby Wolfe, ENTERPRISE INTEGRATION PATTERNS: DESIGNING, BUILDING, AND DEPLOYING MESSAGING SYSTEMS (Addison-Wesley, 2004).

67. See note 5 in this chapter. See also Atul Saini, "Demystifying the enterprise service bus," BUSINESS INTEGRATION JOURNAL, September 2003: 24-27, at http://bijonline.com/Article.asp?-ArticleID=764&DepartmentID=9 (last visited 22 October 2004) and Marty Tenenbaum, "CommerceNet's vision: Millions of interoperable business services," CommerceNet Whitepaper, at http://www.commerce.net/docs/BSN_vision.pdf (last visited 22 October 2004). It is also enlightening to study the changes in product positioning of software vendors like CommerceOne, Ariba, Web Methods, and BEA since the B2B bubble began to burst in 2001. CommerceOne developed the first XML-based marketplace platform in 1999, followed by other vendors who offered similar software that was highly functional and complex and came bundled with a suite of marketplace, supply chain, and auction services. Today the surviving companies have re-implemented and repositioned their software to have a much lighter footprint and to function as more generic service integration platforms; none offers completely packaged "marketplace" software anymore.

68. Nick Wingfield, "In latest strategy shift Amazon is offering a home to retailers," WALL STREET JOURNAL, 24 September 2003. See also Amazon Web Services at http://www.amazon.com/-gp/browse.html/104-5602037-8299135?node=3435361 (last visited 22 October 2004).

69. Talaris Corp., "Services business language (SBL): Supplier integration using SBL," at http://www.talaris.com/technology/SBL_Whitepaper.pdf (last visited 22 October 2004).

70. Above All Software, "Above All Studio", at http://www.aboveallsoftware.com/products/studio.asp (last visited 22 October 2004). Above All Software was founded by Roger Sippl, a Silicon Valley serial entrepreneur who also founded Informix, Vantive, and Visigenix. Just as Informix did nearly 30 years ago with SQL for relational databases and Visigenix did a decade ago with application servers, Above All is making composite services that latest step in an evolutionary trend to raise the level of abstraction to increase the reuse information assets and business logic.

71. Eric Knorr, "Enterprises sketch out service-oriented architectures." INFOWORLD.COM, 26 November 2003, at http://reviews.infoworld.com/article/03/11/26/47FEwsretrofit_1.html?s=feature. (last visited 22 October 2004).

5 How Models and Patterns Evolve

1. Sometimes change takes place slowly and incrementally and at other times it takes place quickly, triggered by some significant business or political event or revolutionary technology breakthrough. And sometimes hindsight shows that a large change that apparently took place quickly actually took a long time, but the incremental changes that led to it were invisible.

2. John F. Kennedy, "Special Message to the Congress on Urgent National Needs" (delivered in person before a joint session of Congress, 25 May 1961), at http://www.jfklibrary.org/j052561.htm (last visited 23 October 2004).

3. David Williams, "The strategic implications of Wal-Mart's RFID mandate." DIRECTIONS MAGAZINE, 29 July 2004, at http://www.directionsmag.com/article.php?article_id=629 (last visited 23 October 2004).

4. Alfred D. Chandler, THE VISIBLE HAND: THE MANAGERIAL REVOLUTION IN AMERICAN BUSINESS (Cambridge University Press, 1977).

5. Oliver Williamson, MARKETS AND HIERARCHIES: ANALYSIS AND ANTITRUST IMPLICATIONS (Free Press, 1975), and THE ECONOMIC INSTITUTIONS OF CAPITALISM (Free Press 1985). Ronald Coase won the 1991 Nobel Prize in economics and is best known for a 1937 article titled "The Nature of the Firm" that introduced the concept of transaction costs to explain the size of firms. Transaction costs are incurred in searching for products and business partners, bargaining to establish price and other terms and conditions, and enforcing them. A very readable introduction to Coase's ideas is Chapter 2 of Larry Downes and Chunka Mui, UNLEASHING THE KILLER APP (Harvard Business School Press, 1998).

6. Carl Shapiro and Hal Varian, INFORMATION RULES: A STRATEGIC GUIDE TO THE NETWORK ECONOMY (Harvard Business School Press, 1999).

7. See, for example, Naomi Lamoureaux, Daniel Raff, and Peter Temin, "Beyond markets and hierarchies: toward a new synthesis of American business history," THE AMERICAN HISTORICAL REVIEW 108 (2003): pp. 404-433; Richard N. Langlois, "The vanishing hand: The changing dynamics of industrial capitalism" INDUSTRIAL AND CORPORATE CHANGE 12 (2003): pp. 351-385; and Walter W. Powell, "Neither market nor hierarchy: Network forms of organization," RESEARCH IN ORGANIZATIONAL BEHAVIOR 12 (1990): pp. 295-336. For an excellent example of new types of supplier relationships, see Susan Helper, John Paul MacDuffie, and Charles Sabel "Pragmatic collaborations: Advancing knowledge while controlling opportunism," INDUSTRIAL AND CORPORATE CHANGE 9 (2000): pp. 443-489.

8. Amazon's book sales in 2003 were over US$2 billion. See the 2003 Amazon.com annual report at http://media.corporate-ir.net/media_files/irol/97/97664/reports/Annual_Report_2003041304.pdf (last visited 18 April 2005). Of course, Amazon.com has made substantial investments in warehouses and distribution centers, but it can optimize them for its online business model, unlike its competitors who are constrained by their existing offline channels.

9. CORBA stands for Common Object Request Broker Architecture, a specification promoted by the OMG to enable distributed object invocation. See http://www.corba.org (last visited 18 April 2005). It requires and benefits from tight coupling and thus is most successful when changes to interfaces can be controlled, usually within a single enterprise. A provocative but flawed proposal to apply CORBA to inter-enterprise applications was made by Jay Tenenbaum, Tripatinder Chowdry, and Kevin Hughes, "Eco System: An Internet Commerce Architecture, " COMPUTER, 30 (5), May 1997, pp. 48-55.

10. Robert J. Glushko, "How XML enables Internet trading communities and marketplaces," GRAPHICS COMMUNICATIONS ASSOCIATION XML 1999 CONFERENCE (Philadelphia, 1998).

11. Peter Dodds, Duncan Watts, and Charles Sabel. "Information exchange and the robustness of organizational networks," PROCEEDINGS OF THE NATIONAL ACADEMY OF SCIENCES, 100(21), pp. 12516-12521, 14 October 2003.

12. Timothy Bresnahan, Alfonso Gambardella, and AnnaLee Saxenian. "Old Economy Inputs for New Economy Outcomes: Cluster Formation in the New Silicon Valleys," INDUSTRIAL AND CORPORATE CHANGE 10(4), pp. 835-860, 2001.

13. Ben Worthen. "Hot Potato!" CIO, 15 January 2003, at http://www.cio.com/archive/011503/potato.html (last visited 23 October 2004).

14. Automakers sometimes have to offer costly incentives to sell some car models because of overoptimistic sales forecasts. At the same time, the buyers of popular models have to wait months to get the car they order from their local dealer, and it can even take two to three weeks for the buyer's order to get from the dealer to the production floor at the factory. See M. Verispej, "Automakers put wheels on supply chains," INDUSTRY WEEK.COM, 1 December 2001, at http://www.industryweek.com/CurrentArticles/ASP/printerfriendly.asp?ArticleId=1174 (last visited 23 October 2004). The exact car the buyer wants could be sitting on another dealer's lot just a hundred miles away, but if all the dealers in a region don't share inventory information, the car might as well be on the moon. Other automation and standards efforts in the automotive industry are discussed in Laurie Sullivan, "Driving Standards," INFORMATION WEEK, 1 March 2004, at http://www.informationweek.com/shared/printableArticle.jhtml?articleID=18201098 (last visited 23 October 2004).

15. Electronic Privacy Information Center, "Radio Frequency Identification (RFID) Systems," at http://www.epic.org/privacy/rfid/ (last visited 23 October 2004).

16. Daniel Machalaba and Andy Pasztor, "Thinking inside the box: Shipping containers get 'smart,'" WALL STREET JOURNAL, 15 January 2004.

17. The growth of this emerging industry called "third-party logistics" is being driven by globalization. See for example, UPS Supply Chain Solutions, at http://www.ups-scs.com/ (last visited 23 October 2004).

18. See Henry Chesbrough, OPEN INNOVATION (Harvard Business School Press, 2003) and Clayton Christensen, THE INNOVATOR'S DILEMMA (Harvard Business School Press, 1997).

19. See Public Library of Science at http://www.publiclibraryofscience.org/, and a collection of articles and editorials about open access publishing at http://www.nature.com/nature/focus/accessdebate/ (last visited 23 October 2004).

20. Stephan Haeckel, ADAPTIVE ENTERPRISE: CREATING AND LEADING SENSE-AND-RESPOND ORGANIZATIONS (Harvard Business School Press, 1999). Randall Hancock, Peter Korsten, and George Pohle, "On demand business: The new agenda for value creation," at http://www-1.ibm.com/services/us/index.wss/xs/imc/a1000745 (last visited 23 October 2004).

21. Make-to-order is the process category term (M2) used in the SCOR reference model; Build-to-order seems to be used more frequently but would be less consistent with the Make process at the highest level of the SCOR model.

22. David Anderson, BUILD-TO-ORDER AND MASS CUSTOMIZATION (CIM Press, 2004).

23. Bruce Silver, The Business Case for Demand Chain Management (Granada Research, 2002). Dell's success has been extensively documented in the academic and trade press. See Kenneth Kraemer, Jason Dedrick, and Sandra Yamahiro, "Refining and extending the business model with information technology: Dell Computer Corporation," THE INFORMATION SOCIETY 16 (2000): 5-21. See also Michael Dell and Joan Magretta, "The power of virtual integration: An interview with Dell Computer's Michael Dell," HARVARD BUSINESS REVIEW (March-April 1998): 73-84.

24. See, for example. Mirko Hager, "Ordering via vendor managed inventory (VMI): Fully automatic delivery chain reduces procurement costs," SAP INFO, 2 March 2003, http://www.sap.info/-index.php4?ACTION=noframe&url=http://www.sap.info/public/en/article.php4/Article-5543e3965105dfd3/en (last visited 23 October 2004).

25. Richard Roehl and Hal Varian. "Circulating libraries and video rental stores," FIRST MONDAY, 6(5), 2001.

26. See http://www.ipv6.org/ for the specification of the IPv6 protocol (last visited 18 April 2005). Also, Chana R. Schoenberger, "The Internet of Things," FORBES, 18 March 2002

27. Larry Downes, "The Information Supply Chain," in THE STRATEGY MACHING (Harper-Collins, 2002).

28. Internet Engineering Task Force, EDI-Internet Integration Home Page, at http://www.ietf.org/html.charters/ediint-charter.html (last visited 15 February 2004). For an example of web forms, see https://www.sterlingwebforms.com/ (last visited 14 February 2004) and Alorie Gilbert, "Wal-Mart project boon for software makers" C/NET News.com, 14 August 2003, at http://news.com.com/2100-1017_3-5064075.html (last visited 10 June 2004).

29. Robert J. Glushko, "How XML enables Internet trading communities and marketplaces," GRAPHICS COMMUNICATIONS ASSOCIATION XML 1999 CONFERENCE (Philadelphia, 1998).

30. This is the definition proposed by the first author in Martin Lamonica, "You Call That A Standard?" NEWS.COM, 28 April 2004, at http://news.com.com/2008-1013_3-5200672.html (last visited 18 April 2005).

31. For the most recent "recommendation" about XML, see http://www.w3.org/TR/2004/REC-xml-20040204/ (last visited 18 April 2005).

32. Chris Moritz, "Beyond the hype," ACTIONLINE (December 2001), at http://www.supplysolution.com/newsroom/dBeyond_the_Hype_december01_p20.pdf (last visited 23 October 2004).

33. UCCNet is a nonprofit subsidiary of the Uniform Code Council, which brings together several business standards efforts and consortia (it began with article numbers for barcodes and now includes RosettaNet). See http://www.uc-council.org/ and http://www.uccnet.org/ (both last visited 18 April 2005).

34. The home page of the SDMX initiative is http://www.sdmx.org/ (last visited 22 November 2004). See also Statistical Commission and Economic Commission for Europe, Conference of European Statisticians. Joint UNECE/Eurostat Work Session on Statistical Metadata Working Paper #11. "Common open standards for the exchange and sharing of socio-economic data and metadata: the SDMX initiative," (March 2002), at http://www.sdmx.org/Data/UNECE_Mar02.pdf (last visited 22 November 2004).

6 When Models Don't Match: The Interoperability Challenge

1. Of course, a web form application also uses document exchange because the form creates an HTML document.

2. The examples we will use in the chapter are based on a simplified version of Universal Business Language (UBL) vocabulary, but we are not attempting to create UBL compliant documents.

3. This is clearly a modeling error or oversight by GMBooks.com because it implies that prices will be interpreted as US dollars. The affiliate is trying to be precise here, but the good deed is being punished by the GMBooks.com system because of the data type mismatch.

4. For many practical examples of EDI to XML translation, we recommend Mike Rawlins, USING XML WITH LEGACY BUSNESS APPLICATIONS (Addison-Wesley, 2003).

5. XML is very flexible in how it encodes content models, and people disagree about best practices in using elements and attributes. Some differences are merely stylistic, while others affect document size, extensibility, and other substantive considerations. For example, programmers often rely heavily on XML attributes because of their familiarity with attribute-value pairs to record or exchange information, but this approach seems less natural to writers and others used to embedded markup.

6. As a related example, in San Francisco we learned the hard way that "No parking between 8 a.m. and 5 p.m. on weekdays" is enforced on holidays in tourist areas and not in residential ones.

7. Natural language processing and text analysis software can probably extract BuildingNumber, StreetName, and Room from the StreetAddress component in Figure 5-15a in many cases. In North America, initial numbers probably form the BuildingNumber, letters that follow make up the StreetName, leaving the ending numbers as the Room. But extracting street names that include numbers, numbers with fractions, post office box numbers, and all the other tricky cases you can imagine suggests that trying to accommodate all the mismatches is the wrong approach. The models are just too different.

8. See Dick Raman, XML/EDI: CYBER ASSISTED BUSINESS IN PRACTICE (TIE Holding NV, 1999).

9. The classic paper in this area is George Furnas, Thomas Landauer, Louis Gomez, and Susan Dumais, "The Vocabulary Problem in Human-System Communication," COMMUNICATIONS OF THE ACM 30 (1987): pp. 964-971. The likelihood of two people choosing the same term to describe a familiar concept is less than 20 percent.

10. We're certain it doesn't really work this way; people who live on oil platforms probably get their mail forwarded from a regular street address or post office box. But there are oil platforms out in the Yellow Sea (see http://www.cnooc.com.cn/english/business/youtian.html), and surely people who work on them need to read books to pass the time. The point of this example is to show how completely incompatible conceptual models can be.

7 The Document Engineering Approach

1. UN Economic Commission for Europe, UN/CEFACT Modeling Methodology, version 8.1 (CEFACT/TMWG/N090R8.1, 2001), Chapter 8. The UMM is a set of metamodels and a prescriptive

methodology for using them in the design of business processes and their associated documents.

2. RosettaNet at http://www.rosettanet.org (last visited 18 April 2005).

3. The BPSS is a metamodel described as an XML schema that can be used to define public business process models as XML document instances. See http://www.oasis-open.org/committees/-tc_home.php?wg_abbrev=ebxml-bp (last visited 18 April 2005).

4. Defining information components as objects rather than data allows the behavior of the component to be attached to its definition. While this has relevance to building reusable programming functions, it is less applicable to loosely coupled document modeling, so we shall focus on analysis of the static component rather than its behavior.

5. The artifacts created by these phases roughly correspond to the business requirements view (BRV) and business transaction view (BTV) in the ebXML BPSS metamodel.

6. See for example Jakob Nielsen, USABILITY ENGINEERING (Morgan Kauffman, 1994), or Deborah Mayhew, THE USABILITY ENGINEERING LIFECYCLE: A PRACTITIONER'S HANDBOOK FOR USER INTERFACE DESIGN (Morgan Kauffman, 1999).

7. The source of the correct quote is "Devotions upon Emergent Occasions, No. 17" (1624).

8. For big ideas about "naturalist" design see William Rouse, DESIGN FOR SUCCESS (Wiley, 1991); for specific case studies, see Dennis Wixon and Judith Ramey, FIELD METHODS CASEBOOK FOR SOFTWARE DESIGN (Wiley, 1997).

9. Any component with a number also has a text title, but it would be a stretch to treat each text title as a label of the type of content.

10. Normalization techniques are taught in almost every database book and course. We recommend the classic text by Chris Date, AN INTRODUCTION TO DATABASE SYSTEMS, VOLUME 1 - 8th edition (Addison-Wesley, 2003).

11. In a complex problem context, the number of possible associations can become unmanageably large, so in practice we need to focus on the most important associations. We might need to simplify the pattern or model somewhat; for example, the most important associations in an organizational model would be the hierarchical reporting relationships, and while some "dotted-line" responsibilities might exist, we might safely ignore them in some contexts.

12. This idea might be implicit in Barbara van Halle, BUSINESS RULES APPLIED: BUILDING BETTER SYSTEMS USING THE BUSINESS RULES APPROACH (Wiley, 2001), but it was first expressed this clearly by Peter Charles and Bob Daly, RULE BASED INFRASTRUCTURE: A DESIGN AND RUN-

TIME SYSTEM FOR ENABLING XML SCHEMA DRIVEN APPLICATIONS (UC Berkeley Master's Project Report, School of Information Management and Systems, 2004).

Analyzing the Context of Use

1. Allison Bloodworth and Robert Glushko, "Model-driven application design for a campus calendar network," IDEALLIANCE XML 2004 CONFERENCE, November 2004. at http://www.idealliance.org/-proceedings/xml04/papers/228/XML2004BloodworthGlushko.pdf. See also Allison Bloodworth, Jeffrey Kahn, and Jon Conhaim, "UC Berkeley Calendar Network: A campuswide event calendar project," BERKELEY COMPUTING AND COMMUNICATIONS, 14 February 2005 at http://istpub.berkeley.edu:-4201/bcc/Spring2005/ucbcalendarnetwork.html (both last visited 16 February 2005).

2. Todd Weiss, "Group seeks calendar, scheduling app interoperability," COMPUTERWORLD, 14 December 2004, at http://www.computerworld.com/softwaretopics/software/groupware/story/-0,10801,98274,00.html (last visited 5 January 2005). The Calendar and Scheduling Consortium's home page is http://www.calconnect.org/ (last visited 5 January 2005).

3. The phrase "Creeping featurism" has been around for a while but probably derives from the "Second System Effect" in Fred Brooks' classic THE MYTHICAL MAN-MONTH: ESSAYS ON SOFTWARE ENGINEERNG (Addison-Wesley, 1975).

4. Design personas were proposed by Allan Cooper in THE INMATES ARE RUNNING THE ASYLUM: WHY HIGH TECH PRODUCTS ARE DRIVING US CRAZY AND HOW TO RESTORE THE SANITY (SAMS, 1999).

5. ebXML Core Components Project Team, Catalog of Context Drivers, 10 May 2001, at http://www.ebxml.org/specs/ccDRIV.pdf (last visited 3 September 2004).

6. Federal Information Processing Standard 55 DC-3, Codes for Named Populated Places, Primary County Divisions, and Other Locational Entities of the United States, Puerto Rico, and the Outlying Areas, 28 December 1994, at http://www.itl.nist.gov/fipspubs/fip55-3.htm. (last visited 16 September 2004).

7. Allan Afuah and Christopher Tucci, INTERNET BUSINESS MODELS AND STRATEGIES: TEXT AND CASES (McGraw Hill, 2000) and Paul Timmers, ELECTRONIC COMMERCE: STRATEGIES AND MODELS FOR BUSINESS-TO-BUSINESS TRADING (Wiley, 1999).

8. Yes, we can count and we know we've not included the System Capabilities context dimension because it doesn't suit our subsequent discussion. But if the Buyer used an Oracle procurement application and the Seller used an SAP ERP system these System Capabilities would certainly be important constraints on the documents they need to exchange.

9. Eduardo Gutentag and Arofan Gregory, "XML-based rules: Automating business context classification to produce semantic interoperability," EXTREME MARKUP LANGUAGES, 2001, at http://www.mulberrytech.com/Extreme/Proceedings/xslfopdf/2001/Gutentag01/EML2001Gutentag01.pdf (last visited 3 September 2004). See also Arofan Gregory and Eduardo Gutentag, "UBL and object-oriented XML: Making type-aware systems work, " IDEALLIANCE XML 2003 CONFERENCE, at http://www.idealliance.org/papers/dx_xml03/papers/04-04-04/04-04-04.pdf (last visited 3 September 2004).

10. Tom Gilb, "Quantifying The Qualitative: how to avoid vague requirements by means of clear specification language," September 1997, at http://www.btt-research.com/quantifying_qualitative_requirements.htm (last visited 18 April 2005).

11. There are many different schemes for categorizing requirements or business rules. A very readable treatment is Tony Morgan, BUSINESS RULES AND INFORMATION SYSTEMS (Addison-Wesley, 2004). Most approaches distinguish constraints on content that are represented in data models from constraints on behavior represented in process models. Other schemes distinguish single-item constraints that must always be true from those that reflect the relationship between two or more items or that can change according to a process context. Finally, constraints can be classified according to the manner in which they are represented and enforced in an implemented application. Our own taxonomy for business rules attempts to synthesize these diverse approaches with a bias toward aligning types of rules with conventional ways of thinking about XML in general and XML schemas in particular. Our approach is consistent with the categories of Interoperability Challenges in Chapter 6 and with the analysis approach we describe in Chapters 9-11.

12. David Ferraiolo, John Barkley, and D. Richard Kuhn, "A role-based access control model and reference implementation within a corporate intranet," ACM TRANSACTIONS ON INFORMATION AND SYSTEM SECURITY, 2 (1999). A comprehensive set of resources on RBAC is at http://csrc.nist.gov/rbac/ (last visited 3 September 2004).

13. UNECE Recommendation 1, United Nations Layout Key for Trade Documents, 1981, at http://www.unece.org/cefact/rec/rec01/rec01_1981_ecetrd137.pdf. See also Annex to UNECE Recommendation 1, Applications of the United Nations Layout Key at http://www.unece.org/-cefact/rec/rec01/rec01_%20Informative%20Annex_2001_%2001cf16.pdf (both last visited 3 September 2004). A brilliant case study of creating technology-neutral formatting specifications for rendering UBL documents to conform with the UN Layout Key is Ken Holman, "Writing formatting specifications for XML documents," IDEALLIANCE XML 2003 CONFERENCE at http://www.idealliance.org/papers/-dx_xml03/papers/04-05-02/04-05-02.pdf (last visited 3 September 2004]).

9 Analyzing Business Processes

1. Clayton Gillette and Steven Walt, "Implied terms," SALES LAW (Foundation Press, 1999). Describes how the customary practices or methods of dealing that are regularly observed within a trade or industry are treated as default provisions in sales contracts.

2. ebXML Business Process and Business Information Analysis Overview v1.0 (11 May 2001). http://www.ebxml.org/specs/bpOVER.pdf (last visited 18 April 2005).

3. We coined this term to convey the corporate sense of a demography.

4. Michael Treacy and Fred Wiersema, THE DISCIPLINE OF MARKET LEADERS (Harper Collins, 1995).

5. C. K. Prahalad and Gary Hamel, "The core competence of the corporation," HARVARD BUSINESS REVIEW, May-June 1990.

6. Benson Shapiro, V.Kasturi Rangan, and John Sviokla. "Staple yourself to an order," HARVARD BUSINESS REVIEW, July/August 1992.

7. UN Economic Commission for Europe, UN/CEFACT Modeling Methodology (UMM) User Guide (CEFACT/TMG/N093 22nd September 2003) at http://www.unece.org/cefact/umm/umm_userguide.pdf (last visited 18 April 2005).

8. Howard Smith and Peter Fingar, BUSINESS PROCESS MANAGEMENT: THE THIRD WAVE (Meghan-Kiffer Press, 2003). Efforts to reengineer and standardize business processes can be traced back to the early 1920s.

9. Todd Datz, "Integrating America," CIO, 1 December 2002, at http://www.cio.com/-archive/120102/america.html (last visited 14 February 2004).

10. Our worksheet format is inspired by ebXML Business Process Analysis Worksheets & Guidelines at http://www.ebxml.org/specs/bpWS.pdf (last visited 18 April 2005), which contains detailed definitions of each section and guidance for filling them out.

11. G. Fitzpatrick, P. Lanner, and P. Hjelm, "SkiCal—An extension of iCalendar," (Internet Engineering Task Force Draft, July 2001) at http://skical.metamatrix.se/skical20010905.html (last visited 18 October 2004).

12. Scott Ambler, AGILE MODELING: EFFECTIVE PRACTICES FOR EXTREME PROGRAMMING AND THE UNIFIED PROCESS (John Wiley & Sons, 2002).

13. See Helmut Wachter and Andreas Reuter: "The ConTract model," in A. Elmagarmid (ed.), DATABASE TRANSACTION MODELS FOR ADVANCED APPLICATIONS (Morgan Kaufmann, 1992): pp. 219-263.

14. Receipts are also sometimes called Acknowledgment Messages or ACKs, but we prefer Receipt because business documents can also serve as acknowledgments and might even have Acknowledgment in the name of the document type.

15. ebXML Business Process Specification Schema, 11 May 2001, at http://www.ebxml.org/-specs/ebBPSS.pdf (last visited 15 January 2005).

16. United Nations Convention on Contracts for the International Sale of Goods (Vienna 1980).

17. We thank David Burdett for this insightful addition to our definition.

18. Jamie Clark (ed.), "ebXML e-commerce patterns v1.0" (May 2001) at http://www.ebXML.org/specs/bpPATT.pdf (last visited 18 April 2005).

19. Paula and Paul Swatman, "Electronic data interchange: Organisational opportunity, not technical problem," in Bala Srinivasan and John Zeleznikow (eds.), DATABASES IN THE 1990s, 2 (World Scientific Press, 1991): pp. 354-374

10 Designing Business Processes with Patterns

1. If the drop shipping retailer wants to hide the fact that a third party distributor is part of their virtual enterprise by controlling every communication with the buyer, this indirection is essential and not viewed as inefficient.

2. "Recipes" for drop shipment are described in "The drop ship guide" at http://www.the-drop-ship-guide.com/ and "Start wholesale drop shipping" at http://www.wholesalemarketer.com/ (both last visited 12 January 2005).

3. Geoffrey Moore. "Darwin and the Demon: Innovation within Established Enterprises." HARVARD BUSINESS REVIEW, July-August 2004, 86-92.

4. Italian Pizza has 114,000 hits using Google and Hawaiian Pizza gets 16,000. But Indonesian Pizza has only 60 on 12 January 2005. For both a fascinating and practical look at recipe patterns principles and experimentation, see Elizabeth Rozin, THE FLAVOR PRINCIPLE COOKBOOK (Hawthorn Books, 1973), republished under the title ETHNIC CUISINE (Penguin Books, 1992).

5. The International Benchmarking Clearinghouse managed by the American Productivity and Quality Center (APQC) categorizes 271 common business processes as part of an extensive repository of best practices and metrics (see http://www.apqc.org). The European Foundation for Quality Management (EFQM) maintains a similar repository (see http://www.efqm.org/). The MIT Process Handbook Repository currently has over 5000 other business process entries at http://process.mit.edu/Info/Contents.asp (all last visited 12 January 2005).

6. Thomas Malone, Kevin Crowston, and George Herman (Eds.), ORGANIZING BUSINESS KNOWLEDGE: THE MIT PROCESS HANDBOOK (MIT Press, 2003).

7. The least-detailed cluster view of RosettaNet is at http://www.rosettanet.org/pips; the most-detailed PIP view is at http://www.rosettanet.org/pipdirectory (both last visited on 13 January 2005).

8. Taxation and Customs Union, "The Single Administrative Document (SAD)," 20 December 2004, at http://europa.eu.int/comm/taxation_customs/customs/procedural_aspects/general/sad/index_en.htm (last visited 31 January 2005).

9. Two representative research papers, both of which use as an example a composite travel service like the one we have described, are Jiang Wang, "Web Service Componentization," COMMUNICATIONS OF THE ACM, October 2003, 46(10), pp. 35-40 and Quan Sheng, Boualem Benatllah, Marlon Dumas, and Eileen Mak, "SELF-SERV: A Platform for Rapid Composition of Web Services in a Peer-to-Peer Environment," PROCEEDINGS OF THE 28TH VLDB CONFERENCE, 2002.

10. In the period from 1878 to 1880 Edison and his associates worked on thousands of potential materials to use for an electric light filament. He finally narrowed his testing to the carbonized filaments of 6,000 different plants, a range that included baywood, boxwood, hickory, cedar, flax, and bamboo. He eventually discovered that a carbonized cotton thread filament began to radiate a soft orange glow. See http://www.ideafinder.com/history/inventions/story074.htm (last visited 13 January 2005).

11. UDDI Version 3 Features List, see http://www.uddi.org/pubs/uddi_v3_features.htm#_Toc10457173 (last visited 13 January 2005).

12. See http://en.wikipedia.org/wiki/Cargo_cult (last visited 13 January 2005).

13. For more information about the "Copy Exactly" factory strategy see Intel's Worldwide Manufacturing Operations Virtual Press Kit at http://www.intel.com/pressroom/kits/manufacturing/-copy_exactly_bkgrnd.htm (last visited 1 November 2004).

14. The university analog to a Forecast would be a student's intent to take courses in future semesters; Inventory Reports would give more precision to the usual "in or out" course registration process; Commitment to Supply requests would ask instructors to commit to teach courses and prevent them from canceling courses.

15. "Channel Assembly: A Lexicon", at http://www.varbusiness.com/sections/98pages/-198chsupp2.jhtml. (last visited 13 January 2005). See also Norm Bogen, "Channel Assembly Gains Favor," ELECTRONIC NEWS, 21 April 1997.

16. For information about UPS Supply Chain Solutions see http://www.ups-scs.com/logistics/index.html (last visited 15 January 2005). See also Aberdeen Group, "Service Parts Management: Unlocking Value and Profits in the Service Chain," September 2003 at http://www.ups-scs.com/logistics/servicepartsre-port.pdf (last visited 15 January 2005).

17. Bob Tedeschi, "Returns are Early, But New Categories of 'Stores' On Amazon.com Show Promise," NEW YORK TIMES, 22 December 2003. See also Edd Dumbill, "Making Web Services Work at Amazon," XML.COM, 9 December 2003 at http://www.xml.com/pub/a/2003/12/09/xml2003amazon.html (last visited 31 October 2004).

18. "Order Management Choreographies," Version 1.0., 15 May 2003 at http://www.xcbl.org/xcbl40/documentation/view/OrderManagementChoreographies.rtf (last visited 27 January 2005).

19. RosettaNet Request Purchase Order (PIP 3A4) Specification 8 January 2004 at http://www.rosettanet.org/PIP3A4 (last visited 15 January 2005).

20. Kenneth Kraemer, Jason Dedrick, and Sandra Yamashiro, "Refining and Extending the Business Model with Information Technology: Dell Computer Corporation," THE INFORMATION SOCIETY, 16 (2000): pp.5-21.

21. See "Fast Moving Consumer Goods: When to Change a GTIN," at http://www.ean-int.org/gtin-rules/Help/When%20to%20change%20GTIN%20basics.htm (last visited 16 January 2005). GTINs can have up to 14 digits and are managed by the European Article Numbering Association (EAN). EAN was created in 1977 to set European standards and controls for the identifiers used on bar codes. The organization has gone global by extending membership to similar organizations on other continents and today has member organizations from more than 100 countries, including the U.S. Uniform Code Council, which also manages the RosettaNet Consortium. In January 2005, EAN announced a name change to GS1, presumably to get European out of its name. See http://www.ean-int.org and http://www.uc-council.org/ (both last visited 15 January 2005).

22. Peter Jones, "Unique consignment numbering: the foundation for a universal tracing and tracking system or an additional obstacle to world trade?", FORWARDERLAW.COM, 3 October 2002, at http://www.forwarderlaw.com/Feature/ucr.htm (last visited 15 January 2005). See also "The World Customs Organization (WCO) and EAN International (EAN) agree continued cooperation on the Unique Consignment Reference (UCR)," press release by the World Customs Organization, 25 June 2004, at http://www.wcoomd.org/ie/En/Press/Joint%20Statement%20WCO%20EAN_36.htm (last visited 15 January 2005).

23. See, for example, RosettaNet Implementation Guide: PIPs 3A4, 3A7, 3A8, 3A9 for Order Management in Japan Business Model Alignment Process, 16 April 2004, at http://www.rosettanet.org/usersguides (last visited 16 January 2005).

11 Analyzing Documents

1. Thomas Malone, "How do people organize their desktops? Implications for the design of office systems," ACM TRANSACTIONS ON OFFICE INFORMATION SYSTEMS 1 (1983): pp. 99-112.

2. Steve Whittaker and Julia Hirshberg, "The character, value, and management of personal paper archives." ACM TRANSACTIONS ON COMPUTER-HUMAN INTERACTION 8 (2001): pp. 150-170.

3. The presentational emphasis of HTML and the accompanying lack of explicit semantics within web pages have motivated the idea of a semantic web. See Tim Berners-Lee, James Hendler, and Ora Lassila, "The semantic web will bring structure to the meaningful content of web pages," SCIENTIFIC AMERICAN, May 2001.

4. One factor in the heterogeneity of narrative documents is copyright law, which treats as infringements new instances that are too similar in content and structure to an existing work.

5. The common patterns are in their purchase orders, not in the books themselves. We know that both Moby Dick and the Bible discuss whales (see the story of Jonah in Matthew 12:40) but there isn't much benefit in proposing a common content component type to capture this fact unless we're designing for a very specialized business model.

6. Governments are especially skilled at this technique with documents that describe deficits, employment, or other economic activity. They also use the related practice of classifying documents as Secret when more accurate categorizations might be Embarrassing, Wasteful, or Likely to Jeopardize Reelection. Some product firms don't create any documents named Bugs or Known Defects, not because their projects have none of them but because they publish these lists as Change Requests, Customer Satisfaction Considerations, or similarly name-obscured documents.

12 Analyzing Document Components

1. A particularly readable and entertaining book on design is Robin Williams, THE NON-DESIGNERS DESIGN BOOK: DESIGN AND TYPOGRAPHIC PRINCIPLES FOR THE VISUAL NOVICE (Peachpit Press, 1994). And we'd be derelict if we failed to remind readers of Edward Tufte's classic books THE VISUAL DISPLAY OF QUANTITATIVE INFORMATION (Graphics Press, 2001) and ENVISIONING INFORMATION (Graphics Press, 1990).

2. According to Webster a sidebar is "a short news story accompanying and presenting sidelights of a major story." So a sidebar is a type of narrative content, but it appears that this semantic distinction has been corrupted by giving it a name that reflects its typical presentation at the side of the more central content.

3. MIL-STD-1472D: Human engineering design criteria for military systems, equipment and facilities, Military standard human engineering design criteria for military systems, equipment and facilities, 14 March 1989, at http://jcs.mil/htdocs/teinfo/directives/soft/ms1472d.html (last visited 23 November 2004).

4. We believe that this is a task best done by people, but this "table extraction" problem is being attacked using a variety of computational techniques; some infer the data model from queries into HTML forms, others analyze HTML tags or the patterns of text and data values, and others employ machine learning techniques to classify tables and web pages. See, for example, Matthew Hurst, THE INTERPRETATION OF TABLES IN TEXT (PhD dissertation, University of Edinburgh, 2000); Alberto H. F. Laender, Berthier A. Ribeiro-Neto, Altigran S. da Silva, and Juliana S. Teixeira, "Surveys: A brief survey of web extraction tools," ACM SIGMOD RECORD, 31 (June 2002); Yingchen Yang and Wo-Shun Luk, "Web mining: A framework for web table mining," PROCEEDINGS OF THE FOURTH INTERNATIONAL WORKSHOP ON WEB INFORMATION AND DATA MANAGEMENT (November 2002).

5. Yalin Wang and Jianying Hu. "A machine learning approach for table detection on the Web," PROCEEDINGS OF THE 11TH INTERNATIONAL CONFERENCE ON THE WORLD WIDE WEB (2002): pp. 242-250. Wang and Hu describe a machine learning approach to classify web tables as either genuine or non-genuine. In their sample of more than 14,000 sites with <Table> tags, only about 10 percent were genuine tables. Content characteristics discriminate better than layout ones.

6. The seminal work in this area is Eleanor Rosch and Carolyn Mervis "Family resemblances: Studies in the internal structure of categories," COGNITIVE PSYCHOLOGY, 7 (1975): pp. 573-605. See also Edward Smith and Douglas Medin, CATEGORIES AND CONCEPTS (Harvard University Press, 1981).

7. United Nations Directories for Electronic Data Interchange for Administration, Commerce and Transport, 7081 Item Characteristic Code at http://www.unece.org/trade/untdid/d01a/-tred/tred7081.htm (last visited 10 March 2005).

8. An initialism is an abbreviation composed from the initial letters of a series of words (like NCAA or BBC). An acronym is a special type of initialism in which the resulting abbreviation is pronounceable (like NATO or ISO). An apocopation is an abbreviation formed by truncating a longer word (such as bicycle to bike or University of California to Cal).

9. See the W3C home page for the semantic web activity (http://www.w3.org/2001/sw) and especially the resource description framework (RDF) and the Web ontology language (OWL) (last visited 24 November 2004).

10. This example comes from J. Brian Farish, "What's in a name," 2002, at http://www.vertaasis.com/articles/whats_in_a_name.htm (last visited 20 October 2004).

13 Assembling Document Components

1. Everywhere except at the extreme narrative endpoint; Melville probably didn't strive for these goals when writing Moby Dick.

2. Much of this subsequent skill and judgment has been successfully captured in rule-based computer programs that generate illustrations automatically from a knowledge base or semantic content provided by the author. See Doree Seligman and Steven Feiner, "Specifying composite illustrations with communicative goals," PROCEEDINGS OF THE ACM SYMPOSIUM ON USER INTERFACE SOFTWARE AND TECHNOLOGY (Williamsburg, VA, November 13-15, 1989):pp. 1-9, and Winfried Graf, "The constraint-based layout framework laylab and its applications, " ACM WORKSHOP ON EFFECTIVE ABSTRACTIONS IN MULTIMEDIA: LAYOUT, PRESENTATION AND INTERACTION (ACM Multimedia '95), at http://www.cs.uic.edu/~ifc/mmwsproc/graf/mm95.html (last visited 3 November 2004).

3. Eve Maler and Jeanne El Andaloussi, DEVELOPING SGML DTDs: FROM TEXT TO MODEL TO MARKUP (Prentice-Hall, 1995). Our comments in this section and its title may imply that Maler and El Andaloussi's book is outdated. But their book contains a wealth of knowledge about project planning, team building, project politics, and other topics that transcend the implementation technology for document models, and we highly recommend it for those reasons.

4. The landmark paper is Edgar F. Codd, "A relational model of data for large shared data banks," COMMUNICATIONS OF THE ACM, 13 (1970): pp. 377-387.

5. The classic and authoritative data modeling textbook is C. J. Date's AN INTRODUCTION TO DATABASE SYSTEMS, VOLUME 1, first published in 1980 and now in its eighth edition (Addison-Wesley, 2003).

6. The Electronics Industry Data Exchange Group (EIDX) develops implementation guidelines for EDI and XML-based vocabulary standards, in addition to publishing recommendations for usage of these transactions and messages (supporting documents). See http://eidx.comptia.org/guidelines.aspx (last visited 23 November 2004).

7. The Society for Worldwide Interbank Financial Telecommunication (SWIFT) offers the financial services industry a common platform of advanced technology and access to shared solutions. See http://www.swift.com/index.cfm?item_id=41946 (last visited 23 November 2004).

8. ASC X12 is the U.S. standards body for the cross-industry development, maintenance, and publication of electronic data exchange standards. See http://www.x12.org/x12org/subcommittees/-dev/index.cfm (last visited 23 November 2004).

9. United Nations Directories for Electronic Data Interchange for Administration, Commerce and Transport, at http://www.unece.org/trade/untdid/welcome.htm (last visited 23 November 2004).

10. OASIS Universal Business Language defines a common XML library of business documents (purchase orders, invoices, etc.). See http://www.oasis-open.org/committees/tc_home.php?wg_abbrev=ubl (last visited 23 November 2004).

11. As of early 2004, courtesy of Robin Cover, at http://xml.coverpages.org/namesAndAddresses.html:

- BS 7666 Spatial data-sets for geographic referencing
- CEN/TC133/WG3 Postal services, Addresses and Automatic Identification of Items
- ECCMA International Address Element Code
- GCA/IDEAlliance Address Data Interchange Specification (ADIS)
- HR-XML Consortium Cross-Process Objects Schemas
- Linking and Exploring Authority Files (LEAF)
- OASIS CIQ TC Name and Address Standard (xNAL)
- SAMPLE: Single Administrative Message for Postal Enterprises
- UK GovTalk Address and Personal Details Fragment
- Universal Postal Union (UPU)
- UN/PROLST
- US FGDC Address Data Content Standard
- US Postal Service
- ASTM E2182: Names in Healthcare Records
- vCard: Electronic Business Card

12. The UN/CEFACT ebXML Core Components Technical Specification 2.01 is available from http://www.untmg.org/artifacts/CCTS_v2.01_2003-11-15.pdf (last visited 18 April 2005).

13. ISO/IEC 11179-1:1999 Information technology — Specification and standardization of data elements — Part 1: Framework for the specification and standardization of data elements is available from http://www.iso.org/iso/en/ittf/PubliclyAvailableStandards/c035343_ISO_IEC_11179-1_2004(E).zip (last visited 18 April 2005).

14 Assembling Document Models

1. What follows is very simplistic treatment of a complex subject. We will not get into any of the debate about data-oriented or document-oriented databases or the representation of XML in databases. See Ronald Bourret, "XML and databases" (July 2004), at http://www.rpbourret.com/xml/-XMLAndDatabases.htm (last visited 6 November 2004).

2. Eve Maler and Jeanne El Andaloussi, DEVELOPING SGML DTDs: FROM TEXT TO MODEL TO MARKUP (Prentice-Hall, 1995), pp. 145-146.

3. Arofan Gregory and Eduardo Gutentag. "XSD type derivation and the UBL context mechanism, " IDEALLIANCE XML 2002 CONFERENCE, at http://www.idealliance.org/papers/xml02/-dx_xml02/papers/05-05-06/05-05-06.pdf (last visited 8 November 2004).

4. Patrick Garvey, Marc Gratacos, Sonia Klemperer-Johnson, and John Leon. "Course project final report," at http://dream.sims.berkeley.edu/doc-eng/projects/COURSE/course-final-report.html (last visited 4 November 2004).

5. This example is inspired by a case study of document automation in an engine assembly plant. John Terris, "Re-use, re-purpose, re-package:A General Engine Products, Inc., case study," IDEALLIANCE XML 2001 CONFERENCE, at http://www.idealliance.org/papers/xml2001/papers/html/04-01-04.html (last visited 3 November 2004).

6. Figure 14-10 uses UML notations for describing dependencies between components. Components are described by a rectangle with two smaller rectangles overlaid on its left side. Dependencies are denoted by dashed lines with open arrowheads pointing from dependent to independent components. In this case the independent components are packages (or libraries) denoted as a large rectangle with a smaller rectangle attached to the top left corner.

7. ELM stands for "enables lucid models," and their notation is described in Eve Maler and Jeanne El Andaloussi, DEVELOPING SGML DTDs: FROM TEXT TO MODEL TO MARKUP (Prentice-Hall, 1995), pp. 34-35.

15 Implementing Models in Applications

1. Eve Maler and Jeanne El Andaloussi, DEVELOPING SGML DTDs: FROM TEXT TO MODEL TO MARKUP (Prentice-Hall, 1995).

2. Eric van der Vlist, XML Schema (O'Reilly, 2002); James Bean, XML FOR DATA ARCHITECTS (Morgan Kaufmann, 2003); Berthold Daum, MODELING BUSINESS OBJECTS WITH XML SCHEMA (Morgan Kaufmann, 2003).

3. Priscilla Walmsley, DEFINITIVE XML SCHEMA (Prentice Hall, 2002).

4. David Orchard, "Extending and versioning XML languages with XML schema," IDEALLIANCE XML 2004 CONFERENCE, at http://www.idealliance.org/proceedings/xml04/papers/248/Extending-VersioningXML.pdf (last visited 10 February 2005); Dare Obasanjo, "Designing XML formats: Versioning vs. extensibility," IDEALLIANCE XML 2004 CONFERENCE, at http://www.idealliance.org/proceedings/xml04/papers/46/VersioningXML.pdf (last visited 10 February 2005).

5. Universal Business Language Naming and Design Rules, 5 November 2004, at http://www.oasis-open.org/committees/download.php/9943/cd-UBL-NDR-1.0Rev1b.pdf (last visited 10 March 2005).

6. The current version of the Berkeley Events Calendar schema can be found at: http://groups.sims.berkeley.edu/EventCalendar/ (last visited 18 April 2005).
7. Some of these are: EDIFIX from GEFEG (see http://www.gefeg.com/en/index.htm), UBLish from SoftML (see http://www.softml.net/jedi/ubl/sw/UBLish/UBLish-1.0/index.html) and Enterprise Architect from SparxSystems (http://www.sparxsystems.com.au/ea.htm) (all last visited 18 April 2005)

8. David Carlson, MODELING XML APPLICATIONS WITH UML (Addison-Wesley, 2001). Carlson's portal for XML modeling issues where hyperModel can be downloaded is at http://www.xmlmodeling.com/ (last visited 10 March 2005).

9. See Ronald Bourret, "Mapping W3C schemas to object schemas to relational schemas," March 2001, at http://www.rpbourret.com/xml/SchemaMap.htm (last visited 20 February 2005).

10. The Schematron can be useful in conjunction with many grammar-based structure-validation languages: DTDs, XML Schemas, RELAX, TREX, etc. Schematron is part of an ISO standard (DSDL: Document Schema Description Languages) designed to allow multiple XML validation languages to work together. For more details see http://www.schematron.com/ (last visited 10 March 2005).

11. Matthew Gertner, Eduardo Gutentag, and Arofan Gregory, "Guidelines for the customization of UBL v1.0 schemas," 22 April 2004, at http://docs.oasis-open.org/ubl/cd-UBL-1.0/doc/cm/wd-ubl-cmsc-cmguidelines-1.0.html (last visited 20 February 2005).

12. BPEL was originally developed by Microsoft and IBM but is now being worked on as an OASIS technical committee; the most current specification can be found at the home page at http://www.oasis-open.org/committees/tc_home.php?wg_abbrev=wsbpel. BPSS was developed in the ebXML initiative (http://www.ebxml.org/) but it is also now an OASIS TC (http://www.oasis-open.org/committees/-tc_home.php?wg_abbrev=ebxml-bp). BPDM is a relatively new effort of the Object Management Group (http://www.omg.org/#BPC). RosettaNet Implementation Framework: Core Specification. Version 2.00.01, 6 March 2002, http://www.rosettanet.org (all last visited 18 April 2005).

13. This idea might be implicit in Barbara van Halle, BUSINESS RULES APPLIED: BUILDING BETTER SYSTEMS USING THE BUSINESS RULES APPROACH (Wiley, 2001), but it was first expressed this clearly by Peter Charles and Bob Daly, RULE BASED INFRASTRUCTURE: A DESIGN AND RUNTIME SYSTEM FOR ENABLING XML SCHEMA DRIVEN APPLICATIONS (UC Berkeley Master's Project Report, School of Information Management and Systems, 2004).

14. Joaquin Miller and Jishnu Mukerji (Eds.), MDA Guide Version 1.0.1, 12 June 2003, at http://www.omg.org/docs/omg/03-06-01.pdf (last visited 4 February 2005).

15. See "The architecture of choice for a changing world: OMG model driven architecture," at http://www.omg.org/mda/ (last visited 20 February 2005).

16. See Ronald Bourret, "XML data binding resources," 12 December 2004, at http://www.rpbourret.com/xml/XMLDataBinding.htm (last visited 7 February 2005); Dennis Sosnoski, "XML and Java technologies: Data binding, Part 1: Code generation approaches—JAXB and more," 1 January 2003, at http://www-128.ibm.com/developerworks/xml/library/x-databdopt/ (last visited 16 February 2005).

17. Somewhat ironically for us, the user's high-level understanding about how an application works that shapes his or her interactions with it is often called a "system model," but this model is a qualitative one that can't be executed or interpreted to run the application. See Donald Norman, THE DESIGN OF EVERYDAY THINGS (Basic Books, 1988).

18. The W3C XForms Recommendation and other useful resources can be found at the W3C XForms Activity Page at ww.w3.org/MarkUp/Forms/. We also recommend a book by one of the editors of the Recommendation: Micah Dubinko, XFORMS ESSENTIALS (O'Reilly, 2003).

19. The home page for the Mozilla XUL project is http://www.mozilla.org/projects/xul/ (last visited 20 February 2005). See also Vaughn Bullard, Kevin Smith, and Michael Daconta, ESSENTIAL XUL PROGRAMMING (Wiley, 2001).

20. "Longhorn" Markup Language (code-named "XAML") Overview. See http://longhorn.msdn.microsoft.com/lhsdk/core/overviews/about%20xaml.aspx (last visited 20 February 2005).

21. "Macromedia Flex: The presentation tier solution for delivering enterprise rich internet applications," October 2004, at http://www.macromedia.com/software/flex/whitepapers/pdf/flex15_-tech_wp.pdf (last visited 10 February 2005).

22. Patrick Garvey and Bill French, "Generating user interfaces from composite schemas," IDEALLIANCE XML 2003 CONFERENCE, http://www.idealliance.org/papers/dx_xml03/papers/03-03-04/03-03-04.pdf (last visited 20 February 2005).

23. Dennis de Baar, James Foley, and Kevin Mullet. "Coupling application design and user interface design," PROCEEDINGS OF ACM CHI (1992): pp. 259-266.

24. Gustavo Rossi, Daniel Schwabe, and Fernando Lyardet. "User interface patterns for hypermedia applications," INTERNATIONAL CONFERENCE ON ADVANCED VISUAL INTERFACES (AVI 2000); Matijn vam Welie and Hallvard Troetteberg. "Interaction patterns in user interfaces," 7th CONFERENCE ON THE PATTERN LANGUAGES OF PROGRAMS (PLoP 2000); Stefano Cerl, Piero Fraternali, Aldo Bongio, Marco Brambilla, Sara Comai, and Maristella Matera. DESIGNING DATA-INTENSIVE WEB-APPLICATIONS (Morgan Kaufman, 2003).

25. Volker Turau. "A Framework for automatic generation of web-based data entry applications based on XML," PROCEEDINGS OF THE 2002 ACM SYMPOSIUM ON APPLIED COMPUTING.

26. Angel Puerta, Michael Michelletti, and Alan Mak. "The UI pilot: a model based tool to guide early interface design," INTERNATIONAL CONFERENCE ON INTELLIGENT USER INTERFACES (IUI'05).
27. Enrico Bertini and Giuseppe Santucci. "Modeling Internet based applications for designing multi-device adaptive interfaces," INTERNATIONAL CONFERENCE ON ADVANCED VISUAL INTERFACES (AVI 2004). Murielle Florins and Jean Vanderdonckt. "Graceful degradation of user interfaces as a design method for multiplatform systems," INTERNATIONAL CONFERENCE ON INTELLIGENT USER INTERFACES (IUI'04).

28. Melody Ivory and Marti Hearst. "The state of the art in automating usability evaluation of user interfaces," ACM COMPUTING SURVEYS, 33(4), December 2001, pp. 470-516.

29. Angel Puerta. "A Model Based Interface Development Environment." IEEE SOFTWARE, July/August 1997.

30. Simon Lok, Steven Feiner, and Gary Ngai. "Evaluation of visual balance for automated layout," INTERNATIONAL CONFERENCE ON INTELLIGENT USER INTERFACES (IUI'04).

31. Carlo Bellettini, Alessandro Marchetto, and Andrea Trentini. "WebUML: Reverse engineering of web applications," PROCEEDINGS OF THE 2004 ACM SYMPOSIUM ON APPLIED COMPUTING.

32. Lisa de Larios-Heiman, "Above All Studio and the Syllabus Project: Generating Data Entry Forms for a Model Based Application." Center for Document Engineering Technical Report, January 2005 (CDE-TR-2005-1).

33. Darrell Raymond and Frank Tompa, "Hypertext and the new Oxford English Dictionary," COMMUNICATIONS OF THE ACM, 31 (July 1988): pp. 871-879.

34. Open eBook Publication Structure Specification, at http://www.openebook.org/oebps/oebps1.2/-index.htm. See Paul Cesarini, "eBooks: A battle for standards," THE WRITING INSTRUCTOR, 2002 at http://www.writinginstructor.com/essays/-cesarini/index.html (both last visited 7 February 2005).

35. Interactive Electronic Training Manual (IETM) Guide (Defense Systems Management College Press, 1999), at http://nsdsa.phdnswc.navy.mil/tmmp/ietm/ietm_DSMC%20acquisition%20doc.pdf (last visited 20 February 2005).

36. John Terris, "Re-use, re-purpose, re-package:A General Engine Products, Inc., case study," IDEALLIANCE XML 2001 CONFERENCE, at http://www.idealliance.org/papers/xml2001/papers/html/04-01-04.html (last visited 9 February 2005).

37. Center for Document Engineering, University of California, Berkeley, Center in a Box 1.0.1 Early Access User's Guide, 2003, at http://cde.berkeley.edu/initiatives/centerinabox/ (last visited 10 February 2004). Center in a Box is a research project to explore model based publishing. It is not a full web portal because it lacks built-in functionality to support user logins or customization by role. It also lacks facili-

ties for WYSIWYG editing, content versioning, or access control that might be found in a complete content management solution.

38. For further discussion of software architecture and technology, see Michael Fitzgerald, BUILDING B2B APPLICATIONS WITH XML (Wiley, 2001); David Linthicum, NEXT GENERATION APPLICATION INTEGRATION (Addison-Wesley, 2004); Gregor Hohpe and Bobby Wolfe, ENETERPRISE INTEGRATION PATTERNS (Addison-Wesley, 2004).

39. David Chappell, ENTERPRISE SERVICE BUS (O'Reilly, 2004).

40. W3C, "Semantic web activity statement,"www.w3.org/2001/sw/Activity (last visited 2 March 2005). See also Tim Berners-Lee, James Hendler, and Ora Lassila, "The semantic web," SCIENTIFIC AMERICAN, May 2001, http://www.scientificamerican.com/article.cfm?articleID=00048144-10D2-1C70-84A9809EC588EF21&catID=2 (last visited 3 March 2005).

41. These two examples are adapted from W3C, "OWL web ontology language use cases and requirements," 10 February 2004, at http://www.w3.org/TR/webont-req/ (last visited 2 March 2005).

42. W3C, "Resource description framework (RDF): Concepts and abstract syntax," 10 February 2004, at http://www.w3.org/TR/rdf-concepts/ (last visited 2 March 2005).

43. See "(XML) topic maps" at http://xml.coverpages.org/topicMaps.html (last visited 3 March 2005).

44. W3C, Web-Ontology (WebOnt) Working Group, at http://www.w3.org/2001/sw/WebOnt/ (last visited 3 March 2005).

45. The British Library defines "creator" as a superset of the Library of Congress definition of "author." See Catherine Marshall and Frank Shipman, "Which Semantic Web?," ACM CONFERENCE ON HYPERTEXT AND HYPERMEDIA, 2003.

16 Management and Strategy in Document Engineering

1. See "Alexander Bain," in The History of Computing Project, at http://www.thocp.net/-biographies/bain_alexander.htm, and "Alexander Bain" in Adventures in Cybersound, at http://www.acmi.net.au/AIC/BAIN_BIO.html (both last visited 27 December 2004).

2. For a useful checklist for resource requirements in web services-targeted projects, see Doug Kaye, LOOSELY COUPLED: THE MISSING PIECES OF WEB SERVICES (RDS Associates Inc, 2003) App A.

3. Carnegie Mellon University Software Engineering Institute, THE CAPABILITY MATURITY MODEL: GUIDELINES FOR IMPROVING THE SOFTWARE PROCESS (Addison-Wesley, 1995). The

Software Engineering Institute no longer maintains the CMM model. See http://www.sei.cmu.edu/cmm/ (last visited 28 December 2004).

4. The SEI's Software Measurement and Analysis site at http://www.sei.cmu.edu/sema/ contains publications, presentations, and other useful resources; the 2004 summary data about assessments is http://www.sei.cmu.edu/sema/pdf/CMMI/2004aug.pdf (last visited 3 January 2005). Some critics suggest that the CMM is easily scammed by software outsourcing firms who claim higher ratings than they deserve to get business. We won't get caught up in that debate because we don't envision using the CMM for that purpose. See Christopher Koch, "Bursting the CMM hype," CIO, 1 March 2004, at http://www.cio.com/archive/030104/cmm.html (last visited 28 December 2004).

5. The Sarbanes-Oxley Act of 2002 requires certain corporate officers of public firms in the United States to certify that they are responsible for establishing, maintaining, and regularly evaluating the effectiveness of internal controls, as well as any disclosures, information in reports and any significant changes or other factors that could affect internal controls. A useful resource about the act is http://www.sarbanes-oxley.com/section.php (last visited 30 December 2004).

6. See, for example, the sophisticated processes and technology of the Federal Enterprise Architecture's Center for Component Reuse at https://www.core.gov/ (last visited 28 December 2004).

7. In some situations where staffing levels are fixed, an alternative justification to cost savings is the benefit of being able to handle more business with the same staff. But if the enterprise is a nonprofit or governmental entity, this may not be a desirable or feasible goal.

8. Our treatment of return on investment and business cases in this paragraph and the remainder of section 16.3 is simplified and mostly qualitative. For a more rigorous treatment of ROI involving net present value calculations, see Gunjan Samtani and Dimple Sadhwani, "Web Services Return on Investment," WEB SERVICES ARCHITECT, 4 August 2002, at http://www.webservicesarchitect.com/content/articles/samtani07print.asp (last visited 2 January 2005). The classic and comprehensive introduction is Stephen Ross, Randolph Westerfield, and Jeffrey Jaffe, CORPORATE FINANCE, (McGraw-Hill, 2005).

9. Larry Downes, THE STRATEGY MACHINE (Harper Collins, 2002).

10. See Todd Batz, "Portfolio management: How to do it right," CIO, 1 May 2003, at http://www.cio.com/archive/050103/portfolio.html (last visited 2 January 2005).

11. Some of these come from Commerce One, How the Business Internet Can Save Your Company Millions. (2002).

12. Fred Metzgen, KILLING THE PAPER DRAGON (Butterworth-Heinemann, 1990), p.111.

13. CommerceOne, ibid., p. 5.

14. John Edwards, "I'm not dead yet," LINE56, May 2001, at http://www.LINE56.com/-articles/default.asp?NewsID=2563 (last visited 31 December 2004).

15. Commerce One, ibid. p. 2. See also Demir Barlas, "E-Procurement: Steady Value," LINE 56, 4 January 2005 at http://www.LINE56.com/articles/default.asp?ArticleID=6246 (last visited 11 January 2005).

16. Kenneth Sall, "How the US Government is Using XML: One Year Later," IDEALLIANCE XML 2004 CONFERENCE, November 2004, at http://www.idealliance.org/proceedings/xml04/papers/150/How-US-Govt-Using-XML-1YL.html (last visited 2 January 2005). This paper and CORE.GOV (note 26) are excellent entry points to numerous case studies and e-government initiatives.

17. Mikkel Hippe Brun. "The Danish approach to standardisation of public sector XML-interfaces and localisation of international standards," OASIS ADOPTION FORUM PROCEEDINGS, 6 October 2004, at http://www.oasis-open.org/events/adoption_forum/slides/brun.ppt (last visited 31 December 2004).

18. Australian Department of Foreign Affairs and Trade, PAPERLESS TRADING: BENEFITS TO APEC (2001), at http://www.dfat.gov.au/publications/paperless/paperless_trading.pdf (last visited 28 December 2004).

19. Polarlake, "Standards-based integration in financial services," April 2004, at http://www.polar-lake.com/en/assets/whitepapers/financial_services.pdf (last visited 2 January 2005).

20. Kazumasa Takeuchi, "Supply chain management (SCM) and traceability," ELECTRONIC COMMERCE PROMOTION COUNCIL OF JAPAN (ECOM) REGIONAL WORKSHOP, 4 September 2004, at http://www.adbi.org/files/2004.09.01.cpp.supply.chain.management.pdf (last visited 6 January 2005).

21. Hong Kong University's Center for E-Commerce Infrastructure Development. Notifiable Infectious Disease Information Messaging System (NIDIMS) Project, June 2004, at http://www.cecid.hku.hk/-newsletter/VOL3Jun2004.php?#Notifiable_Infectious (last visited 6 January 2005).

22. Metzgen, ibid., p.17.

23. Metzgen, ibid.

24. CommerceOne, ibid., p. 9.

25. Linda T. Kohn, Janet M. Corrigan, and Molla S. Donaldson (Eds), TO ERR IS HUMAN: BUILDING A SAFER HEALTH SYSTEM (National Academy Press, 2000).

26. Rhonda Rundle. "WellPoint to pay $30 million for doctors' computers," WALL STREET JOURNAL, 15 January 2004.

27. Most modern container terminals have developed systems for electronic tracking of shipments. For an example the 1-Stop service operating in Australia provides a common platform for industry to report and receive information to and from stevedoring companies. See http://www.1-stop.biz/aboutus.php (last visited 2 January 2005).

28. Jon Hilsenrath, "Beyond surging productivity: The service sector delivers," WALL STREET JOURNAL, 7 November 2003.

29. Australian Department of Foreign Affairs and Trade, ibid., p.19.

30. For an explanation of how OpenTable works, see http://www.opentable.com/info/restindex.asp (last visited 2 January 2005).

31. Lynda Brooks, "ROI reality: How publishers are Realizing true return on their XML investment," IDEALLIANCE XML 2003 CONFERENCE, at http://www.idealliance.org/papers/dx_xml03/papers/03-02-03/03-02-03.pdf (last visited 2 January 2005). For more discussion of the business issues in electronic publishing and content management, see JoAnn Hackos, CONTENT MANAGEMETN FOR DYNAMIC WEB DELIVERY (Wiley, 2002), and Peter Brown, INFORMATION ARCHITECTURE WITH XML (Wiley, 2003). And while its name might make it seem dated, a very crisp discussion of the business case for XML publishing is Pamela Gennusa, "Using SGML: The pain/gain ratio," at http://xml.coverpages.org/gennusaPain.html (last visited 7 January 2005).

32. Among the classic works in software engineering about controlling costs through earlier defect removal are Barry Boehm and Philip Papaccio, "Understanding and controlling software costs," IEEE TRANSACTIONS ON SOFTWARE ENGINEERING, 14 (October 1988): pp.1462-1477, and Tom Gilb, PRINCIPLES OF SOFTWARE ENGINEERING MANAGEMENT (Addison-Wesley, 1988). A more recent paper that discusses the benefits of model-based software development with UML and XML is Martin Soukop, "Model driven architecture: feasibility or fallacy," IDEALLIANCE XML 2004 CONFERENCE, November 2004, at http://www.idealliance.org/proceedings/xml04/papers/200/MDA_Feasibility.pdf (last visited 7 January 2005).

33. The last three groups also have a strategic partnership with the World Trade Organization to promote a free and fair global trading system. An introduction to ISO standards and its standards-making processes can be found at http://www.iso.org/iso/en/aboutiso/introduction/index.html (last visited 7 January 2005).

34. Sean McGrath and Fergal Murray, "Principles of e-government architecture," (Propylon White Paper, 7 July 2003). Available after registration at http://www.propylon.com/ (last visited 7 January 2005).

35. For a careful and comprehensive discussion of intellectual property and standards with an extensive annotated bibliography, see "Patents and Open Standards" at http://xml.coverpages.org/patents.html, last modified 7 December 2004 (last visited 7 January 2005).

36. Ross Altman, "The standards maturity model and plug-and-play integration," BUSINESS INTEGRATION JOURNAL, November 2004, at http://www.bijonline.com/PDF/Altman%20Nov.pdf (last visited 7 January 2005).

37. Henry Chesbrough and David Teece, "Organizing for innovation: When is virtual virtuous?" HARVARD BUSINESS REVIEW, August 2002.

38. Julian Bajkowski, "Customs cargo system delayed again," COMPUTERWORLD, 20 October 2003, at http://www.computerworld.com.au/pp.php?id=957631137&fp=16&fpid=0; Chris Jenkins, Customs busted in $100m overrun," THE AUSTRALIAN, 11 November 2003, at http://www.cbfca.com.au/bulletin/volumeView.asp?VolumeId=29&ArticleId=233; Julian Bajkowski, "Transport heavies choke on Customs system upgrade, ready or not," COMPUTERWORLD, 13 August 2004, at http://www.computerworld.com.au/index.php/id;1318167007;relcomp;1 (all last visited 9 January 2005).

39. From the Australian Customs web site, at http://www.customs.gov.au/site/page.cfm?u=4916 (last visited 9 January 2005).

40. The connection between the telecommunications network and nearly all homes and businesses is referred to as the local loop, or the last mile. This last mile is capital intensive, and has historically been constructed with copper phone lines. See http://www.manymedia.com/futures/bells.html (last visited 17 March 2005).

41. Da Vinci's sketch for his helicopter can be found at http://www.artist-biography.info/gallery/leonardo_da_vinci/27/. (last visited 7 January 2005).

42. Peter Murray. THE SAGA OF THE SYDNEY OPERA HOUSE: THE DRAMATIC STORY OF THE DESIGN AND CONSTRUCTION OF THE ICON OF MODERN AUSTRALIA (Routledge, 2003).

17 Epilogue

1. In a previous draft of this chapter, we also included some examples of the first two cases based on 20th century changes to the names of academic departments and university fields of study, but some reviewers objected to them so you'll have to come up with your own negative examples or take our claim on faith.

2. IBM Global Services, "Service-oriented architecture and web services," at http://www-1.ibm.com/services/us/index.wss/it_services/its/a1002583 (last visited 2 March 2005). See also Ed Scannell, "IBM Delivers SOA Enablers," INFOWORLD, 21 April 2004, at http://www.infoworld.com/article/04/04/21/HNibmsoas_1.html (last visited 2 March 2005). The quotations in this section come from the Scannell article.

3. With the exception of the brave students who've taken the Document Engineering course at the University of California, Berkeley taught by the first author since 2002. It is listed as Information Systems 243 in the current course catalog at http://www.sims.berkeley.edu/academics/courses/is243/ (last visited 2 March 2005).

Glossary

Aggregate Business Information Entity: A structural component in ebXML Core Components terminology.

aggregates: Collections as a whole rather than as parts.

agile modeling: A low-overhead methodology that attempts to minimize risk by ensuring that analysts focus on smaller deliverable units.

ANSI ASC X12: The official designation of the Electronic Data Interchange (EDI) standard for the United States.

apocopations: An abbreviation formed from groups of characters in a set of terms that creates a new word. For example, webcam.

application: In XML-speak, a specific markup language. "Vocabulary" is preferred to avoid confusion with "application" as used to mean software functionality.

application program interface: The interface by which an application communicates with other parts of a system.

artifact: An object made by an activity, such as a model or a document instance.

artifact focused view of modeling: An approach that places a stronger focus on modeling artifacts than on the means for creating them.

As-Is model: A model of the current situation.

ASCII: An abbreviation for the American Standard Code for Information Interchange. ASCII is a code for representing English characters as numbers, with each letter assigned a number from 0 to 127.

ASN.1: An abbreviation for Abstract Syntax Notation 1. An ISO/ITU-T standard for transmitting structured data on networks.

Association Business Information Entity: An association (or more accurately a role in an association) in ebXML Core Components terminology.

association by proximity: Where meaningful associations between components are implied by placing them physically near each other.

asymmetric relationship: A business relationship where one party is able to dictate the terms of the information exchanges.

attribute: A construct used to add additional information to elements to extend their functionality.

auction: A method for establishing prices when market mechanisms don't work well, usually when goods are scarce for one reason or another.

bar code: A printed horizontal strip of vertical bars of varying widths, groups of which represent decimal digits and are used for identifying commercial products or parts.

Basic Business Information Entity: A content component in ebXML core component terminology.

bricks and mortar: Something that exists in the physical world. Used to denote businesses that provide services and products from stores or other facilities.

business: A purposeful, systematized activity to create and exchange value. Can apply to government, educational, and nonprofit entities.

business alliance: A group of companies with the common goal of challenging or defending against the dominant firm or firms in their industry.

business architecture: An abstract model of a business that describes its components and their relationship with each other using hierarchical and compositional structure

business domain view: The partitioning of a business domain into business areas, process areas, and business processes. This view establishes the business context of the process.

business ecosystem: The collection of partners and their organization viewed from the perspective of the enterprise at their intersection or common focus.

business entities: The information components required by a business collaboration or transaction.

business informatics: Combines the modern theory, methods and techniques of business (i.e. organization science) and informatics (i.e. information and computing science).

Business Information Entity: A contextualized component in ebXML core component terminology.

business information model: Specifications for the content of physical documents. These are the lowest level of patterns useful for Document Engineering.

business model: The most abstract, high level model of how a business works

business process: A chain of related activities or events that take specified inputs, add value to the inputs, and yield a specific service or product that can serve as the input to another business process

business process analysis: The evaluating of the effectiveness of an organization's activities and communications.

business process implementation model: A model of a business process that is realized as a document instance suitable for use by software applications.

business process requirements: The requirements that define actions to be applied whenever a given condition or set of information is encountered.

Business Process Specification Schema: A business process implementation metamodel expressed as an XML schema.

business reference model: A hierarchy of generalized business models, describing the ways in which businesses organize their activities.

business requirements view: The view of a business process model that captures the business scenarios, inputs, outputs, constraints and boundaries for business processes and their interrelationships within business process collaborations.

business rule: Constraints that determine the reactions to particular situations in the everyday workings of a business.

business signals: Messages exchanged in a transaction that are not business documents but used for receipts and confirmations of exchanges.

business transaction view: The view of a business process model that captures the semantics of business information entities and their flow of exchange between roles as they perform business activities.

Capability Maturity Model: A model that describes the principles and practices underlying software process maturity intended to help software developers assess and improve their capability to produce quality software.

cardinality: The potential number of occurrences for a component.

channel assembly: An adaptation of the drop shipment pattern so that a distributor, instead of shipping finished goods from inventory, performs some final assembly to customize the inventoried goods.

channel conflict: When a company sells through both direct and indirect distribution channels.

choreography: The description of a business collaboration that may be controlled by any participating party.

Class diagram: A static view of a system including classes, and their associations and attributes.

codes: Sets of possible values that they establish their meaning by reference (or extension) to other values, often by using abbreviations.

collaboration: A set of transactions that have more overlapping context with each other than with other parts of the business process that contains them all.

collaboration properties: Properties (or metadata) that further define the rules of a collaboration to tell the participating businesses precisely what to expect from each other.

Collaboration Protocol Profile and Agreement: Information agreed between two (or more) Parties that identifies or describes the specific Collaboration Protocol that they have agreed to use.

Collaborative Planning, Forecasting and Replenishment: A set of business processes that organizations in a supply chain can use for collaboration on a number of buyer/seller functions, towards overall efficiency in the supply chain.

commerciography: The collective study of businesses, including their size, growth, density, and distribution, as well as statistics regarding establishment, mergers, profitability, and demise. We coined this term to convey the corporate sense of a demography.

community of practice: Organizations composed of individual practitioners who share a concern or a passion for something they do and who interact regularly to learn how to do it better

composite applications: Applications that combine with others to form new services.

composite key: The combination of more than one component to uniquely identify a structure.

composite service: Services that combine with others to form new services linked by overlapping information requirements, business rules, and processes.

conceptual model: A model that represents an abstract or generalized view of the real world. Conceptual models are independent of the physical implementation and are not tied to any particular technology.

confirmation: A signal that informs the sender of the business document's validity according to the recipient's business rules.

connector: Software that uses templates or configurable translations for common physical interfaces to ERP, enterprise database, or messaging software formats.

consumer to consumer: See peer-to-peer.

containment relationships: An association described by the hierarchy of components. For instance an event might contain components for name, location, and time.

content component: Components that contain discrete and atomic values.

content integrity: The requirement to preserve the values of the content (but not necessarily the presentation) of the original document.

context: That which surrounds, and gives meaning to, something else. In Document Engineering we view context as the union of all known requirements.

context dimension: A perspective on the various environmental factors that affect the context of use.

context driver: A way to categorize values for context dimensions. For example, the context dimension known as "business process" may have a context driver known as "procurement."

contract manufacturing: The design and manufacture of products customized to a buyer's requirements.

controlled vocabulary: A fixed set of terms such as used in dictionaries, taxonomies, thesauri and classification schemes.

conversion: To format information into an XML document.

core competency: The activities that are essential to an organization's definition of success.

core component: A building block for the creation of a semantically correct and meaningful information exchange package. It contains only the information pieces necessary to describe a specific concept. In Document Engineering, these are known as generalized components.

corporate culture: Refers to the values, beliefs and customs of an organization.

creeping featurism: The tendency to add more features to a system, especially those driven by marketing considerations or technological possibilities rather than user needs under the (mistaken) idea that more features make a system better than the previous version.

cuneiform: Characters formed by the arrangement of small wedge-shaped elements and used in ancient Sumerian, Akkadian, Assyrian, Babylonian, and Persian writing.

data binding: When code generation techniques turn XML schemas into logically equivalent representations in software.

data mart: Smaller logical units of a data warehouse.

data type: A classification of a particular type of information.

data warehouse: A system used to store large amounts of information regarding an organization's activities in a database. Data warehouses create less formal views than regular database management systems.

database schema: An implementation model for a database management system.

deadheading: The action when a truck returns without a backload on its return trip from delivering goods.

Dell-iversity: A hypothetical university adopting a make-to-order pattern for its courses.

demand chain: When information flows in the opposite direction of the materials and goods, so the demand for products is disseminated up the supply chain to better align production with demand.

dependency: The need for something to be available in order to exist. In Document Engineering we say that if a change to A inherently changes B, then B is dependent on A.

dependent component: A component whose value is functionally dependent on the value of a determinant component.

deployment diagram: A notation of the UML that describes the configuration of processing resource elements and the mapping of software implementation components onto them.

derivative component: A component whose value can be derived from the values of other components.

deserialization: Populating the programming objects that convey a document's content.

determinant component: A component whose value determines the value of a dependent component.

dictionary: A list of words with information about them. In Document Engineering we extend this to mean a list of the terms used in the names of components along with their definitions.

dimensions of context: A means of classifying patterns of business rules and requirements. See also context dimensions.

direct distribution: In which a company sells a product directly to the companies or consumers who buy it.

direct procurement: Procurement of the goods and materials that go into the products an organization makes.

disaggregate: To separate something into its component parts or to break apart.

disintermediation: The removal of intermediaries in a supply chain.

distribution: The commercial activity of transporting and selling goods from a producer to a consumer.

distribution and fulfillment: A collaboration pattern that enables a manufacturer to ensure that the things it sells get to specified places at specified times in specified quantities.

document: A purposeful and self-contained collection of information.

document analysis: Analysis to identify the components of documents or information sources.

document approval: A collaboration where the information added to an original document might be nothing more than the signature (perhaps with comments) of the reviewer.

document component model: Describes the complete set of conceptual information components in a domain, including their structure and their potential relationships. Also known as a Domain View model.

document implementation model: A model that represents the physical view of a document, such as an XML schema.

document inventory: A collection of documents and related information sources along with metadata about their purposes, origins, and other attributes.

Document Type Definition: A set of rules and a schema language for marking up a document in SGML and XML.

down translation: The process of transforming from XML to a non-XML format.

drop shipment: A business model where the seller does not hold any inventory of goods. Instead they place an order with a wholesaler who has the goods delivered direct to the customer.

e-Business: An Internet enabled business model that involves business processes, enterprise applications and organizational structures.

e-government: When governments at both municipal and national levels introduce Web initiatives of various kinds.

e-learning: When academic institutions introduce web initiatives for presenting course materials.

Electronic Data Interchange: The computer-to-computer exchange of structured information. Now commonly associated with specific languages such as UN/EDIFACT and ANSI ASC X12.

element: A component that is one of the individual parts of which a composite structure is made up. In markup languages, an element is identified by an open and a close tag.

enterprise application integration: The use of middleware to integrate the application programs, databases, and legacy systems involved in an organization's critical business processes.

enterprise boundary: The point at which processes that can be controlled by the enterprise are separated from those that can't.

Enterprise Resource Planning: A system designed to support and automate the business processes of medium and large businesses. This may include manufacturing, distribution, personnel, project management, payroll, and financials.

entry point: A structural component in a document component model that will form the root of the document assembly tree hierarchy.

equivalence: The fact of being the same, effectively the same, or interchangeable with something else.

escalating commitment: A collaboration pattern where additional contract negotiations adds progressively stronger obligations.

essentiality: Containing only the essential components and nothing else.

exchanges: A type of marketplace for intangible goods like financial securities where price is the essential attribute.

extensible: A system that can be modified by changing or adding features.

external codes: Code sets from a separate or independent organization.

external model: A model that represents the real world.

facilitator: A party who provides or promotes a broad and commercially neutral perspective in which firms can cooperate to set standards or policies for a trading community.

facilities map: A model of business organization that shows the locations of offices, factories, distribution points, training centers, or other facilities.

fidelity requirements: The amount to which a design must be faithful to the original.

field stocking: Pre-positioning inventory at delivery service distribution hubs near customers.

first normal form: The stage in normalization where every component in a structure can have only a single value.

foreign key: The primary key component of one structure (the determinant one) as a foreign component within another (the dependent one), thereby allowing a link between structures.

formal ontology: The hierarchical structuring of knowledge about things by subcategorizing them according to their essential (or at least relevant and/or cognitive) qualities.

fulfillment: To supply something ordered.

functional dependency: A component is functionally dependent on another when at any given time, the value of a dependant component can only be associated with one (and only one) value of the determinant component.

gateway: A software component that performs the transformation to a required physical interface.

generalization: To make generally or universally applicable.

Global Positioning System: A navigational system involving satellites and computers that can determine the latitude and longitude of a receiver on Earth by computing the time difference for signals from different satellites to reach the receiver.

GMBooks.com: A fictional Internet bookstore abbreviated from GlushkoMcGrathBooks.com.

grammar: The system of rules implicit in a language for generating all structures possible in that language.

granularity: The extent to which a system contains separate components.

Guidelines for Trade Data Interchange: A set of EDI interchange rules published in 1981.

harvesting: To collect or gather something. In Document Engineering we apply this to gathering information components.

hierarchical model: A top-down arrangement of components that has one component known as the root from which an inverted tree structure emanates. All other components in the model are arranged in levels such that each is related to a single parent component in the level immediately above it.

homonym: Components with the same names but different meanings.

hosted drop shipment: Where a third party provides a service for catalog management, shopping cart, and personalization services for a retailer.

HTTP: An abbreviation of Hypertext Transfer Protocol. The client-server TCP/IP protocol used on the World-Wide Web for the exchange of HTML documents.

identifiers: Components whose values uniquely identify specific objects.

implementation: The practical application of a model to fulfill a desired purpose.

implementation guidelines: Published guidelines to assist EDI implementations of the rules of the syntax, and to expand some of the rules contained, often supported by examples.

incremental information trail: A process pattern where documents are created, consumed, added to, and subtracted from as they are passed along from one process to the next.

indirect distribution: Manufacturers selling products through distributors, resellers, and retail outlets to increase their ability to reach customers.

indirect procurement: The procurement of the goods and services needed by an organization to administer its business.

industry group: An organization of businesses in the same industry who work together to promote and protect common interests in trade.

information flow: The who, what and when view of information exchanges.

information goods: A product whose main market value derives from the information it contains. It may also include services (information services).

information model: A formal representation of the structure and semantics of information.

information supply chain: The flow of information that supports a supply chain.

initialism: An abbreviation formed from the first character in a set of terms. For example, EDI.

instance: An occurrence (or an implementation) of a type of document. That is, the actual values for objects the model describes.

integration: The controlled sharing of data and business processes between connected applications or data sources.

integrity: Having everything that is needed.

Intermediary: Organizations acting as a mediator or an agent between for others.

Internet EDI: Using the Internet to transport EDI documents.

Internet Protocol version 6: The most viable candidate to replace the current Internet Protocol. The primary purpose of IPv6 is to solve the problem of the shortage of IP addresses.

interoperability: The condition achieved when information or services can be exchanged directly and satisfactorily between different systems.

ISO 11179: The ISO standard for the specification and standardization of data elements.

ISO 3166: The ISO codes for the representation of names of countries and their subdivisions.

ISO 4217: The ISO codes for the representation of international currencies.

ISO TC 154: The ISO committee charged with the international standardization and registration of business, and administration processes and supporting data used for information interchange between and within individual organizations and support for standardization activities in the field of industrial data.

key information components: Information components that link threads of related document instances within the same business process.

last mile: The connection between the telecommunications network and nearly all homes and businesses is referred to as the last mile.

law of diminishing returns: The tendency for a continuing application of effort or investment toward a particular project or goal to decline in effectiveness after a certain level of result has been achieved.

logical architecture: An abstract or conceptual description of a system architecture.

long-running transactions: Transactions that may take minutes, days or weeks before the outcome of the transaction is known.

loose coupling: An integration approach that does not depend on implementation details or other characteristics at the physical level.

make-to-order: A business model where products are only assembled or manufactured when they are ordered.

make-to-stock: A business model where products are assembled or manufactured for stock.

mapping: To make logical connections between two components.

market operator: A party who provides or co-ordinates a marketplace.

marketplace: A forum which allows people to trade, normally governed by the rules of supply and demand. Marketplaces work by placing many interested sellers in one place, thus making them easier to find for prospective buyers.

markup: Text that is added to the content of a document in order to convey information about it.

mass customization: Where a product is customized to a buyer's requirements by assembling or configuring standardized components.

mass production: The production of large quantities of a standardized article that are held in stock for future sale.

materials management: A collaboration pattern that enables a manufacturer to ensure that the things it buys get to specified places at specified times in specified quantities.

maverick purchasing: When an employee disregards a company's purchasing processes and independently buys indirect goods.

metadata: Information that augments the values of data with additional properties that explain its meaning, organization, cardinality, and other characteristics of interest.

metalanguage: A language or system of symbols that defines other languages.

metamodel: A model of metadata.

methodology: A body of practices, procedures, and rules used by those who work in a discipline or engage in an inquiry; a set of working methods.

mixed content: An element that may contain character data, optionally interspersed with child elements.

mode of exchange: The set of standard procedures, common practices, communication patterns, and norms governing routine behavior in the value chain relationship between a supplier and its customer.

model: Simplified descriptions of a subject that abstract from its complexity to emphasize some features or characteristics while intentionally de-emphasizing others.

model based application: A software application that is configured by information contained in an implementation model.

modeling methodology: An approach to modeling that includes a defined set of activities, a metamodel and possibly a set of notations.

multivalue dependencies: Dependencies that apply to pairs or sets of component values.

namespace: A mechanism for distinguishing the element definitions that come from different vocabularies. In XML environments namespaces allow elements and attributes to be associated with a URI. Generally, they are used to keep track of components and avoid naming conflicts when importing and combining multiple XML Schemas.

network forms: A nonmarket, nonfirm mechanism of coordination.

nonrepudiation: The concept of ensuring that a contract, especially one agreed to via a computer network, cannot later be denied by one of the parties involved.

normal forms: The stages of normalization.

normalization: A series of steps taken to produce data model forms that reduce data redundancy and the chances of data becoming inconsistent.

notations: A set of symbols.

open access movement: An effort to grant access to a large variety of up-to-date information sources for free. Also known as open-access publishing and free online scholarship.

orchestration: The description of a business collaboration that is controlled by a single party.

organization chart: A chart showing the lines of responsibility between departments of an organization.

paperless office: A vision for the office of the future that had paper documents made redundant by office automation. In reality personal computers and related printer technology made the bulk production of paper documents easier.

Pareto Principle: The principle that in nearly all cases, a few (20 percent) are vital and many (80 percent) are trivial. Also known as the 80/20 rule.

parser: A computer program that analyzes the well-formedness and validity of markup in a document with respect to a given schema.

pattern: Models that are sufficiently general, adaptable, and worthy of imitation that we can use them over and over again

peer to peer: Internet-facilitated business relationships between individuals.

persona: The role played by intended users that suggests the characteristics, preferences, and capabilities that influence requirements.

physical model: A model that represents a tangible view of the real world.

physical view: A perspective that yields physical models.

presentation components: Components that express stylistic conventions for formatting information.

presentation integrity: The requirement for preserving the original appearance of a document when it is reimplemented using different technology.

presentation requirements: The requirements that govern the appearance or rendering of an information component.

primary key: A component whose value is unique for every occurrence of the structure that contains it.

private business process: Business processes that are conducted entirely within an organization.

private document exchange: Documents that are exchanged entirely within an organization.

process: The highest level view of a business process, consisting of collaborations, which are in turn constructed from transactions.

proof of concept: A short and/or incomplete realization of a system to demonstrate its feasibility. A proof of concept is usually considered a milestone on the way of a fully functioning prototype.

prototype: A test system designed for demonstration purposes. When the prototype is sufficiently refined and meets the functionality, robustness, manufacturability and other design goals, the system is ready for production.

public business process: Business processes that are conducted between two or more organizations.

public document exchange: Documents that are exchanged between two or more organizations.

pull mode: A situation where the requirement to do something precedes the ability to do it.

push mode: A situation where the ability to do something precedes the requirement to do it.

Radio Frequency Identification: A method of remotely storing and retrieving data using devices called RFID tags. An RFID tag is a small object, such as an adhesive sticker, that can be attached to or incorporated into a product. RFID tags contain antennae to enable them to receive and respond to radio-frequency queries from an RFID transceiver.

receipt: A signal that informs the sender that its business document has been received by the appropriate business application.

reconciliation: A collaboration pattern that brings together information from related transactions to ensure a single consolidated and accurate view.

recursive association: A relationship among data elements where the same items can be both parents and children. For instance, a bill of materials is a list of parts, and each part may be composed of other parts

redundancy: A condition where information can be obtained from other sources.

referential integrity: The constraints that prevent removing information from determinant components without first removing any dependent information.

regular expression: A description of a value pattern using a set of strings of characters.

repackaging: To format a document in a new way for presentation in different media.

representation term: The type of valid values for a content component.

requirements: Constraints on possible solutions that must be satisfied for the solution to be acceptable. In Document Engineering requirements are the way we express the context of our document exchanges.

Rich Text Format: An ASCII interchange format used by Microsoft to indicate the formatting information in a document.

root element: The element that is the outermost element of an instance of a document. A root element has children, but no parent.

Sarbanes-Oxley Act: A US federal securities law enacted in the aftermath of corporate financial scandals that requires firms to implement adequate internal control structures and procedures and attest to their effectiveness.

schema: An implementation model for defining XML documents.

semantic map: A graph or table that represents the semantic relations between components.

semantic requirements: The requirements that define the meanings of components.

semantic web: Metadata standards for the world wide web that allow information to be shared and reused across application, enterprise, and community boundaries.

semantics: The meaning of language created by the use and relationship between symbols and what they represent.

sequence relationships: A restriction on the order of elements in a set of data, for instance, an event needs to be followed by a location and then a time

serialization: Creating document instances from programming objects.

Service Level Agreement: An agreement that defines the roles and mutual obligations with respect to reliability, performance, security, problem resolution, and a host of other dimensions that define document exchanges in a trading relationship.

service oriented architecture: A software architectural concept that considers everything a business does as (potentially) realized by business service components that are combined and recombined as needed.

SGML: Abbreviation for Standard Generalized Markup Language. A standard for creating the sets of elements and attributes in a markup language and specifying the rules by which they combine.

single-source publishing: An information architecture for publishing in which multiple document types or formats are created from a single set of information components.

SMTP: An abbreviation for Simple Mail Transfer Protocol. Used to transfer electronic mail between computers.

software as a service: Treating software as a service, with the customer paying on a subscription or per use basis to access some functionality using Internet protocols.

spreadsheet: The business collaboration pattern of selecting suppliers of goods or services.

standard: Freely implementable specification of patterns developed by consensus among the important stakeholders in some domain, working in a framework that encourages open participation provided by an organization chartered to create standards. It can also mean specifications that businesses can willingly choose to adopt and that are not controlled by a single firm.

straight through processing: Conducting the entire trade process electronically without the need for re-keying or manual intervention.

structural components: Components that are aggregations of other components.

structural integrity: The requirement for consistent assembly of structures in physical or implementation models.

structural requirements: The requirements that define co-occurrence or aggregation relationships between components.

style guide: A specification of editorial conventions followed in preparing text for publication.

styling: The way in which something is presented as distinct from the content of the information.

supply chain: The network of relationships, communication patterns, and distribution capabilities that provide raw materials, components, products, or services to an organization. The Document Engineering perspective on supply chains emphasizes the information flows that accompany the movement of materials and goods.

surrogate key: Components that are artificially created purely for the purpose of unique identification.

syndication: Distribution of content in a number of publications simultaneously.

synonym: Components with different names but the same meaning.

syntactic requirements: The requirements that concern the language in which documents or processes are encoded for implementation.

syntax: The rules whereby words or other elements of language are combined to form grammatical structures.

systems architecture: Describing a business model in terms of its computing platforms, operating systems, databases, and software applications.

table: A convention for presenting information, usually in regular matrix or grid patterns, to emphasize and reinforce the relationships between the content in the cells defined in the structure.

tag: A delimiter in text, often used in pairs to surround or label a text component, that specifies its formatting, structural role, or content type.

third normal form: The stage in normalization where every non-key component in a structure is dependent on the primary key.

tight coupling: A relationship that depends on the complex technology of implementations. Tight coupling may be necessary for maximum performance.

Time to Acknowledge Acceptance: A business signal that specifies when the recipient must send a message confirmation.

Time to Acknowledge Receipt: A business signal that specifies when the recipient must send a message receipt.

Time to Respond: A business signal that specifies when the recipient must send a response document.

To-Be model: A model of the required situation.

traceability: To follow or show a course or series of developments, or be able to be followed back in time or to a source.

trade association: An organization of businesses who work together to promote and protect common interests in trade.

trading community: A trading community encompasses the set of firms that fill the roles in business patterns like supply chains, distribution networks, and marketplaces in order to achieve mutual business benefits.

transaction: The lowest level of granularity in a business process describing the exchange of documents and business signals in a trading or commercial relationship between two parties.

transaction properties: Properties (or metadata) that further define the rules of a transaction to tell the participating businesses precisely what to expect from each other.

transformation: To change the content of an XML document into another format.

translation: The rendering of a document in one formatting language into a different language.

transparency: The ability of a system to change without noticeable impact on existing operations.

UN/EDIFACT: The United Nations standard for electronic data interchange for administration, commerce and transport. Ratified as ISO 9735.

up translation: The process of adding value to information by converting it to XML. See also conversion.

usability engineering: The field of software engineering concerned with the question of how to design software that is easy to use.

usage requirements: Requirements that define the policies or privileges that govern user access to information or applications.

use case: Definitions of the units of functionality or behavior provided by a system from the perspective of external actors.

validation: The process of testing whether an XML document follows the rules defined in an associated schema.

value chain: The generic activities supported by administrative infrastructure management, human resources management, R&D, and procurement. The costs and value drivers are identified for each value activity. The concept has been extended beyond individual organizations.

value-added services: Ancillary services provided to attract participants to a marketplace.

vendor managed inventory: The process where the vendor assumes the task of generating purchase orders to replenish a customer's inventory.

virtual business builder: A software application that interrogates registries of richly described business services, computes some metric of semantic distance to find service combinations with the necessary amount of complementary overlap and then proposes new kinds of virtual enterprises that exploit undiscovered business opportunities by applying patterns to new domains.

vocabulary: The set of words or terms in a language.

Web EDI: Using web forms to create or display EDI based documents.

web services: An interface that describes a collection of operations that are network accessible through XML messaging.

well-formed: Conforms to the rules of the markup metalanguage. For example, a well formed XML document has exactly one root element and no mismatched or overlapped start and end tags.

XHTML: An XML vocabulary that recasts HTML in XML syntax.

XML: An abbreviation for the Extensible Markup Language.

XML vocabularies: A specific set of tags used to markup content into XML

XPath: A language for addressing parts of an XML document.

zombie system: A legacy system not fully replaced by a new one that continues to operate in parallel with its intended replacement.

Index